Mendelssohn

A NEW IMAGE OF THE COMPOSER AND HIS AGE

Mendelssohn
Painting by J. W. Childe
(International Felix Mendelssohn Society, Basel)

Mendelssohn

A NEW IMAGE OF THE COMPOSER AND HIS AGE

ERIC WERNER

Translated from the German
by Dika Newlin

GREENWOOD PRESS, PUBLISHERS
WESTPORT, CONNECTICUT

Library of Congress Cataloging in Publication Data

Werner, Eric.
    Mendelssohn, a new image of the composer and his age.

    Reprint of the ed. published by Free Press of Glencoe,
New York.
    Includes bibliographical references and index.
    1. Mendelssohn-Bartholdy, Felix, 1809-1847.
2. Composers--Germany--Biography.
[ML410.M5W37 1978]   780'.92'4 [B]   78-1750
ISBN 0-313-20302-4

Reprinted with the permission of Eric Werner

Reprinted in 1978 by Greenwood Press, Inc.
51 Riverside Avenue, Westport, CT. 06880

Printed in the United States of America

10 9 8 7 6 5 4 3 2 1

To ERNST

in memory of a beloved Soul

Sighing I turned away; but ere
Night fell I heard, or seemed to hear
Music that sorrow comes not near
  A ritual hymn,
Chaunted in love that casts out fear
  By Seraphim.

WORDSWORTH

Preface

I

TO DO FULL JUSTICE to an artist who stated and lived by the principle that "life and art are indivisible," but who also made it "his inexorable law never to publish anything . . . concerning his own work," requires certain deviations from the orthodox biographical procedure. For one thing, any serious evaluation of the composer Mendelssohn must respect the unity of life and work. Thus, it became the author's task to interweave the historic-biographical facts with the discussion of musical compositions. To elucidate this interaction properly, it was necessary to confront the musical compositions with the original and personal documents of Mendelssohn's life. But such a confrontation had never previously been attempted.

This book, then, was born out of want: the want of accessible documents and testimonies concerning the life and art of Mendelssohn. In a few earlier prolegomena* I have drawn attention to the fact that all previous evaluations of the composer rest upon a number of "censored" and inaccurate

---

* "Two Unpublished Mendelssohn Concertos," *Music and Letters* (April, 1955).
"New Light on the Mendelssohn Family," *Hebrew Union College Annual* (1955).
"Mendelssohn Sources," *Notes* (March, 1955), XII.
"Mendelssohn's Fame and Tragedy," *Reconstructionis* (New York, 1959), XXV, 1.
"Mendelssohn Bartholdy," *Musik in Geschichte und Gegenwart.*
"The Family Letters of Felix Mendelssohn Bartholdy," Bulletin of the New York Public Library (January, 1961).

excerpts from his correspondence. Hence, they are based on faulty premises. Moreover, about 200 hitherto unpublished compositions of the master, which are deposited in the Berlin State Library (East Germany), have remained virtually unknown. This is the cause of an even wider gap in our knowledge. Under present conditions, these works are almost inaccessible to serious study. Rudolf Werner is the only one who has the merit of having examined some of these unpublished works in his excellent study *Felix Mendelssohn Bartholdy als Kirchenmusiker* (Frankfurt, 1932). The general lack of concern with the sources has resulted in a sad state of affairs: no standard biography of Mendelssohn has yet been written.

The published literature on Mendelssohn suffers from another shortcoming: its dependence on the vacillations of musical fashion. First came the Wagner fever; then, after it had abated, there followed the schools of Impressionism, of Neoclassicism, of Expressionism, and of dodecaphony. None of these trends—may we call them styles?—can justly claim Mendelssohn as its ancestor. For he was neither an innovator, a creator of a special style, nor a composer who adhered to a specific school. He happened to be an artist *sui generis*, a champion of old traditions rather than a sower of new seeds. While some of his compositions may still be popular, in our era, "rerum novarum cupida," he is decidedly not fashionable. Until about ten years ago, posterity did not view his name with favor. The reasons for this indifference may be traced mainly to socio-historical developments and radical shifts of musical taste. Compared with these, the infamous banishment of Mendelssohn by the Third Reich and its campfollowers played only a minor part. True, their stupidly insolent defamation of his name and work distorted his image—but equal harm had been done by the uncritical adulation during a part of the nineteenth century.

II

In this book, I have endeavored to present Mendelssohn as one of the focal points of nineteenth-century music. Upon him, many apparently disparate trends converge. Considering the wide scope of his interests, I felt obliged to take into consideration the political, cultural, and social environment of his age. Out of this integration, but especially out of hitherto unpublished documents and compositions, a new image of the man and artist inevitably emerged. Only in the general contour does this new image coincide with the traditional one!

Such a new image may not easily be accepted. Too many preconceived notions and catchwords—those jailers of new ideas—block our view. Foremost in this phalanx we encounter old (though by no means venerable) slogans such as "romantic," "progressive," "original," "reactionary," and the like. Examined critically, i.e., historically or phenomenologically, they prove to be so many vague conventions and popular clichés, born of mental inertia and false traditions. Most dubious seems to me the application of the term "Romanticism" and its derivatives to musical history. It was borrowed from the history of literature, where it has a definite meaning. In music it has, though never clearly defined, served five generations as a convenient label. However, we do not take exception to the undefined term "Romantic" in the history of music because of the ontological delusion that things which are inaccessible to exact definition therefore have no demonstrable existence. Friedrich Schlegel's dictum "Romantic poetry is a progressive and universalistic poetry" is not so much a definition as a postulate. In this and similar maxims (see his *Zentralfragment*) he claimed that Romantic poetry was the final and definite synthesis of all previous trends. He also expressed this idea poetically:

> Der Bildung Strahlen all in eins zu fassen,
> Vom Kranken ganz zu scheiden das Gesunde,
> Bestrebten wir uns treu im freien Bunde.

> To concentrate all of civilization's rays on one point,
> to divide the sound from the unsound
> we loyally strove in free association.

This "older" Romantic school consisted of a group of highly erudite authors who first tried their hands at critical and esthetic speculations about literature, and only later endeavored to realize their theories creatively in artistic forms and expressions. The main principles of this program were acceptable even to the latest writers of that school. In music, such statements were never made, and would, in any case, not have been valid. Hence, we are disinclined to use the term and concept of "Romanticism" in music, for it is derived from another art. There, it is well defined; in music history it is vague and debatable, and, worse yet, is used to describe diametrically opposed manifestations. How can one possibly consider both men of the pairs: Mendelssohn—Berlioz; Schumann—Bruckner; Liszt—Brahms, as champions of the same musical movement? Even if the term "Romantic" were limited to the German composers alone, it would have to cover too many inconsistencies. While, admittedly, poets such as Novalis and R. Wagner may, *mutatis mutandis*, be viewed as adherents of Schlegel's program, in music extremes such as Weber and Hugo Wolf cannot, and must not, be coupled under the heading of "Romantics," just for convenience's sake.

For this reason, I have abstained from an inevitably sterile discussion of the musical representations and conceptions of Romanticism. However, as this foreword is of a somewhat programmatic nature, the following observations may not be amiss.

From the critical writings of A. W. Schlegel, we single out five theses or postulates:

1. "The character of ancient poetry has been designated as classic, that of modern poetry as Romantic."

2. "We understand that the individual entity grows out of the general by limitation and antithesis. In art, which should be considered a general entity, valid for all men, the intrusion of individual and subjective elements would be of limiting and negative character. Abstention from this would be of positive value, for it would make possible the expansion of art in its true scope."

In other words, art is an entity valid for all men. Therefore, subjective and individualistic elements should be limited to a minimum, for they tend to limit or even to negate the universalistic nature of art.

3. Mannerisms constitute an undesirable intrusion of the author's life and individual characteristics into the conception of a work of art.

4. "In order properly to distinguish between the spirit of modern art and that of ancient or classic art, certain thinkers invented the designation "Romantic." It represents an amalgamation of Nordic elements with rudiments of antiquity, whereas the thinking and creation of antiquity was much more of a piece. . . . This opinion, only sketched here, would be much more convincing if it could be shown that the same contrast between the intentions of the ancient and the modern cultures permeates all types of artistic expression—if, in other words, the same contrast could be demonstrated in all arts, such as architecture, music, and poetry. This has yet to be done."

5. "What would be the task of such esthetics? It would have to demonstrate the autonomy of the Beautiful, its essential and categorical difference and independence from the ethically Good; it would postulate the autonomy of art."

It is bewildering for us to recognize that Schlegel's "Romantic" ideas may be deduced from certain assumptions of both rationalist and idealist philosophy. This concept of Romanticism is so totally different from the general and popular idea of "romantic leanings" in music that these philosophical principles either become meaningless or simply cannot be claimed to refer to "Romantic" music. Postulates 1 to 4 can be applied with equal validity to Palestrina, Handel, Mozart, Haydn, Gluck, Couperin, and most other composers. Beethoven, however, violated postulate 3 (autobiographical elements). It is certainly applicable to Schubert, Mendelssohn, Brahms, and Bruckner, but not to Berlioz, Schumann, Wagner, Liszt, and others. Postulate

5 (autonomy of art; independence from the ethically Good) was intolerable to Mendelssohn, but also to many others, including Brahms, Bruckner, Handel, Bach, Haydn, and most other composers before 1900. Even the so-called "Nationalistic Romanticists" of the nineteenth century satisfy Schlegel's postulates only in part.

It is true that Schlegel's concept underwent a constant—or rather never-ceasing—transformation, so that little, if anything, remained valid 50 years later. Even in literature, the term "Romantic" was charged with many contradictions. In music this was even more obvious. Therefore, we shall use the term "Romantic" in a most restricted and often slightly ironical sense. As a sensible designation of musical style or history, it possesses no validity at all, except that of a "rough-and-ready" nomenclature for post-Beethovenian music in Europe up till 1900.

Our final chapter, taking up the problem at this point, will attempt to disentangle its threads.

III

One of a biographer's less enjoyable tasks is the examination and, occasionally, the debunking of the hero legend and of hero-worship. The idol of the Victorian parlor, adored by the German and English bourgeoisie alike, the ever-virtuous, angelic, sentimental Mendelssohn of our grandparents' day is a popular fiction, engendered by that once equally popular, yet very inaccurate book *The Mendelssohn Family*. The inveterate, ultra-conservative enemy of all *Zukunftsmusik* (in the sense of Wagner's cohorts) on the one hand, and the effeminate pietist and weakling, as depicted by that nondiscriminating critic G. B. Shaw, on the other—these and other similar portrayals of Mendelssohn vanish, like so many webs of fantasy, when confronted with the totality of the original sources. There remains this fact, significant in itself: even in Mendelssohn's lifetime, but especially after his early death, his image was controversial and intensely debated.

As to the scope of our presentation: we have limited ourselves mainly to Mendelssohn's own times and have not entered into a discussion of the imputations made by friend or foe concerning the good or bad impact of his music on subsequent generations. Only the last chapter attempts to summarize Mendelssohn's historical position in Western music.

Another methodological problem had to be solved where technical questions of music were under discussion. Although the author is convinced of the truth of Stravinsky's dictum, "What is technique? the whole man," he was not willing to burden the reader with a plethora of musicological jargon. Hence, he had to limit himself to two types of verbal description or interpretation of music (a *contradictio in adjectu*). Either he endeavored to present a serious *morphological* analysis, or, in the discussions of less important works, he contented himself with sketching their historical position in the development of musical form during the eighteenth and nineteenth centuries. In this way, he hopes to have navigated safely between the Scylla of program-note style and the Charybdis of pseudopsychological "associative" criticism, now unfortunately much in fashion. In particular, he has abstained from projecting "messages" into instrumental music.

Problems of musical esthetics were touched upon only in passing; they deserve and demand special studies. The same attitude was taken regarding the still controversial question of the personal and artistic relationship between Wagner and Mendelssohn. We have contributed some authentic material, hitherto unknown, to this old debate, but are still unable to unfold it *in extenso*, as long as the archives of Bayreuth remain inaccessible to the serious musicologist.

On the other hand, the insight into the entire correspondence of the Mendelssohn family and its friends, granted to the author, enabled him to shed new light on the fundamental dilemma of Mendelssohn in his position with respect to Judaism, Jewry, Christianity, and German patriotism. The turbulence of the composer's innermost thinking and feeling on these matters seems to explain a good deal of his posthumous fate.

IV

I feel the deep urge to thank the many helpers whose assistance made this book possible. For the invaluable permission to study and examine the family letters of Mendelssohn in the original,* the author is deeply indebted to the late Professor Joachim Wach and his gracious sister Mme Susi Heigl-Wach; also to Miss Margaret Deneke, M. A., Oxford, and the librarians of the Bodleian Library; and to Messrs. Hugo von Mendelssohn Bartholdy and Max F. Schneider, of the Mendelssohn Society, Basel. They have granted me their unstinted help in every possible way. Most of the illustrations were provided by their kind cooperation. In particular, I wish to express my deep gratitude to Mr. Max F. Schneider, Basel, for his invaluable and always faithful help. Most recently, the collection of Geheimrat Hensel of Erlangen has come to light, but was not accessible to the author. The reasons for its long and hidden slumber are not fully clear.

I am most grateful to Prof. Felix Gilbert, another great-grandson of the composer, for valuable genealogical information; to the Library of Congress, Washington, D. C., and to my friends in it, especially the late Richard Hill, Mr. Bill Lichtenwanger, and Dr. Donald Mintz; to the librarians of the

---

* Now in the possession of the New York Public Library.

New York Public Library, especially Messrs. Miller and Beck; to the officers of the Berlin *Staatsbibliothek;* to Hofrat Prof. Dr. L. Nowak of the Austrian National Library, Prof. Dr. F. Racek of the Vienna City Library, and Mrs. Hedwig Mitringer, Ph.D., of the *Gesellschaft der Musikfreunde,* for their faithful assistance; also to F. W. Riedel, Kassel.

For the final shape of the book I owe deep gratitude to my faithful translator Professor Dika Newlin, to my late friend Eric Blom, C.O.B.E., and to Messrs. Nathan Broder, New York City, and Fred Yeiser, Cincinnati. To Messrs. N. Polsky and F. Freedman, New York City, I am obliged for their encouragement; and to Mr. Edward McLeroy for his editorial work. To my beloved friend, the late Professor Israel Bettan, Cincinnati, I owe many deep insights into the personality of Mendelssohn.

I am obliged to Professor F. Blume and the *Bärenreiter-Verlag*, Kassel, for their permission to quote from my own article "Mendelssohn" in *Musik in Geschichte und Gegenwart.* Also to Professor Orazio Frugoni for his kind permission to peruse the unpublished score of a double concerto by Mendelssohn.

I mention as the last of the list, but the dearest to my heart, my wife Elizabeth, née Mendelssohn, who has helped me with the delicate and fatiguing problems of sifting the rich material with her fine judgment of the milieu, and with the making of the index with patience and love.

E.W.

Venice, 1962

Contents

CHAPTER I *The Ancestors:*
Scholars and Bankers

Daja: He is much esteemed
By all his nation—honoured as a prince—
And yet to hear how he is named by all
Nathan *the Wise*, and not *the Rich*, seems strange.
It often makes me wonder.

Templar: But to them
It may be, *wise* and *rich*—both mean the same.

Daja: It seems to me he should be called *the good*,
So rich a store of goodness dwells in him.

Lessing, *Nathan der Weise* (tr. R. Dillon Boylan)

WHEN a genealogist examines the ancestry of some noble families of Germany or Austria, he will in numerous instances encounter several strange, exotic sounding names, which, on closer scrutiny, turn out to be Hebrew or Jewish. Most of their bearers lived at the end of the eighteenth or the beginning of the nineteenth century. They were usually rich fathers of pretty daughters. An analogous pattern holds true for the patrician intelligentsia of Central Europe; there the Hebrew ancestors were often themselves scholars.

Indeed, during the turbulent history of the German-Jewish symbiosis, the period between 1750 and 1815 witnessed a number of breakthroughs from the legalized ghetto-status of Jewry into German society, before the stone walls of segregation had crumbled. Only two categories of Jews managed to overcome the social and legal barriers which their origin imposed upon them: high financiers and outstanding scholars.

The banker sought his way to the court and the high nobility, thereby following a modernized course of the medieval court-Jew. The scholar had to establish contact with the representatives of contemporary thought in philosophy and science, who, at the time of flourishing rationalism, were

[*1*]

not antagonistic to a more liberal attitude towards the Jewish intelligentsia.

In those days, the Jewish bankers and scholars were often friends and considered themselves to be on the same social level. It was quite natural that their children intermarried. We know of such unions; among their offspring there were frequently persons of great gifts, and the first Jewish representatives in Western science and art. Poets like Heine, mathematicians like C. G. Jacobi, both pioneers in their domains, demonstrated that European Jewry was able and willing to contribute to Western civilization, if the Europeans but permitted it.

The best-known case of such a union of bankers and scholars is that of the Mendelssohn family. It is due to the stature and accomplishments of Moses Mendelssohn and his grandson Felix that the name has acquired international fame. As the grandfather's humanistic spirit remained ever alive for the grandson, we should draw a brief sketch of the life and the main ideas of that remarkable man.

In 1743, the fourteen-year-old hunchbacked and stammering Moses wandered from his native town Dessau to Berlin, like many of his brethren. There he hoped to continue his rabbinical studies with his former teacher, Rabbi Fränkel. He was obliged to work hard in many menial jobs in order to support himself, for his father, a humble scribe, was extremely poor. Moses, handicapped by his physical infirmities and his poverty, and, most of all, by being Jewish, triumphantly overcame all the obstacles in the end. A voracious reader and student, he managed to learn French, English, Latin, and Greek all within five years. Since he could, or would, not give all of his time to earning his livelihood, he had a severely limited income. In later life he recalled how often he had to mark off a loaf of bread into six parts with a pencil, one for every day except the Sabbath. After seven years of privation, better times arrived for him. He became first a tutor, then a bookkeeper, and eventually a partner of a Jewish silk manufacturer. Meanwhile he had attained proficiency in mathematics, philosophy, and literature. It was over a game of chess that he was introduced to the poet Lessing, and their acquaintance soon ripened into one of the immortal friendships of the age. It is not necessary to discuss this phase here, since its results have made history. Lessing's drama *Nathan the Wise*, dedicated to Moses Mendelssohn, personified him in an unforgettable way. At the same time it propagated Lessing's as well as Mendelssohn's ideas on religious tolerance.

As an author, Mendelssohn cultivated the fields of theology, philosophy, and literature. He even tried his hand at a little treatise on the physical and mathematical foundation of music. Moses Mendelssohn's most important contributions lay in his ideas about religion in general, and the Jewish religion in particular. Child as well as champion of eighteenth-century rationalism, he was prone to be "led into the error of confusing religion and philosophy, as if both resulted from pure reason."[1] His religious thinking, however, is highly original and has been well described in these words: "Religion . . . was concentrated in eternal truths, which one cannot be commanded to believe since one must necessarily believe them from proof by reason."[2] Concerning Judaism, he maintained that it was fundamentally no religion at all. It has no dogmas. Rather, it is to be considered a "revealed legislation." At a given time God made His voice heard and gave Israel specific commandments. For Mendelssohn, all great monotheistic religions were emanations of the one eternal truth, however different their respective doctrines and rituals appear to be.

Notwithstanding this universalism, he was most articulate in his concern to preserve the status of the Jewish faith inviolate. In his *Jerusalem* he advised his brethren in solemn words: "Even today the House of Jacob can follow no better counsel than this: Comply with the customs of your country . . . but remain constant to the religion of your forefathers. Bear both burdens to the best of your ability! Hold out and persevere, stand unshakably on the place assigned to you by Providence, and suffer everything, as was predicted long ago by your lawgiver. . . ."[3] (The philosopher Kant saw in this book the proclamation of a great reform of the Jews, which ultimately would spread to other religions as well.)

To act in accordance with the ethical commandments of Judaism was, for Mendelssohn, identical with believing in its entire *doctrinal* tradition. To promulgate this unheard-of thesis among Jews and Christians alike, he set out to translate parts of the Hebrew Bible into German. This experiment was to fulfill a threefold purpose: to educate his coreligionists in the proper use of the German language, to bring up his children in the spirit he deemed the only desirable one, and to prove his thesis to the learned Christians, who were at that time not unwilling to overcome their age-old prejudices. In the preface he made special reference to his children, who were to be "instructed in the *Torah* and to be taught the word of God. . . ."

Most of his works in the realm of pure philosophy are forgotten today, except *Phaedon*, a treatise on the immorality of the soul. This classical work was translated into more than 30 languages. Somehow related to his philosophical works are his contributions to literary criticism. Gotthold Lessing, Friedrich Nicolai, and Moses Mendelssohn comprised the team that edited the *Briefe, die neueste Literatur betreffend* (*Letters about New Literature*, 1759-60). This work, which attacked the unduly strong French influence, cleared the air like a thunderstorm and laid the foundation for the subsequent phenomenal development of German classical literature.

Moses' ideas are somewhat misrepresented in *The Mendelssohn Family*, a book by his great-grandson Sebastian Hensel. Moses was no German nationalist, as Hensel makes him appear, but a good European and a faithful Jew. How susceptible the hunchback from the Dessau ghetto was to all ideas which were "in the air"! During the time of the American Revolution, he wrote a programmatical foreword to an older rabbinic work, using the Revolution as a pretext to set forth his ideas on the separation between Church and State.

His interest in philosophy and literature did not stop at the borders of Prussia. His controversies with the Swiss Lavater, the Frenchman Bonnet, his discussions of Pope and Rousseau, no less than his friendship with Lessing and Wieland, testify to the supranational scope of his thinking. In a widely known monograph, Mendelssohn discussed and championed the legal emancipation of European Jewry scientifically and with great moral fervor. Its results were of historical dimensions.

In consequence of Mendelssohn's championship of the equality of Jews, aimed at all of Europe, the Abbé Grégoire, when introducing the bill for equality of the French Jews, expressly referred to Mendelssohn and his program. This happened four years after Moses' death in 1786. Mirabeau, also an admirer of the Berlin sage, seconded Grégoire's plea in the *Assemblée Constituante*.

As a person, Mendelssohn must have been of irresistible charm. Innumerable anecdotes are told of his ability to turn an adversary into a friend. Two of the best-known stories will suffice to sketch the portrait of the "Jewish Socrates," as he was called by his contemporaries.

When he was summoned by Frederick II (the Great) because of his unfavorable critique of the monarch's poems, he defended himself in the following manner: "Sire, he who publishes poems is like a fellow who enjoys bowling; and whoever does bowl must suffer the criticism of the boy who sets up the pins."

He hoped to win his friend Gugenheim's daughter as his wife. Yet he had no illusions about his chances. For, when the girl met him, she was so shocked by his appearance that she would hardly look at him. Yet Mendelssohn did not lose his courage. He went up to her room and chatted with her; and—skillful dialectician that he was—he managed to guide the conversation to the question of the predestination of marriages. The girl asked: "Do you also believe that all marriages are destined in heaven?" "Certainly," he replied; "and in my case something special occurred. When a child is born, they proclaim in the heavens: 'this boy gets that girl.' When I was born, my wife was named too, but it was added: 'Alas, she will have a horrible hunchback.' Then I said: 'Dear God, a hunchbacked girl will probably be embittered and grim; a girl ought to be lovely. Dear God, please give *me* the hunchback and let *her* be straight, slim, and pretty!'" Hardly had he finished when the girl embraced him—and it became a most happy marriage.

The death of his beloved friend Lessing was a blow to Mendelssohn from which he never fully recovered. In his last publication, he reaffirmed his fundamental beliefs:

I, on my part, remain in my Jewish disbelief . . . and should not even depend upon an archangel's authority, when it comes to issues of eternal truths. On these, man's happiness eventually rests, and therefore I must, in those questions, stand upon my own feet . . . rather, I, too, return to the faith of my fathers, which according to that word's original meaning consists not in belief of doctrine or dogma, but of trust and confidence in the attributes of the Almighty. I trust absolutely in God's omnipotence, that it *could* grant to man the power of knowing the truths on which his happiness rests, *without intermediate authority.* . . . (*An die Freunde Lessings,* 1786.)

Shortly after writing this credo, he died unexpectedly of a cerebral hemorrhage. Many of his descendants inherited this disposition to a sudden, painless death. He was fifty-seven years old when he died in 1786.

While an entire generation intervened between Moses' death and Felix's birth, and tremendous changes had been caused by world-shaking events during those thirty-three years, in one respect the gulf between the two generations was bridged. For Moses was a humanist; this line of thinking was ever prevalent in Felix's mind, even in his art. Humanism stands for evolution, not for revolution. It breeds tradition and prides itself on preserving old heritages. It is certainly no coincidence that Felix pleased Goethe so much, and, in turn, that Goethe, the humanist, remained one of the lodestars of his life and art. In spite of the grandson's adherence to Christianity, the grandfather's spiritual legacy enriched all of Felix's life.

Of Moses' six children, some followed faithfully his doctrine of "a religion of reason"; not so the daughters Dorothea and Henriette (Jette). The former toyed with literature, became the mistress, later the wife of the poet and writer Friedrich Schlegel, changed her religion twice, and eventually joined the Catholic Church with her husband. Jette, a spinster by choice, led the life of a headmistress of a finishing school for *jeunes filles* of the best society in Paris. She, too, was well known in French and German literary circles. Benjamin Constant, the Humboldts, Madame de Stael, and other famous persons of the era were among her friends. Originally "she recognized reason solely and refused all other sources of guidance. Her love of her sister Dorothea was seriously disturbed because of the latter's conversion to Catholicism."[4] Not much later, though, she became converted herself and found her peace in the Catholic Church. Her life may be called a pathetic tragi-comedy, since she vacillated between French and German ideals, between pride in her father and the newly won sodality of the Catholic Church. Yet, in spite of these peculiarities, she was a woman of great intelligence and of remarkable strength of character.

Felix's father, Abraham, was Moses' second son. He was only ten years old when his father died, and was brought up by his mother. He did not have much of a formal education, but his older brother Joseph and his sister Dorothea shared with him a good deal of their learning. Of keen intellect and considerable address in all matters literary and philosophical, he attained relatively early a high level of education. In his twenty-first year he obtained the post of a minor clerk in the banking house of Fould and Co., in Paris. His departure from Berlin was deplored by a society whose member he was and whose name tells more than a whole treatise: *Gesellschaft der Freunde,* a charitable organization for the advancement of the good and noble. This organization was founded by the disciples of Moses Mendelssohn, and its president was, until his death, Moses Mendelssohn's friend Daniel Itzig, a rich banker. It continued until Hitler dissolved it.

On Abraham Mendelssohn's journey to Paris [in 1797] he passed through Frankfurt, where he made the acquaintance of Goethe, then minister of state of Saxe-Weimar. When Goethe learned that Abraham had passed through Jena, where he had taken music by Karl Friedrich Zelter to the poet Schiller, he became very interested in his visitor. "Are you one of Mendelssohn's sons?" he asked. Abraham thanked him for this wording of the question. "It is the first time that I hear my late father's name without an explanatory word or phrase; this is the way I always desired it," he replied modestly.

Goethe invited the young man to his house and inquired about Zelter, his personality and activities, in which he displayed a lively interest. He spoke with great esteem about Zelter's compositions of his own poems. Abraham had to explain to Goethe that he had known Zelter for years; they had met frequently at the house of a highly accomplished, very musical Jewish lady, to whom Zelter was devoted, Mme Sara Levy.

In a subsequent letter to Zelter, Abraham gave a vivid description of the interview and suggested that he take a trip to Jena and Weimar.[5] That meeting inaugurated the intimate connection between Goethe and Zelter, Goethe's longest and closest friendship. It made literary and musical history and ended with the death of both men in 1832. Abraham was, according to his letter, the catalytic agent between the two men.

Those who knew Abraham well in his later years describe him as a warmhearted, highly intelligent man, who loved sharp discussions; he did an enormous amount of charitable work. Eduard Devrient, a close friend of Felix, portrays Abraham as a man of exceedingly clear thought, who, indifferent to established religions, "had discovered the Divine as the highest result of philosophical reasoning."[6] Devrient also maintains that Felix inherited two characteristic traits from his father; his conviction that human life imposes the duty of achievement and incessant striving for usefulness, and his irritability and inclination to quarrel. Abraham's patriarchal and often despotic attitude towards his family was generally known, but it was known too that it was a truly fatherly love which occasionally concealed itself behind the mask of severity. It was also compensated for by Abraham's alert sense of humor.

While Abraham did not have any systematic musical training, he was keenly interested in opera. He recalled with great gusto his presence at the première of Cherubini's *Water-Carrier* and his subsequent interview with the composer, whom he greatly admired.[7] In general, he was more interested in vocal music than in instrumental music; the latter he considered "his wife's department."

While, in his emotional reactions, he was somewhat inclined to clannishness, his thinking was definitely supranational and European in the best sense. He left to Felix the choice as to where to settle permanently, and did not exhibit any special preference for Germany.[8] To a certain extent he sympathized with the French Revolution of July, 1830, which he witnessed in Paris.

In general, Abraham was more than just the "hyphen between his father and his son." In the realm of philosophical thought as well as in the efficient conduct of his business and his family's affairs he was superior to Felix. True, he lacked artistic creativeness; but his firm will, his absolute integrity, his insight and clarity show him a most worthy son of his great father.

Thus far we have contemplated only the philosopher and his children, the paternal side of the composer's ancestors. Yet the maternal ancestry is no less interesting. The peculiar situation of German Jewry just before the dawn of emancipation was characterized by the fact that the few families who had attained a somewhat higher social status knew each other and were frequently related to each other, if not by common ancestors, by marriage. In the case of the Mendelssohn family, both kinds of relationship coincided. For Abraham Mendelssohn's wife was Lea Salomon, the granddaughter of Daniel Itzig, the financial backer of King Frederick II.

This Daniel Itzig (1722-1799) and his wife Miriam (nee Wulff) had sixteen children. According to the prevailing custom, the sons entered the father's business, while the daughters were married either into high financial circles, to rabbinic scholars, or to the Gentile nobility. The male descendants of Itzig assumed, after their father's death, the name Hitzig. One of the daughters, Fanny, married Nathan Adam Arnstein, again a court-Jew, who, some years later, was made a baron by Emperor Francis II. Her sister Caecilia (Zippora) married his partner, the Baron Eskeles.

The Mendelssohn and Itzig families were distinguished long before the eighteenth century. Both are direct descendants of the famous philosopher and glossator, Rabbi Moses Isserles (Cracow, 1520-1572).[9] In addition, they became related to the families Heine, Ephraim, Oppenheimer, Beer, Meyerbeer, the Counts Wimpffen, Széchenyi, and Fries, and the Barons Pereira and Pirquet, to name only a few.

All of Itzig's daughters were handsome and gifted. Music and literature especially were cultivated in his house, as we know from many a description. The family made a "cult of Sebastian and Philipp Emanuel Bach's music," as we hear from the contemporary writer Hennings. This was almost fifty years before Sebastian Bach's music was so momentously revived by Felix Mendelssohn in that memorable performance of the *St. Matthew Passion* in 1829. Indeed, in the lists of subscribers to works of the Bachs at least four of the Itzigs appear unfailingly.

The most colorful, and certainly the most gifted, of Itzig's womenfolk was Zorel (Sara), born 1763, who in 1783 married the banker Samuel ben Salomon Levy *Chalfan* ("money-changer"). Seen against the weird background of a Jewry of which half prayed for emancipation and half despaired of it, fleeing into Christianity, Sara Levy appears as a person of strong character and unusual accomplishments.

She had received an excellent French education and was well versed in French literature, so that Napoleon's ambassador was a frequent guest at her home. Numerous writers described her and her evenings "at home." Here is a brief excerpt from one of them:

> In her salon the old lady [she was then eighty years old] sat, the sweet spiritualized face framed by an old-fashioned lace cap. She and her two companions were reading *A Midsummer Night's Dream* with the various roles distributed among them. Mendelssohn's composition of this drama enchanted all hearts at the time. [The author of this report, a young woman writer, obviously was not aware that Felix Mendelssohn was Sara's grand-nephew.]
>
> Her musical soirées were famous, although at that time no longer as popular as fifty years before, when she and her family championed the music of Sebastian and Philipp Emanuel Bach.
>
> She was deeply grieved by the apostasy of some of her near relatives. "I am like a tree without leaves [*Hier steh ich, ein entlaubter Stamm*, a quotation from Schiller], so many of my relatives are estranged from me by their conversion," she wrote to her friend, the famous Protestant theologian Schleiermacher, who had done his best to proselytize as many intelligent and attractive Jewesses as possible.
>
> She used to say, referring to the then general fashion of conversion: "Since the Jewish belief is, even according to Christian doctrine, the foundation upon which the whole structure of Christianity is erected, how can I be expected to break down the foundations of my house in order to live in its first floor?"[10]

She read the Old Testament regularly and with a scholar's understanding. While her close friend and distant cousin, Henriette Herz, became one of Schleiermacher's favorite proselytes, Sara remained faithful to Judaism in thought and deed. Among the many Jewish charities she sponsored, the Jewish Orphan Asylum in Berlin was her favorite. During her lifetime she donated to it the sum of 20,000 Thaler (today equivalent to more than $150,000).

In her youth this extraordinary woman had been Wilhelm Friedemann Bach's favorite pupil as well as his warm-hearted patroness. After Philipp Emanuel's death, she supported his widow and had a bust of the master made, which, many years later, was placed in the concert hall of the Royal *Schauspielhaus* in Berlin. Her keen interest in the music of the Bach family brought her into contact with Karl Friedrich Zelter, conductor of the Berlin *Singakademie* and later the teacher of Felix Mendelssohn. It seems that it was she who recommended Zelter for the post of the boy's teacher to his mother, her niece Lea. Zelter must have esteemed her for her musicianship, for we find her as harpsichord soloist of the *Singakademie* from 1806 to 1808, occasionally performing in the concerts of that ultraconservative organization. She was certainly among its first instrumental soloists, if not the very first. She remained always on excellent terms with that institution and donated to it her famous musical library.[11]

While the early correspondence of the Mendelssohn family contains frequent references to her and her house, her name fades after 1822; possibly the proud old lady withdrew from her relatives after their conversions. Nevertheless, Felix's sister Fanny attended the first performance of her brother's *Midsummer Night's Dream* in the company of "Tante Levy," together with Professor Steffens, President of the Berlin University. On another occasion, her younger sister Rebecca compared Tante Levy with the last duchess of the Medici: surrounded by frescoes, beauty, and "profound spirit." Sara Levy survived almost all her close relatives, including Felix Mendelssohn. She died childless, in 1854, ninety-one years of age.

Her sister Babette (Bella) Itzig (1749-1824) married the court jeweller Levi Salomon. Their two children, Jacob Salomon Bartholdy and Lea (Lilla, as she was called) were prototypes of those German Jews who desired to be assimilated and absorbed by German society *at any price*. The brother had adopted the name Bartholdy after his conversion to the Protestant Church. Originally, the name belonged to a long-forgotten former owner of a large garden in Bartholdy's possession, which—in spite of the latter's official Lutheran faith—continued to be called the "Jew's garden" by the Berliners.

Brother and sister were well-read and, in the small circle of Berlin's financial Jewry, also well-liked. Lea became an intimate friend of Henriette Mendelssohn, Abraham's sister, and it seems that it was Henriette who played the role of the matchmaker. For, while Abraham liked Lea well enough, he was reluctant to live in Germany, where he, as a Jew, could not enjoy legal equality. He desired that his bride should live with him in Paris, where he held a good position in a banking house. Yet Lea's mother would not hear of her marrying "a clerk" who did not even live in Prussia. At this point, Henriette intervened and wrote to her brother:

I need not tell you how heartily I join in your hopes of a happy result [of Abraham's negotiations], but I must confess that it appears to me nearly impossible that you will succeed under your conditions. And yet, dear brother, this marriage would be the greatest blessing to you in every respect, and I cannot but implore you not to be too hasty, and not to sacrifice too much to your position, which at present may be far from unfavorable, but may become so in the future. . . .

I hope to read in your next letter that you have had a talk with Lilla, and the oftener you speak to her, the more you will observe how unlikely, perhaps impossible it will be that you find another woman like her. Hence I do not approve of your dislike of Berlin having so great an influence upon this most important decision. . . .[12] (See genealogy, preceding p. 299.)

Not only from a financial point of view was Lea a most desirable match for Abraham, but she had had an excellent education. She spoke and read French fluently, was familiar with English literature, and could even read Homer in the original Greek—an unheard-of accomplishment for a Jewish girl of her time. She was a good pianist and had studied with old Kirnberger. She was described as "not beautiful, but most attractive, on account of her sylph-like figure, her sparkling black eyes, and her spirited, intelligent conversation, which never exceeded the boundaries of good taste and refined manners."[13] Her charm was generally praised; it pervades most of her many letters. The "sylph-like figure," however, seems to be a slightly mythical description of her real appearance. For her husband wrote to his daughter Fanny many years later: "Never you mind your plumpness; it constitutes a resemblance with your dear mother. . . . As a young girl she, too, was pretty stout, and will, as I hope, become plump again."[14]

In many respects Lea deserves our interest and our sympathy: for her sparkling, sometimes a little malicious wit, her warm motherly love, her firm rule over her family, her fine musical judgment, even for her weakness. She loved to make acquaintances with aristocratic names (in contradistinction to her republican-minded husband), and was something of a snob. Yet her innate grace conquered even her severest critics. As an intelligent tender mother, she demanded and obtained full respect from her children who adored her.

Thus the philosopher's son had married (in 1804) the daughter and granddaughter of merchants and bankers. From the very outset the young couple was confronted with a burning problem which then concerned most European Jews. Should they, like the many others, wait for the slow, legal fight to attain their aspiration—equality of the Jews? Was such a democratic and general emancipation to be expected in the foreseeable future? Or should they seek their individual release from their despised status by conversion to Christianity? There is no doubt that Lea favored the latter alternative, while her husband was much more reluctant in this question.

It is noteworthy that just at the threshold of the nineteenth century, when decisions of the gravest historical weight had to be made by European Jews, the intellectual initiative was adopted by women, at least in politics and literature. Enlightenment and revolution had undermined the ancient Jewish faith, depriving it of its two splendors: the martyr's glory and the great Messianic hope that had comforted the Jews through many bitter centuries. Now the community seemed to be torn to pieces by centrifugal forces of unheard-of intensity, which alienated the entire Jewish bourgeoisie from its former traditional tenets. Under such circumstances women like Dorothea Mendelssohn Schlegel, Rahel Levin Varnhagen, Henriette Herz, and Lea Salomon Mendelssohn, to name only a few of them, took drastic action themselves, or at least urged their husbands to take it. In the salons they established and held together, enlightened Jew and enlightened Gentile met as peers, nothwithstanding the tremendous gulf between their respective legal positions.

These were anomalous indeed, and demoralizing to the Jews. Thus it could happen that a faithful Jew such as Nathan Arnstein was made a hereditary baron and still was prohibited *by law* to own a house in Vienna;[15] or that the wife of Hofrat Dr. Herz, a physician and disciple of Kant and Moses Mendelssohn, entertained in her house the elite of Prussian society from royalty down, while her husband was still somewhat restricted in his professional activities. This precedence of social equality before legal equality created, as it were, a hothouse atmosphere in the Jewish salons of Berlin and Vienna.

For the time being, no radical decision was possible for Abraham, even if he had considered it. For both Lea's parents and his own mother would have disowned their children had they abandoned the faith of their fathers. All decisions were held in abeyance until, in 1819, a series of events overcame all hesitation.

Notes

1. Kaufmann Kohler, *Jewish Theology* (Cincinnati, 1943), p. 30.
2. Max Margolis and Alexander Marx, *History of the Jewish People* (Philadelphia, 1927), p. 598.
3. Moses Mendelssohn, *Jerusalem* (Berlin, 1783).
4. M. Kayserling, *Die jüdischen Frauen* (Leipzig, 1879), p. 198.
5. The letter, dated Metz, September 1, 1797 is reproduced in the *Jahrbücher der Sammlung Kippenberg* (Leipzig, 1926), Vol. IV.
6. E. Devrient, *Erinnerungen an Felix Mendelssohn* (Leipzig, 1891), p. 10.
7. A. B. Marx, *Erinnerungen* (Berlin, 1865), II, p. 115ff.
8. *Felix Mendelssohn Bartholdy Letters, 1821-1847* (hereafter *F.M.B. Letters*), ed.

Paul and Karl Mendelssohn Bartholdy (Leipzig, 1861), I, letter of February 21, 1832; also the published letters from Milan.

9. Moses, Abraham, and Felix Mendelssohn took pride in this ancestor and cherished his memory.

10. N. Remy, *Das jüdische Weib* (Berlin 1892); also Kayserling, *op. cit.*, pp. 228-29.

11. G. Schünemann, *Die Bachpflege der Berliner Singakademie* (in *Bach-Jahrbuch*, 1928), p. 144; also E. F. Schmidt, *C. Ph. E. Bach und seine Kammermusik* (Kassel, 1930-32), pp. 41-53.

12. S. Hensel, *The Mendelssohn Family*, tr. Carl Klingemann, Jr. (London, 1882), I, p. 78.

13. G. Merkel, *Erinnerungen an Lea Mendelssohn* (unpublished MS).

14. Hensel, *Familie Mendelssohn* (hereafter *F. M.*), 17th ed. (Berlin, 1921), p. 109, letter of July 2, 1819. (Throughout the book most references to Hensel have been taken from this edition, and the first one in three vols. of 1879.)

15. Hilde Spiel, *Fanny Arnstein* (Berlin, 1962), pp. 235ff.

CHAPTER II

Felix's Youth
(1809-1825)

> Happy boy! 'tis true, you will have only a short life, and an ephem-
> eral one, yet love, happiness, and art wove it for you out of light
> and warmth! Go on and droop, if it must be, as everything fair in
> spring. . . .
>
> (Adele Schopenhauer about the twelve-year-old Felix in Weimar,
> in her diaries.)

AFTER their marriage in 1804, Abraham and Lea settled first in Hamburg.
Their house was called "Marten's Mill," and many years later, when Abraham witnessed Felix's triumph at the Düsseldorf Festival in 1833, he wrote
to Lea: "Dear wife, we have a certain amount of joy in this young man,
and I often think: long live Marten's Mill!"

The years in Hamburg were by no means easy, and in 1811 the Mendelssohns were obliged to flee to Berlin on account of the chicaneries and loot-
ings by the French troops of occupation under Marshal Davout. It appears
that Abraham, otherwise exceedingly fond of everything French, had financially aided the coalition against Napoleon, and was sought by the
authorities.

After arriving in Berlin, they did not find conditions much easier. However, the situation improved with the wars of liberation, when Abraham
together with his elder brother Joseph established a modest banking and
import business in Berlin. The firm prospered amazingly and became one
of the leading banks of Germany. It was liquidated during the Nazi regime.

Apparently the French did not molest the Mendelssohns in Berlin: probably the friendship of the French ambassador, Count Saint Marsan, with
Mme Sara Levy, Lea's aunt, was not entirely without effect. Even when
Abraham equipped some soldiers at his own expense for the wars of liberation, he was not questioned by the French officers.

Abraham and Lea had four children: Fanny Caecilia (b. 1805), Jacob

Ludwig Felix (b. 1809), Rebecca (b. 1811), and Paul Hermann (b. 1813). The given names of the children reflect the clannishness of their parents: Fanny was named after the Baroness Fanny von Arnstein and the Baroness Caecilia *"Zippora"* von Eskeles, the favorite aunts of Lea Mendelssohn. The first two names of Felix are reminders of Lea's brother Jacob Lewin Bartholdy; Rebecca was named after her great-aunt Rebecca Veitel, nee Itzig, and Paul bore the "modified" name of his father's uncle Saul Mendelssohn.

Both parents displayed a lively interest in music. Lea, a good pianist and adherent of the Bach school, taught her children the rudiments of keyboard music, while Abraham was more interested in opera; he greatly admired Gluck and his French disciples Grétry and Cherubini.

Fanny as well as Felix exhibited a strong musical talent from early childhood. Although their musical activities were encouraged, the parents were loath to treat them as prodigies. Hence, most careful consideration was given to the children's general education. It was first supervised by their mother, and afterwards by a private tutor, Karl Wilhelm Ludwig Heyse, father of the renowned novelist Paul Heyse. Abraham advocated a well-rounded curriculum and would not tolerate onesidedness. Felix, who did not want to study Greek all by himself, persuaded his younger sister Rebecca to keep him company in this endeavor. This she did with such eagerness that even in her later life she was able to read Homer and Plato in the original.

To people who take the systems of public education for granted, such private tutoring may appear strange. Yet one hundred and fifty years ago higher education was still a prerogative of a small upper class and by no means accessible to every gifted student, let alone a Jewish boy. Private tutors were then a general and accepted institution. Nonetheless, the absence of daily companionship with other children, rich and poor, intelligent and simple, may have added to the already inherent clannishness of Mendelssohn's family life, and increased Felix's sensitivity.

According to present-day standards, the daily discipline of the children was strict to the point of severity. Idleness, in particular, was loathsome to the parents and teachers. Reading, drawing, physical exercise, music, dancing, all these activities were acceptable to them. Leisure, on the other hand, was practically nonexistent during the day. Probably this early and severe order spared the sensitive and sometimes moody Felix empty or unpleasant hours in his later life; it may have been, also, the cause of his perpetual restlessness. In general, however, the children thrived on their discipline, for they knew that it came from loving parents.

Felix and Fanny were instructed in piano by Ludwig Berger, a former disciple of Clementi and Field. He faithfully transmitted his teachers' conception of the "ideal" piano-playing to his charges. Clementi, one of the earliest champions of the modern piano, had evolved the first sound method leading to what was then considered the pinnacle of technique. Field is known as one of the creators of the *cantabile* style of the postclassic period. His nocturnes, which are still heard occasionally, exerted a powerful influence on Chopin, who continued in the lyric vein of Field. Berger thus combined the accuracy and precision of Clementi's school with the noble tone of Field's style, and opened new, if limited, vistas to the piano-obsessed Felix. The study of piano compositions by Bach, Mozart, Beethoven, and Weber was bound to expand the disciple's perspective into a respectable familiarity with the piano literature of the last fifty years. Even composers who were well-nigh forgotten at the beginning of the nineteenth century, such as Scarlatti, Frescobaldi, and the French clavecinists, were not entirely unknown to young Mendelssohn, as we know from his repertory.

Felix began to study the violin under Carl Wilhelm Henning, a respectable member of the opera orchestra, but soon decided, instead, to take lessons from his close friend Eduard Rietz. All through his life he retained the mastery of the viola, sometimes even playing it in public. When his younger brother Paul took up the 'cello, Felix learned its technique also and thus became then thoroughly familiar with the technique and style of all string instruments.

His voice, too, was properly trained. In the singing classes of the *Singakademie*, which he entered in 1819, "he took his place among the grown-ups, still wearing a boy's tight-fitting jacket, cut very low at the neck, over which the wide trousers were buttoned; into the slanting pockets of these the little fellow loved to thrust his hands, rocking his curly head (he had long brown curls) from side to side, and shifting restlessly from one foot to the other."[1] Later on, the systematic choir-singing he practiced for years in his youth enabled the mature composer to write in a most enchanting and effective choral style. Only in this way, not in classrooms, does the vocal composer gather experience, as the cases of Handel, Haydn, Mozart, Schubert, Mendelssohn, and many others show.

Of all of Felix's teachers, it was Karl Friedrich Zelter whose influence upon his pupil proved to be most important. This was not entirely due to the subjects he taught, namely harmony, counterpoint, and composition, a composer's most important disciplines. Zelter was also the strongest personality among Felix's teachers. As we have seen, Zelter was befriended by both parents and their families for many years and was certainly not picked at random by the careful Abraham as his son's musical mentor.

A more suitable tutor for a budding genius cannot be imagined. It is true that as a composer Zelter did not stand out above many of his fellow-craftsmen, but as teacher, conductor, and man of strong character he was extraordinary for his time. It was this strength and robustness that so attracted Goethe, and that to a great extent prevented Felix from becoming a pampered hothouse plant.

Zelter was the son of a mason and, for a time, a mason himself. Not having finished his studies at the *gymnasium* because of his temper and his pranks, he followed his father's trade. Yet, the music theorist Marpurg thought so highly of his talent that he recommended him as a student to Kirnberger and Fasch, the last living representatives of the Bach era. In 1800, after the death of Fasch, Zelter assumed the direction of the Berlin *Singakademie,* where he established high artistic standards, espousing chiefly the smaller works of Bach, Handel, and Graun. Not much later (1808) he founded the first *"Liedertafel,"* which had very much the character of a men's glee club. In 1809 he was appointed professor by the king of Prussia and gave lectures at the Royal Academy and the University of Berlin. Eventually he was chosen as the government's superintendent of church music, and founded in 1819 the State Institute for Church and School Music in Berlin.

An original character in every way, Zelter was wise enough not to impress upon Felix his personal style of composition. On the other hand, the less fortunate traits of Zelter's nature, especially his bluntness, which sometimes was mixed with coarseness, were neutralized for Felix by parental influence. While Zelter ridiculed Weber's *Der Freischütz,* had strong reservations about Beethoven's greatness, ignored Schubert entirely, and compared Gluck with Rossini, sometimes to the latter's advantage, he made no attempt to impose his biases upon Felix. Completely free from servility (a rare trait among Prussians), Zelter was highly respected at court, by the nobility, and in learned and musical circles. To his group of friends belonged the philosopher Hegel, Varnhagen van Ense, Schiller, and foremost of all, Goethe, who was his most intimate friend. This is not the place to speculate on the reasons for Goethe's predilection for this naïve, honest, able, but after all, mediocre artist.

This man became the supervisor of the Mendelssohn children's musical education. He imparted all his knowledge, which was of considerable profundity, to Felix. His teaching was of a standard that towered above the general level of musical education in an era whose taste left much to be desired.

It is hard to imagine two personalities so totally different from each other as Felix and Zelter. The sensitive, high-strung, and intellectual dreamer of dangerously potent imagination was held within bounds by a man who always stood with both feet on the ground, who was not too fond of romantic dreams, a man of action and responsibility, an authoritarian master. Zelter, for his part, soon recognized the immense talent of his pupil and was greatly impressed by, and extremely proud of, so remarkable a fledgling.

His correspondence with Goethe contains so much praise for Felix that the poet, after getting to know Felix personally, wrote Zelter that he envied him for having such a pupil. At the same time the wise teacher did not fail to realize the dangers of the Mendelssohns' all too carefully sheltered atmosphere.

Felix, on his part, was strongly attracted to Zelter and respected him greatly. He occasionally mimicked the blunt and informal manners of his teacher, but without malice. The scion of generations of scholars, he was always amused when listening to the dry and often coarse remarks of earth-bound Zelter. Aware of his own shortcomings, Felix always remained grateful to him, in spite of Zelter's occasionally tactless comments about Felix's own family in the correspondence with Goethe, which was published in 1833-4, after the death of both men.

About Zelter's method of teaching Felix we learn a few details from their correspondence, most of which is still unpublished.

In 1821, when he was twelve years old, Felix submitted a study to Zelter which he intended to send to his friend Rietz.

Example 1a—

Rietz had ridiculed the theme of Mozart's *Jupiter Symphony,* and Felix wanted to demonstrate to him "what could be done with such a theme." By that time Felix apparently had outgrown the elementary study of harmony, which Zelter treated in the dry manner of the "thorough-bass" theorist; but in his defense of Mozart's theme, Felix naïvely overlooked the fact that Mozart himself had amply demonstrated "what could be done with such a theme!"

Felix reported to Zelter about every organ he had the opportunity to play upon. They were usually in very bad condition and Felix gave strongly sarcastic descriptions of such instruments.

Often Felix complained when Zelter was absent and yearned for him, for "there are plenty of poor people who pine for you when they discover parallel fifths here, and false relations there." In the very same letter, of December 13, 1823, Felix gave a modest report on the first performance of his Double Concerto for two pianos and orchestra in E major; a concomitant letter from Fanny waxed enthusiastic about this work—which is still unpublished.

We are given a glance into Zelter's study in the following letter of Felix. His teacher had given him two musical riddles: two counterpoints to themes by Sebastian Bach. It was Felix's task to find and identify the themes. Here is Felix's reply with the solution:

Dobberan, July 30, 1824.

My dear Professor:

Is this the correct solution of your two lovely riddles? Many apologies for the long delay of my answer, but I did not want to write you before I could send you these notes, and the first riddle was tough indeed. The second I solved in a jiffy, and then I tried to solve the first one, and went in my mind through the fugues of Seb. Bach, which I knew, all but the correct one, because it had already been used in the second riddle. Finally I had a brainstorm and I thought I discovered the solution.[2]

Example 1b—

Example 1c—

Zelter had not made it easy for Felix. First, he had transposed the key of Bach's theme from the original B minor to A minor and B-flat minor respectively; then he had arranged the counterpoints in such a manner that one began with three quarter notes and the other with a quarter upbeat, thus leading to the belief that there were two entirely different themes to be looked for; and finally he had added the deception of basing both counterpoints upon one and the same theme.

This was by no means a dry or uninspiring method of teaching counterpoint; it would also familiarize the student with fugue themes of Bach. Many a modern teacher might be proud of such riddles, and even more so of a student who could solve them!

Zelter saw to it that Felix, even as a boy, made the acquaintance of the outstanding musicians of his day. The youngster met Carl Maria von Weber, Cherubini, Paganini, Spohr, Spontini, and scores of professional interpretive musicians. It was again Zelter who took the twelve-year-old Felix to visit the man who made a more profound impression upon him than anyone else save his own father: Goethe.

In his usual coarse way, Zelter had announced their arrival with the words: "It would be something rare [*epes rores,* in mimicked Judaeo-German] if a Jewish boy became an artist." Considering his long friendship with Abraham and the amount of money at his disposal from that source, the remark seems in poor taste indeed.[3]

It is amusing to follow in the parental letters the endless cascade of admonitions, good advice, well meant but somewhat irritating reminders to put his best foot forward. There is no doubt that the parents as well as Felix looked upon the trip to Goethe as the first great accolade bestowed by Zelter upon his pupil. In view of the strict rules of etiquette that were impressed upon the twelve-year-old boy, the relative informality displayed by the great man must have been a relief. So down-to-earth was the tone of the conversation that Zelter could define the game of whist in the succinct statement: "Whist means 'shut up'!"

For the average composer, and even for a prominent one, it was not easy to make Goethe's acquaintance beyond a purely initial stage of courtesy. According to a malicious witticism then current, a composer was only permitted at the court in Weimar when he had first "been given a haircut" by Reichardt or Zelter, Goethe's advisers on music. Not many years before Felix's visit in 1821, Schubert had written a most submissive letter to "His Excellency," enclosing a few compositions of Goethe's poems. The letter, indeed the whole package, was not even acknowledged by Goethe; the name Schubert was entirely unknown to him, for Zelter had never mentioned him. Now the situation was totally different. It was Zelter himself presenting his star pupil, who was thus assured of a hearty welcome.

From the reports by witnesses of the first visit to Weimar, we cite three in addition to Felix's own extensive letters to the family: the account by Adele Schopenhauer (the philosopher's sister) in her diaries, Rellstab's version in his memoirs, and Christian Lobe's report.[4]

The visit lasted sixteen days. All three sources describe Felix as a wild, gay lad, and at the same time as a mature artist who knew exactly what he was doing. At first Goethe, then seventy-two years old, did not take Felix too seriously. In fact, he began by teasing him. He tested the boy's abilities to the utmost, and the first days of the encounter appeared more like a stern examination than a social visit. *Prima-vista* playing of unfamiliar Bach fugues, improvising on strange tunes, playing from Mozart and Beethoven manuscripts, and performances of Felix's own compositions were the order of the day. But by and by the grand old man became very fond of the youngster, and before long Felix kissed His Excellency after each performance.

We may imagine how proud Zelter was of Felix; but his pedagogic wisdom exceeded his pride. The high point of the visit was reached when Felix, together with three professional musicians, performed his Piano Quartet Op. 1. In the boy's absence, Zelter addressed the professional musicians in memorable words:

> His ability as pianist and even more his talent for composition will probably arouse your enthusiasm. . . . Be careful with your praise! For the young fellow is not experienced enough to distinguish properly between a benevolent encouragement and a well-deserved acknowledgment. Hence, gentlemen, if you are stimulated to a hymn of praise, which I always fear and at the same time desire, then intone that hymn in moderate tempo, not too loudly orchestrated and in C major, the least colored key of all. Thus far I have protected him from vanity and conceit, those cursed enemies of every artistic development.[5]

This was indeed Zelter's obsession, and Rellstab's report confirms it. He tells us how Zelter, after a phenomenal improvisation by Felix on a theme unknown to him at that moment, simply remarked: "Well, you must have dreamed of a goblin or a dragon! That was a veritable steeplechase!" (*Das ging ja über Stock und Block!*) He affected indifference in his manner of speaking, as if Felix had done nothing remarkable at all. Doubtless he was motivated by the pedagogic intention of preventing an all too flattering triumph for the boy. Rellstab was indignant about this cavalier attitude and later discussed it with Berger, Felix's piano instructor. Berger was sharply opposed to this treament. To him it appeared unjust as well as poor pedagogy to veil the truth and to minimize his pupil's achievements.[6] To us it seems that Zelter's judgment was wiser than Berger's, for Felix did not lack encouragement or self-confidence. Indeed, Zelter aimed to counterbalance the veiled admiration that even the twelve-year-old Felix was accustomed to reaping from his sisters and friends.

Goethe's forceful personality did not fail to awe the young visitor. In letters to his family Felix gave minute reports of every word Goethe spoke; he impressed the boy much more than the Weimar court, before which he gave two recitals.

"Every morning I receive a kiss from the author of *Faust* and *Werther*, and every afternoon two more kisses from father and friend Goethe. Imagine that!"

And again: "The sound of his voice is tremendous, and he can shout like 10,000 warriors. His hair is not yet white, his gait is firm, his way of speaking mild. . . ." Zelter wanted to curtail their visit in order to go to Jena; but Felix and Adele Schopenhauer conspired against him. "We dragged the professor [Zelter] into the room, and then Goethe began with his voice of thunder to abuse Zelter for wanting to take us to that old nest, as he called it. He ordered the professor to be silent and obey without remonstration; to leave us here, go to Jena alone, and come back again." Of course, Felix was permitted to stay.

The Mendelssohn family were fully aware of the almost unprecedented honor accorded Felix in being the guest of the notoriously aloof Goethe and being treated *en famille* by the court. Considering the boy's age, however, we should perhaps hesitate to attribute too much significance to that first visit to Weimar. What could the great Goethe mean to a twelve-year-old boy, however precocious? And yet, the shadow of the giant as well as his enthusiastic approval never left Felix during his life. He saw Goethe in later years, whenever he had an opportunity, until the poet's death in 1832. These later visits may have taught him more than the first one; but that one left an indelible impression upon the boy: it was his first encounter with genius, commanding and universal.

Before the visitor's departure Adele, an artist with scissors and black paper, gave Felix two charming silhouettes. On one of them Goethe inscribed the verses:

> When up the score and down again
>   Small hobby-horses ride,
> Away o'er music's wide domain
>   Fresh pleasure you'll provide
> As you have done with love and luck.
> We all here wish you: come soon back!
>   (tr. E.W.)

In 1822 Abraham Mendelssohn, the "skilled worrier" as his wife once called him, felt in particularly good spirits. Business had been prosperous indeed, and Europe's peace was assured. He decided, after long deliberation, to take his family on an extended trip to South Germany and Switzerland. Modern men would consider this a grand vacation; yet in those times it was far from our concept of leisure. Long journeys such as this were then undertaken only when necessitated by business, or else as an important part of education. This trip to Switzerland fell into the latter category.

No wonder Abraham's sister Henriette speaks of "Abraham's caravan," for the family with its servants, tutors, and relatives numbered more than twelve persons. Their itinerary took them via Magdeburg and Göttingen to Cassel, where Louis Spohr was conductor of a renowned orchestra. Zelter had provided them with letters of introduction; Spohr received them most cordially and they played much chamber music together, including one piece by Felix. It might have been one of his piano quartets, or his String Quartet in E flat (without opus number), the MS of which is now in the British Museum. In Frankfurt they had a good time and made the acquaintance of Aloys Schmitt and of Nicolas Schelble, the conductor of the fine *Caecilien-Verein*. Schelble had just then begun to perform smaller works by J. S. Bach together with Handel's best-known oratorios. Young Ferdinand Hiller, another *Wunderkind*, was also there, and the boys became fast friends. Their friendship lasted, notwithstanding their critical views of one another, almost throughout their lives.

From Frankfurt the Mendelssohns made their way via Stuttgart, the upper Rhine valley, via Interlaken, to the St. Gotthardt pass, and then began the return journey. We have a long series of letters from both Felix and Fanny to Zelter, wherein the landscapes, the people, the customs and views are described in minute detail. Felix must have enjoyed Switzerland immensely, for he wrote that he "had fallen in love with this blessed country." Drawing and painting then formed a part of the regular curriculum of education for boys and girls; yet while Felix's sisters and brother took their lessons indifferently, occasionally practiced the craft, then neglected it, he developed it systematically. In fact, he possessed a vivid talent for drawing and painting, far above the usual dilettante's level. He drew every view most assiduously, as Fanny told Zelter. In a note to him, the thirteen-year-old boy waxed poetic viewing the great panorama: "The brightest of mornings dawned. The moon shone clear and lit up the snow-chain-Schreckhorn, Jungfrau, and Finsteraarhorn stood out clearly—no clouds in the heavens, and troops of men stormed the Kulm. The sun rose, then the snow caps blushed, while the valleys remained dark as night . . . it was wonderful. . . ." (Zürich, August 4, 1822.)

On their way home they stopped again in Frankfurt, where Felix impressed Schelble with his free improvisations, and visited Weimar again, *en famille*. Once more, Goethe could not hear enough of Felix's music. His discussions with Abraham concerned the youngster almost exclusively. The poet compared himself with Saul, whom young David (Felix) was to cheer with his music. The manliness and the dynamism of Goethe undoubtedly left their mark on Felix. For Fanny, the doting sister, observed right after their visit, and not without a sigh, that Felix's childlike face had disappeared—the long lovely curls had been cut off—and that his figure and poise showed a certain virile handsomeness.

Other trips took Abraham and Felix to Silesia, where the young pianist had a great success with his improvisations on themes of Mozart and Weber. Another time they visited Lea's old uncle Itzig in Frankfurt-on-the-Oder.

Abraham was by no means convinced that Felix's talent sufficed for a truly first-class career. For that it had to be or nothing. His letters of those years display no little doubt as to his son's potentialities. Sometimes he even believed that Felix had no real genius for music, and it might be all the better for him that he had not.[7] In this attitude Abraham was fortified by the letters of his brother-in-law Bartholdy, who strongly opposed any musical career for Felix: "The idea of a professional musician will not go down with me. It is no career, no life, no aim. . . ."[8] Since at that time the professional musician did not enjoy a high social status, and his potential goals were nothing much to be aspired to, Bartholdy was not far wrong. On the other hand, his reasoning was strongly colored by his snobbishness; Felix never forgave him this intervention and, as we shall see, tried in his own way to avenge himself on Bartholdy by minimizing his name and person even after his death.

Meanwhile, young Felix had to maintain himself against three strong men and their influences: Goethe, Zelter, and his father, and it must be considered a major achievement that he succeeded with all of them. Zelter did not esteem Weber highly and ridiculed some of his music; Felix was his fervent admirer. Goethe was strongly critical of Beethoven, the man, and his work; Felix loved his music and knew by heart almost everything he had published; he finally convinced even Goethe of Beethoven's greatness. His father, as we have just seen, did not have full confidence in the superiority of his son's musical gifts and was in doubt concerning his son's career. Fortunately, Felix found just then three close friends, all considerably older than he, who supported him and his plea before his father.

They were, in the chronological order of their appearance in Felix's life: the actor Eduard Devrient, scion of a famous dynasty of actors; Ignaz Moscheles, well-known friend of the aging Beethoven, a pianist and composer in his own right, who met Felix for the first time in 1824; and Adolf Bernhard Marx, a theorist and historian of music, whose acquaintance with the young composer dates probably from 1824 also. Of the three men Marx held by far the strongest attraction for the young composer, and became for a short span (1826-1829) Felix's closest friend and confidant. Their friendship ended in a bitter and spiteful quarrel, about which more later on. The friendship with Devrient and Moscheles, however, lasted all through Felix's life.

These three friends helped Felix staunchly to overcome Abraham's doubts and the persistent effect of Bartholdy's pernicious insinuations.

Moscheles's fight for Felix is dramatically described in his own diaries. There he says: "Felix, a boy of fifteen, is a phenomenon. What are all prodigies as compared with him? Gifted children, but nothing else. . . . Both parents are far from overrating their children's talents; in fact, they are anxious about Felix's future, and to know whether his gift will prove sufficient to lead to a noble and truly great career. Will he not, like so many other brilliant children, suddenly collapse? I asserted my conscientious conviction that Felix would ultimately become a great master, that I had not the slightest doubt of his genius; but again and again I had to insist on my opinion, before they believed me."[9]

Marx and Devrient also confirm the reluctance of the parents. Marx adds here a detail highly characteristic of Abraham's concern for Felix. The father, doubting that his son had the highest gift or genius for composition, suggested that the true genius is *ipso facto* unhappy.

Whatever Abraham's worries and doubts, he desired happiness for his Felix; as for himself, he could rely only on a definite judgment about his son's talent, uttered by a person of commanding authority. Since he knew Cherubini personally from his Parisian days and admired him greatly, he decided to leave it to that master to allay his fears and determine the matter of Felix's profession. Consequently, when family business took Abraham to Paris in 1825, Felix accompanied him.

The sixteen-year-old boy's reaction to what was then generally considered the metropolis of music was unexpected. His sharply worded criticisms in letters to his family and friends are expressed with a violence that is rare in his letters. Notwithstanding the vast difference between his and Berlioz's ideas on music in general, there are a surprising number of parallel opinions in the writings of both artists. Since he met practically every important musician, including Auber, Onslow, Rossini, Meyerbeer, Liszt, Kalkbrenner, and Hummel, all of whom he described most vividly, he certainly had ample opportunity for comparisons.

His bluntly critical attitude towards the entire musical clique in Paris, as reflected in his letters, often took the tone of an impertinent and somewhat immature music critic, true as his observations may have been. The celebrated musical salons wearied him, for they would not tolerate anything serious, and people cared only for "trivial, showy music." Fanny just could not believe that this general deprecation was justified. Whereupon Felix replied to her: "Just consider, I beseech you, are you in Paris or am I? Surely I must know more about it than you." The sad part of the story is that the situation was really as bad as the rash-tempered boy claimed. The music of the celebrated Auber, for instance, "might be capitally arranged for two flutes and a jew's-harp ad libitum." This is essentially true. Occasionally Felix overreached himself to "teach Reicha to love Beethoven and Sebastian Bach." This, of course, was sheer impudence, based upon ignorance, for Reicha had been a close friend of Beethoven's for many years and was a diligent student of Bach. It was also presumptuous, not to say insolent, to parody Cherubini's style in a (lost) *Kyrie* composition, although Zelter winked approvingly at this impish prank.[10]

As for Cherubini, he behaved like a benevolent monarch, to the amazement of all of his friends and pupils. After listening to Felix's Piano Quartet in B minor, Op. 3, which was to serve as the touchstone of Felix's talent, the austere man reacted with great politeness: "Ce garçon est riche: il fera bien; il fait même déjà bien, mais il dépense trop d'argent, il met trop d'étoffe à son habit."[11] Therewith the trial concluded and Felix was vindicated as a professional musician.

We may imagine Felix's sigh of relief after Cherubini's verdict. Nevertheless he described the old man somewhat disrespectfully: "He is dried up and without fire. The other day I heard one of his Masses. It was exactly as gay as he is grouchy, that is, beyond all reason. . . . In sum, I believe he is the only man to whom Klingemann's phrase of the burnt-out volcano is applicable. Sometimes he sends forth a rain of sparks—but he is all covered with cinder and stones." The young Liszt, then the lion of all musical Paris, did not fare better in Felix's letters: "Liszt plays very well; he has many fingers, but little brains, and his improvisations are miserable indeed. . . ."[12]

A few more samples of Felix's descriptions of renowned musicians may characterize his vivid, if occasionally insolent, observations: "Concerning Reicha: this man is dreaded here like the Wild Huntsman (for he hunts nothing but parallel fifths). . . . Meyerbeer gave an instructive discourse on the nature of the French horn in F; I shall not forget it, as long as I live . . . I laughed so hard that I almost fell from the chair. . . . Rossini has an intricate face, a mixture of roguery, boredom, and disgust . . . there you have the great Maestro *Windbeutel* [windbag] . . . !"

The example of Liszt served as a deterrent rather than an incentive to Felix. Henceforth he resisted the temptation of becoming an elegant composer for the salons. Moreover, he was inclined to try his luck with Germany, her ideas, and her emotional climate. To be sure, he had alternatives. The far-reaching connections of Abraham (he had relatives and associates in Vienna, Paris, Brussels, Frankfurt, and other cities) would have greatly helped Felix's settlement in any of those places. His later decision for Germany was certainly not, as has been suggested recently, dictated by sheer patriotism on Felix's or Abraham's part.[13] They were by no means chauvinistic "All-deutsche." More than once, in his later life, Felix decried any kind of flag-waving. Nor was it simply nostalgia for his fatherland that decided the question, although it certainly played an important part. Perhaps Felix's contempt for the state of music in France and the reports of the sad lot of serious music in Vienna, where the aging Beethoven was living in almost entire isolation, buttressed his decision.

Zelter had never doubted the outcome of the Paris examination, as we know from his letters. In fact, in true Masonic fashion he had promoted Felix to "Geselle" (fellow) a year before. On Felix's fifteenth birthday he pronounced him an "independent fellow of the fraternity of musicians; this in the name of Mozart, Haydn, and old father Bach." He then embraced and kissed him. This little ceremony meant more to the usually nonchalant Zelter than appears on the surface. For him it held a higher significance than just a transference of guild customs to the society of musicians. Zelter, like Goethe, was an enthusiastic Freemason, and the ceremony had a clearly ritualistic flavor. In the ensuing year, in the course of which Cherubini pronounced his judgment, Felix matured intellectually and artistically to an astonishing degree. His father, however, considered all these accomplishments mere steps in the proper direction. Hence he saw to it that Felix's general education was not neglected.

The parallel with another famoues father-son relationship comes to mind: that of Leopold and Wolfgang Mozart. In such a comparison, Abraham fares much better as father, pedagogue, and man than Leopold Mozart. He let Felix have, as soon as advisable, full freedom in his travels, in his social relations, and in the choice of his occupation. Nevertheless, it had to be "freedom under the Law." Once a musician, Felix was expected to make at least a decent living and to obtain a proper professional station. Abraham loathed any form of exhibitionism in Felix; he was skeptical of child-prodigies. Leopold behaved in just the opposite way, in addition to keeping Wolfgang in guiding reins far beyond the permissible age. Hence Felix gained his independence without the revolt that was so necessary—and wholesome—in Mozart's career. The older he grew, the more filial affection he showed to the aging Abraham. The father's judgment remained the touchstone of the son's work. Even seven years after the father's death Felix remembered his birthday and directed his family's attention to it.

If one had to rely exclusively on Hensel's book *The Mendelssohn Family* and the published letters for the evaluation of Felix's personality and development, one would be bound to think that in Felix's youth everything went smoothly, exactly as it had been planned, and without a major conflict. Nothing could be farther from the truth. Two problems, closely interlinked with each other, overshadowed his entire youth and early manhood. They were of far-reaching consequence and determined his fate as an artist and as a man.

In order to understand his future course fully we must pay serious attention to the general problem of Jewish emancipation and its effects on the Mendelssohn family. In Felix's mind this problem was closely linked to his relationship with his father. This sounds far-fetched; indeed, if we were restricted to the information carefully meted out by Hensel and the much retouched edition of letters by Felix, there would be no real grounds for a discussion of these issues. The unpublished letters, however, speak a vastly different language. They categorically demand a full airing of the controversy that haunted the family for many years and that was the true reason behind Hensel's selfcensorship. What is more, the personalities of Abraham and Felix, as reflected in this debate, assume new and hitherto unknown aspects.

Notes

1. Devrient, *Erinnerungen an Felix Mendelssohn* (Leipzig, 1891), p. 4.
2. Unpublished letter, Library of Congress, Washington, D.C.
3. *Goethe-Zelter Correspondence*, October 26, 1821; also F. W. Riemer, *Mitteilungen über Goethe* (Leipzig, 1921), p. 208, where he refers to an unpleasant correspondence with Abraham, because of his editorship of the abbreviated edition of the *Goethe-Zelter Correspondence*.
4. Cf. W. Bode, *Die Tonkunst in Goethes Leben* (Berlin, 1912), II, p. 195-207; also Hensel, *F. M.*, I, p. 101-105; and Adele Schopenhauer, *Leben einer Einsamen* (Leipzig, 1921).
5. Bode, *op. cit.*, II, p. 201. (Original version by J. C. Lobe, in Christmas issue of *Gartenlaube*, 1866.)
6. L. Rellstab, *Erinnerungen aus meinem Leben* (Berlin, 1861), p. 140ff.
7. Marx, *Erinnerungen* (Berlin, 1865), II, p. 113ff.
8. Hensel, *The Mendelssohn Family*, tr. Carl Klingemann (London, 1882), I, p. 85.
9. Moscheles' *Diaries*, tr. Coleridge (London, 1873), p. 65ff.
10. *Goethe-Zelter Correspondence*, ed. Max Hecker (Leipzig, 1915), II, p. 334.
11. "The boy is rich; he will do well; even now he's doing well, but he spends too much money and is too elegantly dressed."
12. Unpublished letter of July 24, 1825. None of these roguish, but very funny passages have appeared in print.
13. Petitpierre, *La Romance de Mendelssohn Bartholdy* (Paris-Bern, 1937), where the author does not hesitate to claim Moses, Abraham, and Felix as dyed-in-the-wool German nationalists.

CHAPTER III *Judaism in Transition*

> We have no desire for rights ungraciously doled out; they are
> balanced by an equal number of wrongs. We do not take comfort
> in sympathetic concessions; we loathe clandestine privileges. Only
> in lawful, universal recognition do we find satisfaction; only in
> unconditional equality do we see an end to our sorrow. . . .
>
> Leopold Zunz, Preface to *Die Gottesdienstlichen Vorträge der
> Juden* (1832).

ON A bright spring day in 1819 a royal prince of Prussia stopped Felix
Mendelssohn, then ten years old, on the street, spat at his feet, and
exclaimed: "Hep hep, Jew-boy!"

This carefully suppressed incident[1] occurred during the so-called
Judensturm, a little pogrom that did not amount to more than looting,
booing, and beating of Jews. It did, however, bring to a climax the long-
brewing doubts and anxieties of German Jewry concerning their own
status and the future of their children. Legal as well as social problems
were closely interwoven here, for the outburst of 1819 confirmed their
worst fears: it was, after all, not only freedom of worship to which
Jews aspired. Their very existence, even their lives were not safe. Most
of the mirages of freedom and equality which the Prussian Government
had conjured up since 1806, and which the Jews had watched with impatient hope, had dissolved in empty words and left in their place an
ominous vacuum of fearful insecurity.

Both the legal and the social aspects of the problem were rather
complex and had, moreover, been confounded by vested interests of the
partisans pro and contra Jewish emancipation. The Constitution of the
United States had guaranteed the strict separation of Church and State.
Such a measure was all but unthinkable in Europe; and even the French
Revolution and Napoleon had to come to a "gentlemen's agreement" with
the Church.

Under prevailing conditions the legal position of the Jews was controversial, to say the least. In America every citizen was and is equal before the

law, and, since the Constitution serves as a custodian of the citizen's rights, the Jews are entitled to legal equality; this does not and did not necessarily entail social equality. Conversely, in Europe, social equality of Jews preceded their legal recognition by many years, in some cases by a full century.

In 1791 France had declared all French Jews full citizens; the Austrian policy had vacillated between feeble attempts at "tolerance" together with a moderate recognition by Emperor Joseph II in 1781, and an almost complete reversal and partial withdrawal of Jewish rights in 1815. Following the successful French example, and spurred by genuine humanitarian impulses, the chancellor of Prussia, Prince Hardenberg, finally achieved legal equality for Prussian Jewry in 1812. This law applied only to such families as had previously been in possession of certain privileges and concessions. Even this restricted alleviation did not last very long. Almost immediately after Hardenberg's death in 1822 a royal edict banned Jews from all government positions, be it in a teaching, judicial, or administrative capacity.[2]

From the very outset the legal emancipation was opposed by practically all adherents of the Romantic School. This opposition had many roots. The patriotic reaction against French hegemony and oppression decried the emancipation as a product of the condemned French Revolution. After the wars of liberation (1812-1815) a spiritual climate had evolved in Germany wherein ideas of primitive Christianity mingled with concepts of Teutonic knighthood. The atmosphere became palpably tense and hostile during the years from 1816 to 1835. It was in this atmosphere that the ideal of the Christian-Germanic State emerged.[3] This concept was incompatible with the basically democratic principle of the Jewish emancipation, with the spirit and letter of that law.

Indeed, much had changed since Moses Mendelssohn's death in 1786. There was an inclination to burn the idols that the previous generation had adored: rationalism, cosmopolitanism, the French Revolution, and the enlightenment of a Rousseau or Voltaire. If, in doing so, the basic idea of Judaism could be hit at, so much the better! This was not directly intended as an attack on the Jews as individuals. For many of the leaders of German Romanticism had formed ties of friendship with Jews to the point of intermarriage. But the moral and social tenets of Judaism constituted, in their opinion, a danger to the German nation, since it forced its adherents to form a "state within the state." As early as 1793 the German philosopher Fichte remarked: "There is spread throughout nearly every country of Europe a powerful State which wars continually against all others. . . . This State is Jewry. The only way I can see to give them civil rights is to cut off their heads in a single night and equip them with new ones devoid of every Jewish idea. . . ."

Others saw in the emancipation a danger to the Christian religion itself and warned the governments not to interfere with Divine Providence which had decreed the suppression of Judaism and its followers as an everlasting punishment. Naturally, economic reasons and fears of the mercantile competence of the Jews were not lacking either, if seldom frankly expressed.

The Gentile defenders of the emancipation rose to the challenge. They defended, however, not Judaism or its principles but the Jews, and emphasized the faults of the Christian governments, which had caused the Jewish demoralization and humiliation. They demanded for Jewish citizens true equality before the law, compulsory education by the government, and hoped that a better understanding of history would gradually attain for them what the formal law could or would not do.

The Jewish reaction, also, was not uniform and not entirely affirmative. One attitude was common, though, to the various groups: the representatives of German Jewry, most of them disciples of Moses Mendelssohn's school of thought, watched the fight pro and contra emancipation in utter perplexity. They were not close enough to the inner struggles of the Teutonic soul to appreciate this seemingly unmotivated reversal of all those values which a former generation had espoused. In other respects, and depending upon their social or religious stand, the Jewish reactions ran the whole gamut from enthusiastic acceptance to adamant refusal of the concept of emancipation.

The orthodox group, for instance, was opposed to the ideas of the emancipation, because it would deprive the Jewish communities of their ancient autonomy; the rabbis especially abhorred even the thought of having to waive a large part of their vested rights. A quite different reaction was that of a group of Jewish thinkers, who vacillated between deploring and acclaiming the new status, and indulged in lamentations over the never-ending injustice to and oppression of their fellow-Jews. Entirely different again was the attitude of the "literary set," whose ideas and sentiments were determined not by Jewish ideals but by German and French civilization. They were so deeply stirred by the experience of European culture that in the presence of that glorious new world of literature and art all values of Judaism vanished like "an old garment that is thrown away." So much more vulnerable were they when they began to sense the new anti-Jewish feelings of the young German generation. Spurned love and bitter disappointments were their common lot. Men like the poet Heine and the writer Boerne must be considered typical representatives of this group. The conflict between their Jewish birth and their love of German culture led them often into a *cul de sac,* from which there was no way out but self-hatred and general misanthropy.

Another small group of Jews discovered their affinity for the Protestant theology of Romanticism; these men severed all connections with Judaism and Jewry, becoming champions of Lutheranism, and led it to new aspiration and vigor. They felt that Judaism had served its mission in spreading monotheism and in having given Jesus to mankind. This mission was fulfilled and finished—for them Judaism had no further purpose.

In constructive opposition to the negatives, to the "impeded Germans," to the neo-Protestants, and to all other defeatists and *Weltschmerzler* stood a small but highly articulate group of enthusiasts for the eternal ideals of Judaism. They saw in the scientific exploration of the sources of Jewish civilization the best way of securing a spiritual anchorage for their brethren. Like the humanists of the Renaissance they preached "Ad fontes" and the "science of Judaism" was in their opinion the only means of safeguarding the Jewish position with respect to religion, state, nation, and mankind. This small minority was to survive and eventually to conquer all the other groups; yet it included some men who did not remain faithful to their ideal, like Heine and his friend Eduard Gans, who in later years took the easier way of formal conversion in order to obtain "the entrance ticket to European civilization."

As challenge and reply to the *Judensturm* of 1819 they founded in that very year the *Verein für Kultur und Wissenschaft der Juden* (Society for Jewish Culture and Science). They accepted the emancipation, but considered it only one step in the proper direction. Nor could they identify themselves with the intransigent attitude of Orthodoxy. To them Judaism was a totality embracing all matters of human life, from art to law, from literature to science. They advocated an active and constructive assimilation, but refused to give up their identity as Jews and members of the cultural orbit of Judaism. "To merge is not to perish," wrote Gans.

Their ideas of a real Jewish emancipation were best summarized by Leopold Zunz, the father of the "science of Judaism." In 1832 he wrote:

It is high time that the Jews . . . be accorded, not rights and liberties, but right and liberty; not miserable, humiliating privileges, but complete, elevating citizenship. We have no desire for . . . surreptitious prerogatives. . . . Only in legal status common to all citizens can we find satisfaction; only.in unquestioned equality can we find the end of our pain. The liberty that unshackles the hand only to muzzle tongue and conscience, the tolerance that delights not in our progress but in our decay,[4] the civic position that offers protection without honor, burdens without prospects, these I reject as lacking in love and justice, as baneful elements in the body politic, which can only breed malignant diseases, to the detriment of the individual and the whole. . . .[5]

Beyond and between these clearly circumscribed groups were innumerable opportunists and lukewarm camp followers of one or another group.

In many cases it is extremely difficult completely to identify a person or a family with one of these attitudes; not only were the conditions in rapid flux, but the individual Jew was rarely in a position of being able to define his aims at any given moment. His sentiments and thoughts oscillated between hope and despair, between pride in Jewish culture and contempt of it, between strict observance and utter agnosticism.

The Mendelssohn family found itself caught in these troubled waters and conflicting trends. They and their close relatives, the Itzigs, had contact with all of the Jewish groups as well as with the German intelligentsia. Indeed, by virtue of their name and its great prestige, they lived in the very center of thought and deed, and their attitude was copied by many thousands of German Jews.

When, in 1812, the legal emancipation of the German Jews was decreed in principle, it followed to a considerable extent the pattern set by the French Republic. Henceforth the legal position of the Prussian Jews was clear, if still disputed. Certainly it was not subject to individual decision or modification, unless one chose to take the step to conversion and the full civil equality that was its reward.

Social position, however, remained a matter of the personal status of the individual Jew and its recognition or denial by his Gentile neighbor. It ran the whole gamut from the complete isolation of the ghetto-bound Jew without actual ghetto, as described by Heine, to complete social equality with the highest intelligentsia and even nobility, as we encounter it in the numerous Jewish salons in Berlin, of which the house of Abraham and Lea Mendelssohn was not the least important.

Lea had always sympathized with the radical solution offered by conversion to the Protestant Church. Characteristic of her attitude are the following passages from a letter she wrote long before her marriage to Abraham Mendelssohn. There she expressed herself in unequivocal terms on the controversial subject of conversion:

> Itzig has finished his studies at Wittenberg and is, for the time being, here. What are you going to say if I inform you of his conversion to Christianity? Luther's birthplace and the sacred dwelling of his teachings have influenced him to such a degree that he could not resist the desire to be baptized beneath the image of that great man and thus to be quasi protected by him. By this step for his soul's benefit, he has also attained the worldly advantage of soon being appointed by the government. . . . I hope he will remain faithful to his decision. I cannot even describe how much I wish just this: for most of the renegades [!] have by their own bad behavior made this measure contemptible. . . . If somebody stood forth, who by his integrity, firmness of conviction, and worldly wisdom in his behavior . . . gave an honorable example, a good deal of the all too well founded prejudice by Jews against converts would be invalidated. How I wish that we could do without this

hypocrisy! but the urge for a higher sphere of work than that of a merchant, and a thousand tender sentiments, which the close intercourse with adherents of other religions evokes in young hearts, leave no other alternative [but this hypocrisy]....[6]

Thus, utterly realistically, almost cynically, did Lea assess the Jewish situation, as it appeared to her. The Itzig to whose conversion she referred was her cousin Julius Eduard, who with his conversion accepted the name of Hitzig, an act Heine cruelly ridiculed in verses. Naturally, this piece of studied insult did not exactly augment Heine's popularity with the Mendelssohns or Hitzigs. For nothwithstanding their distant connection with the Heine family, Julius Eduard Hitzig, the butt of Heine's satire, was Lea Mendelssohn's cousin, and rose, as criminologist and jurist, to considerable fame. Seen from our perspective, the entire affair appears rather ludicrous, inasmuch as one convert ridicules the other because of the natural consequences of the conversion.

Much more radical than Lea in thought and action was her brother Jacob Lewin Salomon.

Through him the name Bartholdy came into this branch of the family. He had inherited from his grandfather Itzig a beautiful garden and mansion, nicknamed "Little Sans-souci." Its first proprietor, more than a hundred years before, had been a mayor of the suburb of Neukölln by the name of Bartholdy. When Salomon decided, very much against the will of his orthodox mother, to embrace the Christian faith, he replaced the Jewish Salomon with the Berlinese Bartholdy. Not satisfied therewith, he persuaded his brother-in-law Abraham Mendelssohn to add this name to the Jewish-sounding Mendelssohn. A part of that persuasive letter has been published; together with its preamble, hitherto unpublished, it constitutes a characteristic document of the *sauve-qui-peut* attitude of the upper Jewish classes.

I was not at all convinced by your arguments for loyalty to your name and faith. These arguments have become invalid in our era, for reasons internal as well as external. You say you owe it to the memory of your father; but do you think you have done something bad in giving your children the religion that appears to you to be the best? It is the justest homage you or any of us could pay to the efforts of your father in promoting true light and knowledge, and he would have acted like you for his children, and perhaps like me for himself. You may remain faithful to an oppressed, persecuted religion; you may leave it to your children as a prospect of lifelong martyrdom, as long as you believe it to be absolute truth. But once you have ceased to believe that, it is barbarism. I advise you to adopt the name Mendelssohn Bartholdy as a distinction from the other Mendelssohns.

The letter reflects faithfully the personality of its writer. We may like his reasoning or not; it appears to be logical and full of consideration for his family, if ever so opportunistic. The complete lack of historical understanding of Judaism among the intelligentsia of that emancipation-crazed generation has been noted by many students of the time. Bartholdy shared this shortcoming with his contemporaries. This is the more astounding because he was a capable historian of ancient Greek and Renaissance art. His study on Mycenae (1805) and his diligent collecting of sculpture and ceramics of the della Robbia family secure for him an honorable place among the nineteenth-century scholars of archaeology and history of art.

In spite of these accomplishments, he was despised by many influential people of his acquaintance. Men so different as Baron Gentz, the confidant of Prince Metternich, and the Prussian envoy at the Vatican, von Niebuhr, called him a "demagogic scoundrel" and "a veritable misfortune for [Chancellor] Hardenberg, because of his cleverness that sometimes bordered on unscrupulousness."

Cardinal Ercole Consalvi, who felt obligated to Bartholdy, had obtained for him the position of Prussian Consul General in Rome. His task was to observe, first hand, the political currents and tensions that then pervaded all of Italy. He discharged his duty with sagacity and even courage: his book *The Carbonaria*, about the Neapolitan revolution, shows him, the enemy of all political conspiracy, as a clear-sighted, almost prophetic statesman. Perhaps his obituary in the *Deutsche Allgemeine Zeitung* (1825) characterizes him best:

> He felt entitled to greater position than his birth, his ungainly figure, and his more broad than profound studies seemed to warrant. He felt obliged to force noblemen of ancient lineage . . . to tolerate him in their society; he wanted to be be loved, feared, indispensable, to be everything to everybody, in constant ascendancy, in order to be tolerated. . . . All of this, in order to maintain a place that another man might attain without constantly thinking or worrying about it.

Being a realist as well as a confirmed snob, he was opposed to music as a profession and tried to prevent his nephew Felix from embracing the career of a professional musician, as three sharply worded letters to his brother-in-law show. Small wonder that Felix resented the man who threatened to forestall his musical pursuits.

At first glance it would seem as if Abraham Mendelssohn shared his brother-in-law's views and attitudes towards Judaism and other problems. To believe this, however, would be a serious error; for it is difficult to imagine two persons as different as these two men.

Lea to Felix:

Your father ruins, for him and for us, our good and pleasant life . . . he goes about like a man depressed by grief, gloomy and despondent. Oh God, how happy this man could be and how much happiness he could radiate! Yet he, the soul of a husband and father, is eternally in doubt about something, deep down in his heart. Nor do I know what it is that causes his constant doubts. . . .[7]

Thus his wife describes her husband at a time when his son's fame grew swiftly, when his own business prospered, when everything seemed to be going as well as possible.

Like her brother, Lea preferred in her salon notables of one sort or another, celebrities by birth or by achievement. Her husband mocked this snobbery, teasing her with her "artistocratic inclinations." As for himself, he used to define his position in the famous words: "Formerly I was the son of a father; now I am the father of a son." There is more than a little bitterness implied in this apparently harmless quip. For he felt most keenly the burdensome responsibility of his name. He was one of the few Jews who fully realized the dilemma of their time. Whereas to his wife and his daughters Judaism meant little, and was an old obsolete idea best treated silently or in jokes, he took it very seriously. While he did not sympathize with the then prevailing orthodox forms of Jewish observance, he never allowed himself a Jewish joke or even the slightest hint of a Yiddish-German expression (his wife's letters and his daughters' abound in these). The faithful son's sentiments speak from this letter about his father's hundredth birthday:

On Sept. 10, 1829, the hundredth birthday of my unforgettable father will be blessed and celebrated. The Jewish Community will on that occasion found an orphanage and name it after him. [This was the same institution to which his wife's aunt Sara Levy donated 20,000 Thaler.] The idea appeals to me very much, and I shall contribute to it as much as possible. However, I am becoming every day more and more an enemy of forms, feasts, and celebrations.[8]

Abraham revered his father in a way in which he expected to be regarded by his children. He did everything, consciously or otherwise, to create and foster in the minds of his children a family romance, wherein he and Moses eventually would merge into one image of the "Great Father." In this endeavor he succeeded. The deep dichotomy that existed between his father's thinking and behavior in matters Jewish, and that was uniquely bridged in Moses' case, developed into an open breach in Abraham's life. To him, the conversion was no more than a formality to which he had to submit, since his children all were Christians. In a well-known letter on the occasion of Fanny's confirmation he says:

The form in which your [Protestant] teacher has instructed you is historical and, like all human ordinances, subject to change. . . . We, your mother and I, were brought up by our parents in Judaism and were able, without having to change this form, to obey the God within us and our conscience. . . ."

Years after his baptism he exchanged letters including Talmudic quotations with another convert, the composer and pianist Ignaz Moscheles, Felix's paternal friend. His understanding of Judaism was philosophical and utterly unhistoric. Yet he did not spare his own or his son's feelings in this matter. Proud as he was of the name he bore, he demanded categorically that Felix drop it altogether, for reasons of intellectual integrity and honest consistency. If the name Mendelssohn means anything today in the world of music, it does so because of Felix's insistence on retaining it.

In an extensive letter to Felix, Abraham discusses the entire question of his name and its alteration, as well as his reasons for his conversion to Christianity. This letter is an important historical document; but more than that, it throws much light on Abraham as a human being. Belying the tone of stern paternalism, warm affection for his son speaks in every line. We quote the entire text of this important letter:

Berlin, July 8, 1829.

Dear Felix:—

Today's family sheet will run full without my contribution . . . I will therefore write you separately because I have to discuss with you a most serious matter.

The suspicion has come to me that you have suppressed or neglected or allowed others to suppress or neglect the name which I have taken as the name of our family, the name Bartholdy. In the concert programs you have sent me, likewise in newspaper articles, your name is given as Mendelssohn. I can account for this only on the supposition that you have been the cause.

Now, I am greatly dissatisfied about this. If you are to blame, you have committed a huge wrong.

After all, a name is only a name, neither more nor less. Still, so long as you are under your father's jurisdiction, you have the plain and indisputable duty to be called by your father's name. Moreover it is your ineffaceable, as well as reasonable, duty to take for granted that, whatever your father does, he does on valid grounds and with due deliberation.

On our journey to Paris after that neck-breaking night,[9] you asked me the reasons why our name was changed. I gave you those reasons at length. If you have forgotten them, you could have asked me about them again. If my reasons seemed unconvincing, you should have countered with better reasons. I prefer to believe the former, because I am unable to think of any reasons countervailing. I will here repeat my arguments and my views.

My grandfather was named Mendel Dessau. When my father, his son, went forth into the world and began to win notice and when he undertook the project which can not be too highly praised, that noble project of lifting his brethren out of the vast degradation into which they had sunk, and to do this by disseminating among them a better education, my father felt that the name, Moses ben Mendel Dessau, would handicap him in gaining the needed access to those who had the better education at their disposal. Without any fear that his own father would take offense, my father assumed the name Mendelssohn.[10] The change, though a small one, was decisive. As Mendelssohn, he became irrevocably detached from an entire class, the best of whom he raised to his own level. By that name he identified himself with a different group. Through the influence which wisely and worthily he exerted by word and pen and deed,—an influence which, ever growing, persists to this day,—that name Mendelssohn acquired a Messianic import[11] and a significance which defies extinction. This, considering that you were reared a Christian, you can hardly understand. A Christian Mendelssohn is an impossibility. A Christian Mendelssohn the world would never recognize. Nor should there be a Christian Mendelssohn; for my father himself did not want to be a Christian. "Mendelssohn" does and always will stand for a Judaism in transition, when Judaism, just because it is seeking to transmute itself spiritually, clings to its ancient form all the more stubbornly and tenaciously, by way of protest against the novel form[12] that so arrogantly and tyrannically declared itself to be the one and only path to the good.

The viewpoint, to which my father and then my own generation committed me, imposes on me other duties toward you, my children, and puts other means of discharging them into my hands. I have learnt and will not, until my dying breath, forget that, while truth is one and eternal, its forms are many and transient. That is why, as long as it was permitted by the government under which we lived,[13] I reared you without religion in any form. I wanted you to profess whatever your convictions might favor or, if you prefer, whatever expediency might dictate. But it was not so to be. I was obligated to do the choosing for you.[14] Naturally, when you consider what scant value I placed on any form in particular, I felt no urge to choose the form known as Judaism, that most antiquated, distorted, and self-defeating form of all. Therefore I reared you as Christians, Christianity being the more purified form and the one most accepted by the majority of civilized people. Eventually, I myself adopted Christianity, because I felt it my duty to do for myself that which I recognized as best for you. Even as my father found it necessary to adjust his name to conditions, filial devotion, as well as discretion, impelled me to adjust similarly.

Here I must reproach myself for a weakness, even if a pardonable one. I should have done decisively and thoroughly that which I deemed right. I should have discarded the name Mendelssohn completely. I should have adhered to the new name exclusively. I owed that to my father. My reason for not doing so was my long established habit of sparing those near to me and of forestalling perverted and venomous judgments. I did wrong. My purpose was merely to prepare for you a path of transition, making it easier for you that have no one to spare and nothing to care about. In Paris, when you, Felix, were about to step into the world and make a name for yourself,

I deliberately had your cards engraved: Felix M. Bartholdy. You did not accept my way of thinking. Weakly enough I failed to persist. Now I only wish, though I neither expect nor deserve it, that my present intervention may not have arrived too late.

You can not, you must not carry the name Mendelssohn. Felix Mendelssohn Bartholdy is too long; it is unsuited for daily use. You must go by the name of Felix Bartholdy. A name is like a garment; it has to be appropriate for the time, the use, and the rank, if it is not to become a hindrance and a laughing-stock. Englishmen, otherwise a most formal lot, change their names frequently. Seldom is anyone renowned under the name conferred at baptism. And that is as it should be. I repeat: There can no more be a Christian Mendelssohn than there can be a Jewish Confucius. If Mendelssohn is your name, you are ipso facto a Jew. And this, if for no other reason than because it is contrary to fact, can be to you of no benefit.

Dear Felix, take this to heart and act accordingly.

Your Father and Friend.

The letter was well-meant and written in the spirit of soul-searching honesty; nonetheless it was then as unrealistic as it appears today. For Abraham's contempt of "form per se" had a proper function only as a strictly philosophical concept, borrowed from Kant; it was never applicable to real life.

Felix replied rather apologetically to his father's letter; at any rate, he conducted the four concerts in London under the name Felix Mendelssohn in spite of his father's admonition. It is quite probable that this was an act of hostility against his uncle Bartholdy, who by that time was dead. In this respect Felix was not alone. His sister Rebecca frequently signed her letters as Rebecca Mendelssohn *meden* (Greek for never) Bartholdy.

Abraham was a tragic figure. Of extraordinary intelligence and fine education, widely read, he was the most gifted of Moses Mendelssohn's sons. Radical rationalist and Kantian that he was, he lacked any understanding of the emotional or historical meanings of Judaism. Bereft of deep faith, which so distinguished his father as well as his son, he was capable of sharp, penetrating, and even philosophical speculation upon a critical or phenomenological basis. He viewed only the present and its problems, and these only in their present shape; they dazzled and perplexed him, and thus he paid no attention to any meaning of the past or to a potential future.

His sense of responsibility and an almost gloomy sense of duty show in each of his longer letters. When Felix jubilantly sent home a beautiful letter of old Goethe, addressed to him, his father replied sternly (June 13, 1830):

That letter of Goethe has again made me realize the heavy and responsible obligation which you, my dear Felix, have undertaken, and which you, in your life, will have to fulfill.

This was by no means the way Felix had understood the letter at first glance. But the more the son matured, the more he accepted the ethical views of his father and deepened them by his own intensely religious sentiments. The study of the relationship between father and son, therefore, offers insight of deep significance.

Abraham, the rationalist, might be viewed as a well-developed fore-runner of "Ethical Culture." At the confirmation of his daughter Fanny (Pentecost, 1820) he wrote her a beautifully worded letter, which culminated in these sentences:

> Does God exist? What is God? Is He a part of ourselves and does this part continue to live eternally, remaining immortal, after the other part has ceased being? And where? And how?—I do not know an answer to these questions and have never taught you anything about it. I do know, however, that there lives in me, in you, and in all human beings an everlasting urge towards everything good, true, righteous, and a conscience that warns and guides us, when we go astray. I do know it, I believe it, I live in this faith, and this is my religion. . . .

Felix's thoroughly humanistic upbringing—perhaps the only lasting influence of his grandfather Moses—molded his outlook and his relations to his environment. He revered his father, who most faithfully transmitted the humanistic ideal, yet often enough he feared him more. There is ample reason to believe that these ambivalent emotions determined the son's attitude toward other men, and even more toward women.

Relatively early in life, he selected his own circle of friends and confidants. On the Continent he did not make any intimate friendships after his twenty-second year. He actually shied away, during his many travels and sojourns, from making new friends. Only people who were either related to him or who had been members of that esoteric group of friends which had thronged to his father's house in Berlin could come close to him. This strange reserve, contrasting with the general pattern of his expansive personality, is puzzling, the more so because of his deviations from it. For in England he did permit himself to go out of his way in order to win new friends, and he succeeded. Why this double standard for England and the Continent? Why this general shyness towards men, accentuated by his popularity with the ladies? Why did such a man, gifted with a keen eye, a brilliant mind, a warm heart, and humorous inclinations, confine himself to the narrow circle of relatives and friends of his youth? Felix's propensity for a certain exclusiveness was, of course, no secret. While his father once warned him against this self-sufficiency, his mother sympathized with it and did not find fault in this attitude.

Felix's brother-in-law, the painter Hensel, hinted at this in an allegorical caricature, called "The Wheel." He represented the whole company of the

Mendelssohns as a wheel, the hub of which is Felix, making music like Arion. The spokes are formed by his sisters and friends of the family. The wheel is tightly closed, inaccessible to the outside world, relying only on itself.

Perhaps it would be most accurate if one described Felix's attitude as "defensive." For he had had a number of rather disappointing experiences during his youth and early manhood, and he felt like the proverbial burnt child. Of these shocks a few might be described. Being reared in the dawn of emancipation, in a family whose *mores* were still Jewish in many respects, he met gentiles and Jews on an equal level in the salons of his parents and their friends. But even so, he was a target of prejudice. The insult of the ten-year-old boy by a prince during the "Judensturm" has been mentioned. Another incident occurred in 1824, when Felix was fifteen. The family spent its vacation in Dobberan, a then much frequented watering place on the Baltic. This time both Felix and his beloved sister Fanny were insulted by street urchins, who shouted "Jew-boy" and similar epithets and finally threw stones at them. Felix defended his sister vigorously and staunchly, but seems to have collapsed afterwards. His tutor J. L. Heyse writes tersely about the incident:

> Felix behaved like a man, but after he had returned home could not conceal his fury about the humiliation, which in the evening broke out in a flood of tears and wild accusations.

And for the third time his mental equilibrium was shattered in 1832, when his family, very much against his will, persuaded him to be a candidate for the position of director of the Berlin *Singakademie*. He suffered a severe rebuff; the *Singakademie* would not elect a "Jew-boy," brilliant as he might be. It preferred a mild mediocrity, Herrn Rungenhagen, whose directorship was to a great extent responsible for the stagnation of Berlin musical life during the years 1830 to 1850. An influential writer and music critic, L. Rellstab, friend of Felix, expressed himself more in sorrow than in anger:

> We do hope that the young artist has not been deterred by manifold indignities he had to suffer as reward for his zeal for the good and artistically noble—and that he has not lost his initiative to strive anew for the highest goals!

Notwithstanding this and other attempts at consolation, the public humiliation cast a blight over everything associated with Berlin, and eventually caused Felix to assume a most reserved attitude to all new acquaintances. Is it a pure coincidence that in 1832, the year of the humiliation, he wrote the entire libretto of an oratorio, *Moses,* for his friend A. B.

Marx? Marx refused it, which is understandable, for he was an eager convert, and the libretto has a strictly Old Testament flavor, with which Marx did not wish to identify himself as he desired a more christological interpretation. The existence of this manuscript (first two pages of which are reproduced below) has hitherto been generally unknown.

In contrast to his skeptical father, Felix's nature was deeply religious. It is not only his compositions (psalms, motets, oratorios) that testify to this inherent religiosity, but even more his letters, which breathe a profound faith in God. His religious thinking was deeply influenced by Schleiermacher, whom he knew very well and greatly admired. The sober philosophy of his father, a kind of ethical culture, was not sufficient for Felix, who, like Schleiermacher, desired "to be affected by the Infinite without a practical purpose." For him, as for Schleiermacher, the personality of Jesus was not at all of central importance. Hence, the name Jesus never occurs in Felix's letters; instead he used paraphrases such as "Heavens," and "the Eternal." Somehow his religion was linked with his deep-seated feeling for the fate of Jewry, which was much more positive than that of his father. Of his identification with the Jewish lot there occur frequent indications in his letters. We shall quote from some of them later. Certain philosophical ideas inherent in Judaism also emerge in Felix's correspondence:

> London, May 29, 1833
> God, art, and life are but one. As father always says: to him who works most diligently in the pursuit of knowledge [*in der Lehre*] *for its own sake,* everything will eventually come: good fortune, success, and the friendship of his fellow men as well as the love of his Creator.

What Felix did not know was that Abraham's remark was a literal quotation from the "Sayings of the Fathers," the *Mishna Aboth.* There the passage reads as follows:

> Whosoever labors in the Torah for its own sake merits many things, he is called friend, beloved, a lover of the Lord, a lover of mankind, . . . and it gives him sovereignty and dominion and discerning judgment . . . and it magnifies and exalts him above all things.

He did not mince words in repudiating very sharply a rather tactless letter of his sister Rebecca. She had written to him on June 23, 1829, about a distant relative of Moses Mendelssohn, a faithful Jew, who had succeeded, to her chagrin, in being introduced to the best Berlin society:

> Mr. Dessauer has eventually departed, but not without having presented his sister. I am not hostile to Jews, but this is a bit thick.

Whereupon Felix replied:

> London, July 17, 1829
> What do you mean by saying that you are not hostile to Jews? I hope this was just a joke; otherwise I would take you to task most seriously. It is really

sweet of you that you do not despise your entire family, isn't it? I expect from you a full explanation in your next letter.

Later in his life, Felix had occasion to prove his faithfulness to his grandfather's ideals of humanism. During the years preceding the revolution of 1848, whenever he reflected on issues of a political nature, he invariably took the stand of liberalism against jingoism and sometimes, as in some of his letters to his friends Gustav Droysen and Carl Klingemann, he called himself a "radical."

He also was able to appreciate and to befriend two eminent representatives of that "Judaism which strives to renew itself internally in a pure spiritual way" (as his father had once expressed it in that memorable letter about his name), the scholars Abraham Geiger and Julius Fürst, who advised him on the librettos for his *St. Paul* and *Elijah.*

A comparison of Felix's attitude towards the issues of emancipation and its consequences with that of Heine, his older contemporary, offers a striking picture. This comparison should enable us to view in its true proportions the dilemma that confronted the Jewish intelligentsia.

Heine's Jewish birth became his fate, the cause of his greatness, and the leading motif of his personal tragedy. Until the very last years of his life his sentiments about Judaism vacillated between escape, self-hatred, fierce pride, resignation, and positive acceptance. He embraced Christianity for purely opportunist reasons, yet he viciously denounced all others who did likewise. In 1823 he regarded it as beneath his dignity to be baptized in order to obtain a position in Prussia. In June 1825 he did exactly that. When his friend and fellow convert Eduard Gans had sounded enthusiastic over the new religion, Heine castigated him ruthlessly. "Yesterday a hero and today already a rascal." Later on he regretted his apostasy, yet never returned to Judaism. In his personality the Jewish substratum clashed incessantly with the superimposed ethical tradition of Germany. Eventually he left both spheres, and betrayed both. Yet he never ceased to love these two antagonistic wellsprings of his very being.

Felix Mendelssohn was baptized not because his father considered this the easiest way out of the dilemma, but because he saw in Christianity a "somewhat purer form" than Judaism could offer. Felix never vacillated in his attitude towards Judaism. Its spiritual, nationalist, and ethical teachings had no meaning for him whatsoever, but he felt a strong solidarity wherever Jews as individuals were concerned. Not being familiar with the concepts of Judaism, he never took any positive attitude towards it; the conflict between his native Jewishness and German culture, with which he was so imbued, caused him, no less than Heine, many hours of heartache; yet he never became a self-hater or indulged in *Weltschmerz* and its counterpart *Judenschmerz* (Jewish self-pity). He was faithful to the Christian religion and took it seriously; if he chose a theology that took a most sympathetic view of Judaism, he again demonstrated loyalty to his father's and grandfather's humanistic ideals. And certainly he was a good German, and more: a good European in our sense of the word. In his case the conflict between Germanism and Judaism came as close to a solution as the German nation would permit.

$\mathcal{N}$otes

1. Published only in Varnhagen van Ense's *Denkwürdigkeiten*, Vol. 9, 1819-20.
2. Margolis and Marx, *History of the Jewish People* (Philadelphia, 1927), p. 635; see also Ernst Heilborn, *Zwischen zwei Revolutionen* (Berlin, 1927), I, p. 87.
3. Selma Stern-Täubler, "Der literarische Kampf um die Emanzipation in den Jahren 1816-20," *Hebrew Union College Annual* (Cincinnati, 1950-51), II, p. 171.
4. This is an implicit attack on the policy of the Protestant theologians, who, following Schleiermacher's example, preached tolerance in order to make more Jewish proselytes.
5. L. Zunz, *Die Gottesdienstlichen Vorträge der Juden* (Berlin, 1832), pp. III-IV.
6. Letter of Lea to G. Merkel, in Hensel, *F.M.*, I, p. 94f. (Not in former editions.) And yet even this radical abnegation of all Jewish values did not avail the Apostates full *social* equality. A characteristic, long hushed up scandal, originating in Sara Levy's house, involved the brother of J. E. Hitzig, Moritz, and the well-known poet Achim von Arnim. This scandal turned against the latter and practically ruined his career. In the Appendix (p. 524) we quote the entire ludicrous affair, as described in an unpublished report by Varnhagen van Ense. I am much indebted to Mrs. Margarete Gotthelf, Ph.D., Haifa, for having made the document available.
7. Unpublished letter of October, 1830.
8. Unpublished letter to Felix.
9. In the year 1825 when Felix was sixteen years old.
10. Abraham Mendelssohn seems to have forgotten or not to have known that his father, to the end of his life, used a seal with the Hebrew inscription: "Moses, the Stranger [*Ger*] from Dessau."
11. This alludes to the Hebrew Ben Menahem, an appellative for the Messiah.
12. What Abraham Mendelssohn means by "die neue Form" is not clear. He may have had in mind Israel Jacobson's Reform movement which he happened to dislike, or else orthodox Christianity.
13. This refers to the time when the Mendelssohns were living in Hamburg under the French authorities of occupation.
14. After the Prussian laws of emancipation of 1812. Abraham had by then returned to Berlin.

CHAPTER IV

The Music of the

Apprentice (1821-1825)

> My Felix grows under my eyes. . . . Everything attains solidity,
> hardly lacking are strength and power. Everything develops spon-
> taneously from within, and externals touch him only superficially.
> (Zelter to Goethe)

DURING the eighteenth century the social and intellectual level of the average
musician was not impressive, notwithstanding such exceptional cases as
that of Philipp Emanuel Bach and Handel. The French Revolution brought
about a definite change for the better. It was its reluctant beneficiary, the
nineteenth century, that initiated the gradual ascendance of the composer's
social prestige. This rise was a concomitant of the emerging intellectual
bourgeoisie, which, in turn, provided for a more adequate education of the
citizen. Thus the musicians, avid to obtain a higher education, sought and
established contact with the leading spirits of the other arts and the sciences.
Beethoven, Schubert, and Mendelssohn approached Goethe and other poets.
Gradually the composer created for himself and his music what he considered a proper place in Western civilization. Not since the golden days
of the Renaissance had musicians enjoyed such general prestige as did
Beethoven, Mendelssohn, Chopin, Liszt, Berlioz, and Wagner. They were
intensely aware of their position in the cultural life of their time. Their
aspirations reached high; and yet, many of the composers lacked sympathetic
guidance.

In 1806 the Holy Roman Empire collapsed under Napoleon's assault.
The great dream of a synthesis of European music, so dear to the eighteenth
century, vanished with it. In this sense Mendelssohn was a true child of his
time. His father, Goethe, and even the Prussian patriot Zelter had been
entirely unprejudiced concerning Felix's future place in Europe, but the
young composer tried early to identify himself with the German people
and regarded his music as representative of German culture. Today the
shortcomings of strict nationalistic thought have become obvious to every-

body, in art and statecraft alike. In music especially, much of the so-called "national" school's products are at best provincial. This uncritical exaggeration of musical nationalism, however, did not emerge before the second half of the nineteenth century, after Mendelssohn's death.

The Viennese composers of the preceding generation had been either the employees or the protegés of aristocracy. A definite shift in the social structure of the musical public can be observed during the first third of the nineteenth century. The middle classes began to replace, in ever increasing measure, the aristocracy both as dilettantes and as patrons. And there is no doubt of Mendelssohn's wholehearted identification with the German bourgeoisie.

About the turn of the century the Romantic writers—not composers— had discovered music as a medium eminently suitable to their conception of art, a conception that did not recognize any finite boundaries. To them, music was the "art of infinity." Since they were all striving towards a rather vague goal of boundless dimensions, the art most idealized and glorified was music. In this connection, it is interesting to compare the poetic outpourings of one of those musical phantasts (the novelist E. T. A. Hoffmann, who was also a composer of note) with some of his music. As novelist he writes: "Music is the splendid Djinnistan, the most romantic of all arts, since its essence is the infinite; the mysterious, musically pronounced rune [*sanscritta*] of Nature, filling the human heart with unending yearning."[1] Let us now look at a musical counterpart of his verbal rhapsodies from his Piano Sonata, No. 2:

Example 2

This is a technically well-contrived portion of the development section in one of Hoffmann's piano sonatas. It follows clearly the style of Haydn or the young Beethoven. It does not accord in the slightest with his professed yearnings for the infinite. As a matter of fact, it is rather tame. And yet, there is in his time unmistakable and concrete musical evidence of such dreams. The ideal of "infinite melody," so didactically and insistently championed by Wagner, corresponds to the "longing for the infinite."[2] The following example (from Dussek, Piano Sonata, op. 10, No. 3) presages faintly what was to come:

Example 3

This is taken from one of Louis Dussek's sonatas. Here, over the pedalpoint F$\sharp$ there develops an incessant motion, interrupted only by a deceptive cadence, in order that "infinite" motion should not be concluded before it has run out its course. This tension between clearly ordered artistic thinking and the subconscious, antirational forces in the imagination of the composer was considered by the litterateurs to be the essence of the "Romantic" work of art.

A number of contradictions are discernible in the strict Romantic doctrine. Its adherents in literature were in no way concerned about these contradictions; they thrived on paradoxes. Yet the musicians felt the ever-growing gulf that separated them from the general public. Some of the Romantic votaries were even proud of that isolation. The case of Berlioz is most conspicuous in this respect: he alternately praised and deplored his spiritual loneliness.

It seems more convenient to use the term "Romantic" in a merely chronological sense, to refer to the music of the early and middle nineteenth century than to define so vague and controversial a movement. One important modification, however, ought to be made: Whatever Romanticism stood for, it was not merely a movement of the nineteenth century. For many of the forces and issues that appear typically Romantic emerged long before the dawn of the "romantic" century, as early as in some phases of gnosticism, in certain aspects of the late Renaissance, and certainly in the Baroque. What is more, they have appeared since the Romantic era and are likely to recur again, in some disguise, being age-old impulses and fantasies of man.

It is not possible to discern a real "break" in musical style early in the nineteenth century in the same way, as it had taken place around 1740 under the aegis of Rousseau, C. P. E. Bach, and the Mannheim School. If musical romanticism had carried only a fraction of the older movement's impetus, it would have radically broken with the classic tradition. Yet that was not the case, not in *one* instance. In order to link the romantic style organically with the classical one, the (romantic) critics simply considered Mozart and Beethoven the pioneers of musical romanticism, and thus the continuous flow of tradition was guaranteed thereby. In this sense we must understand much of the musical criticism of the early nineteenth century.

Thus, E. T. A. Hoffmann in his magnificent review of Beethoven's Trios op. 70 and of the Fifth Symphony calls the composer "a pure Romantic (composer), more so than anybody else,"[3] or "a master who takes the listener with him into the spiritual realm of the Infinite."[4] The same reverence was paid to Mozart, at least by the early Romantics. Not only Hoffmann, but many of his literary contemporaries concurred with his judgment. Thus the way to Romantic music was paved by the critic's acceptance of Mozart and Beethoven.[5] The positive attitude towards these composers on the part of the Romantic writers mitigated the drastic change in style, inevitable after Beethoven's last works. The Classicists' lucid musical logic and reasoning, their rational approach to problems of form, were admired by the Romantic authors and, paradoxically, linked with their own craving for the unconscious, the instinctive, in short the antirational in music.[6] By this apparent contradiction the status of the classics was maintained. The link between "romantic" ideas and classical style was provided by Beethoven.

It was the emphasis upon the artist's individualism and autonomy, so often stressed by Beethoven, that was responsible for the widening gulf between the composer and his public. Many of the thoughtful composers watched this development with grave concern. Some of them believed in the remedying power of folk song. It was considered the panacea against the Romantic malady of extreme subjectivism. There emerged a theory, clearly expressed in J. G. Herder's *"Stimmen der Völker in Liedern,"* that all folklore faithfully reflects the true character of its parental nation. If a Schumann firmly believed in this thesis, lesser men were all the more ardent. Rahel Varnhagen had written (in 1822) with reference to national culture: "All artistic production of the various nations will have to be truly national." Yet she had strongly modified this postulate by adding the well-timed admonition: "One may shoot the word 'fatherland' out of guns, journals, books, and what have you; still no country on earth will obtain a national music or national painting . . . in this fashion!"[7] This and similar warnings from Goethe's side were not heeded or soon forgotten. If the Romantics indulged, to a measure hitherto thought impossible, in unbridled subjectivism, they saw in folkish art a vicarious atonement, as it were, for their undisciplined extravagances.

Mendelssohn was an adherent of the older Romantic views on folklore, albeit a moderate one. He wrote *Three Folksongs* and a number of "popular" pieces. Perhaps he yielded here to the public's demand for this sort of music. At one point he even reacted furiously to an overdose of Scotch folklore. In an amusing and interesting letter[8] he expresses his sentiments.

The ideas of the Romantic school in literature, when applied to music, have always appeared either bold, progressive, and forward-looking or shy, conservative, and retrospective, almost in equal measure. The bold half was, even during Mendelssohn's life, interested mainly in the future of the opera, or the music drama, and to a much lesser extent, in the symphony. The conservative half concerned itself chiefly with instrumental or church music, and preferred, in general, the smaller forms. It was also deeply interested in the music of the past.[9]

Undeniably, French Romanticism had a different flavor and a much more radical tendency than the German school. With all due respect to Schumann's fight against the Philistines (as hinted at in titles such as "Davidsbündler"), it seems rather tame in retrospect when compared with the antibourgeois, extravagant, and wayward utterances of a Musset, Saint-Simon, Chopin, or Berlioz. The essential difference between the French and German Romanticists is confirmed by Schumann's own words. Ridiculing the epithet "Teufelsromantiker," he says:

One should stop confusing all issues. One should not suspect the noble intentions of the younger German composers on account of those things which may appear blameworthy in the compositions of a Berlioz or Liszt.[10]

During Felix's adolescence three great composers died: Weber in 1826, Beethoven in 1827, and Schubert in 1828. The fields they had cultivated most assiduously—namely opera, instrumental music, and song, respectively—were now deprived of their champions. Their death left a vacuum wherein only one voice of authority was heard: Cherubini, in some respects the last representative of the classic school, an artist of great versatility, especially significant in the domains of church music and opera. Meanwhile, however, a new tide had already begun to flow: the so-called "Early Romantics."

The composers of that early "Romantic School" are hardly known today. They were eclipsed by Weber, Mendelssohn, Schumann, Chopin, Berlioz, and Liszt. Hoffmann, the poet-composer, and perhaps Prince Louis Ferdinand of Prussia are the only ones who have escaped total oblivion.

Felix's teacher Zelter was by no means fond of the "Romantic School," nor was Gasparo Spontini, the almighty director of the Berlin Opera.

Whether Spontini simply disliked Felix or was jealous of the budding genius is here irrelevant. It is possibly owing to Spontini's antagonistic attitude that we do not possess a full-fledged comic opera from Felix's pen. The young composer certainly tried to familiarize himself with the style of the new *opera buffa*, as we shall see.

Spontini was an adherent of the classic *opera seria;* he and Lesueur were the fathers of the so-called "heroic opera," which continues in the style of Gluck, but prefers great theatrical pomp and splendor. His style mirrors best the glamour of the Napoleonic court. Viewed historically, Spontini is a link in the chain that stretches from Gluck and Cherubini to Meyerbeer and Wagner. The last named praised him highly, considering him "the logical continuation, nay, the fulfillment of Gluck's ideal of the dramatic opera-cantata."[11]

Thus, in the immediate environment of the young Mendelssohn the major influences were conservative to say the least. Indeed, his earlier compositions show traces of only two composers then considered Romantic: Weber and Spohr. Both were personally known to young Felix, and he admired them greatly. Weber's jubilant or lyric outbursts have left their clear mark in the youngster's music. In Spohr's work it was the contrapuntal deftness and harmonic refinement that impressed him.

On the other hand Felix did not subscribe to the Romantic craving for blending various arts, the longing for one universal synaesthetic art. This idea, which attained partial fulfillment in Wagner's *Gesamtkunstwerk*, suggested the fusion of poetry, acting, painting, and music. Again, E. T. A. Hoffmann was a true precursor of Wagner when he wrote: "It is no empty metaphor, no mere allegory, if the musician declares that to him colors, fragrances, rays appear as tones, and that he perceives them in their combination as a marvelous concert."[12] Mendelssohn was certainly no believer in the synaesthetic credo. Although he was a gifted draftsman, painter, and writer, he insisted on keeping these talents strictly separated.

Before we discuss in detail some of Mendelssohn's early compositions, a few words about his attitude towards the established forms in general will not be amiss. For it is chiefly in the realm of form that a clear development of his style can be observed. Tracing the composer's artistic course is not easy. For this very reason it must be undertaken, if the present misconception of Mendelssohn as a stagnant, nondynamic composer is to be dispelled once and for all.

In vocal music he eschewed experiments in form and generally preferred well-trodden paths. It is different with instrumental music. Here Mendelssohn, like most post-Beethovenian composers except Berlioz, did not always excel in the open, expanding form of sonata or symphony. His achievements were more significant in the extended closed forms, as we encounter them in the middle movements, the scherzos, and andantes of his chamber or orchestral music. Only in a few cases did he really fill a large form to the brim without repetition or stretching of his thematic material. Instances are the overtures *A Midsummer Night's Dream* and *The Hebrides,* and the first movements of the E minor Violin Concerto, of the unpublished concertos for two pianos and orchestra, and perhaps of the *Italian Symphony.* Because of his preference for closed forms, Mendelssohn endowed them with a host of lovely details. Hence the many middle movements in Mendelssohn's work that sound like *Songs Without Words.*

Generally speaking, Felix's early works, especially the unpublished ones, display to an astounding degree his pleasure in experimenting. A good many of these unpublished compositions exhibit his contrapuntal deftness. Sometimes he accomplished veritable *tours de force* in such polyphonic enterprises. He was more cautious with respect to form. But even here he toyed boldly with cyclical forms and rhapsodic liberties. According to Henry Chorley, Mendelssohn considered these compositions "rebellious." And so they are. Yet even that conservative critic was obliged to add:

> But they are knotted up, as it were, with close care and pains, not dashed off with insolence. They were the works of a boy anxious to prove himself a man among the double-refined intelligences of those by whom he was surrounded; and parading his science, his knowledge of the ancients, his mastery over all the learning of his Art.[13]

Among the early pieces we find a great many fugues, not only student-like exercises in counterpoint, reeking of the schoolroom, but fugues that appear as living and independent forms of the nineteenth century. And indeed, he comes very near to convincing us. His fugues are seldom naive imitations of Bachian patterns (Mendelssohn was rarely naïve) but melodious, cantabile pieces for the piano or the organ. Here the ideas of Anton Reicha (1770-1836), the friend of Beethoven's youth, were cautiously applied by Mendelssohn, who knew Reicha and respected him.

This interesting man played a double role in the music of the early nineteenth century. On the one hand, he taught a theory of harmony that allowed for highly refined modulations far beyond the actual practice of his time. Reicha foresaw an ever-increasing boldness as well as greater sublety in the harmonic devices of the forthcoming musical generation. His belief that unheard-of progressions would become commonplace was grist for the mill of those musicians who considered themselves Romantic.

On the other hand, Reicha tried to conceive a new type of fugue. His insistence upon "real answers" (instead of the conventional "tonal" ones) in the fugue's exposition led to a considerable expansion of the concept of tonality. It was this insistence on the new fugue that persuaded Mendelssohn, Schumann, Brahms, and even the minor composers of the period to cultivate this obsolescent form in a new spirit and thus to "gather flowers in a field where Bach had once built gigantic forests," as Schumann put it.[14]

Reicha's system of musical education was the last earnest attempt at Classic synthesis and musical universalism. Eventually openly and bitterly opposed to all "Romantic" trends (though he does not use that epithet), Reicha never failed to stress the unity of Classical structure as against the vagaries of the then modern composers. Reicha, Simon Sechter, and Moritz Hauptmann were the leading theorists of the first half of the nineteenth century. All three of them were anti-Romantic. Yet one of Reicha's students was Berlioz; and one of Sechter's was Bruckner!

Forty-four volumes of the autographs of Mendelssohn's compositions bound together by the composer himself, were deposited in 1878 at the State Library in Berlin. They begin with various small compositions of the boy. The first date entered is March 20, 1820, when Felix was only eleven years old. Many of these compositions, perhaps 200 or more, have never been published, although some of them certainly deserve publication today. While this book goes to press, the first two volumes of Mendelssohn's hitherto unpublished compositions have appeared in print under the auspices of the International Mendelssohn Society.

The compositions are not arranged in chronological order, and only where a date is given, can we set them in the proper succcession, until the year 1823. In the following listing we shall adopt a more or less chronological scheme. It is only very recently that some of Mendelssohn's hitherto unpublished compositions have gained the attention of the musical world. The very few works made available to us during the past few years add definitely new traits to the portrait of the master. Two major compositions have been spirited out of the volumes in the Berlin Library. These works, both piano concertos, show him perhaps as a more naïve, less polished character than his G minor Piano Concerto, which used to be in the standard repertory. Yet they convey the image of a sturdy, sometimes even rough boy, exactly as he was described by Adele Schopenhauer during his first Weimar visit.

From these juvenilia we single out those works that demonstrate, either by their originality or their experimentation, the emergence of young Mendelssohn's style.

In general, one can distinguish four phases in his development. The first reaches up to the composition of the overture to *A Midsummer Night's Dream* (1826). The second concludes with *St. Paul* (1835), and the third contains the subsequent works until the completion of *Elijah*. There ensued a short period of two years' length only—to his death—which signalled a new phase in his development. The characteristic traits of each phase merit careful discussion, since they indicate the composer's steady development and growing maturity.

ORCHESTRAL WORKS

IN THIS CATEGORY we shall examine the Violin Concerto in D minor, the two unpublished Concertos for Two Pianos and Orchestra (in A flat major and E major), and the Symphony in C minor.

The "little" Violin Concerto in D minor has only recently come to light, when a copy of the autograph was sold by the family. Yehudi Menuhin, now the owner of the score, was also its first performer. Written for Felix's violin teacher and friend Eduard Rietz, it displays surprising skill on the part of the thirteen-year-old composer as well as a charming ingenuity.

His approach to his thematic material is still naïve. The braggadocio attitude of the first movement stems from the French violin concerto of the end of the eighteenth century, as it was formed by Viotti, Rode, and Kreutzer. Characteristic of this type are the martial, heroic rhythms and figures that reflect the *gloire* of the Revolutionary and Napoleonic era. The first theme of the Violin Concerto breathes just this air:

Example 4

Here we have so robust, so orchestral a theme, that the composer could not entrust it to the soloist, not even in embellished form. The second, lyric theme, however, is more violinistic and is paraphrased by the soloist, but never played by the orchestra. Some rhapsodic elements are solidified by the frequent appearances of the first theme. Development and recapitulation and the other details closely follow the French pattern. Beyond that limited sphere there lie some modulations that must have startled the young composer's listeners:

Example 5

The second movement of the French concerto was almost invariably a "romance." While our slow movement does not bear such a heading, it nevertheless belongs to that category. However, it does not lapse into either the sickeningly sweet or the operatic style, both of which were French favorites. The theme, while in major, bears a distinct resemblance to the main theme of the first movement.

Example 6

This might well be the result of a subconscious process of integration. The embellishments already hint at passages of Mendelssohn's great E minor Violin Concerto.

The French school saved everything of a surprising, witty, exotic, or startling character for the last movement, usually a rondo. "The entrances and in particular the transitional measures before the repetition of the rondo theme were most carefully elaborated and would repay a special study."[15] All these characteristic elements can be found in Mendelssohn's piece. The sharply rhythmic theme is shaped like a gavotte, featuring a special finesse in the anticipation of its first tone in the repetition of the period.

Example 7

The violinistic demands are rather modest. Rarely does the composer go beyond simple runs, arpeggios, or the usual embellishing devices. Simple cadenzas are given for the second and third movements.

The entire work is full of zest and robust vitality but contains nothing that might tangibly be associated with the Mendelssohn we have come to know. For a first attempt of a young student, however, it is a most remarkable achievement. The orchestra is treated with surprising ease and craftsmanship and the few polyphonic passages are entirely free from classroom atmosphere.

When the Concertos for Two Pianos and Orchestra were written Beethoven was still alive. Young Mendelssohn, his fervent and uncritical admirer (in contrast to his teacher Zelter), was unable to escape his magic spell. Yet Beethoven was not the only star Felix looked up to for guidance. Apart from Mozart and Bach, whom he had been taught to consider eternal suns, there were the planets and comets of the then prevalent musical fashion who attracted the boy-composer's attention, foremost among them Hummel, Weber, and Moscheles, all of whom he knew quite well personally. They, too, left their traces in the two concertos.

Mendelssohn's own imagination might have been impaired by so many outside influences. Indeed, the danger of complete eclecticism was not overcome in the E major Concerto (1823). A year later, however, in his second concerto he found his own way, in spite of all these conflicting elements. It is not very difficult to size up these influences in an analysis of the scores. Mozart and Bach are Felix's models for structure; Beethoven and Weber are reflected in his rhythms and harmonies; for specifically pianistic devices he relies on Weber, Moscheles, and Hummel.

The ritornello structure of the mature Mozart concerto is faithfully retained by Mendelssohn. Nowhere does the piano open a first movement, as it does in Beethoven's G major Concerto and in some of its imitations, not to mention Mozart's own early E flat major Concerto, K. 271. The contrast between the *tutti* and the *soli*, framed by a great sonata form with an extensive orchestral preamble, is likewise upheld as a Mozartean legacy. The same holds good for the aria type with or without a second subject, which almost invariably constitutes the form of the slow movements, unless they are variations. It is only in the last movements that young Mendelssohn experiments: *fugati*, thematic combinations in double counterpoint, bold solo *entrées*, and the like. In the first of the two concertos they fail; he is unable to fill the framework adequately. In the second he succeeds admirably.

Thematically, Mendelssohn naïvely traces Bach's or Beethoven's contours, often without realizing their full potentialities. Thus he opens the first Concerto with a Bach-like fugal theme, but sets it out quite homophonically. Not till the very end of the movement does it dawn on him that the theme lends itself most naturally to polyphonic treatment. He then makes two or three rather feeble attempts in this direction, but does not carry them through. In the second Concerto the great rhythm of

Beethoven's Fifth Symphony is clearly heard, and later on even stressed (Double Concerto, No. 2, A flat Major, first movement):

Example 8

In the second Concerto the same master's Septet in E flat casts its net around Felix, and he is caught. He not only copies the bridge-theme in the first movement of the Septet but manages to digest and expand it in his own way. Weber's style is reflected in the initial solo of the first Concerto (Double Concerto, No. 1, E Major, first movement):

Example 9a

(a) First theme

Example 9b

(b) First solo

and in many *tutti* passages of the Second Concerto, such as:

Example 10

Devices of his friends Hummel and Moscheles are occasionally copied also.

In general, the composer follows German patterns, with a single exception: the finale of the first Concerto, where he tries to introduce the elegant verve of the French rondo and fails.

Outside influences apart, the two concertos have certain clearly discernible elements in common. Yet they are fully individualized works, and their differences are at least as important as their similarities.

The first Concerto opens with a *tutti* supported by the two pianos, which Felix terms "principali," in an *Allegro vivace* (originally *Allegro moderato;* the last word is carefully erased). The mood of this movement may be described, however inadequately, as one of bright and elegant lyricism. Towards the end, the contrapuntal possibilities of the first theme are tested, but not very extensively, in a brief *fugato.* The movement ends with a rather spectacular, joyous *tutti* outburst in the manner of Weber, without a cadenza; Mendelssohn had to cajole Moscheles into writing one for the London performance. Since the Berlin autograph shows no trace of it, the composer must have taken with him a clean copy of the original score. That copy may yet be found somewhere in England.

The slow movement (*Adagio non troppo,* 6/8, C major) is a lovely reflection of Mozart's aria-like movements with a *minore* section. The pianos voice the first theme and elaborate upon it. The orchestration, tranquil and yet luminous, displays the amazing craftsmanship of the fourteen-year-old composer.

Well-rounded as this movement is, the finale (*Allegro,* 4/4, E major) is poor. It begins quite presumptuously with a rocket-like solo entry of the first piano, followed by another idea which Mendelssohn obviously considered the rondo subject. It continues without any development and is interrupted by the *tutti,* a noisy operatic tune. Not much goes on after that, except a good many brilliant but rather empty piano passages. After too many repetitions the movement eventually fizzles out like a firework on a wet night. The framework, instead of being filled with organic substance, is merely padded.

The second Concerto, in A flat (1824), stands on a far higher level from the first note to the last. It shows a more elevated artistic ambition and is also of greater length. In it are phrases in which the fifteen-year-old composer attains the kind of mastery that he maintains throughout so accomplished a work as the Octet, Op. 20. Yet the Octet was written only a year after the Concerto, so rapid was the young artist's development. The Concerto opens with the strings and the two pianos announcing the first theme (it sets the mood as well as the pace of the whole movement and might be described as energetic, zestful, and brilliant):

Example 11

This is its later transformation:

Example 12

The slow movement (*Andante,* E major) shaped as an *air varié,* opens with a simple *Lied* theme in the strings:

Example 13

It is expanded in woodwinds and horns and carried to B major, whence the pianos lead it back to its original key. After it is subjected to rather elegant drawing-room treatment, the orchestra turns to A minor and brings the movement to a very serene conclusion, *pp*.

The last movement, a true finale, is a stroke of genius. The *Allegro vivace* opens with an impetuous theme which anticipates the style of Chopin. It is played by the first piano:

Example 14

The subsequent *tutti* reaffirms the energetic rondo subject, topping it off with a lyrical conclusion. The form is a rather complex combination of sonata-rondo, with parts of exposition and recapitulation treated in fugal style. This must be considered a rather bold experiment in musical form. After a restatement of the subject by the orchestra and the two pianos, there ensues a strict four-part fugue on a splinter motif of the main theme. Here Mendelssohn tries another experiment: he inserts in the rapid course of the two-piano fugue the second theme of the movement in the woodwinds, thereby reducing the pace of the fugue. After a full stop the pianos render the second theme homophonically, a truly Mendelssohnian lyric conception. After a highly dramatic and rather agitated development section and recapitulation the orchestra starts a *stretto* with a graceful new theme, whereupon the main theme is repeated by the pianos in alternation. The orchestra, in sheer Weberian jubilation, leads to the repetition of the main theme with and against the pianos and brings the concerto to a brilliant conclusion. This last movement is unquestionably the best of the work. It shows how Mendelssohn had grown in stature during the two and a half months he spent in writing the Concerto.

Of the three symphonies Mendelssohn permitted to be published (neither the *Italian* nor the *Reformation* is among them), two are in a minor key. The Symphony in C minor, Op. 11, written in 1824, represents his thirteenth symphonic attempt, and the autograph of the work, in the library of the Philharmonic Society in London, bears the number XIII. It was first performed in 1827 in the Leipzig *Gewandhaus* and received warm praise, at least from the *Allgemeine Musikalische Zeitung*. Later on, in 1829, Felix conducted this symphony in London for the Philharmonic Society. In his letter of May 26, 1829, he gives a vivid account of the performance, during which the scherzo had to be repeated. This Scherzo is a part of the Octet, Op. 20, and was orchestrated by Mendelssohn, when he inserted it in the Symphony instead of its original Minuetto.

The fact that the intensely self-critical Mendelssohn permitted the publication of this early work should warn us against dismissing it as a "puerile experiment." That it certainly is not. If it does not always display maturity or originality, it already bears the mark of a master craftsman.

Beethoven was still alive when it was written, and his Ninth Symphony had not yet been heard. Young Felix, like most serious composers of the time, was aware of the impossibility of carrying on where Beethoven had left off. Another approach to the symphony had to be found, for Beethoven was—in his way—a monopolist of the symphony. The symphonic writers of three subsequent generations had to struggle against his gigantic shadow.

Mendelssohn's themes are good and sound, but without any characteristic flavor. Nor is his C minor the same as Beethoven's "tragic key." The first theme combines runs and arpeggios and continues in the descending sixth chords that we encounter so frequently in the mature Mozart. Mendelssohn must early have taken a fancy to this device, for in his Symphony in C minor, as well as in the *Hebrides* Overture and other orchestral compositions, we encounter running sixth-chords.

Example 15

The lyrical second theme reminds one somewhat of the young Beethoven, whereas the end of the exposition is sheer Weber of the *Freischütz* Overture—the jubilant C and E flat major, the descending scales, all this is here. The development is brief and uses chiefly the first and last themes of the exposition. The recapitulation ends with a sudden change into a triumphant major. The subsequent coda is pretentious and too long—the ambitious Felix seems to have striven for an effect similar to that of the D flat major in the coda of the *Eroica*. But he does not succeed, and then the end fizzles out. The mood of the first movement is not tragic, not even very serious. It might be best described as zestful and vigorous.

The second movement, a warm *Adagio*, ¾, E flat major, opens with parallel thirds, then very much in vogue. The form is an interesting mixture of sonata and variations. Again the sixth-chords appear and the woodwinds end the pleasant movement. Its orchestration merits attention for its transparency.

The most characteristic and original movement of the symphony is the Minuetto, in 6/4. The theme, in robust C minor, is presented in imitations and sharply syncopated. Its beginning is reminiscent of the main idea of the first movement. The oscillation between G and A flat is the common thematic nucleus. The minuet of Mozart's C minor Serenade for wind instruments is probably the most illustrious of the numerous ancestors of the movement. Its trio, however, is a really original conception. Chorale chords in A flat are quietly embellished by the violins. The return to the minuet is achieved in a thematic fashion all too closely patterned after the passage between scherzo and finale in Beethoven's Fifth Symphony.

The last movement recalls ideas of Mozart (Piano Concerto in C minor, last movement) and Haydn (Symphony in C minor, No. 95). It is a movement full of lively temperament. Once again Weber's influence is clearly discernible, at the end of the exposition. In the development we hear a rather rigid school fugue, which ends (strictly according to old formula!) with a pedal-point and leads back to the recapitulation. We are treated to a fugato coda and a rather forced stretto in C major to provide a triumphant end. Evidently Felix's mind had been captured by Beethoven's *Egmont* and Weber's *Freischutz* and *Euryanthe* overtures. Without any doubt the middle movements are the best and most mature of this work by a fifteen-year-old; and for their sake the work merits performance. It is full of vigor, sounds fine, and would serve as a pleasant curtain-raiser.

CHAMBER MUSIC

The Piano Quartets in C minor, F minor, and B minor, Op. 1, 2, and 3; the Sonata for Violin and Piano in F minor, Op. 4; and the Sextet in D, for violin, 2 violas, 'cello, bass, and piano, Op. 110, comprise a group of five works written by Felix before he attained a more or less consistent approach to chamber-music style. It includes works as different in artistry and maturity as the beginner's overambitious Violin Sonata, Op. 4 and the considerably more sophisticated Quartet in B minor. The Violin Sonata is in itself not interesting, for the thematic material reminds the listener so strongly of Beethoven's Piano Sonata in D minor, Op. 31, and similar works that we almost wonder if the work was not intended as a kind of exercise, patterned after and inspired by Beethoven's sonatas. Its original slow movement saves the work from mere eclecticism.

Of the Piano Quartets the first, in C minor, and the second, in F minor, display more or less the same elements of style and approach. To us they appear almost as little piano concertos with three stringed instruments for accompaniment. Thus the pianist has all the fun, while the other instrumentalists are only occasionally allowed to contribute to it. The third quartet, in B minor, dedicated to Goethe, was written in 1824 and, like the first, performed in Weimar. Here young Felix already shows his power of integration to an amazing extent. The main theme of the first movement recurs also in the scherzo and the finale in these paraphrases:

Example 16

Allegro molto

Scherzo:
Allegro molto

Finale:
Allegro vivace

The scherzos of all three quartets (that of the F minor is called "Intermezzo") fall into one category and one pattern, that of an either furious or polyphonic dance. The scherzo of the B minor quartet is but one of the many *perpetuum mobile* structures that Mendelssohn loved dearly and Wagner attacked venomously.

The slow movements display not only the weakest spots of the quartets, but actually, throughout almost his entire output, constitute Mendelssohn's Achilles heel. To this category belongs especially the Adagio of the Quartet in B minor, which betrays young Felix's fondness for unadulterated sweetness.

The third of the quartets served as the touchstone of Felix's talent before so stern a judge as Cherubini. That austere man, as we have seen, reacted with great politeness. Eight years later, again in Paris, Mendelssohn jestingly singled out the over-sweet Adagio as being in "juste milieu" (i.e. in the established monarchic order) whereas the other three movements represent "mouvement" (i.e. political revolution).

The Sextet in D for piano, violin, two violas, 'cello, and double bass, Op. 110, precedes the Octet, Op. 20 by only one year. Yet the two works are vastly different from each other; while the Sextet pretends to be chamber music, in fact it is again a little piano concerto, which Felix clearly wrote for himself. The lively themes still show a Weberish hue, and in general there are no surprises to be found in this fresh and merry but undeniably mediocre work.

EARLY PIANO WORKS

IF E. M. FORSTER'S DICTUM, that an artist has the right to be judged by his very best creations, is to be complied with, we should, in the case of Mendelssohn, have to ignore many of his piano compositions; in general, they play a minor role in a survey of his work. For it is here that he is most vulnerable, as he well knew. The twenty-year-old composer complained in a letter to his friend, Ignaz Moscheles, about his "own poverty in novel passages [*Wendungen*] for the piano which struck me again very much in the *Rondo brillante*, Op. 29. . . ."

In his piano music Mendelssohn cultivated three strictly circumscribed areas: the brilliant virtuoso style, suitable for the fashionable concert hall or drawing room, the intimate or "domestic" idiom, especially in his *Songs Without Words*, and finally the learned, contrapuntal style, the prototype of which is his Op. 36, the Six Preludes and Fugues. Thus, the emotional compass of his piano music is rather limited, and it became more so the older he grew. He left his major legacy to the pianist in his great *Variations Sérieuses*, Op. 54. With it he anticipated the great development of the variation form in the hands of Brahms, Richard Strauss, and Reger. We shall return to this mature work in a later chapter.

During his youth, Mendelssohn ventured occasionally into radical innovations: in his *Songs Without Words*, where he was successful to the point of danger, and in his Sonata for Piano, Op. 6 (1826), where he boldly but unsuccessfully applied fugal treatment to an instrumental recitative. This basically unsound experiment, spiced with pre-Wagnerian chromaticism, is nonetheless a remarkable attempt at a new form. We quote here only the beginning:

Example 17

Of his brilliant pieces he writes to Hiller (letter of July 17, 1838): "Piano pieces, to be sure, I do not write with the greatest enjoyment, nor perhaps with much success, but occasionally I require something new to play. . . ." The truth of the matter is that Mendelssohn, the lion of the Salons, had to comply occasionally with their demands. This taste cherished brilliant inanities, such as were produced by Henri Herz and Kalkbrenner, of whom Mendelssohn spoke with contempt. Yet his brilliant pieces are better than theirs only in degree, not in principle.

The borderline between the elfin and the brilliant is already reached in his Capriccio, Op. 5 (1825). The spirit of this and similar *presto* or *prestissimo* pieces cannot fail to remind the listener of compositions by Domenico Scarlatti of the eighteenth century. Mendelssohn doubtless knew some of these compositions and they struck a kindred chord in his imagination. To the same category belongs also the little scherzo of the Sonata for Piano, Op. 106, in B flat (1821), an otherwise undistinguished work. But this charming little scherzo that flits by in one minute has been unjustly neglected by pianists. It would be useful as an elegant encore—upon the recommendation of Schumann, who pronounced this early work "exemplary."

VOCAL WORKS

IT WAS MENDELSSOHN'S sad destiny to have risen to fame by the popularity of his instrumental music and his oratorios alone. His strictly liturgical music, that is, music written for a fixed order of divine service, and his cantatas, motets, and other works on biblical texts have been neglected altogether by posterity. And yet he was rightly proud of these works, which testify radiantly to his deep religiousness. More than a third of these compositions have not even been published, and the rest have fallen into oblivion. Why this neglect of some of his most ambitious works?

The reasons are twofold, practical and ideological. Mendelssohn, always praised for the euphony of his choral style, demanded well-trained choruses, usually of five to eight parts. Such choruses are today rarely available, except in large Protestant cathedrals. In addition, the orchestral accompaniment, frequently demanded, makes the cost of such performances virtually prohibitive.

The ideological reasons are no less cogent. In Mendelssohn's time the Protestant liturgy was definitely established in various "Agende," yet often subject to regional statutes (*Landeskirchen*). The growing standardization of the liturgy in Germany worked to the disadvantage of his sacred works, inasmuch as their texts did not become part of the regular service. Moreover, the liturgical trend points in the direction of congregational singing, not towards that of concertizing by professional choirs and soloists. The growing insistence upon community song had to bypass practically all of Mendelssohn's ambitious church music. We shall return to this question in Chapter XVIII.

For the very reason that they are so little known, the church compositions require the biographer's earnest attention. This author is indebted to Rudolf Werner's study *Felix Mendelssohn als Kirchenmusiker*, which evaluates seriously and realistically every church composition of the master.

The twelve-year-old Felix was able to write triple fugues in his sacred music. It is true that in many cases the biblical texts were actually pretexts for exercises in composition, but it is equally true that a large and ambitious work such as the great Magnificat (MS) for chorus, soloists, and orchestra is far more than a talented student's essay. It already interprets the text in a worthy and artistic manner. Thus, the passage *"a progenie in progenies"* (from generation to generations) evokes in Felix the image of a perpetually moving band, which he expresses in this way.

Example 18

The "rolling masses" of the text contrast well with the unmoving pedal-point.

Handel was, in this instance, Felix's lodestar. In others it was Mozart as in the unpublished Kyrie in C minor for eight-part chorus and soloists *a cappella*, written in 1823 (a, Mendelssohn; b, Mozart, *Ave verum*), or in Felix's practically unknown *Salve Regina* for soprano with string orchestra, of 1824 (c).

Example 19a   Example 19b

Example 19c

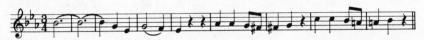

Both compositions are highly expressive, though hardly original. But the latter criticism is no longer true of the great *Te Deum* for eight-part chorus, soloists, and simple accompaniment (double bass or continuo). The work was finished about the same time as the Octet (1825) and shows some affinity to it. Rudolf Werner observes rightly that in purely religious pieces a composer always reaches maturity later than in his secular works. In the *Te Deum*, however, the composer's limitation to eight-part double chorus attests to the profound seriousness with which Mendelssohn approached his task. The type of noisy and spectacular *Te Deum* with trumpets and timpani is here deliberately avoided, possibly under the influence of Thibaut's book *Über die Reinheit der Tonkunst*. Its two climaxes are Numbers 5 (*Te gloriosus apostolorum*) and 9 (*Salvum fac*). Here Mendelssohn deftly handles the intricate technique of a highly polyphonic structure, and approaches his task quite boldly. Passages such as the following should once and for all dispense with the notion of Mendelssohn's lack of harmonic or melodic inventiveness.

Example 20

The astounding progressions of No. 5 (a) are no less admirable than the deeply religious spirit that speaks out of the finely chiselled melody of the *Salvum fac* (b). Especially noteworthy here is the rhythmically richly profiled line.

OPERETTAS AND OPERA

FROM HIS CHILDHOOD on, Mendelssohn was a theatre enthusiast. The merry, intimate atmosphere of his home stimulated the creation of a number of little operettas by the young Felix. He hoped to crown these intimate skits by a veritable opera—his *Wedding of Camacho*. It had only one performance in the Berlin Opera (1827), and Felix ran off before the end of the work, although it was not entirely scorned by the audience. This traumatic experience created strong inhibitions in Mendelssohn and ruined every later operatic attempt. Today the music of these operatic essays (all unpublished) would be entirely inaccessible to us, for they are extant only in the composer's autograph in the Berlin State Library (in the Eastern Zone), were it not for a meritorious study of Professor G. Schünemann,[16] on which the following remarks are based.

Mendelssohn expressed his operatic ideal in these words: "It ought to be German, noble, and gay; be it a Rhenish folk-tale or any other truly national event or fable, or an original character (as in *Fidelio*), I am aiming at the best element in man, the noble, the merry. . . ."[17] Alas, he never came across a libretto that found favor in his hypercritical eyes, and all his operatic aspirations came to nothing.

Yet he had a strong dramatic talent, especially for comic opera, as one may see in his operettas and musical skits, written for parties at home.

His first attempt is a musical joke which takes place at the office of his father and uncle. They sing of their business, of their friendship, but soon father Abraham attacks his brother: "But of music you know nothing, for *Olympia* is miserable." The brother replies: "What? I don't know about music? We shall decide that right away, for *Olympia* is a lovely opera." The allusion is to Spontini's then very popular opera *Olympia*, which Felix detested. The scene is not finished, but merry enough. The librettos of Felix's later operettas were all written by Dr. Caspar, a physician and close friend of the Mendelssohns. The first fruit of this collaboration was *Die Soldaten-liebschaft* (*Soldiers' Loves*). Here young Felix wrote pleasant, melodious tunes but they are without real zest. Only in the cavatina do we hear a melody that anticipates the sweet melancholy of many a later composition.

More successful, because better adjusted to the classroom and *Lausbu-benwelt* (rowdy world) of young Felix, was Dr. Caspar's libretto *Die Zwei Pädagogen* (*The Two Pedagogues*), written in 1821. The overture shows diligent study of Cimarosa, Dittersdorf, and Mozart. Full of comic force is the entrance of the pedagogue, Kinderschreck (Scarechild), and one feels immediately that Felix is personally concerned.

Example 21

I have— of late ma-ny plans made, I spe-cu-late, I have betrayed, by no means bad, re-ver-be-rate_____ hell to be paid.

These are buffooneries which might have been written by the young Rossini. Another (disguised) pedagogue is introduced, and a fight between the schools of Pestalozzi and Basedow unfolds itself very comically. (Pest . . . *vs* Baa . . . !)

Two more of these little operas occupied young Felix: *The Traveling Comedians,* written in 1822, and a real comic opera, *The Two Nephews or The Uncle from Boston,* written in 1822 and 1823. Both works continue the style of the former operettas on a higher level. For the *Two Nephews* Felix gathers all of his now considerable technique and power of invention. The dramatic part of the music is clearly molded by famous patterns of Mozart and Weber. Yet the young composer occasionally shows originality and lovely melodic lines, as in the first piece of the opera:

Example 22

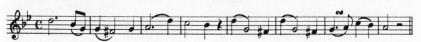

Reminiscences of *Freischütz* and of *The Marriage of Figaro* are to be heard in such pieces from the *Two Nephews* as:

Example 23

This was the last "student's essay" in opera.

This survey of young Felix's first steps in the field of composition shows a surprising versatility on his part and a surpassing speed in learning to handle the tools and techniques of his trade, but, as yet, not much originality. He covered the field of symphony, concert, chamber music, opera, piano solo, and church music. Certainly a wide vista and of an amazing variety for a sixteen-year-old!

However, the major tests and major tasks were yet to come. The apprentice could not handle them. But from his sixteenth year onward Felix Mendelssohn must be considered a master, though a young one, who was willing, and in most cases able, to tackle great tasks and shoulder vast responsibilities.

Notes

1. E. T. A. Hoffmann, *Gesammelte Schriften,* Serapion ed. (Leipzig, 1922), VIII, p. 45.
2. Wagner, *Das Kunstwerk der Zukunft* (Leipzig, 1871; written in Paris, 1850).
3. E.T.A. Hoffmann, *op. cit.,* XIII, p. 192.
4. E.T.A. Hoffmann, *op. cit.,* XIII, p. 89.
5. A scholar of the twentieth century, E. Istel, has shown convincingly that the true Romantic musicians would not accept a distinction between their school and the classic. See E. Istel, *Die Bluetezeit der musikalischen Romantik,* 2nd ed. (Leipzig, 1920), p. 2f.
6. See, however, the remarks on the rationalistic origin of Romantic ideas in Chapter XX.
7. O. Berdow, *Rahel Varnhagen* (Stuttgurt, 1900).
8. Hensel, *F.M.,* I, p. 264 (letter of August 25, 1829). Cf. Chapter VIII, p. 135.
9. In this historical interest grew the first tenuous roots of musicology. R. Hohenemser, *Welche Einflüsse hatte die Wiederbelebung der älteren Musik im 19. Jahrhundert auf die deutschen Komponisten?* (Leipzig, 1901), Chapters 1 and 2; also Alfred Einstein, *Music in the Romantic Era* (New York, 1947), pp. 5; 41-48.
10. Schumann, *Collected Writings* (Year, 1840), "Die Teufelsromantiker."
11. R. Wagner, "Erinnerungen an Spontini," *Gesammelte Schriften* (Leipzig, 1871-72), Vol. V.
12. Hoffmann, *op. cit,* works, VII, p. 344.
13. Henry Chorley, *Modern German Music* (London, 1855), II, p. 408.
14. Schumann was well aware of Reicha's influence.
15. Arnold Schering, *Geschichte des Instrumentalkonzerts* (Leipzig, 1905), p. 170.
16. *Zeitschrift fur Musikwissenschaft* (hereafter Z.M.), (Berlin, 1923), p. 506ff.
17. Devrient, *Erinnerungen an Felix Mendelssohn,* (Leipzig, 1891), p. 245 (letter of April 26, 1845).

CHAPTER V

The Sheltered Years
(1825-1829)

> Never has there been an era when in every respect the old and
> the new have clashed so violently.
> W. v. Humboldt
>
> It is the misfortune of the succession of times that one era always
> influences the other, and now it is not the new that infiltrates
> the old, but the old that influences the new.
> Rahel von Varnhagen

THE HOUSE IN THE *LEIPZIGERSTRASSE*

PROSPERITY shone on the business of the Mendelssohn brothers. In 1825
Abraham and his family moved from their house on the New Promenade
to the palatial mansion at Leipzigerstrasse 3, with which the happiest associations for the whole company were forever connected. The house, with
its large park, many rooms, and subsidiary buildings, resembled a little
castle more than a bourgeois home. The former owners, the Von der Recke
family, had used it as their city manor. The Mendelssohns' friends accused
them of "having moved out of the world," for at that time the house
stood at the periphery of Berlin. Today that section is in the heart of the
city.

To the members of the family this house meant much more than just
a piece of property. They considered it almost a family shrine, representative
of their status in the world. In this sense Felix used the expression "Leipzigerstrasse 3," and in this sense it was understood by the family and its wide
circle of friends. The large garden surrounding the house served as a favorite
gathering place in summer and as an area for physical exercise in winter.
All the letters and memoirs of the Mendelssohn circle abound in tender
references to the house, its atmosphere, and its music. The garden was an
ideal place for merry-making, courting, dancing, athletics (which Felix

[71]

took very seriously), and peripatetic discussions. It even had a journal; called *Garten-Zeitung* in summer, *Thee und Schneezeitung* in winter, it was written by hand, and every visitor was welcome to add his contribution. Founded by Felix and his friends Klingemann and Marx, it became most popular, and even men of international renown, such as W. v. Humboldt or Hegel, did not disdain to write in it aphorisms, anecdotes, or little poems.

The Mendelssohn salon flourished in those years. It would be misleading, however, to define the circle as an exclusively musical one. In the still somewhat patriarchal Berlin, where anybody knew everybody, a salon served a number of functions that in other societies were taken over by the coffee house, the club, the literary or musical association, and even the dance hall. It catered for the activities of three overlapping groups characteristic of the intellectual life of Berlin during the first third of the nineteenth century. It was a meeting place of literary and scientific minds; the admirers of Goethe were always welcome, be they "Hegler or Schlegler," as a contemporary wit remarked. Professors Hegel, Boeckh, Jacob Grimm, Gans, and Ranke represented the various segments of science and the humanities. *Belles-lettres* had no less impressive representatives than Brentano and his equally literary sister Bettina, E. T. A. Hoffmann, Tieck, Heine, Droysen, and Varnhagen. It was also one of the few clearing houses where Jews and Gentiles met in perfect equality. Many of the current religious, legal, political, and social problems were threshed out in that hospitable mansion. And a musical salon it certainly was. Abraham spared no money when it came to hiring additional musicians, purchasing instruments, or engaging music copyists. To conjure up the spiritual climate of that group is not easy. Issues of that day are now unintelligible unless explained at length, the topics of gossip no longer known, the refreshing little scandals irrelevant.

The musicians and scholars of that era need no introduction. Intimate friends of the house were the pianist Moscheles, the violinist Eduard Rietz, the musical scholar Marx, editor of the *Berliner Allgemeine Musikalische Zeitung* the composer Ferdinand Hiller, the revered and a little feared Zelter, with his blunt and often coarse tongue. But any musician of distinction, however tenuous his connection with the Mendelssohns, could also be seen there: C. M. von Weber, the almighty *Generalmusikdirektor* Spontini, then head of the Royal Opera, Spohr, Meyerbeer, and many, many others.

Felix's closest friend was probably the young diplomat Carl Klingemann, no mean musician himself, who in his Biedermeier poems gave Felix songtexts of a respectable "nice-cup-of-tea" quality. Klingemann's unwavering loyalty to the house of Mendelssohn, and his later position in London, where he was secretary of the Hanover Legation, made him the key figure in

Felix's relations with English musical and social life. The most interesting, yet also the most problematic, musician of the circle was certainly Adolf Bernhard Marx, who was fourteen years older than Felix. His influence upon Felix tended to counterbalance that of Zelter to a certain extent. There was no love lost between the two. Thus Zelter poured out his heart to Goethe:

> They are lively boys, rather dilettantes though, and the editor (of their paper) is a certain Marx or Marcus from Halle, who might have been baptized with soda, for his excretions are greenish-grey. They, like flies, stain even the food which they like. . . .[1]

Or:

> Mr. Marx or Marcus, not the evangelist—although he preaches in the new musical magazine the new gospel of bunglers [*Pfuscher*]—brought me greeting from Felix, which I like as much as I dislike the conveyor.[2]

Marx championed not only Bach, Zelter's own domain, but also Beethoven, whom Zelter considered rather critically, and even Spontini, whose grand operas and prestige were respected by the old friend of Goethe. Moreover, Marx had once taken lessons with Zelter, but stopped very soon, since he felt that he "had outgrown his old-fashioned teachings." Small wonder that Zelter took a dim view of Marx's artistic activities. Yet it would be unjust to dismiss Marx with a few sentences, as most writers on Mendelssohn have done. During the years 1826 to 1831 he exerted probably the strongest possible influence upon Felix, until they quarreled and parted company altogether.

Father Mendelssohn disliked Marx intensely. He considered him to be altogether too smart a young fellow, "who will never really produce and may harm a really productive talent."[3] Felix, however, was strongly attracted by Marx's application of critical reasoning to works of music. After their quarrel, indeed after Felix's early death, when almost every one of his compositions was admired uncritically, Marx, being less biased than Wagner, was the first to recognize the more problematical aspects of Felix's talent and work. He deplored the youngster's waste of so much time and effort in the sphere of "small pleasantry and tender sentimentality"; he blamed Felix for being induced to "dwell constantly in this element" by the abundance of homage paid to him.[4] Marx's reminiscences, written long after their quarrel, give us an excellent idea of the intellectual climate in which young Felix and his friends were moving. In Marx's opinion the success of the *Songs Without Words* and similar brilliant drawing-room pieces by Felix distracted the public's attention from his true masterworks.

What Marx with all of his sharp analysis did not observe or appreciate was that Felix was bravely and honestly struggling to find his own way. With the eclectic, if technically precocious, compositions of his boyhood he was no longer satisfied. Felix tried his talents in very different *genres*, sometimes intentionally imitating other composers, sometimes boldly experimenting. The "salon," dominated by his mother, persisted in coaxing him, directly or indirectly, to write "effective," i.e. brilliant, piano or vocal music. At the bottom of his heart Felix resented this interference. And to his father he opened his heart:

> I am now convinced that people expect from me something special, and it must be much, much more than the *Wedding of Camacho*. I know also that I need not disappoint these expectations. But I do not believe that I have to prove this today or tomorrow. . . . In instrumental music alone I have succeeded in paving my own way, but as for the rest I am still far from my goal . . . I know that I shall be able to do well in the operatic realm, but I am no less convinced that even in instrumental music I have barely started. . . .⁵

He expressed horror of all self-appointed geniuses and, even more, of any pretensions to be a genius himself. To him "the highest expression of genius is the greatest truthfulness."⁶ What a strangely anti-Romantic credo, set down during the composition of the *A Midsummer Night's Dream* overture!

Yet his mother continued to prod Felix and turned to his friend Klingemann in London for help. She complained about Felix's reserve. "It is bad enough that Felix has taken it into his head to be heard playing only boring accompaniments, but he now composes only the type of pieces that nobody may see and that can hardly be performed. I consider such pieces stillborn children and I fear that he delves so deeply into this *genre* that nothing fresh, enjoyable, or lively comes forth any more. . . ."⁷

What did Lea mean by her reference to "boring accompaniments"? Nothing less than the fact that Felix introduced in Berlin and Leipzig some songs of the then still unknown Franz Schubert, especially his *Erlkönig*.⁸ Her complaint about Felix's compositions having little chance of being performed refers to his occupation with large compositions for chorus *a cappella* or with orchestra, on austerely liturgical texts.

There can be little doubt that most of her circle, except Fanny, echoed her sentiments. And to keep peace and please the ladies Felix occasionally yielded to their demands and wrote something "enjoyable or lively." He was fully aware of his dilemma. Some of his letters and a humorous poem, written about that time, are very revealing. They bear witness to his striving for spiritual and artistic independence.

If the artist gravely writes,
  To sleep it will beguile.
If the artist gaily writes,
  It is a vulgar style.

If the artist simply writes,
  A fool he's said to be.
If an artist deeply writes,
  He's mad: 'tis plain to see.

If the artist writes at length,
  How sad his hearer's lot!
If the artist briefly writes,
  No man will care one jot.

In whatsoever way he writes,
  He can't please everyman.
Therefore let an artist write
  How he likes and can.
          (Translation by Sir George Grove)

For Felix there was no lack of opportunity to try his hand at any of the styles mentioned. For years the Sunday musicales in the Mendelssohn house provided an excellent laboratory in which to test all kinds of music, old or new, serious or light, conventional or experimental. All this took place in a hall spacious enough to seat several hundred persons. There are many enthusiastic descriptions of these events; that of the novelist Paul Heyse, the young son of Felix's tutor (and Felix's third cousin), is little known:

> An illustrious company filled the large room, yet there was hardly anybody who was not, by his musical knowledge or talent, entitled to his place. Every transient musical celebrity was flattered to be thought worthy of a formal invitation to these Sunday morning concerts.
> Steady guests were Professor Boeckh and old Steffens, once president of the Berlin University. The hall was like a shrine, in which an enthusiastic congregation absorbed every tone with the utmost attention. . . .[9]

During the years 1825 to 1830, Felix spent the happiest time of his life in these surroundings, sheltered in a close-knit affectionate family milieu. A mere boy still, he acquired among the many relatives of his extensive clan, among his friends and the numerous visitors, those urbane manners which later on would enchant the critical Englishmen. His social environment had made him what they most cherished: a highly accomplished "gentleman of leisure." His perfect deportment, his easy poise in the drawing room, were certainly assets in his later life, although the very fact that he had impeccable manners was sometimes criticized by his enemies.

FELIX AND FANNY

AT NO TIME was the bond between brother and sister, always very close, as intimate as in those years during which Felix was in search of himself. Theirs was a relationship that all but exceeded the confines of affection set between a devoted brother and loving sister. It was much stronger than the clannish instincts that meant so much in Felix's intellectual and emotional life, for it rested upon an affinity usually found only in twins, where it has biological causes. Here the element of consanguinity was often sublimated into the spiritual realm, so that sometimes in the correspondence between brother and sister the reader does not know who wrote to whom. Sporadically, though, that consanguinity evoked almost physical impulses and instincts in Fanny, especially before her marriage; they expressed themselves in outbursts of possessiveness and jealousy.

Felix, tactful and affectionate, early became aware of his beloved sister's sentiments, and reciprocated gratefully the spiritual warmth of her love, while carefully guarding himself against a darker, less normal attachment. As a mere boy of fifteen he wrote to Fanny: "If I had not decided not to be tender to you, I could not, after your last letter, vouch for myself. However, I will not be tender, and I am stubborn."[10] Three years later, when Fanny had one of her outbursts of jealousy, he wrote:

> You must get a rap on the knuckles . . . are you the inquisition? Do you spy on me? Is the string, on which I flutter, long, but unbreakable? You were in my room? Prying into my things? . . . Take care, fair flower, take care . . . ![11]

Invariably he criticized her all too romantic sentimentality and its enthusiastic eruptions, sometimes gently chiding, sometimes in language blunt to the point of rudeness. A passage like this is not rare: "I must fairly lash you, my dear Fanny. If, by one of my jokes, you felt 'not concerned but hurt,' there's really no need for you to convey this sensational news across the Channel."[12]

On the other hand, he regarded her as his confidante in all his musical plans, and even more, as a full competent judge of his works. Often he asked for her advice about a composition he was working on. Fanny was the first to know that he had "begun to dream a *Midsummer Night's Dream.*"[13] Felix's affection and respect for her remained undiminished through all his life; he sought spiritual comfort with her after their adored father's death. At that time her sentiments assumed a protective character.

More complex than Felix's feelings were those of Fanny. A few years older than Felix, she had guided the boy's first, uncertain steps in the labyrinth of music. Soon, however, her brother had outgrown her and made her his consultant in his ever bolder artistic ventures. A little jealousy of his surpassing talent she could suppress; it was not quite as easy to share his confidence with others, especially with other women. She adored him, but this was not enough: she wanted to possess him, body and soul. Some of her letters read like passionate declarations of love, yet she herself would have been shocked if somebody had pointed out to her the almost violent nature of her emotions. How can one read without deep sympathy outbursts such as: "I play your *Hora est,* stop before your portrait and kiss it every five minutes, there imagining your presence . . . I love you, adore you, immensely."[14] Fanny was at that time engaged to be married to the painter Wilhelm Hensel. The conflict of her emotional life is often expressed in her letters:

> I was afraid that my engagement would tear me from you . . . but the contrary is true; having gained a fuller knowledge of myself, I have come nearer to you and think even more often of you, if that is possible. . . . It is not possible that your love might decrease, for you know full well that I cannot spare even a jot of it.[15]

On her wedding day, she lost all reserve and confessed to Felix:

> I have your portrait before me, and ever repeating your dear name, and thinking of you as if you stood at my side, I weep! . . . every morning and every moment of my life I shall love you from the bottom of my heart, and I am sure that in so doing I shall not wrong Hensel.[16]

Naturally, Fanny's exaggerated *Schwärmerei* was no secret in the family. Rebecca, Felix's younger sister, and the clown of the family, often ridiculed her sister or mocked her in gentle malice. The mixture of humor and indignation is noticeable in her report: "Last night, in lovely moonlight, during charming conversation, by the side of the most ardent betrothed, Fanny fell fast asleep. . . . Why? Because you are not here."[17]

To all the outbursts and fits of jealousy Felix invariably answered in a calm and moderate tone, almost soothingly. Later, during Fanny's happy marriage and motherhood, these tensions and pseudo-Byronic effusions vanished entirely and were replaced by a deep and devoted affection, combining maternal, sisterly, and comradely feelings of love. The bond between Felix and Fanny became ever closer, and it was her sudden and premature death that broke his own heart. He survived her only six months.

ACADEMIC STUDIES AND INTELLECTUAL CLIMATE

SHORTLY AFTER his return from Paris in 1825 Felix finished his private education in a rather formal manner. His tutor, Dr. Heyse, enocuraged him to write a kind of baccalaureate thesis, according to the custom of German Classical education. Such a thesis could, if it was a creditable piece of work, be recognized by the universities as proof of his fitness for matriculation. In compliance with this suggestion, Felix wrote a translation of Terence's *Andria* in the meter of the original. This most worthwhile achievement did not fail to renew the affection of Goethe, the humanistic sage, for the young artist.

In May, 1827, Felix matriculated at Berlin University. He studied, apparently with great zeal, geography (with Ritter) and esthetics (with Hegel), and attended lectures by Alexander von Humboldt. He also heard some lectures, for that time sensational, on the history of political freedom by the family's friend Eduard Gans, and seems to have been greatly impressed by their democratic idealism.[18] There is no doubt that his interests were far-flung, encompassing a wide scope of intellectual disciplines; yet it is by no means easy to assess their tangible consequences for his creative work.

The formal side of academic life held little attraction for him. In contradistinction to Haydn, Brahms, or Bruckner, he did not overestimate the value of the honorary doctor's degree, conferred upon the twenty-seven-year-old composer by Leipzig University. The only serious reference to this event (which in nineteenth-century Germany betokened a signal honor) is contained in a letter to his friend Klingemann, and the passage does not sound exuberant.[19] In 1831 Felix was offered the newly created chair for music at Berlin University. He declined it, because he felt unqualified for an academic position. Loyal friend that he was, he used his considerable influence to have the chair made available to Marx, who eagerly accepted the offer.

In the circle of his friends, Felix had listened to many an argument about questions of musical esthetics. It cannot be said that he paid much attention to it: general speculation of that sort he considered sterile. Characteristic of this indifference is his criticism of the renowned musical scholar Fétis: "What's the use of talking so much about music? it is better to write well."[20]

Yet Felix had studied esthetics under no less a thinker than Hegel. And even unknown to Felix himself, Hegel's ideas on the subject left definite traces in the mind of the young student. One must take with more than a grain of salt Zelter's somewhat malicious letter to Goethe:

In his lectures, Hegel is just discussing musical esthetics: Felix takes him off very nicely and is able, the dear rascal, to imitate him with all of his peculiarities. Hegel contends that what we do is not real music. It is true (he says) we have made some progress, but we are still far from what he considers real music. Well, we do or do not know this wisdom just as well as he, if he would but explain to us in musical parlance if he [Hegel] has attained "real music."[21]

Yet the question of Hegel's influence upon Mendelssohn cannot be answered by relating gossip. In reviewing the philosopher's ideas, one finds some sentences and principles which indeed seem to be reflected in Mendelssohn's music as well as in some of his letters. Those of Hegel's thoughts on music which seem to have influenced Felix's attitude to music are here paraphrased after the philosopher's published *Lectures on Esthetics* (Berlin, 1838):

1. It is not the function of music to imitate a display of emotion so as to make the imitation seem a natural outburst of passion. The function of music is rather to shape sounds into specific tunes and to imbue those tunes with impressiveness. Music thus lifts the expression of feeling into an element created by art, exclusively for art. In this element, the simple outcry, moving onward, is developed and broadens into a series of tones whose sequence and alternation, attended by harmony, round themselves out in melody. (*Lectures*, p. 192 ff.)

2. Like any other art, music must restrain the emotions and their manifestations lest the music plunge into bacchanalian clamor and whirl into a tumult of passion or get stalled by conflict and despair. Equally amid thrills of delight and amid throbs of distress, music must remain untrammeled and yet in its outpouring serene. (*Ibid.*, p. 193 ff.)

3. What the composer embodies in his work are not feelings that actually exist. They are idealized pseudo feelings (*ideale Scheingefühle*), feelings that, detached from the composer's actual self, abide in his phantasy and appeal, in turn, to the hearer's phantasy, so that the actual feelings of the hearer, as well, remain out of the picture. (*Ibid.*, p. 130.)

4. When intertwined with words, music must not so far subordinate itself that, in order to render completely the verbal characteristics of a text, the music sacrifices its own free flow of movement. Such music, ceasing to function as an art in its own right, becomes an ingenious and artful application of musical devices to something other than music and to contents that are already sufficient without any music. (*Ibid.*, p. 191 ff.)

5. On the other hand, music must not, in the style of recent Italian composers, detach itself completely from textual content, the definiteness of which might seem to fetter it. Music should not aim to approximate utter self-sufficiency. The proper domain of music is essentially that of inward-

ness combined with tone unalloyed (*das reine Tönen*). (*Ibid.*, p. 134 ff.)

6. In music, objectivity abates. Being the essentially Romantic art, music withdraws altogether into subjectivity, as regards both inner meaning and outward manifestation. Its mode of expression dispenses with objects. It presents no sort of object to consciousness. (*Ibid.*, pp. 127, 132, 148.)[22]

It will be demonstrated later that Mendelssohn's music, or rather his conception of music, frequently adheres to these principles, especially to paragraphs 2, 3, and 6. The master's propensity for the musical fairy tale on the one hand, for the "inwardness of tone unalloyed" (*Songs Without Words*), and certainly his treatment of song texts, his adherence to the strophic Lied of the "Berlin School" seem to fall in line with some of Hegel's conceptions. All this might be sheer coincidence, but any doubt about the matter is dispelled by a letter from Hegel to Felix, wherein he replies extensively to the composer's quest for logic in music.

After a lengthy preamble, Hegel settles the question by the following argumentation:

> The emotions evoked by music in the listener's mind belong to the realm of idealized pseudo feelings [*ideale Scheingefühle*] or imagined affects. Hence real logic in music is at least not provable. That this is so can be easily demonstrated by causing an able composer to continue another musician's composition. Most probably he will continue in a way different from the original author's procedure. However, if he masters his craft [*wofern er sein Handwerk versteht*], he will manage to do so in a way that . . . need not be less plausible. . . . Hence, logic in music is a logic of appearance [*des Scheins*] and form, which cannot be tested by comparisons with genuine conclusions pertaining to reality.[23]

In principle, these and similar questions occupied Romantic thinkers a good deal; the problem of logic in music, however, transcends by far the usual tea-table speculations on the essence and function of music. Mendelssohn's letters abound in contemptuous remarks on music esthetics. And yet, this very aversion indicates that he was not naïve enough to ignore the subject altogether.

The years 1825 to 1830 determined the intellectual climate that surrounded him all through his life and work. To be sure, the compass of his interests widened during the subsequent years of traveling, but the tenor and tone of his intellectual taste were firmly set in the neohumanistic mold of Goethe, Lessing, and Shakespeare.

Felix and all the other members of his family were voracious readers. His favorite authors beside Goethe and Schiller were Jean Paul, Shakespeare, and Lessing. The last-named was looked upon in some kind of awe as well as familiarity, being considered a family idol because of his intimate friendship with Moses Mendelssohn. Felix's sense of humor and sentimentality were stimulated by Jean Paul, the poet-philosopher, whom Heine had called "not a star of the first magnitude but a cluster of stars." Especially attractive to Felix was Jean Paul's fluctuation between laughter and tears, between vulgarity and unexpected grandeur. He loved his works dearly and quoted from them even in his later life.[24] Rebecca, too, spoke nostalgically of this author, and as usual, with tongue in cheek: "We all wished to die a little early, just like his heroes, but only 'for a short while!' If I did not know the charms of Jean Paul in our youth . . . I should condemn your copy of his *Hesperus* to an auto da fè."[25]

The magnificent translation of Shakespeare into German by Schlegel and Tieck had but recently appeared. It was read, memorized, and quoted by the company with fervor and enthusiasm. The tremendous impact of his plays upon the Romantic generation served as a wholesome antidote against the *Salonschwärmerei* (drawing-room sentimentality) then in fashion.

A refreshing diversion from the lofty intellectualism of this group of students of Hegel, Humboldt, and Boeckh was provided by the not inconsiderable amount of gossiping that went on. The ladies, especially Rahel von Varnhagen, the *spirituelle*, and Friederike Robert, the lovely wife of Rahel's brother Ludwig Robert, and even Lea Mendelssohn, indulged and excelled in this social pastime. "What one says here about comets and ladies, I'd better not tell you" is a typical gossipy remark of young Felix.

Felix was a fervent flirter and always pined for pretty girls; but he was spoiled, being too much courted by many matrons and maidens. His sisters did not always enjoy this spectacle nor did some male observers, quite understandably. Felix did not care for the intellectual specimens of the female sex, such as the admired Rahel von Varnhagen ("our Jean Pauline") or the sentimental and witty Bettina Brentano Arnim. No love was lost there, and Felix likened such queens of the salons to "Pythias, squatting on their tripods, ever ready to pronounce oracles."

His political interests during his youth encompassed the entire continent plus England, and he was quite articulate on some principal issues, such as liberalism, reforms, or the future of Germany. He was a decided liberal, in many respects a radical. Some of his friends, especially the English ones, loved to tease him on account of his liberalism. Thus Charlotte Moscheles opens a letter with the words: "In order to irk you, the ultra-liberal, I begin with a concert at the Weimar Court."[26] He himself was anything but equivocal in such matters. His letters to his father, to Droysen, Hiller, Klingemann, and Devrient are filled with political observations. Felix sympathized with the French July Revolution of 1830.[27] Any sort of flag-waving patriotism "rubbed him against the grain"; he detested it.[28] He took a strong interest in the emancipation of the Jews in Germany and compared their status with that in other countries, usually to the disadvantage of conditions in his fatherland. [29] Nor did he shun occasional disputes with his brother-in-law Hensel because of the latter's extreme royalism.[30] Invariably he disapproved of the reactionary policy of Prussia.[31] England's internal troubles concerned him, and he referred to Tories like Wellington and Aberdeen as "fellows of that gang" (solches Gelichter).[32] He was forever at odds with what he called "Prussian officialdom, which suits music as a strait-jacket suits a man."[33] In general, his political views were determined by a strong sense of social justice. To him, the born Jew, who was familiar with the century-long oppression of his ancestors, justice constituted the cardinal virtue and the real touchstone of honest government.

For an intellectual of his generation Felix favored a German policy of a rare sort: liberal, anti-Austrian (Kleindeutsch), antichauvinistic,[34] pro-French, pro-English, anti-Russian, and almost republican. Some of his unpublished letters ridicule the fancies of Frederick William IV, his admirer.[35] Felix's indignation about Prussia's imperialistic attitude was articulate and became a matter of public record when he refused point-blank to compose Becker's Rheinlied, Sie sollen ihn nicht haben (They shall not have it [the Rhine]) for Breitkopf and Härtel.[36]

On quite a few issues he was not afraid of being unpopular; his ridicule of "fake art-philosophy, German Catholicism etc." certainly did not correspond with the general trend of the time.[37] On the other hand, he criticized sharply Heine's ambivalent attitude towards Germany. He admired Heine as a poet but despised his "meretricious character."[38]

In his youth he was a willing victim of periodical attacks of wanderlust. Especially dear to Felix were long walking trips in the congenial company of his friends, during which any vehicle, be it freight-wagon or phaeton, came as a welcome relief to the hikers.

Next to Wagner and Berlioz he was certainly the most traveled composer of his time. His linguistic talents rather encouraged his transcontinental trips; besides German, Latin, and Greek he had mastered English, French, and Italian. His talent and faculty for drawing and painting, carefully cultivated, grew more marked in his later years, with the result that he painted water colors and drawings far above the level of a dilettante.[39]

One of those extended hiking trips brought him into contact, in 1827, with the famous Professor Thibaut in Heidelberg.[40] In his treatise Purity in Musical Art (Über Reinheit der Tonkunst, Heidelberg, 1825) Thibaut championed the revival of the "ethos doctrine" which had played so eminent a part in the musical thinking of antiquity. Thibaut wanted this criterion applied to church music. In historical perspective, Thibaut's book is a landmark in the never-ceasing, age-old discussion of music, morals, and religion. His ideal composer is Palestrina; the liturgical compositions of Haydn or Mozart are condemned, not as poor music but as failing to satisfy the author's strict concept of liturgy.

Felix's description of his visit to Professor Thibaut is therefore of special interest. He was greatly impressed by the man's character as well as by his ideas, and summed up his reactions in eloquent terms:

> One Thibaut is worth six ordinary men. . . . I have learned a very great deal from him and owe him many thanks. For he has revealed to me the merits of old Italian music and warmed me with his enthusiasm for it. . . . What I liked best was that he never inquired after my name [!] : I loved music, that was sufficient for him. . . . When I left him, he said, "Farewell, and we will build our friendship on Luis de Victoria and Sebastian Bach, like two lovers who promise each other to look at the moon and then fancy they are near each other."[41]

This introduction to the world of Renaissance music and especially to the so-called Palestrina style left a firm imprint on Felix's musical taste. Henceforth, he made himself ever more familiar with the works of these masters. In his capacity as a conductor he was able to perform their then almost forgotten music, sometimes against considerable opposition. Moreover, the ideas of musical purity linked themselves in Felix's mind with Hegel's and Schleiermacher's thoughts on ethical purity, so that the idealistic young composer viewed his music almost as an exercise in virtue and frequently judged music in terms borrowed from ethics.[42] Early in 1827 another significant trip, this time with his father, took him to Stettin. Carl Loewe, then the city's music director, was known to the Mendelssohns. He was the conductor of one of the most remarkable concerts in the history of musical performance. The first part of the program consisted of the world première of the Overture to *A Midsummer Night's Dream* and of the Second Concerto for Two Pianos in A flat, both by Mendelssohn. The first performance in Northern Europe of Beethoven's Ninth Symphony constituted the second part of this memorable evening.[43]

The first criticisms of these works of Felix's, full of praise, appeared in the *Berliner Allgemeine Musikalische Zeitung* with surprising promptness after the performance. The première had taken place February 20, 1827, and the anonymous critique was published under the date of February 27. Considering the nonexistence of railroad, telegraph, and telephone, the short interval between these dates is somewhat conspicuous. A letter of Felix from Stettin, dated February 17, 1827, did not arrive in Berlin until the 23rd.

Possibly Marx, Felix's friend and the editor of the paper, had written the review in advance, and had held it in readiness while waiting for a personal confirmation of the success of the concert. This, indeed, arrived well in time, for Felix reported that the dress rehearsal had gone very well.

The letter was addressed to his parents and contains the jesting remark: "All of Stettin is topsy-turvy on account of the Beethoven symphony. . . . O Marx! What disaster he has caused! Here one impugns completely his views of the work. . . . Loewe plays the concerto excellently. . . ."[44] Marx had published an elaborate and enthusiastic analysis of the Ninth Symphony (in four installments) in his paper.

The intimacy with Marx was unimpaired, and remained so for six more years. Actually, Marx's influence on the young composer grew in intensity, as may be seen in the controversial history of the two greatest accomplishments of Mendelssohn's early Berlin period: the Overture to *A Midsummer Night's Dream* and the first performance of Bach's *St. Matthew Passion* since the composer's death. Both are milestones in the music of the nineteenth century.

Notes

1. *Goethe-Zelter Correspondence*, letter of May 25, 1826.
2. *Ibid.*, letter of September 26, 1830.
3. Devrient, *Erinnerungen an Felix Mendelssohn* (Leipzig, 1891), p. 94.
4. Marx, *Erinnerungen* (Berlin, 1865), II, p. 134.
5. Unpublished letter of September 24, 1827.
6. Unpublished letter of July 22, 1826.
7. *Klingemann Correspondence* letter of December 28, 1827.
8. Oxford Collection, letter 29: November 27, 1827; see also *Allgemeine Musikalische Zeitung* (Berlin), November, 1827.
9. Paul Heyse, *Gesammelte Werke, Dritte Reihe* (Stuttgart, 1924), Vol. I.
10. Letter of July 17, 1824, Library of Congress, Washington, D. C.
11. Letter of September 20, 1827, Library of Congress, Washington, D.C.
12. Letter of May 15, 1829, Library of Congress, Washington, D. C.
13. Letter of July, 1826, Library of Congress, Washington, D. C.
14. Oxford Collection, letter of July 29, 1829.
15. Oxford Collection, letter of July 10, 1829.
16. Oxford Collection, I, letter 98.
17. Oxford Collection, letter of June 17, 1829.
18. Prof. Felix Gilbert, a great-grandson of the composer, owns Felix's carefully jotted-down notes of these lectures.
19. *Klingemann Correspondence* (letter of March 22, 1836).
20. *Aus Moscheles' Leben* (Leipzig, 1872), I, p. 208.
21. *Goethe-Zelter Correspondence* (letter of March 22, 1829).
22. The author is deeply indebted to Dr. Abraham Cronbach, Cincinnati, for this elegant paraphrase and condensation of Hegel's ideas.
23. Unpublished letter of June 30, 1829.
24. It is interesting to note that Gustav Mahler, too, was spellbound by Jean Paul, at a time when that author was almost forgotten. Mahler's First Symphony was named *Titan* after a novel by Jean Paul.
25. Hensel, *F.M.*, tr. Carl Klingemann (London, 1882), I, p. 129.
26. Oxford Collection, letter of November 27, 1832.

27. Devrient, *op. cit.*, p. 93.
28. *F. M. B. Letters*, II, p. 165; letter of October 29, 1829, Library of Congress, Washington, D. C.
29. Oxford Collection, letter of July 23, 1833; also Eric Werner, "New Light on the Family Mendelssohn," *Hebrew Union College Annual* (Cincinnati, 1950), XXVI, p. 543.
30. Klingemann, *op. cit.*, p. 111.
31. *Ibid.*, p. 151ff *et passim*.
32. *Ibid.*, p. 172.
33. F. Hiller, *Reminiscences of Felix Mendelssohn Bartholdy*, 2nd ed. (Cologne, 1878), p. 109.
34. *F. M. B. Letters*, II, p. 170-71, letter of November 20, 1840; also letter of December 18, 1840, Library of Congress, Washington, D. C.
35. Unpublished letter of October 27, 1840, Library of Congress, Washington, D. C.
36. *F. M. B. Letters*, II, p. 171; also Klingemann, *op. cit.*, p. 251.
37. Klingemann, *op. cit.*, p. 315.
38. Unpublished letters of August 3, 1841 and December 11, 1831, Library of Congress, Washington, D. C.
39. Most of his lovely drawings and watercolors are today in the possession of Miss Marie Wach, Wilderswil, Switzerland, and of Hugo von Mendelssohn Bartholdy, Basel.
40. See also Chapter IV.
41. Hensel, *F.M.*, tr. Carl Klingemann, Jr. (London, 1882), I, p. 138f.
42. Especially the unpublished letters of May 15, 1829, May 29, 1829, and July 14, 1830.
43. For an extensive discussion of the unpublished piano concerto, see Eric Werner, "Two Unpublished Concertos by Mendelssohn," *Music and Letters*, April, 1955.
44. Unpublished letter of February 17, 1827.

CHAPTER VI *A Dream and a Deed*

... the season's heat, one said, worked so strongly on imagination's power, that in those weeks dreams of wild   fancy . . .
visited man. Hence the title of this romantic masterpiece.
L. Tieck, Notes on *A Midsummer Night's Dream*

This Prometheus [Shakespeare] not only shapes human beings, he
also opens the gates to the world of spirits, arouses ghosts . . .
and fills the air with a host of elves and sylphs. These wholly
imaginary beings are so real that when we encounter such mis-
creatures as Caliban, the poet forces upon us the firm conviction
that if they did exist in reality, they would deport themselves in
just this fashion.
A. W. v. Schlegel, *Lectures on Dramatic Literature*

THE OVERTURE TO *A MIDSUMMER NIGHT'S DREAM*

IN 1801 the first sixteen plays by Shakespeare were published in their
definitive German translation by A. W. Schlegel and Ludwig Tieck, the
protagonists of German Romanticism. This translation was enthusiastically
received and is considered a model even today. The champions of the romantic movement hailed Shakespeare as a fellow-Romantic and a spirit akin
to all that was truly Germanic.[1]

In his notes Tieck did not hesitate to call the *A Midsummer Night's
Dream* a "Romantic masterpiece" and added: "Whoever has been denied
. . . the feeling of this poem's originality, the enchantment caused by the
magic of its language and by the lovely kaleidoscope of changing pictures
. . . such a man will not profit either by explanations, critics, or whatever
might be done. . . ."[2] Goethe, while intensely aware of Shakespeare's genius,
took exception to the Romantic coloration imposed upon Shakespeare by
his translators. Utilizing the issue for the expression of his own literary
ideas, he attacked the "whole twilight–sorcery–and dream-stuff" of the
Romantic school.

Yet it was just that "dream-stuff" that so irresistibly attracted young
Felix. The elfin world was not only the general playground of the Roman-

ticists, but it was Felix's special domain, sometimes to his father's displeasure. "I have grown accustomed to composing in our garden; there I've completed two piano pieces in A major and E minor. Today or tomorrow I am going to dream there the *A Midsummer Night's Dream*. It is, however, an enormous audacity. . . ." (*Heute oder morgen will ich dort midsummernights dream zu träumen anfangen. Es ist aber eine gränzenlose Kühnheit.* . . .) Thus did Felix announce the beginning of serious work on the overture, which was to bestow lasting fame upon him. The letter dates from the first week of July, 1826 and is addressed to Fanny. Shortly thereafter (July 18) he wrote her an enthusiastic report on the Berlin première of Weber's *Oberon* Overture, closing with the words: "Since you left, my love for you goes in E minor." This remark alluded to the opening phrases of the *Allegro* of his *A Midsummer Night's Dream* overture.

When Felix, later in life, was asked by Breitkopf and Härtel to recall the associations that had given birth to the overture and had stirred his creative imagination in so lively a fashion, he disclosed nothing that was not previously known.

> . . . it is impossible for me [Mendelssohn wrote] to outline for the [concert] program the sequence of ideas that gave rise to the composition, for just this sequence of ideas is my overture. It follows the play closely, however, so that it may perhaps be very proper to indicate the outstanding situations of the drama in order that the audience may have Shakespeare in mind or form an idea of the piece. I think it should be enough to point out that the fairy rulers, Oberon and Titania, appear throughout the play with all their people. . . . At the end, after everything has been satisfactorily settled and the principal players have joyfully left the stage, the elves follow them, bless the house, and disappear with the dawn. So the play ends, and my overture too.[3]

The genesis of the work is not, however, as simple or incontrovertible as Felix's letters or recollections would indicate. According to the account given by A. B. Marx, the young composer conceived in a brainstorm the idea of writing an overture to *A Midsummer Night's Dream*. Marx warmly approved of it.[4]

"A few days later," Marx writes, "he, the happy and free man, reappeared and brought the score, with the first part already finished." [This means that only the exposition was then completed.] "The introductory chords and the dance of the elves were just as we know them. Then, alas, there followed the overture proper—a merry, delightfully vivacious, altogether pleasant and lovely piece—but I was unable to associate it with *A Midsummer Night's Dream*. As a faithful friend, I felt in duty bound to tell the composer frankly what I thought. He was concerned, provoked, even hurt, and ran away without saying good-bye. I had to put up with it as best I could and avoided his house for a few days; the more so since his mother and Fanny had received me, immediately after our clash, coolly, almost with enmity. . . ." After a few days a messenger appeared with a note from Felix which said: "You are right in every respect. But now come and help!" "I did not fail him, hurried to his assistance and pointed out that such an overture must reflect faithfully and completely the drama of which it was to be the prologue. Enthusiastically and with absolute devotion he took up the work again. Only the allusion to the lover's wanderings in the first motif (E, D#, D, C#) could be salvaged from the original version; everything else had to be rewritten . . . 'Tis too mad, too absurd,' he shouted, when I insisted on his saving a place for the jesters and even for Bottom's ardent braying. But he followed my advice, and the overture took the form we know now. Mother and sister were conciliated by the composer's creative enthusiasm. The father even declared at the first performance in his house that the overture was in fact rather my work than Felix's! There is, of course, no foundation for such a statement. . . . The original idea and execution belonged to Felix; counsel alone was my duty and my part. . . ."[5]

This sounds convincing enough. Devrient, certainly no friend of Marx, testifies to Marx's share in Felix's striking development as a composer since the *Dream* overture: "he boasts rightfully of having urged Felix into a consistently *characteristic* elaboration—thus advertising his system."[6] Here Devrient alludes to Marx's treatise *Über Malerei in der Tonkunst* (On Painting in Music, 1828), whose principles coincide with Marx's ideas on the *A Midsummer Night's Dream* overture. Nevertheless there remain certain discrepancies. To begin with, work on the overture must have commenced not later than July 8, the day after Felix "began to dream the *A Midsummer Night's Dream*." The original score (in the Berlin State Library) bears August 6 as date of completion. The entire alteration therefore probably took place during the fortnight July 12-26, since mother and sister, to whom Marx refers expressly, returned to Berlin on July 22. Moreover, the score does not display any significant corrections or alterations.

The accounts by Moscheles and Hiller do not shed any new light on Marx's tale. For Moscheles heard the overture first as a piano duet in November, 1826.[7] Hiller, not too trustworthy himself, remembers Mendelssohn having told him that he worked on the overture in his spare time between the lectures at the University, concluding with the words: "For a whole year I did hardly anything else." This charming anecdote, however, clashes with the facts, for Felix did not enter the University before Easter 1827. At that time the overture was completed and had been performed at least twice in public.[8]

That Marx did influence the composition of the work is beyond doubt; for the first newspaper criticism, while anonymous, appeared in the *Berliner*

Allgemeine Musikzeitung, whose editor was Marx. The tenor of the review is identical with Marx's recollections and the music example inserted therein shows a familiarity with the work that one hearing could not have established. Since the review covered the world première of the famous work, a few quotations might be of interest:

> Bravo Felix! You have tackled a task that greatly taxed your self-confidence. You have solved your problem in a magnificent way, and, in so doing, vindicated your self-confidence. . . . As by the immortal work of the poet divine, a treasury of fancy, pleasant buffoonery, whim, love's ardor and labor, the reader's soul is surprised and touched alternately, so in the overture a store of musical humor is revealed, the like of which even Corporal Nym—the great expert in humors—did not know. . . . But I will not and cannot anatomize this magic charm . . . it is impossible to "take off" more exactly the dramatic Philistines [Shakespeare's clowns] than in this doltish-saucy fashion:
>
> Example 24a

> . . . Indeed, the clumsy English bass-horn [Mendelssohn's ophicleide] portrays perfectly the boorish Bottom. . . .⁹

The emphasis upon the "characteristic detail," about which Marx had been so insistent, is noticeable in this critique. Hence there cannot be much doubt that Marx himself was the critic.

The overture, while familiar to every music lover, still deserves a few critical remarks. The work ought to be considered in historical retrospect. Thus, one is bound to delineate the strictly musical substance against its programmatic background. Or, did Marx's semiphilosophical insistence on realism, characteristic features, and "objective truth" really disturb the organic flow of Mendelssohn's music? Felix here experiments before Berlioz, Liszt, and Wagner with leading motifs and the idea of a "cyclic" form. The leading motif, four sustained chords in the woodwinds, beloved ever since, introduces the overture. It occurs three times: at the beginning, at the recapitulation, and at the very end. The first theme falls into two sharply contrasting sections: the fairy dance and a march-like tune; it is treated, at least in the exposition, in a perfectly normal manner. The same holds true for the secondary theme and the clown's dance, which forms the "closing group" of the exposition. Thus far nothing has deviated from an orthodox beginning.

The development section is actually a fantasia or a kaleidoscopic vision of a few motifs. Of its 143 bars about 100 are based upon the first two measures of the fairy dance, accompanied by the more robust rhythms of

Example 24b

the clowns. Thereupon follows a thematic pizzicato passage of the 'cellos, in reality an augmentation of a motif presented before.

Example 25

The fantasia ends with the reminiscence of the concluding motif of the secondary theme, which, however, assumes a deeply melancholy cast.

Example 26a

There follows the leading motif and the recapitulation. There, as well as in the development, the elfin character of the fairy dance is disturbed by low, clumsy tones of the horns (*ff* against *pp* of the strings in measures 302-5) and the ophicleide, symbolizing the uncouth Bottom of the play, as Marx rightly believes. The coda, beginning in measure 620, regains an undisturbed fairy atmosphere. It is again interrupted by a double augmentation of the motif that had ended the development; it sings in gentle nostalgia:

Example 26b

The work is concluded by an epilogue of tender beauty, a gentle transformation of the second main theme:

Example 27

and the leading motif fades away *pianissimo*.

Is there anything here that must be considered a serious deviation from an orthodox concert overture? Actually only the following features:

a) The main theme consists of two contrasting halves;

b) the character of its first half is, in the development and recapitulation, distorted by unexpected drones in the bass accompaniment;

c) a conspicuous transformation of the second half of the main theme takes place in the coda; and

d) there is a motto-like ending with the leading motif.

Of these features, only b) and d) can be properly understood as programmatic. The two halves of the first theme represent the fairy dance and the duke's world, respectively. Such a dichotomic structure was a favorite device in contemporary symphonic music; Spohr, for one, made use of it in the overture to *Jessonda* (1823). Both overtures contain another similarity: the four sustained woodwind chords at the beginning.[10]

For this and another reason Mendelssohn did not escape the charge of plagiarism. The closing theme of his overture, in its last transformation (cf. Ex. 27), is for all practical purposes identical with the "Mermaid's Song" from Weber's *Oberon*. It has been established that Felix knew Weber's opera and actually assisted in its performance in the home of old Schlesinger, the music publisher.[11] While the transformation is a perfectly organic one, the resemblance is perhaps too strong to be purely accidental. Possibly Felix intended to pay homage to the memory of the admired Weber, who had but recently died. The absence of written evidence does not preclude this possibility.

In summing up, we are bound to say that the semiprogrammatic features do not impair the structure of the work: neither the motto of the beginning nor the unexpected basses in the development violate Zelter's rule that "one must compose according to strict architectural principles."[12] Indeed, the overture implements this postulate in its hidden thematic relationships. For its entire thematic substance rests upon one descending tetrachord which permeates in many variations the entire overture. The tetrachord appears first in the motto:

then in the first half of the theme:

then in its second half:

again in the transition to the second theme:

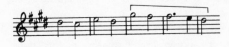

in the second theme itself:

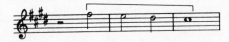

in the clowns' dance, (in the clarinets):

and, finally, in the coda:

It need not be stressed that this admirable unity of the thematic structure is not the result of a calculating intellectual, but of the subconscious choice of the creative artist's mind.

Posterity was justified in viewing the overture as a work typical for its "Romantic" leanings. Indeed, that it is. The love for detail, the minutely elaborated orchestration with its iridescent colors, and the "characteristic feature" of Bottom's braying in ithe midst of the fairy dance make the overture one of the *chefs d'oeuvre* of Romanticism.[13] Never again, though, did Mendelssohn identify himself so unequivocally with romantic maxims. Even here, he did not permit himself to break away from the traditional form-structure as it appears in the overtures of Weber, Spohr, and others.

His musical logic was faultless; and it served his rich imagination well—not to forget his perfect ear—in conceiving the transparent orchestration.

A few words must suffice to sketch the fate of the overture. Mendelssohn's contemporaries loved and cherished it; even the hypercritical Wagner, who usually decried everything coming from Mendelssohn's pen, keeps silent here. Schumann waxed enthusiastic over the work: "The bloom of youth lies over it as it does over hardly any other of the composer's works; in an inspired moment the mature master made his first and highest flight."[14] And Hector Berlioz, himself no mean interpreter of Shakepeare's world, wrote to Felix: "I have never heard anything more deeply Shakespearean than your music . . . I would have given three years of my life to embrace you. . . ."[15] Most eloquent in their admiration were the English: "His inspiration could turn into a volcano flinging out fierce and stormy fire, when the subject was a pagan revel on the *First Walpurgis Night*— or with a wish, could change like a dream, into showers of dew amid the moonlight—bearing the delicate freakish burden of 'a roundel and a faery song,' to the most exquisite faery poetry in the world—that of Shakespeare's *Midsummer-Night's Dream*."[16]

All too little of Mendelssohn's music has withstood the vagaries of taste. Yet even during the almost complete eclipse of his music, between 1890 and 1920, the overture to *A Midsummer Night's Dream* appeared year after year unfailingly on the programs of the great musical centers of the world. Since then, the composer's status has risen again and musicians such as Busoni, Richard Strauss, and Reger have acclaimed the magic spell of the work. The critical musicologists of our generation, such as Alfred Einstein, Paul H. Lang, Sir Donald Tovey, Curt Sachs, and Ernst Bücken have not hesitated to count the overture among the imperishable masterpieces of all music.

Of all Mendelssohn's overtures the *A Midsummer Night's Dream* approaches most closely the concept of illustrative music. Hence it might not be amiss to examine the composer's attitude towards this concept. Felix disapproved of illustrative music in general, even in vocal music:

> To me it seems impossible to compose a descriptive poem; . . . one composer in the *Erlkönig* imitates the rustlings of the willow trees, the wailing of the child, and the galloping of the horse. The other imagines a ballad-chanting minstrel, who recites the gruesome tale quietly, almost in a whisper, as if telling a ghost-story, and this is the more accurate way; still, I do not like it . . . I could indeed have composed the *Nächtliche Heerschau* [*Napoleon's Midnight Parade*, a ballad by Joseph von Zedlitz] in the same descriptive style as Neukomm and Fischhof in Vienna. I might have introduced a very novel rolling of drums in the bass, and blasts of trumpets in the treble, and have brought in all sorts of hobgoblins. But I love my serious strands of

sound too well to do anything of the sort. For this kind of thing always seems to me rather like a joke, somewhat like the paintings in juvenile spelling-books, where the roofs are colored bright red to make the children aware they are indeed supposed to be roofs. . . .[17]

Berlioz took, at least in this issue, exactly the opposite stand. Nonetheless, his concept of a flexible leading motif (*idée fixe*) was not alien to Mendelssohn. The overture, indeed the whole (incidental) music of the *A Midsummer Night's Dream*, to be composed many years later, is permeated by an *idée fixe* (the first four chords); but when it came to the detailed and personal interpretation of the *idée fixe*, the two composers parted company and ways. Mendelssohn's intransigence did not tolerate any compromise in fundamental issues of his art. Berlioz himself knew this severity of Felix well, and, being a great artist himself, respected it.

It speaks well for Felix's integrating ability that many years past his glowing youth he was capable of recapturing the mood of the play as well as his own enthusiasm. When he was commissioned to furnish incidental music for a performance of the play in 1843, the magic world was conjured up again as if by Prospero's wand; Oberon, the fairies, Puck and the clowns, they all arose again. Felix's heart had remained young.

THE REVIVAL OF THE ST. MATTHEW PASSION

IN THE HISTORY of music, many instances are known where initial misunderstandings stimulated great art. The first operas were fancied to be replicas of Greek tragedies; the link between the music of the Renaissance and the world of Classic Antiquity, while based upon error and caprice, was a precedent of the Romantic concern with the music of the Renaissance and Baroque. This concern turned out to be no less fruitful a misunderstanding than the earlier one, which had produced the opera. Actually it was the period of the knightly Middle Ages that had captivated the imagination of the early Romanticists. Yet authentic medieval music was hardly accessible at that time, much as its champions pined for it. So reliable a witness as Rochlitz has emphasized this discrepancy.[18] Under these circumstances one chose what was generally believed to approximate the best medieval music and its spirit: the liturgical music of the sixteenth and seventeenth centuries. This choice seemed eminently satisfactory to the archaizing faction of the literary romanticists.

Characteristically enough, the interest in old church music did not arise among the musical profession. Its pacemakers were the literati, not the musicians. In turn, the literary concern with ancient music may have had its roots in the tremendous change in the style of music, which commenced before 1750. The preponderance of unalloyed instrumental music that characterized the outgoing eighteenth century was perhaps too technical and particular a development to please poets. They began to search for a music that had not yet fully emancipated itself from the word. Thus the mystical inclinations of the early Romantics, coupled with a naive love for the archaic, led them back to the golden age of Catholic church music: Palestrina, Lassus, Victoria, and the glories of the *a cappella* chorus; they added to this pantheon such later composers as Lotti and Durante.

Wackenroder, Tieck, A. W. Schlegel, and E. T. A. Hoffmann were the literary protagonists of this musical trend, which centered on the great Italian composers of the sixteenth and seventeenth centuries. The most articulate champion of this movement was Justus Thibaut in Heidelberg, with whom Mendelssohn had established contact as early as 1827.

The rediscovery of Bach, however, was by no means intended by these littérateurs, nor even by the then ruling circles of the Protestant Church. It was initiated by musicians, and accomplished by musicians. The link between literature and music was provided by the poet-composer Hoffmann's professional article *On Old and New Church Music*, where he termed Bach a "genius of mankind" (*Menschheitsgenius*).

After his death in 1750, J. S. Bach was considered a learned pedant, albeit, a great organist. Essentially his image during the last decades of the eighteenth century did not differ appreciably from that held by his own contemporaries. While occasionally quotations from the *Well-Tempered Clavier* appeared as examples in treatises on counterpoint, not one of his works formed part of regular repertory anywhere in Europe. We need only think of Mozart's interest when he was, for the first time, confronted with Bach's music in 1781. Not one complete work of Bach's pen, except the *Musicalische Opfer* (1761), was printed between 1750 and 1800.[19] Yet, towards the end of the eighteenth century the signs of renewed interest in Bach's output became unmistakable.

One paradox of the many that belong to the Romantic world of thought was the preference for Bach's instrumental works rather than his vocal compositions. One of the reasons might have been the inferior type of poetry for which he created music; this was one of Zelter's misgivings. Another handicap of Bach's vocal works was the feeling of restraint exerted by rational words in comparison with the more indefinite nature of instrumental music. That the same phenomenon occurred in the Romantic attitude to Christianity has been correctly assayed by Alfred Einstein: "The Romantics turned away from all the forms of Christianity to which some element of rationalism clung—away from Lutheranism, from Calvinism. . . ."[20] Likewise, to the Romantic mind it was instrumental music that seemed the perfect manifestation of the intangible, even the mystical, notwithstanding their preference for old choral music.

About 1800 the underground hibernation of Bach's works came to an end. In London some organ and clavier compositions of Bach were published by Kollmann and greatly admired and praised by Samuel Wesley, C. F. Horn, and even by the reluctant Charles Burney.[21] Yet the expressions of this English circle are rather ambiguous, for had Bach not been for decades the embodiment of dull and pedantic rationalism? Now he was being praised as artistic perfection, "a musical Bible," and his name assumed a slightly mystical tinge.

In 1802 there appeared the first biography of Bach, written by Johann Nicolaus Forkel. There the author struck a new note in declaring that "preserving the great man's memory does not merely concern the artists—it concerns the nation." This emphasis upon the German character of Bach's music evoked an enthusiastic echo among the Romanticists.[22]

Carl Maria von Weber uttered a thought shared by many of his contemporaries when he stated: "Sebastian Bach's characteristic attitude was, in spite of its rigidity, clearly Romantic and of fundamentally German character, perhaps in contrast to Handel's more Classical position."[23] Weber's contemporary, the poet-composer Hoffmann, in a similar vein stressed Bach's mystic grandeur. Yet it was one thing to praise him, and another thing to perform his works. Many obstacles stood in the way of practical execution.

Very few of Bach's works had been printed during his lifetime. After his death musical fashion changed direction. The great tradition was kept alive among contrary trends by a tenuous chain of Bach's personal disciples, such as Doles, Kirnberger, J. L. Krebs, Altnikol, and by his sons Wilhelm Friedemann and Carl Philipp Emanuel. Forkel's monograph and Rochlitz's articles were the main literary vehicles of Bach championship in the expiring eighteenth century. In Berlin Karl Friedrich Christian Fasch (1736-1800), a colleague of Philipp Emanuel Bach and Kirnberger, as accompanist to King Frederick II, founded the *Singakademie* in 1791. It then numbered 27 voices. Zelter, who had been Fasch's and Kirnberger's disciple, succeeded the founder as conductor of the *Singakademie*. It was mainly due to him, that Bach's vocal music came again to life. He began, sporadically at first, to introduce a few compositions of Bach into the repertory of the *Singakademie*, which by 1802 numbered over 200 voices. In general, he preferred the motets. He was less familiar with the cantatas and Passions.[24]

By 1820 the most active workers in the cause of Bach's music were Hans Georg Nägeli in Zürich; Nikolaus Schelble, the conductor of the Frankfurt *Cäcilienverein;* and Karl Friedrich Zelter, the leader of the Berlin *Singakademie.* Aside from these professional musicians, a small circle of Lutheran music lovers and clergymen made propaganda for a revival of Bach. Yet none of these champions of Bach was an adherent of Romanticism.

Still, very few of his choral compositions could be performed, simply because the music was not available. Philipp Emanuel and Wilhelm Friedemann Bach had divided between themselves the five yearly cycles of their father's cantatas (in MSS), a treasury of incalculable richness. Publication of these works was generally considered too expensive. Philipp Emanuel's sad experience with the edition of his father's *Art of the Fugue*, of which only thirty copies had been sold by 1756, was a deterring factor for at least two generations. Thus, the few people who did possess manuscripts of Bach rented them to outsiders for inspection or copying. The sole surviving granddaughter of Bach, Anna Carolina, added to her mother's obituary notice in 1795 an advertisement that she would continue industriously the business of renting manuscripts of Philipp Emanuel's and her grandfather's music. Since Wilhelm Friedemann's collection was soon dispersed, a proper performance of a choral work entailed numerous and overwhelming difficulties.

Zelter had set himself the task of presenting Bach's choral music in the face of all obstacles of taste and feasibility. Frequently he poured his heart out to his friend Goethe, once in a lengthy and ardent effusion on Bach's merits. [25] He closed the letter with the proud rhyme:

> Thou gav'st me work with might and main
> To light I did bring thee again.

> (Du hast mir Arbeit gemacht,
> Ich habe Dich wieder ans Licht gebracht).[26]

That Zelter did not himself take the initiative in performing the Passions is understandable in view of the many practical difficulties. He also had a personal reason: his intense dislike of their texts, which he, the friend and admirer of a Goethe, considered atrocious.

Marx gives another explanation, which is at least partially convincing. To Zelter the *St. Matthew Passion* in its entirety had always seemed unpalatable, and the old man had gone so far as to "rearrange" (*umkomponieren*) some of Bach's choruses and recitatives in the then fashionable style of Graun.[27] Nor did Zelter expect so decisive a success as the first performance actually had; therefore he was wary and dubious. In the autumn of 1829 he wrote after a successful presentation of Bach's glorious motet *Sing to the Lord*: "A few persons behaved as if they really liked it."[28]

Here Felix Mendelssohn entered and took the initiative. His links with Bach, direct and indirect, were numerous. The direct line was represented in the persons of his teacher Zelter and his great-aunt Sara Levy, to a minor extent by his mother, a pupil of Kirnberger. Indirectly his membership in the *Singakademie*, his friendship with Nikolaus Schelble, the conductor of the *Cäcilienverein* in Frankfurt, and Felix's many organist friends, some of them real old-timers, kept continually stirring his interest in Bach. Thus, the poetic necrology for Bach, written in 1754 by George Philipp Telemann, assumed unexpected prophetic power:

> . . . Sleep well, then! For thy name, from all oblivion free Remains alive among thy pupils' and their pupils' scores. They shape for you the crown of greater fame. . . .

Actually, Felix was a great-grandpupil of J. S. Bach. The links were: W. F. Bach, J. Kirnberger, Sara Levy, and K. F. Zelter.

Felix had learned, in 1823, that Zelter owned a complete manuscript of Bach's *St. Matthew Passion.* This score was, as we know today, not a Bach autograph but a faithful copy.[29] His grandmother Salomon had a reliable copy made of Zelter's exemplar, written by Felix's friend Eduard Rietz, and presented the score to Felix at Christmas.[30]

During the winter of 1827 a small choir assembled in the Mendelssohn house tried out some pieces of the Passion. The grandeur of the music overwhelmed all the singers. "Felix had so profoundly studied the work—only short of identifying himself with it—that he mastered all its difficulties easily. Thus to us became natural and familiar what heretofore was thought to be a secret language," as Devrient reports.[31]

Devrient's desire for a public performance of the Passion became ever more articulate, the more so because he craved the part of Jesus. The immense technical demands of the composition—requiring a double chorus as well as a double orchestra—seemed to preclude any full-fledged execution. Also Zelter did not budge from his inexorable refusal to try the Passion. Even Marx, Bach's most vociferous champion, and Felix's parents, as well as most members of the *Singakademie*, were skeptical about the realization of Felix's and Devrient's plans. Sometimes in his discouragement Felix derided Devrient's utopian dreams. Yet Devrient remained obstinate.

On January 29, 1829, he harangued Felix so persistently that the latter consented to approach old Zelter once again, with firm purpose.[32] We have a most realistic description of that meeting between Zelter, Devrient, and Mendelssohn, given by Devrient himself. At first, the old maestro was adamant. He enumerated all the difficulties the performance would encounter. The climax came when he exclaimed: "How can I listen patiently to this rot! Much better people than you two have had to give up such a project; and now a couple of brats [*Rotznasen*] appear. They think it is all child's play!"

At this point Felix, already resigned, was beating a sorry retreat; but

Devrient remained steadfast. By applying a good deal of flattery and cajolery he persuaded Zelter finally to yield and to give his consent to a performance by the *Singakademie* under Felix's direction.

Even after this victory the friends were convinced that it would not do to perform the work *in toto*. They began, therefore, to examine the score for possible cuts. The majority of the arias and duets were to be omitted. Of others only the ritornels were to be played. Even the part of the Evangelist was to be shortened. It was during these deliberations that Felix uttered the famous words: "To think that a comedian and a Jew-boy must revive the greatest Christian music for the world."[33]

The rehearsals began. Here Felix rose to his full status as a great interpreter and conductor. Inasmuch as it was not possible, under the provisions of the *Singakademie*, for the conductor to turn his back to the public, he had to turn his back to one of the two choruses. Devrient relates that "this difficult situation was mastered by Felix with a calmness and assurance as if he had conducted ten music festivals," and adds that he, Devrient, being annoyed by the constant beating of time by the conductor, persuaded Felix to agree with his ideas. . . . "Many whole pieces were often 'beaten through' [*durchgefuchtelt*], as it were . . . but Felix . . . as soon as large movements of steady course were running smoothly, dropped his baton and listened with seraphic transport, occasionally beckoning with eye or hand . . . I remember this trait with special satisfaction, since recently it has become the fashion to consider the gesticulations of the conductor as a main attraction of musical performances."[34]

During the rehearsals Felix conducted the whole work by heart. Zelter, who had assisted at the first rehearsals, gradually withdrew, and with praiseworthy selflessness, took a seat with the audience at the rehearsals and the performances. Word had spread about the magnificence of the Passion, and on the day the first advertisement appeared all tickets were sold out; more than a thousand people sought in vain to obtain admission. On the day of the performance, March 11, 1829, within ten minutes the large hall was filled to the last place. As Fanny put it, "a peculiar spirit and general higher interest pervaded the concert, so that everybody did his duty to the best of his powers and many did more." Eduard Rietz and his brother had copied all the instrumental parts for the orchestra and refused any compensation.

Since the concerts were charity affairs, most singers declined free tickets, or else paid for them. For the first concert only six free tickets were given (of which Spontini held two) and for the second performance none. To judge from impartial critics, Felix seems to have conducted the work with surprising calmness and profound devotion. "Twenty years old, he had succeeded where many others had failed."[35] Zelter was jubilant in his report to Goethe, who rejoiced with him.[36]

Some modern scholars have taken exception to concert hall performances. They are not quite justified. There is no evidence whatever that the work was "mutilated . . . that it was no longer the Bach of the Bible, of the Lutheran faith. . . ."[37] It would have been impossible to perform the work as a Divine Service in one of the churches.

It is necessary here to refute certain misrepresentations or simply rumors concerning the "mutilation" of which Einstein spoke. With the exception of the recitative *Der Vorhang im Tempel zerriss in zwei Stücke* (And behold, the veil of the temple was rent in twain), which Felix orchestrated, not one new instrumentation or arrangement was attempted by him.[38] Some solo arias and duets, however, were omitted at that memorable performance, lest the public get restless.

Much was done, within the *Singakademie* and without, in order to discourage Felix and Devrient. These facts are plainly referred to in Mendelssohn's unpublished papers. Truly, the *St. Matthew* Passion was resuscitated in spite of the *Singakademie*, rather than with its help![39] Felix's indignation about the two-faced, not to say treacherous, attitude of the *Singakademie* echoes even in his letters of twelve years later, when the work had attained world fame and the *Singakademie* basked in the glory of having been the institution to give the work its first public performance. In connection with these memories Mendelssohn, infuriated about the bowdlerizations and "emendations" of Bach's work by K. F. Rungenhagen, wrote "Rungenhagen sent me the orchestral parts of the Passion, together with trombones and cornet parts of his own manufacture. . . . What shall I do with the orchestral material (not with the trombones etc.; there I know exactly what to do) . . . ?"[40]

All contemporary witnesses agree on the profound solemnity of the performance, which did not differ essentially from a rendition in church.[41]

The audience was deeply impressed, in particular by the fine dynamic shadings of the choruses, a novelty in those days. The religious momentum of the work stirred the audience to a degree never to be forgotten. So enthusiastic was the response that the work had to be repeated on March 21, Bach's birthday, under Felix, and during Holy Week, under Zelter. By then Felix had left Berlin. Spontini had tried to prevent a further performance; but Mendelssohn and Devrient had appealed directly to the Crown Prince, who thereupon had ordered a second performance.

A humorous incident occurred in Zelter's house after the repetition of the work. Frau Devrient was seated next to a man who irritated her by his troublesome affectation. "Do tell me who is the stupid fellow next to me," she asked Felix. He whispered behind his napkin, "The stupid fellow next to you is the famous philosopher Hegel."[42]

At that time Felix was Hegel's student. Hegel showed a warm interest in Bach, whom he proclaimed as "the master, whose grand, truly Protestant, pithy yet learned genius we have only lately learned to value again properly."[43]

It was to a great extent the result of a well-planned preparation of the public that men of so varied interests as Hegel, the brothers Humboldt, Goethe, the Crown Prince, and many others took so active a part in the revival of Bach's music. This plan was largely directed by Marx and Mendelssohn. The *Berliner Allgemeine Musikalische Zeitung* published, prior to the first performance of the Passion, one large advertisement, five analytical descriptions, and afterwards three reviews, two articles, and two poems. The Leipzig *Allgemeine Musikalische Zeitung*, too, published an article and a review of the performance.

All of this might convey the impression that the victory for Bach's music and all it stands for was decisive and lasting. Such an impression would not fully correspond with the truth. From Königsberg, for instance, where the Passion was performed in 1832, the music critic tells us: "One part of the audience fled already during the first part, another called the work outdated rubbish." The writer identified himself with a third group, which likened Bach's Passion to a colossal Egyptian pyramid. He preferred Graun's *Death of Jesus*, which to him was comparable to the graceful lines of a Greek temple. In Dresden a bold critic maintained that the Passion could stand comparison with most contemporary compositions. In Cassel the performance of the work was forbidden by the Grand Duke as late as 1832,[44] possibly under the influence of Spohr, who generally took a dim view of Bach's vocal music.[45]

Mendelssohn, Zelter, and their circle, on the other hand, recognized the historical significance of the performance. Even long before the actual performance, Fanny wrote: "The work [*St. Matthew Passion*] is being published by Schlesinger at the same time it will be performed by the *Singakademie;* thus, the year 1829 will be of signal importance in the history of music."[46]

History has verified Fanny's prophecy. Yet even well-known champions of Bach's music considered the *St Matthew Passion* an ill-chosen work for the popularization of Bach. Aside from the piece itself, even the monumental style of its performance did not remain unchallenged. One of Bach's most fervent champions, the aforementioned Nägeli of Zürich, published a strongly worded protest against this type of rendition in the *Berliner Allgemeine Musikalische Zeitung*, of which a few characteristic lines may be quoted:

If one intends to introduce the great Bach as magnificently as possible, then it is in my opinion a mistake to begin with great church music in the German language. This excellency of all excellences did not excel as a vocal composer. . . . His melodies for the human voice are not easily singable. He was never fully able to sense how to write well for voices.

Nevertheless, Nägeli offered to put at the disposal of the *Singakademie* some manuscripts of cantatas by Bach, which would present him in a more advantageous light. He closed his offer with the somewhat malicious remark: "If my offer will not be heeded in Berlin, I shall send there instead of the manuscripts a Christian sigh, as it once came from Lavater's mouth: 'One cannot force salvation on anybody.' "[47] This parting shot was a quotation from the Lavater-Moses Mendelssohn controversy, wherein the former had attempted, vainly, to convert Mendelssohn to Christianity.

In 1836 even as erudite a musician as Moritz Hauptmann, later to be president of the *Bachgesellschaft*, had the recitatives radically changed:

> . . . there is really no one here with whom I can discuss the subject quietly: one party is against any alteration of the Passion, the other is passionately in favor of it! I cannot help smiling at the situation . . . the recitatives are not typical of the age, because Handel and many others excelled as writers of recitative; they are merely the recitatives of Bach, who, I suppose, had but rare opportunities of hearing genuine Italian recitative in Arnstadt, Eisenach, Weissenfels, Cöthen, nay, in Leipzig itself . . . I cannot help thinking that the recitatives assigned to Christ, and to the Evangelist, are exceedingly awkward.[48]

Notwithstanding and despite all such misunderstandings, the way was now paved for the systematic publication and subsequent performance of Bach's church music. After the publication of score and piano arrangement of the *St. Matthew Passion* by Schlesinger (under pressure by Mendelssohn and Marx), the voices of the lukewarm patronizers of Bach became more and more silent. Not long before, at the first publication of a cantata by Bach, Rochlitz had stated that Bach had been forgotten before 1800, thereafter overrated, and finally, in 1822, cut down and judged according to his true stature.[49] However, he sponsored further publications of Bach, "since the revolution of things brings to the top again, after a shorter or longer interval, all the main manifestations of the greater human spirits."[50]

How fervently convinced Mendelssohn was of the towering stature of "eternal" Bach is well known; but three less familiar facets of his boundless veneration may be mentioned. To the student and collector of Bach manuscripts, Franz Hauser, Felix sent in 1834 an extensive catalogue of all Bach manuscripts known to him in Berlin; it was never printed.[51] It was Felix's ambition to erect a monument to Bach, for which the necessary money was to be raised by the performance of Bach's own works. Here he succeeded; and the only surviving grandson of old Johann Sebastian, Wilhelm F. E. Bach, then 84 years old, was invited to the unveiling of the monument in 1841 and did attend. Schumann was mistaken when he on that occasion asserted of Bach's grandson that "no one had known of him, not even Mendelssohn . . . who would have eagerly followed up anything connected with Bach. . . ."[52] Felix had repeatedly asked his sister Fanny to get hold of Wilhelm Bach, either in Berlin or in Bückeburg; and eventually she did.[53]

It is not easy to estimate the consequences of the memorable performance on March 11, 1829. A resurgence of an era believed dead, a giant stepping out of his tomb into the mild light of the 1830's, a Romantic misunderstanding—all that and more was the meaning of that signal revival of Bach's most monumental composition. And its repercussions cannot be fully assessed even now, after four generations. As every generation sees Scripture under a new aspect, so it is with Bach. We are in the midst of another "re-interpretation" of his work.

Mendelssohn's own success, however, hardly reached beyond the *St. Matthew Passion*, as Schweitzer justly observed.[54] The work made its way, after Berlin, to Stettin and Frankfurt, still in 1829. In Stettin it was received with enthusiasm and Loewe's direction seems to have merited such acclaim;[55] but the Frankfurt response was noticeably cooler.[56] Thereafter it became part of the repertory of the concert halls of the world, and, at long last, of the churches.

Bach's keyboard music evoked, on the whole, a much livelier response and interest than ever before, a by-product of the Berlin revival. Again, "to estimate the true magnitude of the victory we must look into the scores of the composers of the nineteenth and twentieth centuries. Since Mendelssohn, every composer of any significance has been to school under Bach, not as to a pedantic teacher, but to one who impels them to strive after the truest and clearest expression."[57]

Wagner had, in his *Die Meistersinger*, fallen under the influence of the Bach renascence, at which he had first looked askance. His own school and inclination were superseded, about 1920, by a new wave of rejuvenated Bach. Whenever the best exemplars of German spirit are invoked, the names of Bach and Goethe shine forth.

None other than Abraham Mendelssohn recognized fully the irresistible power Bach's music held over Felix. In a memorable letter to his son written three years after Zelter's death, he linked Zelter's, Bach's and indirectly his son's historical positions with each other.[58]

> I felt more strongly than ever what a great merit it was on Zelter's part to restore Bach to the Germans; for between Forkel's day and his, very little

was ever said about Bach, and even then principally with regard to his
Well Tempered Clavier. He was the first person on whom the light of Bach
clearly dawned. . . . His musical performances . . . were indeed a proof that
no work begun in earnest, and followed up with quiet perseverance, can
fail ultimately to command success. At all events, it is an undoubted fact
that without Zelter your own musical inclination and direction would have
been of a totally different nature.

With the publication of the overture to *A Midsummer Night's Dream*
and the production of the Passion, Felix achieved international repute.
During the four years 1826 to 1829 the composer and man kept pace with
the conductor and organizer. He had advanced boldly. The subsequent
three years of travel all over Europe did much to enlarge the scope of his
artistic and intellectual perspective.

$\mathcal{N}$otes

1. Best examined and discussed by F. Gundolf in his *Shakespeare und der deutsche
Geist* (Berlin, 1920).
2. This strangely polemical hint refers to Goethe's hostile attitude.
3. O. von Hase, *Breitkopf und Härtel Gedenkschrift und Arbeitsbericht* (Leipzig,
1919), II, p. 61.
4. *Ibid.*, Here quoted from *Musical Quarterly* (April, 1933), p. 184.
5. Marx, *Erinnerungen* (Berlin, 1865), II, p. 231ff.
6. Devrient, *Meine Erinnerungen an Felix Mendelssohn* (Leipzig, 1891), p. 32.
7. Moscheles, *Diaries*, tr. Coleridge (London, 1873), November 21, 1826, p. 89.
8. Hiller, *Reminiscences of Felix Mendelssohn Bartholdy*, 2nd ed. (Cologne, 1878),
p. 9-10.
9. *Berliner Allgemeine Musikalische Zeitung* (Berlin, 1827), IV, p. 95. Here reproduced for the first time.
10. They are also in E major and minor alternately!
11. The literature on this controversy is given and the question itself discussed by
Dr. G. Kinsky in *Musical Quarterly* (April, 1933), pp. 178-186.
12. A. W. von Schlegel's letter to Goethe of June 10, 1798 (*Goethe-Gesellschaft*,
Vol. 13, p. 22).
13. Felix's friend Schubring, the librettist of *St. Paul*, relates that during the composition of the overture they took long strolls in the woods near Berlin. "While lying
in the grass, Felix suddenly whispered: 'Hush.' He afterwards informed me that a large
fly had just gone buzzing by and he wanted to hear the sound it produced gradually
die away. . . . After the completion of the overture he showed me the passage . . . where
the 'cellos modulate from B minor to F minor [mm. 264-70] and said: 'There, that's the
fly that buzzed past us at Schönhausen. . . .'" *Musical World* (1866), p. 301ff.
14. R. Schumann, *Ges. Schriften*, Reclam ed. (Leipzig), IV, p. 280.
15. Berlioz, *Musicien Errant*, Tiersot ed. (Paris, 1919), p. 137.
16. H. F. Chorley, *Modern German Music* (London, 1854), II, p. 413.
17. *F.M.B. Letter*, to Baroness Pereira, July, 1831.
18. F. Rochlitz, *Fuer Freunde der Tonkunst*, Doerffel ed. (Leipzig, 1868), IV, p. 351.

19. To be sure, *The Art of the Fugue* appeared in 1751, but its publication had been planned by Bach himself, and he had died before completing it. *Die Musik in Geschichte und Gegenwart* (hereafter *MGG*), article, J. S. Bach, II, cols. 1034-35; also David and Mendel, *The Bach Reader* (New York, 1945), pp. 242ff.

20. Einstein, *Music in the Romantic Era* (New York, 1947), p. 33.

21. Wesley's delightful *Bach Letters, 1808-09* (London, 1875).

22. For a complete bibliography on Bach's position during the late eighteenth and early nineteenth century, see the exhaustive article "J. S. Bach" in *MGG*.

23. Carl Maria von Weber, *J. S. Bach* (Dresden, 1821).

24. A. Prüfer, *Sebastian Bach und die Tonkunst des 19. Jahrhunderts* (Leipzig, 1902).

25. *Goethe-Zelter Correspondence*, letter of June 9, 1827.

26. *Ibid.*, For the entire history of Bach's revival see Schweitzer, *Bach* (New York, 1935), I; also Hohenemser, *Welche Einflüsse hatte die Wiederbelebung der ältern Musik im 19. Jahdt. auf deutsche Komp?* (Leipzig, 1900).

27. Marx, *op. cit.*, II.

28. Devrient, *op. cit.*, p. 56.

29. Ph. Spitta, *J. S. Bach*, 4th ed. (Leipzig, 1930), II, p. 815; also *MGG*, col. 1001-2.

30. This copy, from which the first performance of the *St. Matthew Passion* was conducted, is now in private possession in Oxford.

31. Devrient, *op. cit.*, p. 36.

32. Here Devrient's report is erroneous; for Fanny had already written on December 27, 1828, to Klingemann: "In return for Felix's arrangement of Handel's *Acis and Galatea* the *Akademie* is going to sing the Passion for him. . . ."

33. Devrient, *op. cit.*, p. 56.

34. Devrient, *op. cit.*, p. 59. (The remark was written ninety years ago!)

35. Therese Devrient, *Jugenderinnerungen* (Stuttgart,1903), p. 309.

36. *Goethe-Zelter Correspondence*, letters of March 12, 22, 28, 1829. Goethe's remark (about the choruses of the Passion), "Me seems I hear the roaring of the ocean," has become famous.

37. Einstein, *op. cit.*, pp. 49-50.

38. Hensel, *F.M.*, I, pp. 207-08. That even in this recitative Felix's instinct did not go astray is evident from the fact that many old organs have a special stop, *Terremoto* (Earthquake), constructed just for this moment of the Passion. Kretzschmar, *Führer durch den Konzertsaal*, 4th ed. (Berlin, 1921), II, p. 99. (Hereafter, Kretzschmar, *Führer.*)

39. It should not be forgotten that the directors of the *Singakademie* insisted on the payment of 50 Thaler for the rent of its hall. The concert itself and its two repetitions were for the benefit of underprivileged children.. Nonetheless, Felix had to pay the 50 Thaler. (Hensel, *F.M.*, I, letter of March 22, 1829.)

40. Unpublished letter to Julius Rietz of November 2, 1841, Library of Congress, Washington, D. C.

41. Devrient, *op. cit.*, p. 59-62; also Marx, *op. cit.*, II, pp. 86-7; Fanny Mendelssohn in Hensel, *F.M.* (letter of March 22, 1829), "the hall had all the air of a church; the most solemn devotion pervaded the whole."

42. Therese Devrient, *op. cit.*, p. 309.

43. Hegel, *Aesthetik* (Berlin, 1836), part 3, vol. X, p. 208.

44. Moritz *Hauptmann's Correspondence with Hauser* (London, 1892), letter of November 16, 1832.

45. *Ibid.*, letter of March 19, 1836.

46. Hensel, *F.M.*, tr. Carl Klingemann, Jr. (London, 1882), I, p. 165.

47. *Allgemeine Musikalische Zeitung* (Berlin, 1829), VI, pp. 233ff.

48. *Hauptmann Correspondence with Hauser*, letter of March 19, 1836.

49. Critique of the cantata *Ein feste Burg* by Rochlitz.

50. *Ibid.*

51. Schweitzer, *op. cit.*, I, p. 252a.

52. R. Schumann, *Neue Zeintschrift für Musik* (Leipzig, 1843).

53. Oxford Collection, letters to Mendelssohn of November 14, 1830 and January 15, 1831.

54. Schweitzer, *op. cit.*, I, p. 245. Bach's liturgical works were still frowned upon by K. von Winterfeld in 1847 and a full decade thereafter!

56. The report of the Frankfurt correspondent of the *Allgemeine Musikalische Zeitung* (Berlin, 1829), VI, pp. 245-6.

57. Schweitzer, *op. cit.*, I, p. 261.

58. *F.M.B. Letters*, II, letter of March 10, 1836.

CHAPTER VII

The First Harvest

Without myths every culture loses its natural creative power:
only a horizon surrounded by myths integrates an entire cultural movement in unity. The forces of imagination and of
Apollonic dreams are prevented from aimless straying only by
the mythos. The images of the myth must be the all-present,
yet unobserved demoniac watchmen, under whose guardianship
the soul of the young grows, under whose aegis man expounds
(unriddles) his life and his struggles.

(Nietzsche, *Birth of Tragedy*).

TO ASSESS Mendelssohn's first mature works without comparing them with
the music of his contemporaries would be uninteresting and unfair. Only
by juxtaposing his work with the best of his fellow-artists, shall we be able
to determine whether Felix's pieces represent a common "period-style" or,
if not, to discover what sets them apart from it. By this method we might
also probe into the hidden springs of the master's personal style and observe
its evolution.

While still a youngster, Felix had familiarized himself with much music
of the past and the most significant works of his own time. Beginning with
Bach, there was hardly a composer of note whose principal works he did
not know. And of the music of his own generation he had a most comprehensive knowledge. To obtain this, his father's wealth was of no little help.
For Abraham Mendelssohn could afford to subscribe regularly to all serious
music as it came from the publishers of Germany, Austria, and France. Yet
no amount of money could have purchased for Felix his phenomenal memory, which enabled him to reproduce almost everything he had ever studied
or heard, often at a moment's notice.

Felix had met all of the important composers of his time except Beethoven
and Schubert. Of Beethoven's music he knew everything then available in
print or manuscript copy. As to Schubert, he was not even aware of his
existence until 1827, and then only Schubert's songs were available to him.[1]

Beethoven's *oeuvre* constituted a challenge to every composer of the
nineteenth century. Not only did Beethoven insist on a standard for serious

[*107*]

music equal to that of the greatest creations in literature and philosophy—
an idea unfathomable to a Leopold Mozart and his contemporaries—but he
postulated the utmost autonomy for the composer. This entailed both rights
and obligations for the artist, which the average musician could not easily
accept.

The Viennese master gave frequent expression to this radical attitude,
which maintained that music "is higher revelation than all wisdom and
philosophy. I am dissatisfied with most of my former works; henceforth I
shall pursue a new way." The autonomy Beethoven claimed for himself and
his peers was coupled in his life and work with an insatiable thirst for inner
and outer liberty. His stiff-necked and often truculent personality expressed
itself in an extremely unconventional manner. Freedom from convention,
Beethoven's artistic autonomy, was the secret of his unique power and
originality. Yet we must not overlook the counterpart of these qualities:
strictest economy of means and firm discipline in musical logic, resulting in
a carefully bridled phantasy far from any amorphousness. The passion for
personal originality was a novel phenomenon; and to us, five generations
later, it is highly debatable whether this insistence upon personal originality
was always beneficial to the further course of music.

The young Mendelssohn understood the aging Beethoven in a surprisingly mature fashion. We possess a hoax letter of the sixteen-year-old Felix,
addressed to his sister Fanny, wherein he imitated Beethoven's hand and
signature. Felix pretended to be Beethoven himself, or at least his spokesman.
We quote a few significant remarks from this hoax letter. It is a mixture of
roguish humor and profound poignancy.

Vienna, 8 November 1825.
... some friends reported to me that you, my dear Fräulein, have succeeded
in making a well-educated audience listen to my Concertos in E flat and G;
only a few people seem to have fled. So much applause might almost offend
me and make me doubt the value of my works [*und mich an meinen Werke
irre machen*], were it not for your lovely playing, which certainly must
have its share in the success. ...

It is nothing extraordinary if people like my first trios, my first two
symphonies, and some of my earlier sonatas. As long as one writes such
music as the others do, which means trivial and common stuff, and is young
at that, the people understand and purchase one's music. But I got tired of
this rut and have now written music like Herr van Beethoven; moreover,
at my advanced age and in the solitude of my empty room, things go
through my head which do not please everybody. ...

If I find persons who treat this new music and me, an old and lonely
man, in a friendly manner, then I consider their merit great and am duly
thankful. For such people are my only real friends and I don't have any
others.

I am sending you my Sonata in B-flat (op. 106) as a present on your birth-day, with my heartiest congratulations. I did not write the sonata out of thin air [*nicht des blauen Dunstes willen*]. Play it only if you have ample time, which is indispensable for it. . . .

Where your friendship alone cannot attain full understanding, do not hesitate to ask Marx, the great authority on my music. He will explain everything to you; especially the slow Adagio movement affords him plenty of time to do so. . . .

I am enclosing a poor likeness of mine as a present for you. After all, I am a potentate just as good as any other, who gives away his portrait. I do not in the least consider myself a bad fellow. [*Ich halte mich für gar keinen schlechten Kerl*].

And keep in memory
Your obedient   Beethoven.

Felix's innermost ideas are clearly traceable through the flimsy disguise of the letter: the conviction that a great work of music is not "written out of thin air," that it might express "things that do not please everybody," in short, that all serious music exclusively reflects the composer's personality. The gibe at "mein Kenner Marx" betokens Felix's roguish ridicule of his friend, the professional expounder of Beethoven.

His concern with the person and works of Beethoven, however indicative it might be of Felix's awareness of the master's stature, coincided with the youngster's awakening to the problems most crucial to the post-Classical composer: descriptive or openly programmatic music; chromaticism; the prevailing convention of a sonata form with two contrasting thematic groups; the Romantic conviction that a good piece of music should contain autobiographical elements; and Beethoven's legacy and command, novelty and originality!

All these questions Felix tried to answer—sometimes in words, always in his music. Time and again we shall encounter them in his compositions. As he grew older his views changed, especially after his marriage. As a youngster he approved of descriptive and even of programmatic music. By bold chromatic progressions he stretched tonality to remote boundaries. He repeatedly attempted cyclical approaches to sonata form, neglecting its cat-egorical dualism. Nor did he shun highly original designs. Yet he eschewed anxiously all autobiographical associations in his music, although during his lifetime he could not always prevent his piano pieces, especially the *Songs Without Words*, from receiving fanciful titles.

Mendelssohn's early compositions betray a certain duality. In his in-strumental music he is boldly progressive; in his vocal music he frequently appears archaic. The reasons for this double standard are not hard to detect. Beethoven, supreme master in the instrumental field, was an actual con-temporary of Felix; Haydn and Mozart represented the recent past. On the other hand, the great vocal composers Bach and Handel, not to mention Palestrina, were then being rediscovered—almost like pieces of Classic antiquity. Felix strove to attain the summit of mastery: he would accept as models only the best, the enduring creations. Thus he followed Beethoven in his instrumental music; Bach, Handel, and the old Italian composers in his vocal music. These were the "demoniac watchmen," of whom Nietzsche speaks in our opening quotation.

The main issues on which Felix took a positive stand were:

1. *Descriptive and program music.* All of his so-called concert overtures fall into this category. The *Hebrides, Melusina,* and *Ruy Blas* overtures contain some programmatic, i.e. narrative, elements, though the line of demarcation between the two categories is evanescent. Mendelssohn's approach to illustrative tone poems parallels his drawing technique as painter and draftsman. The contours are firmly drawn: there are no vague lines in the framework of his drawings. Every detail is executed with loving care and painstaking minuteness. The composer works along similar lines. While the *Dream* overture suggests a fairylike and fantastic atmosphere, the determining characteristic of *Calm Sea* is spaciousness and the nascence of movement. Every composer is familiar with the difficult problem of inchoate musical motion, and many solutions have been offered.[2] Mendelssohn's description of rest and motion in space—in this overture—stands out for its classic economy.

Mendelssohn studiously avoids merely illustrative effects. In his mature years he analyzed his opposition to such devices in a letter quoted below.[3] He even frowned upon Cherubini's unnecessarily noisy orchestration. Here the youngster Mendelssohn takes issue with the old master Cherubini, using the classic arguments of economy and moderation.[4]

2. *Extension of tonality; chromaticisms.* In this respect all of the early works of Felix display a boldness and freedom of expression for which we vainly search in later compositions. Especially the first string quartets and an (unpublished) chorale-cantata bristle with chromatic dissonances. Passages of the type that occur in the A minor String Quartet were unheard of before. These are not the languid, melodious chromaticisms of a Spohr; here the pillars of diatonic tonality are trembling!

3. *Strict thematic dualism in sonata form.* In one of his numerous "Grand Mogul"[5] manifestos, Beethoven had proclaimed: "Two principles: A thousand musicians fail to comprehend this." This declaration of the inherent dualism in sonata form, couched in authoritarian diction, pronounced like an order, had its effect. Few composers of stature had the temerity to disregard it. Only as independent a spirit as Berlioz felt the need to "take up music where Beethoven had left it,"[6] that is, to pursue his own aims and to choose his own means. Mendelssohn did not go on record with such proud words. Nor was he independent enough to rid himself altogether of the

towering shadow of Beethoven. Yet in his own way Felix took issue with the all-important principle of dualism in sonata form. Whether this principle was contrary to his nature or to his thinking, his early chamber music as well as the *Calm Sea* overture minimizes the contrast between the two main themes (Beethoven's principles) of sonata form. Here Mendelssohn, like Haydn and others, develops the second theme out of the first, without sharp breaks or dramatic outbursts. The same spirit prevails in the first movement of the Octet and throughout the E-flat String Quartet.

Felix went one step further, in the same direction as Berlioz (whom he did not know as yet). He strove to evolve cyclical forms by using the same theme or complex of themes in a number of movements. This device was not unknown to Beethoven, who had experimented with it in his Sonata, Op. 106, and in two of his last string quartets; but he never went beyond a type of subtle variation of a theme in two or three movements. Schubert, in his Second Symphony, used a variant of the theme of the slow movement for the trio of this minuet (see below, page 133). Mendelssohn, in turn, frequently states a theme, abandons it, and takes it up again in another movement; there he follows older cyclical patterns, such as we encounter occasionally in the concertos of Ph. E. Bach.

4. *Originality of the early instrumental works.* A great many misconceptions have become attached to the term "originality." Today this quality is glorified only by self-appointed geniuses or by amateur critics, preferably of the female sex. Viewed in retrospect, greatness in music does not often depend upon the virtue of being decidedly original. Still it is widely assumed today that personal originality is the *sine qua non* and unfailing criterion of any great composer. It was not always so and, in the last analysis, it is not so even today.

It is erroneous to believe that the nuclear substance of a composition must be the author's original creation. Were this an unalterable rule, no variations on an extant theme would have been written. In the medieval world composers borrowed their thematic substance from the treasury of plainchant, from folklore, or even from each other. During the seventeenth and eighteenth centuries personal inspiration was valued less highly than the systematic *ars inveniendi* and the works of art fashioned according to that rather pedestrian method. Yet Bach thrived on it. Priority of the thematic substance was irrelevant; what mattered was the long-range aim of the composer. In short, subject matter did not matter.

With the outgoing eighteenth century, this system of values underwent a drastic revision. Rousseau's delusive but radiant mirage of a "return to nature" bade the creative artist to express his most subjective impulses. In the ever-fluctuating balance of artistic values personal originality began to outweigh the chain of tradition, often felt as fetters.

This fluctuation might not have produced more than a slight trembling of the scales had not a school of thought, Romanticism (and an "original genius," Beethoven), shaken them so violently that the composers of the nineteenth century were no longer sure of music's true values.

While this craze for more personal originality is not yet extinct, it has lost much of its magic. The many sorts of "objective" devices, such as the twelve-tone method of composition, may be construed as a reaction against excessive individualism.

This does not mean that composers not labeled "original," old or new, did not attain individual styles! They did indeed, but their vehicle was not necessarily the newness of their musical substance. Just as often, and perhaps more impressively, the individual style of a master manifests itself in his treatment of form, or of sound *per se*, or even in his relation to a nonmusical element, mainly the word. Busoni, the keen analyst of the changing musical trends of our century, clearly confronted the issue:

> Is it not strange to demand of a composer originality in all things and to frown upon it with regard to form? . . . Every motif—so I believe—contains like a seed its life germ . . . and in every motif there rests embedded the embryo of its evolved form. . . .[7]

Mendelssohn's claim to originality rests chiefly upon new concepts of form. Otherwise, he was not eager to be original, nor did he consider originality a particular virtue:

> Do you really believe [wrote Felix to his father] that I chase the original, the "inspired" and respect only men who pretend to be original geniuses? . . . Is there any other original genius than that which aspires to truth unadulterated? . . .[8]

Many years later, apropos of a discussion of Cherubini's cautious judgment of Felix's *Tu es Petrus*, Mendelssohn admitted: "I was too eager then to exhibit pettily original touches and was not ready for the truth. Today I recognize the importance of wholeness."[9]

This regard for wholeness was coupled with a strong loathing of anything that smacked of autobiographical music. It is true that Roman ruins, Scotch landscapes, Welsh roses and carnations evoked music in Mendelssohn, and he considered such a fact an intimacy; he would confide it to a friend, but to proclaim it publicly meant to him a rank indiscretion.

Such an attitude sets Mendelssohn apart from many of his colleagues and contemporaries. Romanticism of his time did not normally distinguish the work of art from the person of its creator. Mendelssohn's contemporaries pried curiously into the individual artist's personal life, his views, and even his moral principles. Nonmusical criteria began to invade the field of musical criticism, as most colorfully exemplified in Schumann's often prejudiced writings. How often he judged the man by his work! Even Mendelssohn was not so far distant from such ideas: his word about the indivisibility of art and life approaches the "romantic" attitude.

Of all his fellow-musicians, Mendelssohn was probably unique in his strict insistence upon "privacy" in his art. Scion of an old and famous family, he also valued tradition more than his contemporaries; at any rate, he abstained from deliberately searching for "new paths." As a matter of fact, he dissociated himself from all faddish slogans. In trenchant words he called these gropings for the absolutely new a "confounded demon" (*vertrackter Dämon*) for every artist.[10]

He despises style-copies, but he confesses: "If my music resembles that of Bach it is not my fault; for I have written it in the spirit I then experienced."[11]

Thus we observe in the attitude of the young Mendelssohn a peculiar synthesis of values old and new: He was willing enough to explore the stylistic potential of music in his works, experimenting in the new concepts of substance, form, and esthetics. But in issues of principle, involving autobiographical elements, the pursuit of originality at any price, he displayed a curious sense of caution and reserve.

The principal works of this period are:

The Overture *Calm Sea and Prosperous Voyage;* the String Quartets in E-flat major, Op. 12, and A minor, Op. 13: the Octet, Op. 20.

The Seven Characteristic Pieces for piano, Op. 7.

Twelve Songs, Op. 8 and Twelve Songs, Op. 9, for voice and piano.

Tu es Petrus, motet for five-part chorus and orchestra.

Hora est; antiphona et responsorium for sixteen-part chorus and organ continuo (unpublished).

Christe, Du Lamm Gottes, chorale-cantata for four-part chorus and small orchestra (unpublished).

OVERTURE *CALM SEA AND PROSPEROUS VOYAGE*

THE PROGRAM of the Overture is the celebrated poem by Goethe.

Calm at Sea
Silence deep rides o'er the water
Calmly slumbering lies the main
While the sailor views with trouble
Naught but one vast level plain.

Not a zephyr is in motion!
Silence fearful as the grave!
In the mighty waste of ocean
Sunk to rest is every wave.

Prosperous Voyage
The mist is fast clearing
And radiant is heaven
While Aeolus loosens
Out anguish-fraught bond.
The zephyrs are sighing
Alert is the sailor.
Quick! Nimbly be plying!
The billows are riven,
The distance approaches,
        I see land beyond!

At first blush, the work appears to be a conventional overture in fast tempo (*Prosperous Voyage*), preceded by a customary slow prelude (*Calm Sea*). Yet we know that Felix, "wanting to avoid an overture with introduction, has envisaged the whole in two juxtaposed pictures."[12] The "two pictures," however, are based upon one musical concept. Although there does occur—to appease the othodox—a kind of second theme in the Allegro, it is readily understood as a derivative of the all-pervading first theme. The formal structure comprises:

a) Introduction (with leading motif)
b) *Allegro*, first theme
c) Derived second theme
d) Transition theme and stretto

As observed above, the overture is a study in motion and space. The thematic contours are clearly Beethovenish, especially c), reminiscent of the last movement of the *Eroica* Symphony, as well as the third *Leonore Overture*. The work rests entirely and securely upon a theme developed out of the introduction. The spacing of the sections and their timing are determined by purely musical reasons: music rules, regardless of the program, wholly autonomously.

A few descriptive touches, such as the wave-like motif of the strings, are really irrelevant to the general structure.[13] The rhythmical variety is gratifying, this being a virtue that Mendelssohn did not always cultivate.

Only the coda, with its noisy horns, lusty trumpets, and pounding kettledrums, refers literally to the program: "The distance approaches, I see land beyond!" It is unmistakably the weakest spot in the work, notwithstanding its somewhat contrived thematic unity.

Old Goethe was surely justified when he congratulated Felix upon the completion of the overture: "Sail well in your music—may the voyage always be as prosperous as this!"

STRING QUARTETS IN E FLAT MAJOR, OP. 12, AND A MINOR, OP. 13

THESE TWIN QUARTETS are as different from each other as the biblical twins Jacob and Esau. The first one, Op. 12, in E-flat major (1828), illustrates the singing and sanguine mood of the young composer. The A minor Quartet, however, reveals an entirely new aspect of his music. In it pulses an intense and elemental vitality, the many reminiscences of Beethoven's last quartets notwithstanding. Here the distance between creative emotion and artistic formulation is drastically cut short. Never again was the master able to express the pathos of his musical substance as spontaneously and pithily. His growing reserve, a result of this aristocrat's desire for privacy, forbade any further display of passion. There is reason to regret this development.

In their formal structure the quartets have certain features in common: the persistent endeavor to attain integration by cyclical cross-references between the individual movements. Thus, the first theme of the E-flat Quartet, as well as its companion, is taken up in the last movement. The A minor Quartet is framed by a motto, which cites Felix's lied *Ist es wahr?* (Is it true?)—suggesting a secret program.[14] It prefaces and concludes the work. The second movement (*Adagio non lento*) introduces a fugue, which recurs in dramatic elaboration in the course of the last movement.

The scherzos are replaced by a charming canzonetta in Op. 12 and a lightly woven intermezzo in Op. 13. Felix's preference for feminine endings, together with a certain rhythmic monotony, of which the listener easily tires, mars Op. 12. Few of such flaws are noticeable in Op. 13.

In Op. 13, after the statement of the motto, the first movement breaks forth in passionate vigor. From its inception it is treated contrapuntally, but with an intensity and freedom that leave no association with studiously contrived "learned writing." Harsh chromatic dissonances introduce the second theme. A third and a fourth theme conclude the exposition. The development section deviates from the Beethoven pattern and displays originality and craftsmanship. The recapitulation concludes with a coda, into which a theme of the exposition is forcefully injected.

The second movement (Example 28) has an extremely complex structure. The first theme contains elements of the motto as well as of Beethoven's cavatina from the Quartet in B-flat, Op. 130. The same master's influence is noticeable in the ensuing fugue (cf. the Quartet in F minor, Op. 95,

Allegretto). The fugue abounds in the most excessive chromaticisms ever written before *Tristan.*

Example 28

In a dramatic climax the first violin flies into a recitative, which leads back to the first theme of the movement. The fugal section is inserted in its recapitulation. The movement closes quietly, as it opened, but the over-all impression is that of trouble and turmoil not assuaged.

The piquant *Intermezzo* (A minor, 2/4) opens harmlessly enough and proceeds according to textbook rules: A A A′ A, and the listener expects variations or a conventional trio. Instead the composer surprises him with an elfin trio in lightning speed. There follows the recapitulation of the initial theme, but one more surprise is in store: the main theme and the trio are combined in an utterly charming arabesque-like coda.

The last movement, a *presto* finale, unfolds dramatically with a tempestuous recitative over tremolo chords. Again we are reminded of Beethoven —this time the Quartet in A minor, Op. 132.

Felix is able here, however, to pursue highly individual paths. The entire movement is so charged with emotional energy that it sometimes runs the danger of going out of joint. Whenever such a danger exists, the composer resorts to stricter forms. Thus, Mendelssohn achieves a unique feat: reining in the unleashed forces, he couples the recitative with the main theme of the movement and brings about the recapitulation. How remote this *tour de force* is from the sedate sonata forms of Mendelssohn's contemporaries! The coda of the finale is again a recitative, based upon the fugue theme of the Adagio. It leads back to the restatement of the framing motto, *Ist es wahr?* which concludes the work in a surprisingly modest fashion:

Examples 29a

Example 29b

This is one of the most ingenious of Mendelssohn's compositions. Characterized by a breathtaking poignancy and mastery of integration, it shows him in the unwonted role of a "problematic artist." Indeed, had Mendelssohn been able to maintain the level of this quartet, his name would stand in close proximity to that of a Mozart or Beethoven!

Nowadays the work is heard but rarely, owing to the enigmatic injustice of fluctuating tastes. It would be certain to evoke general admiration today, especially if it were performed by a string orchestra rather than by a quartet. Both its sounds and its proportions warrant a symphonic medium.

OCTET, OP. 20

THE OCTET, OP. 20, and the Overture to *A Midsummer Night's Dream* represent the crown of Mendelssohn's first stage. The Octet possesses both grace and strength, fine musical form as well as lovely individual melodies. It was written with consummate workmanship and presents many new facets of the composer.

In Mendelssohn's lifetime the work was performed in his father's musicales of course, then in Paris in 1832, and frequently in Leipzig with the composer playing the viola. The work was rather popular, so that Mendelssohn arranged it for piano duet. The scherzo was orchestrated by Felix, and very frequently the entire work is performed by a string orchestra of many more than the original eight. However, this practice is in keeping with the young composer's strict direction in the original score: "This octet must be played by all instruments in symphonic orchestral style. *Pianos* and *fortes* must be strictly observed and more strongly emphasized than is usual in pieces of this character." What are the "pieces of this character" to which Felix refers? One may look far and wide in the contemporary literature without finding octets. True, septets, double quartets, and nonets are not too rare, but only Schubert's great Octet and Spohr's Double Quartets have survived, besides Beethoven's Septet. Mendelssohn could not have been referring to Spohr's Double Quartets, since their principle of construction varied essentially from the treatment of an octet. Both he and Spohr were aware of that. Spohr stated in his auto-biography: "An Octet for stringed instruments by Mendelssohn belongs to quite another kind of art in which the two quartets do not concert and interchange in double choir with each other, but all eight instruments work together."[16] There remains then only the Schubert Octet as material for comparison. Yet this work, like Beethoven's and Hummel's septets, requires wind instruments as well as strings. Indeed, Mendelssohn's Octet has remained for almost a century a work *sui generis*. It is the first composition of the sixteen-year-old master in which, from the first to the last measure, everything belongs to him alone. It is futile to search for external influences.

Both cyclical and programmatic principles are discernible in it: the theme of the Scherzo recurs in the finale, and the Scherzo itself tries to recapture the atmosphere of Goethe's Walpurgis Night in *Faust*:

> The flight of the clouds and the veil of mist
> Are lighted from above,
> A breeze in the leaves, a wind in the reeds
> And all has vanished.   (tr. Klingemann)

Fanny writes, apropos of the work,

> To me alone he told his idea: The whole piece is to be played staccato and pianissimo, the tremulandos coming in now and then, the trills passing away with the quickness of lightning; everything's new and strange and at the same time most insinuating and pleasing. One feels so near the world of spirits, carried away in the air, half inclined to snatch up a broomstick and follow the aerial procession. At the end the first violin takes a flight with a feather-like lightness—and all has vanished.[16]

The four movements of the work—*Allegro moderato ma con fuoco*, 4/4, E-flat; *Andante*, 6/8, C minor; *Allegro leggierissimo* 2/4, G minor (scherzo); and *Presto*, 2/2, E-flat—contrast sharply in mood and technique.

The mood of the first movement is one of merry and manly elegance: the first theme (a), flexible as a whip and spirited as a damascene blade, resembles somewhat in its rhythmic and melodic profile the first theme of Haydn's "Sunrise" Quartet, Op. 76, No. 4 (G).

Example 30a

Example 30b

In this first movement, Felix delights in experiments with structure, harmony, rhythm, and scoring. The second theme is actually an offspring of the first, which the composer always keeps at hand, either in its original shape or inverted. A good deal of development takes place in the exposition. We notice, too, that Felix plays with structural retards (a), with piquant progressions (b), with really polyphonic scoring (c).

Example 31a

Example 31b

Example 31c

In the slow movement, a sonorous, elegiac piece, Felix stretches the tonality of C minor to the utmost. He stays in it for only two measures, then leaves it abruptly and returns to it only after an escapade of eighteen measures. At the end of the movement the tonality is once more beclouded: six measures before the end we do not yet know the key in which the composer will reach the conclusion. But it manages to come naturally, without any convulsions. The music satisfies the most rigid demands of musical logic and organic structure. The Scherzo has already been described by Fanny. Little more need be added, except that we encounter here one of Felix's numerous pieces where the finest contrapuntal technique is applied with such a lightness that the uninitiated layman would never suspect the intricacies of texture. It sounds so simple! In this deceptive ease Mendelssohn has only one peer: Mozart. He, too, could write music that conceals its highly complex texture behind a façade of elegant sound.

In the last movement the composer strives for monumentality. This is really a symphonic piece, and its approach is not unlike that of the finale of Mozart's *Jupiter Symphony*. Beginning with a grand fugue, Mendelssohn adds a countersubject and uses many devices of learned writing, such as double counterpoint, inversions, and coupling of themes. As the only contrast to this many-voiced tangle, Mendelssohn offers a stroke of genius: a simple unison theme, full of vigor and energy.

Towards the end we seem to hear chords from Mozart's *Magic Flute*. Yet, nowhere is Felix's originality impaired in the slightest, nor does he permit his polyphony to run dry or become boring. This relatively extensive analysis of the Octet is partly justified by the fact that it was the composer's favorite composition of his young years. Schumann tells us that Mendelssohn always remembered it fondly as a reflected image of his youth.[17] Indeed, it represents a peak in his work, that Mendelssohn did not attain again for some years. When he did, however, it was on an even loftier level.

SEVEN CHARACTERISTIC PIECES
FOR PIANO, OP. 7

IN THE FIELD of musical erudition Mendelssohn had few peers among his contemporaries. He knew much old music, perhaps too much for an unfettered play of his imagination. The three patron saints of Op. 7 are, in the order of their importance: Bach, Domenico Scarlatti, and Beethoven. Although the title of the work promises only seven individual pieces— and individual they are—threads are spun that connect some of them subterraneously, as it were.

Number 1 is a gentle "invention" in Bachian style. We shall encounter its harmonic and even its metrical structure again in Number 6. (Both pieces are also in E minor, a favorite key for Felix.) Number 2 is a fast and furious scherzo, not unlike the Capriccio, Op. 5. Like the latter, Number 2 also "smells of Scarlatti" (as Rossini noticed). Number 3 is an elegant fugue in D major, sounding like a drawing-room Sebastian Bach. It is, however, a graceful and witty piece. Number 4 is entirely *sui generis*: another of the formal experiments of which young Felix was so fond. Here he abandons the traditional dualism of the sonata form, and we are confronted with a monothematic sonata with full development, which sounds in its four imitative entries in alternating tonic and dominant statements like a concealed fugue. Actually it is a combination of sonata form, invention, and *perpetuum mobile*. It serves as prelude to the subsequent double fugue (Number 5) whose first theme can easily be set against the beginning of Number 4. Number 5, the Double Fugue, is a little too academic for our time and taste. It parades its great learning and is a little stiff in its borrowed Bachian dignity. Number 6 sounds almost like a sarabande, but bears the direction "with longing." It is secretly connected with Number 1. Its first part contains nine measures, as does that of Number 1, and the harmonic progressions of the two pieces are all but identical. Are we to look for a secret program? There is no evidence that would lead us in this direction. This "longing" was a well-known "Romantic" *malaise*, which after a while grew to be immensely popular. Originally an outburst of genuine *Weltschmerz* or nostalgia, it served later, to less discriminating composers and listeners alike, as a vehicle of the cheapest sentimentality. That this need for "a good cry" marred much of the serious music of the time was Mendelssohn's misfortune, but hardly his fault. Number 7, in E major, the key of the *A Midsummer Night's Dream*, does not fail to live up to that association. It conjures up in enchanting echoes all the elfin spirits that swarmed through the overture. Since we do not know the exact date of its conception, it might even be a companion piece to the overture. There is also a little link between Number 6 and Number 7: one motif permeates both pieces. The fairy piece ends, surprisingly, in E minor, *pp* once more stressing the common elements of Numbers 1, 6, and 7. Numbers 4 and 7 deserve to be played more often: they are pianistic gems.

SONGS FOR VOICE AND PIANO, OP. 8, 9

THERE IS LITTLE DOUBT that the songs of Mendelssohn constitute the weakest element in his *oeuvre*. The composer's erudition and taste, his generally critical faculties, his "devilish respect for printer's ink," coupled with his true lyrical talent, his sense for a well-rounded melodic line, seemed to presage a great composer of songs. Yet Mendelssohn remained strangely mediocre in this field, granting a few rare exceptions. Sometimes he even stooped to outright banality. How can we explain this discrepancy?

Let us first examine the facts: Who were the poets of the twenty-four songs of Op. 8 and 9? With three or four exceptions, they were personal friends of the composer, such as Klingemann, Droysen (under the pseudonym Voss), Friederike Robert (the Swabian beauty), or other second-rate, older authors. Only two of the poems are of first rank: the folksong *Es ist ein Schnitter* (Yon Reaper Is Death) and *Pilgerspruch* (Pilgrim's Song) by Paul Fleming, the seventeenth-century Protestant poet. With the exception of these two and the *Hexenlied* (also named *Anderes Maienlied*) by Hoelty, the texts of his songs are harmless and eminently respectable pretexts for pleasant melodies. Why did not Felix, while Goethe was still alive, compose some of his poems? That would have been dangerous indeed! Felix's own teacher Zelter was Goethe's most intimate friend and thought he had a monopoly on the composition of music to Goethe's verses. Felix did not dare provoke the old professor's jealousy. Prior to Goethe's and Zelter's deaths, Felix used only the *Calm Sea*—as the program of his overture—and had just begun to sketch some music for the *Erste Walpurgisnacht* by Goethe. Fanny was more audacious: she smuggled her duet, *Zuleika and Hatem* (by Goethe), into the first dozen of Felix's songs. Only some years later did Felix set some of Goethe's verses to music, and one of these songs: *Sonnett, Die Liebende Schreibt* (A glance from eye to eye), is in fact his best lied.

Nowhere do the mannerisms of Mendelssohn appear so conspicuously as in these early songs. Of twenty-four pieces, ten are written in 6/8 measure, a meter fatal to Mendelssohn. The superfluity of feminine endings, of sickening suspensions, condemns most of the songs to well-deserved oblivion.

Although Felix knew some of Schubert's songs (not many) and admired them, he did not deviate from the path shown him by his teachers Zelter and Berger. He was more independent in other forms; why did he follow his master's voice here?

I believe there are three reasons for these disappointing limitations. Aside from Zelter's doctrine of the autonomous melodic line (see Chapter IV), there was Hegel's postulate, too, which pointed to a preference for the simple strophic song, because it does not "like a slave follow the changing steps of its poetic master."[18] Moreover, in Northern Germany the lied had not yet attained the status of a serious work of art, as it had in Vienna. It was considered a stylized folksong, a song for company, or even a couplet, a popular arietta, in short, what would be termed today "functional music." Yet the decisive obstacle lay in Mendelssohn himself. A lied is often a love poem or some form of amatory expression. Now, Mendelssohn was a flirt, not a lover; a husband, but not a Romeo; and, aside from juvenile indiscretions, a paragon of virtue. He still lacked those passions recognized as indispensable for the highest achievement in a medium where subtlety must be at least balanced by spontaneity. During and after his courtship we do not hear of even one love song addressed to his bride, and on his honeymoon he composed a Psalm. Hence, he evaded passionate overtones in the poems he set to music, even in the sedate love poems acceptable to him. It is no coincidence that his songs were favorites of Queen Victoria: they certainly were respectable, virtuous, and proper enough to satisfy her strait-laced court.

With all these inhibitions, the lion's roar, or rather the lark's chant, could not be completely silenced. Of the twenty-four songs, there are three or four worthy of the composer of the *Dream Overture* and the *Octet*. The *Erntelied (Reaper's Song)*, with its simple, modal tune, has the effect of an old German woodcut. The grim vigor of the words finds its match in the music. The *Frühlingslied in schwäbischer Mundart (Spring Song in Swabian Dialect)*, a merry little piece, fittingly reflects Felix, the charmer. The poem *Scheidend (Parting)* by Droysen anticipates, in Felix's setting, a Brahmsian mood in its wayward phrasing. The crown of all these songs, the celebrated *Hexenlied*, is a demonic and dramatic counterpart of the "Witches' Scherzo" of the Octet and a forerunner of the *Walpurgisnacht*. Here the usually monotonous 6/8 measure storms ahead—the constant tremolos obscure the progressions, and the voice assumes the character of a wild ballad singer or rhapsodist.

On the debit side of the ledger we encounter four or five contributions by Fanny, which Felix had smuggled in.[19] Whenever one compares a setting by Felix with one of the same poem by Schubert (and they were occasionally inspired by the same verses), it is to the former's disadvantage. The best-known instance of this is Uhland's *Frühlingsglaube (Spring's*

Advancing), which in Mendelssohn's version sounds fussily agitated, while in Schubert's it is gloriously impatient. It must be added, in fairness to Mendelssohn, that his piano and other instrumental music can well stand a comparison with Schubert's.

CHORAL MUSIC

FOR THE CHRISTMAS SEASON of 1828, all friends received letters and parcels, and in compliance with Klingemann's expressed wish, Fanny attempted to sketch the trend of Felix's music. She wrote:

> On the whole, I feel no doubt that with every new work he advances in clearness and depth. His ideas take more and more a fixed direction, and he steadily advances towards the aims he has set himself, and of which he is clearly conscious. . . .
> I can only watch his progress with loving eyes and, not on the wings of thought, lead the way and foresee his aim. He has full command of all his talents and day by day enlarges his domain, ruling like a general over all artistic means and devices at his disposal.[20]

The last observation, "ruling like a general," is a point well taken. For in his church music, to which she clearly referred, Felix now manifested and even paraded his full technical mastery. None of the works discussed in this section is generally known, nor has any ever been published, with the exception of *Tu es Petrus*. The fate of these pieces is most unjust. It is hoped that the following remarks will arouse public interest in them and bring them to life out of their century-long slumber.

The Mendelssohn we encounter in this music does not in any way fit into the clichés usually pronounced in reference to this composer. The music in question is not only unromantic, but even austere, certainly not easy of access. Yet Mendelssohn was intensely proud of these compositions.[21]

Tu es Petrus

This motet, as well as its companion piece, *Hora est*, belongs to the realm of strictly liturgical music. Impressed by Thibaut's ideas on that subject, Felix eagerly studied the old Italian choral masters of the sixteenth and seventeenth centuries. While Felix's literary friends praised their euphony, the eighteen-year-old student was on the lookout for other aspects, and he found the ideal of linear treatment in the human voice.

This was the technique he used extensively in the *Tu es Petrus*. Not without justice did Fanny call this composition for five-part chorus a nineteen-part motet. For the fourteen staves of the orchestra are treated as independently as the voices themselves. Mendelssohn did not shun even the sharpest dissonances, when two autonomous melodic lines clashed with each other. Parallel seconds and sevenths, stringent conglomerations of persistent contrapuntal threads, are frequent in this work. It culminates in a triple fugue, where the orchestra goes its own way. In rigorous grandeur the composition rises majestically, like the Church, founded upon a rock.

Hora Est, Antiphona et Responsorium for Sixteen-part Chorus with Organ Continuo

The royal *Kapellmeister*, J. Fr. Reichardt (1752-1814), one of Goethe's music advisers and favorites, had brought a sixteen-part Mass by Orazio Benevoli (1605-1672) to Berlin. His colleague, C.F.Ch. Fasch, founder of the *Singakademie*, was very much attached to the work and its style and tried his hand at a *Missa brevis* for a sixteen-part chorus. Both works belonged to the repertory of the *Singakademie*.[22]

Attempts such as these to revive the choral music of the Baroque were lovingly championed by the Romantic school. Yet the advocates of the strict style, as it was called then, were either unwilling or unable to "do likewise," until Mendelssohn's fancy was caught by the grandeur of polychoral writing. His example set the pattern for lesser talents, such as the Berlin masters Eduard Grell and Heinrich Bellermann. While their sixteen-part Masses have been published, Mendelssohn's work remains in manuscript, in the vaults of the Berlin State Library.

Benevoli's conception of many-voiced choral Masses was more inspiring to Felix than the rather dry treatment by Fasch. Writing for sixteen obbligato voices is by no means easy, and it imposes rigid limitations upon the composer's imagination. The division of sixteen voices into four choirs, further subdivisions into smaller and smaller units, collecting them back into massive choruses, requires, on the composer's part, the utmost familiarity with the intricacies of polyphonic choral style.

The operative idea of Mendelssohn's composition is not unlike that of *Calm Sea*, an audio-visual one. It is easily understandable that the text evoked a series of images in Felix's mind.

Hora est, jam nos de somno surgere et apertis oculis surgere ad Christum, quia lux vera est, fulgens in coelo. Ecce apparebit Dominus super nubem candidam et cum eo sanctorum millia.

The hour has struck! Ours it is to rise from slumber and with open eyes to rise to Christ; for He is the true light, radiant in heaven. Lo, thus will the Lord appear, high above a white cloud, and with Him myriads of saints.

This text is recited at matins and, as an ecclesiastical call to rise and pray, it is replete with imagery. Felix's vivid imagination was caught by the conception of a spatial hall, wherein signals come from all sides echoing one another. The refulgence of Christ's sun, the promise of God's reappearance, add a glorious visual picture.

At first, a somber male chorus responds to the incessant calls: "Hora est," almost like reluctant sleepers. Out of the basses a winding figure rises to the highest tenors, a musical expression of physical and spiritual awakening. The second part symbolizes the radiant light. In powerfully polyphonic vision appears the motif

Example 32

led through the four choirs in sixteen canonic entrances, from the highest sopranos to the lowest basses. Majestic progressions mark the conclusion of the impressive piece, which testifies to the vivid sense of tonal color and choral style of its composer. Fanny was especially fond of this work.[23]

Less partial critics than Fanny were also deeply impressed by this ambitious, although austere, composition, and they expressed themselves accordingly after the two performances by the *Singakademie*. The Leipzig *Allgemeine Musikalische Zeitung* praised the work in most glowing terms, calling it "a masterpiece full of spirit and fire."[24] And in the same vein spoke the Berlin *Allgemeine musikalische Zeitung*.[25] After a review of the première of the work A. B. Marx proclaimed in a dithyrambic article:

It is not so much the inventiveness of the piece, nor its tremendous mastery of its sixteen-part setting: the fundamental concept [*die Grundidee*] which has evoked and inspired all this must lighten our heart. It will survive when the paper and canvas of the score will have crumbled away.[26]

In this case, as in many others, Marx proved to be a false prophet. Nonetheless, this work deserves to be published and performed, if only to rectify the current misapprehensions about Mendelssohn.

Chorale Cantatas

Compared with the two mighty achievements just described, the chorale cantatas represent minor efforts. During the years 1827 to 1832, Mendelssohn wrote six cantatas, of which one seems definitely to be lost. The other five have remained in manuscript and continue to gather dust in the archives of Berlin and Frankfurt. With two exceptions this oblivion is not entirely undeserved, for both the form and treatment of the text of a chorale cantata present peculiar problems. Mendelssohn's fine sense of formal roundness could cope with the first difficulty, but failed to overcome the second. We shall discuss these problems elsewhere.[27]

The cantata, *Christe, Du Lamm Gottes* (Christ, Thou Lamb of God), is a quiet and rather idyllic representation of the words of the chorale, which mourns over Christ's Passion. Of this mood, however, there is hardly a trace to be found in Felix's music. Another chorale cantata, in A minor, also of rather sentimental character, is now lost. We know of its existence through references in letters of Klingemann and Charlotte Moscheles, and in one of Felix's letters.[28]

Surveying calmly the values and weaknesses of Mendelssohn's religious music—after the clamor and heat of a now-forgotten controversy—one is inclined to agree with Hermann Kretzschmar's verdict:

The opinion has frequently been expressed that Mendelssohn's greatest accomplishment lies in the realm of church music. This may well be the true answer . . . After a period of rest his compositions will rise again in their full freshness. They are certain to have a great and lasting future, like all works of art in which a real artist's individuality manifests itself in masterly fashion.[29]

Notes

1. O. E. Deutsch, *The Schubert Reader* (New York, 1947), p. 690. Little of Schubert's instrumental music was published before 1830. See *ibid.*, p. 938, "List of Works."
2. It must be emphasized again that Mendelssohn was not a synaesthetic composer. While to him even the ruins of Rome evoke music, he distinguishes clearly between "general" and "musical" music. (Letter to Zelter, December 1, 1830.)
3. *F.M.B. Letters*, to Baroness Pereira, July, 1831.
4. *Correspondence with Moscheles* (Boston, 1888), p. 119.
5. Haydn's nickname for his disciple Beethoven.
6. Even Berlioz acknowledges illustrative effects only under certain circumstances. See Barzun, *Berlioz and the Romantic Century* (Boston, 1950), I, p. 153ff.

7. Busoni, *Entwurf einer neuen Ästhetik der Tonkunst*, 2nd ed. (Leipzig, 1916).
8. Unpublished letter, July 22, 1826.
9. Unpublished letter, March 28, 1835.
10. A. B. Marx, *Die Musik des 19. Jahrhunderts*. Similar passages are found in *Erinnerunger* (Berlin, 1865).
11. Letter to Devrient of July 13, 1831; Devrient, *Erinnerungen an Felix Mendelssohn* (Leipzig, 1891), p. 108.
12. Hensel, *F.M.*, I, Fanny's letter of June 18, 1828. The first idea of the composition originated four years earlier, in Dobberan, on the shore of the Baltic, as an unpublished letter of Felix indicates.
13. Mendelssohn jokes about the illustrative features of the work in his letter to Klingemann of February 5, 1828.
14. The nucleus of *Ist es wahr* occurs in Beethoven's sonata *Les Adieux*, itself a programmatic piece.
15. Spohr, *Autobiography* (London, 1878), II, p. 151-2.
16. Hensel, *F.M.* tr. Carl Klingemann, Jr. (London, 1882), I, p. 131.
17. R. Schumann, *Erinnerungen an Felix Mendelssohn* (Zwickau, 1948), p. 28.
18. Even Nietzsche, with his admiration of Wagner, accepts the older view. "The melody is, then, the first and general element, which without harm may undergo several objectivations in several texts." (*Birth of Tragedy* [Stuttgart, 1921], I, p. 78.)
19. Of Op. 8, Nos. 2 and 3, of Op. 9, Nos. 7, 10, and 12 are compositions by Fanny.
20. Hensel, *F.M.*, *op. cit.*, letter of December 8, 1828, I, p. 163.
21. *Klingemann Correspondence;* see Felix's letter of February 5, 1828, in which he calls the *Tu es Petrus* his "greatest accomplishment."
22. *Musikalisches Wochenblatt* (Berlin, 1791), 8th fascicle.
23. Oxford Collection, letter of June 29, 1829.
24. *Allgemeine Musikalische Zeitung* (Leipzig), Vol. 31, p. 829.
25. *Allgemeine Musikalische Zeitung* (Berlin, 1829), No. 47.
26. *Ibid.* (1830), No. 3.
27. The best chorale cantata of Mendelssohn's "*Ach Gott, vom Himmel sieh darein*", an important work indeed, will be discussed in Chapter X.
28. *Klingemann Correspondence*, April 24, 1829, February 5, 1828; also Moscheles *Diaries*, tr. Coleridge (London, 1873), p. 150.
29. Kretzschmar, *Führer*, II, p. 434.

Interlude:
The Musical
Axes of Europe

IF THERE were such a thing as a philosophy of music history, we would have to consider the beginning of the nineteenth century as one of those periods which is, in the sense of Karl Jaspers, a temporal axis, and, at the same time, a musico-cultural axis. Before 1800, Vienna, Venice and Naples had monopolized instrumental music and opera. Under the pressure of political and cultural re-alignments, two rival axes now appear; London-Paris and Vienna-Naples. How had Vienna lost its hegemony in instrumental music? Since the deaths of Beethoven and Schubert, instrumental music had declined in Vienna; in North Germany, however, instrumental music had come to the fore under the aegis of post-classic composers and there it found its natural home. True, Vienna remained the protector of classical tradition, but the dominant trend was neither classic nor "romantic," but eclectic. This conservative city could never warm to Romanticism, and even Lanner's charming waltz *Die Romantiker* is intended somewhat ironically.

The high Austrian aristocracy, once the patrons of Mozart and Haydn, had lost many of their possessions after the Congress of Vienna and were therefore no longer able or willing to underwrite important composers financially, and none cared to take up again the role of a Maecenas. As they had done a hundred years before, they turned again to the Italian opera.

Since large parts of Italy were newly occupied by the House of Hapsburg, this change in taste was certainly caused in part by culturo-political factors. Lombardy and Venice had now become provinces of Austria, and Hapsburg princes reigned in Parma, Modena, Tuscany, and Southern Italy. Once again a historical principle was confirmed: the conquered Italians began to dominate the manners and the way of life of the Austrian conquerors. Once again, and perhaps for the last time, the Italian opera became the favorite of the Austrian world of fashion.

For those composers who stood outside the pale of Classicism or Romanticism, neither Vienna nor Paris was of special interest. Rather, they were attracted first to Berlin, then to London. And a definite change had taken place in instrumental music. Since the beginning of the nineteenth century, the piano strongly dominated the field of intimate music, often to the detriment of real chamber music. Italy was hardly any longer of serious significance to these composers; for they were interested in writing instrumental music, not opera. Every composer now strove to publish as many popular piano pieces as possible, for only in this field (outside opera) could he enjoy financial and artistic success. The conception of the universal keyboard instrument, which had still been common eighty years before, and which included harpsichord, piano and organ, had been given up long ago. Of the group of composers midway between Classicism and Romanticism, only two were still in a position to do justice to the old conception: Abt Vogler, the oldest of them, and Felix Mendelssohn, the youngest—both outstanding pianists and organists.

The group of "neutrals," traditionally neglected by music history, included many famous names of the day. For instance, there was the notorious Henri Herz, who found a profitable market for his more than 150 "brilliant" and trivial sets of varations, and—like him in spirit—the elegant Kalkbrenner. But lesser masters of solid worth also belonged to this group: Moscheles, the pupil of Beethoven; Pleyel, the favorite pupil of Haydn; Muzio Clementi, the founder of a new piano style; the Berliner Louis Dussek, a highly gifted "crypto-Romanticist" (once the teacher of Prince Louis Ferdinand); L. Berger, the piano teacher of Felix Mendelssohn. They were all overshadowed by two towering figures: Luigi Cherubini (1760-1842) and Mendelssohn himself. Only Cherubini continued the great operatic tradition of Gluck; the others devoted themselves almost entirely to instrumental music, above all to the piano. These basically heterogeneous composers had one other trait in common: they all looked to the West—Paris or London—and many of them settled in those cities.

They all faced the same dilemma: should they serve the highest aims of art, or strive to become as popular as possible? The problem had become acute because of the uncritical worship of all folklike art by romantic poets;

however, real folksongs and popular (folklike) imitations were often confused. Schiller had already recognized the growing conflict and dealt with it in unforgettable words. He wrote:

> At present there is a very great gap perceptible between the élite of a nation and its masses. . . . As a result, it would be in vain arbitrarily to lump under one heading what has long been differentiated. Therefore, a popular poet for our times would have a choice between the simplest and the most difficult of tasks: either to accommodate himself exclusively to the powers of comprehension of the great masses and to do without the applause of the cultivated class—or to bridge the tremendous gap between the two groups by means of the greatness of his art and to pursue both aims at once. What an undertaking—to satisfy the hypersensitive taste of the connoisseur without thereby becoming unpalatable to the great masses—to adapt oneself to the childish powers of comprehension of the people without throwing away any of the dignity of art![1]

About ten years earlier, Mozart had expressed himself in quite similar fashion. He wrote to his father:

> The concertos are . . . very brilliant, pleasant to the ear, naturally without becoming merely empty; here and there, connoisseurs, too, can find real satisfaction—but in such a way that non-connoisseurs must also be satisfied, without knowing quite why.[2]

Among the "neutrals," there were a few who scorned such "popularity": Cherubini, Dussek, Berger. The only one—a proverbial Rock of Gibraltar—who never made concessions to public taste was Cherubini, and he has also remained the only one whose music still lives today. Can that be mere chance? The young Mendelssohn strove to fulfill this high aim of Schiller's thought—the unification of the popular with the classical—without, however, quite being able to reach this goal. We shall have more to say about this in connection with the *Songs without Words.* All the rest of the above-named composers were popular for a short while, but are forgotten today. Schiller was right; only the greatest genius can bridge that gap between classical and popular art. Parenthetically, Mozart succeeded in this great venture, above all in *The Magic Flute,* in the *Entführung,* and in several instrumental works; Beethoven, in the *Busslieder,* the early piano sonatas, perhaps also in several chamber works, and in the Finale of the Ninth; Schubert, in many of his songs, and certainly, too, Haydn and Weber, the darlings of the German bourgeoisie at this time. In contrast to the attitude of the literary Romantics, however, esthetic problems of this sort were far indeed from the thoughts of this neutral group.

These "outsiders" stick to the sonata form of the "middle-period"

Beethoven, and lean towards monothematic or strictly closed forms only in their so-called character pieces. But several of them experiment with cyclic ideas and conceptions. These are, however, quite different in essence from the cyclic ideas of Beethoven, which are all programmatic in function (cf. the self-quotations in his Fifth and Ninth Symphonies). Leitmotifs, too, such as we find in *The Magic Flute* or in *Der Freischütz*, have little in common with these cyclic experiments in instrumental music. Rather, the cyclic efforts of the lesser masters probably stem from the desire to force the dualistic principle of sonata form into manifest unity through the use of mottolike motifs in several movements. As far as I have been able to discover, this principle of integration in absolute music (as one might call it) first appears in Schubert's Second Symphony, in which the Trio of the Minuet and the theme of the variations are built on the same idea. The principle is even more strongly intimated in his Piano Trio in E flat major, the Finale (a) of which recapitulates literally the theme (b) of the slow movement.[3]

Example 33a

Example 33b

In the main, there are four composers of the "neutral" group who operate with cyclic ideas: L. Berger, Dussek, Moscheles, and, of course, the young Mendelssohn. Later we shall return to his attempts at cyclic formation. Dussek plays with such forms in his undeservedly forgotten G minor Concerto, Moscheles in his *Concerto patetico*. It was L. Berger who carried the principle of integration to its most radical extreme, in his C minor Sonata, Op. 18. It is built exclusively on the following one measure motif:

Example 34

Although completed in 1816, it was not published until 1834-5. The most influential musical oracle of Germany at this time, Ludwig Rellstab, was so impressed with the work that this usually rather sober-minded critic, discussing technical fine points of the composition, broke out into the following words of praise:

> That work is not only a masterpiece of contrapuntal skill, in the manifold use of the figure through extension, inversion, changes of rhythm and meter, but also . . . an intimate union of workmanship and fantasy.[4]

Of these artists, only Berger returned to his native city of Berlin; the others settled in Western Europe, either London or Paris. Mendelssohn was related to this group by a certain affinity. Some of them had settled in England; including Moscheles, Clementi, and Cramer. True, he loved Germany as his real fatherland, but England was, for the present, to become his homeland of choice, as it seemed now to offer him much that Germany thus far had denied him. So, only the first goal of the extensive European journey which he was now planning was set: London.

Notes

1. Schiller, Collected Works, *Über Bürgers Gedichte*, written in 1791.
2. Letter of Mozart to his father, December 28, 1782.
3. In the eighteenth century, it was especially C. P. E. Bach who favored such ideas; a persistent motif of cyclical function is traceable in his Harpsichord Concerto in A minor.
4. L. Rellstab, *Ludwig Berger* (Berlin, 1846), p. 20. There, too, we find these daring words: "In our opinion, the sonata could appear under the name of the greatest master and would do him credit." (Egert, *Die Klaviersonate im Zeitalter der Romantik* [Berlin, 1934], p. 106.)

We may perceive an echo of Berger's "idée fixe" in Mendelssohn's piano-sonatas, op. 6, op. 105, and op. 106. The last two were published after the composer's death; all three were written before he had reached his nineteenth year. In the sonata, op. 6, the first and last movements are thematically linked, in the sonata B-flat, op. 106, the middle movements are thematically connected, whereby the passage which links them is derived from the principal theme of the first movement. The finale cites a section of the scherzo. Undoubtedly Berger had been able to interest his disciple in the antinomy between dualistic sonata form and cyclic arrangement.

CHAPTER VIII

*The Journey
to England*

Art and life are not two different things.
(From a letter of Medelssohn to Devrient)

I

SINCE MENDELSSOHN and his work had a significant effect on English music
of the nineteenth century, we shall first sketch the state of English music
at the time of Felix's first visit.

For our purpose, it is unimportant to decide whether Mendelssohn's
influence was beneficial or harmful to English music. The fact of this
powerful influence is not altered by such considerations. Even today, more
than a hundred years after his death, his name is respected and even honored
in broad strata of English society. This is astonishing, in consideration of
the violent attacks and the supercilious scorn to which his music was—
even there—subjected from two directions and for a long time. Not only the
Wagnerians, but also the champions of an autochthonous English music
were his sworn enemies. In spite of all this, Mendelssohn's name and prestige
have assured him a lasting place in the musical repertoire of England.
However, in order to evaluate his effectiveness in England, we must take
into consideration what the musical life of England was like before his
time; also, the principal representatives of English music deserve more
detailed study.

Music in pre-Victorian England present a brilliant façade. Behind this,
however, lay chaos, and the ruins of the structure which had once been so
solid. More than in any other European country, class distinctions determined musical taste. Only the two pillars of English society, the aristocracy
and the upper middle class, were seriously interested in musical life. But even
these two strata were quite differentiated in their spheres of interest. The
opera was almost exclusively, and symphonic music was for the most part,

the domain of the aristocracy and of the developing *upper* middle class. On the other hand, the oratorio, glee clubs, and church music were middle-class domains.

Before the beginning of the twentieth century, the class distinctions were extremely strict, and were rigidly maintained, no less in music than in other areas of life. True, Moscheles, who was often invited to private soirées as a pianist, believed, in his innocence: "The principles which my host (Lord Palmerstone) represents are pure Toryism. Fortunately, art, which I represent, stands on neutral ground."[1] However, reality did not correspond at all to such naïve dreams.

"Patronage" or "protection" were the magic keys which opened all concert halls, tuned all instruments. E. Fétis, the well-known Belgian musicologist, at that time the oracle of European music, wrote, during this period, a very informative letter about the musical situation in England. Among other things, he says:

> Patronage is everything in England, and so convinced are the artists of its power, that they are less solicitous to acquire talent, than to make friends. Whoever has them among the powerful and the wealthy is sure of a fortune....[2]

For Fétis, who was a Jacobin at heart, there exist only two social classes. First, there is the worthy lower class, the great mass of people. In his opinion, this group is always reasonable, diligent, and honorable; but it lacks time for serious music. (When this class finds time, it chooses music only for "light amusement" or for the great choral festivals.) In opposition, he places the aristocracy, which he calls the "pest of England." Ridiculous as it seems to him, it calls itself the "elegant world" and has usurped the arts as its legitimate property. He also describes the behavior of this "fashionable world":

> When fashion attends a concert, it is no way solicitous about hearing music; but there is an opportunity for meeting, and the sound of voices and instruments seems an agreeable accompaniment to its conversation . . . the chattering soon becomes similar to that of a public place or a market, and this lasts till the end of the piece.[3]

Only star singers were not victimized by such insulting bad manners.

Many details in Fétis' report may be exaggerated. But, after all, he was an experienced, if prejudiced, observer and critic, and his picture of London's musical life is not pleasant.

It speaks well for English musicians that those who profited from this organization of patronage were mostly foreigners. For both opera and symphony were controlled by Continental managers and artists. Let us leave aside the question whether this was a consequence of the Georgian preference for German composers and Italian singers, or the result of the blind adoration of Handel and of everything which was even loosely connected with him. Yes, even the question whether dynastic-political interests played a role here (as it often appears) would scarcely be irrelevant. In any case, instrumental music in England during the century 1750-1850 was principally dominated by Germans. On the other hand, despite Weber and Spohr, the opera remained, then as earlier, the domain of troupes of Italian guest artists.

The impresarios of these *stagioni,* who often staked all their possessions, their names and their reputations on success, aimed at presenting a parade of prima donnas in every season. These ladies were, then, the principal attraction—more than that, the real justification for the existence of English operatic activity. Beginning with the famous Pasta, the list of prima donnas contains many once celebrated names: Malibran, Grisi, Rubini, Tamburini, Henriette Sontag of Berlin, the Frenchwoman Viardot-Garcia, then Jenny Lind, the "Swedish Nightingale," and many more. The operas of Rossini, Cimarosa, Bellini, Donizetti, and a host of now-forgotten Italian composers dominated the repertoire. In fact, there was even a strong movement for having all operas, without exception, sung in Italian.[4] For a while it seemed as though this abstruse idea would really take hold in London (and, at the same time, in New York, whose musical taste orientated itself according to London's during this period). A composer like Rossini was praised to· the heavens and was even called "the Voltaire of music."[5] Nevertheless, opera remained strange to wider circles of English life, or was regarded with a certain suspicion. It was not only "foreign," but also light entertainment music, and accessible only to a well-filled purse.[6] Its habitual "patron saints" were always the aristocrats—even if they were not exactly saints!

However, there was no lack of attempts to compose and perform English operas. Today, we know of these efforts and their composers (without exception unsuccessful) only through specialized works of music history. The result of all such experiments remained inexorably the same; an English opera had very slight chances of becoming a repertoire work which would satisfy the demands of the upper class. For, "the upper classes . . . were wholly devoted to the Italian opera and the various *prime donne* who in succession reigned over the fashionable world of London."[7]

If the Italians ruled in the opera, and not always with a light hand, it was the Germans who set the tone in the concert halls.

The parade of German and Austrian musicians who were favored by King George III and the highly musically gifted Prince Regent (later George IV) includes almost all the famous names of music history from the child prodigy Mozart to Liszt. Even late Victorian England more or less followed this example. One of the most noteworthy exceptions to the hegemony of German musicians was, of course, Paganini; but even this devilishly gifted artist was not unanimously hailed as he had been everywhere else in Europe.[8]

The virtuoso's domination of the concert hall begins to become clearly noticeable; opera singers, especially coloratura sopranos, invade the programs of symphony concerts, as do the "wonder pianists." The public reacted to this type of musician much as it does today; more and more, it lost interest in the quality of the music performed, and marveled at the stunts of musical acrobatics.

So the influence of Handel and his school gradually began to disappear under the ceaseless onslaught of new German and Italian composers and virtuosi. However, this development manifests itself only in the 1820's; and one can find only few concert programs of this period which do not pay due tribute to Handel.

Two programs, one conservative, the other more modern, may demonstrate the stylistic potpourri of those years.

I. Antient Concert, April, 1829

Conductor: Earl of Darnley
(in honor of the Earl of Derby)
Act I.

Overture	
Quintet (Flavius)	
Recitative and Chorus from *Deborah*	
Recitative and Aria from *Il Pensieroso*	
Concerto No. 5 (Grand)	G. F. Handel
Aria and Chorus	Guglielmi
Recitative and Chorus	
Recitative accompagnato "Hark, Hark"	Handel
Song "Revenge"	from *Alexander's Feast*
Recitative accompagnate "But bright Cecilia"	Handel
Solo and chorus "As from the"	from Dryden's *Ode to St. Cecilia*

Act II.

Symphony 1st [?]	Mozart
Duetto from *Clemenza di Tito*	Mozart
Glee "Since I first saw"	Ford
Duetto "Quel anelante"	Marcello
Quartet "Sing unto the Lord"	
Chorus "Cry aloud"	Croft

Musette (from Concerto 6th Grand)	Handel
Glee "Through the last glimpse"	Irish melody
Recitative accomp. and Aria	Cimarosa
Grand Chorus: "Gloria in excelsis"	Pergolesi

IV. Philharmonic Concert

Leader Mr. Weischal
Conductor: Mr. Attwood

Act I.

Sinfonia in A	Beethoven
Duetto (from *Barbiere*)	Rossini
Concerto Corno	Belloli
Scena	Pacini
Overture, *Pietro von Albano*	Spohr

Act II.

Sinfonia in C	Mozart
Aria "Il mio tesoro"	Mozart
String Quartet [?]	Beethoven
Terzetto from *L'Inganno felice*	Rossini
Overture to *Lodoiska*	Cherubini

True, each of these programs represents a particular orientation; the second definitely emphasizes Mozart and Beethoven. But concessions to public taste were frequent, and often unavoidable.

The soirées in the city palaces of the aristocracy followed the fashion of the day even more closely. There, it was customary to engage an impresario, who was responsible for both program and performers. The noble hosts often treated the performing musicians in an undignified manner—often, even, with unheard-of insolence. It was quite customary for the gentleman or lady of the house to interrupt the soloist in the middle of a piece with the kind words, "C'est assez, mon cher." ("That's enough, my dear.") The programs of these soirées naturally strove to present the latest operatic successes of the season, with their stars.

The situation in the provinces was entirely different from that in London's musical life. There, Handel's gigantic name still overshadowed all musical innovations. Out of the synthesis of Handel's personal style with that of older English church music, there gradually grew a typical English idiom. It gained its individuality from an influence of many composers now forgotten, from Merbecke (sixteenth century) to Crotch (beginning of the nineteenth century), but Handel remained its center. Such tradition-centered efforts resulted in an unmistakably English and national church and folk music. From it grew the regeneration of English music at the end of the nineteenth and beginning of the twentieth century.

This music, solid, conservative, often somewhat stiff, corresponded to the English middle class in every respect, and was intimately related to it. In this idiom, the great mass of the English people felt entirely at home. The composers of this genre cultivated liturgical music, the oratorio, and the stylized folk song (glee). The tradition of choral folk songs is much older than Handel, who valued it, worked with it, and strengthened it. Perhaps one can trace it back to Dowland, but certainly to Thomas Morley and the Elizabethan madrigalists.

Of the church composers of the pre-Victorian era, Thomas Attwood (1765-1838) should be named first, because he represents a direct connection between Mozart and English church music. Attwood had been a pupil of Mozart, and, in his turn, introduced young Mendelssohn to English church music. As one of the few who had studied on the Continent (and with a great master) he preferred an idiom which was hardly characteristic of classic Anglican church music. It was too lyrical, and took pleasure in imitating the rococo mannerisms of the young Mozart. However, Attwood was an outstanding musician and held the very influential position of principal organist in St. Paul's Cathedral.

The brothers Samuel and Charles Wesley (1766-1837; 1757-1834) composed church music of sterner substance. They were nephews of Dr. John Wesley, the founder of the Methodist Church; that did not prevent them from being champions of the revival of Gregorian chant, and from being equally enthusiastic partisans of J. S. Bach. The son of Samuel, Samuel Sebastian (after Bach), was perhaps the most gifted composer of this noteworthy dynasty (1810-1874). His liturgical music is one of the few towering peaks of English church music of the nineteenth century. Although a thoroughly original artist, he was unable to remain entirely outside Mendelssohn's sphere of influence, as we can sense in his famous *Service in E*. However, there is not a single measure in this work which copies Mendelssohn slavishly. Even in the dangerous vicinity of Mendelssohn's music, Wesley remained true to himself and to his style.

Outside of the great cathedrals and bishops' seats, which produced most of the church music of the Victorian period, the famous old university cities Oxford and Cambridge cultivated an entirely autonomous musical life, stressing especially the music of the collegiate church, oratorio, and glee clubs. The Oxford professor of music was then Dr. William Crotch (1775-1847), from whose once frequently performed oratorio *Palestine* the anthem "Lo, star-led chiefs" is still occasionally sung on Epiphany. A second baccalaureate of Oxford, William Horsley (1774-1858) was known and liked as a glee composer. Several of his popular pieces are still sung today. He and his family became intimate friends of Mendelssohn; and Horsley took the greatest pains to make the young German composer acquainted with the spirit and technique of the glees. These efforts were not in vain. Felix's male choruses, which have so greatly enriched German popular choral music, betray to some extent the stylistic influence of the glees. Also, the organist of Cambridge, Dr. Thomas Walmisley, Attwood's godson (1814-1866), belonged to the circle of Mendelssohn's friends and admirers.

The various genres were represented by a relatively small number of musical institutions. Their names indicate not only their artistic aims but also, in many cases, the social circles from which the organizations customarily recruited their members.

The most important musical institutions of London were:

The "Concerts of Antient Music," which cultivated not only old music but also old orthography. According to their statutes, a work had to be at least twenty years old in order to be admitted to performance.

"The Royal Philharmonic Society," founded in 1813. Its initial ban on soloistic music was given up after three years. The artistic level of the Philharmonic Society was somewhat higher than that of the third great organization:

"The City Concerts," founded in 1818 by Sir George Smart. The statutes of this organization admitted amateurs, both as singers and instrumentalists, but not as composers.

Vocal music was represented by the Caecilian Society (later Sacred Harmonic Society), by the Concentores Sodales, and by the glee clubs.

In 1823 the Royal Academy of Music was founded, which, from its very beginnings, exerted a decisive influence on the musical taste of England. Such outstanding artists as Attwood, Smart, Horsley, Clementi, and Moscheles taught there.

Musical periodicals were, as yet, scarcely developed, and the few magazines of that epoch carried out their difficult task with dignity and decency. They were, so far as these things are recognizable today, completely free of commercial considerations. The *Harmonicon* and the *Quarterly Music Review* were the most significant of these music journals.

All these institutions were centralized in London. But the musical backbone of England was not the metropolis, though many musical nerves grew out from her. The English people found their original tradition most strongly embodied in the great choral associations of the provinces, with their periodic music festivals. Cities like Gloucester, Worcester, and Hereford organized the famous "Three Cities Festivals," in which each of the three cities in turn played host to a music festival. Leeds, Birmingham, Manchester, Edinburgh and many other provincial cities have, and had even then, a centuries-old tradition of music festivals. Their repertoire exclusively cultivated the oratorio, liturgical music, and glees; not until the middle of the nineteenth century did symphonic music invade the program of the choral associations—not without assiduous preparation in this direction on the part of Mendelssohn.

An objective survey cannot leave us in doubt that, in musical affairs, England lagged far behind Germany and Austria; for no garden can be fruitful when it is neglected for decades. Also, the regular visits of foreign artists were not a source of unalloyed pleasure; for not all concertizing Germans or Italians were on the level of a Haydn, Spohr, Weber, or Mendelssohn. There were masses of musical charlatans and "pseudoprofessors," but as in America before 1900, Anglo-Saxon society was profoundly reluctant to believe in the bourgeois respectability of professional artists anyway, especially of musicians. In this respect, too, Handel was an exception. Perhaps through his appearance as a "gentleman amateur," Mendelssohn succeeded in decisively breaching these prejudices.

II

Already as a youth, Felix had considered composition as his aim in life; everything which did not contribute directly to his creative drive was at best a detour, often enough a necessary evil. In this category also belonged his conducting. Because of the resounding success of his performance of the *St. Matthew Passion*, his reputation as a composer had been somewhat dimmed. This unexpected result, the danger of being forgotten as a creative artist, depressed him. He expected fresh stimulus from the forthcoming trip. In September, 1828, several family letters mention the great journey as a definite project, but no reasons are given. Felix feels that "people are tired of me" and he writes, not without bitterness:

> It is a long time since the public has heard something significant from me
> . . . and so I have been forgotten. . . . It was a great sorrow to me to hear
> that the Royal Orchestra declined to play publicly under me. . . . I am
> certain that not a single person would seek out a concert-hall because of a
> composition by me, and I could cite many concerts at which works of mine
> are performed.[9]

Here, one must certainly distinguish between the latent and manifest motives which induced Felix to leave his tenderly loved family for years. Zelter, above all, felt that his favorite pupil had outgrown the provincial circle of musical Berlin. The strictly brought up youth may have been only half aware that he had to get away from the well-meaning despotism of his father, the jealousy of his sister, and the snobbery of his mother, in order to find himself as man and artist.

The reasons given by the family now are, however, at least equally plausible. Father Abraham writes briefly and to the point to Moscheles that Felix will leave his parental home in a few months and go "into the world." He is a musician and intends to devote his life to music. He wants to travel in Italy, France, England, and Germany, in order to acquaint himself with the great works of art and artists on the spot. It is a great relief to Abraham to know that Felix will be under the protection of Moscheles and Klingemann in London.[10]

Felix was not quite so certain of his goals as was his energetic father, and therefore he emphasizes that he does not intend to appear publicly in London. It seemed more important to him to develop and to establish his style and taste. Felix did not yet quite know whether he should choose Vienna or London as the starting point of his European tour. For the first time, the rivalry of the two musical axes of the early nineteenth century—Vienna-Naples versus London-Paris—emerges here. Moscheles, who, after all, had been Beethoven's pupil and therefore knew Vienna, advised London. Now, it was in no way unusual for a gifted German musician to appear in England. Mozart had shone—and studied—there as a child, Beethoven had at least planned a trip to England; Haydn, Spohr, Weber and a host of lesser masters had traveled in England, principally to make capital out of the then highly paid concert tours. German musicians were very popular at this time, as we have seen, and the outlook was favorable.

But no: Felix did not want to make public appearances! He appeared as the brilliant amateur, as the highly gifted musician, but still as the "gentleman of leisure." This aristocratic attitude, repudiating music as a profession, was very popular with England's gentry, and remained so until World War I. In order to understand it, we should think of the distinction which the Englishman still makes between a high-class amateur sportsman and a "pro." The latter may earn much money and may also gain public favor, but the amateur still counts as the only true sportsman.

In spite of all such resolutions, Felix's musical instincts finally gained the upper hand over social considerations. He appeared as conductor, as pianist, as composer. He did not earn money, but then, that was not his intention. What he gained was self-confidence and certainty of direction, qualities which offered rare dignity to the young artist. His letters dispense more and more with the cleverness beloved of the Berlin salons; it had always been a false façade in his case. This development is not manifest in the published letters to his family; they are still full of the usual smart repartee. All the more do we sense the new spirit in the letters to his friends Devrient and Droysen. In one letter Devrient had expressed his fears that Felix, in the mad whirl of his social successes, would forget his true mission. Felix answered rather sharply, though cordially:

I must become rather angry; to be specific, about a passage in your letter which I shall attack most vigorously. You write that my letter "helped" me with your wife, for she was so displeased with my life here, and you, too, were not at all reconciled to it. . . . Should anything "help" me with you and your wife? Nothing should help me or hurt me with you; for I should hope that you knew me by now. . . . What would you say if I asked you nicely not to be dazzled by the brilliance of Spontini's operas, but to cherish good music instead; you would expect me to have more confidence in you. . . . *Life and art are not two different things,* and if I am certain that you don't fear my giving my allegiance here to Rossini or John Bull, then you must not fear that my life here will intoxicate me. . . . Really, Dev., if I become better or worse, I'll send you a special-delivery letter; till then, I don't believe it. Naturally, I refer to what people call convictions.

To the devil with lots of things, among others the whole preceding page, which is no good. But I know very well what I mean.[11]

Only in letters such as this does his true pride appear. In spite of this, he cherished lifelong gratitude to England for the friendly and benevolent reception that the English gave him. He knew very well that many of them understood little or nothing of music, but

I should like right now to play my *Calm Sea,* etc., for the public here, and they would grasp and understand it much better than the circle of cultivated people in our salon. And yet they understand nothing of music. . . . Also, by God, I play better here than in Berlin, and just because the people listen with more pleasure.[12]

It cannot be denied: Father Mendelssohn's common sense and astuteness had discovered the right way to help Felix get over his uncertainty and depression. For all the future, Moscheles and Klingemann, his true friends and protectors in a foreign land, were to be identified in his mind with the adored image of his father. Perhaps for this very reason, they became his dearest and most intimate friends.

III

After a miserable crossing from Hamburg (his father and his sister Becky had accompanied him), Felix arrived in London on April 21 in a state of complete exhaustion. But he became better as soon as he saw his friends Klingemann and Moscheles, who were waiting for him at the pier.

Thus began his years of learning and wandering, which enriched him with new stimuli and new viewpoints. It was not only in London that he exceeded his self-imposed limitations as a "quiet observer"; he also learned to know the variety of British life, in London as in Scotland. At first he was perplexed by the manifold impressions of the metropolis, and in the first flush of this confusion he wrote: "It is frightful! It is crazy! I am confused and head-over-heels! London is the most grandiose and complicated monster that the world has to offer."

And yet, this was by no means the London of our day; there were no airports, no railroads, no automobiles. So, it was a comparatively quiet city. Nonetheless, Felix was shocked by this first impression.

The first days and weeks were occupied with little excursions, visits, and tourist "gadding about." In England, where he could act uninhibited by his usual reserve and by the "correct" Berlin manners with which he had been brought up, he succeeded in making many new friends. And they remained his friends for life. He saw and admired Malibran, then at the height of her popularity, and probably flirted with her a little too. Much as he admired her, he never became a mere languishing Seladon; for, in the musical sphere, his criticism remained untouched by his personal feelings. Mrs. Moscheles took him for visits and promenades in her elegant carriage, and his splendid recommendations gained him admittance to various strata of English society. We cannot describe all his visits, acquaintances, and social circles without becoming either pedantic or gossipy; therefore, in what follows, we shall limit ourselves to the most important experiences and events.

In those halcyon days before Victoria's reign, the social atmosphere in London was anything but Philistine or *petite bourgeoise*. Even such a dyed-in-the-wool bourgeois as Klingemann noted:

> It is unbelievable, the amount of twaddle about frivolities and fads of the day that goes on alongside the seriousness of public institutions and of roast beef—the French are heavy-footed or elephantine in comparison with us.[13]

The theatre season was just at its height when Felix arrived. He saw several operas with Malibran and Henriette Sontag, the famous Berlin *prima donna*. He reports very critically on a performance of *Hamlet* in Covent Garden with the most eminent English actor of his day, Kemble; and also on several French operas, for which he cherished a lifelong lack of enthusiasm. (Perhaps Spontini's cabals had spoiled the whole genre for him?) He visited Parliament, and, like every true liberal of the *Vormärz* (pre-1848 period), was deeply impressed with it. As a "distinguished foreigner" he was a guest at a sumptuous ball given by the Marquis of Landsdowne, and at another by the Duke of Devonshire.

All of this was new to him. He had never seen festivities in such a style and on such a scale before; he marveled at the beauty of the women and the elegance of the rooms. Yet, he did not allow himself to be bedazzled. Clear-sightedly, he recognized the shattering contrast with the pitiful poverty of the masses and the frightful misery of the slums.[14]

News of Mendelssohn's arrival in England was reported as follows:

> ... son of the rich banker of Berlin, and, I believe, a grandson of the cele-brated Jewish philosopher and elegant writer. He is one of the finest piano-forte players in Europe, and though a very young man, is supposed to be better acquainted with music than most professors of the art.[15]

Moscheles found him a modest room with a German ironmonger in Portland Street, and hoped that the young man would be ready "to exchange the attractions of the great city for our rural solitude, where his society will act as a healing balm for our wounded spirits."[16] (Shortly before this, Moscheles had lost a child.)

But already on April 28, a week after Felix's arrival, his friend Klinge-mann wrote that "Felix should not let go of any musical . . . contacts in order to please his close friends . . . and I insist that he should not keep any appointment with me when his profession calls."[17] This attitude also corresponded to Felix's own wishes.

He reports his musical impressions in detail to his parents on April 25. Unfortunately, the text of this letter is so mangled in Hensel's book that the reader must necessarily get a false impression of Felix's reactions.[18]

The secretary of the Philharmonic Society, on whom Felix had called, assumed that Felix would give him one of his new compositions for per-formance, and made a note of his published works. But no definite agree-ment was reached. In the meantime, Felix made the acquaintance of many musicians. Besides the English musicians Sir George Smart, J. B. Cramer, M. Clementi, John Taylor, and Sir Thomas Attwood, he met the singer Henriette Sontag, whom he had already known in Berlin, and, above all, came to know Malibran-Garcia, who, at that time, was creating a universal furor. Felix also came into contact with several members of the high aristocracy, but reacted sharply to rude treatment on the part of Princess Lieven and the Duke of Montrose: "I have had exactly as much of these nobles as I need—namely, the sight of them. . . ."[19]

The "observer" Felix became impatient when, at the end of the first week in May, he had still heard nothing from the Philharmonic Society, and began to think about other possibilities of appearing, although on May 1 he had written:

> The Philharmonic Orchestra offers the best, or rather the only good pos-sibility of having my overture to *A Midsummer Night's Dream* performed; . . . and I shall not play in public, either, till the Philharmonic Orchestra has played something by me.[20]

Finally the ice was broken and the series of misunderstandings resolved; Felix's C minor Symphony was programmed for the concert of May 25. In an unpublished portion of the letter of May 26, of which Hensel, as usual, prints only the triumphant parts, Felix explains the long time of waiting. He had never received an official invitation; when he asked Sir George Smart for an explanation, he was brushed off with many excuses; the season was already too far advanced, there was not enough time to prepare new works, etc. The secretary lied to him, too, for Felix learned that, unexpectedly, a new symphony by Spohr was to be performed in the private concert of Moscheles, as well as in that of Sir George. But the wise Moscheles advised Felix decidedly "not to sell himself too cheaply." It almost appeared that all musical plans would come to nothing. Felix was already dealing with other artists and managers. By chance he met two directors of the Philharmonic Society, in a music store, Sir George not being of the party. Now everything was explained.

Neither Sir George nor the secretary had said a word to the directors about the fact that I had brought music here and wanted to have it played. On the contrary, Sir George had always told them that I really made music *only for fun*, and that "I did not need to do it at all," and that I was here only as a gentleman, not at all as a professor. . . . In a few days I received the formal invitation through the secretary, with the request of J. B. Cramer, who was the conductor of the day, to conduct (the symphony) myself.[21]

We see that everything was not joy and sunshine, and that Felix had awaited the success of his C minor Symphony and of his appearance before he reported to his parents on the preceding difficulties. The success of the work was so great that with one stroke all difficulties dissolved in a flow of engagements and advance contracts. The *Harmonicon* and the *Times* carried extremely favorable reviews. We shall cite just one passage, since it already foreshadows Mendelssohn's popularity in England:

It is not venturing too far to assert, that his latest labour, the symphony of which we now speak, shews a genius for great writing; and it is a fair presumption, that, if he perseveres in his pursuit, he will in a few years be considered as the fourth of that line which has done such immortal honour to the most musical nation in Europe.[22]

Since the program of this notable concert is difficult to come by, we shall give it here. It is a typical program of the time, a potpourri of serious, light, German, Italian, vocal and instrumental music.

Seventh Concert, May 25, 1829

Leader Mr. L. [?] Cramer
Conductor: Mr. Cramer

Act I.

Sinfonia (never performed)   Felix Mendelssohn
Aria, Mr. Rosner, "So reizend hold" (*Zauberflöte*) Mozart
Concertante, Piano and Harp   Kalkbrenner and Dizi
Scena, Miss Paton, "Misera me"   C. M. von Weber
Overture *Euryanthe*   C. M. von Weber

Act II.

Sinfonia in E flat   Mozart
Aria, Mme. Wranizky, "Non piu di fiori"
    (*Clemenza di Tito*)   Mozart
Concerto Violin, Mr. Oury   Kreutzer and de Beriot [?]
Song, Miss Paton "If guiltless blood"
    (*Susannah*)   Handel
Duet, Mme. Wranizky and Mr. Rosner,
    "Amor, possente nome" (*Armida*)   Rossini
Overture *Anacreon*   Cherubini

In his symphony, Mendelssohn replaced the original minuet with the Scherzo from his Octet, arranged for full orchestra. It elicited great applause, and had to be repeated. In a letter, he explains that

the minuet seemed boring . . . and like pleonasm. . . . So I had the Scherzo from the Octet played in the middle, and added some jolly D-trumpets to it. It was very silly, but it sounded very nice.[23]

The friendly, even enthusiastic reception which was accorded to Felix at his first appearance remained unforgettable to him throughout his life. It helped him to overcome the inimical and rude attitude of the Berliners; also, the little hurts caused him by the supervision of his family now seemed important. In a letter written in French, he expressed his deep gratitude to the Philharmonic Society, and later proved it by the dedication of his Symphony to the Society. Thereupon the Philharmonic made him an honorary member. This was the first public and significant honor of his life. He never forgot that he owed it to the English! Near the end of his life he still said that the "universal English applause lifted a stone from his heart." Five days after this performance Felix appeared in the Argyll Rooms, as soloist in a concert directed by Sir George. He shone in Weber's *Konzertstück* in F minor, which, to the amazement of the English, he performed by heart. Another innovation! On June 10, Mr. Nicholson, the first flutist of the Philharmonic gave a benefit concert in which Felix participated. By public demand his new C minor Symphony had to be repeated. Finally, in a concert of the flutist Drouet, he had the longed-for opportunity to perform his *A Midsummer Night's Dream* Overture on Midsummer Day (June 24). Its repetition was demanded, but the concert was not a success, for only 200 persons were present. The Philharmonic played acceptably under Felix's direction, but Sir George had not engaged the right instrument for one part (Felix called it a bass horn), and only in the second performance did things go to Felix's satisfaction. On this occasion, he also appeared as pianist in Beethoven's E flat major Concerto; "Enough of these dry tones, I must play Beethoven again," he parodied Mephistopheles.[24]

His last appearance of the season took place on July 13, 1829, for the benefit of the needy Silesians. This concert has a long preliminary history, which is characteristic of musical conditions in London.

Mme Sontag had planned to give a charity concert for the needy Danzigers at the end of the season, and had asked Felix for his participation. He promised it, too, but the intrigues of Sir George, whom Felix, full of indignation, calls an "intriguing, deceitful and untruthful man," intimidated Sontag, and she abandoned the plan at the end of May.[25] This gave Felix the opportunity to place his newly won reputation at the service of charity on his own initiative. He complied with a request of his uncle Nathan, who suggested that he should try to relieve the sufferings of the Silesians (stricken by severe floods) by giving a charity concert. But he had to swallow his pride and approach Sontag as a suppliant. Since he now belonged to "society," Sontag—who alone could have proposed a charity concert for the benefit of foreigners—was easily persuaded, and consented to participate and also to secure the proper patronage. Finally she and Felix succeeded in winning over several big names of the aristocracy for the plan. After that it was no longer so hard to gain the participation of other artists. The concert program, a real monstrosity, lasted about four hours. There were no vocal soloists, for now everybody wanted to participate and the singers were allowed to appear only in ensembles, so that no one should be insulted.[26]

This time, Felix conducted his *A Midsummer Night's Dream* overture again, and, with Moscheles, played his Double Concerto in E major with orchestra—a work of which we have already spoken.[27] The concert was notably successful and brought 300 guineas (about 6600 gold marks)—a very considerable sum for those days.

In the meantime Felix had not forgotten his old friends. With Klingemann, Rosen (professor of oriental languages), and Mühlenfels he made many excursions in the vicinity of London, and sketched with pleasure the picturesque scenes. They visited new English friends, the Prussian Embassy, where Baron Bunsen received them cordially, and the Hanoverian Legation, where Klingemann had his office. The friends ate German sausage, flirted with German and English girls—in short, lived thoroughly happy days. On this occasion Felix, who was susceptible to feminine beauty all his life long, flirted ardently with Marian Cramer, a daughter or niece of J. B. Cramer, the concertmaster of the Philharmonic. But their fathers knew nothing of i:, and so Felix enjoyed this delightful time to the full.

IV

Only after the fulfillment of his artistic and social obligations could Felix enter with a good conscience upon the long-planned holiday journey. His friend Klingemann was to accompany him to the Scottish Highlands and the Lake District. To avoid trouble, Felix had asked his strict father to permit the journey and a few additional excursions. In order to forestall all possible questions or reproaches, he began with an excuse:

> You seem to think that I live here more or less at random, without real aims and plans. That is really impossible for me anywhere; only, at this distance I cannot tell you about all my little movements . . . but, as Father always says, to him who concerns himself with the study of Knowledge *per se* comes everything, happiness, success, and the friendship of his fellow-men—and now that has happened.[28]

This letter may have been meant as a sort of tribute to his father; Felix wanted to prove that he was still well aware of his father's demand for unconditional obedience.

The journey, by the post-coach or on foot, carried the friends through York and Durham to Edinburgh, where they arrived a week after their departure from London (July 28). There, they saw Holyrood Palace and, as admirers of Schiller, visited the historic places which are connected with Mary Stuart. On the very first day, Felix swam in the ocean, which seemed especially salty to him. Everything in Edinburgh pleased him, including the girls; he promised that if Mohammed's father would become a Christian, he for his part would become a Moslem and settle in Scotland. Another time they visited the ruins of the chapel in which Mary Stuart had been crowned. Felix observes here that he believes he found the beginning of his Scotch Symphony at that spot. And the first sixteen bars of the slow introduction actually were written down at that time; they contain the motto of the first movement. However, it was more than ten years until the symphony was completed; but Felix succeeded in preserving the first creative impulse of the musical atmosphere through all the years.

From Edinburgh they went to Abbotsford, in order to make the personal acquaintance of Sir Walter Scott, who was uncommonly popular in Germany. Unfortunately, the great novelist was just about to leave Abbotsford, and the travelers had to content themselves with staring at him "like a new gate" and were not a little irritated by their bad luck. On the way to the Hebrides (through Sterling, Perth and Inverary) the friends often had opportunity to become acquainted with wild country and wild weather. Felix reacted with delicate sensitivity to this landscape, so strange and unfamiliar to him. This is evident in his charming drawings, and in his letters. Thus he writes once that it was very quiet "in spite of servants' chatter and slamming doors! Quiet and very lonely! I might say that the quietness resounds through the noise."[29]

At the beginning of August, they reached the Hebrides after a strenuous sea-journey, from which Felix suffered greatly, for "he gets along better with the sea as an artist than as a human being with a stomach."[30]

Through Staffa, they came to Fingal's Cave (August 7). From there, Felix sent only a short letter to his family: "In order to make clear to you what a strange mood overcame me in the Hebrides, the following just occurred to me."[31]

The "following" was twenty measures of music, an orchestral sketch for his famous "Fingal's Cave" overture. More than a year was to pass before he had finished the first version of the work, and two years more before he was satisfied with the last (third) version. This is but one of many examples which bear witness to Felix's never resting self-criticism; he himself writes that he has a hellish respect for print.

The journey, which was not interrupted even in rainy weather, continued through Glasgow over the heath to Liverpool. The quiet and loneliness oppressed the wanderers. For ten days they had met no other travelers; they spent their nights in the primitive inns of little villages, in which smoky brandy was the only known drink. How they longed for the sun, which they had not seen for days—for warmth and friendliness! But in spite of the hardships they had suffered through the country, the weather, and poor accommodation, they finally bade a "fond farewell to those Highlands which we criticize and yet love."[32]

In Liverpool the friends parted, for Klingemann's leave was over and he had to go back to London. Felix wanted to make a side trip to Ireland, but thought better of it when he heard that the steamer had spent fifteen hours, instead of six, on the high seas. Instead of this, he decided to accept the invitation of Mr. Taylor to his country estate in Coed-Du (in Wales). But first, Felix wanted to try out the new railway to Manchester, "for fun." He traveled through the two tunnels to the Liverpool harbor and was tremendously impressed by the "crazy speed" of 22 kilometers per hour.

In Coed-Du, with the Taylors and their three pretty and musical daughters, he experienced his first English idyll. He himself reports fully on this visit in letters to his family. From the Taylors and their relatives, the Horsleys, we learn how the young artist was mirrored in the eyes of the young girls. Everything that happens—or, really, does not happen—is purest Biedermeier: amiable, polite, respectable, animated by true feeling, a pleasant and comfortable sense of being together.

We have already spoken of the class stratification of musical taste in England. Thus, we should not be surprised that the Taylor family, with the exception of one daughter, was hardly acquainted with the concert events of the past season, which had brought Felix so much fame. The Taylors, who belonged to the rural gentry, did have their town house in London; but their musical interest was more in the oratorio and the glee than in modern instrumental music. Therefore, we should not be astonished that Anne Taylor, in her letter of recollection written after Felix's death, recalls that on his first visit to Coed-Du the sisters said to each other; "Surely this must be a man of genius . . . we can't be mistaken about this music; never did we hear anyone play so before. Yet we know the best London musicians. Surely by-and-by we shall hear that Felix Mendelssohn Bartholdy is a great name in the world."[33]

In the meantime, Felix had already come into contact with the glees and the various musical dialects of England and Scotland. Contrary to the then-fashionable "Romantic" mode (which had perhaps begun with Haydn) of collecting and arranging so-called "national melodies," Felix felt more repelled by, than attracted to, these folk songs—even though his teacher Zelter had urged him to look out for such pieces and bring them home.[34] Felix, however, exclaims in comic despair:

> But please, no national music! To the devil with all this "folksiness"! Here I am in Wales . . . and a harper sits in the vestibule of every inn and never stops playing so-called folk-melodies, that is, infamous, common, faked stuff. . . . If, like me, you can't stand Beethoven's national songs, then come here and listen to these tunes growled out by harsh nasal voices, accompanied by awkward bungling singers—and don't complain! [In the letter follows a music example with nothing but parallel fifths, possibly a remnant of medieval *organum*.][53]

At first he thought "a glee was a very disagreeable thing," but Zelter admonished him again to study the English choral forms thoroughly. When Felix learned to value them more and more and decided to transplant them to Germany, Zelter agreed with him and called these choral songs "the great serious form for a busy people that constantly lives with great cares."[36]

Amidst pleasant companionship with the Taylors, Felix's creative powers also unfolded in *Trois fantaisies ou caprices*, Op. 16, which were intended to give musical portraits of the Taylor girls. Felix has a great deal to say about the origin of these "fantasies," a rare instance of autobiographical music in Mendelssohn's *oeuvre*.[37] Here we may merely comment that the first piece (representing a bouquet of carnations with a rose) begins not unlike the unwritten Scotch Symphony, but, later on, becomes very conventional. The second piece, which was inspired by yellow trumpet flowers in the hair of Miss Honoria (she was the prettiest of the three), hints at the trumpets—as Felix himself tells us—in an airy, fairy Scherzo. It is unquestionably the best of the three pieces. The third piece was to remind the middle daughter, Susan, of her favorite brooklet, and was therefore called "The Rivulet." It already contains that fatal germ of the "respectable" *Perpetuum mobile*, which, in this case, strikes a sentimental note as well.[38] Many times in his *Songs without Words*, Mendelssohn favored the same sort of elegant but fundamentally meaningless musical chatter. The young man does nothing but flirt here, and in English at that!

On September 10, Felix arrived in London again. This time he was in constant contact with the leading *English* musicians. His first serious judgments on English music now reach his Berlin friends.[39] Reporting on old Attwood, who had received him most cordially, he praises his fine sense of style for church music, organ music in particular. On the other hand, he does not think much of Croft, and finds his eternal *Te Deums* boring. The anthems of Boyce do interest him, but, since he had grown up with the music of Handel and Bach, cannot stir him. Even Purcell often seems to him weak and "occasionally degenerated."

This was not the first time that he had expressed himself critically about Purcell; and these remarks had already placed him in a very awkward position. In one of his letters for the *Revue musicale*, Fétis had committed a grave indiscretion. In this letter he proclaimed (without having asked Felix's permission) that he had been inclined to admire everything from Purcell's pen without ever hearing it. But he was deeply disappointed when, instead of a master-work, he heard "a long string of insignificant phrases, connected together with awkward modulations, with pretentious, but nonetheless 'incorrect' harmonies."

Fétis, distrusting his own first impressions, had turned to his neighbors in St. Paul's Cathedral. "But Mr. Felix Mendelssohn Bartholdy, a young and distinguished . . . German composer, who chanced to be standing next to me, . . . had exactly the same opinion as mine. He felt so uncomfortable that he . . . escaped (*échappé*) before the end of *Te Deum*."[40]

This journalistic churlishness precipitated a little tempest in the English musical world. In a sharp letter to the *Harmonicon*, Mendelssohn was dubbed "Infelix" (unhappy) and called to order as an unworthy, impudent fellow. The affair took on such dimensions that Felix saw himself forced to write a letter to the editor of the *Harmonicon* for publication. There he states, among other things:

> M. Fétis has, it appears, thought fit to drag my name before the public, by referring to some expressions which may have fallen from me in *private* conversation with him, and also to draw conclusions therefrom in corroboration of his censure on a celebrated English composer. . . . While denying the right of M. Fétis thus to quote any private and detached expressions of mine in order to support his own opinions, I must, at the same time, question the justice of your holding me up to the British public as a co-censor with that gentleman.[41]

This episode engendered a lasting tension between Fétis and Mendelssohn, who, as a creative musician, abhorred "professional estheticians."[42] However, the conflict with wounded English pride was settled, and when the Drury Lane Theater offered Felix a contract for an opera (to a libretto of Planchet) at over 300 guineas (about 6600 gold marks), this foolish scandal could do him no further harm.

In deep gratitude for his success in England, he felt the urge to write his old mentor Zelter a moving letter of thanks, a beautiful testimony of the bond between teacher and pupil. If only because of the rarity of human gratitude, this letter deserves complete publication. As a document of his industry, Felix encloses a long list of Handel manuscripts which he had discovered in the King's private library—more than sixty volumes! Even more, he offers to copy for Zelter anything that seems important to him.[45] In his answer, Zelter states the theory that "this heavenly work [*Messiah*] consists of individual parts which were composed at various times."[44] Modern research has confirmed Zelter's supposition.

At the end of his stay in England, he had really bad luck; on September 17 he was knocked down by a cabriolet and hurt his kneecap badly. This accident confined him to bed for nearly two months—a sore test of patience for the hyperactive Felix. The worst of it was that it now became impossible for him to travel to Berlin in order to be present at the wedding of his sister Fanny (on October 3). Both he and Fanny felt this as a source of bitter grief.

Klingemann took care of him tenderly as though he were a sick child; and this generous man praised, in the warmest fashion, the "Englishmen of the lower classes," especially the family of his landlord who, in spite of all the trouble that Felix's accident caused them, were always friendly and helpful. But the aristocracy, too, did not forget the young Berliner in his misfortune; from Felix's letters, we can compile an impressive list of noble visitors who took trouble on his behalf. Sir Thomas Attwood took a special interest in him, and, when Felix could get about once more, he visited the old gentleman at his country seat in Norwood, Surrey, where he passed several beautiful and fruitful days. Back in London, he was melancholy and homesick. Above all, he could not wait to see Fanny again. She had expected that Felix would write a new composition for her wedding, but it was not possible. Instead, Fanny herself, in the end, composed a grand organ prelude "for October 3."[45] At last Felix improved sufficiently to return home. He left on November 29, already preoccupied with planning a *Singspiel* which he hoped to complete for the silver wedding of his parents. It bore a title full of associations: *Die Heimkehr aus der Fremde* (*The Return from Abroad*).

$\mathcal{N}otes$

1. F. J. Moscheles, *Diaries*, tr. Coleridge (London, 1873), p. 73.
2. *Fétis*, "Report on London Music," *Harmonicon* (London, 1829), p. 278ff.
3. *Ibid.*
4. See Ch. Grueneisen: "The 'idea' of an Opera House using the Italian, the best language for singing, for the purpose of executing the works of all masters, *without distinction of country*, was my suggestion as the only system calculated to spread the universality [!] of Art." (Cited by J. W. Davidson in his *Memoirs* (London, 1912), p. 64.
5. In Lady Morgan's *Book of the Boudoir*, reviewed in *Harmonicon* (London, 1830), p. 99.
6. The price of admission for the less aristocratic philharmonic concerts was a guinea *per evening* (21 gold marks). See Davison, *op. cit.*, p. 65.
7. See J. A. Fuller-Maitland, *English Music in the 19th Century* (London, 1902), p. 42. In this connection, we recall the words of John Ella, the most successful impresario of that time: "Of course, every institution supported by the aristocracy must have enemies amongst levellers, republicans and atheists; . . . Now, if we are to ridicule the aristocracy, where must we seek for patronage?" (Davison, *op. cit.*, p. 81.)
8. *Harmonicon* (London, 1829), June.
9. Karl Mendelssohn, ed., *Goethe und Mendelssohn* (Leipzig, 1871), letter to R. Ganz, December 13, 1829.
10. *Letters of Mendelssohn to Ignaz and Charlotte Moscheles* (Leipzig, 1888), letter of December 12, 1828. (Hereafter Moscheles, *Correspondence*.)
11. Devrient, *Erinnerungen an Felix Mendelssohn* (Leipzig, 1891), pp. 76-77.
12. *Ibid.*, p. 79.
13. *Klingemann Correspondence*, p. 54.
14. Briefwechsel mit J. G. Droysen, *Deutsche Rundschau* (Berlin, 1902), letter of November 3, 1829.
15. "Extracts from the Diary of a Dilettante," *Harmonicon* (London, 1829), May, p. 116.
16. Moscheles, *op. cit.*, p. 149.
17. *Klingemann Correspondence*, p. 53.
18. An important (unpublished) part of the letter deals with the interrelation of music and society in England.
19. Unpublished letter of June 5, 1829.
20. Unpublished letter of May 1, 1829.

21. Unpublished part of the letter of May 26, 1829.

22. *Harmonicon* (London, 1829), July, p. 173.

23. Letter of May 29. In this first appearance, Felix introduced the conductor's baton to London; this usage, which C. M. von Weber had caused to prevail on the Continent, found acceptance in England, though only gradually.

24. Unpublished letter of June 28.

25. Unpublished letters of June 28 and July 3.

26. *Allgemeine Musikalische Zeitung* (Berlin, 1829), July.

27. Both works reviewed in *Harmonicon* (London, 1829), July.

28. Unpublished letter of May 29. The saying of Abraham is a literal quotation from the Rabbinical literature. (*Sayings of the Fathers*, Chapter VI.)

29. Some of these drawings are found in Klingemann, *op. cit.*

30. Hensel, *F.M.*, I (Klingemann's letter), p. 251.

31. *Ibid.*, I, p. 256.

32. Hensel, *op. cit.*, I, 261ff.

33. Hensel, *F.M.*, tr. Carl Klingemann, Jr. (London, 1882), I, 225.

34. Unpublished letter of Zelter to Felix, August 9, 1829.

35. Hensel, *op. cit.*, I, 265.

36. Unpublished letter of Zelter, July 5, 1829.

37. Hensel, *op. cit.*, I, 279.

38. Mendelssohn considered it the best of the three pieces, but called it "a little too boringly simple." *Ibid.*, I, 279.

39. The hasty and unfair letter of May 9 to Marx (unpublished), which is preserved for us in a copy in his mother's handwriting, must be understood as an outbreak of his impatience.

40. Fétis, *Revue musicale* (Paris, 1829), June.

41. *Harmonicon* (London, 1829), p. 193 (letter written July 8, 1829; see also pp. 216, 242).

42. Unpublished letter to J. Rietz, February 19, 1841.

43. Unpublished letter to Zelter, July 20, 1829.

44. Unpublished letter from letter, August 9, 1829.

45. The unpublished autograph of this composition is in the Library of Congress, Washington, D.C. Felix's own prelude has also remained in manuscript and is in private hands in Oxford.

Interlude: Return from Abroad

ON DECEMBER 8, 1829, Felix arrived in Berlin. Hardly settled at home, he threw himself head over heels into work. The task of completing the song-play and preparing its performance for the anniversary of his parents was, to him, most important. Today, harassed by atomic fears and disturbed by economic cares, we are perhaps inclined to view this "labor of love" as "love's labor lost"; for the little work was scarcely worth the great effort, since it was not intended for public performance. With it, the good son Felix paid moving tribute to his parents, in a world of peace and of the family idyll. If one remembers this, one will find the musical *Gartenlaube* style of the play—which, Philistine to the marrow, still tries to be "roguish" or "with feeling"—a bit more bearable. Without knowing this, a sound dose of boredom is hardly avoidable. Therefore, let us discuss here only the best-known part of the work, the Overture *To Son and Stranger,* and recount the plot of the song-play, without going into the many details, however wittily conceived.

The Overture begins with a motto "im Volkston," rather slow and sentimental. The real theme of the Allegro

Example 35

has all the melodic charm of the young Mendelssohn, but already shows traces of that rhythmic monotony to which he often fell prey in the *Songs without Words*. Here, however, the danger is avoided, and the delightfully contrasting themes and motifs bring sufficient variety to the well-sounding piece. It ends with the framing motto, which probably had a programmatic significance.[1] As an occasional composition in the truest sense of the word, the overture is of high rank.

The plot of the song-play is as innocent as need be to please the parents and guests. There is a village mayor who is celebrating his fiftieth anniversary in office; but the celebration is marred by the absence of his son (Hermann), who has disappeared. He has a ward (Lisabeth), who has remained true to her fiancé Hermann for many years. Now there comes to the village a swindling shopkeeper (Kauz), who tries to estrange Lisbeth from her Hermann through all sorts of intrigues. At the same time, the missing Hermann reappears and makes himself known to Lisbeth. At night, Hermann wants to wake his Lisbeth with a serenade, but is disturbed by Kauz, who has disguised himself as a night watchman; then Kauz, in his turn, declares his love to Lisbeth, the cause of all this controversy. But now he is arrested by Hermann, who in his turn is playing night watchman. The mayor wakes up and Hermann must let Kauz go again—everyone now retires to rest. The next morning, the general *denouement* takes place; further attempts at deception on the part of Kauz, who pretends to be the vanished son, are unmasked by Hermann himself. So everything ends *in dulci jubilo* with a song of celebration.

For us, the most interesting scenes are those of the "serenade" and "night watchman"; for here, basically, the Beckmesser-Sachs-Walter-Night Watchman scenes are foreshadowed, though without any deeper emotional complications. Here, Mendelssohn abandoned his usual purely lyrical attitude. In the dramatically tinged ensembles, he does not shun sharp dissonances (F in G minor passages; a B that, like Wagner's night watchman's horn, suddenly explodes in the B flat major of the false watchman's song, etc.). There are also leitmotifs, which, after all, were nothing new in opera since *The Magic Flute* and especially since Weber.

Shortly before the performance, which was directed by the routineer Devrient, there was great excitement. Devrient was commanded to attend a soirée of the Crown Prince, and, willy-nilly, could not escape this professional obligation. This *contretemps* threatened to wreck the whole project. Felix, who had set his heart on the affair beyond all reason, broke into a hysterical fit and began to talk gibberish. Only the energetic exhortations of his father succeeded in quieting the maddened Felix and getting him to bed.[2] Devrient's request to leave the princely concert early was granted, and so the performance could finally take place as planned. The completely unmusical Hensel, who sang the part of the village schoolmaster, was given just one note to sing, on which he was "fixed";[3] but he could not even hit this one tone, in spite of the prompting of Felix and his fellow-actors, who laughed themselves sick over it.

The jolly, idyllic little play was so successful that Felix was urged on all sides to try his hand seriously at an opera. He himself felt no less strongly the urge to write a dramatic work. The plan of writing an opera occupies him again and again in the course of his short life. He conducted a very lively, but sporadic correspondence with many poets. In most cases, the scenario of the planned opera was already prepared to the satisfaction of both parties—and then Felix would have nothing more to do with it. Devrient, Immermann, Holtei, Planchet, Helmina von Chezy, Scribe, Bartholomew, Bauernfeld, Birch-Pfeiffer, and Geibel were some of the poets with whom he had dealt in serious fashion. It is shocking to leaf through the correspondence, to follow the enthusiasm of Felix at the beginning of each plan to his courteous, but much too pedantic criticism at the end of the dealings. Perhaps Holtei was not so wrong when he said, "Mendelssohn will never find an opera subject that suits him; he is much too clever for that."[4] His father was of the same opinion,[5] and even Heine, whom one should cite as a musical authority only in case of dire emergency, expressed himself twice in the same sense and with surprising penetration— once in an essay in which he compares Rossini's *Stabat Mater* with Mendelssohn's *St. Paul*, a basically senseless juxtaposition. Nonetheless, he reaches the heart of the problem at the end of the article:

Mr. Leon Pillet has been induced to prepare a libretto by Mr. Scribe, which Mr. Mendelssohn is to compose for the Grand Opera. Will our young countryman undertake the task with success? I do not know. . . . Characteristic of both (Mlle. Rachel Felix, the famous tragic actress, and Mendelssohn) is a great, stern . . . seriousness, a definite dependence on classical models, the finest, most brilliant planning, keenness of understanding, and finally, the complete lack of naiveté. But can there be, in art, originality of genius without naiveté?[6]

Heine could also have applied this question to himself, for no one has ever accused him of naiveté; nonetheless, he truly did not lack originality either. On another occasion. Heine compares the dramatic aspirations of Tieck with those of Mendelssohn. Here, he ventures the prophecy that the master will probably become old and grouchy without having brought anything great to the stage.[7] But Heine himself had to experience the bitter disappointment of failing to win fame as a dramatist—in spite of his *Almansor* and *Radcliff!*

The most eloquent proof of Felix's occasional naiveté is, however, that he was as much in love with his song-play as a Pygmalion might be with his Galatea. Three times he wrote to Klingemann that the song-play was the best thing he had composed up to then, and he was just as conscious of his lack of self-criticism as of his love for the work: "Seriously, however, I am in love with our joint work, more in love than I ever was before, either with music or with a girl. . . ."[8]

It was two whole years before he was able to judge the song-play somewhat more objectively—only then "had he really gotten over it."[9]

The old friends flocked anew around Felix, who rejoiced in this. In 1830, a chair for music (or music history) was established at the Berlin University, and A. B. Marx was appointed to it. The tradition according to which the chair was really intended for Felix and only given to Marx through his influence was widespread is not unlikely. However, I was unable to find any contemporary document in proof of this, with the exception of Devrient's report, from which all other accounts stem.[10] No letter either to or from Felix refers to the affair. Marx, who is otherwise not exactly reticent—in spite of his later breach with Felix—does not say a word about Felix's intervention in his favor. Nonetheless, the story may have a basis in fact, for at this time Felix was still so much under Marx's spell that he wrote to Droysen:

> I can hardly wait for the time when he [Marx] will come out with his big works and put to shame all the dogs and cats who are barking and miaowing at him now. . . . For it is infuriating, the way the mob behaves to the one real musician among them.[11]

It was not long till even Mendelssohn began to doubt Marx's creative powers.

Meanwhile, however, the great European journey which was to be embarked upon had been discussed by Felix and Abraham in all its details. A year earlier, Moscheles, who belonged to the Paris-London axis, had persuaded Felix's father to let him begin in London. Now Felix wanted to get to know the other axis, and its artists and styles, from his own experience.

Zelter, the impatient mentor, writes to Goethe:

> I do not know whether Felix is still there, he was supposed to leave today.
>
> I can hardly wait for the young man to get away from all the mixed-up trivialities of Berlin (*dem vertrackten Berliner Klimperwesen*) and go to Italy, where, in my opinion, he should have gone in the first place. . . .[12]

In March, 1830, Felix finally prepared for the grand tour, after he had been forced to give up his favorite plan of talking his parents on the Italian journey as well. This time it was his mother, who had never cared for traveling and was completely absorbed in her household and her nearer and more distant relatives, who opposed the project most energetically. Shortly before the departure, Rebecca, Felix, and Paul fell ill with the measles, and so it was the beginning of May before the "art-pilgrim" could set forth on his wanderings.

N otes

1. Felix called it "his dedication, his bow of reverence with which he approached his parents." This was meant, however, only for his most intimate circle. (Devrient, *Erinnerungen an Felix Mendelssohn* [Leipzig, 1891] p. 89.)

2. Devrient, *op. cit.*, p. 87.

3. This is an old musicians' joke. It is said that Josquin des Près wrote a motet for the unmusical King Louis, in which the tenor (for the King) always sings the same note. ("Memor esto verbi tui.")

4. Devrient, *op. cit.*, p. 90.

5. Devrient, *op. cit.*, p. 183.

6. Heine, "Rossini and Felix Mendelssohn," *Works*, Part II, XLIII.

7. Heine, *Augsburger Zeitung*, April 25, 1844.

8. Letter to Klingemann, February 10, 1830; also to Rosen, April 9, 1830, and to Klingemann, April 10, 1830.

9. Letter to Klingemann, December 26, 1832.

10. Devrient, *op. cit.*, p. 94; E. Wolff, *Musikerbriefe* (Berlin, 1907), p. 77; Grove, *Dictionary of Music and Musicians*, 4th ed. (New York, 1940), article on Mendelssohn, p. 387.

11. Letter to J. G. Droysen of November 30, 1829.

12. *Goethe-Zelter Correspondence*, letter of May 10, 1830.

CHAPTER IX *Felix's Travels and Reports*

Baccalaureus: "But I, in spirit free, pursue my thoughts
And follow gladly now my inner sight
I wend my way in joyful ecstasy
Toward the light, and darkness lies behind me."
Goethe, *Faust*, pt. II, act 2

THIS IS the proper place to speak of Felix's famous *Reisebriefe* (Travel Letters). We are well informed about his travel impressions through this selection of collective letters to the whole family. But only about his travel impressions! We learn little about Felix's plans and thoughts, and even less about his cares and doubts. This is not his fault, but is caused by the strict censorship of the editors (Paul, his younger brother, and Carl, his eldest son). Whether to spare the feelings of the living or to give posterity as lovable and "respectable" a picture of the young composer as possible, they did not hestiate to mutilate, abbreviate, combine, or completely omit letters, and to alter the text as they saw fit: in short, to do everything to give a portrait of the master which, in many features, is distorted and false. Sir George Grove, the author of the extremely valuable (and up till now the most reliable) article on Felix, in the first edition of his *Dictionary of Music and Musicians*, had to cope with considerable difficulties to get at the source. He was only partially successful in this.[1] Even less successful was Ernst Wolff, to whom we owe the best Mendelssohn biography to date.[2]

Therefore, it will be understood that the author uses the sources which were hitherto unavailable, and only paraphrases from time to time the generally available works: Hensel, *Die Familie Mendelssohn* (F.M.), and Paul and Carl Mendelssohn Bartholdy, F.M.B. *Reisebriefe* (*RB*).

The almost uncensored, but less well-known correspondence of Felix, who was a great letter-writer, with Klingemann, Moscheles, Devrient, Hiller, Droysen, Heydemann, etc., will be referred to more than has been customary in the past. Above all, however, his original letters, which were most obligingly placed at my disposal, will be considered to a far greater extent than was previously possible.

For chronological and practical purposes, the "Grand Tour" may be divided into eight phases:

FIRST PHASE: Berlin-Munich
May 8–End of June, 1830

IT SEEMS SUPERFLUOUS to give a detailed account of the tour. Such an account would not only surpass the limits of this book, but there are also other reasons for avoiding it. What interests us in Mendelssohn is his work and the understanding of his personality—that is, above all, his artistic and human development. Therefore, in the following sections we shall limit ourselves to pointing out and discussing the countries, events and people which were of significance for the young artist. In special instances, Felix's dealings with an artistic, political or philosophical problem will demand our attention. For his active spirit was eager to receive and to assimilate all these stimuli. The very first phase of his journey began with a powerful upbeat; for he traveled through Dessau, the old homestead of Moses, with his father, then to Weissenfels and Weimar.

Like a brilliant star which is setting but still illuminates the heavens, the aged Goethe brightened the spiritual horizon of his time. Certainly he, even more than Zelter and Hegel, determined Felix's esthetic principles. Henceforth, the principles thus established remain the only valid ones for Felix, and he never questioned them—perhaps to the detriment of his free development.[3]

We have already spoken of Goethe's interest in the boy Felix. Now there came a young man, self-assured through his successes in England, burning with the thirst for creation, open to the world of sensations and ideas.

Most important in the last meeting of the young man with the old ·one were the conversations about instrumental and vocal music, and the limits and functions of these genres. In the published letters Felix has nothing to say about this, perhaps with the exception of the remark that every day he has to

> . . . play the piano [for Goethe] for an hour, from all the great composers, and must tell him how they carried on their work; . . . He didn't want to approach Beethoven. But I told him I couldn't help him, and then played the first movement of the C minor Symphony for him. . . . At first, he said; "That doesn't move me at all; that's only astonishing; it's grandiose." Then

he kept on grumbling and finally he said; "That is great, really wild; you'd think the house was about to fall down. . . ." And at table, in the midst of another conversation, he began talking about it again.[4]

The fragmentarily preserved, unpublished diary of Felix observes, however, on the same date: "Long and serious conversation about through-composed songs." He had already written that he had to tell Goethe about Hegel's esthetics;[5] and here we find the connection between these seemingly disparate subjects of conversation. Earlier (in Chapter V) we have spoken of Hegel's esthetics and mentioned its influence on the young Mendelssohn, especially concerning the composition of *Lieder*. Felix did not care to be instructed by the doctrinaire Fétis, but he had the highest respect for the thinker, Goethe, the greatest *creative* artist of the times. We know something of the poet's view on the relationship between word and tone. Like Hegel, he was opposed to the through-composed song, which he considered an aberration. He even believed that through-composing "nullifies the general lyrical character (of the poems) and demands and arouses a misleading interest in the individual details."[6] Also he was prejudiced against any tone-painting: "Imitating thunder in music is no art; but the musician who could make me feel *as though* I heard thunder would be a very valuable person."[7]

Does this not remind us of Hegel's conception of the stimulation of idealized pseudofeelings (*Erregung idealer Scheingefühle*: cf. Chapter V) which, for him, signifies the essence of all musical expression? Goethe had a much more indifferent attitude towards all pure instrumental music. In fact, we might say that he was not able to evaluate it for itself alone, but needed some intermediary meaning in order to understand it—whether a pictorial representation or a poetic idea. Basically, he thought that the new instrumental music was ". . . no longer music. They [the works] surpass the level of human feelings and one cannot add anything to such works [!] from one's own mind and heart."[8]

He freely admits to Zelter: "I lack the faculty for enjoying the thief of fire and clouds [Paganini]—that is, for what is called pleasure and what, for me, always hovers between the senses and the understanding."[9]

In another report on his visit, which, however, was addressed to Zelter, Felix mentioned that the first movement of Beethoven's Fifth had pleased Goethe very much: "He greatly enjoyed the Overture (first movement of the D major Suite for orchestra) by Sebastian Bach; 'at the beginning it is so pompous and noble—you can really see the procession of well-dressed people descending a grand staircase. . . .' "

Again, we note the use of a "visual aid," such as Goethe had also needed for Beethoven.

There can hardly be any doubt: Mendelssohn's avoidance of the through-composed song was the result of the doctrines of Zelter, Hegel, and above all Goethe. Much the same is true of tone-painting—which, after all, was in full swing at this time. Mendelssohn never gets much beyond the mood of a landscape or the mere externals of a human portrait (cf. the portraits of the Taylor girls!). Neither in *A Midsummer Night's Dream* nor in the *Hebrides* Overture (which, nevertheless, enjoys high rank as a landscape painting) nor in the *Fair Melusine* does he ever underscore individual tone-painting details. Later, he abandoned tone-painting entirely.

Goethe seems to have given the young man some counsel concerning association with women, dedicated to him a manuscript page from *Faust II* (then nearing completion) and let him go with his blessing.[10] Earlier, he confirmed

> that his [Felix] presence was particularly beneficial to him, for I found that my relationship to music was still the same. I hear it with pleasure, interest and reflection, but like only its historical side; . . . The principal thing was, then, that Felix has a praiseworthy insight into this stage of development. . . . Tell the worthy parents of the extraordinary young artist all the best, in *weighty words*.[11]

Zelter's reply betrays a little of the sympathy and care with which he surrounded Felix and which are unusual with him; he wrote: "I thank you as much as possible; he can feast on this all during his life. Sometimes I am afraid when I look at the boy's rapid rise. Up till now he has hardly met with any opposition. . . ."[12]

Later, Ottilie von Goethe wrote to Felix how much he was missed in Weimar, and that Goethe wanted to tell him that Felix had done him a lasting service, for only now had many things become clear to the poet.[13] Furthermore, it seems that Zelter had read the long letter of Goethe in its entirety to Felix's parents, for Abraham knew it. But how different was his reaction from the normal one of a flattered father who was proud of his son! Abraham recognized in the words of Goethe only "the grave obligation . . . which you have to fulfill in your life."[14] Lea was not wrong to be annoyed at this cross-grained attitude of her husband!

Felix stopped for a while in Munich. There he was warmly received, and soon felt at home in the circles of musicians and high society. To the first group belonged the splendid clarinetist Heinrich Baermann, with whom he later exchanged the jolliest and wittiest letters;[15] to the second, a group of noble dilettantes and also of professional musicians, like the pianist Delphine von Schauroth, or the Intendant of the Royal Theatre, Baron Poissl. Felix felt very much at home, although he sharply criticized the Munich musical activities. We hear that Haydn and Mozart were valued only as orchestral composers, and that the piano works of Beethoven were as good as unknown; instead, the usual *galant* and *concertante* variations of Herz and Kalkbrenner were diligently played. He was so much in society that he did not do very much work, and so had a bad conscience. Thus we can explain the positively servile letter to his father on July 14. There, he says, among other things:

> Then I wanted to justify myself, dear Father, if you'll permit me—and therefore this stupid letter; excuse it, dear Father, and *also its poor format* . . . I was afraid you'd be angry about the additional days in Weimar— forgive me all that! Also, I wanted to thank you for believing that I have the earnest desire of developing what has been entrusted to me, for I certainly have. . . .[16]

And he goes on in this vein. Earlier, Felix had placed himself in his father's good graces. The latter was in Paris just at the time of the July Revolution. Since Felix was aware of his father's liberal sentiments, he expressed his joy at knowing him at the very source of liberalism in this historic moment. Later, in Salzburg, Felix regretted that he had not rushed to Paris *stante pede*, for he, too, sympathized with the Revolution. Only the fear of his strict father had restrained him; but in reality it was a fairly serious affair of the heart which caused Felix's bad conscience.

Delphine von Schauroth, whom Marx thought "at least sixteen years old," was an outstanding pianist and intelligent musician. In addition, she was brilliant, beautiful, and belonged to a rich, highly regarded family. Felix fell in love with her;[17] and, from various comments, we may conclude that Delphine would have been glad to accept the already famous artist as a husband. On his return from Italy to Munich, this affair came to a climax: threateningly for Felix, who had no thought of marrying. Much later (1834), his mother, worried about some flirtation in Düsseldorf, cautioned him against early marriages.[18]

So, Felix, light of heart, with a tentative contract for an opera from the Royal Intendancy in his pocket, mounted his coach once more and traveled through Salzburg and Linz to Vienna.

SECOND PHASE: Munich-Salzburg-Vienna-Venice
End of June—October, 1830

FELIX HAD no illusions about the duration of his influence in Munich. He was convinced that, after the sudden enthusiasm for Beethoven which he had aroused, the young ladies would return to Herz, Kalkbrenner, etc.[19] Nonetheless, the charm of Munich ladies inspired two of his best piano works, there can be no doubt about it. The first is the well-known *Rondo Capriccioso*, Op. 14, in E ("the thing with sauces and mushrooms"). The second was his First Piano Concerto in G minor, Op. 25, dedicated to Delphine. We shall have more to say of both works.

He had some bad luck in Salzburg, not only because of the usual drizzle (the "Schnürlregen" common to that place) but because he kept thinking that he recognized (probably from a picture) a mysterious "Grande Dame," but always just missed meeting her. As it turned out later, it was his cousin, Baroness Pereira from Vienna (daughter of his great-aunt Fanny von Arnstein), whose house he later frequented.[20]

Not surprisingly, Vienna was a disappointment for Felix. After the achievements of Haydn, Mozart, Beethoven, and Schubert, the Viennese had reverted—doubtless with a sigh of relief—to light opera and, in general, to salon music.

The reminiscences of von Sonnleithner shed new light on a little-known corner of Viennese music history.[21] There, the era of Emperor Franz, during which the Napoleonic Wars and the Holy Alliance (1815) took place, was less memorable to the Viennese for the names of Haydn, Beethoven, and Schubert, all of whom flourished during his reign, than for the little musical soirées of petty bourgeoisie, which began to compete with the aristocracy in musical interests and performances. The foundation of the bourgeois *"Gesellschaft der Musikfreunde,"* the musical evenings in the modest houses of subaltern officials, the insatiable music appetite reflected in the *Schubertiaden,* all these activities testify to the great enthusiasm of the Viennese. Unfortunately, not to their good taste! That had not only declined after Beethoven's death, but had actually taken a plunge. The most played composers were not Mozart, nor even Haydn, but Paer, Rossini, Simon Mayr, Cimarosa, Pixis, etc. Only in the (private) performances of oratorios one may sense the stirrings of a *vita nuova;* there Handel, C. P. E. Bach, Graun, A. Romberg (whose setting of Schiller's celebrated poem *"Die Glocke"* was extremely popular), and Beethoven's "Christ on the Mount of Olives" began to dominate; i.e. the North German or Protestant composers over the Italianized Austrians. Yet even the *professional* musician's organization, the *Wiener Tonkünstler-Societät,* performed no works of J. S. Bach except his Cantata *"Gottes Zeit"* during its entire existence.[22] Sonnleithner's reminiscences, the minutes of the *Tonkünstler-Societät,* and E. Hanslick's autobiography[23] describe a sad state of music in Vienna, especially during the *Vormärz.* All through it mediocrity triumphantly reigned, and its spiteful envy of any great talent found true expression in the actions and reactions of men like Von Eybler and Assmayr, the bosses of musical bureaucracy during those years.

No wonder that Felix called Vienna a "damned frivolous dump," but that did not prevent him from taking part in this lighter style of life. As an antidote, he "retreated into himself," and wrote strict, arch-Protestant music—doubtless as a reaction against the superficial Viennese manner.[24]

Also, he was very much dissatisfied with the local theatres, and sharply criticized the repertoire of the *Kärntnertor* Theatre.[25] Beethoven had written the *Consecration of the House Overture* for its dedication; his *Fidelio* had been performed there, too.

Of the local musicians, the young man speaks in an almost stern tone; he excepts Aloys Fuchs, the Mozart scholar, Joseph Hauser, the faithful Bach enthusiast (later, Conservatory director in Munich), and perhaps the 'cellist Merk. He consigns the others as a whole to damnation:

> By God! these people know nothing better than their boring egos, and that's why they are so tiresome. Czerny, for example, thinks about nothing all day long except himself, his honor, his fame, his money, his popularity. And what's the result? He is not highly regarded in Vienna; he isn't even named any more among the pianists, and although, when he's giving lessons, he always has music paper and writing materials in front of him in order to relieve himself, even the publishers shrug their shoulders at his stuff and remark that it doesn't go over so well.[26]

Felix often met his relatives, the Pereiras, Arnstein-Eskeles, Ephraims, and Count Wimpffen, but he always felt himself a "dyed-in-the-wool bourgeois" and often made fun of the "noble airs and graces" in these families.

Finally, he became acquainted with the theoretician Simon Sechter (later the teacher of Bruckner), "and we showered each other with sweet canonic expressions."

In Graz, on the way to Italy, he completed his cantata *O Haupt voll Blut und Wunden* (unfortunately unpublished) and sketched an *Ave Maria* which he was to complete only much later. Then he traveled through Udine to Venice.

Summing up, we may say that during Mendelssohn's stay in Vienna a very characteristic side of his nature emerged: the insistence on his own principles, which are even reinforced by contrasting surroundings. In arch-Catholic yet light-minded Vienna, he suddenly writes Lutheran church music, which he had not practiced for two years; indeed, he even accepts a gift from his friend Hauser, a book of Luther's sacred poems, in order to draw strength and "true devotion" from it in Italy.[27] This inner resistance against outer influences was to repeat itself several times in his life. Indeed, we may maintain that (according to Zelter) there existed only two people whose opinion on his work he respected and to whose "censorship" he conformed, alas, all too often: Fanny and his father. The latter was then replaced by his wife-to-be, Cecile.

In Venice, he was enchanted by the landscape, and even more by the pictures of Titian and Giorgione. On looking at these works of art, "he was often inspired to think of music." But, again, it is Protestant church music which he plans and later carries out, mainly chorale motets or chorale cantatas. In addition, he was working on the *Hebrides* Overture; he finished the first version and immediately began the revision. Almost everything pleased him in Italy that he had condemned in Munich and Vienna—even frivolity! Doubtless he was prejudiced by the opinion of Zelter and Goethe.

THIRD PHASE: Bologna-Florence-Rome
October 10–November 1, 1830

FELIX's LETTERS from Italy are valuable as intelligent reports from a German traveler of his period, but they tell much more about the letter writer himself. They are true self-characterizations, and their worth is not diminished by the fact that they were certainly not written for that purpose.

The more deeply the classically educated young man penetrates into the ancient land, the more intense is his aversion to anything archeological or archaic, whether in literature or music. Ciceronian or Caesarian reminiscenses leave him completely cold. He values only the monuments of antique art, and, above all, the Italian landscape charms him. He who, with Thibaut, had been enthusiastic about Palestrina and Victoria, shows surprisingly little understanding of Gregorian chant.[28]

Italian opera singing—as he encountered it there—finds him, perhaps, the severest critic of all time; but, in all fairness, he points out that one must go to Paris or London to hear the best Italian singers. Here again, we sense the rivalry of the two musical axes of which we have already spoken. Felix turns definitely away from the Southern axis and towards the Western one.

He admits to being an opponent of the Middle Ages, thus differentiating himself from the dyed-in-the-wool "Romanticists": "Thank God that these highly-praised Middle Ages are past and can never return. Don't show this to any Hegelian, but it is so...."[29]

In other respects, too, we notice his distinct aversion to "schools," especially as he always refuses to belong to any coterie, whether social or artistic.[30] He was and remained an individualist; even cosmopolitan ambitions or ideas are unsympathetic to him:

> But I tell you in confidence that, little by little, I am coming really to hate cosmopolitanism. I cannot stand it—any more than I really like many-sidedness or, actually, believe in it. That which is individual and great and beautiful must be *one-sided*, but this one side must be developed to the utmost perfection....[31]

This opinion is also in contradiction to the then popular synesthesia of the literary Romanticists who tried to blend colors, scents, words, and tones into a total work of art (*Gesamtkunstwerk*)—from Novalis and E. T. A. Hoffmann to Richard Wagner and beyond.

Such clear and well-thought-out opinions are often contrasted, in Felix's thinking, with irrational and unfair prejudices. These are most clearly seen in his meeting with Berlioz, with whom he became acquainted in Rome. What Felix postulated for himself, namely, the unity of the personality of the artist with his work, he does not accept in the case of Berlioz. As a human being, he esteems him highly; as an artist, he would like to "bite him to death."[32] He reports that he had played, with Berlioz, the latter's symphony

> . . . which is called "Episode of the Life of an Artist" and for which a printed program is passed out. In the last movement, the poor artist goes to the devil, where the audience would like to have been long ago. Then all the instruments have a hangover and vomit music, making us very uncomfortable. And yet he is a very pleasant man and speaks well and has fine ideas, and you can't help liking him. . . .[33]

It is understandable that a worshiper of form and of well-rounded melody in the classical sense, as Mendelssohn was, did not know what to make of the bold formlessness and angular melody of a Berlioz. Even more, the *subject* of the Fantastic Symphony must have repelled him—the uncontrolled "artiste," the Witches' Sabbath, and the abrupt dramatic contrasts of the work. And to all this came a feeling of rivalry, doubtless unconscious on Felix's part. This was because he had just begun to compose Goethe's *Erste Walpurgisnacht* in which, after all, the witches also play a certain part. But frankly, alongside Berlioz's monsters à la Felicien Rops (these artists were not accidentally contemporaries!), Mendelssohn's witches seem like seductive sprites of spring.

Since we have already pointed out half-unconscious reactions and contradictions in Felix's emotional life, we must also consider his problematic, very complex attitude towards religious manifestations. Rome confronted him with the wealth and power of centralized European Catholicism. He, a Jew by birth, a faithful Protestant in his upbringing and surroundings, reacted critically to all ritual *forms of expression* of the Church, as far as they appear as esthetic phenomena. But he does not write a word about the fundamental doctrines of the Catholic Church, which are only indirectly related to esthetic questions. If we did not know through Berlioz's memoirs that he provoked the highly sensitive Felix with his Bible criticisms and agnostic (not quite seriously intended) *aperçus*, we should have to assume that, for Felix, only the sensually perceptible forms of a religion were of interest and significance.[34]

Only at one point in his "Roman Letters" do we encounter a sincere and very serious concern with problems of religion. This, however, is neither

Catholic nor Protestant, but arch-Jewish. True, Felix certainly did not know this, but his father would immediately have recognized and identified the doctrine. Felix writes to Klingemann on January 2, 1831:

> The last and the first day [of the Old and New Year respectively] were sad and boring for me again, as always. I was at a few parties on New Year's Eve . . . and had to pay visits on New Year's Day. The way people meet each other then and thoughtlessly or jokingly wish each other a happy future (the most serious wish there is), the way that on this day they open the doors to all sorts of foolish ceremonies and no one seems to think about the real meaning of a holiday, the way they try to get rid of the sadness of New Year's Eve with jokes, drinking, and molten-lead pouring, and can't do it—all of this I find absolutely deadly. The two days are *real days* of atonement, and one should experience them all alone with oneself and not be afraid of these grave thoughts or slink away from them. . . .[35]

No orthodox Jew could have expressed these ideas better. Note also that such sentiments are not formulated like revolutionary novelties but that they formed an organic part of Felix's philosophy. ("The days . . . were sad for me, *as always.*") Whence did these ideas come? Naturally, from his parental home, where the very serious attitude towards the New Year had simply been transposed from Jewish to Christian practice. Expressions of such austere seriousness are otherwise rare in the letters written on his travels. Similar sentiments move him when he hears of Goethe's critical illness. Then he writes to his father:

> . . . in the midst of all merriment I never forget that the core and essence of all things is serious—yes, often tragic. And in serious moments I again think that true seriousness must be gay, and not dark and cold . . . I am convinced of this.[36]

This was certainly after his father's own mind and heart, and entirely Goethean in spirit. In this connection, we cannot help thinking of Giordano Bruno's motto: *In hilaritate tristis, in tristitia hilaris.*

The course of Felix's journey is not exactly adventurous, but it is full of interesting contemporary events which he experienced on the spot. Shortly after his arrival in Rome, Pope Pius VIII died; after a long conclave, the election and coronation of his successor Gregory XVI took place before Holy Week of 1831. Felix did not see much of the Carnival, for the Pope's death and political unrest brought these joyous activities to a premature end. He reports very thoroughly on these events, with a painter's feeling for local color.

Uncommonly interesting, of course, are all his observations on the musical life of Rome. Although Felix lacks scholarly understanding of archaic music, he nonetheless has a well-developed, if limited, sense of style. He takes note of every mutilation of archaic music, although he knew its principles only superficially. His reports on the musical ceremonies of Holy Week, which he sent to Zelter, are masterpieces of critical—if often prejudiced—presentation. Remarkable too is his seemingly unerring memory. Since Mozart's notation of Allegri's *Miserere* from memory, there had been no more such feats of transcription hours after the actual hearing. Even today, his almost phonographically accurate notation of all the many nuances would attract much attention. Because of his fine ear and his innate feeling for style, Felix was an unusually sharp critic of the practice of church music. Yet he never loses his respect for the basic religious idea; therefore, he always closes his criticisms in a tone of respectful wonder at the grandeur and dignity of the liturgical musical ceremonies, qualities which were not lost even in faulty performances.

However, he lacks this reverence when it comes to the practice of secular music. It appears to him "miserable beyond all criticism," "really too bad," "it gives me a toothache," "the whole thing is real cats' music," etc. He feels proud as a German when Spontini's words are cited: "The Germans treat music like an affair of state." He adds: "I accept the omen."[37] He becomes far too sharp and unfair when he compares Italian and German music: "as a *cicisbeo* will always be something common and low for me, so is Italian music."[38] In his *rabbia,* the pupil of Hegel overlooks the fact that he is confusing ethical and esthetic categories here in order to give a rational basis to his cultural patriotism.

Felix was also known in Rome through his own compositions. As his association with the greatest German names was known, he was, so to speak, "accepted" by society. Especially since he came from a wealthy family and bore a famous name, all doors in Rome were open to him. From the Prussian resident minister von Bunsen, a historian of note, who was friendly with the Humboldts, to the Cardinals, from the ducal family of the Torlonias to the French artists and diplomats, from Baini to Berlioz, he ran the gamut of the noble and intellectual society of Rome. Nonetheless, he confronted the Italian high aristocracy with "respect, mingled with aversion." For example, he contented himself with looking at the Napoleonic family, who at that time had settled in Rome, from a distance.[39]

On the other hand, he sought close contact with the Italian musicians Baini and Santini. Zelter had directed him to these musical priests. Both were charmed with him and his music. Abbé Santini, a learned theoretician and admirer of Handel, adapted an observation of Scaliger's on Pico della Mirandola to the young German; he called Felix a *Monstrum sine vitio* (a colossus without faults.)[40] He had hoped that Felix would bring the score of Bach's *St. Matthew Passion* with him; however, he had to content himself with piano excerpts, which the willing and eager youth played for him.

Santini was very much concerned with establishing serious (also Protestant) church music in Italy; and his task was not easy, as we see in Mendelssohn's letters. Felix helped him as much as he could; he got for him, from Berlin, the scores of works by Bach, Handel, Graun, and other German composers, which were, at that time, difficult to obtain. But the earnest efforts of Santini met with no lasting success. In Italy, the opera overshadowed all other musical forms, and even today, performances of German oratorios or church music are actually rarities in the Italian repertoire. Until about 1920, Mozart and Bach found little understanding there, in contrast to Beethoven and Wagner whose pathos the Italian already appreciated much earlier.

With the other maestro, Baini, Felix did not have such a close relationship. This was partly because Baini was a very popular father confessor and had only his evenings free for music and musical studies, if they did not happen to be taken up by rehearsals of the Papal choir. Baini, the first independent biographer of Palestrina, was an ardent admirer of *a cappella* music and considered all instrumental composition as inferior or positively frivolous. Perhaps Felix was not exactly wrong in supposing that *a cappella* fanatic Baini considered him a *brutissimo tedesco*.[41] There seems to have been a certain reserve on both sides, for Felix, too, did not think much of Baini's music. And since he did not have unusually strong historical interests, the great musicological and theoretical knowledge of Baini did not impress him. Here again we see that psychological reaction which we have already observed under other circumstances. In Catholic Rome, he writes Protestant church music; in the history-laden city of the Caesars, he emphasizes the cause of "progress" in the politico-historical sense.

Felix liked to associate a great deal with painters; and Rome was full of them, Germans, Frenchmen, and Englishmen. His favorites were Horace Vernet, at that time director of the French Academy (in the Villa Medici), Schadow from Düsseldorf, and Thorwaldsen, who had already made a great impression upon him with his leonine appearance. As is well known, Vernet painted Mendelssohn in Rome; the mercurial Felix, whose facial expression was constantly changing, is captured well in that portrait, with subtle interpretation and with deeper understanding than in most of his other portraits.

He did not have a high opinion of the German painters; he considered them a bunch of lazy, bearded bohemians, who, as soon as things got even a little dangerous, "shut themselves in and then whine away by themselves."[42] Schadow, however, he does not include with these; he admires the quiet, clear, always respectful way in which he judges masterpieces. This was in contrast to the others, the beatniks of Biedermeier, "who have no respect for their masters"—he feels that he would be doing a good deed if he treated them all to the "heartiest insults."[43]

However, all these distractions seem unimportant when we compare them to the enormous musical productivity of Felix, precisely during his Roman visit. Several significant compositions owe their origin to the fertilizing atmosphere of Rome. Of Protestant church music, there are, first of all, the three pieces in Op. 23. Here we find the chorale motet *Aus tiefer Noth*, and the setting of Luther's poem *Mitten wir im Leben sind*, to which he added a Catholic-tinged *Ave Maria* for eight-voiced chorus. At the same time was written his prayer *Verleih uns Frieden gnädiglich* for four-voiced chorus and orchestra. It became the favorite piece of his father, probably because of the deliberately simple, but strict conduct of the melody in canonic style. Schumann, too, liked this piece very much, and compared it with a "Madonna of Raphael or Murillo, [which] cannot remain concealed for long." Wolff concludes from the faulty declamation of the German text that the composition was set originally to the Latin *Da nobis pacem;* in fact, the setting of the words does fit much better to the Latin text.[44]

Already, Felix had completed a large psalm-composition, *Non nobis Domine* (Psalm 115), which was intended as a birthday gift for Fanny. It is one of his best choral works with orchestra. Children of quite another spirit are the three motets for soli and three-voiced women's chorus with organ accompaniment, Op. 39, which he wrote for the nuns in the church of Trinità dei Monti. Their voices had charmed him—not their music![45] He hit on the ingenious idea of simply sending the pieces to the nuns; he wished, incognito, to hear his music in the church. It is more than questionable whether this wish was ever fulfilled. The texts are all chosen for the Catholic service: *Veni Domine, et noli tardare, Laudate pueri,* and *Surrexit pastor bonus.* Two of these, again, are pieces from the Psalter.

He faithfully reports on most of these works or sketches to his old teacher Zelter; in fact, he even sends him the manuscript of the chorale motet *Aus tiefer Noth* for his criticism and possible corrections. We must remember that Felix, both technically and artistically, stood far above the level of Zelter, so that the desire to be corrected by the latter seems peculiar to us. If we did not know from unpublished letters how sure of himself Felix already was, we should have to question the independence of his artistic judgment and taste.[46] But Felix simply wanted to show his deep respect for the old man, and the means he chose to do so were certainly to Zelter's taste. Felix was no bootlicker, but a grateful and tactful pupil.

Of greater significance for living music are the two secular compositions on which Felix was working in Rome: the *Hebrides* Overture (originally entitled *Die Einsame Insel*—"The Lonely Island") and the setting of Goethe's *Erste Walpurgisnacht* ("The First Walpurgis Night"). Both are masterworks of their genre and belong to the standard concert repertory.

The conception of the *Walpurgisnacht* probably dates back to that last visit in Weimar; in any case, in Vienna, Felix had begun seriously with the composition, "and did not have the courage to write it down."⁴⁷ When the composition is nearing completion, Felix finally takes pen in hand and writes to the poet. In the letter, he says, among other things:

> What has been occupying me almost exclusively for several weeks is the music to Your Excellency's poem entitled *Die erste Walpurgisnacht;* I want to compose it with orchestral accompaniment, as a sort of grand cantata . . . I do not know whether I shall succeed, but I feel how great the task is and with what concentration and awe I must undertake it.⁴⁸

Mendelssohn revised the piece twice more; just as we also have three versions of the *Hebrides* Overture. The first version was completed on July 15, 1831, with the exception of the overture, which was composed only a year later.

In addition, the beginnings and thematic complexes of the Italian and Scotch Symphonies were sketched. These, although completed much later, date back to the Roman period. This is a characteristic of Mendelssohn's creativity; lightning-fast first inspiration and sketch, followed by long-lasting reworking, revision, and super-revision of the finished piece, often even after publication, often delaying publication for years if not preventing it altogether. Thus, till the day of his death Mendessohn was not satisfied with his Italian Symphony and was still tinkering with it. It was first published posthumously, but was completed in 1833.

FOURTH PHASE: Naples-Rome
November 1, 1830—June 19, 1831

IN A JOLLY and congenial group, which consisted of E. Bendemann, T. Hildebrandt, and C. Sohn, Felix journeyed southward. His accounts show us that there he was more of an observer, commentator, and social critic than a musician. Soon he appears to have grasped Metternich's half-cynical remark that Italy is no nation, but a geographical concept. For Felix, the South begins at Terracina, "a different land," and everything reminds him of this difference. The subtropical vegetation surprises and charms the northerner, and he cannot have enough of painter-like descriptions which seem much more colorful and natural than the best photographs. Here, the observation of overpowering Nature takes first place; but the thoughtful young artist says: "What is pleasing in England because of mankind is here pleasing because of Nature."⁴⁹ Shortly thereafter, he formulates his thoughts even more precisely:

> I can continue to enjoy Nature and the blue heavens without thinking of

anything else, for, at present, there alone lies the true art of Italy—there and in her monuments. In spite of this, I am basically enough of a musician to long to hear an orchestra or a full chorus once more.[50]

And he cannot resist the opportunity of giving another of his malicious *aperçus*: "The singers are the worst Italian ones that I have heard anywhere up till now, except in Italy."

In the same connection he denies that Italy has preserved any of her ancient musical glory, and tells that the composer Coccia was valued by serious musicians only because he had studied in *London*.

Felix's social criticisms of South Italy demand our attention. Felix is dissatisfied with himself because the hot scirocco weather keeps him from working.[51] Then it occurs to him that the absence of an active middle class, about which he had already complained, really must be a natural, climatically conditioned phenomenon. The following analysis is so lively, and so naively foreshadows the theories of a Max Weber and K. Mannheim, that we cite it here *in toto*:

> The climate is arranged for a grand gentleman who gets up late, never needs to walk, never thinks (because that makes one feel hot), sleeps a few hours on the sofa in the afternoon, then eats his sherbet and at night goes to the theatre, where, again, he finds nothing to think about but can make and receive visits. On the other hand, the climate is just as suitable for a fellow in a shirt, with bare legs and arms, who also does not need to bestir himself—begs a few grains for himself when he has nothing to live on—in the afternoon, has his little nap on the ground, near the harbor . . . then gathers his own *frutti di mare* from the ocean, then sleeps wherever he happens to end up at night—in short, does whatever pleases him at the moment, like an animal. These, then, are the two principal classes in Naples. . . ."

In the same connection, he adds:

> For that very reason, there is so little industry and competition. Therefore, Donizetti can write an opera in ten days. It is hissed off the stage, but that doesn't matter, for he gets paid for it and can go his merry way. . . .[52]

He would love to have gone to Sicily, but his worried father would not permit the excursion. Felix, obedient as always, complied with his father's dictates, although against his inner conviction. Zelter was not in accord with either the father's prohibition or the son's obedience. He "let the old man know it," too.[53] Goethe was of the same opinion: "Papa was very wrong not to send him to Sicily; the young man suffers from longing without any need for it. . . ."[54] However, it was too late to rescind the prohibition; nor was Abraham Mendelssohn the man to take the advice of others even if they were Zelter and Goethe.

Yet, the renunciation of Sicily had a good result, important to us. Felix worked diligently at his Italian Symphony; he seemed to have completed sketching it in Naples, as he indicates himself.[55] In fact, I found, in the library of the Naples Conservatory, the autograph of a "Concertino" by Mendelssohn, which, however, is nothing else than a short score of the first movement of the Italian Symphony.

Extensive excursions were undertaken to Pompeii, Cumae, the Avernian Fields, and finally Paestum, the southernmost point of the entire journey; these are described lovingly in the travel letters. Then, Felix returned northward. In Rome, he stayed only two weeks, to put his affairs in order, to pay visits, to write an extensive letter to Zelter on the music of Holy Week (it is a treatise) and to book his accommodations for traveling through Florence and Genoa to Milan. On June 19-20, he bade farewell to the Eternal City.

Here, let us add a few words concerning the report on the music of Holy Week. It is astonishing to see how Mendelssohn draws conclusions from its purely physical manifestations as to its spirituality. As objectively— and critically in the positive sense—and as accurately as he registers every nuance of song, the *embellimenti* and other ornaments, although he considers them corruptions, he is just as accessible and sensitive to the great whole, the cultic ceremony. When it is a matter of questions of interpretation and tradition, he is still a true child of his optimistic century with its belief in progress.[56] He does grasp the psalm-tones with his unbelievable memory, but their structure and, above all, their antiphonal manner of performance remain completely mysterious to him. If he had read his grandfather's psalm translation with its learned foreword, then the parallelism of the psalmody would have become clear to him. He is furious about the musical interpretation of "the most sacred, most beautiful words sung to such empty, monotonous tones."[57] The esthetic ideal towards which all Gregorian chant strives is objectivity of expression. Felix feels this intuitively, but like a true Hegelian, he believes: "True, there is no false expression in it, for there is no expression in it at all; but is that not the real degradation of the words?"[58]

From these observations it is clear that Felix did not then (and perhaps never did) fully grasp the true spirit, and, above all, the true *function* of liturgical music. For interpretive expression is, at best, a by-product, not a primary aim of the liturgy. What Felix understands as "expression" is, however, the subjective, interpretive setting or musical symbolization of a liturgical text. It is surprising that, in this Protestant of the first generation, conflicts again arise which once, in the early days of the Church, had moved many spirits and pens. Basically, it is the antinomy of ethos and pathos.

Yet, another complaint of Felix's has lasting validity. For the Passion story, he postulates a "quietly narrating" lesson by the priest. He wishes it to be made so vivid "that I feel as if I were there and were looking on at everything." In other words, there should be "either simple narration or great dramatic, serious truth." Here the question is: Text or interpretation? And perhaps at bottom the problem is whether the liturgy should be understood and performed naïvely or sentimentally in the sense of Schiller. To the present day, this is an open and disputed question; even canonic decisions, for example, the *Motu proprio* of Pius X, neither disposed of the controversies nor solved the problem. Here, therefore, Mendelssohn rightly recognized and indicated an essential problem. In later liturgical works, he had to cope with it often.   ·

FIFTH PHASE: Florence-Genoa-Milan-Geneva-Lucerne-
St. Gallen-Augsburg-Munich   June 20—September 10, 1831

WE LEARN TO KNOW a very different, robust side of our enthusiastic tourist on the way to Florence. There, something happens to him that every traveler in Italy takes for granted: he is cheated. When the coach-owner in Incisa demands four times the usual price for ordinary coach horses, just because she is sure that the *barbaro tedesco* will not find any other travel accommodations, the gentle Felix becomes furious. He demands to see the official coach rates; she shamelessly refuses to let him have a look at them. Ironic at his own expense, Felix now recounts: "The condition of force, which plays a great role here, now set in again; for I grabbed her and threw her into the room." Then he ran to the mayor, and was mobbed by street-arabs. Finally, for a moderate fee, he got a little wagon; he gave an old beggar a few pennies, whereupon everyone yelled "bravo" and wished him a good journey. On the same evening, he attended a masked ball in the *Teatro Goldoni* at Florence.

Via Genoa, Felix traveled to Milan, then the principal city of Austrian Lombardy. There, at the border of Italy, Austria, and Switzerland, he stopped for a week, less because of the city itself, which does not seem to have interested him especially, than in order to draw up, as it were, an account of the Italian journey. From Milan, he wrote a series of important letters, in which he thinks earnestly about his future career and considers various possibilities.

The first thing he does after arriving in Milan is to write a well-thought-out letter to his father. Since this important letter is unpublished, let us at least extract its essence here. Felix regrets that he cannot personally discuss questions of his professional career with his father, and asks him, if possible, to appoint a meeting place. He speaks of his possible chances in London, Paris, and Munich, but he cannot decide

. . . whether I should make new connections there, or turn towards the stationary, quiet existence which I wish to enjoy *only in Berlin*, and which I now see opened to me through the offer of the directorship of the *Singakademie*. But this offer was made to me after the performance of the Passion, and since my return from England nothing more has been heard from me. Therefore, if possible, something significant must happen before my return, so that I can accept the offer with honor. . . .[59]

This is a unique document, because it shows that Felix would gladly have established himself in Berlin. True, when this was written, Zelter was still alive; when Felix returned to Berlin after Zelter's death, he found conditions completely changed, and then wanted to withdraw his candidacy. This, therefore, is the beginning of that sad conflict in which Felix was constantly torn between love and hate, and which certainly contributed to his untimely end.

During these Milan days, Felix wanted to clarify things for himself and his friends. Half seriously, half jokingly, Devrient had thrown the verse from *Don Carlos* at him: "Twenty-two years old, and nothing done for eternity." Carefully he added that one could not become famous with psalms and chorales, even if they were conceived in Bach's spirit, and urgently advised Felix to write operas. He must have been quite surprised when he received a thoroughly philosophical-theological rebuttal. A part of that reply, but not by any means the most important part, is found in the travel letters. Proudly and yet humbly Felix answers that, if God had willed it, he would already be famous at twenty-two. He is not writing music in order to be famous; and as long as he is not exactly starving he feels it his duty to write as his heart dictates and to leave the results to Heaven. In his compositions, he wants to pay less and less heed to conventions or persons: nothing else is of consequence to him. If his music resembles Bach's, that is unintentional, for he wrote it the way he felt: ". . . and if the words sometimes made me feel the same way old Bach did, so much the better for me. For you can't believe that I copy his forms without any content—in that case, I should be so repelled by the emptiness that I couldn't finish a piece. . . ."[60]

Afterwards, in the same letter, he points out to Devrient that he also thinks of the practical side, but adds at once: "But who the devil can write music, which is, after all, the most impractical thing in the world (that's why I like it), and think of practical things at the same time?"

He is eager to write an opera, but longs for a "natural" libretto, that is not only good theatre but also presents believable characters, living human beings.[61] With a certain friendly dignity, in measured fashion, and yet very modestly, he thus rejects Devrient's well-meant admonitions. We see that Felix, as man and artist, had outgrown his youth. In spite of all politeness, warmth, and modesty, all his letters express a clear and firm will, which is certain of its goal, if not always of its way. The last letter cited above also contains an unusually severe criticism of Italian vocal and instrumental music; it emphasizes and praises the Western axis (London-Paris), but reaches its climax with the joyous admission: "The land of artists is, once and for all, Germany. Long may it live!"[62]

In the same view, he writes to his father against the universal Rossini-worship, and adds: "I heartily hate all this fashionable cheapness. Don't blame me for that; you always say, 'No love without hate,' and it was such a strange feeling for me to come upon Gluck with his great figures."[63]

Inspired by such thoughts and feelings, he finished the *Walpurgisnacht*, but could not decide whether to give it a symphonic overture or merely a short introduction, "breathing [or breezes] of spring." His intention to ask the advice of a scholar on this point seems to be not without irony.[64]

In Austrian Milan, he boldly made the acquaintance of Baron and Baroness Ertmann, the loyal old friends of Beethoven. With his charm, he easily succeeded in winning this much older couple as friends; they often made music together, too. Karl Mozart, the master's elder son, was leading the typical life of an Austrian official in Milan. Felix made friends with him, in fact, he grew so close to the lonely man, living in his titanic father's shadow, that he played his *Walpurgisnacht* for him before anyone else. Finally, he found himself in an amusing situation in Como, where the notables of the little city criticized Shakespeare and especially denigrated *A Midsummer Night's Dream*, which, they said, was a foolish piece about witchery and, besides, was teeming with anachronisms. Felix should not bother to read it! He "kept quiet and did not defend it."

Now, with the finished *Walpurgisnacht* in hand, he traveled through Chamonix into Switzerland. His route led him over the Simplon, Brig, Wallis, Weissenburg, Spiez, Unterseen, Grindelwald, Flüelen, Lucerne, Engelberg, Schwyz, St. Gallen, Lindau, and Augsburg to Munich. He had left Milan on July 20, but did not arrive in Munich till September 9-10. This long lapse of time is explained simply by the fact that Felix traveled most of the way on foot, as a real Alpinist—without the help of cable-cars, ski-lifts, automobiles, railroads, etc.; he contented himself with the most primitive sort of shelter at night, and during these months, really live in Spartan fashion. This considerable physical feat clearly shows that Felix was robustly healthy and not in the least spoiled or soft (thanks to his strict upbringing as a child), and that his love of nature spurred him on to the most daring and strenuous expeditions, such as climbing the Rigi, Scheidegg, or Faulhorn. It is instructive to follow his route—which is most exactly described in the travel letters—on the map, remembering that once he was confronted with a severe storm and flood. I believe that only a man who is a thoroughly experienced mountaineer would lightly undertake such a journey today.

The travel letters of those months are literary masterpieces. They will probably live as long as men still go wandering on foot to admire Nature. Again and again he sketches the beloved landscapes (there are over a hundred drawings by Felix) and he assures all his friends, ". . . there is no country like this. All dreams and pictures can . . . not give an idea of what beauty there is here."[65] And he ends with hymns to the beauty of Switzerland: "What green and meadows and water and springs and rocks are—only someone who has been here knows that. . . . I have never felt so completely free, so completely confronted by nature as in these unforgettable weeks. . . ."[66]

He remained true to his resolution always to pass his summer holidays in Switzerland, and retained his deep love for this land throughout his life. Now he had found his three homelands; Germany north of the Main, the land of his birth, the area of his professional life; England, his musical and social homeland of choice; and Switzerland, his refuge.

A self-characterization of quite a different sort than these Swiss letters written by the hand of a poet and painter is a letter to a contemporary composer, Wilhelm Taubert. Felix's nobility, his true modesty, but also the purity of his thought shine through this most unpretentious letter. After a critical observation on the state of music in Italy, he closes the theme with these words: ". . . the latest events which I unfortunately experienced there showed me that it is not only their music which has died out; indeed, it would be a miracle if there could be any music where there are no convictions."[67]

Later, he begs Taubert not to ask him for "instructions or advice"; such requests positively terrify him. He airs his anger when he mentions a "German esthetic journal." The following statement is the essential point of the letter:

The German Parnassus looks just as chaotic as European politics. God help us! I had to digest that supercilious Menzel,[68] who modestly tried to disparage Goethe, and that supercilious Grabbe, who modestly tried to disparage Shakespeare, and the philosophers, who find Schiller too trivial for words! Do you find this new, high-handed, unpleasant attitude, this repulsive cynicism as odious as I do? And do you agree with me that the first qualification for an artist is that he should have respect for greatness and be humble in its presence . . . and not try to blow out the great lights so that his little tallow-candle can shine a little brighter?

But this is . . . a crazy, wild, thoroughly troubled time, and whoever thinks it's all up with art should let it alone, for God's sake! But even though the storm outside may be raging ever so wildly, it does not blow down the houses right away; and if one continues to work quietly inside . . . the hurricane often passes by, and one can no longer imagine how wild it seemed before. . . .[69]

The men named above, who were scorned by Felix, belong more or less clearly to the school of "Junges-Deutschland," with whose chief representatives, Heine and Boerne (but above all with Immermann), he was soon thereafter to come into close but by no means always friendly contact. After he had rested a bit in Engelberg and Lindau and diligently practiced the organ there and in Sargans, he traveled through Augsburg to Munich, where he arrived on September 9-10.

SIXTH PHASE: Munich-Frankfurt-Düsseldorf-Paris
September 10–December 9, 1831

THE SECOND STAY in Munich was important to Felix for three reasons. The flirtation with Delphine had developed into a *grande affaire*, and we know that her mother and probably also Delphine would have greatly welcomed a lasting bond, that is, a marriage. But Felix's family reacted negatively, and Felix had probably not considered marriage either. However, oddly enough, two of his letters from this time are missing, and it is possible that they were later destroyed by Cecile, Felix's wife. How much sensational gossip this affair caused we can see in a suppressed letter from Felix to his father:

> The main thing that the King [of Bavaria] said to me, though, was that I should marry Fräulein von Schauroth; that would be an excellent match, and why didn't I want to do it? That, from a king, annoyed me, and somewhat piqued, I was going to answer him, when he, not even waiting for my answer, jumped to something else and then to a third thing. . . .[70]

For Delphine, the ardent young master wrote his G minor Concerto for piano and orchestra; as he himself says, it was a "rapidly tossed-off thing,"[71] but if the unity of the work is a result of the short time in which it was composed, we might wish that Felix had "tossed things off" more frequently. Although the whole concerto cannot exactly be called deep or original, it is such a good synthesis of "learned" and "popular" music that one has to enjoy it, provided that it is played by an outstanding interpreter.

The work was first performed at a big concert for the benefit of the poor of Munich on October 17, 1831, with Felix at the piano; on the same occasion, he conducted his C minor Symphony and his *A Midsummer Night's Dream* Overture. The applause, which was led by the King himself, was so enthusiastic that Felix, *nolens volens*, had to improvise; the King had given him *Non più andrai* (from Mozart's *Figaro*) as a theme. Although Felix was outstanding in improvisation, he did not like to do it in public; in fact, he considered this practice nonsense. He writes:

I have seldom felt so foolish as when I sat down to produce my fantasy in front of the public. The people were well satisfied. . . . The Queen said all the right things, but I was annoyed; for it displeased *me*, and I shall not do it in public again; it is an abuse, and humbug to boot. . . .[72]

Earlier, Felix had given a little musical soirée at his house, at which many guests, both invited and uninvited, appeared. There, too, he had to improvise. About the following court concert, he says:

. . . you were constantly bumping elbows with Excellencies . . . what I liked best was when the Queen said to me after the improvisation: "That was extraordinary, you really carry the listener away, and one cannot think of anything else during the music." Thereupon I begged her pardon —for carrying her away.[73]

The strongest incentive to his ambition in Munich was the formal contract for an opera which Baron von Poissl, the General Intendant of the Royal Theatre, gave him. In a very polite letter to Poissl, Felix thanks him for the confidence placed in him, and promises to do his very best.[74] At that time, he was thinking of using Immermann's version of Shakespeare's *Tempest* for an opera. It was not his fault alone that, again, nothing came of the plan.

From Munich, he traveled through Stuttgart to Frankfurt, where he stayed several weeks in the circle of old friends. Once more he attempted to present his ideas for his future career to his father, but this time in a much more detailed fashion. This letter of November 13-17, 1831, has remained unpublished until now, although it is much more important than the many gossipy letters in Hensel's collection and many others in the travel letters. The full text is found in the Appendix; here, let us select only the most significant passages.

First of all, he emphasizes that his father's wishes and orders override everything as far as he is concerned, and he would like to know how far his own plans parallel his father's "decisions for him." Also, we learn that his father urgently wishes Felix to stand "on his own feet and [be] independent" after this time of travel. On the journey to Dessau, Abraham had told Felix that the latter had come into an inheritance (from his maternal grandmother) which, in case of need, he could use to establish an independent existence for himself. Now, Felix wants to know clearly when his time of travel is to cease officially and his "independence" is to begin. He also asks whether Abraham wants him to use the inheritance and also the honoraria which he had left in his father's care, or "start without any money except what I earn?" He knows that he can do that and is prepared for both alternatives. But he also knows that he would have to do many things just for money that would not be beneficial to his development, for example, give lessons and concerts. Again, he emphasizes that his father should decide this: ". . . if you think it desirable to start earning from scratch, I shall try to leave the money alone. . . ." He wants to know what his father would think of a position as first conductor and music director *of a theatre,* if such a situation should arise.

Then he speaks of *his own plans.* He considers himself too young at twenty-three to take over a full music directorship, for he lacks outward authority. It would be better for him to apply himself to composition, for he has an opera contract from Munich in his pocket and can easily obtain another one in London. In Berlin, he would not like to be music director if he had to apply for the post, since Spontini's personality has opened the door to intrigue and evil rumors. He mentions other possibilities of appearing in England and also occasionally on the Continent as a guest conductor, and speaks of his opera for Munich as though he would start writing it the next day. But he promises his father to give first consideration to Berlin, "for naturally I'd rather remain . . . where you are, but I must be able to work. . . ."

He reports that Schelble (in Frankfurt) overwhelms him with kindness. He has commissioned a large oratorio for the *Caecilienverein* from him (this was to become *St. Paul*). Felix's genuine feelings come to the fore at the end of the letter, which expresses his inmost belief: "since I have returned from Italy . . . I have felt more clearly that I am really a German and must remain so."

The letter is full of inner contradictions. These, however, are easily resolved when we consider that Felix, who not only feared and loved his father but also knew him very well, had to write diplomatically. It is plainly to be seen that, in spite of all ostentatious obedience, Felix is determined to make his way as a free artist, preferably as an opera composer and guest conductor. His basic intention is, however, cleverly concealed, dressed up with his financial expectations (seen through rose-colored glasses and trimmed with a bit of flattery). Nevertheless, his self-identification with Germany, which is only loosely connected with the rest of the content of the letter, is absolutely genuine and proud. But even today we do not know whether this self-revelatory statement was accepted by his countrymen. It was certainly subjectively true as "inner evidence" in the Kantian sense, but whether it corresponded objectively to the feelings of his environment only the next fifty years will decide.

Unfortunately, his father's answer has not come down to us, but, from a letter of Felix's from Paris (November 19, 1831) we can conclude that his father was sympathetic to the operatic plans of the son. In fact, Abraham even recommended to Felix a French librettist, whose book, translated into German, he should then compose for Munich. But Felix had, on the way to

Paris, stopped in Düsseldorf and approached Immermann for a libretto; he himself had proposed Shakespeare's *Tempest* and Immerman had accepted it. So Felix was in an awkward position, especially as his father did not have the slightest confidence in Immermann as a dramatist or even an opera librettist. Unfortunately, in this matter as in many others the astute Abraham proved to be right. Felix, as a man of honor, felt himself committed, and even criticized his father for the first time:

> Above all, it seems to me as if you approved them [French libretti] more because of the *success* that they have than because of their real *value*. . . . So I shall try it in Germany, and live and work there as long as I can work and maintain myself; . . . If I can't, then I must leave for London or Paris, where things go more easily. However, if I can get along in Germany, I still realize that one is better paid and more highly honored elsewhere, . . . but in Germany one must always progress and work and must never rest. And I shall stick to the latter. . . .[75]

This sharp refutation of his cosmopolitan and, probably, opportunistic father, was, this time, scarcely disguised with excuses for his differing opinion. It shows the beginning of a certain inner emancipation, which, however, he was to attain only to a limited degree in relation to his father. But we have gone ahead of our story. Through Bonn, where he dealt with the publisher Simrock concerning the publication of some of his church compositions, and Düsseldorf, where Immermann consented to write the *Tempest* libretto, he journeyed to Paris, where we meet him in the middle of December, 1831.

SEVENTH PHASE: Paris
December 9, 1831–April 19, 1832

THE PARIS of the decades following the July Revolution saw a hectic social existence—perhaps the most creatively significant of the nineteenth century in France. In literature, it was the era, already legendary today, of the "Titans" Balzac, Daudet, George Sand, Musset, Victor Hugo, Dumas *père*, as well as of many lesser talents. Musical fashion was dictated by Rossini (for friends of opera), Cherubini (for more serious music enthusiasts), and Paganini and Liszt (for the worshipers of virtuosi). Meyerbeer's star had just risen and threatened to eclipse Rossini's; Chopin and Berlioz were scarcely known to the general public, but very well known to musicians. The visual arts were chiefly represented by Delacroix, Gavarni, Daumier, Roys, and Vernet. In science, too, it was one of the greatest periods of French research in all areas—the provinces were scarcely less active than Paris—and there was no dearth of outstanding talents. The seed of equality, sown more than a generation before by the Revolution, had sprouted, and a strong and expansive bourgeoisie everywhere made known its new, still untried strength.

Felix entered this maelstrom of new life rather unprepared, and, we must admit, with the prejudices of a worldly but Puritanical provincial. None of the above mentioned great names are found in his reports, with the exception of Cherubini, Liszt, and Chopin. Instead, he treats his friends and relatives to his immature criticisms of Saint-Simonism, and to accounts of suburban theatres, visits to Parliament, and chamber music performances. He did have contact with some of the German emigrants, but did not sympathize with them—not with Heine, and even less with Boerne, who ". . . with his labored inspirations, his fury with Germany, and his French phrases about freedom, is as repellent to me as Dr. Heine with all his dittos. . . ."[76]

He could not stand either Meyerbeer or his brother Michael Beer, the author of the then-famous play *Struensee*, in spite of Meyerbeer's friendly advances. Here, Felix at least cites reasons, if, perhaps, only rationalizations; his criticism of *Robert le Diable* is merciless, but hits its mark:

> . . . the subject is miserable, confused, and so cold, crazy, fantastic—the music is completely reasonable. It is not lacking in effect, it is always well calculated. . . . Melodies for whistling, harmony for the educated, instrumentation for the Germans, contradances for the French, something for everybody—but there's no heart in it. Such a work is related to a work of art as scene-painting is to artistic painting; in the end, scene-painting is more effective, but when you look at it carefully you see that it's been painted with the feet. . . .[77]

Richard Wagner did not evaluate Meyerbeer very differently, and perhaps not even so severely—he contented himself with calling Meyerbeer's dramatic technique "effect without cause." How deepseated Felix's aversion to his countryman and colleague Meyerbeer was, we may judge from an anecdote recounted by his friend Hiller. Many people thought that they were flattering Felix when they emphasized his external resemblance to Meyerbeer; however, this rubbed him the wrong way. Hiller, too, teased him about this, until Felix suddenly appeared dressed quite differently and, above all, with a ghastly chopped-off haircut. Meyerbeer also heard of the affair, but took it gracefully, with the nonchalance of the man of the world that he was.[78]

When we read Mendelssohn's personal reports in the unexpurgated context, we cannot help wondering why he did not bother to make contact with the great representatives of French literature. There are two complementary reasons for this; he was probably unconscious of both. As in Vienna or in Rome, so in Paris he was by no means inclined to compromise with his principles as an artist—even less with his standards of value—these, however, were in sharp opposition to those of the then-modern French school.

French Romanticism, with its weird, macabre, melancholy, and *"épater le bourgeois"* attitude, did not suit him at all—with scorn, he calls this viewpoint a "weary twopenny melancholy."[79]

If we scan his entire Paris correspondence, we note that he failed to enter either the circle of the revolutionary intelligentsia or that of the new bourgeoisie. Both sides were to blame for this omission. Felix reacted in a provincial, Puritanical way to the wild, new and radical winds that were blowing in arts, sciences, and society. These circles, however, were preoccupied with their own problems, and were less than hospitable to an outsider with conservative priniciples. Where Felix's brother-in-law Dirichlet, a great mathematical mind and a political radical, had found ready acceptance and open doors, Felix's own snobbism prevented him from taking the necessary steps to enter these (often Bohemian) circles. He acted too much the gentleman of leisure!

Perhaps even more significant was his evaluation of his personal chances in Paris. Musically speaking, after the deaths of Beethoven, Schubert, and Weber, Germany was in a period of stagnation. The three most significant composers, Spohr, Loewe, and Marschner, were, after all, no equal rivals for Felix. Schumann and Wagner were still quite unknown to the public, Brahms was too young. In short, in comparison with his German "brothers in Apollo" Felix must have appeared to himself like a second Samson! However, the situation in Paris was quite different. There were living and working masters like Cherubini, Chopin, Berlioz, Liszt and Meyerbeer, all famous or, at least, well known. It may well be that, in his heart, Felix shied away from serious rivalry with these artists. Furthermore, he believed that he had a mission in Germany, as modestly as he may have expressed himself in this respect. In any case, it was in Paris that he first definitely decided to work as a German artist and to share his fate with that of the German people. In this sense, he wrote to Zelter as well.[80]

Indeed, he was poorly rewarded for this decision by German posterity! From the pamphlets of Wagner and his school to the infamies of Nazi *Kultur-Politik*, his name has again and again been degraded and defamed in Germany; but not in France or Italy, not to speak of the Anglo-Saxon countries, and Switzerland, where his name and his work have always remained alive.

In Paris, however, he could not even achieve the aims which he had set for himself; and they were by no means extravagant. He appeared very successfully as a pianist (in the concerts at the Conservatoire), playing his favorite Beethoven concerto, the G major. His *A Midsummer Night's Dream* Overture, too, was played two or three times with moderate success.[81] In more intimate circles, he heard his Octet and his two Quartets in

E flat major and A minor, much to his satisfaction, but the rest is silence. And a very embarrassed silence, for in none of his letters do we find a clear report on the rejection of his Reformation Symphony by the Conservatoire. It is possible that he himself later suppressed or destroyed the letter concerned with this; the only reference to this bitter disappointment is found in a (seemingly) lightly tossed-off remark: "the Revolution Symphony [sic!] has been pushed into the background, because people attacked its workmanship. Who knows whether I shall bring it out again since I have taken a close look at the matter. . . ?"[82]

At the end of February, he was still certain of the world première of the work, for Habeneck, the powerful conductor of the Conservatoire orchestra, had led him to expect eight or even nine rehearsals. We learn about the end of the affair only through Hiller and through a short notice in the Conservatoire archives. From these sources, it appears that already in the first rehearsal, but at latest in the second, the orchestra members rejected the work as "too learned, too many fugatos, too little melody."[83] This was one of the bitterest disappointments for Felix, who had been spoiled by success. Also, he seems to have protested the refusal in strong language, for, during eleven years, the repertory of the Conservatoire remained closed to his works. It would be interesting to find out what went on behind the scenes, for it seems that Fétis and perhaps also Kalkbrenner had intrigued against Felix. In any case, Fétis had criticized him severely in his magazine, and Felix never had any illusions as to Kalkbrenner's loyalty.[84]

However, he speaks in tones of high admiration for the orchestra of the Conservatoire, and he certainly learned, from its organization and training, decisive methods for his activity of reformation at the *Gewandhaus*. Wherever it is a question of purely musical matters, he always knows what he is saying; he is often sharply critical, but never blasé or arrogant. Concerning his musical associations in Paris, we learn more from Hiller than from any other source. Felix, who had already made the acquaintance of Chopin in Berlin and had met him again in Munich, was a great admirer of the Polish genius. He defended him against the patronizing judgment of a Kalkbrenner, and thereby made the latter his enemy.[85] He had great respect for the "old, gruff" Cherubini, and esteemed him as an outstanding master; but his music seemed to him too cold and poor in emotion. He could not fathom that a great composer should be devoid of all human warmth, all lively feeling. It was scarcely clear to young Felix that a mature, introverted artist like Cherubini did not choose to express himself autobiographically in his music; therefore, Felix misunderstood him, believing that the old master "did everything with his brain."

The news of two deaths disturbed his spirit and filled him with grief. One was that of the friend of his youth, Eduard Rietz, the "fidus Achates" of the St. Matthew Passion; the other was the passing of Goethe. He wrote a

warm-hearted epitaph for Rietz in the Adagio of his Quintet, Op. 18
(*Nachruf*). He could not escape memories of Goethe when he finished
the Overture to the *Walpurgisnacht*. He called it "Saxon" (probably because
of the struggles of the Lower Saxons against Christianity). Also, he predicted the early death of Zelter as a result of Goethe's passing. "Only old
Zelter doesn't weep for him, but will follow him in death [*Stirbt ihm lieber
nach*]," they were saying in Berlin. And it was true. A few weeks after his
friend's death, Zelter, in his home, ironically bowed before Goethe's bust
with these words: "Your Excellency naturally has the precedence; but I
shall follow soon." Indeed, he died not quite two months after his worshiped
poet-friend.

To all this grief was added a violent cholera epidemic, which descended
upon Paris and poisoned or suppressed all social life. Felix, too, fell victim to
the epidemic, but recovered from the attack. However, in the literal sense,
this turned Parisian life—which he had always observed from the periphery,
as a moralizing outsider—into a plague for him. After a short convalescence,
he hastened to flee to his beloved England.

So the stay in Paris ended not only with a dissonance, but even with a
negative balance. Felix was not the man to deceive himself about this. On the
positive side, we find his clear recognition that he, as a German artist, must
make his way in Germany; the completion of the *Walpurgisnacht*, of the
Hebrides Overture, of the first *Songs Without Words;* and several worthwhile connections with French music publishers. On the negative side were
the failure of his Reformation Symphony, and his aversion to the great
creative wave which was then fertilizing France's intellectual life.

EIGHTH PHASE: London
April 23–June 22, 1832

NOT LONG BEFORE his departure from Paris, he had received the formal
commission of the Frankfurt *Caecilienverein,* which suggested an oratorio
with the Apostle Paul as its central figure. Now we must remember that
Mendelssohn also had a firm opera contract for Munich in his pocket, so
that he was going to start two large works. In addition, there were London
performances, the completion of more than a dozen larger works which
he had begun on his travels, and even more far-reaching plans for Berlin.
All these works ripened to maturity—except the opera. We shall have more
to say about the strange fate of all his operatic plans.

For the second time, and not for the last, London lavished balm on the
wounds which Paris and the death of loved ones had inflicted on him. In
Paris, the news of Goethe's death had reached him; in London, he was to
learn of Zelter's death. He reacted to this occurrence, so sorrowful for him,

in a way which, in spite of all his grief, shows his serious manliness; yet at Goethe's death he would have liked to "break out into loud wails."[86] This strengthening of his spirit is certainly attributable to the London atmosphere. How well Geheimrat Bunsen, his Roman mentor, understood him is shown by a letter from this intelligent and spirited statesman and scholar. Here, among other things, he says:

> Nothing would make me happier than the news that he [Felix] was going to settle himself and his art in England, *at least for several years.* He has to fight a hard battle in order to save his best talents from an age that is threatened with barbarism in spite of flashy mechanical capacity and skill. The composer of our times has no more dangerous enemy than the virtuoso. . . .[87]

But it was precisely with the virtuosi that he had to do again in London; and it speaks well for Felix's *savoir vivre* and his politeness that he, the antagonist of the Kalkbrenners, Herzs, and their like, nevertheless was always able to avoid scandalous scenes *à la* Berlioz.

Felix's spiritual condition during the three months of his second London visit contrasts sharply to his more passive, almost exclusively receptive attitude in Paris. These few weeks in London are packed to the brim with the joy of creation and artistic activity, with the society of his old friends Klingemann, Moscheles, and Rosen, whom the Horsleys now joined as new and lifelong friends. The great warmth with which all of England, not just the musical world, took him to herself always filled him with new strength and deep joy. Therefore, we notice none of the prejudices which had estranged him from the social world of Paris.

Beginning with the memorable occasion when the orchestra members of the Philharmonic recognized him at a concert (in which he was not participating) and greeted him with a spontaneous ovation before the program could begin, his disappointments were forgotten. His mood, darkened by the deaths of his dear friends and masters, was now brightened. He began once more to dedicate himself to life and the present with full force, as he had always been accustomed to do.[88]

Soon afterwards (May 14) he had the satisfaction and pleasure of hearing his final version of the *Hebrides* Overture played by the Philharmonic Orchestra. "It sounded very strange among lots of Rossinis"; but was accepted with great enthusiasm.[89] The *Harmonicon* cannot praise him enough:

> . . . unity of intention is no less remarkable in this than in the author's overture to *A Midsummer Night's Dream*, and indeed is a prominent feature in all he has produced. Whatever a vivid imagination could suggest, and great musical knowledge supply, has contributed to this, the

latest work of M. Mendelssohn, one of the finest and most original geniuses of the age; and it will be but an act of justice to him, and a great
boon to the frequenters of these Concerts, to repeat the present composition before the conclusion of the season. Works such as this are like
"angel's visits," and should be made the most of.

On May 28 and June 18, he played his G minor Concerto; on May 25,
his new work, written for London, the *Capriccio Brillant* in B minor with
orchestra.[90] He himself conducted the *Hebrides* and the *A Midsummer
Night's Dream* Overtures in Moscheles' concert evening (June 1) and, with
Moscheles, played Mozart's Double Concerto, for which he had written new
cadenzas. His own "Munich" Concerto was so successful that "the people
went crazy and thought it was his best piece." Before a distinguished audience, he played the great organ in St. Paul's Cathedral; the reports on this
performance are filled with admiration and astonishment, especially at his
extraordinary ability to improvise in double and triple counterpoint. Although he was otherwise highly opposed to public improvisation before a
large audience, he certainly gave both his hearers and himself pleasure with
his polyphonic fantasies on the organ. All his life long, he preferred this
instrument to the piano *for this purpose.*

He published his first volume of *Songs Without Words* with Novello,
under the title *Original Melodies for the Pianoforte.* We shall have more to
say about this in the next chapter. Finally, he received a commission from
the publisher Ewer to write two large pieces for the Anglican service; later,
too, he wrote several works for the Church of England, which were published in England only.

Perhaps his greatest achievement during these days in London is the
third (and final) version of the *Hebrides.* Sir Ernest Walker still believed
that only two versions of the work exist;[91] but even the published travel
letters point to a third version, the original one, which he discarded in
Paris.[92] It seems that the autographs of the various versions are in Oxford
with Miss Margaret Deneke, Fellow of Lady Margaret Hall, with the Sterndale Bennett family, and at Corpus Christi College, Oxford. The last version
bears the date June 20, 1832, exactly five weeks after the first performance
of the work. It is nearly identical with the subsequently published score,
corrected by Mendelssohn himself.

He often met his old and honored mentor for English music, Sir Thomas
Attwood. Indeed, when he got the news of Zelter's death, he fled to Attwood's country house in Surrey; for he feared that he would become
"seriously ill" from the bad news.[93] He felt the urgent need of collecting
himself and meditating seriously on his dead teacher, as well as on his own
future. Two "father-images," besides his "great father" Abraham, had
played an important part in his life: Zelter and Goethe. Now they were

both gone, and his real father was too far away to offer comfort and support. Is it not significant for young Felix's need to lean on father-figures that he now flees to Attwood, as a "substitute father," in order to find comfort, to collect and refresh himself!

The subsequent hypothetical ideas originate in certain depth-psychological principles. Although they are still disputed today, they have shed new light on many problematic personalities. I am convinced that Felix's deeply rooted bond with the father is also manifest in his music. It seems to me that the dominant personality of Abraham had absorbed all of Felix's capacity for hero-worship. This might explain the absence of all heroic traits in his music and his lyric inclination even in fast and passionate movements. Even in his *Athalie* and *Antigone* music, the heroic element is not really convincing. Only in his last years, in *Elijah* and in the last works, did he find true heroic accents. All his earlier efforts to do so failed. Wherever he tried to master the father-complex by artistic means (which implies the heroic liberation from the yoke of Oedipus, as a prerequisite) he did not succeed. His *Moses* did not get past the libretto; his *Tempest* (Prospero) was not even begun, and in his *St. Paul* he shies away (consciously or unconsciously) from the great father-figure of Rabban Gamaliel, Paul's teacher; in fact, he does not even introduce this dominant personality. As he comes close to the heroic in *Elijah*, so eventually he tries to dissolve the bond with the father on an artistic level: in his (unfortunately, merely begun) oratorio *Christus*. Mozart, who also had to emancipate himself from an unusually strong bond to his father, was able to succeed in doing this once and for all, in *Don Giovanni;* the Commandant is the father-image and, at the same time, the warning conscience.[94]

But Felix's father did not leave him alone, on the contrary; he urged him, in ever more pressing letters from Berlin, to apply seriously for the vacancy in the directorship of the *Singakademie* caused by Zelter's death. Here we see the true nobility of Felix's character. Far from wanting to conform to the wishes of his father, who was ambitious on his behalf, he was most unwilling to "jump into" the vacant place. Zelter, during his last days, appears to have expressed the wish that Felix should take over the Academy.[95] Felix merely wants to "relieve Zelter of any extra work, as long as he wanted me to; for that would naturally be my duty." Further, he says: "Anything else would seem to me to be wronging him. . . ."[96] He would be even better pleased if Zelter got well and could make out without his help. A few days later he writes to Fanny in the most determined manner that was possible between brother and sister so closely linked:

You write, dear Fanny, that I should hurry back twice as fast in order to get the position at the Academy if possible. But I shan't do that. I'll come back as soon as I can, because Father wants me to. . . . But that's the only reason; the other affair would, if anything, prevent me from coming. . . .[97]

From the very beginning, he opposes the idea of *becoming a candidate* for the *Singakademie* position; if it is offered to him, he believes that he must accept it, even jointly with Rungenhagen.[98] Even this he was willing to do only because he had promised it three years ago to the Board of Trustees of the *Singakademie*: "To repeat my 'Yes' once more is not necessary; for, if I've once given it, I'll stick by it. However, I can do so [i.e., repeat it] even less because that would mean *offering myself* for what was once *offered to me.*"[99]

In addition, he refers to a letter from Paris in which he emphasizes that Berlin is the only large city of Germany which he does not yet know well. He was—rightly, as soon proved to be the case—very skeptical concerning his chances in Berlin, but positively *distrustful* of the musicians and music enthusiasts there. In the letters which he wrote to England after the performance of the St. Matthew Passion, he had already shown a similarly pessimistic attitude toward the Berliners.

However, his family's pressure did not cease. As long as Felix was not exposed to it personally, and could take the advice of such well-meaning and wise friends as Klingemann and Moscheles, he remained adamant in his negative attitude. Even in his last travel letter from London, he is aware that his way is the right one. He writes:

I'm afraid that your next letter will scold me because I *don't want to* aspire to the Academy position . . . the way I feel now, I don't want to tie myself down to a fixed position in the next few years. . . . I must get back to this country [England] soon again, and have some very special plans along this line . . . it's very nice to be here, and nowhere will you find such friendly people and such lovely girls as here. . . .[100]

Here speaks a good son—but also a man. As long as Zelter was still alive, Felix was much too proud to take on a sinecure under his protection; he wanted to stand on his own feet. Not only his pride, but also his judgment of men which had matured in these years of travel, warned him that a candidate must necessarily expose himself, that he loses some of his dignity, and that, in some instances, he must accept whatever is offered. If only he had remained firm! He would have spared himself the greatest disappointment of his life, a disappointment from which he recovered only in his last years.

But he was not spared this, and since up till now both his biographers and the *Singakademie* have kept quiet about it, we shall expose all the moves in the affair with their motivations, insofar as these are still traceable. They do no credit to the *Singakademie*, but the Mendelssohn family, too, made serious tactical and human errors, the results of which were even to embitter the lives of the next generation of the family. We shall take a closer look at this crisis in Chapter XI.

The London visit produced far-reaching artistic and human results, which for Felix were always indivisible. Mendelssohn's success was undisputed. He was treated with special respect, and yet like a native of England —something which had not happened to any Continental musician since Handel, not even to Haydn or Clementi. He found a society congenial to him, and even a real friend in Charles Edward Horsley, the son of the well-known choral composer William Horsley. The Horsleys belonged to the "gentry," the small country nobility, the backbone of the English nation.

The Mendelssohn who finally arrived in his family home on June 25, 1832, was sure of himself, confidently looking to the future, successful, and widely known in Europe. He had changed a great deal, and the most striking witness of this is to be found in the works which he wrote during his time of travel. Our next chapter will deal with these.

Notes

1. Charles L. Graves, The Life and Letters of Sir George Grove (London, 1903), p. 128ff.

2. Wolff, Musikerbriefe, Felix Mendelssohn Bartholdy (Berlin, 1907), p. XIII; "The editors of this two-volume collection [Mendelssohn's Letters] dealt with the rich material available to them in most arbitrary fashion."

3. Mendelssohn's remark to Jenny von Gustedt: "Who knows what would have become of me without Weimar, without Goethe?" (Wolff, op. cit., p. 80.)

4. RB, pp. 5-6 (May 25, 1830). Goethe and Mendelssohn, p. 61.

5. RB, p. 4 (May 21, 1830).

6. F. F. Blume, Goethe und die Musik (Kassel, 1948), p. 32.

7. Ibid., p. 36.

8. Eckermann, Conversations with Goethe, 1823 (concerning the quartets of the twelve-year-old Mendelssohn).

9. Goethe-Zelter Correspondence, letter of November 9, 1829.

10. Goethe-Zelter op. cit., letter of June 3, 1830.

11. Ibid.

12. Ibid., letter of June 15, 1830.

13. Unpublished letter of June 8, 1830.

14. Unpublished letter of June 13, 1830.

15. Some of these letters are found in the Library of Congress, Washington, D.C.

16. Unpublished letter of July 14, 1830.

17. In order to quiet Fanny's jealousy, Felix compares her with Delphine in a letter, and makes a sort of declaration of love to her.

18. Unpublished letter of Lea, January 21, 1834.

19. Letter to Klingemann, August 6, 1830.

20. Unpublished letter to his father, August 9, 1830.

21. *Oesterreichische Musikzeitschrift* (Vienna), February-April, 1961.
22. C. F. Pohl, *Denkschrift zum 100-jährigen Bestehen der Tonkünstler-Sozietät im Jahre 1862 (reorganisirt als "Haydn"-Verein), Vienna, 1871.*
23. Hanslick, *Aus meinem Leben* (Berlin, 1894), I, pp. 79-99.
24. The dark piece *O Haupt voll Blut und Wunden* originated, as Felix writes, under the influence of a picture by Zurbaran which he saw in Munich. (Unpublished letter of August 22.)
25. Letter to Devrient of September 5, 1830.
26. *Ibid.*
27. Letter to Zelter of October 16, 1830: "The people around me [in Vienna] were so trashy and worthless that I took a spiritual turn and behaved like a theologian among them."
28. To give but one example, we cite Felix's completely mistaken criticism of the *Tenebrae:* "I cannot help it—it infuriates me to hear the most sacred, most beautiful words sung to such empty, monotonous tones. They say it's *Canto fermo*—it's Gregorian —that's all the same to me. If, in those days, they did not feel it differently or could not do it differently [!] we can do it better today. . . ." (Letter to Zelter of June 16, 1831.)
29. *RB*, p. 23 (May 28, 1831).
30. *RB*, p. 66.
31. *RB*, June 6, 1831; see also *RB*, December 11, 1831 (concerning Santini).
32. *RB*, March 29, 1831.
33. Unpublished letter to his father, March 12. In Chapters XV and XVI, we shall have more to say about this twofold relationship of the arch-Romanticist Berlioz to the "mannerist" Mendelssohn.
34. Berlioz, *Correspondence inédite* (May 6, 1831). "All that I heard of him [Mendelssohn] ravished me; I firmly believe that he is one of the greatest capacities of the age. . . . Mendelssohn is one of those candid souls such as one so rarely sees; he believes firmly in his Lutheran religion, and I scandalized him sometimes by laughing at the Bible. He gave me the only bearable moments that I enjoyed during my stay in Rome."
35. Letters to Klingemann, December 26, 1830, and January 2, 1831.
36. Unpublished letter to his father, December 14, 1830.
37. *RB*, January 17, 1831.
38. *Ibid.*
39. *RB*, March 15, 1831.
40. *Goethe-Zelter Correspondence,* letters December 22-31, 1830.
41. *RB*, December 7, 1830.
42. *RB*, March 1, 1831.
43. *RB*, December 11, 1830.
44. *Wolff, op. cit.,* p. 90.
45. Letter to Goethe, March 5, 1831; "not to speak of the operatic arias which the nuns produce—the nonsense is too annoying. . . ."
46. Letter to Zelter, December 18, 1830.
47. *RB*, February 22, 1831.
48. The full text of the letter is found in the *Goethe-Jahrbuch*, XII, p. 93. It is strange that Dr. Blume, in his book *Goethe und die Musik,* completely ignores the correspondence between Goethe and Felix concerning the *Walpurgisnacht.*
49. *RB*, April 13, 1831.
50. *RB*, May 17, 1831.
51. Letter to Klingemann, December 20, 1831: "I had one of those unpleasant moods when one is dissatisfied with oneself; this nearly always happens to me when I have not composed for a long time."
52. *RB*, June 6, 1831.
53. *Goethe-Zelter Correspondence*, letters of June 10-15, 1831.
54. *Ibid.,* letter of June 28, 1831.

55. *RB*, April 27, 1831.

56. "For, as a musical tradition is a chancy thing, I don't know how a five-voiced piece can be transmitted by hearsay." (Unpublished letter from Rome, June, 1831.)

57. See note 28.

58. Unpublished letter from Rome, June, 1831.

59. Unpublished letter to his father of July 7, 1831.

60. Letter to Devrient of July 13, 1831.

61. Letter to Devrient of August 27, 1831.

62. Letter to Devrient of July 13, 1831.

63. *RB*, July 14, 1831.

64. *RB*, July 14, 1831.

65. Letter to Devrient of August 27, 1831.

66. *Ibid*.

67. *RB* to Taubert, August 27, 1831. The expression "latest events" refers to the tyranny of the mob, of the Maffia, and of the *carbonari*, all of which Felix abhorred and scorned.

68. Wolfgang Menzel, the notorious critic of Goethe.

69. *RB*, August 27, 1831.

70. Unpublished part of the letter of October 18, 1831. Wolff has the following information about the then seventeen-year-old Delphine: "Adolphine von Schauroth, later Mrs. Hill Handley, born in 1814 in Magdeburg, was a pupil of Kalkbrenner. . . . At an advanced age, she still played the work [Mendelssohn's G minor concerto] on February 4, 1870, at the Mendelssohn festival in the Leipzig *Gewandhaus*. . . ." R. Schumann devoted one of his most delightful reviews to the C minor Sonata of Delphine Handley.

71. *RB*, December 28, 1833.

72. *RB*, October 18, 1831.

73. *RB*, October 6, 1831. There, too, is an unpublished, very malicious observation: "Who talks a lot and washes little? Who pulled an opera subject out of her coat pocket right away? Why, La Chezy!"

74. Unpublished letter to Baron Poissl, November 4, 1831, Library of Congress, Washington, D. C.

75. *RB*, December 19, 1831.

76. Unpublished letter of December 11, 1831.

77. Letter to Klingemann of December 20, 1831.

78. Hiller, *Felix Mendelssohn Bartholdy* (Cologne, 1878), p. 21.

79. Letter to Klingemann of December 20, 1831. It is not without irony that Richard Wagner criticized Mendelssohn's music because of its excess of melancholy (in *Das Judentum in der Musik*).

80. *RB*, February 25, 1832. Zelter understood this very well and reported on it to Goethe. (*Goethe-Zelter Correspondence*, February 19-27, 1832.) He adds a few mildly malicious remarks about Abraham Mendelssohn's Francophilia.

81. So we read in Felix's reports; actually, however, the work seems hardly to have had any success, as Liszt, witness, reports. (*Briefe an eine Freundin*, ed. La Mara, No. 65 [Prague, 1858] April 21.)

82. Unpublished letter of January 7, 1832. This lame excuse for the symphony's failure refers to the July Revolution of 1830 and the subsequent riots.

83. Hiller, *op. cit.*, p. 19.

84. *RB*, March 15, 1832.

85. He even took active part as a pianist, along with Liszt and Hiller, in Chopin's debut (February 26, 1832) in the Salle Pleyel.

86. Unpublished letter, April 3, 1832.

87. Unpublished letter to Hensel (Rome, January 19, 1832), Library of Congress, Washington, D. C.

88. *RB*, May 11, 1832: "And I had to . . . climb up to the orchestra and thank them. You see, I shan't forget this, for it was dearer to me than any medal."

89. *Harmonicon*, 1832, p. 142.

90. Written for Mori's concert, but played by Mendelssohn himself. (See Moscheles, *Diaries*, tr. Coleridge [London, 1873], May 25, 1832.)

91. Ernest Walker, "Mendelssohn's 'Die einsame Insel'," *Music and Letters*, July, 1945.

92. *RB*, January 21, 1832. The original version bears the date, "Rome, December 16, 1830," and seems to be identical with the version that was in the Heyer Museum in Cologne. See also Grove, 4th ed. article on Mendelssohn, p. 387.

93. *RB*, May 25 and June 1, 1832.

94. Rank (in Reich, *Bekenntnis zu Mozart* [Lucerne, 1945]).

95. Unpublished letter by Abraham Mendelssohn, May 9, 1832.

96. *RB*, May 18, 1832.

97. *RB*, May 25, 1832.

98. *RB*, June 1, 1832.

99. *Ibid.*

100. Unpublished letter of June 15, 1832.

CHAPTER X

Mature Works:
The Product of
The Years 1830-1832

> "... words seem to me so ambiguous, so vague, so easily misunder-
> standable in comparison with genuine music, which fills the soul
> with things a thousand times better than words. Ideas expressed by
> a beloved music are, to me, not too indefinite to put them into
> words, but on the contrary, too definite. ..."
>
> Mendelssohn letter to André Souchay of October 15, 1842

ONE OFTEN reads that Mendelssohn did not undergo a real development
as a composer. This is usually said by authors whose lack of knowledge of
Mendelssohn's works becomes clear when they go into details and comparisons. It is not our purpose here to discredit such views. We shall undertake a comprehensive evaluation from a historical viewpoint. In doing this,
we shall often find opportunity to marvel at the astounding coherence and
integration of his work in every phase.

The first phase of Mendelssohn's creative life took a course between
serious, elegant music and salon music. We shall discuss here the second phase
of his creativity, which shows quite clearly his turn away from what is
merely pleasing. He had already set foot on this path in the chamber music
of his earlier years, especially the Quartets, Op. 12 and 13; however, these
works were still in the minority when compared with half-academic student
works on the one hand and musical *causeries* on the other. He had now left
this no man's land. As artist and as man, Felix now undergoes a transformation the goal of which he does not know, but the course of which he sees
before him.

We shall begin with a survey of the most significant works of the travel
years 1830 to the end of 1832.

[*198*]

VOCAL MUSIC

1. *Die erste Walpurgisnacht*, Ballade for soli, chorus and orchestra, after verses by Goethe
2. Psalm 115 ("Non nobis, Domine . . .") for soli, chorus and orchestra
3. Chorale Motet *Aus tiefer Noth* for four-voiced chorus *a cappella*
4. *Ave Maria*, for eight-voiced chorus and organ
5. *Mitten wir im Leben*, for eight-voiced chorus and soli
6. Three Motets, for women's chorus and organ
7. *Verleih uns Frieden gnädiglich*, for chorus and orchestra
8. Songs for Soprano, with piano accompaniment

Mendelssohn cultivated with equal zest both small and large forms. In his instrumental music, the small forms are mainly piano compositions such as the *Songs without Words, Albumblätter*, Preludes and Fugues, Caprices, etc. In his vocal music, small forms are used for the secular choruses, the individual motet, and the songs and hymns. His large forms are concertos symphonies, quartets, oratorios, etc.

If we ask ourselves which one of these sets established his position in musical history, we can without hesitation point to the large forms. The same conclusion would be reached if we set as a valid criterion the amount of *living* music, i.e., pieces of the concert repertoire, by Mendelssohn. Again, unlike the cases of Chopin or even Schumann, the large forms prevail by far over the miniatures.

It cannot be denied that talent, originality, and a good germinal idea (*Einfall*) count for much in the smaller forms. The larger forms also require these components, but in addition, they demand a certain gift of integration, and, perhaps most important, a tenacious intention and aspiration towards the monumental. We shall have to cope with this question in another connection. For the "rules" of large forms are *essentially* (not merely in degree) different from those of miniatures. The crucial postulates for large forms demand economy of means, and the wise and balanced governing of rest, motion, and their intermediate stages. Large vocal forms do not require the same strictness in the use of the thematic material as do the large forms of instrumental music; for the progression and continuity of the text in themselves safeguard a certain unity. In instrumental music, this unity has to be attained by musical means alone. In the post-Beethovenian era, the generally accepted device for securing unity was thematic development. Even in so radical a deviation as Berlioz' *Symphonie Fantastique*, the principle of thematic unity and development was not abandoned.

We see, at this time, that Mendelssohn paid more attention to vocal music than to instrumental music. In the vocal category, he permits himself much more freedom than in instrumental music. In Chapter VII, we pointed out that the progressive, experimental element in his style belongs to his chamber and orchestral music, the more traditional, not to say conventional, to his vocal music. This is still true, with one important exception, the *Walpurgisnacht*. It is typical of the young man's urge to expansion that, in the midst of a nearly three-year-long journey, he writes no chamber music, but only works of larger scope, aside from the smaller religious occasional pieces. The degree of archaizing in the vocal music is perceptibly less than before; we sense that Felix, in this realm too, is looking for a style suitable for him. But he did not yet find it. Only the *Walpurgisnacht* is, already in the first version (1832), quite free of archaizing elements. This may have to do with its slightly parodistic, in any case "secular" character.

Felix tirelessly strives for renewal and closest integration of musical form. Regrettably, his *formal experiments* were ignored by most of his contemporaries. He held a thankless position between the battling "traditionalists" and "innovators." If one did not appear such a bold innovator as Berlioz in his orchestral works, or Chopin and Schumann in their piano works, it was not easy to draw the attention of musicians, or laymen, to the less conspicuous *internal* innovations in structure. But we do not mean to say that Mendelssohn's creations of these years remained unnoticed. All his life long, he was not lacking in successes. However, up till now, many otherwise sensitive observers have overlooked his brilliant attempts to free the sonata, symphonic, and piano forms from their post-Schubertian limitations and find new formal principles for them.

We have already spoken of the modest experiments in cyclic form which we occasionally meet in the early works. Now, we encounter two large symphonic movements which grew from a single motif; the first and third movements of the Reformation Symphony, which are both built on the "Dresden Amen" cited as a leitmotif: Something similar happens in the Overture to the *Walpurgisnacht*. Here, the traditional second theme almost disappears. Instead, we find a (programmatically conditioned) large coda. This contrasts most strongly with the principal portion; in expression, it is completely different, but in thematic material, it is related. We find cyclic ideas in the Piano Concerto, but there, they are clever play rather than a constructional principle. However, the Concerto no longer has pauses between the movements, and also dispenses with the classical orchestral ritornelli. Beethoven, in his Fourth and Fifth Piano Concerti, already let the second movement proceed without transition into the Finale, but preserved the pause after the first movement, and also used the orchestral ritornello. It is not impossible that, as Schering suggests, Mendelssohn followed, transforming them for his own purposes, the formal principles of Bach's concerti.[1] In any case, the G minor Concerto inspired many imitators—more, perhaps, than its artistic worth would lead us to expect. As a new formal type, it was of considerable significance.

When we spoke of the lack of attention to Mendelssohn's *formal innovations*, the *Songs without Words*—and, indeed, all his piano works—should be excepted from this statement. For these pieces suited the taste of the time almost too well, and so became overpopular. Nonetheless, in them, too, we can sense the joy in formal experimentation. All forty-eight pieces in this category are written in the three-part song form; yet what a wealth of variety pulses within this seemingly limited medium! Mendelssohn's colleagues were slow to notice this: not so, the publishers. The first volume appeared in 1832; after a year, only forty-eight copies had been sold, after four years, only 114. Mendelssohn threw away his rights for the first and third volumes of the *Songs without Words*, three Preludes and Fugues for organ, and the three chorale motets for women's chorus which he wrote in Rome, to Novello for a lump sum of £35—the equivalent of 700 marks in those days, or about three times that amount today. But even if we call it DM 2000, we must say that it is a ridiculously low price.[2]

Die Erste Walpurgisnacht

In sacred music—in fact in the entire realm of vocal music—Mendelssohn generally moves much more carefully, one might also say, more traditionally. Naturally, the *Walpurgisnacht* is excepted from this rule; for there was no tradition yet in existence for this "Ballade," as its creator called it after considerable hesitation. In reality, this is an extended secular cantata, like Bach's "jolly" compositions *Der Zufriedengestellte Äolus* or the *Coffee Cantata*, which have a merry, parodistic tone. Handel's *L'Allegro ed il Pensieroso* could have stood godfather to the later work, if Mendelssohn had known it. It was probably a good thing that he did not know these works, or he would have fallen into archaizing here too. As it was, however, he felt himself to be almost a pioneer of quite a new genre—and rightly so! For this poetic category was a creation of Goethe, who, at first, wanted to call such works "conversations in songs," but later classified them, in his collected works, as cantatas. There were only three of these works: *Idylle*, written in January, 1813; *Rinaldo*, written in May, 1811; and *Die erste Walpurgisnacht*, which Goethe already mentioned on July 30, 1799, in his diary.[3]

Already in August, 1799 (in other words, almost immediately after its completion) Zelter had received the poem directly from its author. At that time, Goethe had added: "This production came from the idea that one might develop dramatic ballades in such a way that they would give the composer material for a larger vocal piece. . . ." But he then says: "Unfortunately the present [Ballade] does not have enough dignity to deserve such a great outlay of means."⁴

Zelter, embarrassed, replies: "*Die erste Walpurgis-Nacht* is a very original poem. The verses are musical and singable. I wanted to send it along to you set to music, and have worked at a good bit of it, but I cannot reproduce the atmosphere of the whole thing and so I had better leave it alone for now. . . ."⁵

Three years later, Zelter excused himself again to Goethe: "*The Walpurgisnacht* remained unfinished because the old worn-out cantata uniform kept imposing itself upon me. . . ."⁶ But the poem continued to occupy his mind. Thirteen years after the first abortive attempt, Zelter asked for historical information about the subject of the *Walpurgisnacht*: "Some time ago I have started to set the poem to music, and have satisfied myself as to its necessary form. . . ."⁷ Goethe gave some information but could not remember his historical sources. In detail, he said:

Now one of the investigators of German antiquities wanted to justify the witches' and devil's ride on the Brocken, which has been known in Germany for ages, by giving it a historical origin. It seems that the German heathen priests and patriarchs, after they had been driven out of their sacred groves and Christianity had been forced on the people, retreated, with their faithful disciples, to the wild and inaccessible Harz Mountains, in the early days of spring. There, according to ancient custom, they offered up their prayers and their fires to the incorporeal God of Heaven and earth. To protect themselves against the spying, armed missionaries, they thought it good to disguise several of their number, in order to frighten away their superstitious opponents; and, thus protected by devils' masks, they carried out the purest service of God. . . .⁸

Zelter, however, was not up to such an assignment, and never completed his composition of the piece. This honorable modesty should not be construed as lack of understanding, as Einstein does when he says: "Zelter, *of course*, did not know what to do with it."⁹ Zelter did not lack good will and intelligence; that he gave up such a difficult undertaking speaks rather well for his self-knowledge.

We do not know when Felix became acquainted with the poem. But, in a letter to Fanny of February 22, 1831, he says that for months he had been planning to compose a cantata. In Rome, he took heart and wrote the grand old man in Weimar about his plan. Goethe answered in especially cordial fashion, and addressed Felix as "My dear son." No one else of the younger generation could boast of having been addressed by him in such moving and intimate tones. In this letter, too, he gives his interpretation of the poem; it may be called historical, though it leans toward the philosophical. He says:

Really, it is intended highly symbolically. For, in world history, it must occur again and again that something old, well-established, well-tried, and comforting is pushed aside, and, if not extirpated, cramped into the least possible space, by innovations that crop up. The intermediate period, where hate still can and does have its countereffect, is presented here pregnantly enough, and a joyous, indestructible enthusiasm flames up once more in glory and truth.[10]

The "dramatic Ballade," as Goethe first called the poem, is firmly on the side of the Germans or Celts who were devoted to the old beliefs and customs, and who, "protected by devils' masks, carried out the purest service of God [the incorporeal Universal Father]." Therefore, it is a mild satire on medieval churchly bigotry, and sets a pure monotheism, derived from natural philosophy, against the superstitious usages of the early European Church. Born of the spirit of the Enlightenment, the work far surpasses the limits of a superficial Rationalism and, in its own way, foreshadows ideas of Nietzsche. It is a humanistic poem in the deepest sense.

There can be no doubt that both Moses and Abraham Mendelssohn would have enthusiastically acclaimed Goethe's vision. And the inner conflict which accompanied Felix throughout his life—the conflict of a Jew, proudly conscious of his origins, who was deeply and honorably devoted to the Protestant Church—comes to light clearly. The hymn, praising the unity of mankind, which forms the end of the *Walpurgisnacht* was set to rousing tones by Felix:

> Und raubt man uns den alten Brauch,
> Dein Licht, wer kann es rauben?

> And if they crush our olden ways,
> Whoe'er can crush Thy light?
>   (tr. John Storer Cobb)

Here, he succeeded in resolving the inner conflict between pure monotheism and belief in the Church. The medium which he used, with the insight of genius, to present and resolve the conflicts was the humoristic element. The *Walpurgisnacht* is one of the rare great works in which humor, spirit, majesty, and charm are interwoven. Only Haydn's *Seasons*, on a much larger scale, might be compared with the *Walpurgisnacht*—yet, on the whole, this comparison is invalid. Both works do have in common a subtle humor.

The Overture in A minor, whose first motif reminds us a little of the (then incomplete) Scotch Symphony, represents "bad weather." Its most beautiful and important section is the slow "turn towards spring" in E and A major. Wagner seems to have known this transition, for the same turns of phrase are found in *Die Walküre*. The epilogue of the Overture introduces the first chorus, *Es lacht der Mai* (May is laughing), a charming, highly characteristic spring song. Stormy, lovable and daring elements are combined here in a piece of irresistible brilliance. Now the priest adjures the multitude to thank the Universal Father with him (chorus: *Die Flamme lodre durch den Rauch*—[Amid the smoke shall gleam the flame]), and the music soars to a joyous, yet solemn mood. The Christian missionaries and watchers are to be deceived and frightened.

> Diese dummen Pfaffenchristen,
> Lasst uns keck sie überlisten!
> Mit dem Teufel, den sie fabeln,
> Wollen wir sie selbst erschrecken. . . .

> Let us in a cunning wise,
> Yon dull Christian priests surprise!
> With the devil of their talk
> We'll those very priests confound.

Everything rushes towards the work's central number, the chorus *Kommt! Mit Zacken und mit Gabeln* (Come with prong and come with fork); with the greatest realism, it represents the spectres which drive the watchers into panic flight. This chorus caused Mendelssohn a great deal of trouble; he mentions it three times in his letters and finally decides: "I must get back to my witches; the whole letter hovers in uncertainty, or, rather, I do, as to whether I should use the bass drum or not. *Zacken, Gabeln und wilde Klapperstöcke* really drive me to it, but moderation dissuades me . . . I am convinced, Fanny says yes, but I still can't make up my mind. In any case, a great noise must be made."[11] Full orchestra, with bass drum and shrill flutes, characterizes this grotesque-humoristic piece, whose wild fantasy represented unheard-of daring in Germany. Of his contemporaries, only Berlioz went far beyond this; it was no accident that the *Walpurgisnacht* appealed to him especially and that he valued it highly. The harmonic style of this movement, too, by no means avoids harsh dissonances which Mendelssohn rarely uses otherwise. Towards the end of the movement, the listener hears a foreshadowing of the elves' choruses of the much later *A Midsummer Night's Dream* music; but here, the imaginary witches are presented humoristically and grotesquely.

Upon the crude joke, there follows the real ceremony. In simple, devout tones the Druid sings:

> Doch ist es Tag,
> Sobald man mag
> Ein reines Herz zu Dir zu bringen.

> Yet when 'tis day,
> To Thee we may
> A heart unsullied bring.

The chorus answers with the festal songs of the Walpurgis ceremony. Now for the first time the Christian watchers appear. They flee, frightened and confused:

> Hilf, ach hilf mir, Kriegsgeselle!
> Ach, es kommt die ganze Hölle!

> Comrades, quick! your aid afford!
> All the brood of hell's abroad!

This scene is, throughout, in the caricaturing tone of the Italianized *opera buffa;* it affords an amusing contrast to the ceremonial song. The latter is now heard once more, this time in triumphal tones:

> Die Flamme reinigt sich vom Rauch;
> So reinig' unseren Glauben!
> Und raubt man uns den alten Brauch,
> Dein Licht, wer kann es rauben?

> As from the smoke is freed the blaze,
> So let our faith burn bright!
> And if they crush our olden ways,
> Whoe'er can crush Thy light?

With this, the work closes. Mendelssohn had no models for his undertaking; therefore, here he is completely himself, free of imitation, original, bold, and as subtle as he is robust. No wonder that the *Walpurgisnacht* has remained the most significant secular oratorio of the nineteenth century.

The Sacred Vocal Music

All vocal works of these three or four years have in common a significant refinement of the feeling for sonority, indeed, of the "sound-ideal" (*Klang-Phantasie*). The abstract-academic element of the immature apprentice disappears; the polyphony becomes free and easy; the choral texture is exceptionally well-sounding, transparent, and, where desired, massive and majestic. We meet with no formal experiments, but rather, studies in choral sonority. To this category belong, for example, the three motets for women's chorus, as well as the chorale motet *Aus tiefer Noth* for four-voiced chorus *a cappella*, and the unpublished motet *Herr Gott, wir loben Dich*. Basically, the last-named works take up again a very old form, the *cantus firmus* variation. Eduard Grell, an older pupil of Zelter's and a contemporary of Mendelssohn's, whose important vocal music is unfairly forgotten today, may have attracted Felix's attention to the great *cantus firmus* style of the motets of Lasso or Victoria. Felix had heard some of them in Italy, and the acquaintance with Baini and Santini, as well as his tireless searching through the

Italian music archives, must have led him to many forgotten motets of the *cinquecento* and *seicento*.

Just before he turned to his "strict" cantatas, Mendelssohn bade farewell to "experimental" writings for the church in his (unpublished) motet *O Lux Beata*, in which we encounter some of the most "tristanlike" progressions before Wagner:

Example 36a

Before we go into some of these works individually, let us give a survey of Mendelssohn's sacred music from the years 1830-33.

Chorale Cantatas (for soli, chorus and orchestra) on the following chorales: *Vom Himmel Hoch; Ach Gott, vom Himmel sieh' darein; Christe, du Lamm Gottes; O Haupt voll Blut und Wunden; Wir glauben all an einen Gott.* None of them has been published, although at least the second (*Acht Gott, vom Himmel*), and the fourth (*O Haupt voll Blut*) are to be considered mature, fully formed works.

Psalm Cantatas on whole Psalms (for soli, chorus and orchestra): Psalm 115.

Chorale Motets (soli, four- or eight-voiced chorus, *a cappella* or with organ): *Aus tiefer Noth; Mitten wir im Leben sind; Ave Maria;* Three Motets for women's chorus (*Veni domine, non tardare, Laudate pueri, Surrexit pastor bonus*); *Hymn* (for mixed chorus and orchestra): *Verleih uns Frieden gnädiglich.*

PSALM 115

This large-scale work is clearly inspired by Bach's cantata form. It may be assumed that Mendelssohn, who composed the arch-Protestant piece "defiantly," as it were, in Rome, originally set it to the Latin text. This supposition is based on the somewhat faulty declamation of the German text. The declamation becomes beautiful and natural as soon as one underlays the music with the Latin text:

Example 36b

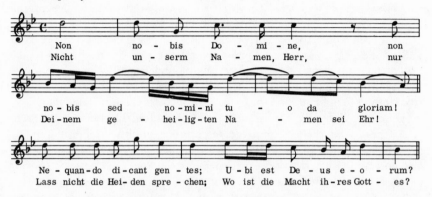

Or, even more clearly, in the countertheme of the opening fugue:[12]
Example 36c

The work begins with a powerful double fugue, which, in a strangely excited tone, simultaneously gives thanks and disputes with God. A fanatical seriousness, such as we find otherwise only in *Elijah*, dominates the whole piece. Even the following, somewhat sentimental duet in 6/8 cannot wipe out the vision which has been summoned up. In chorale-like, lapidary rhythms the eight-voiced chorus declaims: *Die Toten werden Dich nicht loben, Herr* (The dead praise not the Lord). This leads to a monumental ending.

It was soon pointed out that Mendelssohn's own church music is rather under the aegis of Handel than that of Bach. Kretzschmar even sees Mendelssohn's model in the psalms of Marcello.[13] In any case, models have always been looked for. But Moritz Hauptmann already pointed out that Mendelssohn knew (with the exception of Handel) no model which he could have imitated with profit. When we study his teacher Zelter's miserable efforts

along these lines and, in addition, look into some of the North German composers of the eighteenth century, we still find nothing that could have served
Felix as a model; perhaps a slight influence by Reichardt's psalms and hymns
may be conjectured.

In Psalm 115, we already find all the strong and weak points of the
master's sacred music. The following general observations are valid for all
of his church music; for while his technique and artistic conception of sacred
music did change, his power of expression never changed. His greatest weakness in this area lies in the complete lack of understanding of all mystical-
transcendental experience. He knew this himself. He had already written
from Italy: "I could not find the tone of the incomprehensible, the unearthly;
it's good enough for me if it has understandable and earthly beauty."[14] Reverence, fear of God, the sense of praise, of gratitude, of bitter complaints and of
pride in one's faith, all these lay in his personality; but he could comprehend
and portray neither mystical experience nor the "cry of creature" (*Schrei
der Kreatur*). Might we sense here the effects of the world of ideas of his
father and grandfather? Be that as it may, Mendelssohn was never untrue
to the rationalistic theology of Protestantism, as expounded by Schleiermacher.

His greatest strength lies in the choruses, which serve to express hymnic
praise, love of God, and religious indignation. These choruses express the
devotion of the Christian trusting in God.

He has great respect for the Biblical Word; but he permits himself all
too frequent repetitions of words or sentences. The extensions caused by this
heighten the artistic effect, but contradict the truly liturgical spirit. In spite
of all his critical gifts, Mendelssohn never understood or even recognized
the difference between liturgical and sacred music. He generally lumps
together all works of a sacred nature as "church music," or *Geistliche Musik*,
no matter whether they are to serve the real church or an ideal one. That
is the principal reason, aside from lesser practical considerations, why his
music was never accepted as truly liturgical. Even later, when he was of a
mind to make concessions to Lutheran neo-orthodoxy, his *a cappella* choral
music intended for the Berlin Cathedral Choir fell on barren ground, this seed
never grew. Mendelssohn himself soon recognized the fruitlessness of his
efforts. In 1835, he wrote to his spiritual adviser and friend, Pastor Bauer:

A real church music, that is, for the Evangelical service . . . seems impossible
to me. This is not only because I cannot see at what point of the service
the music should begin to function, but also because I simply cannot imagine
this point . . . Up till now I do not know . . . how it is to be brought
about that music should become an integral part of the service, and not
merely a more or less edifying concert.[15]

In the concert hall, however, his Psalm 115 will always enthrall and uplift the listeners, perhaps even fill them with enthusiasm.

AUS TIEFER NOTH

As we observed above, Mendelssohn here returns to the classical chorale motet of the Renaissance. In contrast to Bach's motets, which use the chorale more for "interpretation" of the Biblical text, or dispense with the chorale altogether, here the chorale, note for note, forms the basis of the work.[16] Also in its choral texture and structure, *Aus tiefer Noth* differs from Bach's type; the counterpoints of the chorale themes change in every strophe, but the *cantus* itself remains almost unchanged. Such treatment harks back to earlier models, perhaps the late Netherlanders or the Roman school of the sixteenth century. Mendelssohn differs from these models in his very fluent and yet harmony-bound polyphony. The limitation to four-voiced *a cappella* chorus, in conjunction with the *cantus firmus* technique, made a transparent linear style mandatory. Indeed, one might cite the work as a model of pure counterpoint from the late Baroque, for passages like this scarcely corresponded to the harmonic language of Mendelssohn's musical environment:

Example 37

This is a matter of conscious archaizing, a tendency which has always clung to church music and which was always dear to devotees of that movement which is, however vaguely, termed Romanticism.

There is no doubt that Mendelssohn took the chorale very seriously. Here, too, we sense the influence of his father, who still wrote to him in 1835: "One should not trifle with the chorale."[17] That was a rule which young Mendelssohn never broke; only later did he allow himself occasional liberties in the citation of the chorale. When Felix wrote the motet, he first inquired from Zelter whether it would be all right to lengthen the first note of the chorale![18] Unfortunately, Felix observed the Phrygian character of the piece only in a single strophe; the others are in pure minor.

MITTEN WIR IM LEBEN SIND

This motet was composed at almost the same time as the foregoing piece. It is conceived for eight-voiced chorus with organ, and is of far greater worth than its sister motet. The piece, with its austere power, has the effect of a medieval woodcut. Deliberately, it turns away from the tonal language of the early nineteenth century. The work was written in Rome (again "for spite," as it were). Mendelssohn was certainly well aware of its value.[19] It is rather antiphonal than polyphonic. The text is divided between male and female choruses, and only towards the erd of the first two strophes does adroit imitative work enhance the effect. However, the last strophe is basically a homophonic chorale, set in lapidary style.

AVE MARIA *for eight-voiced chorus*

In contrast to the antiphonal technique of the motet *Mitten wir im Leben sind,* Mendelssohn experiments, in the *Ave Maria,* with responsorial forms, and finally unites both types in the Three Motets for women's chorus. Since we shall often have to speak of these formal principles, a short explanation may eliminate possible misunderstandings which often occur. A responsorial piece sets off one or two soloists against the whole chorus; the latter "responds" to them. In the antiphonal form, we find, not a soloist, but two choruses which alternate with each other. The contrast is even more intensified when one choral group is small, the other large.

The *Ave Maria* is a skillfully written, but excessively "sweet" piece. It was evidently conceived as a pilgrimage song; the tune of the solo singer is repeated, line for line, by the chorus. Not until the end, at the "Sancta Maria," does Mendelssohn go over to antiphonal technique; he separates the male and female choruses, and ends the piece in polyphony of the grand style. The beginning motif (from the Gregorian tradition of the *Magnificat*):

Example 38

Ave Maria, gratia plena!

contains a favorite turn of phrase of the composer. This already occurred in the middle section of Psalm 115. Often, especially in the *Lobgesang*, it becomes an obsession, particularly since the composer, for whom it doubtless had a personal significance, often harmonizes it identically.

THREE MOTETS FOR WOMEN'S CHORUS

Of the three motets for the nuns of *Trinità dei Monti*, Nos. 2 and 3 are noteworthy. In the second, *Laudate pueri*, Mendelssohn uses the Gregorian antiphon *Assumpta est* as the basis of the composition, and works it into a delicate polyphonic fabric. The third of the motets, *Surrexit pastor bonus*, crowns the whole work. Here a solo quartet is set off against the chorus and the text is performed antiphonally. Mendelssohn remained close to the meaning of the text, and turned the beginning into a pastorale of the "good shepherd." The following duet, "Tulerunt dominum meum," is, as Mendelssohn's solo movements often are, a bit too sentimental, though the euphony of the whole piece is entrancing. The hymnic ending, sung by all voices, is expressive; but it remains on the earthly plane and does not approach heavenly regions, as the text "Surrexit spes mea" demands.

ACH GOTT, VOM HIMMEL SIEH' DAREIN

Of the unpublished cantatas, we can speak only briefly as copies or photocopies are only obtainable with great difficulty. (Here, I must thank Dr. Köhler of the *Deutsche Staatsbibliothek* [formerly *Preussische Staatsbibliothek*], Professor Dr. H. Chr. Wolff of the University of Leipzig, and Max F. Schneider of the *Internationale Felix Mendelssohn-Gesellschaft* for their kind helpfulness, without which I could not have become acquainted with these works.[20]

This unjustly neglected work is the most important of the five unpublished chorale cantatas. As Rudolf Werner already emphasized, these works grant us "the fullest insight into Mendelssohn's attitude to the Protestant chorale."[21] In a brilliant analysis, the author points out the dilemma inherent in the chorale cantata: the composer must do violence either to the text of the chorale or to its musical line, that is, he may either insert recitatives or arias on new texts, or leave the text untouched and set stanzas of the chorale for solo voices or use freely invented choruses. The conflict lies in the evaluation of the chorale melody in contrast with the chorale text.

Schweitzer formulated the problem even more forcefully and comprehensively. Since the abovementioned duality was inherent in the structure of the chorale cantata, with which every composer had to deal according to his inclination and understanding, Schweitzer's words on Bach are valid for Mendelssohn also:

> Strictly speaking, this form of cantata is a mere medley, since a strophic song is not in place in the text of a work with solo pieces The whole species invites the criticism that a new patch does not suit an old garment. . . .[22]

In all of his chorale cantatas, Mendelssohn chose to preserve the integrity of the text rather than that of the melody. In the cantatas *Christe, du Lamm Gottes* and *Wir glauben all,* he dispensed with all additions which did not belong to the chorale. In the others, he took a few liberties with the chorale melody (never the text!) and inserted "free" solo pieces on chorale or Bible verses. Basically, therefore, he follows the structure of Bach's later cantatas.[23] He carefully avoids recitatives on chorale texts, unconsciously following the principle of J. A. Hiller, who had expressed the viewpoint that "one should entirely dispense with the recitative style."[24]

By far the strongest and best section of the cantata, *Ach Gott, vom Himmel sieh' darein,* is without a doubt the opening chorus, which uses the chorale lines 1-4. Already the beginning, with its harsh dissonances, its constant chromaticism which never becomes excessively sentimental, is far indeed from all other works of that period. In contrast to the old melody, the harmonization is positively revolutionary, and foreshadows chords from *Tristan*:

Example 39

Amid the close-knit polyphony, the chorale then enters powerfully; for the fourth strophe, Mendelssohn constructs his own chorale, which is conceived according to older patterns. There follows an aria (C sharp minor, ¾), preceded by a recitative (which was written later); it offers the desired contrast to the closing figured chorale of the last strophe. This, interrupted by triplet motifs and accompanied by the full orchestra, ends with a strict Phrygian cadence.

The aria, which one might rather call a spiritual song, is infelicitous in its declamation and otherwise not noteworthy in its invention. Only the opening chorus is on the level of a masterwork, and is distinctly worthy of publication.

HYMN: VERLEIH UNS FRIEDEN GNÄDIGLICH

Of all Mendelssohn's church compositions, this piece, as anemic as it is well-sounding, most distinctly betrays the influence of the contemporary "Nazarene" painters. The piece, a modest four-voiced chorus, set with refined simplicity, is accompanied by the full orchestra.

Example 40

The discrepancy between the somewhat insipid thematic material, *Verleih' uns Frieden gnädiglich, Herr Gott zu unsern Zeiten* and the rich background is striking, and hurts the piece; its style would be purest with a simple organ accompaniment. Schumann, however, was of quite a different opinion; let us give free rein to his enthusiasm:

A uniquely beautiful composition, of whose effectiveness one can hardly form an idea after merely looking at the score. The little piece deserves to be world-famous, and will be in future; Madonnas of Raphael and Murillo cannot remain hidden for long.[25]

Later, with wise insight, Mendelssohn entrusted all such "sacred verses" to the *a cappella* choir exclusively. Without question, this is the most suitable medium.

INSTRUMENTAL MUSIC

1. *Hebrides* Overture ("Fingal's Cave")
2. Reformation Symphony in D minor
3. Piano Concerto in G minor
4. Songs without Words, first volume (Nos. 1-6)

The Hebrides Overture

For a long time, this overture has been recognized as a high point of Mendelssohn's art. Even Felix's arch-enemy, Richard Wagner, characterized it as "one of the most beautiful works of music that we have."[26] He had good reason to value it highly! Not a little of its mood and sound turned up effectively again in *The Flying Dutchman*.

We have already mentioned the three different versions of the work. In its themes and tone-color, the "silly middle section" was inconsistent with the sound of the original conception: strange, for those days almost exotic. Paradoxically enough, Felix wrote the famous first theme of the work shortly *before* he visited "Fingal's Cave."[27] It is significant for the psychology of the creative artist that he left his first two versions alone for nearly three years before he undertook the radical alterations of the final version.[28] These alterations seem to have caused him a great deal of trouble; for Moscheles, to whom he gave the old Roman score of the work, remarks with admiration that "his things, already in the first version, seemed so beautiful and well-rounded that I could not conceive of any change, and we discussed this point again today. However, he stuck to his decision to change it. . . ."[29]

The "sense of space" which so noticeably characterizes this work has often been pointed out. The representation of wide space in music was not successfully achieved by many composers—not even by Debussy in *La Mer*. In this respect, we may detect certain similarities between the Prelude of the third act of *Tristan* and the present work. Here, we cannot go into the esthetic problem of how one recreates a landscape musically. Suffice it to say that the rich modulations, the free rhythm, and the ceaselessly changing colors certainly contribute to the impression of a bleak and agitated sea, under a wide and empty sky.

Yet, the principal theme is neither spacious nor long-breathed, but short and pregnant. Felix's mastery shows itself in the way that he recognized the good qualities, but also the weaknesses of the theme. He avoided tiresome repetitions in three ways: 1) through the introduction of autonomous countersubjects against the theme; 2) through a broad-winged second theme; 3) through strongly modulating variations, e.g., the great G major episode of the development.

The success of the piece was assured after the première (London, 1832). Even the distinctly cooler Berliners judged the Overture with good will and not without respect. But precisely the freedom of thematic workmanship, which gives the Overture its imperishable charm, was misunderstood or even blamed by the German critics. Rellstab, whose attitude was certainly benevolent, wrote about it, in closing: "Many details surprise; structure, flow, form, in the customary sense of the word, are hard to follow. Perhaps the mistake of the composition is simply that it needs a commentary."[30]

Reformation Symphony

Today, it is hard to read Rellstab's review of this work without an ironic smile. Here, let us simply quote the statements from it which seem most striking today:

> We should like it better if the composer did not insist so much on colossal features, as beautiful as they may be; if he did not orchestrate so over-richly; and, finally, if he gave melody precedence over the beauties of daringly combined harmony. Too, he rarely shows us smiling heavens; it is nearly always stormy and thundery.[31]

The composer himself had nothing good to say about this work. His sharply self-critical observations on it are numerous. He calls its first movement "a fat bristly animal." Fanny used to say, "It's a cross animal, and there's something strange about it."[32] Later he "cannot stand it any more, would rather burn it than any other of my pieces; it should never come out."[33] He caps the climax with the words, "a complete misfit."[34] In truth, he never intended this piece for publication. Is such a harsh judgment justified by the facts, or are there reasons unknown to the composer himself which caused him to damn his own symphonic work? Music history teaches us not to take the self-judgment of an artist too seriously, since he often lacks distance from his own work. So it seems to be in this case, for this symphony is one of the few works of Mendelssohn which have risen in public favor during the last thirty years. Of course, this can never be the decisive criterion for the worth (or lack of it) of a work of art; but purely objective analysis, too, shows long stretches of brilliant inventiveness. From the formal standpoint, the Reformation Symphony may be placed beside Berlioz' *Harold in Italy* as a cyclic structure.

It appears that Felix's feelings toward the work were negative for two reasons: first, he had suffered a severe loss of prestige with it in Paris because it was not performed, and second, at least in the first movement, he had tried a wild experiment in instrumentation of which he was probably ashamed afterwards. We hear from Devrient that the composer, without even sketching principal motifs or leading voices, orchestrated the first movement measure by measure from top to bottom.[35] In fact, many passages of the movement sound a bit rough and demand careful dynamic retouches on the part of the conductor. This experiment bears witness to Mendelssohn's incredible power of memory, but also to his somewhat childish joy in this virtuosity. Even as the later Mendelssohn damned public improvisation at the piano (except for cadenzas of concerti), so, too, he probably condemned this *par force* experiment, for both artistic and moral reasons. For him, the latter were decisive. In view of this contradictory judgment of the symphony, we consider it necessary to pick out its most important elements, at the risk of having to go into technical musical questions from time to time.

Fifty years ago the inner unity of the symphony was defended. A. Heuss and W. Tappert, approaching it from different directions, proved that the first three movements grew from a common germ-motif, the so-called "Dresden Amen."[36] The following observations are partially based on these studies.

The first movement consists of two parts: a slow introduction in D major and a fiery Allegro, 2/2, in D minor, which are thematically interrelated. The introduction works with Mendelssohn's favorite turn of phrase, the psalmodic beginning,

Example 41

the *Magnificat* of the Third Tone, whose basic motif also belongs to the *Nunc dimittis* and other canticles. The introduction, developed in a fugato, ends with the "Dresden Amen," a formula known to many church musicians.

Example 42

The phrase is familiar to us through Wagner's *Parsifal* where it is the Grail motif. As Tappert proved, it was considered, in the Saxon liturgy, as a symbol of the Holy Ghost. Now, a more suitable motto for a Reformation Symphony can hardly be imagined. From this motif of the stepwise-rising fifth, there arose the principal theme of the first movement, which contains this characteristic interval as the skip of a fifth.

Example 43a

Also, the second theme is derived from the germ-motif; at the end of the exposition, we even meet the principal motif of the *Hebrides* Overture:

Example 43b

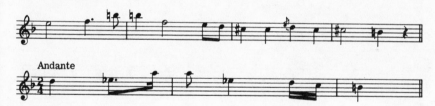

and the coda transforms the basic motif with syncopation:

Example 43c

The second movement (Scherzo, B-flat major, ¾) includes only fragments of the "Amen" (in the Trio):

Example 43d

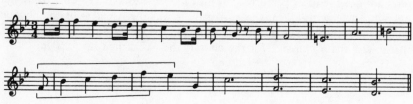

The third movement (Andante, G minor, 2/4) is set for strings alone, to heighten the contrast with the following Finale. It brings in the "Amen" in a variant (second theme of first movement); in addition, it contains a beautiful instrumental recitative. Without pause, there follows the fourth movement (G major, 4/4). An unaccompanied flute now intones the chorale *Ein veste Burg*, the first verse of which is immediately developed in fugato fashion. The transition to the second theme and this theme itself are flabby, almost vulgar. The development deals with the second verse of the chorale and culminates once more in a fugato. In this, the brass ensemble, including three trombones, blares forth the chorale as *cantus firmus*. Unfortunately, Mendelssohn allowed himself to be seduced into a brilliant coda, which paraphrases a motif of *Der Freischütz* and then brings the work to a rather noisy end in *tutti*:

Example 44a

Example 44b

Even the peroration, the chorale in whole notes, cannot help out the weaknesses of the last movement. But this does not mean that the symphony does not deserve to be performed! Three movements are well-conceived and bubbling over with inventiveness. Again, it was the problem of the chorale which Mendelssohn failed to solve, as also in the cantatas. We shall later see that it was the preference for the chorale that weakened his *St. Paul*.

G *minor Piano Concerto*

It is unnecessary to go into all of the details of this well-known and beloved work. The cyclic ideas (resumption of second theme, reminiscence of middle movement, etc., in the Finale), the absence of pauses and orchestral ritornelli, etc., are so striking and at the same time so out-of-the-way for the period that they called forth well-merited attention and endless imitation. Yet, it seems that the time for these innovations was overdue; for even such a conservative critic as Rellstab found nothing to object to in them. His criticisms were limited to the "predominance of the orchestra over the fortepiano" in the first movement.[37] The idea that the fanfares which lead from the first to the second movement should also fulfill the same function before the third movement obviously seemed organic or at least "sound" to him; at least, he wasted no words on this brilliant detail—neither he nor any of his contemporaries.

In addition to these well-known facts, let us emphasize two characteristic elements of the present work: the weakness of the slow movement and the trim structure of the whole work. Beethoven's slow movements are varied hymns; Mozart's and Schubert's are, basically, quiet sonata forms or simple aria forms with or without *da capo*, sometimes also leaning towards variation form. The slow movement of the G minor Concerto really belongs to none of these categories; it is a "Song without Words" with *concertante* figurations. It possesses neither the long, quiet breath of a Beethoven middle movement nor the seemingly refined simplicity of a Mozart or even Schubert one—though it does display the outward elegance of the latter. Only in several of his chamber music works did Mendelssohn succeed in writing broad, deeply felt and organically flowing Adagios. This was an innate defect of most composers in the post-Beethovenian era. Only in exceptional cases did they succeed in writing a good slow movement. The mature Brahms and Bruckner are again masters of this art.

On the other hand, we must admire the power which can draw the entire thematic material of an extended sonata movement out of two themes. These, indeed, are formed in sharp contrast to one another and are introduced in dramatic fashion. When we consider that the Concerto was tossed off in a few days, we can understand the respect, but also the envy of Mendelssohn's brothers in art who had not been so richly favored by the Muse.[38]

Songs without Words

In 1839, Mendelssohn writes to the publisher Simrock:

But they are not Songs without Words [that he is planning to write].

I do not plan to publish anything more of that sort, let the Hamburgers say what they will. If there were too many of these creatures on the face of the earth, nobody would like them any more. And really, such a mass of piano music of this kind is composed today; one should try something different, I think![39]

Should we regret that he did not remain true to this resolution? Opinions on this are divided. But it is not true that connoisseurs are on one side and amateurs on the other; whether one scorns or loves the *Songs without Words* has nothing to do with one's technical musical knowledge. It is very difficult to achieve impartial judgment, for most music-lovers of older generations have strong personal associations with the individual pieces. Perhaps the younger generation today (in Germany, at any rate) will have a clearer judgment since Mendelssohn was forbidden during their childhood or, at least, looked at askance.

However, we shall try to seek out the historic, stylistic, personal, and cultural conditions determining the nature of the *Songs without Words;* then we can answer questions of musical esthetics in general and in particular.

The name "Song without Words" is first found in a letter from Fanny to Klingemann in 1828. She says: "Felix gave me three things: a piece for my album—a Song without Words, of which he has written some very lovely ones recently—another piano piece . . . and a big work, a piece for four choruses . . . [*Hora est*]"[40]

This shows plainly that the name originally meant the same as "Album Leaf"; that is how it was understood by Fanny. Only later did the name "Song without Words" serve as a cover for all manner of musical and unmusical impulses. Such an album leaf always had an especially intimate character which linked it closely, artistically and humanly speaking, with the person to whom it was dedicated. In this connection it is significant that, of the six volumes that appeared during Mendelssohn's lifetime (the other two are posthumous), five bear dedications, all to ladies of the elegant world: Elise von Woringen, Rosa von Woringen, Sophy Horsley, Clara Schumann, and Sophie Rosen, Klingemann's fiancée. Thus, the pieces are principally intended for "the ladies," as Mendelssohn made clear in an unpublished letter to Fanny.

In shape and mood, the pieces are highly differentiated. Formally, however, all forty-eight are transformations of one and the same principle: that of the closed ternary form ABA. Here, B is not to be understood as an entirely new idea, but as a continuation of A. In this framework, the manner of the retransition from B to A naturally plays an especially important role. Long before Felix's time, there had been piano pieces in this form; some of Beethoven's *Bagatelles* seem to have served him directly as models. Probably, he hardly knew Schubert's *Moments musicaux;* they conform in principle to the same artistic idea of the small, intimate, closed "cabinet piece." Admirable, and completely different from the *Bagatelles,* is the detailed individualization of each *Song without Words,* in spite of the strict unity of their formal type.

Partial as Schumann was to all kinds of miniature pieces, he knew exactly where to draw the dividing line between aimless improvisation and strict form:

> Who has not sometimes, at twilight, sat at the piano and, while improvising, unconsciously sung a soft melody? Now if, by chance, one can link the accompaniment with the melody in one's hands alone, and if, most of all, one is a Mendelssohn, there come forth the most beautiful Songs without Words. . . .[41]

This charming *causerie* best characterizes the Biedermeier nature of the *Songs without Words.* Here we find hints of poetic mood, sophisticated form, respectable attitude (no wild passion or hot eroticism), a certain intimacy, and maybe, too, a good dose of sentimentality. All this applies to these pieces. Here are the strengths and weaknesses of all Biedermeier art—in its means, its expression, and in the emotional realm it was strictly limited. But, on the other hand, in every bourgeois home there was a music-loving daughter (or one who had been forced into music). To this Biedermeier bourgeoisie, the far-reaching individualization of the *Songs without Words* was extremely welcome; the many nicknames (not Mendelssohn's own) of at least twenty-eight Songs testify to this. No wonder such popularity summoned up flocks of imitators! As we have seen, Mendelssohn was well aware of this; he recognized, too, that "too many of these creatures" would spoil the whole type for the public. How right he was![42]

From the first two volumes, let us briefly analyze some of the characteristic pieces; in a way, these are prototypes from which most of the *Songs without Words* deviate but slightly. Schumann already recognized and identified these four types.[43]

Vol. I, No. 1. This delightful piece ("Sweet Remembrance") belong to the first of the four categories which we find in the *Songs without Words.* These are as follows: 1) solo melody, surrounded by homophonic broken chords; 2) imaginary duet with similar accompaniment; 3) chorale-like, compact melody, harmonized in chorale style, occasionally interrupted by slight figuration; 4) pianistic "character piece" without imaginary voices or chorus. The form of No. 1—in most pieces, of great charm and deceptive simplicity—may be described as follows:

A: 2 measures of introduction; 4 + 9 measures of principal melody, which culminates in the dominant. B: 4 + 1 + 8 measures of slightly contrasting, modulatory continuation of the principal idea. A: 4 + 8 + 1 + 3, varied repetition of the principal idea; coda, on a quiet tonic pedal-point, 5 measures. The melody moves mainly in quarter-notes, and, in the last section, is sometimes varied by eighth-note passages. The harmony is simple, most varied in B, where it modulates slightly; the rhythm is often somewhat too monotonous, but this does no great harm in view of the brevity of the piece.

No. 9 ("Consolation") belongs to the third category, the imaginary choral song. Its form is as follows: 2½ measures of introduction; A, 4 + 4, principal idea; B, 4 + 2, continuation in the dominant; A¹, 4 + 1 + 1 + 2, repetition of A with climax; 3 measures of postlude (= introduction). The melody is compactly harmonized, moving in quarter-notes and eighth-notes; the rhythm is hardly ever varied.

No. 6 ("Venetian Gondolier's Song") is one of the three barcarolles, which, alas, were so often imitated by incapable hands.[44] The pieces is noteworthy for its charm of sound, which, paradoxically, is caused by the sparseness of its chordal structure. Nowhere does Mendelssohn surpass a three- to four-voiced setting; the piece begins with three voices and ends, *con due pedale*, with two:

Example 45

Form: A, 7 measures (!) of "motto" or "call"; 4 + 6, principal idea; B, 8 measures of continuation + 1 of retransition; A, 4 + 1 + 7 "motto." In its way, it is a real gem of intimate music, comparable only with Chopin's Preludes.

No. 24, the crown of all the *Songs without Words,* is a highly original pianistic *tour de force.* In it, the modesty of the thematic-melodic material stands in starkest contrast to the brilliant and complex harmony which fills the piece. Already in the first measure (*Molto allegro vivace,* 6/8, A major) "the rule is set and then followed." From the very beginning, the middle voice of each chord resolves into its feverishly pulsing lower minor second. At the climax, where this is doubled, very sharp dissonances are produced:

Example 46

This idea stimulated three generations of composers for the piano, from Liszt to Bartók. Such *tours de force* are scarcely expected in the *Songs without Words,* so often dismissed as "all-too-innocent"! And, indeed, this is practically the only one of its kind.

Form: Rondo-like; A, 8 + 8, principal idea; B, 8 + 8, continuation; A¹, 8 + 8, variation (principally harmonic) of A; B¹, 8 + 8, variation of B; A, 8 + 8, return of the theme, B², 8 + 8, strongly varied version of B; cadencing crescendo, which leads to a dramatic high point (with the dissonances), 1 + 1 + 1 + 1 + 4; coda, 4 + 1 + 4 + 4 + 1 + 4 + 2 measures of postlude. The eight-measure regularity of the melodic-rhythmic structure is most cleverly interrupted three times by means of extensions or repetitions. Toward the end, the dissonant changing tones resolve into a quiet bass trill, but right at the end the composer does not deny himself a daring, witty, and yet thoroughly logical "point."

Do we not seem to hear the faint echoes of King Mark's hunting horns in the prelude to the second act of *Tristan?* This ending is highly piquant, and was a bold stroke not merely in pieces of lighter nature, but anywhere!

Example 47

Very soon after their appearance, the *Songs without Words* caused esthetic controversies. These should not be taken too seriously, but do mirror the Classic-Romantic conflict. In connection with Mendelssohn's own esthetic credo, we shall later return to these controversies and the discussion caused by them.

$\mathcal{N}$*otes*

1. A. Schering, *Geschichte des Instrumentalkonzerts* (Leipzig, 1905), p. 189.

2. *Moscheles Correspondence* (Leipzig, 1888), pp. 65-66.

3. According to the information of Prof. K. Heinemann in the Goethe edition of the *Bibliographisches Institut*, Leipzig and Vienna, Vol. I, pp. 377, 393, 394.

4. Bode, *Die Tonkunst in Goethes Leben*, Vol. I, p. 235.

5. *Goethe-Zelter Correspondence*, letter of September 21, 1799.

6. *Ibid.*, letter of December 12, 1802.

7. *Ibid.*, letter of November 18-21, 1812.

8. *Ibid.*, letter of December 3, 1812. In the meantime, investigation has revealed Goethe's sources. They were Honemann's *Altertümer des Harzes* (Vol. I, 1754-55), and *Archiv der Zeit* (December, 1796).

9. Einstein, *Music in the Romantic Era* (New York, 1947), p. 174.

10. F. W. Riemer, *Mitteilungen über Goethe* (1841), Vol. II, pp. 611ff.

Felix wrote Goethe about his enthusiasm: "Permit me to express to you my thanks for the heavenly words . . . one hardly needs to make music to them, for the music is already there, everything already sings; I always sang the verses to myself without thinking about it." (In a letter to Goethe for his birthday, August 28, published in *Jahrbruecher der Goethe-Gesellschaft*, XII, p. 98.)

11. Hensel, *F.M.*, I, p. 343ff.

12. Wolff maintains that Mendelssohn composed the work on the Latin *Vulgate Text*. Felix, too, mentions the Psalm by its Latin title. (Letter of November 16, 1830.) The autograph has the Latin text in ink, the German written under it in pencil.

13. Kretzschmar, *Führer durch den Konzertsaal*, 4th ed. (Berlin, 1921), II, p. 434.

14. Letter of April 4, 1831.

15. Letter to Pastor Bauer, January 12, 1835.

16. The lost Latin motets of Bach cannot have used the chorale, for a Gregorian *cantus* would have probably been found offensive by the authorities. See Spitta, *Bach*, Vol. II, pp. 429-443.

17. Letter from Abraham to Felix Mendelssohn, March 10, 1835.

18. Letter to Zelter, December 18, 1830. Rudolf Werner points out that Bach cites the chorale in just the same way as Felix.

19. Letter of November 23, 1830. "The Chorale *Mitten wir im Leben sind* . . . is probably one of the best church pieces that I have done."

20. We also urgently recommend Rudolf Werner's useful work *Felix Mendelssohn als Kirchenmusiker* (Frankfurt, 1930-31).

21. R. Werner, *op. cit.*, p. 65.

22. Schweitzer, *J. S. Bach* (London, 1923), Vol. I, pp. 80ff.

23. See also Spitta, *J. S. Bach*, Vol. II, pp. 285ff.

24. J. A. Hiller, *Beyträge zu wahrer Kirchenmusik*, 2nd ed. (Leipzig, 1791), p. 7.

25. Schumann, *Gesammelte Schriften*, Vol. III, p. 40.

26. *Gesammelte Schriften*, X, p. 149.

27. On the different versions and manuscripts of the *Hebrides*, see G. Kinsky, *Heyer Musikhistorisches Museum*, IV, p. 332; also G. Abraham, in the *Monthly Musical Record*, September, 1948, and, finally, the *Amerbach-Bote* (Almanach 1949, pp. 140ff.) According to the latter, there are even four versions; however, the last two are nearly identical.

28. He still writes his family from Paris on January 21, 1832; "I cannot present the *Hebrides* here, because I do not consider it . . . ready. The D major middle section is very silly. The whole so-called development tastes more of counterpoint than of whale-oil and seagulls and cod-liver oil, and it ought to be the other way around."

29. *Aus Moscheles' Leben* (letters and diaries), May 1, 1832. In Felix's unpublished letter to his mother of November 28, 1833 (Düsseldorf), he says, "In the last days I have made the score of the *Hebrides* ready for publication. The Overture became much better through *threefold revisions*. . . ."

30. Rellstab, *Gesammelte Schriften*, Neue Folge, VIII, p. 217.

31. *Ibid.*, pp. 212-213.

32. Klingemann *Correspondence*, pp. 82-83.

33. Letter to Rietz of June 20, 1838.

34. Letter to Rietz of April 13, 1841.

35. Devrient, *Erinnerungen an Felix Mendelssohn* (Leipzig, 1891), pp. 92-93.

36. See Dr. A. Heuss, "Das Dresdener Amen," *Signale*, 1904, p. 201; also W. Tappert, "Das Gralthema aus Wagners Parsifal," *Musikalisches Wochenblatt*, 1903, No. 31-2.

37. Rellstab, *Gesammelte* Schriften, X, p. 213.

38. Not many colleagues were as free from envy as Schumann, who wrote about the Concerto· "Then you should have seen Meritis [Schumann's nickname for Mendelssohn] play the Mendelssohn Concerto! He sat down as innocently as a child at the piano; now he enthralled one heart after the other and had them all flocking after him, and when he let them go, we knew only that we had flown by a number of Greek islands of the Gods. . . ." (R. Schumann, *Schriften über Musik*, Vol. I, "An Chiara.")

39. Letter to Simrock, March 4, 1839.

40. Hensel, *F.M.*, Vol. I.

41. Schumann, *Schriften über Musik*, Vol. I, "Felix Mendelssohn, Sechs Lieder ohne Worte (zweites Heft)."

42. *Ibid.*, Vol. II, p. 227. Therefore Schumann had to exclaim: "Finally a volume of *real* Songs without Words!" (In contrast to the many imitations.)

43. *Ibid.*

44. H. Tischler ("Mendelssohn's Songs without Words," *Musical Quarterly*, 1947, p. 15) is in error when he concludes, from the similarity of the "Gondolier's Song" No. 29 to No. 6, that there is no development in Mendelssohn's style after 1832. Certainly not in the *Songs without Words!* But this form was already "set" and not capable of development. One could as well say that Beethoven's style did not develop between the *Bagatelles* and the *Rage over a Lost Penny*.

CHAPTER XI

Berlin Rejects,
Europe Invites

A prophet is without honor in his own country.

I

DURING his great journey, Felix had tasted and enjoyed freedom. He had met important people, and he had followed the musical, literary, artistic, and political trends of the time with alert senses. Finally, he had been in Paris and London, the centers of Western civilization. In contrast with their turbulent drive, Berlin must have seemed provincial and small to him. Nonetheless he was resolved to see and find his mission in Germany. So he began to adjust himself to the narrower *milieu* of his family, his friends, and the *Singakademie*.

Here we remember that serious letter of November 13, 1831 (see Chapter IX) which Felix had written in Frankfurt, and in which he doubts that he has enough authority for a music directorship. Already at that time he was very skeptical about Berlin as a possible domain for his activities; but, for the sake of peace, he added, "for naturally I'd rather remain . . . where you are, but I must be able to work."

Meanwhile, Zelter had died, and there was fierce competition to succeed him in the *Singakademie*. From the very beginning, Felix had resisted *becoming a candidate* for this position. If it were offered to him, he would accept it, even if he had to share the authority of the directorship with Rungenhagen. He was firmly convinced that his standpoint was the right one—but he had not reckoned with the powers of persuasion of his family, his friends, and, above all, with the decisive mandate of his father. So, against his inmost convictions, he let himself be prodded into becoming a formal candidate for the directorship of the *Singakademie*. He regretted the error; it induced the severest trauma of his life. The wound in Felix's soul never healed fully, and the unpleasant consequences for the family did not cease even after his death.

From the moment that he became a candidate, Felix grew bitter, sarcastic, and cross; and his creative power seemed to dwindle. His letters faithfully reflect this state of affairs. First, it turned out that the opera libretto on Shakespeare's *Tempest* which Immermann had promised was completely unfit for use. Felix had the unpleasant task of sending the work back to the poet. How he did it, we do not know; but it must have been a masterpiece of diplomacy, for Immermann, who was well-known to be haughty and vain, seems not to have held the rejection against Felix.[1] In August, 1832, he already feels that he has no real chance to be chosen as Zelter's successor; and his letters become very troubled, for instance, the one to Pastor Bauer, in which he calls the Fall of 1832 "the bitterest time which he can imagine and which he has ever experienced."[2] The saddest thing is a letter to Klingemann in which Mendelssohn tries to explain his condition to himself:

> . . . for several weeks I have been so unspeakably depressed and in such a bad mood that I cannot describe it to you. . . . The death of beautiful Mrs. Robert took away a whole piece of my youth; I, too, was physically unwell and still am, suffered terribly from pains in my ears and, since then, from headaches, but that always goes together; then comes great apathy and indifference in the midst of this excited time, then the whole stagnating Berlin dump, then the dealings about the Academy—with which they torture me more than is decent, in order finally to choose their Rungenhagen or God knows whom. And my poor head, which nothing pleasant can enter—Oh, the devil with the whole time. I never had it so rough.[3]

Nevertheless, he forced himself to work, and what he undertook was not insignificant: three public concerts in Berlin for charitable ends, the edition of Handel's *Solomon*, the *Morning and Evening Service* for the Anglican Church, and, finally, the *Italian Symphony*. In none of these works can we sense his bad mood or "spleen" as Felix often called his condition. Nevertheless, he makes no bones about his scorn for the Berliners' praises of the three successful concerts.[4] And yet, he had no reason to complain about this. Rellstab, then the most influential critic in Berlin, did not fail in praise and recognition, and used expressions which are rather unexpected in the work of this cool and conservative judge; for example, "These three musical evenings (Mendelssohn's concerts) were more significant for art than a whole year of the usual concerts. . . ."[5]

What so discouraged and irritated Felix was the period of uncertainty which lasted from the moment of his return from London to the decisive election of the *Singakademie* on January 22, 1833. As painful and even insulting as the outcome of this was for him, nevertheless afterwards he felt that he had regained his freedom of action.

Meanwhile, a bright ray of light had come from London: on November

5, 1832, the Philharmonic Society had resolved to give Mendelssohn a definitive, very well-paid commission. He was to write for them "a symphony, an overture, and a vocal composition"; the performance rights of the three works would belong to the Philharmonic exclusively for two years. The honorarium was more than £100, in other words, about 720 Rheinthaler (equivalent in buying power to about DM 8000, or $2000). Now Felix feels that "the fog is beginning to lift. . . . See, I have lived through a very bad time . . . but now joy takes it all away."[6] Once more he begins to take up creative work in full force.

There had reached him at this time an invitation from Moscheles to come to London and be godfather to his awaited child. Now he would once more see "the dear, old, smoky nest" (London); and he cared little for the outcome of the *Singakadamie* intrigues. His idealistic zeal for the revival of Handel was ill-repaid by the *Singakademie*. He had been lucky enough to ferret out Handel's original score of *Solomon* and had brought along the copy to Berlin. But the *Singakadamie* could not sing it to the English text, so Felix begged good old Klingemann to whip up a German poetic translation of the text that would fit the music.[7] However, when it arrived, the *Singakademie* had already decided to sing the oratorio in prose, with some bad "improvements" in Handel's instrumentation. Felix reports on this in several unpublished letters to Sir Thomas Attwood and to Moscheles; here, the anger about his and his friend's wasted work is mingled with indignation at the audacity of wanting to correct a Handel score.[8]

Aside from the concerts, Felix, in this "winter of his discontent," appeared also in the concert of the singer Milder, the clarinettist Bärmann, the music director Möser, and also of lesser-known musicians, whom he was always glad to help out. The variety of his repertory as a pianist, the maturity of his compositions were finally recognized and admired outside of England. At this time Leipzig began to take a lively interest in the promising artist. But first, Felix was to undergo two severe challenges to his character and his art. The first came from the *Singakademie*, the second— for which Felix was infinitely thankful—from London.

II

Now, fruitless though the subject may appear, we must deal in more detail with Felix's rejection on the part of the *Singakademie*. Two reasons make the elucidation of the true circumstances indispensable: 1) The almost universal, embarrassed silence of all Mendelssohn biographers, and, indeed, of most of the sources about this event; and 2) the *traumatic* effects on Felix, which were catastrophic for him and of which he was at first unconscious. When a man of Felix's intelligence and maturity writes eight months later: "On earth I have nothing in common with the Berlin *Sing-*

akademie—indeed, nothing anywhere, since it does not exist in Heaven . . ."[9], we feel that he had been stricken to the heart. All attempts at making amends on the part of the *Singakademie* could not heal this painful inner wound.

What are the facts? Of printed source material, there are really only four works: Devrient's memoirs, the Mendelssohn-Klingemann correspondence (both these naturally take Mendelssohn's side), and the two large documented histories of the *Singakademie*, a) the one by M. Blumner, which goes to 1891, and b) the more extensive one by G. Schünemann, which gives a complete account of the development of the institution from its founding till 1941.[10] Besides these, there are unpublished letters of Felix, or papers which were directed to him; these, I could see, while the (unpublished) minutes of the *Singakademie* were not available to me.

As has already been mentioned, Felix—quite against his instinct, his personal wishes, and his completely realistic evaluation of the true state of affairs—allowed himself to be persuaded to become a candidate for the position of director. Immediately, there began a series of bickerings among the parties involved. *Geheimrat* Lichtenstein and Devrient, who took Felix's part, were (as is hinted in personal papers) defamed as propagandists "paid" by Abraham Mendelssohn; other candidates, among them Carl Loewe, declared themselves, but never had a real chance. For its part, the election commission considered C. G. Reissiger from Dresden, F. Mosewius from Breslau, N. Schelble, the director of the Frankfurt *Cäcilienverein*, von Neukomm, and Eduard Grell, who later stepped in for Reissiger; finally, Fr. Schneider from Dessau was also mentioned as a potential candidate. Felix was in agreement with the compromise proposition that he should share the directorial duties with Rungenhagen, the principal candidate of the conservatives; but Rungenhagen flatly rejected this proposition. After this rejection, Felix thought that the election of Rungenhagen as sole director was certain, and was inclined to withdraw his candidacy. Again it was Devrient and Felix's family who dissuaded him from the only right step.

From the very beginning, the argument had been raised that the *Singakademie*, an institute for Christian music, "should not have a Jew-boy imposed on them as director." This, at least, was a clear point against Felix even though he and his family had long been Protestant church members. However, the affair was complicated by certain material interests of the *Singakademie* involving their unusually valuable manuscript collection. For this collection consisted mostly of gifts from Abraham Mendelssohn and Sara Levy, his wife's aunt. Zelter had showed his deep gratitude to Father Mendelssohn for these valuable gifts,[11] and the trustees did not want to be disobliging to generous donors.

While these manuscripts were given to the Academy, the Bach collections of J. Pölchau and even of Zelter had to be purchased. Doris Zelter even went so far as to bring the dispute into court and before the King; she received 1000 *Rheinthaler* from the *Singakademie*.¹² We may well imagine that Mme Levy and Abraham Mendelssohn viewed the decision of the *Singakademie* as a foolish and ungrateful action. Immediately before the election there was a somewhat obscure dispute between Felix and Grell, which turned them into lifelong opponents. From an unpublished letter of Felix's mother it seems that Grell intrigued against Felix behind his back; however, we should not take too much stock in Lea Mendelssohn's gossip.

The final election took place on January 22, 1833, and its result did not surprise Felix, though it certainly did surprise his family and friends. With 148 votes for Rungenhagen and 88 for Mendelssohn, plus 4 for Grell, a clear verdict was given against the "young Jewish musician," as Schünemann calls him (not insignificantly from the viewpoint of the *Singakademie*). If Felix had not become an official candidate, he would have been spared this bitter disappointment, which poisoned Berlin for him the rest of his life. Already before the election, his mistake was clear to him. To his intimate friend Klingemann, he writes, in December, 1832:

> They are still hesitating between Rungenhagen and me, and four months ago I was stupid enough not to beg them right from the start please to leave me unshorn. Now they shear me to their heart's content and ruin my wool in the process; everyone who meets me knows some new bit of gossip.¹³

After the election, the *Singakademie* offered him the post of vice-director. The politeness of Felix's refusal astounds us. From the letters to Klingemann we learn that, for his birthday, he received a few very precious music manuscripts, among them an ". . . almost touching letter from Mozart in which he applies to the Vienna Municipal Council for an unpaid post, and mentions that his musical talents are known abroad. . . ."

This letter made him feel thoughtful, and humble, and so he merely wrote "with polite expressions, that they could go hang themselves."¹⁴ Not long before Mendelssohn's death, the *Singakademie*, which had become wiser through the damage it had sustained at Rungenhagen's hands as well as because of Felix's world fame, tried to make good its error, which had taken on historic dimensions.¹⁵ It named Mendelssohn an honorary member, performed several of his works regularly—but Felix could not forget the shame and humiliation which the *Singakademie* had caused him. The relationship remained one of chilly politeness, even when the King named him *Generalmusikdirektor*.

The candidacy for the *Singakademie* had somewhat paralyzed Felix's plans for the future; as long as it was in the offing, he could not plan anything serious, aside from short engagements. But, in January, 1833, already in possession of his London commission and more or less certain of his rejection on the part of the *Singakademie*, he finally begins to think of the more distant future; he mentions Munich (for which he was to write an opera), Vienna, and Switzerland (as a place of rest).[16] Hence he cannot have known anything about an offer from the Rhineland which must have reached him at the end of February. This invited him to conduct the Lower Rhenish Music Festival of 1833. Who were the men who entrusted to him so honorable and so responsible a task? The official representative of the Lower Rhenish Music Festival, who conveyed the invitation to him, was *Regierungspräsident* von Woringen from Düsseldorf; but it seems that Immermann and the Düsseldorf painters vigorously championed Felix,[17] for they wanted somehow to bind him to the local theatre, where Immermann was intendant.[18]

This richly compensated Felix for his Berlin defeat. The London invitation, coupled with the promising invitation to Düsseldorf, finally showed him a "way out," and he speedily took advantage of it. Now he worked busily and tirelessly on his *Italian Symphony*, which he wanted to bring along in fulfillment of his London commission, and also finished his so-called "Trumpet Overture." The last-named work was not really new, it came from the years 1825-26, but the ever self-critical Felix thought it necessary to revise it thoroughly. He acts consistently when he balks at performing one of his double concerti for two pianos with Moscheles in London. He looked over this juvenile work, but finally concluded that it "is quite impossible to play it now."[19] But he is ready to "throw together a jolly piece" with him. From this desire grew the brilliant variations on the Gypsy March from Weber's *Preziosa*—a monumentally insignificant occasional piece.

Meanwhile, Moscheles' longed-for son had been born, and Felix sent a charming congratulatory letter (with drawings) to his godchild and his parents.[20] The son was named after Felix; and the godfather hastened to London. This time he went by way of Düsseldorf, where he spent several days in negotiations about the music festival and the immediate future. On April 25, he was in London. On the first of May, he appears in Moscheles' concert to perform with him the hastily "thrown-together" variations; these were received with great applause.

On May 13, the Philharmonic concert took place which heard the first performance of Felix's *Italian Symphony*, and at which Felix appeared as a pianist in Mozart's D minor Concerto. Originally, he had thought of playing a concerto of his own, but "alas, I don't yet know which one." This leads to the conclusion that, besides the G minor Concerto, he had another one ready; but no trace of it remains.[21]

The symphony was received with real enthusiasm. While working on it, Felix had felt uncertain. But now he believed "it has turned out to be a good work; be it as it may, there is progress in it, and that is the important thing."[22] Musical London sensed this immediately. After a detailed description of the work, the *Harmonicon* writes:

> M. Mendelssohn's symphony . . . is a composition that will endure for ages, if we may presume to judge such a work on a single performance. . . . And, to be brief, the manner in which the whole work was received by the most critical, the best qualified audience that London (now full of eminent foreign musicians) could assemble, bears us out in what we have said. . . .[23]

Even the very reserved Paganini was full of praise and invited Felix to play Beethoven violin sonatas with him. Naturally, Felix was on fire with enthusiasm for this suggestion.[24] But nothing came of it, for Paganini had to undergo a serious and painful jaw operation.

IV

On the following day (May 14) Felix returned to Düsseldorf in order to direct the remaining rehearsals for the music festival. The program of the first day consisted of Mendelssohn's Trumpet Overture and Handel's *Israel in Egypt* in the first European performance of the original score.[25] The second day offered Beethoven's Pastoral Symphony and *Leonore* Overture No. 3, a cantata by a Thuringian composer (forgotten today) E. W. Wolf, and finally, Peter von Winter's then-popular oratorio *Die Macht der Töne* (or *Timotheus*). The last two works barely attain the status of mediocrity.

Here, we may well ask why Mendelssohn allowed two such insignificant works to remain on the program. The answer is simple enough: they were already rehearsed and there was no more time to study something else. We must, too, consider the significance of these music festivals, as well as the life of the times, which was not yet corrupted by mechanized music and in which means of transportation were limited to Rhine boats and slow mail-coaches. In general, music festivals were regionally limited: for example, the English Three Choir Festivals of Gloucester, Worcester, and Hereford, or the old festivals of the Viennese *Tonkünstler-Societät*, in which Mozart had still participated. The first itinerant music festivals were organized by the *Allgemeiner Deutscher Musikverein* (from 1859 onward). Many others, especially international performances of contemporary music, followed in the footsteps of these. But even today, institutions like the *Biennale* of Venice, the May Festival of Cincinnati, and many other concentrate either on a particular style-period or a particular type of repertoire, from which they only exceptionally depart.

Of the German music festivals, only the Lower Rhenish one (founded in 1817) achieved towering significance. Among its conductors, we find Mendelssohn seven times, F. Hiller twelve times, Liszt once, Brahms twice, R. Strauss once, H. Richter four times; also K. Muck, H. Abendroth, R. Schumann (together with Hiller), Gade, A. Rubinstein—in a word, the resounding names of the nineteenth and beginning twentieth centuries. With the exception of Liszt and Rubinstein, however, the Wagner school is not represented.[26] From this fact we may recognize the rather conservative tendency of the Lower Rhenish Music Festivals; this was brilliantly and sympathetically characterized by such a man as Otto Jahn, himself an arch-conservative.[27]

Father Mendelssohn visited Felix in Düsseldorf in order to gain a "clear" picture of the capabilities of his son at the music festival. But the astute, skeptical, often hypercritical Abraham was so overwhelmed by these events that he took refuge in his sense of humor—which he lacked no more than did his great father Moses—in order to preserve his inner equanimity. Therefore, his letters from those days are so valuable, because fatherly pride, skepticism, irony, and perhaps a bit of resignation, "intimately linked" in him, produce a rather faithful picture of events. We shall compare his reports with those of the completely unprejudiced critic of the *Westfälischer Merkur* and of a French correspondent, in order to gain a somewhat objective judgment.

Abraham writes:

> But I have never yet seen anyone carried around on a silken cushion as Felix is here. He himself cannot sufficiently praise the zeal of all who are participating in the festival, and their confidence in him; and, as everywhere, he astonishes and moves everyone with his playing and his memory. . . . This afternoon . . . at three o'clock is the principal rehearsal of the whole *Israel*, which, Felix believes, will last till about eight o'clock. . . . Tomorrow there are morning and afternoon rehearsals, Sunday and Monday the concerts, Tuesday a grand ball and then still a third concert, in which, I hope, all five or six Beethoven symphonies will be given one after the other, Decker will sing, Felix will play and then a few more things will happen. I shall suggest that this begin about 10 in the evening and last through the whole night. There's a lot in favor of this. . . .[28]

(There follow some ironic observations.)

> Besides this active furthering, many hindrances are lacking here. There is no court here, no mixing-in or interference (Abraham's pun "*Einstörung* [kommt von Einfluss]" is not translatable). from above, no *Generalmusik-direktor*, no royal this or that. [Here the old republican speaks quite bluntly.] It is a true folk festival! . . .
>
> During the intermissions . . . everyone rushes into the garden. Masses of sandwiches and May wine . . . are consumed and the whole thing is

rather like a *kermesse* . . . A loud fanfare resounds from the orchestra, whereupon everyone quickly . . . returns to the hall. Tardy or thirsty ones are summoned by a second fanfare, and Israel cries once more to the Lord. . . .

Now since a director belongs to a music festival, I must tell a bit . . . about this year's, one Mr. Felix. Dear child! We have a certain amount of joy in this young man, and I often think: long live Marten's Mill![29]

Yesterday evening was the dress rehearsal of Felix's overture and *Israel.* . . . The Overture pleased greatly; but the last chorus of the first part, "He rebuked the Red Sea and it was dried up," and then the first one of the second part with its frightening ending: "The horse and its rider hath He thrown into the sea," excited such tremendous enthusiasm and excitement among the listeners and performers as seldom occurs; it was a good quarter-hour before everything had quieted down again. . . .[30]

Here, unexpectedly, a real Old Testament enthusiasm breaks forth in the "enlightened Kantian" Abraham Mendelssohn. (Felix sensed something similar when in full fervor he emotionally experienced the enthusiasm in Psalm 114, "When Israel out of Egypt came." It became his best religious work.)

Yesterday morning in the rehearsal Woringen . . . announced that, for the first time since the existence of the music festivals they planned to give a third concert . . . and the proposition was generally greeted with the greatest applause. So the concert was given yesterday with the following program:

First part: Felix's overture, scene from *Der Freischütz* (Mme Decker), *Concertstück* by Weber (Felix), arias from *Figaro* (Mme Kufferath).

Second part: Overture to *Leonore*. The second part of *Israel*. The performance was splendid throughout; the orchestra and chorus vied with one another in a way to arouse enthusiasm, and the last chorus from *Israel* was executed with real fury—I can't call it anything else.[31]

The musical part of the festival ended yesterday and today everything is being rehashed. These were a few very beautiful days, unforgettable to me . . . which I owe first of all to Felix, then to you, who talked me into it, and for which I am very thankful.

From tomorrow onwards I shall see everything that is to be seen here, and shall talk with Felix about his future, which seems to shape itself according to my wishes. . . .

The last sentences make us take notice. The father rejoices that everything goes according to *his* wishes (those of Felix were not discussed); and we see again that the patriarchal style of life still seems perfectly right and proper to the old man. Only on the following journey to London did the father begin to moderate the tone and content of his "orders of the day or the year" concerning Felix.

At the end of Abraham's Düsseldorf letters, we hear more precise information about the dealings at which he had hinted. He writes:

> Felix has been appointed director of all musical activities (municipal and private) here for three years ... with a salary of 600 thalers (corresponding to about 800-900 th. in Berlin) and a yearly vacation of 3 months. ... [32] His municipal duties consist in the direction of the church music, his private ones in the direction of the choral and orchestral societies which exist here ... and in the organization of four to eight concerts a year with these two societies, with the exception of the actual music festivals. [33]

Abraham praises the "wise and noble manner in which Felix behaved" and is happy that Felix will not have a title, but will have a real office, while so many have titles without offices.

Alongside this account, let us place two excerpts from the most important German and French musical journals, in order to gain that detachment which is necessary for a factual judgment of Mendelssohn *in the eyes of his own time.*

Four of his works are reviewed rather superficially in *Caecilia.* Only the first volume of *Songs without Words* is treated thoroughly and accorded high praise. The lukewarm eulogies of the G minor Concerto begin with the hymnic exclamation, "How different Mendelssohn is from the army of other fashionable musicians!" but beyond this statement, hardly anything of importance is said. [34]

The *Revue Musicale,* whose editor, E. Fétis, can hardly be called a friend of Mendelssohn, brings a highly laudatory review of the first performance of the *Italian Symphony* in London: "The symphony . . . is a very estimable work . . . the scrupulous exactitude . . . and the perfect taste excited the admiration of the audience." [35]

V

As he had agreed to, Felix returned to London after the completion of the music festival, on June 3. But this time he brought his father along. This "wise Memnon," as he called himself in irony at his own expense, had been persuaded without much difficulty to accompany Felix to London. The season was drawing to a close, and so this visit was devoted more to pleasure than to business. Again, we can draw information from two sources: from a prejudiced one, the father, whose letters bubble over with wit and common sense, and from the Horsley girls, who most accurately describe their activities and especially their association with the Mendelssohn circle (Klingemann, Moscheles, Dr. Rosen, and Felix himself). Unfortunately, they spread themselves endlessly on the most boring trivialities. Their letters represent the style of life, thought, and writing of the "gentlewomen" of the nineteenth century, with all its good and lovable features, but also with its indescribable narrowness and prudery. Nonetheless, they give a very fresh and critical portrait of Felix, undistorted by any hero-worship. They are true documents of a period.

Soon after his arrival, Father Mendelssohn sustained a painful leg injury and Felix, always a good son, was somewhat tied down to the patient. Nonetheless, he visited the Horsleys' house as often as he could.

Through their letters, we become acquainted with a milieu that has been pictured with unsurpassable clarity and fidelity to life by Jane Austen in her novels. In fact, she portrays it even better than a real collection of letters could do! However, in order to preserve some of the comments of these dear girls, who were very unconstrained with the already famous Felix, we shall note a few of their microscopically detailed observations.

Mendelssohn's emotional state: Felix was extremely subject to sudden changes of mood. Within an hour, he could turn from a clown into a melancholy introvert.

Mendelssohn's outer appearance: in spite of his careful grooming, it could happen that he was offered soap and a nail-brush. But Miss Fanny is shocked because men, "these dirty pigs," [sic!] mention it when they want to take a bath.

His relationship with his father: they sometimes had vigorous philosophical disputations in which they both became very excited. That was not surprising, for Abraham was a Kantian, Felix an Hegelian.

They are greatly embarrassed when a strong gust of wind lifts up Mamma's skirts so that her petticoats show; they prevent Felix and Klingemann from approaching Mamma, for it "was distressing to the female mind."[36]

At this time we hear from Klingemann that Felix was grieving over Delphine from Munich, now lost to him through marriage. He saw her again "and was quite crushed. . . . Mr. Klingemann told us that he [Mendelssohn] had been much struck with Delphine, she however, being another's, is quite out of the question."[37] In the meantime, we hear from quite another source that Felix does not go out of his way to avoid adventures with less prudish ladies. There was a young girl-friend of Rosen, gifted in painting, whose temperament, aggressive in the erotic sense, charmed Felix. He seems to have had success with her, too. In any case, he was by no means prudish, though his father and Klingemann inclined in that direction.[38]

The old gentleman sent home his brilliantly critical observations on the big city; he did not at all share Felix's enthusiasm for London. From the climate, which he made fun of, to English cooking and English social customs which he respected but which were strange to him, he gives us a lively picture of pre-Victorian London. Here, too, we can select only a few observations.[39]

Abraham's humor:

> Furthermore, I speak Italian with Horsley, for he speaks neither German nor French, and at least *both* of us don't speak Italian.
>
> He is annoyed because his second son-in-law, the celebrated mathematician Dirichlet, "did not write him about the birth of his son. At least he could have written $2 + 1 = 3$!"

Difference between Paris and London:

> In England . . . foreigners are quite ignored. There really must be no foreigners, there are only Englishmen. The foreigner must completely deny his birthright, must denationalize himself . . . in order to attain any kind of existence. In Paris, Germans, English, Chinese . . . can live . . . without giving up a jot of their individuality and nationality.

Impressions of Malibran: the old man, who, three years earlier, had followed his son's enthusiastic reports about her with mistrust, now falls completely under her spell:

> What exuberance of mind and spirit, of caprice and ebullience, of passion and *esprit* . . . surges from this woman, whom I, too, now appreciate!

He raves about her for more than a page, and speaks of her "inexhaustible powers of genius."

Social conditions: Social contrasts are much greater than in Berlin; in London it can happen that the wife and two children of an Irish workman can literally starve, while Abraham, the foreigner, lacks for nothing. "I hope that this observation . . . will not be fruitlessly forgotten." In fact, after his return, Abraham established a charitable foundation for the free feeding of the sick.

Felix played the great organ in St. Paul's Cathedral: The organ blowers were no longer there, so that Klingemann and two other friends had to replace them. Felix played Attwood's Coronation Anthem in the presence of the composer, his own Prelude and Fugue, and three great fugues of Bach. Abraham spent some time in Attwood's home, where the two old gentlemen became very friendly.[40]

Felix's concern for his suffering father: Here Abraham is full of the most extravagant praise for the worried Felix and his tender care. "He deserves my best thanks." Furthermore, we should mention that Felix did not fail to attend the parliamentary discussions on the Jewish emancipation in England. He writes about it to Berlin:

This morning they have emancipated the Jews; that pleases me tremendously. After a number of Jew-baiters, Mr. Finn, Mr. Bruce . . . and Inglis had twaddled unctuously, Mr. Robert Grant, the sponsor of the bill, concluded with the question, whether they believed they existed in order to fulfill the prophecies of Scripture . . . and stated that he himself followed the word "Glory to God and good will to men." Thereupon followed ayes 187 and noes 52. This is quite noble and beautiful and makes me proud.[41]

Meanwhile, the father's injury was healed, and on August 25 they traveled together to Berlin. On this occasion, the old Mendelssohn could not resist the adolescent prank of announcing at home that he would bring along a young friend, a French painter, Alphonse Lovie. His wife was annoyed, because she had looked forward to the reunion with Felix; naturally M. Lovie was none other than Felix himself.[42]

On September 13, they finally reached Berlin. For Felix, this return also meant the farewell to the parental home, and, as much as he delighted in his newly won independence, he greatly regretted the separation from his dear ones. But he arrived in Düsseldorf in good spirits on September 25, and began to settle in there.

VI

Felix was music director now, but what did he have to conduct? The contract had been made with the Düsseldorf Music and Theatre Society, which, at this time, was a municipal institution. Felix had to direct its rehearsals and concerts, and, besides this, to "supervise" the church music, which, today, in the Rhineland, is mainly limited to Catholic services. Important, too, is his relationship to the music festivals. The Düsseldorf Society was a constituent member of the Lower Rhenish Music Festivals, but it neither wanted to nor could impose its newly minted director on that great institution. Felix was quite clear in his mind about the somewhat delicate situation, and hesitated to take the slightest step towards being invited to conduct at the next music festival (which took place in Aachen).[43] In 1832, Ferdinand Ries, Beethoven's pupil, had been invited, and he was to lead the festival in 1834 also. Nonetheless, gossip and the usual intrigues seem to have been busily at work, as we learn from the following facts:

Felix considered it necessary to give a concert with Ries in order to eliminate all grounds for the malicious gossip that one was "the pope, the other anti-pope."[44]

In connection with the fifteenth music festival (Pentecost, 1833) we encounter a very strange notice in Fétis *Revue musicale*, which was not exactly devoted to Mendelssohn. Here we read the following news from Düsseldorf:

A musical society of some 500 members has existed and flourished here for some years. . . . In recent times it has gone backwards from day to day, and now it is in a state of almost total ruin. . . . Steps towards the revivification of this organization have been undertaken, and Mr. Anton Schindler has been entrusted with their execution. . . .[45]

What is this mysterious "musical society?" And why is a notice about it published in the *Revue musicale* on the very eve of the Düsseldorf music festival and linked with the name of Anton Schindler, the old friend of Beethoven? Was Schindler perhaps Mendelssohn's rival candidate for the post of conductor? Perhaps this question can be cleared up some day.[46]

It is almost equally strange that this time (1833) the Lower Rhenish Music Festival is not even mentioned in the *Allgemeine Musikalische Zeitung, Caecilia,* or the *Revue Musicale,* while those of the preceding and following year are extensively reviewed.

All these facts indicate that Felix, at least in the beginning, did not find an easy situation. It was above all his overwhelming success as conductor of the music festival which helped him over the initial difficulties.

As church music director of a Catholic domain, he basically represented the ideas of J. B. Thibaut; that is, he did what he could to revive the old Italian church music of the Renaissance and the Baroque in the liturgy. So he rummaged through the libraries and archives of Cologne, Bonn, and Elberfeld and found what he was looking for, namely, Masses and Motets by Palestrina, Lasso, Lotti, Leo, Allegri, and Pergolese. Against all opposition, he strove to introduce these into the churches, and was finally successful. In this connection, he felt that real church music had originated only in the sixteenth century.[47] He even finds Masses of Haydn "scandalously gay."

On the other hand, he did not incline towards archaizing in his secular duties, but he also dared not appear too modern. (We must remember that Beethoven had been dead for only six years and Mozart was still regarded as an "innovator.") In the concerts he especially emphasized Handel (*Messiah, Alexander's Feast,* and *Judas Maccabaeus*) and Beethoven (Piano Concerti, *Eroica,* etc.), as well as Weber (*Oberon* Overture, *Leyer und Schwert* for male chorus), Gluck (Overture to *Iphigenia in Aulis*) and Cherubini (Mass in C, Overtures). He was obligated to direct six concerts and where possible, as a representative of Düsseldorf, also to appear elsewhere in the Rhineland. He faithfully fulfilled this obligation, although he refused any honorarium, for he had vowed at the beginning of his career never "to arrange concerts for his own benefit."[48] So, in the first weeks and months he was not overloaded with work.

Meanwhile, Immermann had recognized Felix's great talent and thought that he would put it at the service of his ideal of a great national theatre in

Düsseldorf. He persuaded the young artist to conduct several operas, as "model performances" of classical or modern works. As this expression was rather unhappily chosen because of its ill-concealed arrogance, it was necessary at least to justify it by a special effort.

Therefore Mendelssohn conducted Mozart's *Don Giovanni* only after twenty ensemble rehearsals, and the town gossip, sufficiently active during the rehearsals, had done its bit; in short, there was a real riot in the theatre at the first "model performance." But all the vociferous scandals could not intimidate Felix. On the contrary: as always when he encountered a mob, he became furious, and "would rather throw his baton at the fellows' heads." But the people gradually became quiet, and the riot turned into a victory. Furthermore, the instigator of the disturbance was discovered (a government secretary) and now "justice took its course." For his superior, the *Regierungspräsident*, was none other than Felix's benefactor and friend, Herr von Woringen. The sequel can be imagined! The repetition of *Don Giovanni* was a triumph in the theatre. There were further little disputes, but in general the "model performances" had established themselves.

But there were plenty of irritations in the spoken drama, too. During the rehearsal of Beethoven's *Egmont* music, which was to be performed with Goethe's play, Felix became so excited that he tore the full orchestral score in two "out of annoyance at the stupid musicians, whom I positively spoonfeed with the 6/8 measure beaten in subdivisions and who still need more and more 'pacifiers'."

. . . also they love to beat each other up in the orchestra—but with me, they are not allowed to do that, and so from time to time I must stage a furious scene. . . . Then for the first time I tore a score in two, and thereupon they immediately played with more expression.[49]

The description of this incident shows us that Felix was quick to anger; but as soon as he got home he smirked with pleasure, as though he had "arranged" the scene. Furthermore, he was not exactly enchanted with the *Egmont* music; only the Overture, the March, and a pantomime of Klärchen were written to suit him.

Felix was quite a theatre fan, but only as a spectator. Now a new theatre was to be founded in Düsseldorf, financed by shares, and already, he, as "music intendant," was involved in a whirl of activities of which he had not previously dreamed. That was life "behind the scenes." At first he took pleasure in it; this, however, was not to last long. First there were unpleasant conflicts of jurisdiction with Immermann, which led to aggressive letters between the two and finally to an open break. Of this affair, which did little credit to Felix, we possess his version, which paints his actions in unduly rosy colors; we also have the sharp reproach of his father (who had learned the true state of affairs from Woringen), the report of the theatreman Devrient, and several notices from the contemporary journals.

It is true that, according to Devrient's words, Felix was simply unsuited for the administration of the Opera (which he had assumed along with his musical duties). Certainly, too, the destruction of many illusions about theatrical life which Felix had previously cherished played an important part. When one is the all-powerful Herr Opernintendant, whom every unemployed chorister views as a half-god, in whom every pretty singer sees an unscrupulous debauchee, then a sensitive, honorable idealist like Felix soon loses his appetite for such a position. In the beginning, he enjoyed his position of power; perhaps he would have liked to keep it if corrupt compromises and unworthy people had not been forced upon him. And so he expresses himself rather bitterly:

> I shall never become an Intendant again, and shall always remember those few weeks. Pfui, to the devil with it! To quarrel with people about two thalers, to be strict with the good ones and indulgent with the bad ones, to make noble faces so that they won't lose the respect which they don't even have, to act angry without being angry—these are all things which I can't do and don't want to be able to do. . . . You could bring me Spontini's position on a silver platter and I wouldn't accept it now. . . .[50]

Nonetheless, he should never have abandoned the position in so irresponsible and abrupt a manner as he did. This is the only time in Mendelssohn's life that he simply discarded an obligation which he had assumed and on which the existence of many people depended. It is even sadder that he did not have the courage to tell his family, especially his father, the full, unvarnished truth. But this was as follows: as opera Intendant and principal conductor, he had to be responsible for the regular and undisturbed sequence of operatic performances. For this, he was responsible to the board of trustees of the theatre company and probably also to Immermann personally. But, from one day to the next, he simply threw away this position and responsibility, without caring much about the consequences to those affected.

Fortunately, Felix had engaged a reliable assistant or second conductor before the conflict broke out. The latter received the salary which was Felix's right as theatre Intendant and which he turned over to his *adlatus*. His name, Julius Rietz, will not surprise us greatly; for he was the younger brother of the friend of Felix's youth, Eduard Rietz, who had copied the *St. Matthew Passion*. Julius Rietz fitted into the situation with astonishing speed and, after Felix's departure, took over the leadership of the opera company, so that its collapse was averted.

It is not without irony to confront Felix's letter to Rietz, in which he offers him the post of conductor in Düsseldorf, with his own actions. The proud Mendelssohn, inclined to quick anger, warns the much calmer Rietz "that all Rhinelanders are difficult, easily insulted, very stubborn and somewhat headstrong," in spite of their amiability in other respects. Therefore, one must have much patience with them. In addition, we learn Felix's plan for the operatic repertory: *Titus*, Rossini's *L'Italiana in Algeri*, two or three operas by Bellini, Marschner's *Hans Heiling*, and, naturally, as much Weber as possible.[51]

In spite of his great love for his son, Abraham Mendelssohn was far too just a man to be able to approve Felix's actions and his subsequent maneuvers of concealment. Two letters from Abraham, of which only one is published,[52] speak very clearly indeed. In the first, he reproaches his son for his hasty action and self-righteous attitude:

> He is furthest from the ideal of virtue who most relentlessly demands it of others. Now, it cannot be denied that up till now you have not been able to free yourself of a certain gruffness and violence, of grabbing things quickly and dropping them just as quickly. Thus you have put many obstacles in your own way, from a practical viewpoint. . . .[53]

He expresses himself even more sharply in a later letter:

> Through your own calamitous stubbornness you have done yourself more harm than you yet know. But—and this is more important—you could have brought misfortune on a whole institution which you yourself encouraged and now have thoughtlessly deserted.[54]

But it was too late. A highly gifted, but still very young artist had given a deadly insult to the generally respected and admired poet who was his superior and who, furthermore, was thirteen years older than he. In addition, as Intendant, Felix had gotten Immermann into an embarrassing situation. Until Immermann's death (1840) they remained unreconciled enemies.

However, Felix had a certain respect for the poet, for he composed incidental music to Immermann's translation of Calderon's *The Constant Prince*. But Klingemann's influence overcame his hesitation. For without a doubt it was the quiet, polite, rather shy Klingemann, who, during his visit in Düsseldorf, persuaded Felix to give up the Intendancy. Felix writes to him: "Without your being here I should certainly have wished this decision throughout the winter, but not taken it; and so, I am more grateful to you than you can know."[55]

Half a year earlier, at Pentecost of 1834, the sixteenth Lower Rhenish Music Festival had taken place in Aachen, this time under the direction of Ferdinand Ries. Since Düsseldorf was taking an active part in it, Mendelssohn could take advantage of the opportunity to see old friends once again. Above all, he spent his time with Hiller and Chopin. They made music, talked politics, and had long discussions. Hiller had translated Handel's *Deborah* and completed the fragmentary instrumentation of the original. His arrangement had been accepted by Ries, and he brought Chopin along to the music festival.[56] For his part, Felix now invited the friends to Düsseldorf, where they met with all the painters of the Academy, especially Schadow. Felix praises the music of his friends, but cannot keep from inserting a critical observation:

> Both suffer somewhat from the Parisian sickness of despair and quest for passion, and have often lost sight of tact, quietness, and what is truly musical. I, on the other hand, have perhaps paid too much attention to these latter things, and so we complemented each other and, I think, all three learned from one another. I seemed to myself a bit like a schoolmaster, and they seemed to themselves a bit like *mirliflors* or *incroyables*.[57]

Does not the Classicist speak here against the French "avant-gardists"? Nonetheless, Felix mentions Chopin's pianistic art with greatest admiration; it puts everything else in the shade.

On the occasion of that music festival in Aachen, Felix had the opportunity to get even with Fétis. Since that first encounter in London, in 1829, the two had come no closer. True, Fétis had published a laudatory sketch on Mendelssohn in the *Revue musicale*,[58] but scolded him for his "mistakes in composition, which are evident in the Overture to *A Midsummer Night's Dream*."[59] According to Fétis, "one should not take these mistakes too seriously, for Mendelssohn comes from a school in which one does not think too strictly about such things."[60] When Fétis and Mendelssohn met in Aachen, the former came up to Felix with outstretched hand and friendly smile. But Felix "cut him dead; nodded slightly and turned about. Let him curse me and criticize me; in such matters I like blunt sincerity and wish to let my behaviour show my sentiments, in this case: 'Let him go hang himself!' "[61]

In this case, Felix was indisputably in the right; for not only Fétis's arrogance and love for intrigue, but above all his frequently untrue and gossipy reports were bound to repel Felix. Years later, Fétis claimed that, at the Aachen music festival, there had been a scene between Mendelssohn and Ries, provoked by the younger man.[62] There is not a word of truth in this assertion; worse yet, it was made when Felix and Ries were dead and could no longer call the "biographer" to account.

However, Felix's resentment did not stem merely from a personal aversion—as he may have believed himself—but had a much deeper and more impersonal cause. Not in vain had he learned from Goethe to mistrust pseudo-philosophical esthetics; from youth onwards, he was an enemy of journalism. There are numerous passages in his letters where he expresses this conviction.[63] Felix was no friend of the daily press. Fétis embodies, for him, two unsympathetic disciplines: namely, a dictatorial music esthetics and an often unscrupulous journalism. We shall later have occasion to see this idiosyncrasy of Mendelssohn's at work; it often harmed him externally, but, on the other hand, protected him all his life long from corrupt compromises or unhealthy seeking after sensation.

Felix's attitude towards an *applied* critical esthetics was quite different. For this, there are many interesting indications in his extended correspondence, and no critic of those days could compete with his father in stylistic sensitivity. One of several such critical contributions has been published: that of March 10, 1835. From another unknown one, let us select a passage which literally hits the nail on the head. It deals with the use of the song *Ein veste Burg* in the last movement of the *Reformation Symphony*. Abraham observes tellingly:

> When you use chorales, you must carry them through quite consistently; and it is not easy to find artistic contrasts to them without disturbing their inherent spirit; the best contrast would be another, quite different chorale. You did not do it this way, and the last movement suffers from the somewhat too "popular" counter-theme.[64]

Felix generally bowed to the opinion and criticism of his father; he breaks out in admiration of the latter's observations on his *Ave Maria*, quite rightly, and cannot understand how a man can have such good judgment about music without himself being musically educated (in the technical sense).[65] Indeed, the recognition of an unsuccessful passage (to which his father had called his attention) had annoyed him at first, but then again "he was pleased that such clarity of feeling is present in music," and that his father understands it.[66] There can be no doubt that the father understood the essence of Protestant church music much better than did the son; and his dictum "The highest aim of the chorale is that the people should sing it in the pure form accompanied by the organ—everything else seems to me vain and unreal," would, considered and taken to heart by Felix, have spared the latter many disappointments and controversies, especially in connection with *St. Paul*.[67]

Alongside such orthodox Lutheran observations in Abraham's letters, we find others from considerably older sources, as, for example, the Talmudic statement in the same letter: "Nothing that is begun seriously and quietly . . . can remain without consequences." And Abraham thinks quite in the spirit of his great father Moses when he, referring to *St. Paul*, hopes that, in it, Felix "will resolve the problem of uniting old meaning with new means."[68] From such a mentor, Felix could learn much. Nonetheless, he grimly remains at a distance from theoretical esthetics, and writes: "A philosopher, I am not . . . not even an esthetician—in spite of Hegel . . . I become more and more furious with these fellows."[69]

And soon thereafter he makes fun of their "funereal esthetics," closing with the powerful words:

Really I can do without all these estheticians, reviewers [!] and whatever they are called. . . .[70]
  Yesterday they offered me, from Leipzig, a professorship at the University which would be created for me; but I rejected it. I cannot read lectures on music if my life depended on it.[71]

This was the second time that he rejected an offered University professorship. He agreed with Goethe's word: *Bilde, Künstler, rede nicht!* (Create, artist, do not talk!).

Working with religious music was a deeply felt need for him. In the correspondence with his father, but only with him, he goes beyond liturgical questions and into theological problems. But this happened seldom, for Felix shied away from theological speculations. In connection with a successful performance of Lessing's *Nathan* in Düsseldorf, with which he himself was delighted, there arose a violent dispute between his friends and the Catholic Schadow, who was "too annoyed about it." But Felix "did not join in the controversy; for when one is so far apart on matters of principle, it comes to nothing."[72] Though he did not think as rationalistically as his father about the religious experience, his Protestantism was more closely bound to Hegel's and Schleiermacher's philosophy than to Luther's anti-Catholic dogmatism. As we have seen, he directed the Catholic church music in Düsseldorf; later, he gladly accepted the commissions to compose a *Lauda Sion* for the Eucharistic Congress in Liège, and to write solemn liturgical music for the dedication of the Cologne Cathedral. Alas, he could carry out only the first project—death struck him down too soon. His religious thinking and feeling was deep and sincere, but far removed from mystery or ecstasy. Yet, he had an inclination towards precisely those characters in whom the miracle, the incomprehensible, takes place—St. Paul and Elijah. However, when it comes to the point, he was unable to present a mystical experience convincingly. He sensed this contradiction but dimly, and his age was probably unaware of it.[73]

While the artist eschewed religious disputations, the man, intelligent and open to all stimuli, took a lively interest in all ideas which stirred his age. Foremost among these ideas there stood, before 1848, political questions and problems. His correspondence, especially with Klingemann, is, at that time, full of references to English and also some Prussian politics. His and Klingemann's circle were convinced liberal Whigs and anti-Tories; "Wellington and the rest of the gang" is one of his standard expressions, and he considers himself a "reformer" by conviction.[74]

Concerning German politics, Mendelssohn was without doubt a "liberal

Little-German," opposed to a Greater German Parliament; in other words, he was, in principle, in agreement with the "Göttingen Seven," whom he regularly supported following their dismissal.[75] He agreed, too, with Droysen and the other liberals, who turned away from Austria and saw their salvation in the North German Customs Union. If he had lived to experience the 1848 Revolution, he would have "fallen between two stools." While rejecting the liberalism of the nationalistic student societies (*Burschenschaften*), he would also have opposed the Frankfurt Parliament. On the other hand, he was a liberal and democrat; therefore, after Frederick William IV's abdication, he would have had to bite into the sour apple of a Bismarckian Prussia. At least, he was spared this.

Though political thinking determined his social life to a certain extent, in Düsseldorf he associated principally with painters, and there developed his considerable talent for drawing. But basically, he put trust only in his father and Klingemann, and, concerning musical matters, in Fanny. In this maelstrom of thoughts and sentiments, he was, after all, fundamentally lonely. He complained about it often, but only to Klingemann.[76] He felt most at home with the Woringens; we find the expression of his gratitude in the dedication of two volumes of *Songs without Words* to the ladies of the house. His repeated complaints that there are no nice girls in Düsseldorf are not to be taken seriously. He had a close relationship with a widowed aristocratic lady, but neither he nor she seemed to have viewed it as a lasting one. Since Felix was an intellectually demanding partner, her exclusively physically oriented love could not suffice him. On the other hand, because of his upbringing, he was too puritanical in his feeling to be content with a mistress for a longer period. So, soon after the first blaze of passion, it seems to have come to serious conflicts and, after some time, to a cool separation.

Felix had been highly discreet, and it must have surprised him to know that his mother (probably through the Woringens) had gotten wind of the affair. Thereupon she writes him a very private letter, ending with the remarkable tirade:

> On the theme of the marriage recommended to you, you could have chosen Father's phrase, *"Don't marry, or you will get a beating!"* . . . Oh, dear artist, don't impede the free flight of your wings—in spite of all bad examples and riotous evenings of other people's sons. And don't let your self be married off [*schatchanisieren*] or turned itno a Catholic [*Katholisieren*] by Schadow . . . be warned in time. . . .![77]

But Felix was miles removed from such plans.

The parting from his lady friend was externally accentuated by Felix's departure for Berlin, where he spent the late summer of 1834 with his family.

On his return, the first feelers were extended from Leipzig. But Felix replied noncommittally and diplomatically; he demanded that there should be no further negotiations until he had received the binding assurance that he was "in no case thwarting another candidate."[78] Indeed, making such a condition was a noble action which, then as now, would have amused most of his colleagues as a *Don Quichotterie*.

Nonetheless, Felix already knew in December, 1834, that he would not stay another year in Düsseldorf.[79] He was invited to direct the Seventeenth Lower Rhenish Music Festival in Cologne, and accepted the invitation for Pentecost, 1835. He already knew that he would go to Leipzig, and sensed that this represented an important step. So his testimonies from this time bear a unique mixture of great seriousness and joyous optimism. A new phase of life lay before him.

Notes

1. A short account of this in Devrient, *Erinnerungen an Felix Mendelssohn* (Leipzig, 1891), p. 136; also Klingemann *Correspondence*, letter of July 25, 1832.
2. Letter of April 6, 1833, to Pastor Bauer.
3. Letter to Klingemann, September 5, 1832.
4. Letter to Klingemann, December 5, 1832: "Now, when two of them are past, the people shower me with honors. . . . but now it brings me no more pleasure."
5. Rellstab, *Kritiken und Erinnerungen* (Berlin, 1861), p. 217.
6. Letter to Klingemann, December 5, 1832.
7. For the details of the planned *Solomon* version, compare letter to Klingemann of August 15, 1832.
8. Unpublished letter to Fanny, March 31, 1835. "So they want to change or even to improve Handel, but they can't even do that properly. . . . Now they added oboes in F sharp minor to fill out the lower register, which will make every oboist's heart shudder! and one miserable bass trombone! it sounds like an old comb. They want to orchestrate G. F. Handel, but they would be cowering under the table with fear if the forceful old gentleman were still alive. . . ."
9. Unpublished letter to his mother, November 28, 1833 (from Düsseldorf).
10. M. Blumner, *Geschichte der Singakademie* (Berlin, 1891); and G. Schünemann, *Die Singakademie zu Berlin, 1791-1941* (Regensburg, 1941).
11. See Schünemann, *op. cit.*, pp. 71ff. Blumner calls this part of the collection the most valuable, because of the many manuscripts of the Bach family; *op. cit.*, p. 91.
12. Schünemann, who discusses this ticklish affair thoroughly, published his book during the Nazi regime. Nonetheless, the Jewish Maecenases appear there in a much better light than the others. Schünemann's historical-political presentation often reminds us of walking on eggs; it would be amusing if it were not so sad.
13. Letter to Klingemann, December 26, 1832.
14. Letter to Klingemann, February 4-6, 1833.
15. It is perhaps not purely accidental that, with the failure of Mendelssohn, the *Singakademie*, the most important Protestant choral association, lost its hegemony in Germany. From then on, the important music festivals shift to the Rhineland, to Frank-

furt, and finally (in the case of operatic festivals), to South Germany: Bayreuth, Munich, Salzburg.

16. Letter to Klingemann, January 16, 1833.

17. Letter to Klingemann, February 20, 1833.

18. It seems that just at this time the Lower Rhenish Music Festivals had reached a crisis. J. Alf, who knows most about this institution, writes concerning 1832: "The festival was in a crisis. The reports about it in the press sound weary." (J. Alf, "Die Niederrheinischen Musikfeste," in *Düsseldorfer Jahrbuch*, 1942, Vol. 3.)

19. Letter to Klingemann, April 10, 1833.

20. Text and facsimile in Moscheles-Mendelssohn correspondence. To this belongs, also, a Cradle Song, later published as Op. 47, No. 6.

21. Unpublished letter of May 7, 1833.

22. Letter to Bauer, April 6, 1833.

23. *Harmonicon*, 1833, p. 134.

24. Unpublished letter of of May 7 and 13, 1833.

25. The *Singakademie* had already performed the work in 1831, but in a radically shortened and altered version.

26. On the Lower Rhenish Music Festivals, see A. Becher, *Das Niederrheinische Musikfest* (Cologne, 1836); also *Blätter der Erinnerung an die fünfzigjährige Dauer des Niederrheinischen Musikfests* (Cologne, 1868); and, more recently, J. Alf, *Geschichte und Bedeutung des Niederrheinischen Musikfests in der ersten Hälfte des neunzehnten Jahrhunderts* (Freiburg, 1940). Because of German racial laws in force at the time of its appearance, the latter, otherwise thorough work, was forced to minimize the influence of Mendelssohn, Hiller, etc.

27. See O. Jahn, *Gesammelte Aufsätze über Musik*, pp. 166, 181ff. See also E. Bücken, *Musik des 19. Jahrhunderts*, p. 3: "The tendencies towards restoration in this epoch could be realized . . . in the music festivals, for these took up the tradition . . . of the great English Handel performances. And, furthermore, the Lower Rhenish Music Festivals became . . . ardent promoters of the Bach renaissance inaugurated by Zelter, Mendelssohn and Schumann."

28. Hensel, *F.M.*, Vol. I, letters from Düsseldorf of May 22, 26, 28, 1833.

29. Marten's Mill, it will be remembered, was the house in Hamburg where Felix was conceived and born.

30. Compare here the report of the *Westfälischer Merkur*. "What can be achieved by good will and a clear mind . . . combined with an endurance in the many strenuous rehearsals such as I have *never* yet seen in my artistic career, was shown there in such a way that one must have seen and heard it to believe it possible." (J. Alf, *op. cit.*, p. 175.)

31. It is interesting to observe that, in this "extra concert," Mendelssohn made no more concessions. Neither P. v. Winter nor Wolf are represented. However, Father Mendelssohn lists the program wrongly. The works performed were: Beethoven, *Fidelio* Overture; Weber, scene of Agathe from *Freischütz;* Weber, *Konzertstück;* Mozart, aria from *Figaro;* Beethoven, duet from *Fidelio;* intermission; Beethoven, *Leonore* Overture; Handel, various choruses from *Israel*.

32. In the letter of May 31 to Klingemann, Felix speaks only of a two-year contract with Düsseldorf.

33. Hensel, *F.M.*, I, p. 363. Oddly the theatre is not mentioned here. Perhaps Immermann wanted to wait and see how Felix would settle down before engaging him for the Opera.

34. *Caecilia*, 1834, Heft 64, pp. 259ff. With this very summary review, compare the enthusiastic six pages (with music examples), which I. R. von Seyfried, the friend of Beethoven, devotes to a boring piano concerto in E flat major by Aloys Schmitt.

35. *Revue Musicale*, Vol. VI (1833), p. 168; on p. 391, *Ibid.*, is an extensive biography of Felix.

36. *Mendelssohn and His Friends in Kensington*, ed. R. B. Gotch (London, 1934), p. 72.

37. *Ibid.*, p. 78; and unpublished letter from Klingemann, May 7, 1833.
38. Unpublished letter from Rosen to Mendelssohn, June 13, 1833.
39. Hensel, *F.M.*, I, pp. 366-386.
40. *Musical Times*, December, 1900, pp. 792 and 800.
41. Unpublished letter of July 23, 1833.
42. Why did Abraham choose this name? He had often heard the famous Jewish cantor Lovy in Paris. The latter had died in 1832, and it is possible that the recollection of him suggested the name to Abraham.
43. Letter of December 28, 1833.
44. Letter to Mrs. Moscheles, May 11, 1834. At that concert, Ries and Mendelssohn played, among other works, Beethoven's *Kreutzer* Sonata, a favorite of Felix.
45. *Revue musicale*, May 25, 1833, p. 135. The Düsseldorf *Singverein* then had 120 active members. See Hiller, *F.M.B.*, pp. 40-41. On Schindler and the Lower Rhenish Music Festivals see A. Moser, *J. Joachim*, p. 46.
46. In 1833, Anton Schindler was cathedral conductor in Münster, Westphalia.
47. Letter of January 12, 1835. We shall say more about Mendelssohn's everchanging attitude towards church music.
48. Letter of April 16, 1835.
49. Letter of February 16, 1834.
50. Devrient, *Felix Mendelssohn-Bartholdy*, 3rd edition, pp. 176ff.
51. Unpublished letter of August 2, 1834, Library of Congress, Washington, D. C.
52. Letter of December 5, 1834, from Abraham Mendelssohn.
53. *Ibid.*
54. Unpublished letter of Abraham Mendelssohn, December 4, 1834. Felix, in his unpublished letters of this period, expresses himself hatefully and arrogantly about Immermann.
55. Letter to Klingemann, November 30, 1834.
56. See Hiller, *Felix Mendelssohn-Bartholdy*, pp. 32-33: "At that time, in Aachen, people did not yet seem to divine his significance; only twelve years later did they decide to entrust the leadership of a music festival to him."
57. Letter of May 23, 1834. *Mirliflors* and *incroyables* were types of Parisian dandies.
58. *Revue musicale*, 1833, p. 391.
59. *Ibid.*, 1832.
60. A. Jullien, *Airs Variés*, 1877 ("Mendelssohn à Paris").
61. Unpublished letter of May 28, 1834.
62. Fétis, *Biographie universelle*, second (!) edition, Vol. 6, p. 79. But it is true that Felix was not in agreement with the Aachen program; see correspondence with Moscheles, May 11, 1834.
63. See for example, the letter to Klingemann of April 3, 1834, and to Moscheles of June 26, 1834.
64. Unpublished letter of December 3, 1834.
65. Letter of March 23, 1835.
66. *Ibid.*
67. Letter from Abraham Mendelssohn, March 10, 1835.
68. *Ibid.*
69. *Ibid.*
70. Unpublished letter of January 3, 1835.
71. *Ibid.*
72. Unpublished letter to his father, February 19, 1834. I assume it is known that "the wise Nathan" was an embodiment of his grandfather Moses Mendelssohn.
73. This lack was probably first recognized by W. H. Riehl in *Musikalische Charakterköpfe* (Bach and Mendelssohn from the social viewpoint) and Otto Jahn, *Aufsätze über Musik* (*St. Paul* and *Elijah*).
74. Letter of December 23, 1834.
75. See passage concerning this especially in Droysen's correspondence, Stuttgart, 1929. The so-called *Göttinger Sieben* was a select group of outstanding professors

at the University, which then was under the jurisdiction of Hanover. For their liberal convictions and utterances, they were illegally expelled. Prominent among them were the Grimm brothers.

76. Klingemann, letter of April 10, 1835, "Deep loneliness."

77. Unpublished letter from Lea to Felix, January 11, 1834. The expression "schat-chanisieren" is a play of words on the German-Jewish "Schadchen" (marriage-broker).

78. Unpublished letter of October 9, 1834.

79. Unpublished letter to his father, December 11, 1834. "Above all things I want to avoid giving the slightest appearance of applying for posts which are occupied by others. In this sense I wrote to Leipzig . . . and left it entirely up to them . . . eschewing any application on my part."

CHAPTER XII *The Turning Point: Düsseldorf–Cologne–Leipzig*

Res severa verum gaudium.
To create true joy is a severe task. (Seneca)
(Felix's motto, which was placed on the *Gewandhaus*.)

I

THE NEGOTIATIONS with Leipzig began in October, 1834, and lasted till April, 1835. Felix kept them strictly confidential, and only with his father did he discuss the various contractual questions. Even to his close friend Klingemann he betrayed only that he had resolved not to stay in Düsseldorf, but "to go elsewhere"—he did not as yet know precisely where.[1] However, Felix knew very well he would go to Leipzig. The affair weighs on his mind and actually in the next letter he reveals his secret to his friend in a markedly nonchalant manner in which we seldom find him; he had "let himself be talked into going to Leipzig next winter. . . . The Leipzigers believe that I should and will settle there. . . ."[2]

But the matter was not so simple; for two personal conferences and a very detailed exchange of letters preceded the final contract. The father was always kept up-to-date on the affair, and every important question was discussed in a letter. The conditions which Felix stipulated do him the greatest honor as a man and artist: Under no circumstances should a predecessor or another candidate be driven out by his coming.[3] He would prefer a private institution to an official one. He insisted on five or six months of free time for his creative work. Finally, he will have no part of benefit concerts for his profit (which were very fashionable at that time), and categorically refuses to organize or to give such concerts.[4] Here, he refers to the wish of his parents that he should practise his art as a profession, and

[252]

should earn his living by means of it. Long before, he had discussed this question in an (unpublished) letter to his father.

His heart is not exactly set on going to Leipzig; he would rather have undertaken another two-year trip as a free artist. But it was clear to him "that one can only gain pleasure and reputation thereby, but that one matures less on journeys than in a fixed position." Munich, too, had offered him the position of opera director, with a salary of more than 2,000 fl.—much more than Leipzig could offer.[5] But, rightly, his father reminded him of his Düsseldorf theatrical experiences, and demanded that Felix should finally become aware of his own sympathies and antipathies; therefore, he earnestly dissuaded him from Munich, and recommended Leipzig to him most warmly. This advice must have been decisive, for at the end of April the contract was signed.

But what about his principal condition? Is it really true that no one was driven out or even inconvenienced because he was summoned? This question, so important for the Mendelssohns, can be answered only after thorough study of musical conditions in Leipzig. The city contained five well-known musical institutions: St. Thomas' Church and its choir; the *Gewandhaus* orchestra; the *Singakademie;* the Opera; the popular "Euterpe," a nonprofessional orchestral and singing society.[6] The orchestra of the *Gewandhaus* was, like many others, directed by its concertmaster; only for the performance of oratorios or other vocal works did it require a conductor. At that time, the conductor was Christian August Pohlenz (1790-1843). But he was only "a little light," as a modern historian has called him.[7] Richard Wagner judges him much more harshly; his malicious description of Pohlenz's incompetent direction of Beethoven's Ninth is well-known.[8] The concertmaster was Heinrich A. Matthäi (1781-1835); however in the Fall of 1834, he already seemed hopelessly ill. So Conrad Schleinitz, the president of the *Gewandhaus* Board of Governors, spoke the truth when he assured Felix that no one would be hurt by his coming. But Felix insisted on a suitable compensation for Pohlenz; only when this had been arranged did he accept the position. He even felt obligated to employ Pohlenz as singing teacher at the newly founded Conservatory (1842); but the latter died before he could step into the position.[9]

Felix's salary consisted of 600 Rth. (1800 gold marks) for the first two years; therefore, it can certainly not be called extravagant. In spite of all his ethical conduct and his strict integrity in every phase of the dealings, the resolution to engage him seems to have met with some opposition. For the *Leipziger Musikalische Zeitung* was still defending Pohlenz's position at the end of May, when the contract with Felix was already settled; it ended its article with words which demand that Pohlenz should be rewarded rather than dismissed: "so the affair [which one, is not mentioned] is still a real mystery to us, and we can only say that it grieves us. . . ."[10]

We have seen that Felix was determined to give up the position in Düsseldorf. What reasons motivated this decision? In the first place, it was probably the insoluble conflicts of authority with Immermann and the aversion towards the darker sides of the theatrical business which embittered his life in Düsseldorf. Then there were two other reasons: the undisciplined state of the local orchestra—whose members often got drunk and then beat each other up—and the Catholicism of the Rhineland, which often caused conflicts of conscience in the Protestant Mendelssohn.

Leipzig was more agreeable to the young master because of its short distance from Berlin and his parents, but above all because of its old and great musical tradition, which included St. Thomas' Church and J. S. Bach. It promised him far greater opportunities of development. Since he was a humanist by upbringing and inclination, the old and famed University there also represented a distinct advantage to him; he expected intellectual stimulation from its proximity. True, he had rejected its offer of a music professorship, but he had reason to believe that the University would be understanding and benevolent in its attitude towards his artistic efforts. This proved to be the case.

Mendelssohn was to assume his position in Leipzig in the Fall of 1835. But before that, he had to direct the Seventeenth Lower Rhenish Music Festival, which, this time, took place in Cologne. In order to avoid future conflicts and unpleasantness, he planned to introduce a rule forbidding the conductor to perform his own works. Although the suggestions was not accepted, he stuck to it in Cologne and did not place any of his works on the program.[11] In consideration of the demanding program, Felix had taken the trouble to assemble a large orchestra; and, in fact, the orchestra consisted of 91 violins, 33 violas, 26 'celli, 17 double-basses, 19 woodwind instruments, 16 brass instruments, bass drum and kettledrums. The chorus was massive; it had 118 sopranos, 101 altos, 120 tenors and 137 basses, as we learn from contemporary documents[12]—an unusually large ensemble for those days. Although in general the nobility and the proletariat stayed away from the festivals, this absence did not prevent the bourgeoisie, as the leading group, from carrying the festivals far beyond their regional significance and giving them an international reputation.

The program contained, as principal works, Handel's *Solomon*, Beethoven's Eighth Symphony and *Consecration of the House* Overture, Op. 124, J. F. Reichardt's *Morgengesang* (on a text by Milton), Weber's *Euryanthe* Overture, and Cherubini's *Marche religieuse* and *Hymn*, written for the coronation of Charles X.[13] With the exception of the Beethoven compositions, all the chosen pieces reveal Mendelssohn's personal taste. He had already occupied himself with Handel's great oratorio during the Italian journey, and he wrote his own organ part to it for the first German performance.[14] Reichardt's *Morgengesang* was a favorite piece of the Berlin

Singakademie; for the "rejected" Mendelssohn it evoked the days of his youth. Weber was one of his favorite composers, while in Cherubini he honored the greatest living composer of France (along with Berlioz), who was also his old benefactor.[15]

Klingemann contributed his bit to the success of the festival; the German translation of the oratorio was his work. Felix wrote him a concise report on the festival, though Rebecca thought it was as impossible to describe a Rhenish Music Festival as a Swiss glacier.[16] Again, we miss any detailed criticism or reportage in the professional journals. The *Allgemeine Musikalische Zeitung* in Leipzig finally condescends, in September (!) to bring 14 whole lines about the great Lower Rhenish Music Festival in Cologne.[17] From the entirely laudatory text it emerges that the reviewer could take only passing notice of Felix as the new musical director of Leipzig. On the other hand, the much less significant Elbe Music Festival was evaluated in two extensive articles. The *Revue musicale* took notice of the Lower Rhenish Music Festival only insofar as it once again used the opportunity to spread a few rumors about personal feuds of Felix. Behind all this gossip there is not a word of truth, as Dr. Julius Alf, the meritorious historian of the Lower Rhenish Music Festivals, assured me in a letter. Neither the official documents nor contemporary handwritten accounts of noteworthy events contain even a hint which would justify these rumors.

But as far as we can learn from the contemporary sources, the Cologne music festival was an important artistic and organizational success of Felix's. This was true in spite of the fact that the relationships between the various participating choruses were not always friendly; for instance, the choruses of Cologne and Düsseldorf were not on the best terms with one another.[18]

Spohr visited Felix in Düsseldorf and Cologne and expressed himself in tones of high esteem for the program and execution of the festival. Other musicians now hastened to echo the praise of the old master—for instance, Aloys Schmitt, Heinrich Dorn, and others. The principal work was indubitably Handel's oratorio; this master's mighty choral epic played a predominant part in most German music festivals. When two such different, yet such outstanding authorities as Alfred Einstein and Hugo Riemann agree that "the greatest and most important result of this epoch of music festivals is unquestionably the full appreciation of the art of Handel; this heralded its reception into the common consciousness for the first time,"[19] then an important fact has been established: a single giant, Handel, possessed the primal power to inspire and carry whole groups of music organizations "in his name." Today, these organizations are 150-200 years old and many of them are still flourishing.

Felix's family prepared to journey to Cologne, to acclaim the triumphant young man. The joy of reunion was great. The parents accompanied Felix back to Düsseldorf, where he wanted to wind up his affairs. Incidentally, the Rhinelanders remained loyal to Felix throughout his life; his repeated direction of the Lower Rhenish Music Festivals is the finest proof of their devotion. Of his family, Rebecca alone got to know his lady friend, and, to put it bluntly, she was not charmed with the liaison; however, she was moderate in her letters and only observed at the end: ". . . I have seen what a good thing it is that he is not married."[20]

Felix planned to accompany his parents to Berlin. Shortly before his departure, the family got an unexpected fright: his mother seems to have had a slight stroke. In his letters, Felix does not express himself quite clearly on the subject, but Elise Polko, who revels in reminiscences, knows more precise details. After the crisis, the jolly Rebecca (inclined to practical jokes) sewed the coat of the sleeping Felix to the sofa. On waking up, Felix was in a comic state of embarrassment: the joke had succeeded![21] (A real Biedermeier idyll, hard for us to appreciate today!)

The journey to Berlin was—because of the sick mother—strenuous and exciting, and the good son thanked Heaven when he saw Steglitz and the *Gendarmentürme*. After their arrival, no visits were made or received. Besides, he felt miserable and highly dissatisfied in Berlin, which he calls a "highly revolting nest."[22]

He feared the loneliness which he foresaw in Leipzig. He had already tasted this in Düsseldorf, where, at least, the Woringens, his lady friend, and the painters occasionally alleviated his "spleen." Nonetheless, he wanted to depart at once for Leipzig, but he did not have the heart to leave his aging parents alone in their big house. So his departure was postponed until August 30. He left with a lighter heart, and the certainty of finding a mission adequate to him in Leipzig must have made the journey even easier for him.

II

Mendelssohn was already well known to the Leipzig musical public, mainly through his concert overtures, which had been performed there a number of times. His enthusiastic partisanship of Bach, whose name was still not forgotten there, and his growing significance for European musical life were well known to the editor of the *Leipziger Allgemeine Musikalische Zeitung*, Gottfried Wilhelm Fink (1783-1846). Although he, a worthy musical Philistine, was rather mistrustful and lukewarm towards these tendencies—Schumann characterized his criticisms as "paintings done in honey"—his newspaper naturally had to take notice of them.

Leipzig's musical life was almost as well known as the two most famous institutions of the city, the Fair and the University. Each of them was, in its way, a pioneer of European internationalism. Through their many foreign visitors, they had a powerful influence abroad.

In contrast to Düsseldorf, where musical culture was still *in statu nascendi,* Leipzig had an old, well-established musical tradition. Since 1479, the *Rathspfeiferei* (town pipers) were an established institution; only in the nineteenth century did they blow their last chorale.[23] The cantorship of St. Thomas' School, which was occupied by men like Calvisius, Schein, Kuhnau, J. S. Bach, J. A. Hiller, Doles, and Schicht, played a leading role in the Protestant church music of all Germany. To this were soon added the *Collegium musicum* of the University, the regular "Motets" of the *Thomaner* on Saturday afternoons, the *Singakademie,* founded in 1809, and the *Gewandhaus* orchestra, founded in 1781. Popular music was served, in the *Vormärz,* by the concert society "Euterpe," which also ventured into serious contemporary music, and the very popular "Trombone Choir" of Queisser. This was an outstanding band which, surprisingly, was patronized not only by the lower middle class, but also by the aristocracy.[24] The municipal theatre presented opera, but it was not on the same level as the other musical institutions of the city.[25]

The *Gewandhaus* Orchestra, in 1831, shortly before Mendelssohn's directorship, comprised eight first and eight second violins, four violas, three 'celli, three basses, two each of flutes, oboes, clarinets, bassoons, horns, trumpets, and two percussionists including kettledrums (trombones did not belong to the standing ensemble).[26] The members of the orchestra were rather badly paid, and had to take employment in the nearby spas or even beer gardens outside of the concert season. Since neither a court nor a state supported the *Gewandhaus,* the social classes which carried it consisted exclusively of the well-to-do bourgeoisie and the resident patriciate. In his memoirs, Spohr points out that the orchestra, maintained by merchants, yet does not belong to the category of better dilettantes but has and deserves a very respectable reputation as a professional orchestra.[27]

A concert in the *Gewandhaus* was often described as a "rendezvous of cultivated circles." But we must note that the expression "cultivated" had undergone a certain change of meaning since the middle of the eighteenth century. For the brothers Grimm, it was still the translation, at least the equivalent of the French *poli.*

In Mendelssohn's time, the word already embraced a much larger circle of ideas: that of the individual—and perhaps also collective bourgeois—interest in art and scholarship.[28] This not yet industrialized or highly capitalistic, but honorable and artistically interested bourgeoisie furnished the right soil in which Mendelssohn could grow as a composer and conductor, as a musical guide and leader. He knew it well. We shall see how the repertoire of the *Gewandhaus* unfolded, gained in breadth and depth (certainly not in all dimensions and directions), for Mendelssohn was a man who thought well of his judgment—and his prejudices! Nonetheless, the *Gewandhaus* attained world fame under his leadership.

The traditional concert program of the period immediately before and, in part, during Mendelssohn's directorship consisted of two sections, more or less according to the following scheme:

> Overture or classical symphony
> Opera aria with orchestra
> Concerto for one (or two) solo instruments with (and often without) orchestra
> Quartet, chorus or finale from an opera
> > Intermission
> Smaller symphony or overture
> Aria with orchestra
> Concert piece for the whole orchestra—often with soli and chorus (or a large symphony)[29]

Here, the rise of virtuosity is already discernible; for this "model program" demands at least one solo singer and one instrumental virtuoso. In the second half of the nineteenth century, the participation of the soloists in a *symphonic concert* grows beyond all bounds, often to an absurd extent. Already from Mendelssohn, but even more from Wagner and Berlioz, we hear complaints about the silent orchestral musicians who, for long periods, have nothing to do but twiddle their thumbs and stare at the instrumental soloist or the singer.

Mendelssohn endeavored repeatedly, and in various ways, to enliven or at least to vary the monotony of the inherited scheme. The orchestra which he took over did not consist of artists, but of solid, experienced musicians, used to playing with one another, who really formed an organized body of sound. Even though these musicians were no artists, they brought along enthusiasm worthy of the best artists. Often, they gave many extra rehearsals free, in order to do justice to the work to be performed.[30]

With the death of Matthäi, the post of first concertmaster had become vacant, and Mendelssohn succeeded in securing his old friend Ferdinand David for the post. This outstanding violinist and teacher felt the time was ripe to present the Leipzigers regularly with chamber music in model performances by professional musicians. We must not forget that, at that time, chamber music was still the musical type principally cultivated by the dilettantes—until the piano gained the favors of their growing daughters. Already in Beethoven's time—as we hear from him and from Schuppanzigh—professional musicians had concerned themselves with chamber music in Vienna; in Berlin, Karl Möser performed classical chamber music in public concerts, and we hear similar reports, though more rarely, from Paris. In Leipzig, David's introduction of this practise must have been new, for it was attentively evaluated by Schumann as well as by his antagonist Fink in the *Leipziger Allgemeine Musikalische Zeitung.* Coming from Vienna and Berlin, these "professional" chamber music evenings conquered the concert halls of the whole world through the consolidation of special ensembles (David, Joachim, Hellmesberger, Rosé, etc.) Perhaps this favored the development of a higher level of taste, but it certainly hurt amateur chamber music, the life expectancy of which was thereby diminished.[31]

Felix undertook a second effort to vary the concert pattern with two series of "historical" concerts, in the 1837-38 season, as "extra" presentations. The repertoire of the four evenings can scarcely be called "historical"; rather it is a selection of noncontemporary compositions regarded as "classics." It consisted of works of the following composers:

    I.   J. S. Bach, Handel, Gluck, Viotti.

    II. Haydn, Cimarosa, Naumann, Righini.

    III. Mozart, Salieri, Méhul, Andreas Romberg.(!)

    IV. Abt Vogler, Beethoven, Weber.

The second series (in 1841, partly under David's direction) brought works by:

    I.   Bach, Handel.

    II. Hadyn.

    III. Mozart.

    IV. Beethoven (Ninth Symphony).[32]

With this, the "historical" character of these evenings had, in fact, completely vanished. Mendelssohn never had the taste or inclination for purely historical-musical studies or stylistic experiments. Bach was living music to him, and so was Palestrina—if certain liturgical assumptions were granted. But neither of them was comprehended historically by him. He seriously believed, true to his concept of progress that, in certain respects, his age knew more and could achieve more than past centuries had done.

It is not uninteresting to observe the outer and inner attitudes of the *Gewandhaus* public. Leipzig was a wealthy city; but in its "representative" concerts all outward show was ostentatiously avoided. Still in 1847, the *Grenzboten* reports: "the democratic character of Leipzig is quite manifest; at least, diamonds and tailcoats are rare here." The concerts usually began at 6 p.m.; not until 1841, when, under the shadow of irresistible industrialization, the daylight hours became ever more precious, was it decided, *nolens volens*, not to begin until half-past six. It remained this way till well into the 1880's.

The attitude of the public towards Mendelssohn underwent many changes. Until his death, and even up to the middle of the nineteenth century, it followed him willingly and enthusiastically "as the great teacher."[33] With the era of Wagner and his cohorts, this attitude changed rapidly. However, the "academic" circles of the conservatory founded by Mendelssohn clung stubbornly to a so-called "Mendelssohn" tradition which, created by them, would probably not have appealed very much to their patron saint. We shall discuss these and similar questions in the chapter on "Mendelssohn and Posterity."

On the other hand, this is the place to deal with Mendelssohn as conductor, in the specific and the broad senses of the word.

Today the worth and effectiveness of an outstanding conductor—aside from fashionable stars—is judged not only by his power of interpretation but also by his abilities as a trainer and teacher of the orchestra. Today, the international repertoire of the great orchestras is always more or less standardized; the conductor may have his favorite pieces, but, in general, he will have to follow a prescribed path. He has also to take into account the unionization of the orchestra members. In Mendelssohn's time, things were still quite different. A conductor was first of all a time-beater and crammer, only secondarily an interpreter. His taste determined the repertoire to a great extent, though not exclusively. Beyond this, a really good conductor of the nineteenth century often looked after the material welfare of his musicians. In all these conceptions—still strange to the early nineteenth century—Mendelssohn preceded his contemporaries as a pioneer. How he took over from the time-beating concert-master and became an orchestral pedagogue, master interpreter, benevolent administrator; how he made the worthy, but hardly outstanding orchestra a model instrument of Europe— all this has been described thoroughly and precisely.

Although Mendelssohn was well aware of his own merits in this respect, he could not stand boasting, exaggerating praise, or inflated publicity; he was no star conductor and did not wish to be one. There can hardly be a more moving testimonial to this, touching in its modesty, than his letter written when he was overwhelmed with offers to have a portrait of him "on the grand scale" painted for the Cologne festival. He answers very simply:

It is now run-of-the-mill for unknown or mediocre people to give out their pictures, in order to become somewhat better known . . . I wish that in my case it would not happen until I had achieved something which, in my opinion, deserves this honor. But, up till now, that is not yet the case, and so I should like to postpone such an honor until, according to my own conviction, I am worthier of it. . . .[34]

Otherwise, too, Felix ducks all outward honors whenever he can; there are many witnesses to this. But he was not without consciousness of his own worth, and often of an exaggerated sensitivity which was by no means justified.

Now let us discuss specific characteristics of his conducting.[35] In studying a new work or one that had not been played before Mendelssohn was polite to the musicians, but relentlessly exact. He demanded from them most precise obedience to the prescribed phrasing, dynamics, and tone-color. As a conductor, he embodied "the pure style," and is fond of fast tempi. That he gave Beethoven too flowing a character is maintained by opponents, but has not been proved.[36] He abhorred equally pantomiming and "just beating time through" a work. On the other hand, H. von Bülow and R. Wagner—the former in an objectively friendly manner, the latter in a subjectively hostile manner—bear witness that Mendelssohn was always inclined to brisk tempi, although he objected to rushing through his pieces.[37] Bülow goes far in his admiration of the conductor Mendelssohn:

". . . that Mendelssohn, in his capacity as a conductor, did not form a school . . . cannot be regretted enough. The fault lay not in the master, but in the disciples. . . ."

There ensues an enthusiastic description of the world première of Schubert's great C major Symphony under Mendelssohn's direction.[38] Joseph Joachim, who had still played under him, likewise praises his

almost unnoticeable, but extremely lively language of gesture . . . through which it was possible to transmit the spirit of his personality to chorus and orchestra, to set little deviations aright once more with a flick of his finger. . . . He loved lively tempi, was, however, miles removed from a superficial gliding over the surface such as . . . Richard Wagner attributes to him; and he had an inimitable freedom of rhythm.[39]

In great detail, brilliantly and with fine frankness, Berlioz, for whose music Mendelssohn had absolutely no understanding, describes the Leipzig ensemble and admires the patience, but also the lack of compromise, with which Felix directed the many rehearsals.[40] Even Wagner, in retrospect—Wagner, who scarcely suppresses any malicious remark that he might make at Mendelssohn's expense—saw himself forced to admit, in a slightly ironic tone, the change of taste of the Leipzigers which had set in with Mendelssohn's directorship:

. . . the friends of music in Leipzig had undergone a change of taste which I could not overcome even with the so-skillful combination of my six trumpets.[41]

The famous fast tempi of Mendelssohn, which are certainly no legend, may be explained in various ways and may be justified in general but not in particular. Schumann seems to have divined what was rationally explicable: ". . . one must help out the lack of resonance through driving tempi" (in connection with the review of Beethoven's Fourth Symphony under Mendelssohn).[42]

Wagner gave another explanation, and, in doing so, cited an alleged utterance of Mendelssohn; now, we know that the reader should use some caution with Wagner's so-called "quotations." According to him, Mendelssohn censured slow tempi because they do much more harm than fast ones. For really perfect performance is so very rare that one notices the imperfections least when one marches over the difficult terrain in quick-march tempo.[43] Basically, the two explanations do not exclude each other, but complement each other. To the "perfectionist" Mendelssohn, a performance was hardly ever commensurate with his (or the composer's) ideal, and so he tried to make the weaknesses disappear, tried to make them inaudible through fast tempi. Be that as it may, we believe that besides this very plausible reason still other very elemental impulses, unknown to the master himself, played a role. They reveal themselves in the wealth of extremely fast tempo-designations chosen by Mendelssohn for most of his compositions. *Presto, Molto Vivace, Molto Allegro con Fuoco*, etc., are regularly recurring tempo designations. Though a perfect performance by a great orchestra can be attained only with the expenditure of much trouble, time, and cost, this is not true of chamber music or piano pieces! But there, too, we find a preponderance of very fast tempi. Does not this have its origin in the eternal restlessness of the master, which he learned in his parental home? More: is it not the expression of a mysterious emotional unrest, even insecurity, the origins of which are to be sought in regions which are accessible only to the conscientious depth-psychologist? We leave the question unanswered.

We must also mention Mendelssohn's care for the material welfare of his musicians. He seems to have been the first conductor who demanded, and eventually also got, a fixed pension for the permanent orchestra members.[44] True, every larger orchestra had a so-called "pension fund," but this was dependent on voluntary contributions of the members, on gifts, and on the income of the statutory concerts for the benefit of the fund. Aside from this social-political activity, Mendelssohn was always at hand with his personal funds when any misfortune or need struck one of his musicians. In Oxford (in the so-called "green books," the collection of many letters directed to Mendelssohn), a large number of letters of thanks from Leipzig musicians are found. Without exception, however, Mendelssohn imposed the condition that others should not learn of his help.

However, the enlargement of the orchestra under his direction is to be understood on purely musical grounds. The stylistically correct performance of the large Beethoven symphonies and the steadily increasing demands of contemporary composers made the step an absolute necessity. We have seen that before and during Mendelssohn's time the orchestra consisted of about 40 regularly employed musicians; the string section included 26 men. In the season 1838-39 it was increased to 31, and the whole orchestra to 48-49 men. Finally, we must refer again to that change of taste in the Leipzig program which had set in under Mendelssohn. The most frequently performed composers shortly *before* he took over were: Eberl, von Seyfried, Clementi, Hummel, Reissiger, Fesca, Neukomm, F. Ries, Lindpainter. Nine symphonies and a number of concert pieces by Friedrich Schneider of Dessau, then a highly regarded composer, were performed, though seldom repeated. After Mendelssohn's coming the composers most performed (among living contemporaries) were Spohr, Cherubini, Moscheles, Gade, Rossini, Liszt, Chopin, Thalberg, Schumann, Mendelssohn.[45] By far the most played composers were Mozart and Beethoven; considerably behind them came Haydn, but also Bach and Handel. This seemingly unfair preference on Mendelssohn's part has sometimes been misunderstood and foolishly criticized. It was generally overlooked that neither the scores nor the parts of many Haydn symphonies and Bach orchestral works (e.g., the Brandenburg Concerti, etc.) could be obtained or even seen.

But we have gone far ahead of our story and we now return to Mendelssohn's assumption of his position in Leipzig. After only two orchestral rehearsals, Felix presented himself to his public on October 4, 1835, with the following program:

A

Mendelssohn: Overture, *Calm Sea and Prosperous Voyage*
K. M. von Weber: Scene and Aria from *Freischütz* (Mme H. Grabau)
L. Spohr: Violin Concerto No. 8 (Music Director Gehrke from Berlin as soloist)
L. Cherubini: Overture and Introduction to *Ali Baba* (with *Singakademie* and St. Thomas Choir)

B

Beethoven: Fourth Symphony in B flat major

In his own report to his family, Mendelssohn mentions that the pieces by Weber, Spohr, and Cherubini did not go as well as his own overture—for "one rehearsal was not sufficient," but that he was fully satisfied with the performance of the Beethoven symphony.[46] Furthermore, he felt wonderfully well and completely at home in Leipzig. Even in later statements he always views Leipzig as his choice of home; there "all winter long he has no irritating day, practically no annoying word in connection with his position, and many joys and pleasures."[47] And, in a grand style, he states that it is a real satisfaction to him to have become well established in Germany and not to have to seek for recognition abroad. This pleasant change in his status he owes above all to Leipzig and his acceptance there.[48]

In general, Felix had a good instinct for the genuineness or lack thereof of the sentiments expressed to him. In the case of Leipzig, he certainly did not deceive himself. The two musical magazines, Fink's opportunistic *Allgemeine Musikalische Zeitung* and Robert Schumann's *Neue Zeitschrift für Musik*, greeted the new music director most warmly, each in its own way. In the former magazine, we read the following statement: "Immediately on his appearance as director, the most lively pleasure of the gathering in the well-filled hall was unequivocally expressed in enthusiastic applause. . . . Everything went splendidly. Everything was honored with applause." After additional enthusiastic commentary, the review ends somewhat too sanctimoniously with the words: "And so let this undertaking be blessed! And it will be so, if everything under the leaders goes in a spirit of unity and in devoted love of art, without small-minded self-seeking. . . ."[49]

Quite different, and much more personal and cordial, is Schumann's reaction. For him, Mendelssohn was, all his life, the "master of his age"; he called him F. Meritis after a musical organization in Amsterdam and greeted him with these words:

> F. Meritis stepped out. A hundred eyes flew towards him in the first moment . . . F. Meritis conducted as though he had composed the overture himself [it was *Calm Sea and Prosperous Voyage* which he *had* composed himself! This is just one of the many examples of Jean-Paul-like or Schumannesque fun] and the orchestra played accordingly. . . . For my part, the baton disturbed me, and I agreed with Florestan, who thought that in the symphony the orchestra should be like a republic . . . but it was a pleasure to see how F. Meritis foreshadowed with his eye every spiritual nuance of the composition, from the most distant to the strongest, and how he, the blessed one, swam far ahead of the common herd. . . .

The tempo of the scherzo in the Beethoven symphony was too slow for Schumann; the concerto of Spohr seemed to him to be played "too barely and starkly."

> That a change of administration had taken place, everyone believed that he had recognized in the choice of pieces. While, in the past, in the first Firlenz [Leipzig] concert Italian butterflies had always fluttered around German oaks, this time the latter stood all alone, powerful and dark. A certain party saw a reaction in this; I consider it rather accidental than intentional. We all know how necessary it is to protect Germany against the invasion of your darlings [this means contemporary Italian operatic arias]. . . .[50]

Here began a relationship between two lofty spirits, who, however, both personally and artistically, followed quite different paths. It was never an intimate friendship, but a mutual respect and esteem. To this was added, in the case of the highly romantic and enthusiastic Schumann, a purely personal "Schwärmerei"—one has to call it a real "crush"—for the somewhat cooler and justifiably reserved, but so irresistibly charming Felix. We shall discuss the relationship between the two masters and friends in greater detail in Chapter XVI. Unfortunately, first the Wagnerians and then the Nazi historians spun many malicious and often infamous lies about the relationship between the two. For these gentlemen could not accept with equanimity the fact that a real German honored one who was racially completely Jewish! So there was an attempt to falsify or corrupt the sources. The great master of the art is indubitably Dr. Wolfgang Boetticher, who, in his edition of the writings and letters of Schumann (carefully sifted on racial-political grounds) did not hestitate to commit wild distortions, omissions, and even forgeries.[51] Thus, we read the following versions of the first meeting between Schumann and Mendelssohn.

Boetticher	Photostatic copy of the memoirs issued by the Schumann Archive
p. 107. ". . . In August first saw him in the *Gewandhaus*. [Henrietta] Voigt if I am not mistaken, first introduced us. At the end of September he moved completely to L."	p. 62. "In August, 1835, first saw him in the *Gewandhaus*. The musicians played him h[is] Overture "Calm Sea." I told him that I knew all his compositions well; he answered something very modest. The first impression was that of an unforgettable human being. Voigt, if I am not mistaken, first introduced us. At the end of September he moved completely to L."
p. 110. "To everyone he wishes steady solitude with himself and his art: his own direction alarms him, lest it become one-sided."	p. 71. "To Gade he wishes steady solitude with himself and his art; his direction alarms him, lest it become one-sided."
p. 114. "Founding of the Conservatory and his attitude that he wanted to be regarded as director."	p. 35. "His ideas ab [out] the Conservatory, that he wanted to do the musicians a service." "Founding of the Conservatory, and his attitude that he wanted to be regarded *only* [*nur*, word could also be *nie* (never)] as director."

Naturally notes of Schumann such as the following were sedulously suppressed:

"Spreading joy and blessings everywhere" (p. 40); "his praise was always of the highest value to me—he was the highest, final reference" (p. 44). "Strictest fulfillment of his duties towards God and man" (p. 51). "Mendelssohn was true in everything" (p. 58). "He was free of all weaknesses of vanity" (p. 61). "Highest moral and artistic maxims; therefore, incorruptible, seemingly often gruff and inhuman" (p. 77).

And so on! Is it not sad and shameful that the sources on Mendelssohn have been corrupted by both sides, his friends and his enemies? If it is true that legend is always stronger than historical scholarship, then the latter must always forestall the formation of myths and legends, or, if that is not feasible, at least deprive them as much as possible of the soil in which they can grow.

III

THE WORKS OF THE DÜSSELDORF YEARS

In contrast to the works of the great journey, among which choral works predominated, choral compositions now seem to recede in importance. But this is only apparently so, for their absence is explained, or, rather, put in the correct light, through Mendelssohn's work on the oratorio *St. Paul*, which was finished in 1836. Instead of these choral works, we now find the master's songs. Symphonic music is represented by two larger works, piano music is carefully cultivated, and we miss only chamber music, for which Mendelssohn at this time wrote only smaller occasional works. Here, we give a survey of his compositions in the years 1832-1835.

Orchestral Music

SYMPHONY IN A, SO-CALLED "ITALIAN"

Mendelssohn himself gave this symphony its nickname "Italian" for he wrote it mostly in Italy.[52] In fact, in the library of the Naples Conservatory there is a manuscript entitled *Concertino* which contains the first movement of the symphony in short-score form (written in four staves, but only the first two pages in Mendelssohn's hand). It shows a few slight deviations from the final version, most clearly in the retransition to the principal theme. The master regarded his work with great self-criticism; he was never quite satisfied with it and never released it for publication in his lifetime. We know that he was dissatisfied with many details of the first movement, but we do not know which ones. In a letter to Moscheles, he reports on his alterations in the second and third movements of the work, and also on his dissatisfaction with the first movement.[53] But the printed version following the original score bears the date March 13, 1833. It was not possible for me to ascertain what has become of the manuscript revised in Düsseldorf; it appears to be lost.[54]

The symphony consists of the following movements: 1) *Allegro vivace,* A major, 6/8; 2) *Andante con moto,* D minor, 4/4; 3) *Con moto moderato,* A major, 3/4 *(Menuetto);* 4) *Presto,* A minor, C *(Saltarello).*

First Movement: Although Mendelssohn was often a "victim" of 6/8 meter, here he remains sovereign throughout. The theme is free of lyricisms; it is like a simple call, so that it is thoroughly suitable for symphonic treatment. Mendelssohn's critical understanding of art prevented him from succumbing to the temptation which seduced Schumann and Chopin (in the concerti): to use a self-contained theme as symphonic raw material. If the theme appears in a perfectly finished form at the beginning, there are scarcely any new possibilities for its development. Schumann's E flat major Symphony suffers from this in the outer movements, Chopin's F minor Concerto in the opening movement.

Immediately after the appearance of the theme, Mendelssohn brings in a miniature development section; only then does the *tutti* take over the theme. After a skillful transition, a real second theme is presented in contrast. The development is far more than "a clever game," as Einstein unfairly calls it, but, rather, a brilliant interplay among the principal theme, the "bridge," and a new theme in minor which is sharply contoured both rhythmically and harmonically. It leads to a *fugato* and, with the inclusion of the principal theme, to a magnificent "written-out ritardando" (Riemann) on the beginning of the principal theme, now doubled in note-values:

Example 48

In the reprise, a literal repetition never occurs; everything is brilliantly and elegantly varied. The coda takes up the new theme of the development (in minor), but, in a mighty crescendo reaches A major once again and closes the movement with jubilant calls.

Second Movement: Oddly, no one seems to have pointed out, up till now, the striking similarity of the theme to Zelter's *Es war ein König in Thule;* it is usually described as an "elegiac processional." It is possible that Felix, with this movement and its theme, wanted to remember his dear old Zelter.

Example 49a

The song melody begins darkly in the oboes, bassoons, and violas, accompanied only by pizzicato 'celli and basses. It is a rarity for a slow movement to be intoned in two voices! The whole movement develops from a tiny basic cell:

Example 49b

This idea was later done to death by others (principally by Tschaikovsky, but also by Mahler in his Fifth Symphony). A short countertheme in march tempo contrasts with the "König in Thule," but cannot come into its own. Here, too, the master achieved a splendidly rounded form. It is best diagrammed as ABA,A₁ (A₁ is a slight variation of the principal theme.) The movement closes with the elegiac *pp* D minor pizzicato of the low strings.

Third Movement: This minuet-like *Con moto moderato* is praised highly by most commentators; to us, it seems the weakest movement. It is a Biedermeier Minuet: merry, lovable, but without the power of a Haydn, without the winged, noble grace of a Mozart—a real bourgeois minuet! The finest section is the close, where the Trio knocks at the door once again but is gently turned away, and the Minuet theme softly closes the movement.

Fourth Movement: This movement, conceived in the spirit of a Neapolitan *saltarello*, is nearest to the familiar Mendelssohn of the elfin scherzi. But it has a much longer breath, and, above all, is a real symphonic *tour de force* in that the entire development is one single crescendo from *pp* to *ff*. The retransition is based on an unusual pedal-point. At the very end, we hear the beginning call of the first movement, now turned to minor. The symphony, which had begun in radiant A major, ends in a frenzied (yet soft) and macabre A minor. A strange ending, unusual both then and now! Rightly, Tovey speaks of the completely singular position of this symphony in the whole literature of Classic and Romantic music.

Though its ideas deviate from the textbook, the instrumentation is, even today, a model of well-sounding and characteristic linear writing. The beginning, where woodwinds (which must not cackle!) accompany the principal theme, is famous. Brilliantly successful is the middle part of the *saltarello*, leading from a mere whisper in the orchestra to a whipped-up *ff*. The crowning glory of the work, however, is the involvement of the principal theme in the *fugato*, above the new theme in the development of the first movement. Here, the orchestra is so transparent that one can almost see the two thematic complexes dancing with one another!

Both older authors (Reissmann, Dahms) and more recent ones (H. Botstiber, A. Einstein) present the viewpoint that the *Italian Symphony* lacks inner unity and that its reprises do not bring the themes back on a higher level than at their first appearance. Since there are some outstanding scholars among these critics, the present writer considers it necessary to invalidate such views with a short analysis:

The second theme of the slow movement is harmonically linked with the theme of the third movement. Another relative of this thematic family is the second theme of the first movement.

The "new" theme of the development of the first movement clearly foreshadows the key, meter and mood of the last movement. In reverse, a reminiscence of the first movement appears at the end of the last.

One can go so far as to reduce the basic motifs of the whole symphony to a common denominator. The author is aware of the controversial nature of all such reductions to an *Urlinie*, but would like to call attention to the possibility of its existence in this case. The following relations appear:

Example 50a

1st movement

2nd movement

Example 50b

Example 50c

The musical examples elucidate the close relationship of all these motifs. We do not consider this relationship as the result of a conscious process of creation, but, rather, as the outcome of the certainty of the "selective instinct." Schumann felt this very precisely when he spoke of "the intimate relationship of all four movements" and established that "the melodic leading in the four different movements is related."[55]

OVERTURE, *The Fair Melusine*

After everything we have heard about Mendelssohn's "zeal for revision," we are not astounded that the *Melusine* overture shared the fate of most of the other compositions of the master, to be revised again and again. Sir Thomas Attwood possessed the first version, Klingemann the second, on which the première of the work was based (in the absence of the composer, 1834). It did not exactly win enthusiastic applause. Klingemann carefully conveys this to his friend, not without citing a few excerpts from the most important reviews, probably as consolation. The *Atlas* emphasized the similarity to Beethoven's *Egmont* Overture (!); the *Times* found points of similarity with Beethoven's Pastoral Symphony, indeed, it felt that the mantle of the dead master had fallen on Felix's shoulders. The reception of the work was cool, in spite of all words of praise. Moscheles, the conductor, seems to have been partly to blame for this, for (according to Klingemann's report) he took the tempi too slowly. Mendelssohn, spoiled by success, received these reports with great equanimity. His reaction reminds us a little of Mozart's cavalier response when Emperor Joseph II observed that *Don Giovanni* was not the right food for his Viennese. In the same sense, Mendelssohn (metaphorically) shrugged his shoulders. "Didn't the people at the Philharmonic like my *Melusine?* So what, I shan't die of it. . . ."[56] He had sent Klingemann and Moscheles whole series of dynamic and instrumental corrections; finally, in 1835, a year later, he began the "final" revisions. Before he allowed this version to be printed, he begged Klingemann to burn the old (second) score, "because it always seemed only half-done to him."[57] Of all his overtures, it was then his favorite.[58]

Schumann praised the work beyond all bounds; inspired by fantasy, he raved about "flashing fishes with golden scales, pearls in open shells, etc." Such extravagancies imposed upon music went against Mendelssohn's inmost nature. He defended himself against such interpretations, at the risk of being considered ungrateful. In delicately ironic and sober fashion he answered the question as to what *The Fair Melusine* was about: "Hmm—a *mesalliance.*"[59]

The overture is organized in a novel form, already foreshadowed in Beethoven and Weber. Strictly speaking, it is a sonata movement (S) in F minor, framed by an introductory and a closing section in F major. These (A and A¹) naturally use the same thematic material. Thus the form is: A (F major)—S (F minor)—A¹ (F major).

Example 51

The F major introduction (see music Example 51) brings the "magical wave-figure" (Schumann) which Wagner then took over literally for the *Rheingold* motif. Not unjustifiably, the third measure of the theme has been criticized for its rhythmic weakness, but since both the introduction and the epilogue are concise, the rhythm does not become monotonous. Again, it is a measure in 6, this time, 6/4. Fortunately, in the F minor section Mendelssohn is able to derive some clever effects from this meter, through the following divisions:

$$3 + 3; 2 + 2 + 2; 3 + 1 + 2; 2 + 1 + 1 + 2.$$

The marvellously transparent "water-clear" orchestration has always been admired. Contemporaries and critics praise the trumpet entrance on the dominant seventh (in the 18th measure); Schumann calls it "a tone from age-old times." The serene idyll is presented enchantingly and simply; and the defiant F minor section has as a countertheme another idyllic melody of great charm. So it is no wonder that this, of all the master's overtures, pleased the connoisseurs the most. The absence of a brilliant ending emphasized the unity with the spirit of the fairy-tale and of the themes, and made the work all the more lovable.

Vocal Music

SONGS FOR SOLO VOICE WITH PIANO ACCOMPANIMENT, OP. 19, 34

Among these twelve pieces we find only six "hits"—a meager haul. Who are the poets of the successful pieces? H. Heine (4), Goethe (1), Ulrich von Liechtenstein (1); the other poets are Egon Ebert and Klingemann. Felix succeeded in finding better texts, but he was still at home in the Biedermeier style—and that is where we usually find him. Only when he escapes it (all too hesitantly) does he succeed in creating some pieces that have become famous. We have already pointed out, in Chapter VII, the esthetic and personal reasons for this weakness. Now we shall examine somewhat more closely the forms of his songs, and then his relationship to the German poetry of his age.

Only late in his life, and then reluctantly, did Mendelssohn use the freely through-composed song form as he found it in Schubert. His best piece in this vein is Goethe's sonnet *Die Liebende schreibt*. Otherwise, however, he is freer than Zelter, but distinctly more restricted in his form than Schubert. He was inclined to write strophically constructed songs with more or less free closing sections. Good examples are *Auf Flügeln des Gesanges* (sung to death, alas!) or that inspiration of genius, *Neue Liebe* (Heine). A weakness of his song composition is his indifference to correct declamation of the text. While such violations of prosody are unpleasant in choral music, in solo performance—especially in comparison with Wagner's, Wolf's, and Mahler's strict observance of the rules—they strike us as directly contrary to the style. A few examples may justify this criticism:

> *Frühlingslied* (Ulrich von Liechtenstein)
> ". . . blühen gén des Mayen Schein"
> *Frühlingslied* (Klingemann)
> "Es bréchén im schállénden Reigén"
> *Auf Flügeln des Gesanges* (Heine)
> "Es liegt ein rotblühender Gartén"

Zuleika (Goethe)
"Freudigés Gefühl von beiden"
Reiselied (Heine)
"Und wie ich *reite*, so réitén mír die Gedanken voraus"

His piano accompaniment parallels the voice exactly. Only in his best songs does he throw away the crutches; then, as in the *Reiselied* or *Neue Liebe*, he wins the spurs of a master.

We must say a word concerning his relationship to contemporary poets. The period between 1830 and 1850 is characterized by the rise of *Junges Deutschland*. Oskar Walzel, an authority on this movement, says of it: "The *Jungdeutsche* is anything but a regional artist; above all, he is a writer for the day. . . . The will to create from the day for the day is the strength and the weakness of the *Jungdeutschen*. The *Jungdeutschen* are the founders of German journalistic writing of the 19th century."[60]

We have already seen with what mistrust (to say the least) Mendelssohn regarded the journalism of all countries. The Francophile trend of the *Jungdeutschen* was completely antipathetic to him, the disciple of Goethe and Zelter. His letters are not lacking in negative judgments on the *Junges Deutschland*. He asks his father to tell him what he thinks of this movement:

I have something about it in my heart; they are scoundrels—especially von Gutzkow.[61] One thing is certain: I don't want to have anything to do with anyone who associates with such scoundrels (Gutzkow and Company). . . . They are such shameful wretched people—characterless and talentless— the whole *Junges Deutschland*; on top of that, they love me, but very unhappily.[62]

Even so, he could not resist the verses of Heine; otherwise, however, the poets of his songs are conservative, respectable, or "pseudo-old-German." The latter were, at that time, the preferred mode of the solid, well-capitalized bourgeoisie.

All in all we seem still to hear the warning voice of Hegel, who cautioned Felix against sacrificing the autonomy of music (and of melody) to the poet and his form. In principle, Mendelssohn followed this warning all his life— to his disadvantage—for where he disregarded it he succeeded in writing his best songs.

LIEDER IM FREIEN ZU SINGEN (Songs of the Open Air)

Fanny had questioned the "genuineness" and "spontaneity" of four-voiced folk songs, and expressed her preference for one-voiced folk song settings. Felix replied that his way seemed to him the only right way to write folk songs, for all piano accompaniments smacked of the chamber and the music-cabinet.⁶³ He knew this method from the *Singakademie* (Zelter's *Liedertafel*) but above all from the English glees. Not a little of their technique and their spirit entered into these choruses; it is this that brought them so near to the German bourgeois—indeed, to the German people as a whole.

Oddly, here the master is much more selective in his texts than in the solo songs. The first volume contains poems by Platen, Heine, Hölty, and Goethe. Inexact declamations, unfortunately, also occur here, for example:

> In weiter Ferne sei mein Herz
> dír Vaterlánd und Vaterhaus (Heine)
> Bé-gég-nen un-sérm Láuf (Goethe)

Formally, the composer is much freer than in the solo songs. Nos. 2, 3, and 4, grouped together by Heine under the title "Tragedy," are real folklike pieces. On the other hand, Nos. 1, 5, and 6, gems of the secular choral song, are easy to sing and reach great artistic heights with simple means.

INFELICE, CONCERT ARIA FOR SOPRANO WITH ORCHESTRA

This composition was commissioned by the London Philharmonic Society. In it, Mendelssohn hardly surpasses emotionally the usual elegy of the "Abbandonata" aria, which was the showpiece of Baroque opera. The feelings of the beloved deserted by the hero are experienced here in elegiac fashion, but are not presented convincingly either dramatically or emotionally. The antiquated style of the *opera seria* which Felix had to imitate here did not suit him at all. Nonetheless, from a purely musical viewpoint, the piece is successful—above all because of its noble melodic line planned on the grand scale, then, too, because of the orchestra, which often goes its own way. But it is not a living piece of music.

Piano Music

Of these compositions, the three *Capriccios*, Op. 33, deserve only a few comments, the *Rondo brillante* in E flat major hardly that much. The title "Capriccio" is, in this case, a designation thought up for want of a better one; for these pieces neither come near stylistically to the old, polyphonic form, nor do they resemble a Chopin Scherzo (which one might also call a Capriccio) in content or form. They most resemble fast sonata movements; as such, however, there is little that is characteristic about them. The thematic material is rather unrewarding, and the pianistic treatment is elegant enough, but completely unoriginal. Of the three pieces, the third (in B minor) is probably the most successful—above all because of its slow funereal introduction; the *Presto con fuoco* borrows a bit from the last movement of Beethoven's *Appassionata*, without coming anywhere near it in force, power, contrasts, and execution. This is one of the "rip-roaring" pieces of Mendelssohn which show temperament enough, but what is first taken for a cannon soon proves to be a series of salvoes with blank cartridges.

The second piece (E major), which pleased Schumann so much that he compared it with a chapter of the *Flegeljahre* of Jean-Paul (a favorite author of both masters), interests us only because of the connection between its theme and the motifs from the *Melusine* Overture.

The *Rondo brillante* in E flat major with orchestra was written for Moscheles and was often played by him. It is brilliant, empty, and was once very effective. That is all we can say about this work, which differs from similar compositions of Kalkbrenner only in its solid technical mastery.

However, the six Preludes and Fugues, Op. 35, are on quite different level. The twelve pieces were written at various times between 1827 and 1837; therefore, they cannot be regarded as "occasional compositions."

Anyone who has written a four-voiced fugue for piano knows how dangerously dependent the playability of the piece is on the theme and its counterpoints. It is much easier to compose fugues for string quartet than for piano. This difficulty must have challenged the experienced contrapuntist Mendelssohn to try his hand in this little-exploited area. The work bears witness to the artistic integrity of the master as few others could do; for, in this field, not much fame or profit could be reaped at a time when the name of Bach did not have a good reputation with publishers or with the piano playing public. A fugue was condemned in advance as "learned stuff," and pianists preferred a brilliant rondo a hundred times to a fugue. After all, it is not so different today.

Aside from the technical challenge which confronted the master in this work, on a higher level he encountered a problem of quite different dimensions, namely, the stylistic question. Did not a fugue automatically have to imitate Bach's models? Ought Mendelssohn to follow the interesting, yet sterile experiments of Reicha, who had postulated complete tonal freedom for the fugue? Might it be possible completely to avoid the baroque style, in which the fugue had created its most magnificent monuments, without, on the other hand, falling into the anachronistic and arid academic fugue?

Felix thought a great deal about all this, and expressed some of his ideas (in letters to Fanny). He knows that this opus will not be much played, but he cares nothing for that.[64] He feels that the strict discipline of the fugues, after all the *Songs without Words*, will do him good.[65]

The result is impressive, but uneven in details. He succeeded in freeing himself from mere imitations of Bach—unlike the two fugues in Op. 7 (the *Charakteristische Stücke*), these enter upon virgin territory. Indeed, he succeeds in achieving a creative synthesis of the polyphonic tradition with post-classical, free piano style; we sense no archaic or "academic" mannerisms. It is astonishing to see how certain of his formulas and structural ideas recur in Reger, who had undertaken something similar. In some sections, Mendelssohn foreshadowed Reger, who, though he came much later, was distinctly related to the earlier composer in spirit.

Of the six Preludes, the most important are Nos. 1, 4, and 6. A Song without Words, No. 5 calls for a very light touch; No. 2 is a rather conventional "Invention," while No. 3 is a furious Capriccio. In No. 1, he succeeds in developing a really new pianistic idea: the melody is surrounded by the arpeggio accompaniment, which is distributed between the two hands. Otherwise, he is always complaining, and rightly so, about his dearth of truly pianistic conceptions. Harmonically, the Prelude is reminiscent of the Songs without Words No. 21. No. 4 resembles the Songs without Words No. 18 (also in A flat major) but is more finely organized. In its accompaniment, No. 6 slightly suggests Schubert's *Ave Maria;* it is a noble, well-developed piece.

Of the Fugues, we consider No. 1 (E minor), No. 3 (B minor), and No. 6 (B flat major) the best. The theme of No. 1 is utilized both in its original form and in its inversion, and, after a great crescendo intensified by stretti, culminates in a (free) chorale with figured bass, which distinctly reminds us of *Was mein Gott will, das g'scheh allzeit.* After this fortissimo high point, the piece ends quite softly. In No. 3 contrapuntal artifices are exposed: inversions, double stretto, canonic episodes, etc., overwhelm the listener. Nonetheless, the fugue never sounds forced and is of monumental stature. Finally, No. 6, a piece of brilliant virtuosity, is many years ahead of its time. The sharply separated rhythms are blended together only at the very end of the fugue. Perhaps Nos. 4 and 5 promise more than they fulfill. An uncommonly sonorous piece, No. 2 never allows one to feel the strictness of the form; it is practically a fugued Song without Words. Therefore, Schumann could justifiably write:

> So one could give many a young lady the last part of a fugue—for example, the second one—as a Song without Words. . . . In short, they are not just fugues worked out with the brain and according to a formula, but pieces of music, originating from the spirit and carried out in poetic fashion.[66]

Notes

1. Letter to Klingemann, May 14, 1835.
2. Letter to Klingemann, June 26, 1835.
3. Letter to K. Schleinitz, January 26, 1835. Both father and son demanded this; but the father knew that, in so doing, he was following a cardinal principle of Jewish ethics (one is forbidden to apply for another's position).
4. Letter to Schleinitz, April 16, 1835.
5. Unpublished letter to his father, January 15, 1835.
6. See Schumann, *Schriften über Musik*, Vol. II.
7. W. Vetter, in *Festschrift, zum 175. Jubiläum des Gewandhauses;* article *"Res severa . . ."*
8. R. Wagner, *Mein Leben*, Vol. I, pp. 75ff. (1911).
9. This must be said quite clearly, since even such an author as Ernest Newman, in his Wagner biography, makes observations like "Pohlenz was dismissed from his post to make way for Mendelssohn." (*Life of Richard Wagner*, Vol. I, p. 177.)
10. *Allgemeine Musikalische Zeitung* (Leipzig, 1835), May, No. 10.
11. Unpublished letter of February 26, 1835.
12. See Adam Carse, *The Orchestra from Beethoven to Berlioz* (New York, 1919), p. 60.
13. Originally, Mendelssohn had wanted to perform one of the great revolutionary hymns of Cherubini, but then received from the latter the manuscripts of the works which were performed. See Hiller, *F.M.*, p. 37.
14. Letter of April 3, 1835; see also letter to Klingemann of June 26, 1835. According to the proceedings of the Music Festival, Mendelssohn's suggestion of an overture by J. S. Bach was turned down as possibly harmful to the attendance.
15. See the extensive memorandum of Mendelssohn to the committee of the Lower Rhenish Music Festivals, written on April 10, 1835. The manuscript (unpublished) is in the Library of Congress, Washington, D.C. The correspondence of the Lower Rhenish Music Festivals, at present in Cologne, reveals that it was Mendelssohn who insisted upon the performance of a symphony by F. Ries.
16. Letter to Klingemann, July 6, 1835.
17. See *Allgemeine Musikalische Zeitung*, September, 1835, No. 35, pp. 580ff.
18. Letter to Klingemann, March 26, 1835.
19. See Riemann, *Geschichte der Musik seit Beethoven*, p. 213; Einstein, *Music of the Romantic Era*, pp. 177-178; also Kretzschmar, *Führer*, 3rd edition, II, 2, pp. 109ff.
20. Letter to Klingemann, July 17, 1835.
21. E. Polko, *Erinnerungen an Felix Mendelssohn* (Leipzig, 1868), II.
22. Letter to Klingemann, May 14, 1835.
23. For the musical history of Leipzig, see R. Wustmann, A. Schering, *Musikgeschichte Leipzigs* (2 vols., only till 1723); A. Dörffel, *Festschrift zum hundertsten Jubiläum des Gewandhauses;* E. Kneschke, *Die hundertfünfzigjährige Geschichte der Leipziger Gewandhauskonzerte*, 1956. (Especially W. Vetter, *Res severa verum gaudium: Die Tradition des Gewandhauses.*)
24. See F. Schmidt, *Das Musikleben der burgerlichen Gesellschaft Leipzigs im Vormarz*, Langensalza, 1912; also A. Carse, *op. cit.*, p. 134. (Schumann calls Queisser "Trombone God," II, p. 97.) See also Edward Holmes, *A Ramble Among the Musicians of Germany*, 1828, pp. 254ff.—an outstanding sourcework by an unprejudiced American.

25. Holmes, *op. cit.*, p. 248. Chorley calls the theatre "small and shabby."

26. Dörffel, *Festschrift zum Hundertsten Jubiläum des Gewandhauses.*

27. Spohr, *Memoiren*, I. (1804).

28. Schmidt, *op. cit.*, pp. 32ff. See also W. H. Riehl, *Musikalische Charakterköpfe*, 5. Auflage (1876), pp. 100ff: "Mendelssohn was the first musician who really made music for 'fine society'—in the good sense of the word. He was not the pithy German burgher, keeping himself to himself, like Bach, but a culturally well-rounded, socially skillful, wealthy, well-mannered man, personally known almost throughout Germany, sought-out in all distinguished circles. . . . So Mendelssohn wrote in the spirit of this cultivated society, which now, equalizing and mediating, spreads over all ranks. . . . Therefore, Mendelssohn is a personality no less characteristic in cultural history than Bach was for his time. No other art could show a man who, in his artistic creation, stood so firmly in the midst of the social life of our cultivated circles, and, in turn, was so well understood and valued by them as Mendelssohn. . . ." So it was, once upon a time!

29. Schmidt, *op. cit.*, pp. 64ff.

30. Dörffel, *op. cit.*, p. 32.

31. Mendelssohn was aware of the possible harm caused by professional chamber music. In his unpublished letter to F. David of September 3, 1841, he says: "As hard as I try to present the masters in good performances, I would not want to pull the rug out from under amateur music—even if it's my own *Songs without Words*. 'For they did them wrong, may God forgive them!' "

32. According to Schmidt, *op. cit.* Letter to Klingemann, January 14, 1841: "I think it is a good thing for us to accustom the paying public to taking part itself on occasion—that gives the institution more of a social than a public tone." Accordingly, he used volunteers for the Beethoven Ninth.

33. Schmidt, *op. cit.*, pp. 38ff.

34. Letter of May 18, 1835, to *Regierungs-Sekretär* Hirte in Cologne.

35. On Mendelssohn as conductor, see G. Schünemann, *Geschichte des Dirigierens*, 1913; Dörffel, *Geschichte der Leipziger Konzertdirektion;* Berlioz, *Memoirs;* Schumann, *Schriften über Musik*, W. Chorley, *Music in Germany.*

36. A. Weissmann, *Der Dirigent im 20. Jahrhundert*, pp. 39-40.

37. H. von Bülow, *Ausgewählte Schriften* (1896), p. 406.

38. *Ibid.*, p. 335.

39. E. Wolff, *op. cit.*, pp. 123ff.

40. See H. Berlioz, *Memoirs*, ed. H. Scholz, pp. 299ff., with the marginal observation: "But he still loves the dead a bit too much."

41. R. Wagner, *Mein Leben* (Munich, 1911), Vol. I. p. 125. Wagner suddenly identifies himself with old Pohlenz, whom he had criticized severely not long before (p. 73). On the delicate subject "Wagner and Mendelssohn" see Chapters 15 and 20.

42. Schumann, *Schriften über Musik*, I, p. 137.

43. R. Wagner, *Über das Dirigieren.*

44. Dörffel, *op. cit.;* also letter to Moscheles of November 30, 1839.

45. Schmidt, *op. cit.*

46. Letter of October 6, 1835.

47. Letter of January 30, 1836 (completely distorted in the published edition). For Felix, so sensitive to atmospheric conditions, this was a criterion of real well-being.

48. Letter of June 1, 1836.

49. *Allgemeine Musikalische Zeitung* (Leipzig, 1835), October, No. 41.

50. Schumann, *Schriften über Music und Musiker*, I, "Schwärmbriefe."

51. Wolfgang Boetticher, *Robert Schumann in seinen Schriften und Briefen* (Berlin, 1942).

52. Letters of February 22, 1831; April 27, 1831; January 21, 1832.

53. Letter to Moscheles on June 26, 1834, in which Felix observes that, from the fourth measure on, he *would have to alter the whole first movement* if he once set to work seriously at revision! See also letter to Klingemann of June 26, 1835.

54. The date of the "revised" score of 1837 is deceptive. Scarcely anything is changed. But see letter to Klingemann of February 16, 1835: "It must become quite different in any case."
55. Schumann, *Schriften über Musik* (1840), III, pp. 145 ff.
56. *Aus Moscheles' Leben* (Diary), p. 278 (by his wife).
57. Letter to Klingemann, December 14, 1835.
58. Letter of October 26, 1833; letter to Klingemann of December 14, 1835. Actually, the overture was written to an opera of Conradin Kreutzer which Felix had heard but which had "displeased him especially." See letter of April 7, 1834.
59. In Schumann's *Schriften*, I, p. 158.
60. O. Walzel, *Die deutsche Dichtung seit Goethes Tod*, 2nd edition (1920), pp. 43-44.
61. Unpublished letter of October 30, 1835.
62. Unpublished letter of November 13, 1835. Mendelssohn, who had been brought up puritanically, was displeased by the new slogan of the "emancipation of the flesh" which the *Jungdeutschen* propagated.
63. Letter of April 7, 1834.
64. Letter to Hiller, January 10, 1837.
65. Unpublished letter to Devrient, January 14, 1837.
66. Schumann, *Schriften über Musik*, II, p. 46 ff.

CHAPTER XIII *Sorrows and Successes:*
The Life's Companion

Mit der Freude zieht der Schmerz
Traulich durch die Zeiten . . .
Joy and grief go side by side
Closely through the ages
J. P. Hebel, *Neujahrslied,* composed by Mendelssohn

I

MENDELSSOHN was *Gewandhaus* director, a secure and leading position!
Many an artist of today, grasping for "security," would be satisfied with
such a position, and then, too, there were many important musicians who,
once they had landed in the safe harbor of a "position for life," would sit
back and leave well enough alone.

But Felix was not one of this complacent sort. On the contrary, he enjoyed little peace and quiet throughout his life. We shall still have to
evaluate this striking trait when we concern ourselves with his personality.

During the years 1835-37 Felix had several painful experiences, which
would normally have left behind no deeper traces. In any case, the sudden
death of his beloved father would have forced them into the background for
the moment; later, though, they embittered Felix's sorrow, for they struck
him where he was most vulnerable: in his relationship to beloved friends.

The first wound, which never quite healed, was the break with his friend,
A. B. Marx. Unfortunately, we know the story of the estrangement only
from Marx's side, aside from a few critical observations of Felix in his
letters. Besides, Marx does not give the real reasons in his memoirs; these
were made known only after his death, by his wife.[1] What had poisoned the
old friendship?

We remember Felix's aversion to all journalism, and, above all, his scorn
of all abstract, i.e., "non-applied" esthetics, for which he finds eloquent, if

unflattering, words. Now, Marx had dabbled in both these areas, much to Felix's displeasure! Nonetheless, he would have forgiven the older man escapades of this sort, if, as a composer, he had fulfilled what he promised and what Felix was still expecting from him in 1832. When nothing but dry, uninventive stuff issued from Marx's pen, Felix began to think about the aversion of his father and Zelter—about which neither of them had ever remained silent—and seriously to question the worth of his friend.

Then came two episodes, insignificant in themselves. Mendelssohn and Marx had agreed to write oratorio librettos for each other. Marx wanted to write an oratorio "Moses"; and Felix, even then, was fascinated by the character of the Apostle Paul. So Felix wrote the text for *Moses* and Marx that for *St. Paul*. As might have been expected, both felt deeply disappointed in their respective librettists and it came to an unpleasant scene between them. Soon thereafter, Marx became engaged and demanded a substantial loan from Felix. He received it, too, with friendly good wishes, but never made any attempt to return it. Instead, Marx kept producing more and more authoritative esthetic-journalistic manifestoes, along with very weak music. Felix was quite unpleasantly impressed by all this, and turned away from Marx. But we cannot conceal that his mother, with her gossipy and often malicious letters, did everything to widen the breach. Felix, far away from these events in Düsseldorf as in Leipzig, hardly looked into the truth of these rumors. So, gradually, it came to a complete estrangement, under dramatic circumstances. In 1839, Marx had finished his *Moses*, and would have liked to entrust its première to Mendelssohn. Making up his mind, he got on the train to Leipzig with the score in his trunk.

> "If he performs my work there, success is assured." With the plea, "help me, my work is finished," he came to his friend. Both sat down at the piano, and Marx sang and played the first part of the work from the score. After he had finished, Mendelssohn got up and said coolly, "Don't hold it against me, but I can do nothing for this work . . ."
> Marx left without another word. . . . The hopes which he had set on Mendelssohn's help were blasted, the last bonds of friendship broken. This sorrow continued to hurt him for a long time—indeed, he never got over it during his life. . . .[2]

Soon after the return from Leipzig, Marx in blind anger, destroyed all Mendelssohn's letters to him. With the end of this friendship, a part of Felix's youth died.

The publication of the Goethe-Zelter correspondence poisoned memories of his youth which were especially dear to him. Zelter certainly valued Abraham Mendelssohn, the old friend of his youth, and always held him in high regard; the fact that he had almost unlimited credit with him doubtless helped the friendship along! But he loved Felix with all his heart, like a father. His "loyalty," though, belonged to but one man;

the Great Friend in Weimar. When Zelter wrote his letters to Goethe, both of them were far from thoughts of publication. Only in the last years of their friendship did such an idea come into being. Zelter was quite uninhibited in personal observations; he knew that Goethe admired this gift of trenchant and free speech in him, and so he wrote many things which he did not intend for publication. Unfortunately, the delicate task of the publication of the correspondence was given to a narrow-minded, embittered schoolmaster, a poetaster and factotum of Goethe's, Professor Friedrich Wilhelm Riemer. This man lacked any feeling of tact towards those still living as well as any discretion concerning the memory of the dead.

Therefore, there remained many observations of Zelter concerning the Mendelssohn family and their friends which hurt Felix and made his family look ridiculous. He was determined to get even with Riemer for his tactlessness when he had the chance. Even the Weimar Chancellor von Mueller writes to Doris Zelter: "I will not deny that I wish that Riemer had left our many names; but he feared that this would take away the piquancy of the letters. . . ."[3]

The reaction of the one for whom the profit of the publication was meant, Doris Zelter herself, was quite different. In a letter to Reimar, she said: "As far as the personality of Zelter is concerned, I have the whole synagogue on my neck, and I hardly think that the old temple will hold up under all the weeping and wailing. . . . The Mendelssohns are behaving strangely enough. . . ."[4]

This Doris had been treated by the Mendelssohn family as one of their own children; she had been taken on many trips and Abraham had planned to provide generously for her on the occasion of her wedding. But it never came to that; she remained unmarried, an old maid with an evil tongue. It should be said that none of the remarks of Zelter, which were meant rather humorously, is really discreditable to the Mendelssohns; it is simply a matter of small indiscretions. But these mean little breaches of confidence by Zelter would have been forgotten, although Abraham and Felix were indignant about them and duly inveighed against them in their unpublished letters. It seems, however, that the excitement connected with this caused the sudden death of Abraham. The family papers leave hardly a doubt of it. The following seems to have occurred:

Father Mendelssohn was annoyed by one or two critical remarks of Goethe concerning Hensel's talent and art. Perhaps some one in the immediate family called Riemer to account anonymously. Riemer suspected that Abraham had written this letter, and answered in a rude sarcastic tone. Abraham was very indignant and began to formulate a sharp reply. The next morning, he felt a little unwell, and shortly thereafter died of a stroke, just as his father Moses had died: easily and without pain.[5]

In 1841, seven years after Abraham's death, Riemer was vicious enough to publish the following lines: "Let us hope, however, that the good father-in-law [of Hensel] will have obtained satisfaction from the guttersnipe stuff poured out in sight of the whole nation by Heine and Boerne! In this, he, too, would find his revenge [*mitgerächt*] or, as he might put it, his smell! [*Mitgerochen.*]"[6] (The pun is untranslatable.)

Such and similar infamies, in which this memoir of a Goethe indulges, already foreshadows a poisonous anti-Semitism of a *racial nature*. For example, we read the following:

> The fundamentals from which the whole nation [of the Jews] has proceeded, and on which it has acted . . . are *ineradicable*. So let us not think that we can wash Moors white, not even with Christian baptism, as, in the middle ages, they thought they could eliminate the *foetor judaicus* (Jewish stink). . . .[7]

For the third time in his life, Felix was brutally reminded that, basically, he was and would always remain a stranger who was merely tolerated. If the Prussian prince who spat on him (as a sign of his truly noble character) could not bring the lad to turn in upon himself, if the rejection by the *Singakademie* could not force the youth to think about himself, will the infamy of the Goethe circle, which nastily reminded him of his ancient Jewish race, be able to free the man of cherished delusions?

The question must remain unanswered; for with Abraham he lost the focal point in which all his affections and ideals converged and by which they were yet linked, on a still higher level, with his grandfather Moses. The reaction of the deeply shaken son with many letters testifying to his grief, expressed itself in twofold fashion, indeed, on two levels. On the one hand, there was a conscious and intentional purification of his religious thinking and feeling, that is, in a turn towards the positively experienced Christianity of Schleiermacher; on the other hand, there was a strongly emphasized identification with the ancient people of his forebears. For this only seemingly paradoxical antinomy of feelings, there are many bits of evidence; here, we shall present only a few.

Nothing was more important to Felix now than the completion of *St. Paul*, the work, with the growth of which his father was familiar in every detail and of which he had a high opinion. All Felix's letters of this time speak of his zeal, his truly holy devotion to this task, as a double tribute to Christianity and to his father. The figure of the Apostle, who was born a Jew and, after his conversion, always remained a friend of his people, must have struck a deep chord in Felix.

During this very time, an orthodox Jew from Russia, a virtuoso on his own homemade *rebeck*, was making a grand European concert tour. This strange man, Gusikow by name, filled Felix with quite unusual enthusiasm.[8] This extraordinary artist, who put his orthodox Judaism on display, was called a "splendid fellow" and a "genius" by Mendelssohn.[9]

It is interesting to compare the various reactions of Felix's family to this performer with his enthusiasm.[14] Fanny writes with cool admiration, but not without irony:

> I have seen him and can confirm that he is an uncommonly handsome man. He flirts with strict Judaism in dress and way of life, and makes a good thing out of it at court. . . . I have heard the phenomenon and assure you, without being so charmed as many, that he turns all virtuosity topsy-turvy . . . he certainly seems to be a first-class fox. . . . We all agree that Father would have been highly interested in him, if he had heard him. . . .[15]

Lea writes quite differently:

> Gusikow visited me yesterday; what an interesting physiognomy! . . . He does not lack a certain coquetry in his costume, which I thoroughly approve of; the lock on his forehead, the little tilted cap, the picturesque clothing! . . . He speaks of you with due appreciation. . . . If dear Father could have heard him . . . how much he would have discussed and argued with him!

Later, she tells of the appearance of Gusikow in the *Gesellschaft der Freunde*, a social organization of assimilated Jews with charitable and artistic aims:

> He is, as you rightly say, a phenomenon . . . it is self-evident that the whole Old Testament is gathered together and feels very much at home when he plays. The chief rabbi, they say, was recently in the opera house. . . .[16]

Fanny, on the other hand, is now very critical:

> This affair of the Polish Jew [Gusikow] is very good . . . the fellow is creating a furore here—but the fuss is finally exhausting my patience. . . .[17]

Why this irony and impatience in Fanny? Why the expression "fellow"—against which she would otherwise have emphatically protested—for an artist? The answer is simple. Unlike Felix, she had begun to be ashamed of her Jewish origins: More than that, her shame had turned into that pernicious self-hatred which, alas, became a characteristic of many German Jews. What is a natural, friendly reaction in Felix, who invites Gusikow's friends, all

Orthodox Polish Jews, to his home, becomes, in her, irony and—in spite of all her admiration—scornful hatred.

Now for the other side of the coin: almost at the same time, Felix decided to make a second, truly Christian offering to the memory of his father. In Frankfurt (substituting for Schelble, who was ill), for the first time he performed Bach's funeral cantata *Gottes Zeit ist die allerbeste Zeit.* A year later, he asked the conductor Friedrich Schneider in Dessau to have a plaque placed over the door of the house in which Moses Mendelssohn had lived; however, he wanted first to ascertain that the present owners of the house and the inhabitants of Dessau in general knew how to value such a memorial.[10] If *St. Paul* and the performance of Bach's funeral cantata bear witness to Felix's purified Christianity, the enthusiasm for Gusikow and the remembrance of the great ancestor emphasize his loyalty to the old race. In this way, Felix deals "cathartically" with the principal problem of his life.

Returned from the funeral of his father, Felix first began to feel how lonely he was in his sorrow—far from his family and his friends. Now he longed to finish *St. Paul* as soon as possible, for, as he himself says,

> the last letter of my father prodded me to it, and he very impatiently awaited the completion of the work; I feel that I must now make every effort to complete *St. Paul* as well as possible, and then imagine that he is taking part in it.[11]

Felix planned to have the first performance of the new oratorio among old friends, at the Lower Rhenish Festival in Düsseldorf. Originally, it was to be performed by the Frankfurt *Caecilia*, but the serious illness of its director Schelble made any such hope illusory. So, before the beginning of May, Felix had to get score and parts of the large work into performable condition. Only by summoning up all his strength—then still fresh and untapped—could he fulfill the task that he had set himself.

Before this, after he had worked in Leipzig only half a year, he had the satisfaction of seeing his services to the musical life of that place recognized in an authoritative quarter. The University conferred upon the 27-year-old the honorary Doctorate of Philosophy—an extraordinary honor for so young an artist. The diploma of March 20, 1836, reads as follows:

> Vir clarissimus Felix Mendelssohn Bartholdy, concentus musici director, ob insignia in artem musicam merita
> Honoris Causa
> Philosophiae Doctor et Bonarum Artium Magister Creatus.

(The illustrious Felix Mendelssohn Bartholdy, symphony director, is because of his outstanding services to the art of music, named Honorary Doctor of Philosophy and Master of Fine Arts.)

II

After the death of his father, life in his lonely room in Leipzig had become very depressing for Felix. During the sad Christmas season of 1835, his mother had extracted from him the promise to look around soon for a "suitable wife," but it seems that he sought in vain in Leipzig.[12] Only rarely does Felix let himself go as in the letters to Klingemann from these days. Among other things, he says:

> Only gradually do I begin to feel the frightful change which has taken place in my life . . . it is the certain feeling that my youth was over with that day (of father's death), and everything that belonged to it was over with it. . . . That . . . makes me serious for ever and instills the wish to become like my father and to live up to what he expected of me. . . .

Here we find one of the many observations in which Felix shows his self-knowledge. Felix, quite in the Jewish spirit, strives to honor the memory of Moses and Abraham. This striving shows itself outwardly as well. He did not permit a gilded iron cross to be placed on his father's grave, as Hensel had planned; he demands strictest simplicity, as *"our principles"* demand.[13]

He describes his day's work about as follows. He usually got up early and worked till noon on his compositions; then he customarily went for a walk till 1 p.m., following which he lunched with friends in some good inn. In the afternoon he played the piano (he scorned the idea of "practising"); towards evening, he worked again, and then he ate supper with friends, privately or in the hotel; this generally lasted till 10 P.M. A few pleasant changes brought some joy and color into this monotonous existence. Already, before his father's death, Moscheles and Chopin had visited him; the former had even gone to Berlin with him to visit his parents. In March his mother and sister Fanny visited him to cheer him up a bit. At that time, they ran into Ottilie von Goethe, who insisted that her son Walter, who had musical inclinations, should study with Mendelssohn. Beyond this, she seems to have tried to console the good Felix in another way; but he victoriously resisted this and similar temptations. He appeared in public as violist in the performance of his Octet, as he writes, "not without palpitations." In the midst of all his workaday duties, he longs for nothing so much as the restoration of his "inner serenity." This expression is thoroughly characteristic of Felix; it should never be confused with thoughtless merriment. This is basically the

serenity which he had so admired in Goethe, and which was so indispensable
for the poet.

Every free hour was, in the meantime, devoted to *St. Paul*, and Felix
was completely absorbed in the oratorio. He let himself be advised by his
friendly critic Fanny, but did not by any means always follow her suggestions, especially when she, the unconditional archaizer, characterized the recitatives as "too modern." A creative artist of Mendelssohn's rank naturally had
to exclude such thoughts, in spite of all his respect for the past. When the
oratorio was nearly finished, the problem of the first performance still
remained acute. There had to be a long correspondence with the Düssel-
dorfers, and, above all, the decisive protestations of his mother, who had to
remind him most emphatically of his father's wishes, in order to extract
from him his consent to the first performance at the Lower Rhenish Music
Festival. Then, however, he concerns himself with all details of the performance in lively and energetic fashion. The worst part of the inner crisis
was overcome. Thus, he can report to his mother with satisfaction:

> It gives me great pleasure to be able to write you that I have now prob-
> ably established myself firmly in Germany, and will not have to wander
> abroad to make a living. This has been clearly evident for only a year—
> namely, since my position in Leipzig—but I certainly believe that it is so.[18]

III

It is hard for us to be fair to *St. Paul*. The work is laid out and intended
on a grand scale, but it did not turn out monumentally like *Elijah*. Probably
for this reason, it has nearly disappeared from the concert repertoire. It is
significant of the unevenness of the work that, already a hundred years ago,
the critics could not agree on the worth of the oratorio. But in most cases,
after more than a century, one can tell whether and why a great work lives
or is dead. In the latter case, the historian may protest against the unfairness
of posterity; thus he may bring about the performance of at least parts of
such an important work of art—even if only on records—and so confront the
modern audience with it. Did not Mendelssohn himself do music such a
service by reviving Bach's *St. Matthew Passion*? In our time, has not Cherubini's *Medea* been awakened to new life? In such cases, to which one might
also add the revival of Monteverdi and older masters, with the newly performed work a whole previously forgotten style has been resurrected.

But with *St. Paul*, the problem is basically different. For, if it were
to be revived, no forgotten style would be revived with it. The much
stronger and stylistically purer *Elijah* eclipses *St. Paul*, though it was written
by the same master and is animated by the same style. But a much surer

hand formed *Elijah*. Therefore, we must try anew to examine the strong and weak points of the earlier work, in order perhaps to justify artistically, and to rescue, at least parts of it.

The text of the oratorio was compiled from the Bible by Schubring, with the help of J. Fuerst. The story tells of the martyrdom of St. Stephen, who was stoned by Jews who were fanatical adherents of the Law. Among them was Saul of Tarsus; he planned to attack the Christian community in Syria. Yet, on the road to Damascus the miracle occurs; he sees the light of Jesus, loses his sight, and becomes converted to Christianity. Cured, he repents his former sins and becomes one of the missionary leaders of persecuted Christianity. With this, the first part ends. The second part shows Paul and Barnabas as missionaries to Jews and heathens. Both groups turn against the Apostle, and he decides to leave Ephesus and return to Jerusalem, in full knowledge that he is going to his martyrdom. With his farewell to the Ephesian Christians, the work closes.

The second part is poor in dramatic events. Mendelssohn and Schubring let three highly dramatic situations escape them: the wonderful rescue of Paul and Silas from prison, the confrontation of Paul with his erstwhile master Gamaliel before the Synhedrion, and, finally, the mighty tribunal scene in Caesarea before the Roman Governor Festus and the King of Judea, Agrippa II. Each of these situations would have given the composer splendid opportunities to depict the character of his hero "under fire." Mendelssohn does try to conceal the dearth of action of the second part with a plethora of lyrical and homiletic pieces; but he did not succeed in this, and, on hearing these insertions, the listener does not escape either occasional boredom or annoyance at some all-too-sanctimonious texts.

A further cause of the inner weakness of the text is found in the choice of Bible passages. Neither Schubring nor Mendelssohn succeeded in bringing the listener closer to the irrational element—one may also say the very mystery—with which the Apostle constantly struggled anew. The fact that the teachings of the living Jesus were scarcely of importance to the Paul of the Epistles, that for him the sacrifice, the crucifixion, and resurrection of Christ were the decisive moments, points to the central position of the mystery in Paul's career. Yet, in *St. Paul*, we find only three passages which do justice to this sense of mystery and wonder: the vision of St. Stephen at his stoning, the scene of Paul's conversion on the road to Damascus, and, already considerably weaker, the miracle of his eyesight recovered through the intervention of Ananias. This emphasis on rational aspects was completely in the spirit of Schleiermacher, but it neglects the very complex, prophetic-visionary character of Paul in favor of his limited missionary activity.

Now let us turn to the music of *St. Paul*. Here, Mendelssohn writes in a hybrid style the elements of which he takes over from Handel, Bach, and the Italians of the seventeenth century. The models of his form seem above all to be the *Messiah* and the *St. Matthew Passion*. Bach's influence is shown most clearly in the chorales, which, from the very beginning, appeared out-of-place, even anachronistic, to the critics. In Bach's Passion, the chorales escape this criticism, for the work was intended as liturgical music on Good Friday. The *Messiah*, again, is an exception in the history of the oratorio; for, since Kretzschmar, we know that

> the cantatas for the whole festival time from Advent to Trinity can be taken continuously from the first and second parts of the *Messiah*. The idea has a certain justification, for there is an intentional relationship between the organization of the *Messiah* and the sequence in which the so-called ecclesiastical year follows . . . the history of the Saviour.[19]

Both the works which he used as models pursue liturgical aims, but *St. Paul* does not. This discrepancy in itself gives rise to stylistic conflicts.

When Mendelssohn had composed several chorale cantatas during his Italian journey, he had turned to Zelter for advice and criticism, especially because of the freer treatment of the chorale. Only now has Zelter's answer come to light, and we shall see that Zelter had very clear ideas about the chorale problem, but that Mendelssohn, after his master's death, disregarded the latter's principles. We cite the passages concerning this problem from Zelter's original manuscript:[20]

> The old chorale in itself, as the song of the whole congregation, containing the Gospel, is, according to its first cause, the dividing line between the Catholic and Protestant forms of worship, because, through it, the congregation becomes an active participant in Divine Service. In the Catholic worship, there is really no congregation, for each one may take part in the worship for himself, quietly. . . . In the Catholic service, the open practice of worship is the duty of the priests only, as a community of saints. With the Protestants, the laity is not excluded; all of Christianity is included and the Protestant church chorale is the uniting principle, that is, the congregation becomes an active factor in Divine Service.
>
> So long as the chorale is a song of the whole congregation, it had better remain as we have it; insofar as we use it as the motif of a free composition, the relationship is the same as that of the text to the sermon, the title to the book, and you have a free hand. . . .

Zelter would admit the chorale only as the "song of the whole congregation," as which, however, it cannot occur in an oratorio. Furthermore, Zelter points to the worship of saints in the Catholic Church. The logical implication would then be that a saint would not be a suitable subject for an oratorio; and, in fact, neither Bach nor Handel ever used the lives of the saints for their oratorios or liturgical compositions, not excepting the poetic *Ode for St. Cecilia's Day*.

In particular, the function and attitude of the chorus gives occasion for misunderstandings. O. Jahn already recognized the threefold significance of the choruses in St. Paul and gently criticized it. The chorus appears in active, narrating and reflective capacities, and it is not always easy for the listener to adjust himself to its function of the moment. Besides this, however, the chorus also sings chorales, but these are part neither of congregational activity nor of a ritual.

In comparison with the problematic function of the chorus, the other structural problems of St. Paul more or less disappear: the carrying of the narrative continuity by different voices and characters, the rigorous preservation of an epic, nondramatic recitative which does not deny its origin in the opera seria, and the admixture of free solo songs like cavatina, aria, duet, ensemble with chorus, etc. The defenders of Mendelssohn have compared the role of the chorus in St. Paul with that which it plays in Greek tragedy.[21] This comparison is wrong, in my opinion. For, in the tragedy, the chorus does not take part in the action, but is the traditional announcer of the feelings and thoughts which should move the onlooker. In particular, Mendelssohn had been warned against transplanting the chorale into an oratorio; but he clung to his belief that this typically liturgical form of the Lutheran Church was suitable for every text of the New Testament. Unfortunately, Schubring advised him badly here.[22] However, it is not only the threefold role of the chorus, or the use of the chorale, which make St. Paul appear lacking in unity, but the all-too-free mixture of divergent styles.

True, a scholar of the rank of Einstein sees the root of all evil in the "hybrid" (mixed, impure) form of the oratorio.[23] But the validity of this judgment is more than doubtful. For he himself calls Elijah "a work of the greatest stylistic purity, of the highest nobility, of the loftiest spirituality, this time more Classicistic than Romantic." There, the dangers of the mixed form seem to have been overcome; but this cannot be said of St. Paul.

Before we mention individual, especially characteristic pieces, let us comment on the treatment of sonority, melody and rhythm in the whole work. Mendelssohn handles orchestra and chorus with greatest sensitivity; he is no "al fresco" painter like Handel, no mournful visionary like the Bach of the St. Matthew Passion, but rather a precise and careful designer. (This observation also holds true for his real drawings and paintings, in which the linear-drawing element also predominates.) His choral polyphony is always carried by clear lines; therefore, it is seldom massive and sounds particularly beautiful. Where he takes over older models of style, as in the aria "Jerusalem," he succeeds in preserving his independence from the model with little, completely individual touches; often, thereby, he shows the model in the correct light for the first time. On the contrary, the recitatives are often monotonous in effect, and are not always well declaimed. Many of the fugal choruses would gain in force through energetic cutting. The total sonority attracts us more through its harmonious, noble lines than through bold coloration.

The overture intones, in dark, gradually brightening strains, the chorale *Wachet auf*, the "program chorale" of the whole oratorio. There follows a great fugato, which, at the end, goes into a triumphal double fugue above the chorale and closes the overture in a glowing orchestral *tutti*. Of the following pieces, we single out No. 4, recitative and entrance of the false witnesses; here, Mendelssohn indubitably follows Bach's model. In motives of fanatical monotony the zealous Jewish people are depicted in No. 5, "Now this man ceaseth not." With No. 6 (address of Stephen and chorus of the zealots) Mendelssohn reaches his first high point. The speeding-up of the tempo from the Andante of the recitative to the Presto of the chorus, and its slowing-down to the Molto Adagio of Stephen's vision, is of the most penetrating dramatic force. Rightly, Mendelssohn inserts here a reflective point of-rest, the lofty and beautiful aria "Jerusalem" (No. 7), the noblest solo song of the work. In its melodic structure, it harks back to Italian *bel-canto* models, which Handel, too, often followed. The rhythm is very common in Handel, but its association here with newly entering voices is quite novel. Admirable, too, is the concise but very effective ternary formation. This is one of the pieces which should certainly be rescued for the concert-hall. The following chorus No. 8 ("Stone him to death") seems all the more monumental and forceful after the exalted repose of the preceding aria. It, too, is quite in the spirit of the great Handelian oratorio choruses; it is impressive and furious in effect. If the chorus carried the action here, in No. 11 ("Happy and blest are they") it is a sorrowful observer. The piece itself is the most beautiful choral elegy before Brahms. The euphony of the choral sound, combined with the independent motion of the orchestra and the highly individual intonation of the principal strophe, make the movement "specifically Mendelssohnian," as Kretzschmar emphasizes. He recognizes its function as the old *gratiarum actio*, which customarily occurred in the closing section of Passions.[24] With this splendid piece, the Stephen episode closes.

In No. 12 ("Consume them all") Saul is introduced in an angrily thundering aria, the only weakness of which lies in its all-too-symmetrical melody. Although it is planned as a contrast to Saul's fury, the following piece (No. 13, recitative and aria, "But the Lord is mindful of his own") is quite inferior to the foregoing, above all because of the sentimental nature of the melodic invention; it reminds us of a weak passage in Beethoven's Violin Concerto. No. 14, in the scene of Saul's conversion on the road to Damascus, drives towards a new climax. When the work was new, much was written about the women's chorus as representative of the voice of Jesus. To us, the chorus seems an entirely legitimate means of eliminating the anthropomorphic or all-too-individual element from the voice of Jesus. The piece fulfills its task with noble simplicity. The following chorus (No. 15, "Rise up! arise!") is an imposing piece, which, in its orchestral ritornello, already reaches a climax which the chorus cannot surpass. It is somewhat too long, especially in the fugue, "Behold, now, total darkness covereth the kingdom." All the more refreshing is, then, the version of the chorale *Wachet auf* (No. 16) with trumpet fanfares inserted regularly at the end of each line. The broken pride of Paul is magnificently portrayed in No. 18, the aria "O God, have mercy upon me," again a high point of the oratorio. The melodic line of the aria, which again reminds us of Handel, is broken, like the heart of Saul, by inserted highly dramatic recitatives. As a whole it is, both musically and psychologically, a splendid piece. The aria with chorus (No. 20, "I praise Thee, O Lord my God") appears as an attempt on the grand scale to grasp musically the inner state of Paul stricken with blindness. But here Mendelssohn's empathy was insufficient, for the aria itself is too sentimental and the comforting chorus too sanctimonious to be able to move seriously the hearer of today. The following recitative, No. 21, portrays the miracle through which Paul regains his sight. With short and trenchant motifs it is presented in the orchestra, and finally this foreshadows the opening theme of the following chorus (No. 22, "O great is the depth"). The chorus itself, though beautifully planned, is at a disadvantage through its great length and the somewhat worn out thematic material. A few cuts would do wonders here.

With this closes the first part of the oratorio, rich in action. What now follows consists of genre scenes from the first missionary activity of the Apostle. That Mendelssohn, after the fugal closing chorus of the first part, begins the second part with a great double fugue, must be regretted because of the wasted effect of this splendid choral movement, which far surpasses its predecessor. Quite aside from the mighty art manifested in the more than a dozen stretti of the fugue's great sweep, the impulse of the melodic structure is admirable. This is one of the pieces which certainly should be rescued, perhaps through being provided with a new text. After two less significant pieces, the chorus sings the famous "How lovely are the messengers," once a very popular piece (No. 26). It is a pastorale in tone and mood, and a real point of rest in the midst of events. However, as (unfortunately) so often, Mendelssohn did not always escape the dangers of his beloved 6/8 time, and one sometimes cannot get away from the impression of a gentle musical rocking. In sound, the chorus is of enchanting euphony. In sharp contrast to this is the Jews' chorus No. 20 ("Is this he who in Jerusalem") with its hissing, slanderous, poisonous orchestral motif. It is as genuine a character piece as No. 26 was an idyll. Surprisingly, this Jewish storm is answered by a splendid chorale paraphrase, "Oh Thou, the true and only Light!" in which the orchestra, with independent motifs, acts as an equal partner of the chorus. It is unquestionably the most beautiful chorale of *St. Paul*. Here, all critical voices are silenced, for the function of the chorale in this case is not liturgical, but purely psychological; it is felt as a prayer of the persecuted Christian community.

Paul and Barnabas now travel in heathen lands. In an almost merry, sunny chorus (No. 33, "The gods themselves as mortals have descended"), the composer portrays the enthusiasm of the heathen. No. 35, "O be gracious, ye Immortals," takes a slightly comic turn. Rightly, Kretzschmar recognized here the *opera buffa* element of the constant "salaaming" and bowing. The recitative in which the reaction of the apostles is depicted is again quite lively; it culminates in a complaint of Paul which reaches its high point in a monumental adaptation of a chorale. The five-voiced chorus fugues the text "But our God abideth high in heaven," while the second soprano, supported by oboes, horns and trombones, throws in the chorale *Wir glauben all' an einen Gott* as *cantus firmus*. The piece is of impressive effect, but in no way indulges in sound effects for their own sake; rather, it is austere, gloomy, and strict. After a chorus of the Jewish zealots, "This is Jehovah's temple" (No. 38), which, basically, is simply a reprise of the earlier "Stone him to death," the voice of Jesus speaks to Paul in "Be thou faithful unto death" (No. 40), a cavatina with obligato 'cello. It was once a favorite piece of the nineteenth century, but to us it seems somewhat too sentimental and melodically uncharacteristic. Paul takes leave of the community of the faithful, and they implore him to look after himself in the lively chorus "Far be it from thy path" (No. 42), full of real feeling. We encounter the same world of feeling in the farewell chorus "See what love hath the Father," in which the master often makes use of "learned" contrapuntal means. These, however, are unnoticeable on a first hearing because they are organic. The final chorus does not end the work mournfully or elegiacally, but with a hymn to God's greatness ("Praise ye the Lord," No. 45), in a fugue which is somewhat too lengthy but sounds brilliant and triumphant. Thus, an at least outwardly satisfying ending is guaranteed.

Even if we disregard the weaknesses of text and plot, our cursory observation shows so many musical and stylistic uneven elements of the work that probably only parts of it can be rescued for the concert hall or for church music. This was not at all, however, the judgment of Mendelssohn's contemporaries. Wherever the work was performed, it had a definite success. Of all the enthusiastic judgments, we shall first quote one which was published in the London *Athenaeum*, an arch-conservative journal in every respect:

> For his oratorio [*St. Paul*] it would be difficult for us to say too much in its praise—simple, massive—every note of it full of expression: written in the spirit of the great ancients, but not according to their letter. We should be disposed, unhesitatingly, to rank it next to the immortal works

of Handel, being persuaded that every subsequent hearing must bring its truth increasingly home to every listener. It includes no difficulties crowded together for the production of great effects, (the resources of second-best genius); the airs are as easy as they must be delightful to sing; and the orchestra, though, when it is required, as rich and figurative as a master's hand, guided by a master's mind, can make it—is kept in its proper place— that is, working together with the vocal parts, neither predominating over them, nor lagging behind. . . .[25]

In addition, we possess a number of contemporary reports and criticisms of the Lower Rhenish Music Festival and the performance of *St. Paul;* we might especially mention the report of Mendelssohn's friend Hiller (*Erinnerungen*, pp. 44 ff.), the very belittling criticisms of the Frankfurt daily papers, and the highly enthusiastic one of Schumann. Let us briefly refer here to the views of two philosophizing musicians or music historians of those days, both of whom have a positive attitude towards Mendelssohn's work; we are thinking here of Moritz Hauptmann, later Thomas Cantor in Leipzig, and Otto Jahn, the first great Mozart biographer. The former especially praises Mendelssohn's choral style as incomparable and sees, in *St. Paul*, the organic connection of the Bach and Handel style with the idiom of Beethoven. Rightly, Hauptmann considers the chorus "Happy and blest are they" a musical gem which will defy all the onslaughts of time. Otto Jahn, on the other hand, especially praises the

seriousness of feeling, which strives to rise above the subjectivity of the individual, to grasp the universal and to bring it to light with the mastery of the artist. . . . By this, we mean to say that the musical expression is always simple and noble; and in the very truth and simplicity of the elements from which the master builds his works of art lies the universal impression and the clear understanding of these. . . .

All the more noteworthy is Devrient's criticism:

In the second part, things get flatter and flatter, and the second part has nothing comparable to moments like the stoning and blinding. . . . The second part lacks something interesting . . . could it not be shortened for the performance? The material is barren, and, with oratorios, I have usually had the feeling that the little cycle of religious sentiments is soon worn out. I must come back to my old complaint that the oratorio . . . is an indefensible hybrid form. . . .[26]

When we add to these contemporary observations a noteworthy comment by R. Rolland, it seems to us that, without unduly citing the indiscriminate flatterers (of whom there were many), we have given several of the representative statements of Mendelssohn's contemporaries and posterity. In closing his discussion of Mendelssohn's oratorio, R. Rolland says: "Mendelssohn strikes the right note there; he gives his characters a tragic accent and puts dramatic truth even into his choruses. In all his sacred music . . . it seems to me that Jewish feeling comes to his aid and animates him with the breath of the ancient prophets of his race."[27]

Viewed from a theological observer's stand, *St. Paul* is the first testimony of a spirit that quickened the new thought of Protestantism and culminated in the living and fighting "Professing Church" of our days. Its champions, K. Barth, R. Niebuhr, and others, are strongly stressing this ever-actual and ever-present problem of the believing Christian. Of this movement, Mendelssohn's is a lofty precursor.[28]

The program of the Lower Rhenish Music Festival contained, besides *St. Paul*, the following works: Beethoven, *Leonore* Overture Nos. 1 and 3, and the Ninth Symphony; Mozart, *Davidde penitente;* Handel, Chandos Anthem, No. 3.

The first *Leonore* Overture, at that time still quite unknown, was greeted enthusiastically; on the other hand, the Ninth Symphony was by no means universally applauded. Fanny, who knew the work only from the score, writes about it:

This colossal Ninth Symphony, which is as great and in part as frightful as only the greatest man can make it, went as if executed by one man . . . a colossal tragedy with an ending which is meant to be dithyrambic, but, at its climax, turns around and falls into the opposite extreme: the burlesque.

Mendelssohn himself still wrote to Droysen, on December 14, 1837:

It is hard to speak about this music at all . . . the instrumental movements belong to the greatest things that I know in art; from the moment where the voices enter, even I do not understand it, i.e., I find only individual details perfect, and when that is the case with such a master, the fault probably lies with us. Or with the execution. . . . In the vocal movement, however, the writing for voices is such that I know of no place where it could go well, and perhaps that is the reason for the incomprehensibility up till now. . . .

In other words, Felix blindly trusted Beethoven's mastery. He, otherwise such a critical listener, mistrusted his own judgment and hoped for the impossible from a "perfect" performance of the work. This humility in the face of a work which displays obvious technical faults has something of religious belief; it shows that Felix seriously believed in the absolute value of a work of art.

The anthem of Handel was an importation from England, for these pieces were scarcely known in Germany. Here, too, Mendelssohn is a pioneer; and the same holds true of the performance of *Davidde penitente*. As is known, the oratorio of Mozart's is a reworking of his great, unfinished C minor Mass. Neither the latter work nor the oratorio derived from it belonged at that time to the usual repertory of the concert hall or even of music festivals. So we are quite right in saying that Mendelssohn championed otherwise unknown music when he was convinced of its worth or of the *absolute mastery* of its composer. He held this prejudice all his life, and so he often neglected important works of his own time.

IV

At the music festival, Felix had the pleasure of seeing Fanny and Klingemann again; the sister even sang in the chorus of *St. Paul* and saved a dangerous situation at the première. Both preserved, in lively reports, their remembrances of the lovely days in Düsseldorf. Naturally Mendelssohn met many old acquaintances and friends made during his earlier activity there, above all the Woringens. Immermann is not mentioned anywhere, not even in a single word; shortly thereafter, Felix expressed himself very unfavorably about his long novel *Die Epigonen*. Here, personal resentments certainly played a significant part, for Felix was never able (except in the case of Berlioz) to separate personal and artistic sympathies or antipathies.

From Düsseldorf Felix went directly to Frankfurt, where he directed the "Caecilia" for six weeks during Schelble's severe illness. He did this not only to help Schelble but also to keep the slowly growing choral tradition in Frankfurt from withering away. The permanent leadership of the "Caecilia" was even offered to him, but he declined it for several reasons, not the least being his loyalty to Schelble. Also in Frankfurt he met old friends and relatives. Dorothea Schlegel, his aunt (the eldest daughter of Moses Mendelssohn) was living there after the death of her second husband Friedrich Schlegel. He saw her often and this brilliant woman became a true friend at this time. His old friend Hiller was staying in Frankfurt, too, and had even visited him during his triumph in Düsseldorf. Through these people and the members of the choral society, he also came into social contact with many circles in Frankfurt.

In the meantime, he directed the rehearsals, performed selections from Handel's *Samson* and Bach's B minor Mass, and gave a concert the heart of which was Bach's funeral cantata *Gottes Zeit ist die allerbeste Zeit;* he had intended this work as a requiem for his father. Quite naïvely, he took pleasure in his growing fame: "I'd never have believed what a powerful creature I have become for the people here, through my overtures and songs."[29]

His impartial judgment in matters of art was once more put to the test, this time in amusing fashion, through his meeting with Rossini. We have often seen what a low opinion Felix had of this last gourmet of music and musician of *gourmandise*. His earlier acquaintance with him had been only a superficial one. Now, however, Rossini turned the full force of his irresistible charm on the young German, and Felix, himself a charmer of no mean rank, could not resist the wit, the lively intelligence, and even the satirical irony of Rossini. He observes condescendingly in a letter to his mother: "That will be too beautiful for words, when Rossini has to admire Sebastian Bach."[30]

But he was completely captivated by the Italian: "I really know few people who can be so amusing and clever as he can when he wants to. . . . Intelligence and vitality in all his features and in every word, and whoever doesn't think he is a genius must hear him preaching once—he will soon change his opinion."[31]

Rossini insisted on hearing as much as possible of Mendelssohn's music played by himself. Among other things, he played some of his earlier *Capriccios* for him, and heard Rossini murmur in French: "That smells of Scarlatti's sonatas." He was no little annoyed by this. Why? Because Rossini had hit the nail on the head and, with unerring insight, had recognized the style which dominates Felix's early piano works. It is noteworthy that Rossini remembered Mendelssohn later in accents of genuine admiration, indeed, not without a trace of melancholy.

V

The feeling of loneliness which darkened Felix's life in Leipzig and which is expressed in all his letters of those days was pleasantly interrupted, if not entirely removed, by the music festival in Düsseldorf and the following activity in Frankfurt. The stay in Frankfurt was of decisive significance for the lonely man; for there, he found his life's companion. He met her in the "Caecilia" and also socially, for her family belonged to Frankfurt's patriciate, which views itself as one big family and is generally so viewed by the outside world as well. The families of Jeanrenaud and Souchay belonged to the Huguenot aristocracy of the city. From Petitpierre's book *The Romance of the Mendelssohns* we learn the interesting earlier history of this clan—for such it certainly was. It seems to have been a closely knit family, which, in its structure, was very similar to the Mendelssohn clan, however different it might be in such points as origin, religion, tradition, and language.

The Jeanrenauds were an old Huguenot family who resided in the vicinity of Neuchatel from the sixteenth century onwards. The men had an inclination towards fine mechanical work: they were clock makers, clock dealers, and merchants. The father of Cecile Jeanrenaud, Mendelssohn's wife to be, became a Reformed pastor in Frankfurt after he had finished his theological studies in Basel and Geneva. In 1810, he was chosen as pastor by the Reformed congregation of Bockenheim-Frankfurt. As a strict Calvinist, he could sympathize neither with the Napoleonic regime nor with the "liberal" direction of the Protestant Church under Schleiermacher's leadership. In 1811, he became the principal pastor and married Elisabeth Wilhelmine Souchay, the granddaughter of his predecessor.

The Souchay family came from the Loiret and had fled to Geneva in the seventeenth century under the pressure of the Edict of Nantes and of the following persecution of the Huguenots. Their grandchildren then turned to Hanau and Frankfurt, where they soon reached the rank and status of principal merchants, and married into the families of the patricians. The son of Pastor Daniel Souchay, Carl Cornelius, the father-in-law of Pastor Jeanrenaud, was a great man of business—which did not keep him from strictly ruling his household until his early death. When, after a long illness, Pastor Jeanrenaud also died in 1819, leaving his wife with three minor children, it was Mme Souchay who most energetically took the reins into her hands. She let her daughter feel bitterly their moral and financial dependency, and would have been inclined to take over the same role with Felix Mendelssohn; but there, she came up against the wrong man!

From his early youth, Felix had come into frequent contact with women, both in and out of the family. He was accustomed to be pampered and spoiled by young and not-so-young ladies, and took this more or less for granted, without becoming vain or dissolute because of it. He was a charmer and a flirter, but certainly anything but a "man about town." The rules of life and morals that had been impressed upon him in his father's house were too strict for that—not to mention the century-old patriarchal tradition of his Jewish ancestors.

Was Felix's attraction for Cecile love at first sight? Hardly, nor yet at second, but very soon thereafter. Since we learn very little from printed sources, it seems important to us to explore the letters as far as possible in order to evaluate these deep emotions and relationships with the proper understanding. This is all the more desirable as the influence of Cecile Jeanrenaud in the life and on the creative work of the master has by no means been properly evaluated.

The following manuscript sources were available to me:

All Felix's family letters; the letters of his nearest relatives to him; a few letters from Cecile. Shortly after Felix's death, she destroyed her correspondence with him from before and after the wedding.

A few fragments from Felix's diary. The greatest part of this priceless document was not available to me, although Petitpierre had seen the diary.

Along with these, there are the reminiscences of Moscheles, Klingemann (in the letters), Hiller, the sisters (in Hensel's *Die Familie Mendelssohn*, to be read with the greatest caution!), Elise Polko, Schubring, Devrient, Chorley, Davison, and others.

*Fanny Hensel, nee Mendelssohn
Drawing by Wilhelm Hensel
(International Felix Mendelssohn
Society, Basel)*

*Abraham Mendelssohn
Drawing by Wilhelm Hensel
(National Gallery of the former
State Museum, Berlin-Dahlem)*

Lea Mendelssohn
Drawing by Wilhelm Hensel
(National Gallery of the former State Museum, Berlin-Dahlem)

Garden-house at 3 Leipzigerstrasse
Water color by Sebastian Hensel
(Dr. Cecile and Fanny Hensel Erlanger)

Adolph Bernhard Marx
Drawing by Wilhelm Hensel
(National Gallery of the former
State Museum, Berlin-Dahlem)

Sophy Horsley
Drawing by Wilhelm Hensel
(National Gallery of the former
State Museum, Berlin-Dahlem)

Eduard Devrient
Drawing by Wilhelm Hensel
(National Gallery of the former
State Museum, Berlin-Dahlem)

Cecile Mendelssohn, nee Jeanrenaud
Painting by Eduard Magnus
(International Felix Mendelssohn
Society, Basel)

*The Spanish Steps, Rome, with
the Casa Bartholdy on the right
Drawing by Mendelssohn
(Miss Marie Wach)*

*Carl Friedrich Zelter
Drawing by Wilhelm Hensel
(National Gallery of the former
State Museum, Berlin-Dahlem)*

Jenny Lind
Painting by J. L. Asher
(Stockholm National Museum)

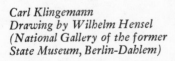

Carl Klingemann
Drawing by Wilhelm Hensel
(National Gallery of the former
State Museum, Berlin-Dahlem)

*Geheimrat Carl Josias von Bunsen
Drawing by Wilhelm Hensel
(National Gallery of the former
State Museum, Berlin-Dahlem)*

*Friedrich Wilhelm IV of Prussia
as Crown Prince
Drawing by Wilhelm Hensel
(National Gallery of the former
State Museum, Berlin-Dahlem)*

Queen Victoria
Drawing by Wilhelm Hensel
(National Gallery of the former
State Museum, Berlin-Dahlem)

Prince Albert
Drawing by Wilhelm Hensel
(National Gallery of the former
State Museum, Berlin-Dahlem)

Unterseen by Interlaken
Drawing by Mendelssohn
(International Felix Mendelssohn
Society, Basel)

Death mask of Mendelssohn
(International Felix Mendelssohn
Society, Basel)

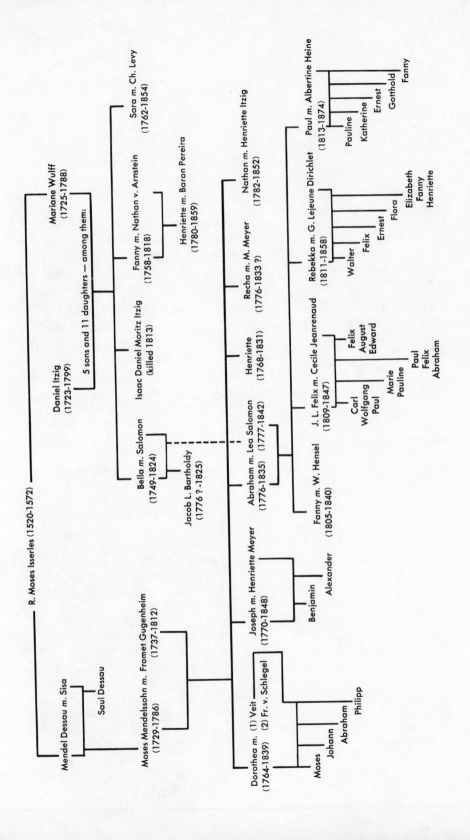

The first mention of "an especially beautiful girl whom I should love to see again" is found in a letter to his mother of July 13, 1836; as yet, he mentions no name. In the same letter, he does mention his Aunt Dorothea Schlegel, *née* Mendelssohn, and calls her there "the most brilliant, lively and lovable one in the whole family." The good mother did not like this association. Because she and her sister-in-law did not understand each other at all, she wrote: "Father regarded life, under all conditions, as the supreme good, the gift of the Creator—on which point he can come to no understanding with that Schlegel woman, who thinks quite differently."

Parenthetically, here the dogmatic conflict between Judaism and the Catholic Church is expressed in somewhat too simple a fashion, but is nonetheless clearly recognizable. Here, Abraham represents the Jewish standpoint, Dorothea the arch-Catholic. On the other hand, after the mother had assured herself of the seriousness of Felix's sentiments, she encouraged her son as only a tender concerned mother proud of a famous son can: "I repeat: *don't be too modest;* for if the dear girl has not already given her heart elsewhere, I—and not only I as a mother—see no reason why she should not be happy to belong to you."

In contrast to this gently veiled warning, Dorothea writes her nephew an uncommonly understanding and sensitive letter—beautiful in its modesty —about the mystery of marriage. Again in parenthese: Dorothea had originally been married to a Jewish merchant named Veit, but had left him in a famous elopement which was to have significant (at that time, even scandalous) results in the history of German literature, in order to live in a free relationship with Friedrich von Schlegel. To please him, she became Protestant. When both of them, following the trend of the time, came under the spell of Catholic mysticism, she became a Catholic along with him; furthermore, she threw herself with enthusiasm into the writings of the Catholic mystics—Dorothea, the favorite daughter of Moses Mendelssohn, who had once declared war on all obscurantism and everything antirational! Very noteworthy are her thoughts on modesty. Once she had been the wild and passionate heroine of Schlegel's *Lucinde,* and had enthusiastically agreed with Schleiermacher's postulate of a new "innocence" of the flesh (by which he understood spiritual, not physical modesty). Later, she told that defender of the painfully indiscreea *Lucinde* that Protestant Christianity meant more to her than Catholicism; for the latter greatly resembled Judaism, "which she abhorred." Richard Huch, who judges this remarkable figure with understanding, expresses herself in her fine book *Die Blütezeit der Romantik* with the well-measured words:

> That she talked easily, much, and in lively fashion, possessed a gift of rapid comprehension, and was also clever enough not to say anything stupid . . . made her appear more brilliant than she was. . . . As independent as she

could be in action, in thought she was completely dependent. . . . Schlegel
had always missed feeling himself so unconditionally worshipped; . . . She
should have given him wings; instead, in the belief that she was furthering
his interests, she powerfully pulled him down to earth.[32]

At the end of July, 1836, Felix was all but sure that he loved Cecile.
On her part, he might at least hope for understanding, but that is all he
knew. And now something strange, even ludicrous, happened. Felix, who
had never avoided a flirtation before, did not want to fall victim to a passing
infatuation this time. He had to be quite certain of his own feelings, and
tore himself away from the presence of the beloved girl. He traveled to
Scheveningen ("in the cheese country") for an extended cure at the baths
with Schadow, his Düsseldorf friend, and Schadow's son. The letters from
this time are really tragi-comic, for Felix was fully aware of the anomaly
of his situation. He was bored to death, for he had to teach young Schadow
Latin. He knew now that he would always love Cecile, and yet he could
not get away from Scheveningen. After finishing his self-imposed quaran-
tine, he still made a stop in Horchheim with Uncle Joseph; first to have
a good rest, then to drink to Goethe's birthday, finally to ask the blessing
of the head of the family (*in loco parentis*). Naturally, this was granted
him with pleasure.

Now he knew that his feelings would not change any more; he must
win his bride. In spite of the strict atmosphere in which she had been
brought up, the lovely girl was a true daughter of Eve, "dedicated to the
higher motherland, Nature" (K. Kraus), and knew very well that Felix
loved and desired her. She, too, first had to overcome a hindrance; it seems
that Felix had first paid court to the still very attractive Mama Jeanrenaud
before deciding definitely on the daughter. At least, that is how the affair
appeared to the Frankfurters, although Felix had never seriously thought
of Mme Jeanrenaud. A friendly discussion seems to have taken place between mother and daughter; only then was Cecile, if she had ever had
her doubts, sure of her Felix.

Sensitive as always, Felix did not explain himself first to the confidante
of his youth, sister Fanny, but to the younger sister, Rebecca; he understood Fanny's possible jealousy very well, and kept everything decisive
from her and his mother.

On August 6 he writes to Becky (under the motto "All right") that he
does not know anything definite yet about Cecile's attitude, but that "she
has given me the first happy hours," and that her house, with the many
relatives, had most pleasantly reminded him of his family and happy childhood. He answers his sister's questions point for point: "How she looks?
Very, very good. Speaks? German and much French. . . . Walks? like a
somewhat spoiled child; musical? no, not at all. . . ."

This is in contrast with Petitpierre's belief that Cecile had significant musical interests—Felix is the better authority here. On August 9, he still objects to the designation "fiancée,"

> Up till now I really know her very little and she does not know me well either, so I cannot write to you about her as you wish. I can only say that her presence has given me very happy days in Frankfurt, at a time when I badly needed them. . . .

At the same time he observes, in connection with sea-bathing: "People keep asking me for a new *Calm Sea*, whereupon I answer that I have probably gotten out of the water and away from the fairies forever—an adage which you probably know."

This observation refers to his dead father's wish that he should avoid the spirits of water and forest and stick to solid ground—a wish which Felix faithfully obeyed except in his second *A Midsummer Night's Dream* music. (All the above citations come from the family letters.)

Finally, on September 9, Felix formally tells his apprehensive mother of the engagement to Cecile: ". . . I feel so tender and happy." In following family letters, Felix keeps coming back to the "beautiful old recollections from the *Leipzigerstrasse*," which puts him in a joyous and happy mood. He portrays his fiancée as a "childish nature, in spite of all her refinement." (The few letters of Cecile give us some insight into her thinking and feeling and are written in a German which makes full use of all the fashionable clichés of the day.) He tells his mother that when near Cecile he enjoys a quiet happiness such as he can remember only from his childhood.

Before we turn to Cecile's personality, we should try to understand what the happy memories of childhood and their association with her meant to Felix. Certain ideas force themselves upon the unprejudiced reader of the letters. Many people remember their childhood with joy and longing. The sense of being protected and cherished, the intensity of the feelings of bliss which those of adults can never equal, the feeling of "belonging," at home, of being surrounded with love—most normal human beings associate these with youth. How much more so in the case of Felix, who was spoiled and almost worshiped by his sisters, who was always "cock of the walk!" So we cannot be surprised that he was boundlessly happy when "sitting and chatting between two sisters on the sofa, as in the old days." But this time he means his fiancée Cecile and her sister; he is again "cock of the walk." Still another connecting link was the similarity of social structure in the Jeanrenaud-Souchay and Mendelssohn families. In both cases, there rules the law of the clan. The absolute dependability and loyalty of the members of the clan in relation to it, the great number of these members—all this was thoroughly familiar to Felix and gave him a feeling of home. It speaks well for the emotional maturity of Felix that such feelings could extend into the erotic-sexual sphere, that he could associate a family structure which had been familiar to him from childhood with the object of his erotic choice without any inner conflict.

It is much harder for us to evaluate the personality and character of Cecile understandingly and fairly—indeed, even to comprehend it. As mentioned above, few letters from her are preserved. Neither Felix's sisters nor his mother express themselves in their letters to him otherwise than in friendly, but completely meaningless phrases. That was quite natural, and would not be any different today. Since Felix's sisters lived with his mother, here, too, there is no correspondence which would present Cecile to us more objectively. Therefore, if we want to form our own judgment, we are entirely dependent on Felix's remarks, Hiller's, Klingemann's, and Moscheles's observations; and a few sparse letters between the sisters.

From the portraits, we recognize Cecile's enchanting beauty. From her letters, we sense her thoroughly domestic, conventional temperament. In one instance, Felix, who was otherwise a devout soul, mentions that he had to warn Cecile "not to bother the good Lord with bagatelles." The regular orthodox prayer of the Jeanrenaud family finally got on the nerves of the Schleiermacher pupil. The sentimentality of Cecile speaks from every one of her letters as a young girl; it is expressed much more seldom in the letters of the mature woman. She was and remained always polite, but equally reserved, even in the letters to her sisters-in-law. She spoke from the heart only to her mother and (probably) to Felix. She was very elegant, of gracious presence, and was greatly interested in fashion news, but probably can not be regarded as a "grande dame." She was not widely read; this was quite to the taste of Felix, who could not stand blue-stockings. She had no great understanding of music, as we know from Felix himself. In social matters, she seems to have been quite experienced, and an especially gracious hostess; but in her judgment of people and things she betrayed great naiveté. She became a splendid housewife and mother, and a beloved companion for Felix, to whom she brought joy, beauty, and goodness. Unfortunately, however, it seems as though in other respects she exerted a restraining influence on the master. Perhaps he always inclined somewhat to the traditional and conventional, although the works of his youth definitely contradict such an assumption. Now, however, during his marriage, a certain conventionality appears more and more distinctly, by no means to the advantage of his music. It can hardly be proved that it was Cecile who furthered this conventionality, but many indications point to it.

Finally, we must ask ourselves what drew Felix, who had been spoiled by the most beautiful and cultivated women, so strongly to Cecile that he remained totally dependent on her.

The women with whom Felix usually associated—the mothers and

daughters among the closest relatives, the sisters, the ladies of Rahel Varnhagen's salon, the many acquaintances whom he made on his journeys—all
these fell into one of three categories: relatives, the intellectual or the
artistic, and flirts. In Cecile, he found a type of woman new to him: the
ingenue who was elegant, but domestic, naive, but by no means stupid,
attractive, but not provocative or coquettish. To this was added the slightly
exotic aura which always surrounded the Huguenots in Germany, and
which made them the natural intermediaries between Central and Western
Europe. The circle to which Cecile belonged was new to Felix, but by no
means unsympathetic to him; it had many similarities to the enclaves which
the Jews of the Emancipation had formed.

In all his letters from this time, he never tires of emphasizing that Cecile
alone can summon up the happiness of the days of his youth for him; a
lost Paradise, which now regained, seemed accessible to him once more.
For him, she was sweetheart, wife, and sister. In her beauty, she far surpassed Fanny, though she was on a lower level intellectually and culturally.
And so it came about that the world-traveler finally found the ideal wife,
even though she was not an equal partner in his thoughts and intentions.[33]
Perhaps he deceived himself on this point at first, especially during the
wedding journey, but he soon recognized Cecile's strong and weak points.
Therefore, it became an especially happy marriage; it was a good bourgeois
household, not a mere adventure. This destiny contrasts so strongly with
the "romances" of his contemporaries that we must call special attention
to it. In comparison with Berlioz's tragic vagaries, with Liszt's escapades,
with Chopin's worldly lady friends, with Wagner's unscrupulous adventures, even with Schumann's problem-laden relationship to Clara Wieck,
Felix's marriage was really "pure Philistinism"; indeed, he called himself,
not without self-irony, an "arch-Philistine " Perhaps this points towards
the strict tradition of his Jewish forebears, a tradition which takes sexual
matters with the utmost seriousness, especially in marriage. The strong
sensuality of the artist and man was held within strict bounds by clearly
formulated and sensible restrictions. This tradition of careful moderation
triumphed in Felix Mendelssohn's life, beyond a doubt. Should we assume
that a more permissive attitude in matters of sexual passion would have
been to the advantage of himself and his music? We think not—and point
to the lack of inner discipline in most of the poems of Heine, who was
inclined to give in too easily to such urges.

But all difficulties were not yet overcome. The two clans mixed like
water and oil. The concerned mother Lea read between the lines with
exaggerated worry, and chased down every rumor; and when the Jeanrenauds visited Felix in February and March, 1837, immediately before the
wedding, he tried to persuade his mother not to come to Leipzig at the
same time.[34] Did he want, perhaps, to avoid an encounter that could be

unpleasant? It almost seems so; for the Jeanrenauds promised to come to Berlin (from Leipzig), but every time that they were ready to go, Madame Jeanrenaud became ill, three times in succession. Felix became quite furious about it and placed the blame, probably correctly, on Cecile's grandmother, the "family dragon," Madame Souchay. About her, he writes: "Madame Jeanrenaud lives in complete dependence on her parents, namely Madame Souchay, who lets her feel it thoroughly."[35]

Finally, however, his mother came to Leipzig, to hear *St. Paul* in the *Paulinerkirche* (March 16). Before this, Felix assures her: "She [Cecile] will also make a nice wife, I am sure of that."[36]

He reports that Madame Souchay was equally feared by her daughter and granddaughter.[37] Lea answers resignedly that she would come to Leipzig, but Felix "need not worry about a long visit."[38] After the meeting of Lea with the Jeanrenaud ladies, she decides not to come to the wedding. We should not misunderstand this; Lea was elderly, was often ill, and had always hated journeys of all kinds. It is far more significant that no one from Felix's immediate family was present at the wedding; only the old aunt Dorothea Schlegel represented his family. This seems to have been a well-calculated policy, especially with a family which, like the Mendelssohns, traveled often, liked to travel, and, besides, always clung together as closely as possible. Petitpierre speaks of the magnificent wedding, at which the equipages of the Mendelssohn Bartholdys, who are described here as "faithful parishioners," rode forth among the Frankfurt patricians. Not a word of it is true! And this conspicuous absence had not only its cause, but also its consequences; years passed before the mutual jealousies and tensions were laid aside.

Already in May (shortly after the wedding, which took place on March 28), both sisters consider Felix "definitely altered"; but Felix defends himself against this insinuation, and maintains that the sisters must be mistaken —for otherwise he would have to despise himself! And he closes with the somewhat diffident words: "I must beg you once again—don't believe in any change, don't read it between the lines, don't hear it in people's conversations, but believe that I shall love you all my life . . . and cannot do otherwise. . . ."[39]

But he had changed, without a doubt! Never before would he have thought, let alone written, what he now explains quite openly: "The concerto [in D minor] is nothing special as a composition, but the last movement is so effective as piano fireworks that I must often laugh and Cecile cannot hear it often enough."[40]

This from the man who sarcastically scorned Kalkbrenner and the young Liszt! Already, his self-judgment, otherwise so strict, was compromised; the wish to please and impress Cecile weakened his artistic integrity. And so it remained until 1845, two years before his death.

Even Hensel, who carefully suppresses all scandalous matter, cannot help hinting at traces of ill-humor in the family. He expresses himself politely: ". . . a bad mood had set in with my mother [Fanny]; she thought that some opportunity could already have been found to bring Cecile to Berlin."[41] In the late autumn of 1837, she wrote to Cecile in Leipzig: "It is another thing, and annoying, that it stood written in the book of fate that we do not live together, but that he [Felix] should have had, for eight months, a wife whom I do not know."[42]

This was a mild reproach, but it had no direct result. So, willy-nilly, Fanny had to make up her mind to travel to Leipzig on her own, in order finally to get to know her new sister-in-law. She did it with considerable reluctance. For, in her notes and little letters to Rebecca, she airs her feelings and expresses her ill-humor without mincing words.

The meeting of the sisters-in-law restored, at least outwardly, the old solidarity of the family. However, we must henceforth remember that Felix had emancipated himself from the power of his family, but in favor of a new dependency which was no less bound up with a family. Only when he himself became a father was this imbalance agreeably resolved. Only then began a really warm relationship between Cecile and Felix's family.

He, immediately after the Leipzig performance of *St. Paul,* traveled with bride and mother-in-law to Frankfurt for the wedding, and from there they departed on the wedding journey. In a time without railroads, people could not and did not want to get too far away from headquarters. So they traveled into the upper Rhine Valley, through Worms and Speyer, and through Strasbourg into the Black Forest, to Freiburg, Rastatt, Heidelberg, Darmstadt. From there, the young couple returned to Frankfurt, but only for a short rest. They then traveled through another circle with Frankfurt as the center; Oberad, Kreuznach, Bingen, Koblenz, and then to dear old Düsseldorf, which they reached in the middle of August, 1837. There, Felix got ready for his fifth visit to England.

They painted and sketched a great deal on the long quiet wedding journey. They even kept a joint travel diary, which is filled with Biedermeier drolleries, serious reports, and drawings by both of them. Unfortunately I had no opportunity to see this interesting document in the original; however, charming excerpts from it are found in Petitpierre's book.

Their honeymoon seems, from all we know, to have been animated with idyllic beauty and with serene joy. Felix's creative powers were tremendously stimulated. A whole series of larger and smaller works was sketched on the wedding journey, and carried out soon thereafter: Quartet in E minor, Piano Concerto in D minor, three Preludes and Fugues for organ, a volume of Songs without Words, and even a large-scale Psalm for chorus, soli, and orchestra on the text "As the hart panteth after the water brooks" (Psalm 42). Hiller was the first, but not the last, who approached this spiritual sublimation of the honeymoon with amazement and mistrust. But soon he came to the conclusion: "The blessed trust in God and the muted emotion which . . . sings itself out in certain sections may well be reconciled with the feeling of deepest joy which surged through him [Felix] at that time."[43]

That may be true; but it is equally true that the composer has no inkling of the religious melancholy or the wild longing for God of that magnificent text. But more of this in the next chapter.

VI

Already in April, 1837, Felix had accepted the invitation to lead the festival in Birmingham. Hesitantly and reluctantly, he prepared for the journey, and left Düsseldorf on August 24. He reached London on the 27th, in a miserable, positively furious mood: "This time England and fog and beef and porter taste terribly bitter to me . . . I wish that I were sitting by my Cecile and had left Birmingham to itself."[44]

The first London days became a tragic experience for him through the sudden illness and death of the friend of his youth, Professor Rosen. To this was added the complete uncertainty of the position of Klingemann, who had had the ground cut out from under him by the death of King William IV. We remember that Klingemann was Legation Councillor of the "Royal German Chancellery" in London; this institution had significance and justification so long as the personal union between the King of Hanover and the King of England existed. Since William's successor according to English law was Victoria, but, according to Hanoverian law, was Ernst August, Duke of Cumberland, the personal union fell apart; with this, the Hanoverian Chancellery in London had lost its real function as a diplomatic intermediary between Hanover and London.[45] Finally Klingemann did succeed in establishing his position in London, but it was years before he could feel secure in it.

All these events depressed Felix, who spent many hours at the sickbed of his friend Rosen; he was not present at his death, because just at that time he had to hear his *St. Paul* in Exeter Hall. The next morning he traveled to Birmingham, following a call of duty which, this time, he would all too willingly have escaped.

During these London days, he met with a number of musicians, principally organists. He had never neglected his organ playing, and now he played in St. Paul's Cathedral and in Christ Church, Newgate Street, both times before a throng of enthusiastic organists. In St. Paul's, the organ-blowers let the air out of the pipes while Mendelssohn was playing the great A minor Fugue of Bach—they had become angry because no one wanted to leave and they had to work too much![46] In Christ Church he improvised fugues on themes which old Samuel Wesley played for him, and added further extemporaneous material. Grove, who personally knew Chorley, Gauntlett, and other witnesses of those days, observes:

> He was the greatest of the few great German organ-players who had visited this country, and the English organists, some of them no mean proficients, learned more than one lesson from him . . . he brought out a number of Bach pedal-fugues which were not known here. . . . He was the first to play the D major, the G minor, the C minor, the short E Minor, etc.[47]

Immediately after his arrival in Birmingham, he had his hands full with rehearsals and arrangements. The program of the music festival did not spare him. On the first festival evening, he played on the great organ fantasies on themes from Handel's *Solomon* ("Your harp and cymbals sound") and from Mozart's D major Symphony (principal theme of the first movement). These two works had already been performed that day, so the themes were still familiar. Besides, he once again conducted his *A Midsummer Night's Dream* Overture. On the second day, he directed his *St. Paul;* on the third, he played and conducted his Piano Concerto in D minor; on the fourth, he again played on the organ—the great E flat Major fugue (so-called "St. Anne") of Bach. From the organ he sprang into a coach and arrived in London about midnight; continued to Dover, which he reached about nine in the morning. There he took a Channel steamer, which, after a five hours' miserable journey, brought him, not to Calais, but to Boulogne. Through Lille, Cologne, Koblenz he traveled over bumpy roads to Frankfurt. He had been on the road six days and five nights, on top of ten days' strenuous work in Birmingham. In Frankfurt he rested two days and then traveled to Leipzig with his Cecile, this time in a comfortable coach and with several rests *en route*. He finally arrived there on October 1, exactly four hours before the first *Gewandhaus* concert of the season, which, of course, he had to direct. A real escapade and at the same time a *tour de force!*

Fanny was not so wrong when, troubled, she exclaimed in a letter to Cecile: "If only I could once hear about Felix that he gets away from this eternal unrest; this eternal mad rush in which he lives year in and year out, makes me, who lives in deepest peace, breathless every time I think about it. . . ."[48]

The fifth English journey of Mendelssohn, the shortest of his career, had brought him artistic triumphs in London and Birmingham, but also great exertions and excitement. So he decided to enjoy his own fireside now and to dedicate himself to the *Gewandhaus* and to his wife. Since

Cecile was expecting a child in early 1838, Felix, a good husband and father, did not want to leave her or to expose her to the risks of a journey. Felix himself loses, for a few years, his uncompromising self-criticism. Now he becomes conventional and apolitical; he does not care for the newspapers; he scarcely dares any more experiments. At least as a composer, he becomes somewhat too smooth, and only his inborn taste and his technical mastery save him, in the following years, from sheer mediocrity. These observations hold true only for the *general level* of his creations from the years 1838-1844; a few masterpieces tower above this and make us feel all the more painfully the difference between them and the other works. A little statistical study shows that, before 1838, almost every third work is a masterpiece. Afterwards, this is true of only every fifth work. Only towards the end of 1844 does Mendelssohn rise out of this artistic slump and reach his earlier standard once more.

Is it not sad that the creative spirit had to pay for his private, innocent joy as a human being with a diminution in the value of his achievement?

$\mathcal{N}otes$

1. See E. Devrient, *op. cit.*, p. 94; A. B. Marx, *Erinnerungen,* and, above all, Therese Marx's, *A. B. Marx' Verhältnis zu Felix Mendelssohn* (Leipzig, 1869), pp. 14, 16, 19, 20-24.

2. Therese Marx, *op. cit.* (directed against Devrient's inaccurate and subjective account), pp. 22ff.

3. Max Hecker, "Zelters Tod," *Jahrbuch der Sammlung Kippenberg VII* (1927-8), pp. 111ff.

4. *Ibid.*

5. Letter to Schubring, December 6, 1835.

6. Riemer, *Mitteilungen über Goethe* (1841), I, pp. 427ff.

7. *Ibid.*, p. 440.

8. Many letter of Mendelssohn and recollections of the family, as well as the memoirs of Hiller and Moscheles speak of him.

9. Hensel, F. M., II (Fanny's letters to Klingemann of February 8 and 12, 1836). See also Hiller's letter to Meyerbeer of October 14, 1836, and Moscheles' correspondence (Felix's letter of July 20, 1836; also his letter of February 18, 1836).

10. Hensel, *F. M.*, II, pp. 4ff.

11. Hensel, *Ibid.*, II, p. 5.

12. Unpublished letter of April 18, 1836.

13. Letter to Felix of April 24, 1836 (unpublished).

14. Unpublished letter by Felix in private hands.

15. Letter to Schubring, December 6, 1835.

16. Hensel, *F. M.*, II, p. 29.

17. Unpublished letter of Lea, January 26, 1836.

18. Letter to his mother of June 1, 1836.

19. Kretzschmar, *Führer durch den Konzerstaal,* II, 2 (Oratorio, p. 204).

20. Presently in private possession in New York.

21. For example, Otto Jahn, in "Mendelssohn's Oratorium Paulus," in *Gesammelte Aufsätze über Musik* (Leipzig, 1867), pp. 17ff.
22. *Briefwechsel Mendelssohn-Schubring*, ed., Julius Schubring (Leipzig, 1892).
23. Einstein, *Music in the Romantic Era* (New York, 1947), p. 172ff.
24. Kretzschmar, *Führer*, II, 2, pp. 331ff.
25. Chorley, in *Athenaeum* (1837), p. 708.
26. Unpublished letter of January 22, 1837.
27. In Lavignac, *Encyclopédie de musique* (2nd edition), "L'école romantique."
28. See Eric Werner in *Amor Artis Bulletin*, Vol. 1, No. 2, March, 1962, New York.
29. Letter of July 14, 1836.
30. Letter of July 14.
31. *Ibid.*
32. R. Huch, *Die Blütezeit der Romantik*, I, pp. 21ff.
33. All Leipzig took and interest in his marriage. The management put the Finale of *Fidelio* on the program of December 12, 1836; the passage *wer ein holdes Weib errungen, mische seinen Jubel ein!* "Let him who has won a lovely wife join in the rejoicing!" won such universal applause that, afterwards, the master had to sit down at the piano and improvise freely on this theme.
34. Unpublished letter of January 27, 1837, to Felix's sister Rebecca.
35. *Ibid.*
36. *Ibid.*
37. Unpublished letter of February 18, 1837.
38. Unpublished letter from Lea, March 5, 1837.
39. Unpublished letter to mother and sisters, June 8, 1837.
40. Unpublished letter of July 22, 1837.
41. Hensel, *F. M.*, II, p. 52 (Letter of October 4, 1837).
42. *Ibid.*
43. Hiller, *op. cit.*, p. 82.
44. *Ibid.*, p. 88.
45. It is significant for the uncertainty of the early Victorian days that Klingemann speculated as follows: "finally our King [of Hanover] . . . is supposedly the heir to the throne; [of England] . . . if the good little Victoria should meet with bad luck and die before her time[!], our chancellery will come to life again." (Letter of June 30, 1837.)
46. See Dr. Gauntlett's report in *The Musical World* of September 15, 1837, p. 8.
47. Grove, *Dictionary of Music*, 4th ed., article "Mendelssohn," pp. 396-97.
48. Hensel, *F. M.*, II, letter of October 5, 1837.

CHAPTER XIV

The Tranquil Years
(1837-1841)

Medium tenuere beati.
(Vergil)

ACTIVITY IN LEIPZIG

WE MAY OFTEN ask what may motivate a creative spirit in science or in art to set itself tasks and goals in the areas of organization and administration. Such resolutions demand a division between pragmatic and artistic activity which is by no means without dangers. As long as the composer interprets his own original creation, he remains true to his mission; Bach and Handel as master organists, Mozart, Beethoven, or Chopin as outstanding pianists, were principally interpreters of their own works. Purely organizational work is something else again. We must probably go back to Lully to find a precedent for Mendelssohn's administrative efforts, which, indeed like those of Lully, served above all the purpose of *establishing a style.* For the composer, the central question remains: is it worth the trouble of taking him away from his proper field of endeavor? If we recall that a towering genius like Newton gave many years of his life to the service of the Royal Mint (not compelled to do so, but gladly) or that Goethe freely took on the burdens of a high administrative officer, it seems inadmissible to complain about such a division of effort. But *non cuivis viro adire Corinthum*—only a few succeed in attaining this goal! In the case of Mendelssohn, who possessed neither the elemental strength of these spirits nor their physical vitality and longevity, one might well complain about the heavy administrative responsibilities placed on him in Leipzig and then in Berlin. They certainly cost him many years of his life, and many works never ripened to fruition because of this. Was it worth it?

Mendelssohn himself posed this question; at first, he answered it in the affirmative, but, in the last years of his life, definitely in the negative. Why, then, did he subject himself, at least till 1843, to all the troubles and harassments which inevitably accompany administrative and organizational activity?

The discernible reasons are twofold. Mendelssohn felt that his mission was to direct a concert institution that would set the pace for all of Central Europe; further, he was concerned with propagating a particular trend, a specific kind of taste in art. He attained this goal through the creation of a clearly defined "*Gewandhaus* Tradition." Then, he wanted to assure the continuity of this tradition; that was one of the tasks of the Conservatory which he founded. But less than ten years after his death, both aims had undergone radical modification. Other trends, often diametrically opposed to his, were now to be served.

In this chapter we shall, therefore, examine the practical and organizational activity of Mendelssohn more thoroughly, in order to determine the precise nature of his artistic aims; we shall also try to assess to what degree his efforts were crowned with *lasting success*. Only then can we decide whether the end result was "worth the trouble."

We do not rely too much on statistical tables in music history. However, when Robert Schumann makes a modest effort at such a thing, we should accept it thankfully; for, to him, the numbers of performances of composers did not stand for absolute values, but rather served as indications of the artistic taste of his time. In his *Rückblick auf das Leipziger Musikleben im Winter 1837-38* Schumann gives a welcome survey of the majority of the works performed in the *Gewandhaus* concerts. According to this, Mozart holds first place, Beethoven second, Weber third; only then come Haydn, Cherubini, Spohr, Mendelssohn, and Rossini. Still later follow Bach, Handel, Cimarosa, Méhul, Abt Vogler, Onslow, and Moscheles; trailing them we find Naumann, Salieri, Righini, Fesca, Hummel, Spontini, and Marschner. Of contemporary composers, the following should be named: Hiller, Lachner, Reissiger, Molique, Rosenhain, Sterndale Bennett, Taeglichsbeck, Burgmueller, and Gaebrich. It would be difficult to find a composer of renown who is not included in this list. And yet—three names are conspicuous by their absence—Chopin, Liszt, and Berlioz. Mendelssohn was a great admirer of Chopin, but he always liked to hear him playing his own music, and so it was 1844 by the time he reconciled himself to performing Chopin's concerti without Chopin. Liszt, to Felix, was a Paganini of the piano, and although he soon revised the bold judgment of his youth, "Lots of fingers and little brains," he could not warm to his compositions, which he viewed as brilliant but empty tinkling. However, he did not experience Liszt's stylistic change to "serious" music, and so his judgment remains biased. On the other hand, he opened all doors in Leipzig for the great pianist Liszt, as we shall see. Mendelssohn had no use at all for Berlioz's music. Nevertheless, in 1843 he placed the *Gewandhaus* at his disposal for the performance of an all Berlioz program. "Mendelssohn still sincerely disliked Berlioz's music and Berlioz knew it. Yet Mendelssohn helped to rehearse and produce it, and Berlioz no less sincerely admired and praised his friend's works till his death and after."[1]

Schumann's orchestral works were mostly introduced by Mendelssohn himself, greatly to the delight of the composer. Although everyone of fame in continental music was represented in the *Gewandhaus* concerts, a definite tendency to prefer certain styles and reject others is immediately recognizable. It is in contemporary music that the preference for certain styles is most evident. Hiller, Sterndale Bennett, Spohr, Schumann, Chopin, Méhul, Lachner, Moscheles, Marschner, and Kalliwoda are accepted: rejected or at least neglected are Hummel, Rossini, Donizetti, Meyerbeer, Berlioz, Liszt, and Wagner.

And yet, a dry compilation of the concert programs or a list of the performing artists and works performed does not do justice to the activity of Mendelssohn in Leipzig. We shall understand its spirit better and also the ruling musical taste, which Mendelssohn did help to form (but to which he often had to adapt himself), if we choose and discuss several outstanding programs from the five concert seasons 1837-1841. We must qualify the expression "outstanding"; it does not refer to the historic significance of those concerts as we see them today, *but to their evaluation in Mendelssohn's time.* From the apparent divergence between our modern evaluation, the opinions of Mendelssohn's time and Mendelssohn's real intentions, a picture of Mendelssohn's educative aims and methods and an image of the musical fashions of his time will result.[2] We have chosen eight programs (in chronological order) which were most discussed at the time. Here we give the most important documents and some explanatory comments.

Clara Novello

Mendelssohn had already heard the young singer in England and, at the very beginning of her career, had invited her (from Frankfurt) to Leipzig.[3] She and Mrs. Alfred Shaw were the English woman singers whom he valued most highly. Both enjoyed great success, but Miss Novello won the hearts of even the most severe critics. She appeared quite regularly in Leipzig during the seasons 1837-1839. Schumann became positively poetic in his review of her Leipzig engagement.[4] Especially he praised her "most noble interpretation, her simple and modest art, which allows the work and its creator to shine." Mendelssohn, too, was very much prejudiced in her favor. In his letters to Hiller he expressed very friendly feelings towards her; but to his intimate friend Klingemann he shows considerable emotional reservations because of her lack of warmth.[5]

After her marriage to an Italian count, she retired from her concert career for some time; however, eventually she appeared in public again, and we have a quite impartial evaluation of Novello by Wasielewski.[6] Under Mendelssohn's direction, she sang the soprano part in *Messiah* at the Lower Rhenish Music Festival in Düsseldorf, in 1839. An ear witness, Elise Polko, has only words of praise for her.[7] Alas Novello also took pen in hand; in her memoirs she shows none of that modesty which Schumann praised in her. For instance, she says: "For me Felix composed 'As the hart pants.' I was struck by the entire want of knowledge of Handel's music evident in Germany, his times, etc., quite mistaken even by such scholars as dear Felix. . . ."[8] From every page of her memoirs there speaks the soul of a silly, often unbearable snob. Mendelssohn seems to have been well aware of Novello's limitations, for, in a letter to her brother Alfred, he expressed himself in a gently ironical manner:

> I am sometimes afraid she must find the place [Leipzig] very small and dull, and miss her splendid Philharmonic band and all those marchionesses and duchesses and lady patronesses who look so beautifully aristocratically in your concert-rooms, and of whom we have a great want. But if being really and heartily liked and loved by a public and being looked on as a most distinguished and eminent talent must also convey a feeling of pleasure to those who are the object of it, I am sure that your sister cannot repent her resolution of accepting the invitation to this place. . . .[9]

It is unbelievable, but true, that Mendelssohn's irony in this letter was observed neither by the addressee nor by the editor of the memoirs. In general, Miss Novello's tone is rather condescending when she speaks of Mendelssohn. But then, he was no Italian count like her husband, whom she had to support!

World Première of Schubert's C Major Symphony

Years before Mendelssohn had championed Schubert's songs both in Leipzig and Berlin.[10] In his correspondence with Moscheles he praises the symphony as the best symphonic music to have appeared in many years,[11] and in his family letters he calls the works "immortal." Schumann, who had discovered and unearthed it in Vienna, in a pile of Schubert manuscripts at his brother's house, brought it to Leipzig. His enthusiastic essay about the work and its first performance belongs to the classic literature of music history.

Everywhere, Mendelssohn's achievement in bringing the long work to its first performance (March 21, 1839) was acclaimed; in this connection, one should remember that Schubert's instrumental music was, at this time, virtually unknown—not even the "Unfinished" had been discovered! The

Leipziger Allgemeine Musikzeitung, which was ordinarily not exactly fond of "novelties," managed to squeeze out the following sentences:

> If the tremendously gifted and popular composer had not died so young, he certainly would have shortened his work himself and thereby made its many attractive features even more attractive. Already the beginning with the horn solo prepossesses us in its favor. . . . The performance, under Dr. Mendelssohn-Bartholdy's direction, was as masterly as if the work had already been performed many times.[12]

But we have better witnesses. Fortunately, Hans von Bülow heard the Schubert symphony under Mendelssohn:

> I recall the impression—never again so powerful in subsequent performances —which was made on me by Schubert's C major Symphony under Mendelssohn's direction. At that time it was not yet fashionable to install Schubert on the heights of Mt. Olympus; he was loved, admired, and enjoyed as a *minorum gentium,* but there were complaints about the expansiveness of his forms and the monotony of his rhythms. But, under Mendelssohn's baton, one was not aware of these faults. Without using the blue pencil—simply through his elastic sensitivity and the magnetic eloquence of his gestures—the brilliant leader was able completely to conceal the abovementioned deficiencies. What wonderful nuances of color, what intelligently thoughtout shadings of tempo he used! How easily he caused us to glide over the varied steppes of the "endless" Allegretto, so that, at the end, the hearer had no conception of the duration of the acoustical phenomenon! For we had just dwelt in eternity, in a timeless world. . . .[13]

In foreign countries, too, this world première made a significant impression. Here, let us simply cite a short observation taken from the *Revue Musicale* (which, under Fétis's editorship, was hardly friendly to Mendelssohn): "In the concerts in the *Gewandhaus,* under the superb direction of a master like Mendelssohn, there was performed a symphony by Franz Schubert which enjoyed very great success. We hope that the music-lovers of Paris may soon have the opportunity of hearing this beautiful work in one of the concerts of the Conservatoire. . . ."[14]

Franz Liszt

Here, we shall let Mendelssohn speak for himself, since the letters from which we quote have remained unpublished up till now. As a fresh lad of sixteen, he had dismissed Liszt in a brief and malicious phrase. Later, in Paris, he had become friendly with him, chiefly through their mutual friend and artistic colleague Hiller. Now, in March of 1840, Liszt came to Leipzig.

Before we let Mendelssohn tell the story, we must make a few explanatory remarks. It seems that Liszt, who was in the height of fashion at the time, was under the thumb of a rather unscrupulous manager, who was determined to make as much money as possible as fast as possible—for who knew how long Liszt would remain in vogue? So admission fees to his concerts were suddenly raised, with unpleasant results (crude pamphlets attacking Liszt's greed were published). The Viennese, too, had struck out rudely at him in a magazine (of which we shall have more to say later), and he was forced to reply in the press. In this statement, he said, "I was richly recompensed by the flattering recognition in both cities [Dresden and Leipzig], the honor graciously accorded me by Dr. Mendelssohn, of whom I think so highly, with the cooperation of the outstanding Leipzig orchestra and chorus. . . ."[15]

The following letter to sister Fanny has been previously published only in parts. It should be compared with the letters to Felix's mother of March 30, 1840, printed in the "official" edition; this letter, too, has been "cut to size." In the letter to Fanny, we read the following:

Liszt was here for two weeks and caused a devil of a scandal—in the good and in the bad sense. His playing and his technique are magnificent, and his personality, too, pleases me greatly; in my heart I consider him a good artist and human being. But the newspapers! There was such a flood of explanations and counter-explanations, and reviews and lawsuits, and this, that, and the other that has nothing to do with music, that his visit caused almost as much irritation as pleasure. . . . But his way of dealing with the public didn't please me at all—basically, they are both wrong. . . . Since he cares a lot about these things, I gave him a soirée for 350 people in the *Gewandhaus*, with orchestra, chorus, bishop, cake, *Meeresstille*, Psalm [Mendelssohn's 42nd Psalm], Bach's Triple Concerto (Liszt, Hiller, and me), choruses from *St. Paul*, fantasy on *Lucia di Lammermoor*, *Erlkönig*, the devil and his grandmother! . . .[16]

Thirty-three years later, Hiller still remembered this scene exactly:

"When he played Schubert's *Erlkönig*, half the public stood up on their seats. The *Lucia* fantasy turned everyone's heads. Some other pieces, however, were less successful. This was true of Mendelssohn's D minor Concerto, which had just appeared and which he neither sight-read nor found time to study somewhat more thoroughly. People thought that the composer played it better. Also, it seemed unsuitable for him to play part of the Pastoral Symphony in a hall where it had been heard so often in its variegated orchestral garb. In a foreword to his transcriptions of the Beethoven symphonies, Liszt calmly yet boldly proclaims that everything can be reproduced on the modern pianoforte. When Mendelssohn read this, he said,

"I'd just like to hear the first eight measures of the Mozart G minor symphony, with the light viola figure, on the piano the way they sound in the orchestra—then I'd believe it."

That Liszt was honored as much as possible is self-evident. Mendelssohn organized a huge soirée in the hall of the Gewandhaus, to which about two hundred people were invited. It was half a rout, half a concert; Liszt played a great deal and was as amiable as possible. I had the honor of participating in a performance of Bach's concerto for three pianos. . . .[17]

Finally, let us cite a few significant observations of Schumann on Liszt's appearance in Leipzig:

. . . it was not Liszt's fault that the public was made uneasy by the advance announcements, and annoyed by mistakes of the concert management. . . .

He began . . . with the Scherzo and the Finale of the Pastoral Symphony. The choice was whimsical enough, and unfortunate for many reasons. In the privacy of one's own room, this very painstaking arrangement may make us forget the orchestra; but in a larger hall, where we have so often heard the symphony in its orchestral perfection, the weakness of the instrument was all the more noticeable. . . .

Meanwhile, a musical feast was prepared for him—one which will probably remain unforgettable for Liszt himself as well as for all those who were present. The host [Mendelssohn] had chosen for performance only works which were unknown to the guest: the Schubert symphony, the psalm, Wie der Hirsch schreit, the overture Meeresstille, the triple concerto by Seb. Bach. The latter was played by Liszt, Mendelssohn and Hiller. Everything seemed to spring from the inspiration of the moment, nothing seemed prepared; there were three joyous hours of music such as one does not experience otherwise for years at a time . . .[18]

Mendelssohn did not think much of Liszt's compositional talent; he expressed himself on this point to Moscheles, carefully and with admirable restraint.[19] However, he did not live to experience the later works of Liszt; but we may venture to suppose that Liszt, the composer of programmatic symphonies, would have been even less acceptable to Felix than the elegant Liszt—not to mention the church composer Liszt, who certainly would have been a horror to Mendelssohn.

Gutenberg Festival and Hymn of Praise

It was natural that Leipzig, the city of the book and of books, would, on the occasion of the four hundredth anniversary of the invention of printing, honor the inventor, Gutenberg, in especially sumptuous style. Thus, a most pompous festival was planned in June of 1840. Mendelssohn took part in the two most important musical festival performances; the third was the première of Lortzing's comic opera *Hans Sachs*. For the musical open air demonstration before the Gutenberg monument, Mendelssohn—unfortunately!—composed a festival chorus. This work, for male chorus and band, is based on a silly and often tasteless text, which is a weird mixture of Protestant chorales with outpourings such as *Gutenberg, der deutsche Mann, zündete die Fackel an* ("Gutenberg, the German man, lighted the torch"). The very "learned" composition, into which Mendelssohn wove chorale melodies contrapuntally, was not considered worthy of publication by him, and was printed only after his death.[20] However, the program of the real festival concert, in St. Thomas' Church, included Weber's *Jubelouvertüre* (which, as is known, weaves in "God Save the King"— *Heil Dir im Siegerkranz*), Handel's *Dettingen Te Deum*, and the world première of Mendelssohn's *Hymn of Praise*, written for that occasion. As a motto for the work, he had written into the score Luther's saying, "But I would see all the arts, especially music, in the service of Him who gave and created them." The title *Lobgesang* is his own; the designation *Symphonie-Kantate* comes from Klingemann; in England and America, the work is known as *Hymn of Praise*. Mendelssohn thought a great deal of this work, much more than we do today. More of this later!

The première was a great success, and in England the piece has remained popular, at least in part, till the present day. Hans von Bülow expressed himself in characteristic fashion concerning the work and its performance in the London Crystal Palace on the occasion of the thirtieth anniversary of Mendelssohn's death:

> It was a consecrated evocation of that master who, today, remains unrecognized except by anachronistically Schumannizing conservatory students, and whom Mr. Richard Wagner—in conversation at least—was accustomed (sic!) to designate as the "greatest specifically musical genius" who had appeared in the world since Mozart. Granted that, in the course of his development, even this genius descended to the rank of a talent—in the *Lobgesang*, we find, alongside much that is faded and barren of inspiration, quite enough sections upon which the stamp of genius is indelibly impressed. . . [21]

Schumann, who attended the première, gives the following judgment:

> The form of the whole could not be more happily chosen for this purpose. The whole stimulated enthusiasm, and certainly the work, particularly in the choral movements, is to be accounted one of his freshest and most charming creations. . . . We shall not emphasize details; and yet—that duet, interrupted by the chorus, *Ich harrete des Herrn*, after which there broke forth in the audience a whispering which counts for more in the church than loud applause in the concert-hall. It was like a glimpse into a heaven of Raphael's madonnas' eyes. . . .[22]

Because of the much disputed genesis of this work, we shall return to it later.

Organ Concert for the Benefit of a Bach Monument

As is generally known, Mendelssohn was an outstanding pianist. But his favorite instrument was the organ; and here, almost like Liszt on the piano, he set a new standard. For not only did he have a thorough technical mastery of the organ (that was self-evident for a Bach enthusiast like Felix) but he had taken great pains to ascertain Bach's preferred organ dispositions and his art of registration. In contrast to the organ taste of the nineteenth century, Mendelssohn cultivated the baroque organ and its typical registers; he thought highly of mixtures, *Schnarrstimmen* and *Gedackte*. We know this from his letters to Attwood and Buxton. It had long been a favorite idea of his to "play together" the money necessary for a monument by giving Bach concerts. He had already toyed with this idea in 1838, as we know from a letter to Klingemann.[23] After the end of the concert season, Mendelssohn took time for thorough preparation and then played the following all Bach program in St. Thomas' Church:

> Prelude and Fugue in E flat major ("St. Anne")
> Chorale Prelude, *Schmücke dich, du liebe Seele*
> Passacaglia in C minor
> Prelude and Fugue in A minor
> Pastorale in F major
> Toccata (?—The reports on this are unreliable)
> Free fantasy on *O Haupt voll Blut und Wunden*

The master had practised his pedal studies so diligently that he could "hardly stand upright any more, and walked down the street in nothing but organ passages."[24] The concert brought in 300 thalers profit, and after another similar undertaking, the memorial bust could be placed in 1843 directly under Bach's windows in the *Thomas-schule*.

In its day, little was said about this concert, which, after all, had only local interest. Schumann, naturally, praised it to the seventh heaven; the Berlin newspapers looked on the affair as more or less a curiosity, but the *Leipziger Allgemeine Musikalische Zeitung* published a very positive review:

Through the performance of several magnificent compositions of Sebastian Bach, and through the rendition of a free fantasy, Mendelssohn once more proved himself a distinguished organist and great artist; it was a truly splendid artistic treat, for which we are all the more thankful as it is offered to us—alas!—so seldom. . . .[25]

The patriarch of the music critics, old *Hofrat* Rochlitz, who had still heard the Thomas Cantor Schicht play, embraced Felix after the concert with tears in his eyes and said, "Nunc dimittis."[26] As the strongest of witnesses, we once more present Hans von Bülow, who had heard the master at the organ. He writes:

> Here, above all, we enthusiastically recall Mendelssohn, whose delicate constitution, unfortunately, did not often allow him to offer his admirers this treat—especially as, once he was at the instrument, he forgot himself in his art and entirely neglected to spare his nerves. His style of playing had a definitely modern character; it was interesting and poetical, whereas the style of the organists who could not play the piano was hard without energy—in short, dry and leathery. . . .[27]

The English, too, especially Chorley and Davison, could not find enough praise for Mendelssohn's organ playing.[28]

Moscheles's Concert

Although Moscheles was besieged with requests to give a regular concert in the cycle of subscription concerts, he could not make up his mind to it; for he was on his way to Prague and expected to leave from one day to the next. However, it turned out differently; he was forced to wait from October 10 to 20. In order to divert him during this time, his old friend Felix organized many parties for him; also, the pair busily made music together. Among other events, the Schumanns gave him a private soirée, with Clara Schumann at the piano. Mendelssohn, too, gave one for him, and later, as in the case of Liszt, a semi-public one in the *Gewandhaus*. For this occasion he had thought up the joke of sending Mrs. Moscheles, in London, a printed invitation card, which read, in part, as follows: "Please show this card on entering the hall. If this card is not shown, Professor Moscheles should be sent to London to collect the applause which can only be incomplete here. R.s.v.p. by return mail."[29]

The program of the fête (October 19, 1840) consisted of the Leonore Overtures Nos. 2 and 3, Mendelssohn's Psalm 42, Moscheles's *Hommage à Händel* (performed by Felix and Moscheles with "brotherly enthusiasm"), Mendelssohn's *Hebrides* Overture and Moscheles's G minor Piano Concerto. But that was not enough! More and more encores were demanded. So the guests also heard Bach's Triple Concerto with Clara Schumann, Felix, and Moscheles, and, finally, Moscheles's Concert Etudes.[30] In his letters to Klingemann from these years, Mendelssohn gives a vivid picture of the social whirl in which he had become involved.[31]

Bach-Handel Concert

The experiment of "historical concerts" in the previous year had been successful beyond all expectations; therefore, at the beginning of 1841, Mendelssohn could report to Klingemann about his historical programs for the current year. He defines "historical concerts" as organized "according to the chronological order of the great masters from 100 years ago to the present time." He adds that the dilettantes of Leipzig were in such fierce competition to be allowed to sing in these concerts that it was a real joy. "But I think it is a good thing for us to accustom the paying public to participate with us from time to time—that restores to the institution a social rather than a public aspect. . . ." What a good idea this was we can realize today, when music is mortally threatened byov er-mechanization.

The Bach-Handel evening presented the following gigantic program on January 21, 1841:

> Bach, Chromatic Fantasy and Fugue (Mendelssohn)
> Bach, Motet for two choirs a cappella, *Ich lasse dich nicht*
> Bach, Chaconne for violin solo (F. David)
> Bach, *Crucifixus, Sanctus, Resurrexit* from the B minor Mass
> Handel, Overture to *Messiah*
> Handel, Recitative and Aria from *Messiah* (Sophie Schloss)
> Handel, Theme and Variations ("The Harmonious Blacksmith")
>   for piano (Mendelssohn)
> Handel, Four large choruses from *Israel in Egypt*

The venture of placing the solo chaconne next to the monumental choruses seems to have been successful, for the critics praised everything. Schumann was not so wrong when he maintained that Mendelssohn knew Bach and Handel better than any other contemporary musician. In fact, hundreds of Bach manuscripts had passed through Mendelssohn's hands. His largely unpublished correspondence with F. Hauser, Aloys Fuchs, and George Cooper (of the Royal College of Arms, London) bear witness to his thorough familiarity with Bach's compositions. Cooper had sent Mendelssohn a catalogue of Bach's works written by Philipp Emanuel Bach. I was not able to discover what has become of this priceless document. Since his childhood, Felix had come into contact with Bach manuscripts. His great-aunt Sara Levy possessed a considerable quantity of them; and I cannot resist quoting a significant passage from Hiller's memoirs, in which Felix's irritation at a missed opportunity breaks through.

Several years before Felix' birth, Mendelssohn's father, who was friendly with Zelter, gave him a great number of Bach cantatas in the original manuscript. [Their fate has already been mentioned above, in connection with Doris Zelter and the *Singakademie*. Most of the manuscripts were gifts of Madame Levy.] During Mendelssohn's student years, Zelter from time to time led him to the closet in which these treasures were stored and showed them to him. "There they are," he said, "just think of everything which is hidden there!"—but not even a peep into the works was vouchsafed to poor Felix, who stood thirstily before the precious drink and was not allowed a sip of it. In any case, these things would have been better taken care of in Mendelssohn's hands than in those of Zelter.[32]

It would probably be a worthwhile task to trace the manuscripts which Mendelssohn saw (and copied) and to recount their history.

Beethoven Concert

The program, given on February 11, 1841, was as follows:

Leonore Overture No. 3
Kyrie and Gloria from the C major Mass
Violin Concerto (M. Gulomy)
Adelaide (Madame Schroeder-Devrient)
Ninth Symphony

Just at this time the eminent English critic Henry Fothergill Chorley was visiting Germany. His descriptions, although too enthusiastic in Mendelssohn's favor, give a very lively picture of conditions in Leipzig. In connection with the Beethoven program, which Schumann calls "one of the richest evenings of music, such as we may, perhaps, hear but seldom in this world," we quote Chorley's report on the noteworthy performance of all three *Leonore* Overtures plus the *Fidelio* Overture. He writes:

I cannot pass over the performances of Beethoven's four overtures to "Fidelio" on the same evening, to afford the curious means of comparison: or the series of three or more historical concerts, in which the effect meditated by Spohr, in his strangely incoherent symphony, was produced by progressive selections of instrumental music, beginning with Bach and Handel. We English are still too far from being ripe for such performances as these—too largely apt to treat all public exhibitions as mere aimless amusements, where the most piquant novelty is the one thing best worth pursuing.[33]

But, when it is a matter of serious art, he claims that no other orchestra can compete with Leipzig's, and finally breaks out with these emphatic words:

Never, indeed, did I hear the Symphonies of Beethoven so intensely enjoyed as at Leipsic and never so admirably performed. As regarded those works of the Shakespeare of music, I felt, for the first time in my life, in 1839, richly and thoroughly satisfied beyond reserve or question. There was a breadth and freedom in their outlines, a thorough proportion in all their parts, a poetical development of all their choice and picturesque ideas, which fully compensated for the occasional want of the hyper-brilliancy and the hyper-delicacy, on the possession of which my friends in Paris pride themselves so vain-gloriously.[34]

Furthermore, Chorley gives us a lively portrayal of social and musical life at that time. Especially interesting to us are his remarks on the arrangement of seats in the old *Gewandhaus;* this was criticized on at least two occasions by Germans and foreigners. However, Chorley's judgment is mild. Today, we would condemn the Old *Gewandhaus* as a firetrap; at that time, people were not aware of the danger inherent in such cramped spaces. This danger, nonetheless, was ever present:

> The *Gewand-haus*, a moderately-sized room, was, in 1839-40, infinitely too small for the audience who crowded it, paying their sixteen *groschen* (two shillings) for entrance. . . . The ladies of the place occupied the center of the room, sitting in two *vis-à-vis* divisions—that is, sideways to the orchestra. Behind them crowded the gentlemen so thickly that any one going as late as half an hour before the music struck up, run no small chance of being kneaded into the wall by the particularly substantial proportions of those before him, whom no good-natured wish to accommodate a stranger can make thin.[35]

When the King of Saxony, Friedrich August, visited the *Gewandhaus* and wanted to express his appreciation to Mendelssohn, he had to force his way through the masses of men and then march through the rows of ladies before he could reach the Maestro, who himself had no greater freedom of movement! At this time, even the Leipzig newspapers began to observe that the available space had long ceased to suffice, and that the concert hall was urgently in need of enlargement. Miss Novello expresses herself even more drastically in her memoirs: ". . . the benches are arranged that one sits as if in an omnibus—and no lady and gentleman ever are allowed to sit together here or in their churches. So that the women sit in rows opposite one another staring at each other's dress which is celebrated for being as ugly as the men and women—the men standing round looking at you through an immense eyeglass the whole night."[36]

We must date the world fame of Mendelssohn from approximately the year 1839. In the years 1839 and 1840 major articles on him appeared, more or less simultaneously, in the leading journals and magazines of France, England, and Germany. Even Vienna joined—though hesitantly—the universal chorus of recognition. The *Revue Musicale* published an extensive editorial on him and his *Verleih uns Frieden gnädiglich*, which was reproduced as *Dona nobis pacem;* in fact, it even lithographed the entire manu-script score of the work and gave it to its readers as a supplement.[37] The *Athenaeum*, the *Musical World*, and the *Manchester Guardian* published long essays on Mendelssohn, in which he was generally referred to as the heir and successor of the great Viennese tradition. Through his leanings towards the music of Bach and Handel, he had brought a certain spiritual trend into what had been completely secularized music. Also, the *Allgemeine Musikalische Anzeiger*, Vienna's leading music journal, began to call the attention of its readers to our master. However, it cannot be said that its editor, I. Castelli, was fair to Mendelssohn.

THE MUSIC FESTIVALS

DURING THE YEARS 1838-1840, Mendelssohn directed several music festivals: the Lower Rhenish Music Festivals in Cologne and Düsseldorf (1838, 1839), the music festival in Brunswick (1839), and the Schwerin Festival (1840). In England, he directed the festival in Birmingham (1840). What favorably distinguished the festivals under his direction from all other contemporary ones was, above all, the well-balanced programs, which pleasantly combined old and new, heavy and light, grave and gay.

Lower Rhenish Music Festival in Cologne

The following program was presented at this Festival in 1838:

> Ferdinand Ries, Symphony in C minor
> Handel, *Joshua*
> J. S. Bach, *Himmelfahrts-Kantate*
> Mozart, Symphony in D major ("Prague")
> Cherubini, Overture to *Les Abencérages*
> Beethoven, *Preis der Tonkunst* (revision of the cantata
>   *Der Glorreiche Augenblick, oder Belle Alliance*)

Also, solo selections from operas and oratorios and piano selections.

The symphony of Ries was intended as a memorial offering, for the composer, an old pupil of Beethoven, had died in January, 1838. We have already considered the ugly rumors which Fétis had spread concerning the supposed rivaly between the two masters. Now, Mendelssohn himself had chosen the above program; thus, we see that there was no word of truth in the gossip. Nonetheless, Fétis was not ashamed to include the following passage in the second edition of his *Biographie Universelle*—more than 25 years after Mendelssohn's death:

There was a certain rivalry between Felix and Ries, because they took turns directing the Lower Rhenish Music Festivals. . . . Mendelssohn spoke about the conducting of his rival in rather crude terms, which, however, were soon reported to Ries. Ries told me of the anger which the improper mode of expression of his young rival had caused him.[38]

Shortly after the death of Ries, Fétis published the canard that Mendelssohn had succeeded Ries with the Frankfurt *Caecilia* Society.[39] However, it was not long till even Fétis had to recognize Felix's significance. He did this in a very polite letter (unpublished till now) the most important passage of which I cite here: "Vous grandisez chaque jour et vous acquirez d'une manière incontestable la position de chef de la musique en Allemagne. . . ."[40] (You are becoming greater every day, and you are incontestably acquiring the position of musical leader of Germany. . . .)

Mendelssohn performed Handel's oratorio with the organ accompaniment intended by the composer, much to its advantage; however, the Berlin *Singakademie* still stuck to its "damned tedious trombones." The *Himmelfahrtskantate* was the first Bach cantata to be performed at a music festival. It was highly praised. It may at first seem strange to us that Mendelssohn performed such a poor work as Beethoven's *Glorreiche Augenblick*, for he must have realized what a miserable piece it is. However, we should not forget that he could not always perform a Mass, and that he wanted to include a large but little-known work of Beethoven. Later, in such cases, he chose the Fantasy for orchestra, piano, and chorus, the forerunner of the Ninth.

Lower Rhenish Music Festival in Düsseldorf

The program was:

> Handel, *Messiah*
> Beethoven, *Eroica* Symphony
> Beethoven, C Major Mass (German text by F. Rochlitz)
> Mendelssohn, Psalm 42
> Julius Rietz, Concert Overture
> Mozart, *Jupiter* Symphony

Also: Mozart, *Magic Flute* Overture; arias and duets by Mozart, Rossini and Bellini; Scottish folksongs; *God Save the Queen* and *Heil dir im Siegerkranz*.

Three outstanding female singers took part in this festival which took place in Düsseldorf in 1839. The most important was Miss Novello, the "star" of the music festival; the others were Auguste von Fassmann and Sophie Schloss (the latter was to make a great career under Mendelssohn's aegis). On the third day of the festival Mendelssohn, as usual, played one of his new compositions; this time, it was his Second Piano Concerto, which was greeted with deafening applause.

Music Festival in Brunswick

On the evening of the first day of this Festival, which took place in September, 1839, the master was fêted with a serenade. On the evening of the third day, Mendelssohn had dedicated the concert to the benefit of the orchestra's pension fund; this was followed by a festive ball in the ducal residence, at which Mendelssohn was honored with a giant laurel wreath.

Thanks to the accounts of Chorley, who was a guest there, and thanks to the prolific reports of the music journals, which did not have much new material to write about in the early autumn, we have very full accounts of this festival. The Brunswick correspondent has this to say about *St. Paul:* "It is the fiery outpouring of a great spirit, possessed by the idea of eternal beauty, which has nourished and strengthened itself at the holy springs of religion for the noble song of praise to the victory of God's kingdom!"

He closes with the pious wish alas, not to be fulfilled: "May this great representative of art protect and preserve *the German Spirit of our ancestors.*"[41]

Various musicologists during the years 1925-45 felt quite differently on this point—especially H. J. Moser and Ernst Bücken, who, of course, slavishly followed in the footsteps of Richard Wagner when it came to the "case of Mendelssohn." It is pleasanter to read what Chorley has to say about the cordial spirit which prevailed at the Brunswick festival.[42]

The program was as follows:

(First day)
Mendelssohn, *St. Paul*
(Second day)
Weber, *Jubelouvertüre*
Spohr, Adagio for Solo Violin and Orchestra
Fr. Schneider, Psalm 24
Beethoven, Fifth Symphony
Handel, Hallelujah Chorus (*Messiah*)
(Third day)
Overture, *Calm Sea and Prosperous Voyage*
Arias from *Don Giovanni*
Molique, Violin Concerto
Beethoven, Seventh Symphony
Mendelssohn, Serenade for Piano and Orchestra

Schwerin Music Festival

This smaller festival (July, 1840), was actually a continuation of the Gutenberg celebration. Two oratorios were performed: Mendelssohn's *St. Paul* and Haydn's *Creation*. We know that the "North German Festival," as Mendelssohn called it, afforded him great pleasure, because ". . . one knew that one was among upright, honest souls, who speak as they think, and sing as they feel—that is, honorably and decently."[43]

On the evening of the second day, a ball again took place, with Mendelssohn as guest of honor. It seems that he had an especially good time on this occasion, and danced most energetically; he was known as a skilful and elegant dancer.

Music Festival in Birmingham

Very soon after the great success of the *Hymn of Praise,* Mr. Joseph Moore, manager of the Birmingham festivals, had invited Mendelssohn to conduct the work at the 1840 festival to take place in September. Mendelssohn was rather seriously ill, for the continual inroads which he was making on his delicate constitution were bound to have their effects. Since 1838 he had been having frequent migraine headaches with disturbances of sight and hearing, yet he overcame all these handicaps with enormous strength of will and self-discipline. His doctors recommended that he take a lengthy cure of the waters; but they permitted him the Birmingham Festival. On July 21, Felix decided to accept the invitation, and wrote of his plans to Klingemann as well as to Mr. Moore. Originally he had hoped to be able to bring Cecile along, but she was pregnant and he did not dare to expose her to the risks of the long and difficult journey. He was prepared to perform the *Hymn of Praise* in English, and gave the organizers a choice between his well-known 42nd Psalm or the new 114th Psalm. Finally, he wanted to perform some Bach works and his own new organ compositions on the great organ.

On the evening of September 17, he reached London. It was his sixth visit to England. He stayed only two days in London, visiting old friends—Klingemann, the Chorleys and Moscheles; with the latter, he traveled on the new railway to Birmingham.

The program for this festival was:

Handel, *Israel in Egypt*
Handel, *Messiah*
Handel, Selections from *Joshua* and *Jephtha*
Mendelssohn, Overture to *A Midsummer Night's Dream*
Mendelssohn, Piano Concerto in D minor

Mendelssohn, *Lobgesang*
Rossini, *La gazza ladra*
Grecco, *La prova*   Both operas condensed to one act each

Handel's *Israel* was given with the famous Lablache. However, the great solo in the *Hymn of Praise* was performed by Mr. Braham, an older, but distinguished musician, much to the satisfaction of the composer.

The *Hymn of Praise* was preceded by works of Fasch, Handel, Palestrina, and Mozart. At the end of the *Hymn of Praise* with the triumphal closing chorus, the whole audience rose spontaneously, a tribute otherwise paid only to Handel's Hallelujah Chorus. Afterwards, Felix still played the organ a long time for his friends and colleagues, as freshly "as though his day were just beginning," this after trying rehearsals and the conducting of his own work. The doctors were not so wrong after all! Still later on the same evening, he played his G minor concerto for a large audience. However, the master was not satisfied with the performance of the *Hymn of Praise* in Birmingham; soon thereafter, he revised the second part of the work so radically that the parts engraved for Birmingham became completely useless.

When England once takes a foreigner to her heart, he can do no wrong. So it was in Mendelssohn's case; the *Hymn of Praise*, certainly one of his weaker works, was praised to high heaven in England. Only he himself, its creator, was never quite satisfied with it. But, as a mother is especially warm, loving, and tender to her crippled child, so Mendelssohn loved this work.

On the way home from Birmingham, he played on the organ of St. Peter's, Cornhill; however, as the season was already far advanced, it was no longer possible for him to arrange the charity concert which he had planned to give in London. After a week's stay, Mendelssohn, accompanied by Moscheles and Chorley, undertook the tiresome return journey, at the prospect of which he always shuddered. On his arrival in Leipzig, he made his friends acquainted with Cecile, and they passed several happy days together.

THE VIENNESE PERFORMANCE OF *ST. PAUL*

THE TRAGI-COMEDY of Mendelssohn's "nonappearance" in Vienna has been hushed up, as if by general consensus. We shall here refer only to Mendelssohn's correspondence and to local Viennese sources.

The Vienna *Gesellschaft der Musikfreunde* had performed *St. Paul* during Lent in 1839 with rather surprising success. Always on the lookout for possible "gala productions," the vice president of the *Gesellschaft der Musikfreunde*, Baron Vesque von Puettlingen, a noble erudite man of excellent musical judgment who had studied music under Sechter, and composed several operas as well as church and chamber music under the pseudonym J. Hoven, invited Mendelssohn to Vienna to conduct his *St. Paul* at a grand music festival during the late fall. Almost immediately Mendelssohn replied in the affirmative. Moreover, he announced his intention of giving a charity concert in Vienna, as he usually did in England; this time its yield was destined for the widows and orphans of musicians. He also acknowledged Vesque's suggestion that I. Castelli, the editor of the *Vienna Musikalischer Anzeiger*, poet, music lover, and general busy-body, should be the go-between in making all the arrangements. In August Mendelssohn replied amiably to the news that the Emperor had granted permission to use the ample *Reitschule* for the concert. Again he mentioned his plan of a concert for the benefit of the *Tonkünstler-Societät*. And for the first time he posed, albeit most delicately, the question of expenses. He wrote (August 16, 1839):

> Such a journey, especially in these days, will run to manifold expenses; and I should like to know, whether the *Gesellschaft* that sponsors the festival will be able to reimburse me for these. . . . If you have in the past engaged musicians from afar, and settled with them in concord with certain statutes, I should be obliged to you, if you could advise me of these precedents, and I shall be glad to abide by them. . . .[44]

Baron Vesque seems to have replied in a somewhat evasive way, for Mendelssohn, while still confirming his intention of appearing in Vienna, added in his reply the following remarks (September 14, 1839):

> Concerning the question of expenses: I should be happy to follow your suggestion that we discuss this point personally during my stay in Vienna, if I did not know all too well that I shall be absolutely unable to negotiate such matters personally. However, many difficulties which will emerge just at the appointed time, force me to suggest an agreement on this point right now.
>
> In order to avoid a cumbersome and tedious itemization of expenses, also to prevent any misunderstandings, I ask you to grant me the amount of 100 (hundred) Louis d'or.[45]

This was an extremely magnanimous offer, for Mendelssohn had to pay for his private coach both ways, and had to have a good hotel in Vienna. Obviously he did not expect a fee for his own labor.

Shortly thereafter three ugly incidents, all related to his prospective appearance in Vienna, infuriated him to such an extent that he reversed his decision to come to Vienna. These were:

(1) The lack of discretion on the part of Vesque and Castelli concerning the pending question of expenses, which resulted in a shabby press campaign. For the Baron and his negotiator broke the confidence Felix had

put in them, and Castelli did not hesitate to publish in his own magazine
and in other journals nasty remarks on Mendelssohn's "materialism" and
greed.

(2) The refusal of the *Tonkünstler-Societät* to participate in a concert which Mendelssohn intended to give *for its own* charitable purposes.
As the minutes of that session (September 11, 1839) have disappeared, we
may rely on the remarks of E. Hanslick, who had seen that memorable
document:

> Mendelssohn had offered to give a concert of his new compositions for
> the benefit of the *Tonkünstler-Sozietät*, and also to appear as pianist at
> that occasion. . . . This magnanimous and flattering offer was refused "for
> various and sundry reasons." One does not trust one's eyes if one reads
> the minutes of September 11, '39. The venerable *Tonkünstler-Sozietät*
> seems to have been interested in cash only. . . . The Messrs. Court-
> conductors etc. apparently did not appreciate the fact that a concert of
> Mendelssohn was as good as cash in their funds. . . .[46]

(3) The decision that Demoiselle Caecilia Kreutzer would sing the
soprano part. Miss Kreutzer, daughter of the composer Conradin Kreutzer,
had a nice, well-trained soprano, but was at that time beyond her zenith.
Moreover, an aristocrat, supporter of the *Gesellschaft der Musikfreunde*,
whose mistress she had been, insisted on her appearance in *St. Paul*.

Now Mendelssohn, quite the *grandseigneur*, cancelled his visit to Vienna,
and wrote rather patronizingly (October 10, 1839):

> I confirm receipt of your kind letter of Oct. 1 . . . I was, however, obliged
> to read in the daily journals the reaction of the *Gesellschaft* to the con-
> tents of my last letter and its details a fortnight ago. It seems to me that
> this matter, as long as it was pending between us, should also have been
> discussed solely beween us; furthermore that it required the strictest dis-
> cretion, while I did not yet know your ideas or suggestions in this respect.
> I cannot deny that this fact by itself would have made it very difficult
> for me to come to the festival. . . . Yet the recent accouchement of my
> wife and certain considerations connected therewith render it impossible
> for me to leave Leipzig right now; thus I would in any case be unable
> to travel to Vienna. I am therefore obliged to forego this pleasure and
> also the direction of the festival. . . .[47]

In an unpublished letter to Fanny, Felix aired his true feelings:

> What's new on the Rialto? One thing: I do not go to Vienna, but "remain
> at home and earn my bread honestly." When I, at last, posed the question
> of expenses (as they never wanted to touch the subject), they proved to
> be somewhat stingy, and I got somewhat rough, and they put articles in

the newspapers . . . and they thought I would now be weary and give in, and wrote politely again. But I answered even more politely "I'll remain at home." Seriously speaking, they behaved damn shabbily; but did me a service, after all, for now to leave Cecile and the children alone would be as bitter for me as all hell! (*würde mir wie Teufelsdreck schmecken*)[48]

Mendelssohn's refusal embarrassed the *Gesellschaft der Musikfreunde*, the more so, as all the journals had made a lot of noise *pro* and *con* Felix. In all fairness it must be said that the *Gesellschaft der Musikfreunde* was innocent of the brewing scandal. The first alarm was sounded by Castelli's organ, the *Allgemeine Musikalische. Anzeiger*: "The *Gesellschaft der Musikfreunde* has been treated badly, but thank God, we have here in Vienna quite a few well-trained musicians and good conductors, who will be able to conduct the work—even without the composer's assistance—perfectly well."[49] By now the matter had become—still before the concert—public gossip, and Schumann poured oil onto the flames by reporting on the first (March) performance of *St. Paul* in Vienna:

> The Viennese is, in general, suspicious of outlandish musical talents (except Italians). . . . Moreover, there flourishes a clique here, the successors of those who booed *Don Giovanni* and the overture to *Leonore!* This clique seriously believes that Mendelssohn composes only in order to confuse them; they fancy that they can darken Mendelssohn's famous name, even if they have to use sticks and pitchforks for that purpose—in short: a clique so miserable and ignorant, so incompetent in its judgment and achievement as any might be in hicktown. . . .[50]

Finally the festival took place, naturally without Mendelssohn, on November 7 and 10, with almost 1000 participating singers and instrumentalists. We shall cite here only the most characteristic passages from the *Allgemeine Musikalische Anzeiger, Sammler, Theaterzeitung, Zeitschrift für Kunst* (called "*Modenzeitung*") and the "*Humorist*."

Allgemeine Musikalischer Anzeiger, before the concert: "All of you, who are honest lovers of art, rally around this Mendelssohn—Paulus, pay him homage gratefully and sincerely. . . ."[51] The same, after the concert: ". . . It cannot bear comparison with the masterworks of Bach, Handel, or Haydn; it is more a skilful mosaic-work than a real whole, broken out from the towering heights. . . ."[52]

Der Sammler: "It is a great delight to watch the start of so gigantic a talent, which harkens . . . only to the divine call of the Muse. . . ."[53]

Theaterzeitung:

> Now we have heard the *St. Paul*, we must beg humbly the composer's forgiveness for having put him in the same category with the composers

of the new romantic school. There is an enormous distance between the composers of those hardly intelligible overtures which mean to be 'fantastic,' and the composer of *St. Paul;* for he is both in spirit and form, a truly *classic* composer . . .⁵⁴

Zeitschrift für Kunst, Literatur, Theater und Mode, "Modenzeitung." (By far the best accounts of all performances of *St. Paul,* both in spring and fall, were given in the *Modenzeitung.* The reviewer, writing under the pseudonym "Carlo," was a fine musician (Karl Kundt, d. 1852), a friend of Aloys Fuchs. The first review went very much into details and comprised five full double-columned pages. It was enthusiastic beyond measure, but nevertheless sensible and of fine musical judgment. The review of the *Festival* is interesting because of the following passages):

Demoiselle Kreutzer, though not at ease in the grave atmosphere of this work, received for some soli encouraging applause . . . Mendelssohn's humility, charity, and total lack of pretension (in matters financial, not artistic!), are well known. He often dedicates his concerts to charitable institutions, provided that he approves of the execution and the interpreters in both personal and artistic respects. This approbation could not be granted to this performance . . .⁵⁶

Der Humorist: (The editor of this periodical was none other than Mr. I. Saphir, whom we met many years (and chapters) ago in Berlin. He had certainly no reason to praise Mendelssohn, for his family (and he himself) were eager to get rid of him in Berlin. Yet he revenged himself most nobly. The spring performance of the oratorio elicited a veritable dithyramb on the composer, and the *Festival* was greeted with the words): "If in music this decade had produced nothing but *St. Paul,* we should call it a blessed one . . . The master was prevented from appearing in person by various circumstances which are not exactly to our liking. . . ."⁵⁶

Leipziger Allgemeine Zeitung: (We quote finally from the report of the Vienna correspondent of this newspaper one significant sentence): "The overjoyed audience praised their good fortune, and all literary journals speak in the same vein. . . ."⁵⁷

Shades of Gustav Mahler, of Beethoven, and, above all, of Karl Kraus—how well you knew, loved, and scorned Vienna! For Mendelssohn met the same fate as you; he was just another of the countless "cases" which Kraus immortalized with his deathless prose and deadly satire. First, a great fuss about "culture"; then, negotiations; then, stinginess; then, vilification in the press; then, a proud look backward at the "glorious Viennese tradition" (which let Mozart perish miserably); finally, general jollity under the motto: *Wean bleibt Wean!* Vienna remains Vienna: so be it!

If we wish to look for a particular artistic trend in the afore-mentioned programs and performances, we must first admit that the master, for all his "tolerance" of contemporary music, had a strong preference for older music. Among composers of Mendelssohn's time whose works are still living today, he performed only Schubert, Cherubini, Chopin, Schumann, Spohr, and—later—some Wagner, while he gave Liszt and Berlioz merely the opportunity to perform their compositions themselves. Aside from the mediocrities of the day, whom he had to permit to be heard *faute de mieux*, there were only two famous composers of the period whose works he had to perform regularly in spite of his lack of sympathy for them: Rossini and Meyerbeer, both of whom were vigorously demanded by the public. We shall have much more to say in Chapter XVII about his attitude to them and other contemporaries.

Many critics have maintained that Mendelssohn thought little of Haydn and did not perform him often. This is absolutely untrue, as a look at the programs in Doerffel's *Geschichte der Gewandhauskonzerte* will show. However, the accusation of belittling Hadyn, though untrue of Mendelssohn, is substantiated in the case of Schumann. When it came to historical understanding of music, Mendelssohn was far superior to Schumann. To begin with, Mendelssohn was no uncritical believer in progress, but rather inclined to skepticism in his philosophy of history; not in vain had he been a pupil of Hegel. Then, he *knew* much more music, both old and new, than did Schumann. This was because of his incredible joy in studying; he left no library unvisited that he could possibly reach. He spent many hours in copying and making excerpts from older music. The catalogues of his Handel collection which he wrote out (partly for his own use, partly for Zelter's) comprise more than fifty large closely written pages.[58] Finally, Mendelssohn lived in a musical continuum which embraced old and new without admitting any basic qualitative differences between them. Schumann and especially Wagner were concerned with the "Music of the Future"— Mendelssohn was not.

DOMESTIC AND SOCIAL LIFE

MENDELSSOHN did not want to be merely an artist and a social being—he had very strong family instincts. He loved to see himself, too, in the role of *pater familias*. In February, 1838, his first son and heir was born, who was christened Carl Wolfgang Paul after the three guiding stars of his life.[59] (Carl after Klingemann and Zelter, Wolfgang after Goethe, Paul after the Apostle). Cecile had no easy time with the birth, and was dangerously ill in the following weeks. In the fall of 1839 he became a father again—this time of a daugher, Marie Pauline Hélène (the names were chosen from the family circle of Cecile). His second son, Paul Felix Abraham, came into the world in January, 1841. Felix's intimate and moving descriptions of family life are most delightful and fresh when read in the exchange of letters with Klingemann, whom he kept informed of all these matters.

With the births of Mendelssohn's children, Cecile's relationship to Felix's family had distinctly improved. Amid charming and chatty letters from Fanny and Rebecca to Cecile we do find a bit of "needling," but on the whole she understood how to make her sisters-in-law into friends. She was not so successful in the case of her mother-in-law. As always in such cases, the fault was on both sides. Cecile's reserve with Lea, and her fear of her, often expressed itself in strange symptoms which we would probably call "psychosomatic" today. Several times she had "nervous attacks," each time shortly before a planned journey to Berlin to visit her mother-in-law. Also, her brothers-in-law were none too friendly to her; her extreme reserve and her often exaggerated piety seem to have gained the upper hand over her charm and her lovable nature. Nevertheless, Felix spent the summer of 1838 with Cecile in the parental home in Berlin in the most intimate family circle, and Cecile became accustomed to the way of life prescribed by Lea.

With all of this, Felix's indestructible humor, which bridged all conflicts, was a great help: let a little piece of it, a joke canon for brother Paul, testify to it. Its text reads: "My brother does not write, and I am also a poor writer."

Joke Canon

Indeed, he had need of this happy disposition, for he had many irritations and upsets to cope with, whether in his professional life or in his family. Cecile was especially oppressed by the "melancholy and domineering nature of grandmother" (Mme Souchay), as her sister recounts.[60] Admirable, too, are Felix's physical and psychic powers of resistance and resilience. which allowed him to recover from strenuous exertions in a few days. Thus, he writes after the very exhausting Brunswick Music Fesival that, in order to recover, he must first "catch up on eating, drinking, and sleeping."[61] The expression "catch up on drinking" requires a little explanation here. From his early years, Felix was accustomed to drinking wine and could take a great quantity. In his papers we find, neatly bundled together, the wine bills of each year. Since he ran a large household, he ordered two hogsheads of wine per year, and several hundred bottles. He preferred Rhine wine, Moselle, and white Burgundy. He abhorred drunkenness, like every other excess. Furthermore, he had the gift of enjoying the most modest treats beyond all measure. One of his favorite foods was rice pudding, which was always served him at Devrients'. In London, he greatly enjoyed German sausages, and, of course, English roast beef. Once he wrote to Beckchen: "I am still childish enough to take pleasure in such a cake [a Jewish-style butter-cake] for a whole evening. Moses must have been a great law-giver. Cecile insists on knowing if such a cake can be baked only by Jews, and why?"[62]

He was a master of sleeping, that is, he could take a catnap at any time and in nearly any place, and was refreshed by it as if after a long rest. Nonetheless, from his childhood he was accustomed to a rigorous discipline of work; his working day generally lasted from 6 a.m. to 11 p.m.

His particularly attractive social manners were well-known and made his house a center of social life in Leipzig. His wide reading and culture, his intelligence, his lively wit (which was sarcastic only in his youth), his gift of mimicry, which often seduced him into imitating well-known personalities—all of these were, understandably, points of attraction. But occasionally it happened that Mendelssohn, enlivened by wine, would make a mocking remark about this or that person and, of course, these never remained a secret! In general, however, he was the soul of discretion. For example, in the exchange of letters between him and Julius Rietz, there are many remarks on the big and little scandals in which Richard Wagner was involved; however, Mendelssohn never makes use of these in other letters or communications. Although he abhorred affairs with women, he was worldly enough not to judge artists by their sexual activities.

Many Leipzig families were friendly with Felix or Cecile; we mention the names of Schleinitz, Dr. Frege, Porsche, Professor K. F. Guenther, but there were many more. Professionally and socially, he had a great deal to do with the great publishers, above all Raymund Härtel, and the senior directors of the Kistner and Simrock firms. Of his colleagues, he most often saw Ferdinand David, his concertmaster, and Robert and Clara Schumann(although they did not live in Leipzig very long). When Schumann traveled to Berlin, Felix wrote his mother the following letter of recommendation:

> I am very fond of him, and since my first coming here he has been unalterably good and friendly to me . . . , he is the fiancé of Clara Wieck and will seek her out in Berlin now, since her father here remains in constant opposition to the union . . . ; he is rather quiet and turned-in upon himself, but a friendly, extremely talented and very good man at heart, and so I ask you again to give him a very good reception. . . .[63]

Certain German scholars, who during the Nazi period, believed that they should be ashamed of the Schumann-Mendelssohn friendship, hit upon a simple way out; they either denied the facts of the intimate relationship between these artists or at least tried to diminish its importance. We shall later return in detail to the connection—quite a complex one—between the two men.

Mendelssohn's daily activities—one might say, the rhythm of his life—are best described in detail by Hiller in his memoirs. Since he lived for several weeks in Felix's house, he was very familiar with the workaday life of Mendelssohn and we may believe his account. In the following paragraphs we give a few short excerpts from those memoirs.

On rising, which was usually at six, he did paper work on one or another of his projects. Breakfast was at eight; for Felix, coffee and white bread which he broke up and "dunked" as he had done since childhood. Thus fortified, he was ready for a rehearsal, some administrative business, or failing these, he wrote letters or composed. Lunch at one, accompanied by wine, was light and took little time. Dinner, on the other hand, lasted for hours and was usually a very jolly affair.

The afternoons were spent, as in the morning, in composing, writing, reading, and all the manifold tasks that must occupy a man in Mendelssohn's position. He played the piano a great deal, but never practiced. As a score reader and player from score he was incomparable, as many contemporaries report. When he composed, he rarely used the piano, nor could he endure having another person in the room at such times. If he had thought it necessary, he could have composed at any time—"but that he was often doing it when people least suspected it is certain." His correspondence certainly took up much of his time. It is incomprehensible that he could find time for his many thousands of letters, all neatly written and carefully folded. Once he reported to his mother that he had written 35 letters in a day, aside from his other work; and this without any secretary! His favorite authors, whom he could always re-read with pleasure, were Goethe, Shakespeare, and Jean Paul. Especially when he was in the limelight of world fame, his modesty assumed absurd forms. He forbade his portrait to be printed on programs; he did not permit the publisher to call his second 'cello sonata "Grand Sonata." When and how he "actually managed to work in the midst of such manifold distracting conditions, would be hard to understand, if he had not possessed what I should call a marvelous spiritual equilibrium." He often said of himself:

> When from time to time I am so very dissatisfied with myself, I think
> of this one and that one who are friendly with me, and I tell myself,
> "you can't be so bad if such men love you."

He had little use for pathos—actually, only in the theatre and in lyric poetry. As has been said above, he was by no means a believer in progress.

> I do not speak of machines and railroads . . . I ask if you believe that
> in the course of time men become better, more noteworthy?[64]

In letters and conversations he often called himself a Philistine; but he was a deadly enemy of all Philistines in art. He was convinced that his time had overcome Philistinism in art; but he feared that "even more danger threatens our art from the other side."

Mendelssohn was a socially conscious man. We have already noted his intervention in favor of his orchestra players, and on many occasions he tried anew to better the lot of practising musicians as well as that of composers. In contrast to his mother, who was an adherent of the "ancien régime" and made much of class distinctions, he, an aristocrat by birth and feeling, would have nothing to do with class distinctions. Very noteworthy in this respect is a report which he gave his friend Julius Rietz concerning an intervention on his behalf with the publisher Hofmeister. It reads, in part, as follows:

> . . . In the real old-fashioned niggardly way, Hofmeister began to sing the same old song that bored and annoyed me more than anything else . . . before he signed the contract, he would have to have a copy of the score, for that was customary when publishing piano reductions. Here I became *very rude* [underlined by Mendelssohn] and told him that he need not think he could play around with me as with his ordinary customers or push me around to his heart's content . . . I added a few other malicious remarks . . . But I fear you may answer his queries with a mere "Damn it all!" if you are not warned in advance about his leech-like ways . . .[66]

The letter goes into many other details of the conference with Hofmeister—all in favor of Rietz! He undertook similar enterprises for many other composers and conductors, generally with good success.

Beyond this, Felix had the philanthropic tendencies which were hereditary in his family. In his papers we find countless begging letters, most of which were answered favorably. He helped many boys of St. Thomas' School, Marx, Dohrn (who called him his lifesaver), Lobe, and a legion of musicians who are forgotten today. Humanitarian organizations were supported by him regularly, without religious or national discrimination. As a curiosity, we may mention the following case, which has remained unknown until today, since Felix could never tolerate that his name should become known as a benefactor. In the community of Schwaz in the Tyrol, the master had an ardent admirer, Herr Christiannel. This man approached him with the proposition that he should designate some work, perhaps a hymn, for performance in Schwaz alone, and should dedicate the profits of every performance to the benefit of the poor of the town of Schwaz. Felix took up the proposition enthusiastically, and from his correspondence we learn that the work which he composed for Schwaz was performed there regularly during his life-time, with considerable profit to the poor of the town.[67]

Mendelssohn's social consciousness manifested itself in quite another way when he was asked by Droysen and by his brother-in-law, the great mathematician Dirichlet, to support the "Göttingen Seven" who had just been dismissed from their teaching posts. This *cause celèbre* has a long history, which is, however, immaterial to the understanding of Mendelssohn's willingness to help. As we have seen earlier, Mendelssohn inclined towards a "little-German" liberalism of Rankian tinge; the Göttingen Seven, however, by no means all shared these views. All, however, were enthusiastic liberals—especially Dahlmann, the Grimm brothers, and the great Orientalist Heinrich August Ewald. The unconsidered and foolish actions of Ernst August, King of Hanover, embittered Mendelssohn beyond reason, and he hastened to help these men. He supported them faithfully until they found other teaching positions. As indignant as the master was about the "arrogance of officialdom," he had serious doubts that the bourgeois population would take an effective stand for the Göttingen Seven and their viewpoint. Essentially, he was right. But he expected, in the foreseeable future, a violent clash between the extreme elements of both parties—the "Ultras" on the conservative side and the "Fire-Eaters" on the liberal side. There can be no doubt of his liberal sympathies, and if he had lived till 1848 he would probably have become involved in political affairs to such an extent that conditions might have driven him into exile. At least, his premature death spared him this.

In another way, too, politics poisoned his life. The nationalism of "Young Germany," which was ever-increasing during the forties, was, for many reasons, not at all to Felix's taste. The so-called "Rheinlied" ("Oh, they shall never have it, the free and German Rhine") which, at that time, inspired old and young alike to patriotic demonstrations, seemed completely undignified to him. Here we may best let him speak for himself:

About the abovementioned *Rheinlied* I could write you a long complaint. You have no idea what a fuss they make about it here, and how repellent this whipped-up enthusiasm in the newspapers is to me. Then the whole idea of making a noise about the idea that others shouldn't get what we have! That is worth real noise and real music! But not a single tone should be sung when it is simply a question of not losing what one has. Little children and timid people shout about that; but real men make nothing of what they have—they have it and that's that . . .[68]

To Klingemann, he writes in a similar vein, but adds:

. . . Naturally, the musicians are falling on it in a frenzy, and composing their way to immortality with it. Leipzig composers have created no less than three melodies to it, and every day there is something about the song in the newspapers. Yesterday, among other things, they said that my composition of this song has now become known—whereas I never dreamed of setting such defensive enthusiasm to music . . .[69]

There was a modicum of truth behind the rumors. Two famous publishers—their firms still exist today!—offered him large sums if he would set the *Rheinlied* to music. Mendelssohn definitely declined both offers, but then, responsive to public opinion, did give one performance of Konradin Kreutzer's setting of the song.[70]

Hand in hand with Mendelssohn's aversion to this artificially nurtured nationalism went his negative attitude towards all militaristic "exhibitions," as he called them. Thus, he refused to appear in the box which was reserved for officers of the guard: "blessed is the man . . . that sitteth not in the seat of the officers of the guard (Psalm 1;1.)" This Psalmist's reference is to the scornful and ungodly; the man who does not associate with them is praised.

Also, he could no longer tolerate the "old-German fuss and feathers" (which he had once supported); he made no secret of his feelings toward W. von Zuccalmaglio, one of the standard-bearers of this "woodcut old Germany." He expressed himself confidentially to his mother concerning this correspondence:

But I cannot compose his songs; they were patriotic and old-German, and I am just not in the mood now for patriotic songs. Too many misunderstandings can occur—and the way it is now, when they are beginning to sing songs against the French *at the very moment* when they see that the French don't want to fight them—well, I won't set it to music . . .[71]

To this "medieval" mannerism he even preferred some representatives of "Young Germany," though he could hardly respect them otherwise because of their journalistic activities. Thus, Laube suddenly appears in Felix's correspondence—indeed, he even addresses him with the familiar *Du*. I could not discover how he came to this new friendship. Perhaps Devrient was the intermediary here, as always when it was a matter of opera libretti. It is astonishing to find Felix (who was already very reserved at this period) using the brotherly *Du* to a new acquaintance; even stranger is the interlocking here of art, greater-Germany politics, and personal friendship. Apart from such individual cases, Devrient spoke after Felix's own heart and earned his enthusiastic agreement when he explained, in opposition to the new wave of enthusiasm for nationalistic art: "Germany is the consciousness of Europe."[72]

Operatic Plans

The vain search for a suitable opera libretto extends throughout Mendelssohn's adult life. It brought him into contact with almost all living German playwrights, not to mention the dead ones, and with many English and even French authors as well. But the same process constantly repeats itself: after a promising and acceptable scenario, the author begins to work out his material, and Felix immediately becomes hypercritical. Sometimes the characters do not please him, another time he misses dramatic contrast, or tension; but all too often the language of the authors displeased him.

Here we cannot go into detail concerning all the projects and dealings which Mendelssohn undertook from the time he was twenty-one in order to secure a libretto that suited him. The fate of Immermann's *The Tempest* was to be repeated, with greater or lesser variations, again and again. In order to discuss all the projects, an entire monograph would be necessary; this would afford us noteworthy insights into the dramatic literature of Germany. Here, it may suffice to select the three principal projects and give a short sketch of their fate.

However, let us try to find the deeper reasons for Mendelssohn's hypercriticality. For, after all, he set masses of very mediocre verses to music, and, if anything, we can reproach him with being too uncritical rather than too critical in literary matters. Why, then, did he demand the utmost for the theatre? Here is the basic antinomy which sabotages Mendelssohn's operatic creation from the outset:

Mendelssohn wanted to compose a poetic drama for the theatre, but when the theatrical aspect appealed to him, the poetry displeased him, and when he found pleasure in the poetry, it was never "real theatre" in his estimation. This operatic dilemma, for which Wagner had found brilliant solutions in his best dramatic creations (*Meistersinger*, Act I of *Walküre*, Act I of *Tristan*), blighted all of Mendelssohn's operatic plans in the bud. It cannot be denied that King Frederick William IV displayed outstanding judgment of Mendelssohn's capacities and inclinations, for, among the many commissions for the royal theatre which he gave the master, we find only great poetry—which, however, was by no means always suited for the modern theatre: e.g., Racine's *Athalie* or Sophocles' *Oedipus at Colonus*. Mendelssohn never tried to make operas out of these plays, but he wrote good, and in many cases splendid, incidental music for them; e.g. *A Midsummer Night's Dream* and *Antigone*. Here he did not need to indulge in those compromises which the theatre categorically imposed on him, and before which he retreated; he could simply depict the poetry in tones. We cannot satisfy ourselves with the simple explanation that Mendelssohn possessed no dramatic talent. His youthful opera *Die Hochzeit des Camacho* shows unmistakable traces of theatrical talent, and his *Singspiel, Die Heimkehr aus der Fremde*, also contains many delightful details. Does not *Elijah*, too, offer magnificent dramatic moments? But one cannot compose an opera and at the same time demand the highest and purest poetry for it. Even with a Goethe or a Schiller, this combination succeeded only in individual cases, and then the problem of opera was not even included in the poetic work!

Mendelssohn was in contact with a legion of authors. To give the reader an idea of Felix's irresistible urge towards opera, we shall name only the following: Scribe, Planché, Birch-Pfeiffer, Holtei, Raupach, Laube, Devrient, Immermann, Tieck, Klingemann, Droysen, Chezy, Geibel, Atterbom, Benedict, Bartholomew, Lumley. Of all these plans, three reached the stage where Mendelssohn would have had to go to work immediately if he had considered it worthwhile. J. R. Planché was a playwright, not a poet; for he came from the living theatre. For years the manager of the Vauxhall musical plays, author of Weber's *Oberon* (after Wieland's famous work), he was a genuine theatre enthusiast. The subject which he chose for Mendelssohn, "The Citizens of Calais" (the siege of Calais under Edward III) was theatrically effective, but otherwise rather worthless; above all, this choice showed no understanding of Mendelssohn's lyrical tendencies and gift for subtleties.[73]

A second plan goes back to an idea of Wieland, with whom Mendelssohn has more in common than we may recognize at first glance. Here we are dealing with the verse narrative *Pervonte*, which Klingemann wanted to dramatize. It is the old motive of the three wishes, here dressed rather bombastically in romantic Italian scenery. Wisely, Klingemann did not start with Wieland's original, but with Kotzebue's dramatic version of the idea. The scenario had already been accepted, and whole scenes had even been worked out by Klingemann, before Mendelssohn gave up the plan, on the grounds that the plot was not interesting enough and the characters were not clear enough.[74]

In the last years of his life there again crops up the plan of bringing out Shakespeare's *Tempest* (in a "modern" English version) as an opera. Felix was at first on fire with enthusiasm for this idea—just as formerly in Düsseldorf, where he was also considering *The Tempest*. This time, the entrepreneur was Mr. Benjamin Lumley (really Levy), also a theatre manager, who was in a position to interest such an experienced playwright as Scribe in his plan. As we shall see later, this idea fell through.[75] I do not believe that posterity was deprived of a significant work thereby. However, we must regret that Felix rejected Droysen's *Nausikaa;* this would have been splendidly suited to a secular oratorio. It is a lasting pity that Mendelssohn was discouraged by Droysen's skepticism from setting to music the beautifully organized scenario and the partly completed poem. And in this case we shall take the liberty of speculating on the problem "Mendelssohn and the Theatre" beyond all historical evidence.

Felix was a fan of the theatre all his life. How is it possible that he shrank back from the creative "theatrical act" each time, as though its consummation would be a sin? We remember, too, that already in Düsseldorf he had withdrawn from active theatrical life, and on rather flimsy grounds; that he rejected the position of a court conductor in Weimar principally because he did not want to live "in constant contact" with the theatre. What inhibitions, conscious or unconscious, stood in the way of the expressed and certainly sincere operatic intentions and impulses of Mendelssohn, and crippled his creative powers where he most longed to use them? The antinomy between theatre and poetry perhaps suffices for a rational explanation of Mendelssohn's attitude as he himself may have understood it. But it does not penetrate to the fundamentals of his being and feeling. Perhaps a contemporary of Mendelssohn's, a philosopher this time, may help us to explain these contradictions.

In Kierkegaard's profound interpretation of Mozart's *Don Giovanni*, we find these words: "But as the totality of the opera cannot be thus self-reflective, as in the case of drama proper, so this is also the case with the musical situation, which is indeed dramatic, but which still has its unity in the mood."[76]

In many other passages of his *Either/Or*, Kierkegaard emphasized the role of the demonic in every good opera: ". . . the sensual assumes the form of the demonic in aesthetic indifference."[77]

Schiller illuminates the same problem from quite a different angle. For him, there are two extremes of the drama

. . . between which truth and nature lie. The characters of Pierre Corneille are icy observers of their passions . . . in England and Germany . . . they unveil Nature in all her nakedness, enlarge her flaws and liver-spots under the magnifying-glass of uncontrollable wit; the whimsical fantasy of fiery poets inflates her to a monstrosity. . . .[78]

It was precisely this serious attitude towards the demonic and towards passion which the theatre demands, and which was denied to Mendelssohn; he could not and would not grant this seriousness to the theatre. If we follow his correspondence with Klingemann attentively, we are amazed to notice, amidst all the operatic plans and discussions, that Felix is completely indifferent to his characters, whom, after all, he is supposed to make believable in his music. They may die or live, laugh or cry, thrive or not; it is all the same to him. For his nature could never fulfill itself in the theatre, since, fundamentally, he did not take the theatre seriously. Whatever demonic power he possessed belonged to the sphere of religion. Here, and only here, was it given him (sometimes, but not often) to express in tones the

> Pain of the pining breast,
> Rapture of God possessed!   (Goethe)

We may understand this disposition through his upbringing during the emancipation of German Jewry and the Puritanism which is associated with it. In spite of all emancipation, enlightenment, and assimilation, the cultured Jew could not take the theatre so seriously as did the German, for instance Lessing or Schiller. For him, it was not a "serious" form of expression. Even less could he bring himself to share his deepest, most essential feelings, which were dedicated to the One Ineffable God, with the theatre. Such an equalization would have seemed to him, in his inmost heart, nothing less than blasphemy. Therefore, it was not only rational and aesthetic considerations that hindered Mendelssohn from writing an opera. Much deeper feelings, ancient in origin, unconscious yet very powerful, religious and ethical in nature, and associated with the prophetic set of values, did not permit him ever to consider the theatre as essential to life.[79]

Since we have already presented Kierkegaard as principal witness for the demonic in opera, we shall close these observations with a passage in which he defends Mendelssohn's ideal of value. In his article "The Balance of the Aesthetic and the Ethical in the Development of the Personality," he says:

> The ethical absolute does not rob life of its beauty; rather, it alone makes life beautiful. It gives life security and peace, for it is always calling to us: *quod petis, hic est* [What you are seeking is here]. It protects us from all weakening sentimentality; it gives the soul health and strength. . . . The main thing in life is to gain oneself to merit one's soul.

$\mathcal{N}otes$

1. Jacques Barzun, *Berlioz and the Romantic Century* (New York, 1950), I, pp. 434-435. See also our Chapters XVI and XVII.
2. A full statistical table (made at the time) of the *Gewandhaus* concerts, 1836-1841, is found in the *Leipziger Allgemeine Musikalische Zeitung*, 1841.
3. Unpublished letter to Novello, June 19, 1837, Library of Congress, Washington, D.C.
4. Schumann, Writings, *Rückblick auf das Leipziger Musikleben 1837-38.*
5. Correspondence with Klingemann, pp. 226-27.
6. Von Wasielewski, *Aus siebzig Jahren*, p. 146.
7. E. Polko, *Reminiscences of Felix Mendelssohn Bartholdy* (English ed.), p. 70.

8. Clara Novello, *Reminiscences* (London, 1910), p. 63. (Psalm 42 was intended and composed for Felix's wife Cecile.)

9. *Ibid.*

10. O. E. Deutsch, *The Schubert Reader*, p. 690.

11. Correspondence with Moscheles (English ed.), p. 190.

12. *Leipziger Allgemeine Musikalische Zeitung* (1839), col. 256.

13. v. Bülow, *Ausgewählte Schriften* (Leipzig, 1896), pp. 335 f.

14. *Revue Musicale* (Paris, 1840), p. 19.

15. *Leipziger Allgemeine Musikalische Zeitung* (1840), p. 60.

16. Unpublished letter to Fanny, April 7, 1840.

17. Hiller, *op. cit.*, p. 145 ff.

18. Schumann, "Franz Liszt," *Schriften über Musik* (1840).

19. Letter to Moscheles, March 21, 1840.

20. Of the *Festgesang*, No. 2 was provided with a Christmas text by Dr. W. H. Cummings and is still popular in English-speaking countries as the Christmas hymn, "Hark, the Herald Angels Sing." Mendelssohn, however, was anything but delighted with this revision and considered his music "completely unsuitable" for such a text. See *Musical Times* (December, 1897), p. 810.

21. Hans v. Bülow, *op. cit.*, p. 371.

22. Schumann, "Gutenbergfest in Leipzig" (Writings, 1840).

23. Letter to Klingemann, January 7, 1838.

24. Family letter of August 10, 1840.

25. *Leipziger Allgemeine Musikalische Zeitung* (1840), col. 863.

26. E. Polko, *op. cit.*, p. 87.

27. Hans v. Bülow, *op. cit.*, p. 137 ff.

28. Chorley, *Autobiography* (London, 1873), Chapters IV and V.

29. Moscheles *Tagebücher*, edited by his wife, II, pp. 67ff.

30. *Ibid.*

31. Letter to Klingemann, October 26, 1840.

32. Hiller, *op. cit.*, p. 156.

33. H. F. Chorley, *Modern German Music* (London, 1854), II, p. 31, footnote.

34. *Ibid.*, p. 32.

35. *Ibid.*, p. 34.

36. A. M. Grieve, *Clara Novello* (London, 1954), p. 50 (from Miss Novello's diary).

37. *Revue Musicale* (Paris, 1840), p. 197.

38. Article "Mendelssohn," *Biographie Universelle*, 2nd ed. (Paris, 1875). A scrutiny of the proceedings of the *Niederrheinische Musikfeste* (at present in Cologne) reveals a total absence of such a rivalry. In fact, Ries refers to "Mendelssohn's young Masterhand."

39. *Revue Musicale*, February 11, 1838.

40. Unpublished letter of Fétis, April 16, 1842.

41. Brunswick correspondent in the *Leipziger Allgemeine Musikalische Zeitung* (1839), col. 791ff.

42. Chorley, *op. cit.*, I, Chapter V.

43. Unpublished letter of August 1, 1840.

44. Unpublished letter of Mendelssohn to Baron Vesque von Puettlingen in the possession of the *Gesellschaft der Musikfreunde*, Vienna.

45. *Ibid.*

46. Hanslick, *Geschichte des Konzertwesens in Wien* (Vienna, 1869), I, p. 17.

47. Unpublished letter of Mendelssohn in the archives of the *Gesellschaft der Musikfreunde*, Vienna.

48. Unpublished letter of Mendelssohn to his sister of October 9, 1839.

49. *Allgemeiner Musikalischer Anzeiger* (1839), p. 230.

50. R. Schumann, "Paulus in Wien," in *Gesammelte Schriften über Musik;* first published in 1839.

51. *Allgemeiner Musikalischer Anzeiger* (1839), XI, p. 67. E. Hanslick remarks on

this periodical in the following way: "Even the worst trash was discussed in this periodical with loving care. . . . Later on the reviews of concerts were given more space, but remained miserable, just as everything else therein. . . ." (*Geschichte des Konzertwesens in Wien*, I, p. 320).

52. *Ibid.*, XI, p. 242.

53. *Der Sammler* (1839), p. 119.

54. *Wiener Theaterzeitung* (March 1 and 17, 1839).

55. *Modenzeitung* (1839), I Quartal, pp. 252ff; IV Quartal, pp. 1118ff. It seems that Aloys Fuchs, who was in constant contact with Mendelssohn, had given some confidential information to the reviewer, Mr. Kundt, who was one of his best friends.

56. *Der Humorist* (1839), 45, pp. 178ff; 56, p. 223; 224, pp. 698ff.

57. *Leipziger Allgemeine Zeitung* (1839), November 13 and 14.

58. See also the unpublished letter to Breitkopf and Härtel in which Felix reports on on the discovery of Bach's *Orgelbüchlein*. (Library of Congress, March 26, 1840). In the same year, he severely criticizes the first edition of Bach's G minor Prelude and Fugue for organ. (Unpublished letter to Peters, Library of Congress, January 6, 1840).

59. Baptismal poem by Dr. Clarus:

Im Phaedon wie im Paulus   "The spirit was transfigured
Hat sich der Geist verklärt—   In Phaedon and Paul of old—
Des Hauses jüngstem Sprössling   May the family's youngest scion
Sey zweifaches bescheert.   Receive their gifts twofold!"

60. Letter from Julie Schunck to Mendelssohn, November 3, 1838.

61. Unpublished letter of September 11, 1839.

62. Unpublished letter to Beckchen of February 6, 1839.

63. Unpublished letter to his mother of September 12, 1839.

64. Hiller, *Erinnerungen*, p. 155.

65. *Ibid*, p. 153.

66. Letter of 1840 to J. Rietz (Library of Congress; unpublished).

67. See Hiller's unpublished letter in Vol. V of the family letters, Oxford: "Christannel found it remarkable that you, as a *Hebrew*, had handled this material so magnificently—but I reassured him that you had been a Christian for years . . ." Further letters concerning the remarkable affair appear in Vols. V and VI. The letters of Mendelssohn and a composition remained in the family of Mr. Christannel's descendants until 1940 when they were lost in the Southern Tyrol.

68. Letter to Paul Mendelssohn-Bartholdy, November 20, 1840.

69. Letter to Klingemann, November 18, 1840.

70. Letter to the family, November 20, 1840.

71. Unpublished letter, December 18, 1840.

72. Unpublished letter of Devrient, October 3, 1843.

73. Planché, *Recollections and Reflections* (London, 1872), I, 279-316.

74. *Correspondence with Klingemann*, pp. 120-166.

75. B. Lumley, *Reminiscences of the Opera* (London, 1864).

76. Søren Kierkegaard, *Either/Or*, tr. David F. Swenson and Lillian Marvin Swenson (Princeton), I, 96.

77. *Ibid.*, p. 73.

78. Schiller, *Über das gegenwärtige deutsche Theater* (1782).

79. In this connection let us note the remarkable fact that the Jewish people, in spite of their great love for the theatre, never produced a single outstanding dramatist or operatic composer. This striking lack of talent in spite of constant contact with the stage and in spite of the mimetic gifts of the Jews may be traced back to similar causes.

CHAPTER XV   *The Works of*

1837-1841

Arcadia in Sparta's neighborhood
(Faust II, Act 3.)

DURING the years of 1837-1841, fourteen major compositions were written, as well as many smaller ones. This is a considerable achievement for a very busy conductor. But in these works we see that the creative powers of the master often display more breadth than depth. Of these fourteen larger works, only five can withstand the more critical view of posterity, along with two or three of the smaller ones. A list of the works written during these years will confirm the observation.

Vocal Music: Psalms 42, 95, and 114; *Lobgesang* (Hymn of Praise); *Lieder im Freien zu singen*, Op. 41, 48, 59, 88, 100, and Male Choruses, Op. 50, 75, 76, 120; Songs for one voice, Op. 34, 47.

Instrumental Music: Overture to *Ruy Blas;* Piano Concerto in D minor, Op. 40; Three String Quartets, Op. 44; Sonata for 'Cello and Piano, Op. 45; Trio for Piano, Violin and 'Cello, Op. 49; *Variations sérieuses* for Piano, Op. 54; Three Preludes and Fugues for Organ, Op. 37.

Of lasting worth are the following: Psalm 114, D minor Trio, *Variations sérieuses*, Three Preludes and Fugues for Organ, E flat major Quartet. Of the songs: *Es ist bestimmt in Gottes Rath, Auf Flügeln des Gesanges*, and *Die Liebende schreibt;* also several Songs without Words.

We shall attempt to justify this evelution, not on the familiar basis of popularity, but through the inherent musical values of these compositions. As in every other art, in music there are changes of taste and fashion, even distortions of esthetic criteria, which we must by no means regard as "eternal principles." Therefore, we shall explicitly list the criteria on which we base the following analyses and judgments: Freshness and power of invention; Thematic integration (unity and contrast); Economy of means; Rational relationship between substance and size of form.

[*345*]

These are ideal postulates which, apparently, result from the observation of *classical masterworks*. But, by the same token, they are indissolubly linked with "classical" structure and viewpoint, and the attitudes expressed in the nineteenth century towards many of these postulates frequently differ from those of classical aesthetics. Hence, the author must show his colors. He rejects on principle the idea of understanding and judging the works of any master *only* "with reference to his times." He employs the same criteria in judging the music of his own time. After all, there have not been so many changes in the last hundred years of Western music history that we, familiar with the world of Stravinsky, Schoenberg, Bartók, and Hindemith, may dare to throw out everything that was written before 1900, simply because we consider it "old-fashioned." If we believed this, there would be no sense in music history; for its (often unspoken) basic axiom is and remains the assumption of real continuity in Western music. Only on the basis of this preconception can we justify the criteria above.

VOCAL MUSIC

Surrounded by the lovely Italian landscape, the young Mendelssohn becomes conscious of his duty of adding to the heritage which the great masters had left him. This is how he explains himself to his mentor Zelter. Never did he fulfill this aim better than in his Psalms, which—regarded from a purely artistic viewpoint—certainly present his own style of religious music in its purest form. Here the ideal of the early literary Romanticists is attained; the fusion of the old Italian *bel canto* with the power of Handel, so desired by Wackenroder, E. T. A. Hoffman, the Schleiermacher. Of the three Psalms under consideration, Psalm 42 is the most sentimental, Psalm 95 the most suitable to the needs of the liturgy, and Psalm 114 by far the strongest. In fact, next to *Elijah*, it seems to us to be altogether the best sacred work of Mendelssohn.

Psalm 42

As has been mentioned, Psalm 42 was written on Mendelssohn's honeymoon journey. During the master's lifetime, it was the most popular of all his Psalms and also (probably for personal reasons) Mendelssohn's own favorite. It cannot be denied that, in a number of spots, this work was composed without too deep a consideration of the text. One need only compare the Psalm text (whose German translation already weakens the wild passion of the original text) with its musical interpretation. Here everything that impresses itself upon the reader of the verses with strong words and passionate images and recollections is softened and toned down.

The insertion of recitatives, of antiphonically treated sections, and of responsorial ensembles in contrast with the chorus, does bring a degree of color and variety to the work. But the passion and power of the text is watered down to sentimentality in the music. Of the choruses, the first, in spite of a few weakish spots, is the best. The middle section, too, contains some fine details. At the close, however, Mendelssohn takes a liberty which might make sense in a liturgical work, but is out of place in one intended for the concert hall. He adds to that text a *Preis sei dem Herrn* (Praised be the Lord), obviously borrowing from the idea of the Catholic doxology of the *Gloria Patri*. Not only do those "optimistic" words of praise stand in contradiction to the problem-filled text, but the music belonging to them has an unpleasantly unctuous character which reminds us of bad preachers. Here, Mendelssohn has not composed the psalm, but a trivial theological tirade with an operatic flavor.[1] This discrepancy has best been explained and evaluated by Rudolf Werner:

> The wonder at the majesty of God and the submission to His power, the praise of His greatness and the thanks for His mercy . . . and even the cry for His help—all of these feelings melt together into the basic tone of hymnic exaltation. His sovereignty has also conditioned the form; the original personal *subjective* address of the psalm-singer to his God is broadened to a song of praise and thanks, a prayer and plea of all humanity. . . .[2]

Schumann considered the Psalm Mendelssohn's best religious work; indeed, he even presents it as the ideal towards which modern church music must strive.[3]

Psalm 95

This composition hews to a strictly liturgical line which touches the *concertante* sphere only in its ensembles. Even more than in Psalm 42, we notice here the influence of the Italian church composers of the Baroque, especially Leonardo Leo, Durante, and Marcello with whom R. Werner has compared the master.

Important to the understanding of the work is the liturgical formal organization, which makes extensive use of responsorial and antiphonal techniques, unison singing, and stylized recitatives. Without exception, the choral sections here are better and more significant than the soli or ensembles. Only the final "Today if ye will hear His voice" remains free of softness and sentimentality, and inclines toward a grave seriousness which fits very well into the liturgical framework. Probably, there was some negative reaction to this elegiac mood; therefore—contrary to the intentions of the composer—

in England, a brilliant chorus "The sea is His" was allowed to close the work. However, this chorus was not planned in the final version of the Psalm; it appears as an intrusion in the whole.[4] Even Grove's seal of approval cannot alter the state of affairs. The chorus, which Mendelssohn may originally have planned for the Psalm but which he then dropped, does give the work a brilliant close, but spoils the liturgical simplicity, strictness and objectivity of the preceding sections.

Psalm 114

Of a basically different nature and intuition is Psalm 114, Mendelssohn's most powerful and integrated church music. In contrast to the preceding Psalms, it contains no single solo part; in fact, from beginning to end it is written for compact eight-voiced chorus. Here we see the will to collective expression, to de-individualizing monumentality. This aim is still further reinforced by the clear formal divisions of the work, by its splendid polyphony, its massive contrasts and its harsh harmonies which eschew the soft and the sentimental. This magnificent work deserves careful evaluation. Although, for practical reasons, we cannot give this in its entirety here, let us at least explain the structure and layout of the choruses.

The work is divided into six sections, which flow into one another organically without pause and are interwoven. (I) Verses 1 and 2; "When Israel out of Egypt came," *Allegro con moto maestoso, Allegro moderato,* G major, C. (II) Verses 3 and 4: "The sea saw, and fled," G minor, C. (III) Verses 5 and 6: "What ail'd thee, thou sea?," *Grave,* E flat major, 3/4. (IV) Verses 7 and 8: "At the Lord's coming ye trembled," *Allegro maestoso e vivace,* C major, C. (V) Verses 1 and 2: "When Israel out of Egypt came," *Allegro con moto e maestoso,* G major, C. (VI) "Hallelujah! Sing to the Lord forevermore!" G major, C.

Sections I and V correspond to the principal theme of a sonata form; II and III are contrasting themes; IV is a bridge-passage, and VI is a double fugue which works with two already familiar themes. It uses a text which does not belong to the original Psalm. Again, Mendelssohn added the verse freely; this time, it fits perfectly, and rounds off the splendid composition majestically.

The Psalm begins with the men's chorus in unison, singing the archaically strict theme "When Israel out of Egypt came." The women's chorus joins in with trenchant harmonies. With "Then was Judah his holy place," the polyphonic working-out begins. At first, its scope is modest; it is limited to the imitation of short phrases. On the dominant, D major, there then begins stretti and inversions which lead to massive dissonant clusters of sound.

In Section II, "the Jordan begins to rush," all external illustration is

Example 52

avoided, except for a wave-like motif in the orchestra, which pervades this section. Once again, "living waters" inspired the master! The chorus is now in a more declamatory style; with the description of the driving-back of the Jordan, there begin new imitations, which lead to forceful, hammering pronouncements of the chorus against the surging background of the orchestra playing *fortissimo, unisono*. With a Phrygian cadence, the wave ebbs away on G. In breathless wonder, the chorus declaims *pianissimo* (*a cappella*, E flat major), "What ail'd thee, thou sea?" The following orchestral *tutti*, *fortissimo* with organ and the full chorus give the shattering answer: "At the Lord's coming ye tremble"; on the word "Lord's" there occurs a *fortissimo* outburst of the chorus and orchestra of truly magnificent effect. Now, three themes are interwoven polyphonically, and with majestic tread there unfolds a kind of musical procession. The passage "who turn'd rocks into standing waterpools" is *not* interpreted illustratively, but elevated to a level of nobility, of awe before God. Now, the composer repeats the opening verse of the Psalm, with slight variations, and then goes directly into the Hallelujah verse. For this, all the arts of counterpoint are called into play, without, however, compromising the naturalness of the musical flow in any way or distracting the listener from purely spiritual enjoyment. This part culminates in an eightfold stretto on the words "Sing to the Lord forevermore." (Example 53.)

Amidst enthusiastic cries of "Hallelujah" by the chorus, all voices recall the opening verse, which is repeated in broad, full chords and closes the wonderful work.

It is understandable that this work, which is exceptional even for Mendelssohn and which differs in many respects from his usual style, has attracted special attention. From Sir George Grove to Rudolf Werner, many writers have associated this work with the spirit of Handel, on the one hand, and with Mendelssohn's Jewishness on the other. In Grove, we find the following observation, which has often been quoted: "The Jewish blood of Mendelssohn must surely for once have beat fiercely over this picture of the great triumph of his forefathers, and it is only the plain truth to say that in directness and force his music is a splendid match for the splendid words of the unknown psalmists."[5]

At its first performance, January 1, 1840, in Leipzig, the work inspired great admiration, the echo of which is heard in the daily newspapers of the time. It is noteworthy that Grove's intuition guided him in the right direction, for Felix reports to his mother on the progress of work on the Psalm in the following remarkable words: "It often seems to me that I hear great pinions rushing by over my head; in the Psalm, they really force themselves upon me. . . ."[6]

Example 53

Sing to the Lord for - e - ver - more

Lobgesang (Hymn of Praise), a Symphony-Cantata

Although Grove correctly senses the creative impulse of Mendelssohn in his Psalm 114, on a similar occasion he misinterprets the intentions of the master. He, like other biographers, believes that at this time an independent symphony in B flat major was ripening towards completion. In this sense, he interprets various letters to the Philharmonic Society in London, to Fanny, to Ferdinand David.[7] However, there is no trace of sketches or of concrete references to this symphony. On the contrary, we read in a detailed letter to Klingemann:

> The piece for the festival here was no oratorio, but, as I called it in German, "eine Symphonie für Chor und Orchester," and was entitled *Lobgesang*—first, three symphonic movements, followed by 12 choral and solo sections. You already understand that first the instruments sing praise in their fashion, and then the chorus and the individual voices. . . .[8]

He speaks even more clearly a half year later:

> Strange, that when I first conceived the idea I wrote to Berlin that I wanted to write a symphony with chorus; afterwards, I didn't have the courage for it, because the three movements were too long for an introduction, and yet I always had the feeling that there was something lacking in the mere introduction. Now the symphonic movements will come in according to the *old plan*, and then the piece will come out . . . I do not believe that it will *really* lend itself to performances, and yet I love it so much. . . .[9]

Besides this and other letters, there are still other clear indications which lead us to the conclusion that the *Lobgesang* was not originally planned by the composer in the form that we know today. We do hear of a symphony in B flat major,[10] but also of a choral work for the Gutenberg Festival Week in Leipzig.[11] This did not mean the "Gutenberg Hymn," of which we have already spoken in the preceding chapter. The *Lobgesang* was written for the Gutenberg Festival and was later only "expanded," as Felix himself reports.[12] We do not know exactly when Mendelssohn decided to combine instrumental and vocal pieces. But when we look through the score for the germ cells of the work, we come upon a surprise: the cyclic theme ("All that has life and breath, sing to the Lord") which introduces and closes the work, was not and is not organically built into the rest of the work. We deduce this from the following facts:

　　a) The first movement is built entirely on the cyclic theme.

　　b) The second movement, in the Trio of the Scherzo, contains the theme as a middle voice. It seems to have been added subsequently as a counterpoint to the chorale—the principal motif of the Trio. (Score, p. 60 ff.)

　　c) The third movement does not contain the theme at all; obviously, it was already a finished symphonic movement, in which nothing could or should be altered.

d) In the nine choral numbers of the cantata, the theme appears only in the first chorus and again right at the end, as a brilliant close.

This survey leads us to the assumption that Mendelssohn had completed the first three symphonic movements (perhaps with the exception of the Trio of the Scherzo) before he thought of a choral ending. Then, he recognized the unifying power of the first theme, and associated it consciously with the idea of a hymn of praise; in the vocal closing section he devoted the first chorus entirely to the development of his favorite theme, and finally cited it at the end, like a motto.

Mendelssohn clung to his *Lobgesang* with special love. Soon after the first performance, there had risen critical voices which took particular offence at the structure of the work, in which they perceived the sacrilegious attempt to surpass Beethoven's Ninth. The most sincere expressions of opinion came from Moritz Hauptmann, Robert Schumann, and A. Reissmann. Not quite so unprejudiced was Richard Wagner, who called the work "a foolishly uninhibited piece."[13] In his evaluation of the *Lobgesang* —which was not intended for publication—Hauptmann used the word "mannerism," which was considered as a term of unfavorable criticism at that time. He did try to moderate this judgment, and sincerely admired the symphonic parts of the work, but the associations with the word "mannerism" sharpen our ears.[14] Hans von Bülow's judgment is not exactly the same, but basically similar; he, too, accepted only the instrumental portion.[15] Even Mendelssohn's admirer, Hugo Riemann, brushed off the work as "an unsuccessful effort on the whole."

Without becoming uncritical we must do justice to the strong parts of the work. Mendelssohn himself was far too intelligent not to recognize and fear the dangerous proximity with Beethoven's Ninth. Therefore, he extended the choral part so greatly that, in comparison to it, the three preceding symphonic movements really appear to be merely a festive prologue. Of these sections, the first is the most compact and strongest; the Scherzo can no longer maintain itself on this level, and the slow movement shows a distinct decline.

The choral second part contains three high points. The inserted section (No. 6) "Watchman, will the night soon pass?"; the brilliantly figured Chorale, "Let all men praise the Lord" (No. 8); and the fugal beginning of the final chorus (No. 10), "Ye nations offer to the Lord." The duet "I waited for the Lord" (No. 5) has an unpleasantly unctuous tone, and does not avoid banalities. The chorus "The night is departing" (No. 7) is pompous, but unconvincing in its melodic and rhythmic invention. The duet "My song shall be always thy mercy" (No. 9) begins beautifully and warmly, but is carried out at far too great a length; radical cutting of this section would restore the duet to effectiveness. The long final chorus after the magnificent fugal introduction turned out to be somewhat dry, not to say academic. The choral development of the cyclic theme "All that has life and breath, Sing to the Lord" (No. 12) is planned on a grand scale, but grows only in extent, not in depth—the composer repeated himself too often here. Paradoxically, the work shows no unifying line, and cannot maintain the level of the best movements.

Lieder im Freien zu singen and Male Choruses

With the small pieces for mixed chorus Mendelssohn entered upon a field which had already proved fertile. In the Italian Renaissance, there had been the madrigal; in Germany, the artistically stylized folk song; in France, the chanson; and in England, the glee. Through their folklike tinge, these smaller choral forms had transmitted important impulses to art-music. Composers like Orlando Gibbons, Luca Marenzio, Hans Leo Hasler gave of their best in such pieces. At the end of the eighteenth and the beginning of the nineteenth century, these "convivial" forms were dying, pushed aside by humorous canons, operatic finales, or lascivious street-songs. Here, too, Gresham's Law proves itself: bad money drives out good money.

The *Berliner Liedertafel* and its sister organizations had striven since Zelter's time to counteract this decline of social choral singing; but somehow the compositions of Zelter, B. Klein, Romberg, etc. did not become popular. None of these composers was a real melodist. Schubert (who, however, accompanies his choruses with piano) was unknown in North and Central Germany. Here, Mendelssohn could fulfill what Zelter had initiated; he brought to his task the necessary equipment of melodic inventiveness and special familiarity with *a cappella* choruses.[16] This explains the tremendous success of his little choral songs; while most of them are forgotten today, some of them became real folk songs and live on as such. There is no greater honor for a composer than when one of his songs becomes a folk song; his name is forgotten, but his work lives on.

Somewhat different conditions prevailed in the field of the male chorus. We have already called attention to the *Liedertafeln* (singing societies), for which even a Goethe did not consider it beneath his dignity to write songs. However, after the deaths of Zelter and C. M. von Weber, this garden of song, neglected, withered away or became a wilderness. Basically, the male chorus had degenerated into a mere accessory to the academic Philistinism of the "Old Boys" or to the less academic mob patriotism or nationalism.[17] Even in our generation, we can clearly trace these two roots of modern German male chorus-writing. Mendelssohn felt uncomfortable with both Philistinism and nationalism. Also, we cannot claim that he was enthusiastic about the male chorus, with its poverty of sound effects. On the contrary! He was rather unsympathetic to these singing societies.[18] Nonetheless, he cultivated this field as well, and with lasting success, true to his motto "Res severa verum gaudium."

In the following we shall discuss briefly all the secular choral songs of the master, as a definite stylistic development is not discernible in them (in contrast to his other works). Hence, the chronology of these pieces is irrelevant.

Of the *Lieder im Freien zu singen* (Songs of the Open Air), the following have become well-known and loved: *Es fiel ein Reif* (There Fell a Frost, No. 3), which has "inspired" countless imitators; *Auf dem See* (On the Lake, No. 6), the beautiful and artful musical construction of which lets the listener forget the frequent mistakes in declamation; the charming *Lerchengesang* (Song of the Lark, No. 10), a double canon of enchanting melodic quality; the atmospheric beginning (in C minor) of the *Herbstlied* (Autumn Song, No. 12), which, unfortunately, sinks into complete banality in the second part. The most famous pieces are these: *Abschied vom Walde* (Farewell to the Forest, No. 15) has become a model for many hymns in Germany and England; the exquisitely worked *Nachtigall* (Nightingale, No. 16), a jewel of melodic and folklike polyphony; J. P. Hebel's modest and intimate *Neujahrslied* (New Year's Song, No. 19), the text of which was written after Mendelssohn's own heart.

The pieces for male chorus show the master in an unaccustomed light. Here he gives free rein to his humor, to his whimsicality, even to his satire. The charm of his personality shows itself undisguised here, and naturally wins the listener.

Among the first six songs, we find three delightful pieces: No. 1, Goethe's *Türkisches Schenkenlied* (Turkish Tavern Song); No. 2, Eichendorff's *Der Jäger Abschied* (The Hunter's Farewell)—for good or ill, a landmark for the German male chorus, since it has been imitated *ad nauseam* by every Tom, Dick and Harry; and No. 5, Goethe's *Liebe und Wein* (Love and Wine; "to be sung in a drunken tone"). The second volume contains Goethe's *Trinklied* (Drinking Song), a light, mocking composition, which is congenial to its famous text. The third volume contains Heine's satire *Das Lied vom braven Mann* (The Song of the Worthy Man), which Mendelssohn, with comic solemnity, turns into a bitterly humorous parody; No. 4, Hoffmann von Fallersleben's beautiful *Comitat* (Comradeship) which glorifies the spirit of the "Old Boys," and which became famous through Mendelssohn's composition. The last volume brings us Goethe's *Zigeunerlied* (Gypsy Song) in a very temperamental interpretation; the piece is extraordinary in sound, but not easy to sing.

If we glance at the poets of Mendelssohn's best choruses, we find the following names: Goethe, Heine, Eichendorff, Lenau, Hebel, Hoffmann von Fallersleben. It is certainly no accident that his best choral songs are written to texts of these poets.

In closing, let us touch on two basic problems with which Mendelssohn had to deal in his choral songs. The first is that of the "folklike" song (*not* the folk song). In a similar connection, we have mentioned Schiller's penetrating discussion of this problem.[19] Mendelssohn inclined more towards the reflective-artistic than to the naïve-folklike element; as a born aristocrat, he did not care much for the man of the mass. So, on the whole, he tended more to stylization than to "folksiness." Nonetheless, a good many of his choral songs attained popularity among the common people, although in considerably simplified versions.

In several of these songs, Mendelssohn strikes the patriotic tone of the Fatherland. As we saw in the case of Becker's *Rheinlied*, the master was reluctant to champion emphatically patriotic ideas; all the more surprising is his chorus *Deutschland* (Geibel). For the poem expresses the impatient hope for the early return of the German Emperor, who will bring home the bride, Germany.

> When will you wake her with drums so loud
> And bring her home, my Kaiser?

Mendelssohn wrote electrifying, fiery music to these verses. The nearer the year 1848 drew, the easier it seemed for the "Little-German" (*Kleindeutsch*) Mendelssohn to accommodate himself to the "Great-German" (*Grossdeutsch*) concept of the *Reich*. Herwegh's *Rheinweinlied*, too, speaks, though half in fun, the same language which Mendelssohn had censured in Becker:

> He is not worthy of his wine,
> Of German wife or German home,
> Who will not gladly swing his sword
> To smite the enemy. . . .

There is a mitigating circumstance for this crass contradiction. Mendelssohn loved Rhine wines above all; he set great store by a well-cared-for and well-stocked cellar. Thus, we may excuse such patriotic extravagances on his part. That he was a good German, or at least felt himself to be one, is evident a thousandfold, and is not a matter for discussion here.

Songs for One Voice

Among the twelve songs, only three have been able to survive the changes in taste and the development of the German song. These are: the (alas, now hackneyed) *Auf Flügeln des Gesanges* (On Wings of Song; Heine), Goethe's *Suleika*, and the folklike poem of Feuchtersleben, *Es ist bestimmt in Gottes Rath* (It is Forsooth in God's Counsel). The less-known *Blumenstrauss* (Bouquet; Klingemann), a tender, fragrant, and melodious piece, deserves to be added to this list.

It would be vain to seek for new ideas or treatment of text in these pieces; they do not pretend, either, to reveal deeper emotions in tones, as do many songs of Schubert, Brahms, Hugo Wolf, or Mahler. Rather, they serve principally to fulfill the requirements of decent, often modest domestic music.

With respect to form, *Auf Flügeln des Gesanges* is a noteworthy creation. For, in it, we find—not for the first time in Mendelssohn—a real *Barform*: two *Stollen* and an *Abgesang*.[20] We encounter the same structure in the settings of Heine's *Neue Liebe*, Lenau's *Schilflied* and Eichendorff's *Nachtlied*. Mendelssohn probably became acquainted with this ancient form in a number of Protestant chorales. In any case we can say that Wagner was not the only one to rediscover this unusual form, but that, here, Mendelssohn "imitated him in advance" (*vorgeahmt*), to use an expression of Karl Kraus's.

Mendelssohn's most beautiful song had already been written at this time, but was published only after his death (Op. 86, No. 2). It is Goethe's sonnet *Die Liebende schreibt* (The Loving Girl Writes). Mendelssohn was truly blessed with inspiration when he set this poem to music. The strict form of the sonnet confronts the composer with a difficult alternative: either he follows the rhyme scheme exactly—that is, he cadences after each rhyming pair—or he ignores the rhyme and simply sticks to the (equally restrictive) metre. In the first instance the melody often becomes monotonous—in the second instance, the rhythm. Mendelssohn tried the first possibility, with excellent success—the bugbear of monotony is avoided. Of the rhyming pairs

1	2	3	4
a	a	c–c	
b	b	d–d	
b	b	e–e	
a	a		

he pays attention to *b, c, d* and *e,* but ignores *a* entirely. His metre follows that of the poem up to the seventh line, but then takes wings on its own, until, in a spirited and fervent cantilena, it reaches a climax on the words *Gib mir ein Zeichen!* (Give me a sign!). The beauty of the melodic line, the depth of emotion and the perfection of form will always continue to bring purest pleasure to attentive listeners.

INSTRUMENTAL MUSIC

Overture to Ruy Blas

In ADDITION to the three symphonic introductory movements of the *Lobgesang*, Mendelssohn completed, during these years, only one orchestral work: the Overture to Victor Hugo's *Ruy Blas*. And even this was not much more than an occasional piece. However, we must not forget that he had been polishing the Scotch Symphony for years; but it was published only in 1843.

In the case of the *Ruy Blas* overture we once again encounter the inner contradictions in Felix's character. For he considered Hugo's play "quite ghastly and completely devoid of dignity."[21] Nevertheless, he fired off his overture in three days—and it is fiery enough; and, as he himself admits, the composition of the work brought him "unspeakable pleasure."[22] How is the contradiction to be explained? The composer himself gives a part of the explanation: he "was vexed," because people supposed that the composition of an overture would take him months. The blood of a youthful bohemian still boils in his veins; he will show the gentry what he can do when he wants to. Are his artistic principles, then, sacrificed for a gesture of bravado? Not entirely, for the play *Ruy Blas* was, for Mendelssohn, not much more than an excuse to write a concert overture. If the play had been something else and he had felt like writing an overture, the result would probably have been much the same. We might wish that he had saved a bit of this naïve, uncritical attitude for his operatic plans as well. But no! Then there arose a thousand impediments as soon as the first scenario had been presented.

Actually, the *Ruy Blas* overture scarcely sounds the tragic note; it is, rather, somewhat bombastic, but very fluent, and still effective today as a curtain raiser for the theatre.

Piano Concerto in D minor

Another work with orchestra, of which we have already spoken, was his Second Piano Concerto, Op. 40. It is hardly worthy of his name. Its superficiality and empty brilliance bring it dangerously near to the French salon composers Kalkbrenner, Herz, and Thalberg, whom the master otherwise so scorned. The concerto is justifiably forgotten today. Mendelssohn himself was probably well aware of the weaknesses of this salon concerto, for he wrote to Hiller: "You would, I think, abhor my new Piano Concerto."[23]

Three String Quartets

Children of quite another spirit are the three quartets in D major, E minor, and E flat major. As the Second Piano Concerto is far inferior to the First, so these quartets, as a whole, do not reach the heights of originality and inspiration of their forerunners Op. 12 and 13. Nonetheless, they are mature works of a master, and especially the Quartet in E flat major stands at the peak of Mendelssohn's art.

The themes of the first movements of the E minor quartet immediately remind every listener of the Violin Concerto in the same key (which, at that time, was not even *in statu nascendi*); only the jerky rhythm of the first movement of the Quartet mars the resemblance. The middle movements, an elegant sparkling Scherzo and a *cantabile*, canzonet-like *Andante*, are the best parts of the work; for the Finale, despite its impetus and brilliance, declines somewhat into the trivial.

Of the three quartets, the D major was Mendelssohn's favorite. Here, too, the middle movements are most successful: a Minuet in D with a floating Trio in B minor, and an *Andante espressivo* in B minor, markedly elegiac in mood and wonderfully beautiful in sound. Again there follows a brilliant, but rather empty Finale, which, because of its thematic weakness, seems too long in spite of its relative brevity.

The E flat major Quartet contains the strongest contrasts, and is also the most carefully worked-out. It is deserving of detailed analysis.

The first movement (*Allegro vivace*, C, E flat major) is built on a single theme, the four motifs of which are worked out separately. Already the theme itself is conceived quite according to the spirit of the string quartet, and created out of the very nature of the stringed instruments. As in other movements, Mendelssohn here spins out the exposition into a little development. The secondary theme is really only a variation of one of the motifs from the principal theme. The development is characterized by especially transparent thematic work; the climaxes are prepared and reached with the highest art. The retransition into the recapitulation occurs almost unnoticeably. The Coda, again a little development, is based on original pizzicato effects.

The second movement, a Scherzo (*Assai leggiero vivace*, 6/8, C minor), begins with a *staccato* motif which starts in one voice but is soon taken up by all four instruments. Polyphonic devices are piled one on another: canon, stretto, fugato, counter-themes. But the verve of the piece is not diminished by all this; on the contrary! The coupling of the first theme with the fugue generates a whirling double fugue which carries the movement to a magnificent climax; a coda, rich in surprising deceptive cadences, closes the piece *pianissimo*.

In the third movement (*Adagio non troppo*, ¾, A flat major), the master shows his best side. A deeply felt chromatic theme, with hymnic characteristics, opens the movement. Soon it grows into a *crescendo* of orchestral effect; a second theme is contrasted with it. Here, in the changing interplay of the two themes, the movement unfolds in full beauty. The dualism of sonata form is used to better effect here than in the first movement. The second theme vividly reminds us of the unforgettable melody of the slow movement of Schubert's B flat major Trio, that most beautiful lullaby of chamber music literature. But Mendelssohn's movement was to exert its influence far into the future. Especially, we hear its echo in the *Andante* of Smetana's Quartet "From My Life," in Dvořák's A flat major Quartet, in the Waltz from Tschaikowsky's *Swan Lake,* in the slow movement of Brahms' Second Piano Concerto. The basic idea reminds us of a passage in Mozart's E flat Quartet (the A flat major movement).

The last movement (*Molto allegro con fuoco,* C, E flat major) uses a little motif of the preceding movement as a contrast to the somewhat too "free-and-easy" principal theme of the Finale. Only Mendelssohn's sovereign artistic insight and mastery of the quartet style save him from superficiality here. Thus, he succeeds in striking sparks from the somewhat arid thematic material, and the splendid work ends in spirited style. It is the last instrumental composition in which Mendelssohn still operates with cyclic ideas. That is regrettable, for to few composers after him was it given to spin threads from one movement to another so easily.

Sonata for 'Cello and Piano

Closely related to the Quartets in its diction is the 'Cello Sonata in B flat Major, Op. 45, which Felix wrote for his brother Paul. The slow middle movement which unfolds from a short, rhythmically pregnant motif, seems to me the best part of the pleasant work.

Trio for Piano, Violin, and 'Cello

In this great D minor trio, Op. 49, Mendelssohn presents himself in more brilliant fashion than in his 'Cello Sonata. Of all his chamber music, the Trio has probably become the most popular, perhaps to the detriment of his other, deeper works in this genre. Since the Trio is still often played today, a detailed discussion is unnecessary. However, we should like to call attention to a few fine details which are often overlooked.

In the recapitulation of the first movement, the violin introduces a charming counterpoint to the main theme. In the slow movement, the hovering accompaniment figure of the piano should veil the somewhat monotonous steps in the bass; it calls for careful balance of the sound. The elfin scherzo requires the fastest of tempi, and exact staccato; the last movement, which begins most promisingly but does not work out its theme thoroughly enough, would benefit by some cuts, especially towards the end.

The piano part of the work was, at the behest of Hiller, "polished up" by the composer; that is, it was equipped with many brilliant passages, so that it makes a *concertante* impression.

Variations sérieuses

Among Mendelssohn's piano composition, the *Variations sérieuses,* Op. 54, stands on a lonely height. Quite unlike the Second Piano Concerto, which is a mere façade, the series of variations is of exemplary significance and had a profound historical effect. The work was created in the summer of 1841. The master's naïve confession is quite moving: "I vary every theme that occurs to me. First I did eighteen serious ones, then six sentimental ones; now I want to do ten graceful ones, and then some with and for orchestra. [Too bad that he did not execute this plan!]. . . . The *Variations sérieuses* start in D minor and are peevish."[24] This ironical observation is meant to make the gravity of the theme a bit ridiculous; such was always the fashion in the "elegant world" of assimilated Jews in Berlin, who did not like to take themselves too seriously or present themselves too seriously to others.

Enthusiastically he reported to Klingemann:

> Do you know what I have just been composing passionately? Variations for piano. I started right off with a theme in D minor; and I had such a heavenly time doing it that I went right on with new variations on a theme in E flat. . . . It seems as though I had to make up for never having written any before.[25]

In no other form is the stylistic attitude of a composer displayed in such open and unadorned fashion as in that of variations. Mendelssohn is no exception to the rule. Therefore, we shall seriously examine his handling of the variation form; thus, we shall discover the true criteria of Mendelssohn's self-chosen position between the conservatives and the "radical progressives" of the post-Beethoven era.

At first it must seem strange that Felix, the admirer and champion of Beethoven, appears not to have been intimately acquainted with his great variations. After all, the C minor Variations, the *Diabelli Variations*, and the many variation movements in his chamber and piano music belong to Beethoven's most characteristic creations in the realm of original forms. And we should assume that Mendelssohn would have understood the problems posed by the *Diabelli Variations*. A. B. Marx calls special attention to them in his composition textbook, and openly says that "no one went further in this field than Beethoven, or even as far."[26] We may perhaps suppose that up until this point, Mendelssohn had remained unaware of the strict demands which the form makes on the artistic integrity of a composer. Let us not forget that the fashionable music of his time was flooded with "Variations brillants," which are at the opposite pole from Beethoven's great variations. Mendelssohn heartily scorned these tinklings of Herz, Kalkbrenner, and young Liszt, and made no bones about his feelings. For this very reason he emphasizes in the title of his first and best effort in this genre the epithet *sérieuses*, with openly polemic intent. He himself did not consider the two following, much weaker sets of variations. Op. 82 and 83, worth publication; they appeared only posthumously. A much earlier occasional work, the Variations for 'Cello and Piano, Op. 17, still belongs in the "brilliant" category.

In fact, the *Variations sérieuses* represent a turning point in Mendelssohn's artistic direction. Brilliant, superficial, but also atmospheric elements retreat more and more into the background, and the master turns to classicistic formalism. In its weaker moments, this degenerates into academicism, but in his best creations, it leads to the finest achievements of his art. We know of only one return to the world of his Romantic inclinations—a return greatly to be prized: in the incidental music to *A Midsummer Night's Dream*.

Since Beethoven—perhaps since Mozart's piano concerti—we may distinguish between *strict* and *free* variation. By *strict* variation we mean the dissolution of the thematic contour into ornamental or figured brilliant passages (or also contrapuntal alteration); *free* variation signifies the transformation of the theme into almost independent character pieces, which are often only loosely connected with the theme. Beethoven's C minor Variations belong to the first category, his *Diabelli Variations* to the second. But only seldom are the two categories so clearly distinguished; they melt imperceptibly into one another and it is not always easy to tell them apart.

If we may use the terminology of the old theorists, in the first category only the theme itself is a *res scripta*, while the variations are *res factae;* in the second category every variation is "scripta." Rightly, Martin Friedland calls attention to the fact that the strictest variation form contains only a paraphrase of the meaning of the theme, but no new interpretation of it.[27] Perhaps the extreme types of variations may be most sharply symbolized by the concepts *kaleidoscope (strict variation)* and *metamorphosis (free variation)*. In the kaleidoscope, all possibilities of development are predetermined, and surrounded by a fixed framework; the constituent motifs simply exchange places with respect to one another, in each case. In the metamorphosis, both framework and motifs are variable.

If the essence of a variation is determined by its relationship to the theme, we must establish still another basic antinomy which appears more clearly in variations than in any other musical form: the polarity of the spiritual and the sensual. We cannot identify one or the other of the two types of variations with one of the two poles. However, in principle, we may say this: the variation which thrives merely on sonorities has a lower artistic rank than that which lives on the *spirit* of the theme, not just on its *sound*. Therefore, the variation-style of a composer may perhaps be explained by his basic attitude to this "spirit-sound" antithesis. Fully aware of this, Beethoven set the two extremes of the variation form and then traversed all the intervening space. Between his variations on *Nel cor più non mi sento* (G major) and the *Diabelli Variations* we find a multitude of variation forms, which incline now to one side, now to the other. Understandably, Beethoven, growing deaf, found himself attracted rather to the spiritual metamorphosis of a theme than to its sensual manifestation in sound.

Here Mendelssohn could not follow him—not only because of his love for euphony but above all because of his aversion to all "abstract" music, that is, music which was not conceived for *one and only one* specific medium. In the last works of Beethoven, we often sense comparative indifference to the specific instrument.

As has already been recognized, in Mendelssohn the theme itself can often be added as counterpoint to the variation of the moment. That is correct, and, in the case of variations where such a congruence takes place, the strictly classicistic attitude of the composer is manifest. Nevertheless, we cannot simply dismiss Mendelssohn's variation technique as "kaleidoscopic." Very often we find transformations, autonomous pieces in imitative style, or variations which far surpass the original framework of the theme.

The masters whom we might call "godfathers" of the *Variations sérieuses* were the Beethoven of the C minor Variations and C. M. von Weber. In the freer variations Mendelssohn follows Weber; in the stricter, Beethoven (but not the model of the *Diabelli Variations*). However, our composer always followed his own guiding spirit; nowhere did he simply copy older models. This must be clearly maintained in contradiction to Martin Friedland's unproved assertions. His thesis of the nonexistence of stylistic development in Mendelssohn is neither new nor at all tenable. Friedland closes his evaluation of Mendelssohn with the sage observations that

these transformations do not surpass certain limitations of expressive power—this lack is not to be explained by lack of power of formal organization, but by the peculiarity of Mendelssohn's emotional life. His was a creative nature which, in spite of great intellectual activity and flexibility, can bring forth its manifold forms in tone, only within the circle of its spiritually limited artistic individuality.[28]

Friedland's criticism does justice neither to the stature of Mendelssohn nor to the basic question concerning the function of a set of variations. Let us set aside the problem of how far Friedland correctly recognized the spiritual limitations of the master. At any rate, it is doubtful that these can be discerned in strict variations.

Finally, we come to the work itself. (Example 54) The theme is chromatic and broad-winged; suppressed pathos quivers in it.

The fourth variation presents the theme as a two-part canon, the fifth develops it over a pedal-point, the tenth takes a motif out of the theme and unfolds it in a fugato; in the fourteenth, it appears with broad and full harmonies, in D major. The fifteenth piquantly accentuates the weak beats of the theme; the eleventh is a real character variation, which reminds us of

Example 54

Schumann's piano pieces. Also very clever is the thirteeth variation, in which
the theme takes the middle voice, surrounded by flighty staccati in the right
hand, against the quarter notes of the bass. At the very end there appears
a sort of apotheosis of the main idea, in whirling passages which mark the
principal tones. The same Mendelssohn who complained to Hiller that he
had no individual or new piano style, now writes a work which is hardly
brilliant, but is pianistically effective and new. From it, Brahms, César
Franck, Reger, Busoni, and even Bartók drew inspiration. For example,
the percussion-like repetition technique of Bartók is clearly foreshadowed
here. With respect to rhythm, too, the work is filled with a variety which
Mendelssohn attained only in a few pieces.

A word should be said about the three closing cadence measures. Jack
Warner called attention to the minor cadence which frequently occurs in
Mendelssohn. Probably correctly, he traces it back to an ancient cadence
of synagogue music, which was intimately familiar to German Jews from
the High Holydays. He cited no less than ten examples of this rather unusual cadence which may be found in Mendelssohn's music. It closes the
Variations sérieuses, as well as the duet (No. 2) from *Elijah,* and, in especially striking association, "Hear ye Israel."[29]

Quite different from the Variations are Mendelssohn's first published
organ works. They are dedicated to his old friend and patron Sir Thomas
Attwood and written about the same time as the Six Preludes and Fugues for
piano, Op. 35. We should emphasize the fact that, of the Three Preludes

and Fugues for organ, it is the Preludes, not the Fugues, which seek and find new ways. Since Bach, there had been no organ composer of standing in Germany. Again, it is Mendelssohn who begins with Bach's organ style but places it at the service of the softer, more *cantabile* sound-ideal of the nineteenth century. Today, the Three Preludes and Fugues belong to the standard repertoire of every good organist. Without them, the organ pieces of Brahms and Rheinberger, and certainly the monumental works of Reger, are inconceivable; indeed, at many points these are directly linked with Mendelssohn, as he was linked with Bach.

All three pairs (Preludes and Fugues) are characterized by a seriousness befitting the medium. They consistently avoid cheapening excursions into the territory of "pretty" melodies. Schumann's judgment of the Six Preludes and Fugues for piano, Op. 35, is also applicable to these organ works:[30] "that he rather let the melodic character of the *cantilena* dominate, while clinging to Bach's form, is also quite like him."

Prelude and Fugue in C minor

The Prelude combines Bach's art of wide flung imitation with Beethoven's "atomizing" technique of sonata development; with this synthesis, it attains an unexpectedly strong effect before the resumption of the full theme Already in this piece we note Mendelssohn's striking preference for *stretti* at short intervals of time, which gives many of the polyphonic compositions a certain feeling of breathless unrest. The fugue avoids the dangers of 12/8 time (always risky for Mendelssohn) by means of frequent ties; it is also characterized by fine voice-leading.

Prelude and Fugue in G major

The Prelude is a Pastorale in polyphonic style, and remains within the elegant framework of a three-part song form. The second theme enters in G minor, touches C minor, A flat major, and C minor again, and then returns to G major. Then, without any "bridge," it goes into the varied reprise of the first theme; in the Coda, there is one more surprising glimpse of the second theme. The Fugue, in 4/2, begins quietly; it does contain some highly chromatic turns, but remains conventional throughout, a disappointment, considering the beautiful and promising theme. Naturally, it, too, from the standpoint of craftsmanship, is flawless, but it lacks the spark of genius which the theme really seems to promise.

Prelude and Fugue in D minor

The 23 introductory measures really have nothing to do with the rest of the Prelude, but do anticipate the theme of the Fugue both rhythmically and melodically. The Prelude itself gives the impression of being heterogeneous and not organically developed; for it falls apart into a large fugato, a toccata-like section, and a homophonic, compact section. The seams are painfully obvious; a) abrupt change from hasty motion in triplets to eighth notes; b) equally abrupt return to triplets and sixteenth notes in A minor; c) sudden slowing-down from sixteenth notes to quarter notes. The most subtle but most important art of a composer, that of instigating or liquidating movement, of keeping careful balance in movement, is notably lacking here. Also the Fugue, the theme of which is derived from that of the B flat minor fugue in Part I of Bach's *Well-Tempered Clavier*, is somewhat monotonous and without impulse, in spite of its many contrapuntal devices.

Regarded as a whole, however, the Three Preludes and Fugues take an important step in the direction of the future German organ style, which is linked to the Baroque without being archaistic. The sense of continuity, which was always awake and alive in Mendelssohn, should not be confused with the inclination of other composers to make pseudoantique stylistic copies. Mendelssohn wrote few works "in olden style." Much of what he did is derived from long-standing tradition, but everything breathes the air of its time and often we sense "Neoclassical" tendencies.

Notes

1. Here, R. Werner finds similarities with the Finale of Act I of *Lohengrin*.
2. R. Werner, *Mendelssohn als Kirchenmusiker*, p. 77.
3. R. Schumann, *Musikalische Schriften*, II, p. 166.
4. R. Werner, *op. cit.*, p. 86.
5. Grove, article on Mendelssohn in Grove's *Dictionary of Music and Musicians*, 4th ed.
6. Unpublished letter, June 4, 1839. Such an experience can be reproduced only in music or poetry of high rank. We find an analogous example in the beautiful verses of Karl Wolfskehl: (*Die Stimme spricht*, p. 17)

> Immer wieder, nun und immer wieder,
> Samml' ich meines Volks verworfne Glieder
> Zu der Zeltnacht meiner Passahstunde,
> Schlag und schone, treu dem ewigen Bunde,
> Ziehe immer wieder, wieder immer
> Vor Euch: Tags Gewölk und nächtens Schimmer,
> Nächtens Schimmer!

(Evermore, now and evermore, I gather the scattered remnants of my people to the tent-filled night of my Passah. I smite and protect, true to the eternal covenant. Evermore I travel on before ye: cloud by day and shimmering glow by night!)

7 Grove, *op. cit.*
8. Letter to Klingemann of July 21, 1840.
9. Letter to Klingemann of November 18, 1840.
10. Letter to Klingemann of January 1, 1839.

11. Unpublished letter of August 10, 1840.
12. *Ibid.*
13. R. Wagner, *Das Kunstwerk der Zukunft.*
14. Letter to Hauser of December 10, 1841.
15. H. von Bülow, *Schriften*, p. 371.
16. Letter of July 3, 1839; letter to Klingemann of August 1, 1840.
17. Concerning the patriotic-dynastic statutes of the *Berliner Liedertafel*, see Einstein, *Music in the Romantic Era*, p. 101.
18. Letter to Klingemann of August 1, 1840; letter to his mother of October 27, 1840. "God help us, what a tiresome thing the German fatherland is when you look at it from this viewpoint. I vividly remember how Father hated the singing-societies. . . ."
19. See above, Chapter X.
20. See A. Lorenz, *Das Geheimnis der Form bei R. Wagner;* see also H. Leichtentritt, *Formenlehre*, 4th edition, pp. 24, 155, 402.
21. Letter of March 18, 1839.
22. Unpublished letter of March 14, 1839.
23. Letter of December 10, 1837.
24. Unpublished letter to Rebecca of July 31, 1841.
25. Letter to Klingemann of July 15, 1841.
26. A. B. Marx, *Die Lehre von der musikalischen Komposition*, 2nd ed. (1848), Part 3, p. 567ff.
27. Martin Friedland, *Zeitstil und Persönlichkeit in den Variationswerken der Romantik* (Leipzig, 1930), p. 13.
28. Friedland, *op. cit.*, p. 73.
29. Jack Warner, "The Mendelssohnian Cadence," *Musical Times* (1956), Vol. 97, pp. 17ff.
30. See above, Chapter XII, p. 276.

CHAPTER XVI *Composer in Royal Service*

Berlin is one of the sourest apples to bite into, and yet it must be bitten. . . .

F.M.B. to Klingemann

As A STRONG CURRENT quickly burns through a weak connection, so the constantly increasing flood of artistic, administrative, and pedagogical activity prematurely exhausted the weak body of Mendelssohn. His death at 38 was the inevitable consequence of the drain he put on his physical and psychic resources in the years 1841-44. In order to have a clear idea of this, it is necessary to compile a list of the principal activities of those years.

1. As a composer, he completed: four major works of theatrical music; ten religious works (for chorus with organ or orchestra); a symphony; six organ sonatas; twelve duets, twenty songs, many choral songs; a violin concerto; a piano trio; a sonata for 'cello and piano; and many piano pieces.

2. As a conductor: he headed the *Gewandhaus* Orchestra, the Berlin Cathedral Choir and the subscription concerts of the Royal Orchestra, for which he was artistically responsible even though he did not personally direct every concert. Beyond this, he directed two German music festivals (in Düsseldorf and Zweibrücken) and two English music festivals; in addition, he took a very active part in two London music seasons.

3. As an administrator: He made vain efforts towards the founding of a music academy in Berlin, but saw his efforts for a similar institution crowned with success in Leipzig.

4. As an editor: He made several Handel oratorios available to the world of music in proper and stylistically correct form.

5. As a teacher: At the newly founded Conservatory in Leipzig, he taught piano and composition, although not always regularly.

How did this tremendous expansion of all his artistic and organizational activities come about? To this must be added the many journeys and the endless correspondence, the writing of which consumed many hours since, in general, the master did not use a secretary.

In a time when people lived much more quietly than today, such restlessness is hard to understand. For Mendelssohn wanted mainly to compose, not to administer and not to travel! He was not dependent on the income which his tours brought him. He hated administrative work of all kinds. He abhorred the intrigues that always flourish in courtly circles. Why, then, did he flee repose and enter circles in which he did not feel comfortable and in which he was not at home? In short, why did he not grant himself inner or outer peace?

There are two possible answers to this question. The first is hypothetical, the second offers reasons; however, both are necessary to the understanding of the master. From the correspondence of Mendelssohn, the attentive reader must gain the impression that he considerably overestimated his strength. Along with this, we always sense his feeling that he had to fulfill a mission; to make Germany the undisputed center of all European music. After the opening of the Leipzig Conservatory, when students from all countries streamed to Leipzig, this obsession became even stronger.

The second source of his restlessness may be traced to the interference of the King of Prussia, who spurred him on to new deeds. The works which we owe to this interference did not satisfy him entirely—with two exceptions: the music for *A Midsummer Night's Dream* and for *Antigone*. It almost appears as though he resented his weaker creations because they were products of his office as his Royal composer; they remained a thorn in his flesh, constantly provoking him to attain that fulfillment which Berlin— now for the second time—would deny him. How did it happen that the Prussian King was interested in the Leipzig musician?

In 1840, Frederick William IV ascended the throne of his ancestors as King of Prussia. He has gone down in history as the "Romanticist on the Royal Throne." Whence does this expression come? Does it correspond to his nature? If we believe the judgment of the most far-seeing and superior statesman of that time—Prince Metternich—Frederick William IV often showed himself to be "a weak reed in the wind." The following observations of Metternich present a devastating judgment of the monarch:

"I do not think I am wrong when I make a distinction between what the King still wants today and what he will do tomorrow," and "The basic evil of the day in Prussia is the eccentricity of the King in his well-meaning ideas. . . ."[1]

If a double-dyed legitimist could feel this way, what must the liberals have thought! The friend of Mendelssohn's youth, Gustav Droysen, who gained fame as a historian, expressed himself in unusually drastic fashion concerning the King; we hear that he battled chimeras, founded orders such as the very romantic Order of the Swan and the poetic-religious Order of

Mary, that he neglected foreign policy in a most dangerous manner, that he simply ignored developments in Austria and France, etc.[2] Most bluntly for his time—and therefore, for us—spoke a theologian. No one recognized as clearly as he did the weak points of this King, who, in many respects, reminds us of William II.

But how was it possible, in that censor-ridden time, to criticize a reigning Prussian King openly without the author and the work in question falling victim to the police? Nonetheless, one man succeeded. True, he went about it very cleverly, and with a strong sense of his responsibility, with wit, and with profound erudition. Perhaps he was a little too clever; for only educated readers could understand the dynamic nature of his satire. The famous theologian and historian David Friedrich Strauss claimed to be criticizing Julian the Apostate in his essay *Ein Romantiker auf dem Throne der Caesaren*. In reality, however, he meant Frederick William IV. The epithet "Royal Romanticist" probably comes from D. F. Strauss. Though he was very critical, this author was fair enough not only to admit that the King's aims were good, but also to evaluate them properly. But the road to revolution, too, is paved with good intentions. With all the good will in the world, the King not only did not hold back revolution, but with his vague plans completely estranged from reality, he actually provoked it.

Not many good things can be reported about his court. Perhaps every court reflects the personality of its monarch in a distorting mirror, as La Rochefoucauld believed. In that case, this King must have been a strange mixture of lofty flights of intellect, true love of the arts, anachronistic knightly ideals, and incompetence to rule. Or, if it is correct that all courts of a given period are alike in their inmost essence, then we should have to call this time a worthy one; for, while the King may have had foolish, short-sighted, unworldly and even incompetent advisers, neither they nor he lacked integrity of viewpoint or good will.

From the very beginning, the King showed a lively interest in culture. Wilhelm von Humboldt was one of his ministers; the noted Orientalist Josias von Bunsen was one of his closest advisers. The painter Cornelius, the Grimm brothers who had been driven out of Göttingen, the poet Rückert, were all invited to Berlin. Music, too, was to be illuminated by the sun of royal grace. The best-known German composer of the time was, without a doubt, Mendelssohn. Therefore, the court began its dealings—at first, with Mendelssohn's family in Berlin—very carefully, in order to be sure of acceptance. For our master was anything but a nobility-loving snob and, as we know, definitely inclined towards liberal ideas, which were naturally abhorred at court.

Who, then, really brought about the summoning of Mendelssohn? From the sources and family archives, we can fairly accurately reconstruct the individual steps which led to this move. Although the King knew Mendelssohn personally from Düsseldorf, the idea of summoning him to Berlin did not originate with him. In reality, the initiative came from Freiherrn von Bunsen and from Wilhelm von Humboldt. These facts are not yet generally known, and therefore we shall attempt to follow the plans of these distinguished men in detail.

Bunsen knew Mendelssohn from Rome and also from England, where he had long been Prussian ambassador. Humboldt had been friendly with the whole Mendelssohn family for years.[3] On October 30, 1840, Bunsen wrote to the King:

> Your Majesty's personality will also easily resolve the difficulty—of which I am fully aware—concerning Felix Mendelssohn's positions. Even if the two principal musical positions were not now occupied by Spontini and Rungenhagen, Felix would not want either of them and would probably reject both, the former most definitely. But fortunately, neither man is doing exactly what Your Majesty . . . has in mind. It is a matter of reintroducing the most beautiful and noble music into life—not only into the general life of the people, but also into the social life of the higher and highest classes of the most musical people in the world. It seems to me that this can come about if three aims that are now entirely unfulfilled can be realized:
>
> 1. An outstanding educational institution for all music, especially on the higher levels.
> 2. Performance of really appropriate music for the Divine Service, according to Your Majesty's directions.
> 3. Performance of great old and new oratorios, as a future branch of the theatrical productions—for the present, as royal festivities and celebrations.
>
> Is that not enough for one man and master? I rather think it would be too much for anyone but Felix Mendelssohn. . . .[4]

As can easily be seen, the summoning of Mendelssohn had already been considered in the King's circles. That Humboldt was actually the instigator of such plans we see from a letter of Bunsen to Humboldt, which he wrote the very next day. Here, Bunsen carefully weighs the chances of Mendelssohn's opponents in Berlin, and takes their disfavor into consideration. Then: "*Your* idea of a conservatory I find splendid; however, I should like to associate two items with this which you will surely not exclude."

There now follows the enumeration of exactly those points which he had already presented to the King. The end of this letter amusingly combines the traditional stinginess of Prussian officialdom with a quite astonishing prudishness: "The most magnificent musical creations must come to life . . . as a State institution. . . . But just think of all we can save on the opera and the horrid ballet, the barbarity of which has always shocked me!"[5]

Bunsen was no sentimental optimist. In his next letter to Humboldt, he foresees a "thorny path" for Mendelssohn in Berlin, but relies on the "proven sure-footedness" of the artist. As we see, this was all very beautifully and nobly conceived. But "thoughts live easily together . . ."; if Mendelssohn had had to do only with these two scholars and truly noble men, the Berlin project would indeed have developed splendidly. Unfortunately, however, the master came under the jurisdiction of a department—the minister of which was Von Eichhorn, a dull, unimaginative, and reactionary bureaucrat. The man with whom Mendelssohn dealt directly, and who was responsible for him, His Excellency von Massow, was an official whose attitude was noble but who was greatly handicapped by his position between the King and the Minister. He did try to ease Mendelssohn's path, but without initiative or courage and, therefore, without visible success.

The obstacle was, however, always Eichhorn, at least during the noteworthy *first* attempt.[6] Actually, Felix, exactly as Bunsen has proposed, tried three times to carry out the King's wishes and ideas: 1) as director of the music class of the Royal Academy of Arts; 2) as composer for the Royal Theatre and director of the Royal Orchestra; 3) as conductor and reorganizer of the Cathedral Choir, as general musical director of Evangelical church music, and as composer of works of sacred music which were mostly commissioned by the King.

THE FIRST ATTEMPT

It CANNOT be our task to go through the heaps of memoranda, reports, and documents concerning Mendelssohn in his official position. This would only stir up dust which already "smelled bad" in those days, as Felix observed. But we shall try to explain the rather confused affair as clearly as possible, in order to do justice to both sides.

First of all, the Academy of Arts was to be divided into four classes: painting, sculpture, architecture, and music. In its turn, the music class was to form the basis for a large conservatory, and then to be expanded into a center for German composers. Mendelssohn, who already had some administrative experience, declared himself ready to take over the direction of the —*de facto* still nonexistent—class, and asked von Massow to send him the existing statutes and the constitution of the class. When he received these, he was amazed. For ". . . Of the eleven subjects which they have set up, seven are actually useless, in fact, absurd. . . . From time to time I have read about these things in the *Staatszeitung* and laughed about them; but when a serious minister sends them . . . to one, then it's something to weep about."[7]

In order to achieve a real reform, Felix wrote a large *Pro-Memoria* for

Eichhorn, in which he sought for "a thorough change from the ground up, or a reform" of existing conditions, and mentioned many concrete details. This document, a far-seeing reorganization of higher musical studies, was pigeonholed by Eichhorn, without answer. Felix was irked, but von Massow succeeded in calming him down and getting him to make preparations to transfer his family to Berlin, for "once he is there his influence will take hold."[8]

But again there were difficulties. Felix, who had never chased after titles or decorations but knew his Berlin musicians well, demanded the official title of a Royal *Kapellmeister*, in order to be equipped with the necessary outward authority. (Inner authority meant nothing to the Berliners). He had been named *Kapellmeister* by the King of Saxony, but that did not count in Berlin. Eichhorn, however, denied him the title, and Felix grew stubborn. Again, von Massow acted as intermediary, and the title was granted, but all further efforts of the master to build up the Music Academy remained fruitless and were smothered "in the sand," as Felix calls it. Already here, he feels the senselessness of the undertaking. There had been promised him the position of a director in the Academy of Arts, a salary of 3000 thalers, and ample leave; but the directorship existed in name only, and, concerning his salary, he writes that he has not yet received a penny of it.[9] He no longer abandoned himself to any illusions: "the affair with the Conservatory is in the most distant field, that is, if it is in any field and not just in the air."[10]

To Klingemann, who tries to urge him to patience and recognition of his mission, Felix vents all his disappointment and anger. Above all, he defends himself against the idea that Leipzig was easygoing and his work found no echo, while in Berlin he could work for all Germany. "Really, it is exactly the opposite. . . . There in Berlin, all efforts are private efforts, without any consequences in the country at large—and these we get *here*, even though it is a little place. I did not move to Leipzig in order to have a quiet life. . . ."

Further, Mendelssohn emphasizes that he would have nothing against teaching activity in Berlin if he could remain a private individual. In that case he would just compose and live quietly. But the strange duality in Berlin life would ruin all such plans: "Big plans and tiny realization; big demands and tiny achievements; perfect criticism and miserable musicians; liberal ideas and the court servants out in the street."[11]

The result: the plan of a musical section of the Academy was, for the present, shelved, but the King did not let Mendelssohn go. More than ever, he clung to his project of setting up, in Berlin, a musical center for all Germany. Hensel, describing this first attempt, cannot suppress his indignation, and he is essentially right. For, during more than 25 years after Felix's memorandum, the founding of a Music Academy in Berlin remained stuck in the sand. But eventually, Mendelssohn's preparatory work came into its own; it played an important part in the organization of the *Staatliche Hochschule für Musik* in Berlin.

After this first failure, Mendelssohn could hardly wait to get back to Leipzig. But a *modus operandi* was arrived at. Felix would "place himself at the disposition" of the King for another year; during this year, the Academy question would be clarified and, if possible, resolved. So ended the first attempt.

THE SECOND ATTEMPT

STILL DURING these fruitless dealings, two people went into action who had been passive up till now; the King himself and his reader, *Hofrat* Ludwig Tieck. The latter had once chosen to read Sophocles' *Antigone* in the translation of Professor Boeckh. The King, who up till then had seen or read no Greek tragedy, was, as Bunsen reports, "delighted as with a new and brilliant discovery." Now nothing would do but that the King should see a Greek tragedy performed in its entirety.[12] Here, Bunsen's description contradicts the usually reliable report of Devrient, but agrees with Mendelssohn's own recollection. The latter wrote to David "Everyone was talking back and forth about it [Antigone] and no one wanted to get started. They wanted to put it off till late next year . . . and since the magnificence of the play took hold of me so, I got after old Tieck and said, 'Now or never!' And he was very nice and said 'now.' "[13]

According to Devrient, Tieck favored the postponement, but here we can probably depend on Mendelssohn's personal testimony. On the other hand, a marginal note of Devrient's deserves attention, for it indicates a conflict which could easily have wrecked the whole project.[14] We learn from Bunsen that Tieck praised *Antigone* to the pietistically tinged King as a drama "presaging Christianity." The scholarly Boeckh, however, was upset by this anachronism, and it came to an excited exchange of words between him and Tieck. This difference of interpretation of the play and the polemics following upon it are still reflected in Boeckh's explanations of the new edition and its music.[15] In contrast to the Romanticist Tieck, the great philologian derived the humanitarian ideas of the tragedy from the cultic practices and ideas of the Greeks, without saying a word about the Christian element.[16]

After overcoming the technical and intellectual difficulties, Mendelssohn set to work composing the music for *Antigone*. He was thoroughly aware of the problems which any musical treatment of the work must raise, and first began to experiment with the choruses. Since we shall speak of the work itself in the next chapter, we shall return to Mendelssohn's intentions on that occasion. Devrient has given us a vivid picture of these experimental attempts, which we may refer to here. "Not without careful testing of the task did Felix go about its solution."[17] Here, let us cite briefly the chronology of the work's composition. On September 9, Felix began to compose it; on October 10, the first reading rehearsal took place; on October 26 was the dress rehearsal, and on October 28 there took place the first performance at the Potsdam court theatre, in the presence of the King.

If we ask what is the significance of the work today, as living music (it has long been absent from theatre programs), only one answer is possible. The humanist Mendelssohn was directly touched by the tragedy, which places universal human feeling above all laws of cult and kingdom. But he was not the only one to feel this way; in general, the German educated public, and, thereafter, its English equivalent, felt a spiritual kinship with the ideas and principles of antique tragedy. We find ourselves at the beginning of that epoch which, in the works of E. Rohde, of Jacob Burckhardt and above all of Nietzsche, introduced quite new conclusions—differing from Winckelmann's and Goethe's idealized conception of Greek culture—concerning the origins of tragedy. Wagner, too, for whom Nietzsche's *Birth of Tragedy from the Spirit of Music* was a revelation, belongs to those who learned much from this generation of new humanists. Basically, Mendelssohn was following in the footsteps of his truly humanistic grandfather Moses Mendelssohn.[18] Devrient was probably right when he maintained that Mendelssohn's music had revived Greek tragedy in the grand style for the theatre public.[19]

But the Berlin critics and the Berlin public, as usual, were not on Mendelssohn's side. Rightly, he was annoyed by the well-meaning, patronizing, yet almost unbearably pedantic judgment on the part of that old fossil, Rellstab. The satirist Glassbrenner was, at least, more honest and straightforward. He poked fun, in the form of a parody, at the forced style of Donner's translation and at the whole idea of the revival of Greek tragedies. This satire had a political background insofar as many liberals complained that the King was trying to dictate the artistic taste of the public from above.

The *Antigone* effort had its scholarly consequences, too. All the daily newspapers had engaged philologists as critics, and a conference of the classical philologists (in Kassel) concerned itself with the new edition. The most outstanding scholars, among them Boeckh, Droysen, and Toelken, sided with the composer. In his detailed review, Boeckh gave a few additional suggestions which Mendelssohn took into consideration before the work went into print.

What was really the point at issue in this lively debate? It is hard to believe that the educated German public was interested in details such as, for instance, the treatment of the ancient metres; and the same is true of the instrumentation of the choruses, in which Mendelssohn distinguishes carefully between strophe and antistrophe. The essential problem was and remained the "modernization" of the tragedy in scenic, musical, and choreographic aspects. Basically, it is still the same today; modern French and American authors, as well as Hofmannsthal and Richard Strauss, everyone who dealt with ancient subjects had to cope with the same questions.

Droysen's rebuttal, directed against Rellstab, rejects the notion that the drama should have appeared on the stage exactly as it had long ago in Athens. In that case, Antigone would have been enacted by a man, the actors would have had to appear with tragic masks, and the like. But above all:

> Insofar as what is old belongs only to ancient times, one cannot revive it. But it has something that is great and important at all times, something immortal, and that should come to us in fresh and lively fashion today. . . . Mendelssohn speaks to us in strange and yet understandable tones; it is not antique music, but gives us the impression of antique music as it revealed itself to him. . . .[20]

Mendelssohn himself remained silent in the midst of the controversy. Indeed, when Professor Dehn, the editor of an important music magazine, asked him to say something about his own work, he declined the invitation, politely yet definitely. He had made it an unbreakable rule never to write anything concerning music for public magazines or "directly or indirectly to bring about the publication of an article on his own achievements." He realizes that this principle works to his disadvantage, but he cannot abandon it.[21] How differently Wagner would have acted, and did act, in a similar situation! Here, Mendelssohn's inborn aristocratic character speaks clearly. He did what he thought was right, without consideration for the howling of the mob, and kept quiet about it. In intimate circles, however, he spoke out. There, he emphasized that he did not want to write the kind of music which the ancient Greeks might have had. His music was to build a bridge between the antique play and modern man.[22]

As official composer to the King, Mendelssohn wrote three more works of incidental music: to A Midsummer Night's Dream, to Racine's Athalie, and to Sophocles' Oedipus at Kolonos. A fifth commission, to compose the choruses to Aeschylus' Orestie, he rejected after serious consideration. With that, his "theatrical mission" for the King was ended. We shall return again to this break, for that, in effect, was what it was.

While Athalie and Oedipus carried on antique tragedy in the French or Greek sense, A Midsummer Night's Dream is by no means a revival of a forgotten play, but, theatrically speaking, a new staging with music especially composed for that occasion. This time, it was not a matter of tragic ideas and effects, but of fantastic and comical ones.

Even more than in the case of the other works of incidental music, Mendelssohn was dependent on Tieck's understanding cooperation if the commissioned work was to succeed. Therefore, we shall attempt to look more closely at the relationship between these two "royal" artists.

Although he was personally enthusiastic about *Antigone* as a tragic drama, Mendelssohn was skeptical about the attempt to revive it: "The Berliners will be tired of Grecian culture for the time being. Now Tieck wants to feed them *A Midsummer Night's Dream*. Well, I'm all in favor of it and have written some music for it. . . ."[23]

Quite a jump on Tieck's part, from *Antigone* to *A Midsummer Night's Dream*! How to explain it? Here, the simplest interpretation seems to be the best: *Antigone* was revived to please the King, but Shakespeare's fantasy-comedy to please Tieck. And there can be no doubt that Shakespeare was nearer to the inmost nature of Tieck than all Greek tragedians lumped together.

Tieck's poetic significance and style must be considered if we wish to properly evaluate his role as a partner of Mendelssohn. All literary historians agree in crediting Tieck with being a *musical* poet *par excellence*. This is the judgment of F. Strich, O. Walzel, and Marianne Thaelmann. The latter explains:

> There exists [in Tieck's work] that mixture of reason and fantasy about which Gottsched and the Swiss [poets of the eighteenth century] already disputed. This always presents itself to the educated citizen either as critical reasoning or as fantastic obsession. In the musical empathy of the Romantic poets, it becomes a distinctly productive capacity.[24]

Now, Tieck had not only taken an active part in the sympathetic translation of the original work, he was also the director and responsible for the staging of that noteworthy performance of the play with Mendelssohn's music on October 14, 1843, in the *Neue Palais* in Potsdam. Aside from the court, only invited guests were admitted; only when the success of the play was beyond all question was it performed publicly in Berlin in the Royal Theatre—mostly before sold-out houses.

Like Wieland in his *Oberon* and Weber in his opera of the same name, Tieck and Mendelssohn experienced this "back to the original" as a return to the land of their youth, of early Romanticism.

> *Noch einmal sattlet mir den Hippogryphen, ihr Musen,*
> *Zum Ritt ins alte romantische Land!*

> Once more saddle the hippogryph, Muses,
> And carry me back to romantic domains!   (Wieland: *Oberon*)

All the magic of youthful reminiscences is poured over this wonderful work. Shakespeare had already given an important part to music in his stage-directions, but Mendelssohn went far beyond what was required. We shall discuss the details of his composition in the next chapter.

The first performance brought certain irritations. Tieck did not keep his promise to Mendelssohn; he divided the play into three acts, while Felix, who had followed Schlegel's four-act version, had composed three entractes. These splendid pieces now had to be played on an open stage on which nothing was happening. Then there was a long intermission, during which, in the Royal box, tea was served and court was held. David, who had come to the first performance with a large contingent of Leipzig friends, reports that during the whole introduction to the third act, the clatter of teaspoons and the courtly chatter caused so much disturbance that Mendelssohn flushed, then grew pale, and had to exercise utmost self-control in order not to break off furiously and run away.[25] To this was added the impertinence of several orchestra members, who allowed themselves some crude jokes. Already on the occasion of the *Antigone* performance, the master had been forced to realize that the Berlin musicians still did not take him quite seriously. Thus, we find very blunt observations about the Berlin musicians in his unpublished letters. He calls them "fawning, fresh, and servile"; only after the King had named him *Generalmusikdirektor* and given him other substantial honors did the behavior of the musicians improve. "Now they have taken up flattery and foot-scraping which is worth just as little." However, he did not put up with any nonsense, and had the jokesters severely fined at every provocation.[26] In short, Mendelssohn, even after the unqualified success of *A Midsummer Night's Dream*, was "very mad" again, and, at least from time to time, was trying to get away from Berlin.

Also, the narrow-mindedness of the Prussian nobility, whom he could not avoid in Berlin, upset him so much that he lost his sense of humor; especially when he had to listen to remarks like this: "What a shame that you wasted your beautiful music on such a stupid play!"[27] Felix answered in ice cold, malicious fashion, but in the family circle he raged with anger. Fanny's report, too, mentions this lack of understanding on the part of the higher ranks.[28] This was the reception which the most popular creation of the supposedly "always happy" Mendelssohn got in Berlin.

LIFE IN THREE CITIES

A DETAILED CHRONOLOGY of the journeys, visits, and concerts which Mendelssohn conducted, and the conferences in which he took part, would both confuse and even bore the most interested readers. Here, we shall confine ourselves to his most important guest appearances. The many journeys of these years would not be as time-wasting and strenuous today, in the age of jet planes, as over a hundred years ago. For the modern conductor, they have become more or less an occupational hazard which he endures with equanimity. For a creative musician, however, this craze for traveling is not the norm even today; and one can scarcely escape the prejudice that works which are conceived on a journey must somehow bear the stigma of unrest. But how can one recognize this stigma in the *Scotch* Symphony, the Violin Concerto, the incidental music to *A Midsummer Night's Dream?* Anyhow, Felix liked traveling, for all his moaning and groaning about it in his letters.

Mendelssohn spent his time, during the years 1841-1844, in Berlin, but also frequently in Leipzig. In between fall two extended visits in England (1842 and 1843), a long summer in Switzerland, many visits to Frankfurt, to which he was drawn ever more frequently, and professional activity in Düsseldorf (Lower Rhenish Music Festival, 1842), Zweibrücken (Music Festival, 1843), and Dresden (end of 1842), where he received the royal authorization for the founding of the Leipzig Conservatory.

How did his life in Berlin go? We can get a good idea of it from a letter to David:

> Last Wednesday, Thursday and Friday was *Antigone,* afterwards on Friday a concert for the King, Saturday Ernst's *soirée* with my trio, in between endless rehearsals and conferences, tomorrow again Ernst's soirée with the Kreutzer Sonata of Beethoven, Saturday again a concert for the King in Potsdam, Monday again a concert here with the *Lobgesang,* and Wednesday, Thursday and Friday again *Antigone.*[29]

Already at the beginning of 1842, the King had commissioned him to conduct a series of symphonic and choral concerts. Mendelssohn began with his *St. Paul* in the Royal Theatre; soon afterward, he directed the same work in the *Singakademie.* The critics of both performances hold the line between respectful appreciation and conservative opposition. In April, he directed his *Lobgesang* and played his own piano pieces. He might be criticized for having placed too many of his own works on his Berlin programs; and the attitude of several critics suggests the idea that they did not always want to accept this "royally" approved music without opposition. We are in the midst of the *Vormärz;* and certainly, antimonarchistic-liberal resentments played a role in the opposition to the Royal Court Composer. This situation did not get any better when the King decorated Mendelssohn with the highest civilian order, *Pour le Mérite,* and later named him *General-musikdirektor.*[30]

The irony of the situation is that Mendelssohn was a convinced liberal, and characterized himself as such; he wanted nothing to do with "noble society," that is, the courtiers, and often made fun of them. That did not hinder him from being quite fond of the King, in spite of the latter's aimless cultural and artistic policies. But his bitterness against those who surrounded the King, whom he quite rightly considered responsible for many of his difficulties, grew even more intense. It must have made him seem intolerably querulous to those gentlemen, who were accustomed to quite a different tone. Mendelssohn's bitterness is often expressed in tones of great pride, as, for example: "The whole court was in the Royal box, we were in ours"; or, "We do not need to sit where the officers of the guard and their like sit (Psalm I, Verse I)" The psalm quotation refers to the seat of the scornful and of the sinners.[31]

But not everything in Berlin was work, annoyance, and bitterness. He was together with his whole family again, saw his mother daily, met many old friends, among them Devrient, and, both as a listener and a participant, enjoyed Fanny's especially successful Sunday musicales. Besides Felix, artists like Ernst, Mme Pasta, Ganz, and Mlle Ungher-Sabatier took part in these; they performed before an audience of the choicest spirits of Berlin, among them Cornelius, Boeckh, Lepsius, Bunsen, von Humboldt, and many more. Liszt, too, who was in Berlin at this time, played once or twice in the Mendelssohn house, but the relationship between him and Felix had become somewhat strained. Mendelssohn severely condemned "the stupid jokes which he [Liszt] now plays with music itself."[32] He scorned the untrammeled exhibitionism of the mere virtuoso. David, who is of a single mind with Felix on this point, goes a step further and asks ironically; "Isn't Liszt giving concerts in the *Hasenheide*, for the regimental guardsmen, for a silver sixpence admission? He can have a real success there. . . ."[33]

Liszt's servile adulation of all nobility by birth seemed "miserable and unworthy" to Felix; it stood in sharp contrast with his own very reserved attitude, which was, indeed, one of rejection. As he himself says, his aversion to associating with the nobility had, if possible, increased since his coming to Berlin.[34]

At home, too, in the family, there were certain difficulties and friction, especially, among the women of the house. They began when Felix's brothers-in-law, perhaps at the instigation of their wives, objected to having Cecile constantly in the house. That was the principal reason why Felix this time (1842) took his wife to the Lower Rhenish Music Festival and to England; for Cecile objected to staying alone in the house with her mother-in-law and Fanny.

The Lower Rhenish Music Festival, again in Düsseldorf, presented a monster program:

First Day:	Fifth Symphony	Beethoven
	Israel in Egypt	Handel
Second Day:	Symphony *Lobgesang*	Mendelssohn
	Solemn March from *The Ruins of Athens*	Beethoven
	Overture *Hero and Leander*	Julius Rietz

	Motet [?]	J. Haydn
	Harvest Cantata	C. M. von Weber
Third Day:	*Egmont* Overture	Beethoven
	Aria from *Robert le Diable*	Meyerbeer
	Duet from *Israel*	Handel
	Overture [?]	J. Müller–Düsseldorf
	Aria from *Titus*	Mozart
	Piano Concerto in E flat Major	Beethoven
	(played and conducted by	
	Mendelssohn)	

In the chorus, over 400 persons sang; in the orchestra, 170 men played; and six soloists appeared.

It cannot be denied that Mendelssohn's concert programs take on a certain rigidity, in that practically all composers except Bach, Handel, Beethoven, Weber, and Mendelssohn are neglected. Granted that the three last-named were universally popular; but the neglect of Mozart, Haydn, Spohr, Schumann (whom, however, he always performed in Leipzig), not to speak of composers like Berlioz, Chopin, or Méhul, is obvious. Mendelssohn acted as if there were no French masters of importance. Rietz, whom Felix performed in Düsseldorf, was a personal friend of his and a local celebrity; his music, however, is thoroughly mediocre and boring. This is the front on which Wagner and his myrmidons were later to attack Mendelssohn; the one-sidedness of his direction and of his taste.

In the summer of 1842, he made his seventh visit to England, which lasted four weeks. First, in the Philharmonic Society, he performed his new symphony, the *Scotch*, to jubilant applause. Later, he conducted his *Hebrides* Overture, which had to be repeated, and played his G minor Piano Concerto. Meanwhile, as usual in England, he gave himself and his admirers a treat by playing and improvising on the organ. We hear of four or five such occasions, on which he always carried away his audiences with the power of his splendid polyphonic improvisations.[35]

He enjoyed an exceptional triumph at a concert in Exeter Hall which he was attending. When he was recognized, the public, consisting of over 3000 listeners, gave him an enthusiastic ovation under the leadership of Sir Robert Peel. He felt obligated to acknowledge this tribute at the organ. On a similar occasion, at a concert of the Sacred Harmonic Society, he played Bach's great triple fugue in E flat Major (*St. Anne* Fugue) with its prelude, and closed with improvised variations on Handel's *Harmonious Blacksmith*.[36]

The high point of the English journey was his invitation to Buckingham Palace, where he made music with Queen Victoria and the Prince Consort. Hensel gives a detailed account of this occasion; we cite a few of his observations and add some previously unknown details.

The King of Prussia had given Felix a letter of recommendation, in his own hand, to Prince Albert. The latter then invited the master to visit him in Buckingham Palace. On the second visit (July 9), there was an animated musical conversation between the Prince and Mendelssohn. Suddenly the Queen appeared alone, and immediately began to tidy up the room: the two enthusiasts had hauled out all manner of volumes of music. Then Prince Albert played a chorale on his organ, very neatly and musically, and the Queen listened "with great pleasure." Then Felix played, and improvised on themes from *St. Paul*, whereupon the royal pair joined in the chorus. Now, the Prince wanted the Queen to sing some of Mendelssohn's songs; but the music could not be found, although the Queen looked for it busily. The distinguished group then adjourned to the Queen's parlor; there, a volume of Mendelssohn's songs was finally found. And the "pretty, delightful Queen, who is so girlish, shyly friendly, and polite, and speaks German so well" now sang a song "quite delightfully, . . . cleanly, in strict time and with very nice interpretation." Actually, it was a song of Fanny's, and Felix told his listeners so. Then the Queen sang another of Felix's songs, after which Prince Albert performed Felix's song *Es ist ein Schnitter, heisst der Tod;* finally, Mendelssohn had to improvise again, on the *Schnitter Tod* theme.[37] The distinguished company wanted to hear as much as possible about the courts of Berlin and Dresden; "but I wasn't a very good storyteller, for I know little of court life," Felix observes at the end.

Later, in 1844, he was once more a guest of the Queen. This visit is little-known. Of it, he writes:

> Recently, I once more spent a few hours with the little Queen and Prince Albert all alone; we made music, chatted, and I amused myself superbly. I invited her to come to the Philharmonic, and the way she accepted immediately without letting anything stand in her way was delightful. Now she is coming next Monday with the whole appendix of potentates and court, and you can imagine what a tizzy the Philharmonic directors are in. . . .[38]

Already, he had asked permission to dedicate the *Scotch* Symphony to the Queen.[39]

Without a doubt, Prince Albert was the *spiritus rector* of this unusual invitation. The Prince had a great deal in common with our master, in spite of all social differences. First of all, he was a good musician; he played the organ and composed solid church music. Then he was the "intellectual" in the Royal family and in the English court. In this respect, he was far superior to the cabinet ministers; only Sir Robert Peel could compare with him in culture and understanding.

As we know, the Prince had to suffer greatly from the mistrust of the English nobility, directed against him as a German; all his life, he was regarded and treated as an "outsider." We shall return to this truly important man.

Cecile was warmly accepted by Felix's friends, Klingemann, Moscheles, and the Horsleys, who had not met her before. Her gentleness and beauty won the admiration of all, and especially Mme Moscheles grew very fond of her. This was all very different from conditions in Berlin, and Felix enjoyed the change of atmosphere to the full. On July 10, the happy pair left London and went to Frankfurt, where they spent some time with Cecile's relatives. Then they traveled to Switzerland, where Felix met his brother Paul and the latter's wife Albertine. Again Switzerland gave balm to his body and soul, and became his true refuge. In his letters he praises this "country of countries" as incomparably beautiful. There he sketched and painted to his heart's content, free of all cares, and was happy and light of heart.

The crass contrast between the atmosphere of understanding and appreciation which he had breathed in London and the stiff, rude tone at the Berlin court caused Felix to regret his return. He simply could not get used to Berlin again.

At this point, the increasing keenness of political thought in the whole Mendelssohn family must be mentioned. The personal documents of this time are full of bitterness and complaints about the growing reaction which was spearheaded by Eichhorn and the Prussian Junkers. Felix "jumped with joy" over the contents of the work *Vier Fragen, beantwortet von einem Ostpreussen* (Dr. Jacoby, who was sentenced to two and a half years in prison for writing it, but who was later acquitted). On the question of Jewish emancipation, Felix agreed with Jacoby's criticism, and he closes with the resigned words:

> However, the work has been forbidden, and we shall now see in how far it is merely a single lofty spirit which expresses its views here, or in how far this spirit has really permeated and warmed the whole nation. . . . Again, a melancholy feeling has overcome me, when one sees so clearly . . . that the way is open, paved, and clearly delineated which would lead all Germany to a transformation such as it has never had—and yet, no foot is ever set upon this path. . . .[40]

Just like Fanny, he was furious about the confiscation of Herwegh's writings and his banishment. They found this arbitrary prohibition infuriating and humiliating. Even the conservative Boeckh was "quite wild" about this foolish step of the reactionaries.[41]

If the obstructions of bureaucracy, the cool attitude of the public and the reactionary atmosphere in Prussia spoiled the Berlin position for him, intimate conflicts in his family also made his life more difficult. Fanny and Cecile loved one another at a distance, but not at close quarters. Cecile was not only jealous of Felix's sister, but of every woman who made eyes at her famous husband—and there were plenty of them. In Berlin, she really had no basis for this attitude, for Felix scarcely bothered to answer the occasional "propositions" of society ladies. The affair with Miss Louise Bendinen in London was something else again. Felix took such obvious pleasure in her company that his friend, the critic J. W. Davison, had to warn both parties against too obvious manifestations of their feelings.[42] Let us be fair; it would have demanded the self-sacrifice of a saint to resist the definite advances of many beautiful and also clever women. Thank goodness, Felix was not the plaster saint that his well-meaning friends have tried to make of him; he loved beautiful women and flirting with them. How far the flirtation may have gone in each individual case, we cannot know, and it is not really important. But Cecile had a certain right to be jealous from time to time, as she admits herself: "Well, I think it's a good thing that I am not there [in Berlin], at least for my jealousy. You must tell me so much—must keep nothing from me—until your lungs are worn out. . . ."[43]

For all these reasons, Felix was determined to leave Berlin as soon as possible, and to give up his duties to the King. He wrote attempting to take leave of the King, explaining the difficulties of his situation to him and asking permission to resign. But things turned out quite differently than he expected. In his explanatory letter to von Massow, he chiefly mentions the technical administrative difficulties which had gotten in the way of his work. He closes with the expression of his conviction that for him, in Berlin, there is no possibility of any musical activity of consequence.[44] Too, he mistrusted the assurances of Eichhorn that he was working on a definite improvement of the situation. Felix did not want to misuse the King's trust any longer with inactive waiting; therefore, he begged the King to grant him the privilege "of living and working for the present in some other place, where he could take an active part at once, and of awaiting his commands there."

At the same time, the master requested an audience. He had not taken this step lightly; as we hear from Fanny, he was deeply moved, wept, and with self-control waited for his dismissal. Nevertheless, he hoped to be released in the good graces of the King.[45]

Of this audience, we possess a lively account by Felix himself. From it, we learn essentially the following facts. Massow had told Felix that the King was very much upset about the request to resign. To everyone's surprise, however, the King showed himself very amiable, trustful, and understanding. He expressed his regret that Felix, through his departure, would leave a gap which the King could not fill again. And now Frederick William explained his personal plans to our master. They went like this: the King wanted to create an elite chorus, place the Royal Orchestra under Felix, and have both ensembles perform church music and oratorios in the

Cathedral, but also in concert halls. Also, Felix was to compose church music for the King, that is, for the Cathedral chorus. It would be the King's concern to establish the chorus and the orchestra, but he must be certain that Felix would want to play on the instrument created for him. Until this had happened, Felix was to have full freedom of action. He could go to Leipzig or also to Italy; only, the King must be able to count on his readiness. This, however, could be expected only if Felix stayed in his service.

This was a truly magnanimous offer, and Felix simply could not refuse it. Therefore, he accepted it, but asked the King to reduce his salary to 1500 thalers. However, Felix confesses in his report: ". . . to tell the truth, I thought more about my dear little mother than about anything else."[46] Thus began the third attempt.

Massow was beside himself with joy and could not get over the sudden change. He kept repeating, "No, really, if you still think of leaving. . . . !"[47]

To equip Mendelssohn with the necessary authority, the King, soon after this audience, named him *Generalmusikdirektor*. With this title, in theory, he was entrusted with the leadership and supervision of the Protestant church music of Prussia. But, in practice, things were quite different.

THE FOUNDING OF THE CONSERVATORY

FOR THE MOMENT, pending the reorganization of the Cathedral choir and the orchestra belonging to it, Felix found himself free. He used this respite to travel to Leipzig and there to dedicate the new *Gewandhaus* hall. First, however, he had to resign from the service of the Saxon King; relations between Prussia and Saxony were such that a Royal Saxon *Kapellmeister* could not at the same time be a Prussian *Generalmusikdirektor*. However, at the audience in Dresden during which he was released from Saxon service, he obtained permission to use Blümner's legacy of 20,000 thalers, which was at the disposal of the King for the founding of a conservatory. He now received assurance (for a conservatory in Leipzig which he had long planned) in a letter from Minister von Falkenstein, that the Saxon administration would take the institution under its protection and support it with important privileges.

So the Conservatory (on the official prospectus it is still modestly called "Music School") was provisionally opened on March 27, 1843; finally and formally, on April 3, in the *Gewandhaus*.[48] Felix, otherwise so enlightened, here succumbed to a superstition that may amuse us; he wanted to avoid opening on April 1, which he considered an unlucky day.[49] The historic "first faculty" consisted of the following teachers: Mendelssohn (for piano and ensemble, later also composition); Robert Schumann (piano and composition); Moritz Hauptmann (Thomas Cantor), one of the most important music theoreticians of the nineteenth century (music theory and counterpoint); Ferdinand David (violin); K. F. Becker (organ); L. Plaidy (piano); E. F. Wenzel (piano). C. A. Pohlenz, who had been appointed as singing teacher, died before the school opened and was replaced by Frau Grabau-Bünau and F. Boehme, who taught solo and choral singing. Not until 1846 did Mendelssohn succeed in securing his friend Moscheles as teacher of the highest piano classes in the Conservatory. Afterwards, Moscheles, with typical loyalty, served the Conservatory until his death.[50]

The opinions on Mendelssohn as a teacher vary widely. Alongside enthusiastic evaluations by E. Naumann, H. von Bülow, and von Wasielewsky, we have reports by Otto Goldschmidt (later to be Jenny Lind's husband) and Rockstro, which somewhat contradict that favorable picture. Mendelssohn himself did not take great pleasure in teaching, nor did he ascribe to himself real pedagogical talent: "Through repeated experiences I have convinced myself that I lack . . . real teaching talent. Whether I take too little pleasure in it or do not have the patience for it—in short, I do not succeed in it."[51]

Opposed to this is the testimony of H. von Bülow, according to which Mendelssohn "consented to give the boy [Bülow] a piano lesson of several hours," with incomparable patience. The impression gained on this occasion, the power of the hypnotic personality of the master to help the comparative immaturity of the chance pupil, understandably, "remained alive."[52]

Von Wasielewsky and Naumann likewise emphasized the wealth of stimulation they received from Mendelssohn. But when they go into details, they give a rather colorless picture of Mendelssohn as a teacher. Quite different, however, are Goldschmidt and Rockstro. They present the irritable master in lively fashion, yelling angrily, "You crazy fellow, the cats play like that!" or sardonically criticizing the Englishman, "This is a very ungentlemanlike modulation."[53] As a composition teacher, he inclined—wiser than any of his contemporaries and successors—to the method of style imitation as practised by aspiring composers (e.g., Haydn, Mozart, Beethoven, and Bruckner) for over 250 years. So, Mendelssohn advised his pupils to copy the form of a Haydn quartet exactly, and observed, "My teacher Zelter did the same thing with me."[54] This method, however, contradicts the Romantic ideal of originality at any price, of "blazing new trails." Mendelssohn seems less of a pedagogue when he interrupts two students who are enthusiastically playing Bach for him with the words, "Please let me come to the piano—I can do it better." Naturally he could do it better! But presumably this performance was more than he could take.[55] His influence as a pedagogue came, in general, more from his personality than from his actual teaching. Indisputable, however, is Mendelssohn's vision as an administrator. A purely external expansion of the Conservatory meant very little to him, and his wise moderation still deserves our respect. Thus, he says in one of his reports:

> . . . the students all want to compose and theorize, while I believe that solid practical activity, solid playing and keeping time, solid knowledge of all solid works, etc. are the principal things that one can and must teach. From these, all other knowledge can be derived automatically; anything further is not a matter of learning, but of God's gift. That I, in spite of the above, do not want to make a mere craft out of art goes without saying. . . .[56]

In the Conservatory, Mendelssohn's official rank was not quite clear. From the sources nothing definite can be learned, and the various documents seem to contradict each other. From the letters to Moscheles, it seems that Mendelssohn had neither been appointed as director of the Conservatory nor regarded himself as such.[57] On the contrary, he thinks of Moscheles as director of the institution. From the strictly legal standpoint, Conrad Schleinitz was the *de jure* director of the Conservatory, as Moscheles also reports.[58] In this sense, too, Schumann reports in his *Erinnerungen an Mendelssohn*: "Founding of the Conservatory and his attitude that he never wanted to be considered as director."[59]

Three months after the opening of the Conservatory, it numbered 33 male and 11 female students; these groups were strictly segregated from one another, even in teaching. Since Mendelssohn had already been accustomed at home to charity as a duty of mankind, he saw to it that there were six full scholarships available; thanks to his personal help, the number of these constantly increased. The same spirit is revealed by his urgent request to the council of the city of Leipzig, in which the master asked the city officials for increases in salaries for the *Gewandhaus* musicians. After some hesitation, it was granted—the second raise in eight years![60]

In December, 1842, his mother died, as easily and suddenly as his father. Though the mourning for her was not so hopelessly desperate as that for his father, her death broke many bonds which tied Felix to the paradise of his youth, the parental home, and thus to Berlin. He inherited the family home in common with Paul, but he left it to his sisters and brothers-in-law to decide if they wanted to live in it or not. To him, the beloved house seemed deserted and empty now. He found comfort in "half-mechanical work" (the revision of the *Walpurgisnacht*). The diligent work on the score gripped his attention, and helped him through the worst days.[61] Nonetheless, he, aged only 34, shows a tendency to quick fatigue and resignation which bodes no good; the letters to his brother, to Fanny, and to friends all sound tired and dispirited. This condition did improve, but the lack of vitality is shocking for the reader of the letters today.

In early 1843 there came two concerts with which the master was very concerned. He performed Niels Gade's C minor Symphony and was so taken with it that he wrote an enthusiastic letter to the composer. On the other hand, he underrated the appearance of Berlioz, whose music always remained foreign to him. In both cases, music history proved him wrong.

From Weimar, Berlioz had carefully inquired whether his visit in Leipzig would be welcome. Mendelssohn, thereupon, had most graciously invited him. Berlioz was sincerely thankful and was happy to see Felix again.[62] In his *Voyage Musical* and in his *Memoirs,* he set down several characteristic incidents of his Leipzig visit. The old acquaintances, who had not seen each other for twelve years, were a bit shy at first; but soon they understood each other better than ever.

> Mendelssohn was charming, attentive—excellent—in short, a wonderful young man in every respect. We exchanged our batons as a sign of our friendship. He is truly a great master. I say this in spite of his enthusiastic compliments for my *Romances* (for orchestra and violin) . . . for he never said a word about my symphonies, my overtures, or my Requiem. . . .[63]

In closing, he says, "Mendelssohn helped me like a brother; . . . his patience was inexhaustible."[64]

The letter concerning the exchange of batons caused quite a to-do among the musical Philistines of that day. In reality Berlioz intended with this gesture a parody on tht style of James Fennimore Cooper's Indian novels. This was in order to avoid sentimental outpourings of feeling, which Mendelssohn abhorred.[65]

On parting, he wrote in his friend's album: *Donec eris Felix, multos numerabis amicos.* (As long as you are Felix [happy] you will count many friends.) The clever joke of interpreting the word *felix* as a proper name here was fully appreciated by the real Felix.

With all his admiration of Mendelssohn's talent and his artistic integrity, Berlioz had one criticism: "He loves the dead much too much." How much more Berlioz would have sighed over Felix's "necrophilia" if he had remained in Leipzig! For Mendelssohn crowned his efforts to revive Bach with a concert on the occasion of the unveiling of the monument for which he, in earlier days, had raised the money through concerts of Bach's organ music. There were performed the *Ratswahl* cantata, the D minor harpsichord concerto, the D major prelude for violin solo (played by David), and the *Sanctus* from the B minor Mass. At the unveiling itself, the boys of St. Thomas', led by their cantor Moritz Hauptmann, sang the motet *Singet dem Herrn ein neues Lied.* Shortly before, Mendelssohn had celebrated the hundredth anniversary of the *Gewandhaus* concerts with a historical concert.[66] Leipzig was becoming quite an exciting place under the stimulating leadership of the master. The City Council recognized this thankfully by naming Mendelssohn an honorary citizen of Leipzig on April 13, 1843. Not quite a hundred years later, towards the end of the "Thousand-Year" Reich, his statue was removed and his citizenship was disallowed *post mortem.* Now, however, his name is again mentioned with honor in Leipzig. . . .

Suddenly, into his tightly planned program of work, there burst a command of the King of Prussia to arrange the Chorale *Herr Gott Dich loben wir* for chorus and orchestra. . . . "And that is the longest chorale and the most tedious work!" All this was for the thousandth anniversary of the Holy Roman Empire of the German Nation in Berlin. Here the historical irony is that, when this Empire still existed, Berlin either scarcely bothered about it or tried to destroy it. Felix set to work quite irritably; with no greater pleasure did he rehearse and conduct the performance of the work, or, as he called it, "the Thousand-Year Reich," in the Berlin Cathedral.[67] Scarcely returned from Berlin, he received the official news that the King had ordered the performance of *Antigone, A Midsummer Night's Dream,* and *Athalie* for September. The scores of the last two works were not even ready for the copyist, and Mendelssohn had "a gruesome amount of work to do" in order to finish the pieces in time. As usual in such cases, Felix had let himself be "put on the spot" unnecessarily. *Antigone* only needed a revision, and *Athalie* did not come to performance at all that year. So the master could have concentrated quietly on *A Midsummer Night's Dream.* He could hardly handle all the Royal wishes or commissions any more. Now the King of Saxony wanted to hear *St. Paul* under Mendelssohn's direction in Dresden, and the composer had to obey.

MENDELSSOHN AND WAGNER

To THIS DRESDEN performance we owe the first documentary testimony of Richard Wagner's relation *at that time* to Mendelssohn. Since Wagner had long forgotten about it, he could not let it disappear in the comfortable depths of his typical "theatrical" memory—as he did with other letters or documents. By chance, the manuscript of this report by Wagner was found in Berlin in 1898. As is well known, Wagner and his disciples tried to veil the real situation and his relation of those days to Mendelssohn behind an artfully painted curtain of racially influenced *Weltanschauung.* It will be necessary to evaluate the known and unknown documents of the two opponents *de novo.* Here, we must limit ourselves to what actually went on between the two masters from their acquaintanceship in 1835 to Mendelssohn's death in 1847, without going into the *ex post facto* constructions of Wagner and his cohorts from a much later time.

For this purpose, an enumeration and citation of a few documents suffices.

From the previously unpublished letters of the two masters let us select just one which Wagner wrote to Mendelssohn after the above-mentioned *St. Paul* performance. We must never forget that our information on the meetings of the two men is very one-sided: we are informed only through Wagner. A real service would be done to the music history of the nineteenth century with the publication of the previously unknown documents. In the above-mentioned letter, Wagner pays court to the composer of *St. Paul*, and ends with the words: "I am proud to belong to the nation which produced you and your *St. Paul*."[68]

The report of Wagner on the *St. Paul* performance was directed to the Intendant von Lüttichau and reads as follows:

> The last Psalm Sunday concert must be called one of the most brilliant, and left a deep impression with the unusually numerous listeners. Mendelssohn Bartholdy had been invited to direct the performance of his oratorio *St. Paul* in this concert. Through his willingness to respond to this invitation he brought us an exceptional pleasure—that of hearing a classic work reproduced under the personal direction of its creator. We had already become acquainted with this masterwork in two public performances, and yet it seemed as though we came to a real understanding of it only now, when the direct personal leadership of the master filled each of the executants with special devotion and made them so enthusiastic that the worth of the performance almost reached the heights of the work. . . .
>
> In this way, Mendelssohn Bartholdy showed us, in all perfection, a work which is a testimony to the highest flowering of art. The reflection that it was composed in our times fills us with justified pride for the age in which we live. . . .[69]

Here let us mention that Wagner, in his autobiography, does not say a word about the report to Lüttichau or the letter to Mendelssohn. In Berlin, Wagner often met Mendelssohn, as the following letter[70] shows:

> My dear, dear Mendelssohn,
>   I am really happy that you like me. If I have come a little closer to you, that is the nicest thing about my whole Berlin expedition.
>   God luck to you!
>   Your Richard Wagner
> Berlin, 10 Jan., 1844.

In Leipzig, too, Wagner enjoyed Mendelssohn's hospitality,[71] and entrusted his *Tannhäuser* Overture to him for the performance in the *Gewandhaus*.[72] Even in his *Judenthum in der Musik*, Wagner calls him a "Jew of the highest, most refined sense of honor" and praises his "richest specific abundance of talent."[73] In addition, the two masters met in 1843; then, rivalry is clearly sensed for the first time. On July 7, 1843, a statue of Frederick August I was unveiled in Dresden. On this occasion, Wagner, later to be a fighter on the barricades and a revolutionary, and Mendelssohn, the convinced liberal, composed festival songs. Wagner's opus has subsequently been published, while Mendelssohn's has remained in manuscript, and rightly so. Both compositions are monumentally mediocre. Wagner observes in his autobiography that "the effect of Mendelssohn's daring combination completely missed fire," while Wagner's "simple song seems to have made quite a good impression at a distance." (Mendelssohn had used the Saxon national hymn, a *contrafactum* of *God Save the King* with the text *Heil Dir im Rautenkranz*, as a *cantus firmus* in his composition.) However, Mendelssohn thanked Wagner in writing for the careful directing of his composition, and, in any case, paid the tribute which politeness demanded.[74] This is not the place to go more deeply into the extremely complex relationships between these two opposites. We may, however, say this much: when we study the contemporary sources, one fact emerges clearly: the opposition between the two, which Wagner later bolstered up with philosophical reasons, really depended on the irreconcilability of their personal natures and temperaments. The artist of the religious and the ethical, Mendelssohn, is opposed to the protagonist of passionate pathos, Wagner. Neither had understanding or even respect for the sphere of the other. However, in many artistic and political matters, Mendelssohn and Wagner took very similar stands.

BETWEEN LEIPZIG AND BERLIN

BERLIN KEPT INSISTING that the incidental music for the theatrical productions should be ready by September, 1843. This increased Mendelssohn's work load even more, and he decided to move back to Berlin. At first, he went there alone, in order to prepare the most important rehearsals. Then there began the familiar traveling back and forth:

To Berlin:	September 16
To Leipzig:	before October 1
To Berlin:	about October 10
To Leipzig:	October 22
To Berlin:	November 25, now with the whole family.

In between, there were weeks during which he "sat at his desk from early in the morning till late at night and wrote scores until his head was burning."[75] During this time came the performances of *A Midsummer Night's Dream*, the first *Gewandhause* concert of the new season (October 1) under Hiller, in which Felix played his Piano Concerto in G minor, and much more. On October 31, Clara Schumann, Hiller, and Mendelssohn were the soloists in the performance of Bach's Triple Concerto. On November 18, a farewell concert was tendered to the unwillingly leaving master; on this occasion, his Octet was performed. The casting of the instrumental parts was unique. David and another orchestra musician played first and second violins, Moritz Hauptmann and *Kapellmeister* Bach third and fourth; Gade and Mendelssohn took over the two violas, and the 'celli were entrusted to ⊍ewandhaus musicians.[76]

The experiment with Hiller as vice director harmed the Mendelssohn and Hiller friendship. Hiller wanted to feature too often the artistry of his wife, an experienced singer. However, her singing pleased neither Mendelssohn nor the Leipzig public. Then there was the inexperience of Hiller as a conductor, plus his lack of familiarity with the orchestra. The estrangement between the two friends lasted till Mendelssohn's death.[77]

Finally, on November 25, 1843, the master moved "with bag and baggage, wife and children to Berlin." This move was even harder for him than the first one. He did, however, have a secret consolation: his intention of accepting the invitation of the London Philharmonic Society, which had engaged him to direct six concerts. But this escapade would not take place until after Easter, 1844. Until then, he had to "submerge in Berlin" again.

Besides composing incidental music for the theatre, Mendelssohn, as we recall, also had to serve his King as director of the Cathedral Choir and of the subscription concerts of the Royal Orchestra. The preparatory organizational work and rehearsal of the choir had been carried out for the most part by Eduard Grell, the refined but excessively purist connoisseur of the Italian *a cappella* style. The task was hard, but artistically rewarding. Mendelssohn could not guess that he, the devout and sincerely believing Protestant, would clash with the clergy (or rather, with several personalities thereof), because of his church music. The bone of contention was the use of instruments, and the limitations which the Prussian *Agende* placed on Protestant church music even in the Cathedral. Nonetheless, Mendelssohn served his church and his King with his finest powers, and with the integrity which is characteristic of him. A series of worthwhile compositions for the Protestant church is Mendelssohn's legacy to the Berlin Cathedral Choir. We shall take a closer look at these works in the next chapter.

It seems to have been mainly the court preacher G. F. A. Strauss who made trouble for Mendelssohn. This orthodox-reformed clergyman, for whom "the *Agende* was the ideal liturgy,"[78] tended, in his sermons, to a "heated pathos,"[79] as his friends called it. But he did not want his thunder stolen by a musician. Through him, Felix had his troubles, above all because of using the harp in the 98th Psalm; probably because of its use in the street and tavern music of those days, the harp was considered the most profane instrument.

This time, the activity with the Royal Orchestra was more satisfactory. After the retirement of concertmaster Moeser and *Generalmusikdirektor* Spontini, its direction had been turned over to the conductors Henning and Taubert, with concertmasters Ries and Ganz. Actually, Mendelssohn was an intruder here, but he was on good terms with the leading musicians, and he was supported by the authority and the trust of the King. Ten concerts were given by the orchestra in the season 1843-44. Mendelssohn directed seven of these, and the success was significant; the great hall of the *Singakademie* was overcrowded, and about a hundred listeners had to be seated in the anteroom. It was no different in the Cathedral on holidays; even Fanny could hear her brother's music only by regularly renting a pew there. The programs of the orchestra were one-sidedly conservative; but one should not reproach Mendelssohn with not having tried to make the programs livelier and more varied. This effort, however, always broke down because of the lethargy of the public and the press, which was now completely under the thumb of the fossilized Rellstab. He took a stand against all modern music and against the participation of instrumental soloists; singers were a real thorn in his flesh.

The frequent performances of his stage music, of the Cathedral Choir, of the Royal Orchestra, and the Sunday musicales arranged by Fanny, gave Felix a wealth of variety in his work. In fact, he had acclimated himself in Berlin much better this time than before. This may have been partly due to his steadily growing, now international fame and the resulting increase in his self-confidence. Certainly the inner and outer satisfaction with his success in winning over the cold, hypercritical, and cynical Berliners gave him new wings. So Fanny could tell Rebecca about Felix's splendid mood and his irresistible charm. Not even the official and clerical difficulties could spoil his good mood this time.[80] He had no lack of society, either. Here, Felix was infected by the *genius loci* of Berlin, which the typical Berliner Fontane has called "the lack of sense of solemnity." His reports from this time are full of humorous observations.

He was courted by the English ambassador, Lord Westmoreland, who was an amateur composer; he had to put up with a great deal of his music. He did this with such good humor that Fanny was horrified, "nearer to crying than laughing." Finally, too, Mendelssohn begins to laugh at the musical public, and does not take it so tragically as in years gone by.

The regular Sunday musicales of Fanny were in their highest glory, and everybody flocked to them. "Liszt and eight princesses in the room . . . then came the *Walpurgisnacht*. . . ."[81] The high points of this brilliant season, which had begun with the first performance of *A Midsummer Night's Dream*, were the grandiose performances of Handel's *Israel in Egypt* and of Beethoven's Ninth Symphony. The former, given in the *Garnisonskirche*, was presented with a chorus of 450, orchestra, and organ (the part of which

Felix had already edited). Both performances had a far-reaching success; even the "granddaddy of critics," Rellstab, was enthusiastic. Meanwhile, the London season was advanced, and Felix hastened to fulfill his obligations there.

THE EIGHTH VISIT TO ENGLAND

IN NOVEMBER, 1843, Mendelssohn's friend Sterndale Bennett had invited him to direct the Philharmonic concerts. Mendelssohn could hardly wait to get back to his "dear old smoky city." He wanted to help out the Philharmonic Society, which had had severe deficits in the last few years, by lending the force of his name and personality. And this mission was a thoroughgoing success. Instead of a deficit of £300 there was a profit of more than £450 after Mendelssohn's departure.[82]

But he could not get away from Berlin without annoyance. The King had several times expressed the desire to have Aeschylus' *Eumenides* performed with music. He had expected Mendelssohn, who had solved this problem so beautifully in *Antigone*, to turn his hand to it this time as well. However, Mendelssohn's healthy artistic instinct revolted against this monstrous undertaking, and he merely promised to *try* to compose the music. But this was not good enough for his protector Baron Bunsen; he, who had recommended Mendelssohn to the King, felt personally injured by this lack of cooperation. He wrote Mendelssohn a preachy letter—a form of persuasion which was not unpopular in Victorian Europe. But Mendelssohn was too certain of his instinct and watched over his independence too carefully to take such a sermon quietly. He replied politely, but in a positive, firm tone, that he always wanted to obey the wishes of the King "but if I cannot do it with a *good artistic conscience*, then I shall try honestly to express . . . my objections, and if I do not make my point then I must go."

He closes the very energetic letter with the warning that "he cannot remain under such unstable conditions."[83] This hints at the resolution which he carried out in November of the same year. He would serve the King only for special performances and compositions, but for the rest would bring his stay in Berlin to a close.

The letter had been written in Frankfurt, on the way to England. Mendelssohn had left Cecile and the children with her family in Frankfurt, and so he traveled happily to England. This was his eighth and surely his most brilliantly successful visit to the island kingdom; he himself called the season "splendid," "a mad whirl," "the wildest sort of life." This is natural when we consider that the domesticated and "housebroken" Mendelssohn hardly ever got to bed before 1:30 a.m. on this trip. He enjoyed this vacation from the confines of court and marriage, and other fetters, to the utmost, and was proud to be able to report that he had made more music in these two months than previously in two years.

The concerts under his direction began with a monster program for which the master was not responsible, as he emphasizes.[84] (It must have given the hearers acute musical indigestion):

Part I

Symphony in C	Mozart
Aria "La Gita in Gondola"	Rossini
Concerto for Pianoforte in G	Beethoven
[Mendelssohn as soloist]	
Air "Ere Infancy's Bud"	Méhul
(*Joseph*)	
Concerto for Violoncello	Kummer
Overture and Suite in D	J. S. Bach
(First performance in this country)	

Part II

Symphony in B-flat	Haydn
Air "C'est un Caprice"	Adam
(*Cagliostro*)	
Concerto for Violin in A	Molique
Scene "La Religieuse"	Schubert
(accompanied by Dr. Mendelssohn)	
Overture *Egmont*	Beethoven

The most interesting parts of this musical feast in eleven courses are the Bach Suite (then performed for the first time) and the mysterious "Scene" by Schubert. Can this title conceal the *Ave Maria*, whose text is by Walter Scott? Was it perhaps performed as a pantomime or a melodrama? The English critics were very friendly to Mendelssohn, though very negative to Bach—as was the orchestra.[85] The leading critic, J. W. Davison, observed:[86] "The overture and *suite* of Bach must be regarded rather as a curiosity than a specimen of musical beauty. The first and longest part is an elaborate and fugued movement in the style of some of the overtures of Handel, but more obscure and less effective."

As a great German novelty, the master thought he would present Schubert's C major Symphony to the Londoners; but "the rude members of the band laughed so much at the repeated triplets in the last movement that he indignantly set it aside. . . ." (It was first performed by the Philharmonic in 1871, under Crusius.)[87] A smaller work of Schubert, the overture to *Fierabras*, was dismissed as follows by the musical oracle of London, Mr. Davison:[88] "[The work is] literally beneath criticism. . . . Perhaps a more overrated man never existed than this same Schubert. He has certainly written a few good songs, but what then? Has not every composer that ever composed written a few good songs?"

Mendelssohn was again so "mad" about such insolent stupidity that he withdrew his own overture, *Ruy Blas,* which had never been heard in England; no entreaties would change his mind; not until after his death could the piece be played in England. He had better luck with his other importation; he introduced his protegé Joseph Joachim, then thirteen years old, to the London public. Now, the Philharmonic had a statute forbidding the appearance of "child prodigies." But, on Mendelssohn's behalf, it was simply ignored. Though Bach and Schubert had displeased Mr. Davison, he was delighted with Joachim's playing. His criticism "No master could have played it [Beethoven's Violin Concerto] better" opened all the doors of the English musical world to the boy; thenceforth, he was loved and honored there just as Mendelssohn was.

> As conductor, he turned to the young soloist . . . so as to follow him dutifully, Mendelssohn's own subordinate position appearing to give him a degree of amusement. But it was very beautiful to see the pleasure it gave him to regard the boy at his side, not only with admiration, but with honor.[89]

Not content with this, the master reported in detail to Joachim's relatives on the wonderful debut of the "Posaunenengel" [angel of the trombone]. He closed with the plea that they should take him out of public life for the next two years and let him mature quietly, both physically and spiritually. The relatives followed this wise counsel.[90]

Spurred by Mendelssohn's concern for a reliable text of Handel's oratorios, the English Handel Society commissioned him to take charge of a critical edition of some of the great oratorios. Mendelssohn accepted and, while still in England, began with the critical examination of the autograph and the first editions of Handel's *Israel.* As he insisted upon the bare *Urtext,* the members of the Society were not too pleased; this was a time when one tried to "improve" on Handel, Bach, Gluck, and a number of other composers.

Of his own compositions, Mendelssohn performed his Scotch Symphony, the revised *Walpurgisnacht,* and the new music to *A Midsummer Night's Dream* (which, by popular demand, had to be given in two successive concerts) at the Philharmonic. In other institutions, he presented *St. Paul* (twice), the Scotch Symphony, quartets and quintets, and much more. In this period falls his acquaintance with Charles Dickens, the Alsagers, and the Ayrtons, all of whom he got to know through his old friends in the English gentry. Indeed, Klingemann did not exaggerate when he wrote that never before had a German artist been so loved and honored in England. In fact, Mendelssohn came into closer relationship with the Victorian middle class, so typical of England, than any other foreigner.[91]

Since he lived in the house of his intimate friend Klingemann and, therefore, saw him every day, we lack notes of events from this season. Such notes would have been of great interest. In spite of all *Erinnerungen* and *Recollections* of others, Mendelssohn himself is quiet about the musical and social details of his journey, and the letters of Benedict, Macfarren and other musicians scarcely mention anything interesting. Moscheles's *Diary*, too, mentions only social affairs and the appearances which he and Mendelssohn made together.[92]

On July 10, he crossed the Channel once more, and on July 15 he was happily reunited with his family in Soden (near Frankfurt).

There followed an idyll in the otherwise restless life of the master. He let the world go by, had a fine time with the children, ate lots of strawberries, and associated a great deal with the politically like-minded Hoffmann von Fallersleben, Freiligrath, and Lenau, who all lived nearby. That was a life to his taste: "Without dress coat, without piano, without visiting-cards, without carriage and horses; but with donkeys, with wild flowers, with music paper and sketchbook, with Cecile and the children—twice as good!"[93]

But he worked—now calm and certain of his goal—on his Violin Concerto, on *Elijah*, on the Organ sonatas, and also on a new symphony of which no trace has been found,[94] and he wished he could live this way for half a year. Giving and conducting concerts no longer pleased him, and he decided only reluctantly to travel to the Zweibrücken Music Festival (July 31-August 1) which was under his direction.

He need not have worried. For the whole round-trip sounds, in Felix's report, like a great wine journey in the heart of summer, interrupted only slightly by music. He performed his *St. Paul* and *Walpurgisnacht*, Beethoven's Fourth Symphony, and Marschner's *Bundeslied*. The rest is laughter, jollity, pleasure, and, above all, wine!

The fall began, and Felix braced himself for the decisive audience with the King. Ever since Bunsen had scolded him, he had been determined to get out of the Berlin situation, which he considered undignified. This appears in a draft of the answer to Bunsen, in which Mendelssohn already makes it quite plain that he is not tired of the King, but of Berlin conditions, and would withdraw at the first opportunity.[95]

On September 30, he came to Berlin and presented his request to the King. The latter, weary of the difficult, critical, sensitive, yet famous man, gave him full freedom on the condition that in the future he would be available for special commissions of the King and occasional festival performances in Berlin—for a salary of 1000 *Rheinthaler*. This princely generosity seems to have surprised Felix somewhat; but he rejoiced, accepted, and—had to stay, because the King 'had counted on him for the first orchestra concerts and, besides, wanted to hear *St. Paul* again. So things went on for a while, during which Felix, melancholy, bitter, but glad of the freedom he had won, could prepare for the farewell from his beloved sister. It was very difficult for both, and the diary notice of Fanny on this occasion must be understood from her loving heart. Somewhat exaggerating, Felix had congratulated Devrient on being summoned as *Oberregisseur* to the Royal Court Theatres in Dresden: "The first step out of Berlin is the first step to happiness."

And so, the noble experiment of a King who thought sentimentally and romantically, but took Schiller's ideas seriously, had failed. But it had not been in vain. Besides *Antigone* and church music, it resulted in the music to *A Midsummer Night's Dream*. This alone, we believe, would have justified the experiment. On November 30, 1844, Mendelssohn left Berlin for Frankfurt.

Once more he was free.

ℕotes

1. Prince Clemens Metternich, *Denkwürdigkeiten* (Munich, 1921), II, p. 385
2. Read Fanny's account of the celebration of the Order of the Swan (Hensel, *F. M.*, III, p. 110). Her word "Gefühlsschwobelei" [sentimental rubbish] strikes at the heart of the matter.
3. Wilma Hoecker, *Der Gesandte Bunsen als Vermittler zwischen Deutschland und England* (Göttingen, 1951), p. 94.
4. *Josias Freiher von Bunsen aus seinen Briefen, geschildert von seiner Witwe* (Leipzig, 1869), II, p. 142.
5. *Ibid.*
6. See Fanny's letter of September 4, 1844 (in Hensel's *F. M.*) in which she says: "this person, Eichhorn, really seems to have sworn death to any free intellectual activity; he is afraid of every mouse. . . . He is, however, only a tool; the whole difficulty comes from above. The eternal forbidding and suspecting . . . has really reached an extent which is quite insufferable."
7. Hensel, *F. M.*, II, p. 244.
8. Unpublished letter of von Massow of May 3, 1841.
9. Unpublished letter, August 28, 1841. ("Therefore everybody tells me that I am now entirely theirs. . . .")
10. Letter to F. David, in Hensel, *F. M.*, II, p. 249ff.
11. Letter to Klingemann of July 15, 1841.
12. Bunsen, *op. cit.*, II, p. 261.
13. Letter to F. David, October 21, 1841.
14. See Devrient, p. 212: "This play is nearest to modern-Christian understanding."
15. August Boeckh, *Des Sophokles Antigone, Griechisch und Deutsch* (Leipzig, 1884), p. 259ff.
16. W. Kraegenbrink, *Tieck als Vorleser* (Koenigsberg, n. d.).
17. Devrient, pp. 212ff.
18. With all admiration for Theodor Haecker's thoughtful essay—representative of Western civilization in the best sense—*Vergil, Vater des Abendlandes* (Fischer, 1958),

I cannot possibly subscribe to his aphoristically pointed sentence which proclaims: "A humanism devoid of theology is not tenable. Today, we are frantically seeking for 'Man,' but we seek something that does not exist: Autonomous Man." Haecker nowhere qualifies the nature of the postulated theology; for him, it was exclusively that of the Catholic Church. But one can also easily imagine a humanism with a Protestant, Jewish, Islamic, or Buddhist basis; furthermore, such humanism has existed and still exists today!

19. Devrient, *op. cit.*, p. 218.

20. G. Droysen, *Kleine Schriften zur alten Geshichte*, II, pp. 146ff.

21. Letter to S. Dehn of October 28, 1841.

22. Hensel, *F. M.*, II, pp. 241ff.

23. Letter of August 19, 1843, in Hensel, *F. M.*, III, p. 19.

24. Marianne Thaelmann, *Ludwig Tieck* (Bern, 1955), p. 38. See also F. Strich, *Der Dichter und die Zeit*, pp. 355ff., and O. Walzel, *Vom Geistesleben Alter und Neuer Zeit* (Leipzig, 1922), p. 105ff. "Tieck belongs, in Schiller's sense, to the musical poets."

25. David, *Briefe, op. cit.* p. 187.

26. *Ibid.*, p. 156ff.

27. Unpublished letter to Rebecca of October 29, 1843.

28. See Hensel, *F. M.*, III, p. 73. Characteristic of the degree of education of the Prussian high aristocracy is the following letter (unpublished of October 21, 1842): "Honored Herr Kappelmeister! [sic]. On behalf of Her Royal Highness, the Princess of Prussia, I have the pleasure of sending the enclosed material about the young Herr von Goete [sic], where Her Royal Highness will have occasion to speak, this summer, with Your Excellency, with the request that you return it to me at your earliest conveniennce [sic]. Respectfully yours, Countess Schweidnitz, Oberhofmeistern of Her Royal Highness the Princess of Prussia."

29. Letter to David, *op. cit.*, p. 177ff.

30. The civilian order *Pour le Mérite* was created on May 31, 1842. Mendelssohn, Meyerbeer, Rossini, and Liszt were the first Knights of the Order.

31. Unpublished letter, July 30, 1841.

32. David, *Briefe*, p. 146.

33. *Ibid*, p. 165.

34. Unpublished letter to Rebecca of December 23, 1843.

35. *Athenaeum* (London, June 18, 1842).

36. *Atlas* (June 18, 1842); *Musical World* (June 23, 1842).

37. See Hensel, *F. M.* I, pp. 26off.; *Goethe and Mendelssohn* (English ed.) p. 141; letter of June 22, 1842. Also we have used some unpublished material here.

38. Unpublished letter of June 7, 1841. In sharpest contrast to the noble attitude of the English royal family is the rude behavior of the Prussian Queen. She had asked for the piano reduction of the *Lobgesang;* the master prepared it in ten days. He received neither an acknowledgment nor a word of thanks from the Queen. (Unpublished letter of von Massow of October, 1841.)

39. Oddly, a written consent of the Queen is not to be found either in the Royal Archives in Windsor or in the British Museum; it is also lacking in Felix's correspondence.

40. Letter of March 3, 1841.

41. On the admittance of a Jew into the Royal Prussian Academy, which became the subject of a controversy, Lea reminds her son, in most sarcastic fashion, of a family story: "You know that this Academy once elected your grandfather, and Frederick II did not confirm the election, whereupon Moses said: 'Better than if the King had appointed me and the Academy had not confirmed me.'" (Unpublished letter of Lea of June 22, 1842).

42. *Grüne Bücher*, Vol. 16, pp. 160-61 (Oxford).

43. *Ibid.*, Vol. 15, October, 1842. Cecile's fearfulness is illuminated by the following passage: "Do you still sleep alone? I am terribly afraid every evening, and open and close all possible doors."

44. Letter to von Massow of October 23, 1842.

45. Diary of Fanny, entry of November 2, 1842.

46. Letter to Klingemann of November 23, 1842.

47. Ibid.

48. Festschrift zum 75. Bestehen des Kgl. Konservatoriums (Leipzig, 1918).

49. Letter from M. Hauptmann to Spohr of February 6, 1843.

50. Riemann-Einstein, Musiklexikon (article on Moscheles). See also Moscheles's diaries and letters (1846-1850).

51. Letter to Professor Naumann of September 19, 1839.

52. H. von Bülow, Gesammelte Schriften, III, p. 404.

53. Grove's Dictionary, 4th ed., article Mendelssohn.

54. Von Wasielewsky, Aus Siebzig Jahren (Stuttgart and Leipzig, 1897), pp. 35-36.

55. Ibid., p. 35. See also M. Hauptmann's letter to Hauser of June 13, 1843.

56. Letter to Moscheles of April 30, 1843.

57. Letter to Moscheles of April 15, 1843.

58. Aus Moscheles's Leben, letters and diaries, II, p. 131.

59. It seems that the editor of the Erinnerungen an Mendelssohn erroneously read the word nie (never) as nur (only). Dr. Boetticher simply leaves out the questionable word, so that quite another meaning emerges: "Founding of the Conservatory and his attitude that he wanted to be considered as director." This is exactly the opposite of the sentence in the letter to Moscheles and the correct reading of Schumann's text. See also the letter to Moscheles of December 20, 1845, in which it is very clear that Mendelssohn was not director and never wanted to be.

60. Request of Mendelssohn to the council of the city of Leipzig, October 3, 1843.

61. Letter to Klingemann of January 17, 1843.

62. J. Barzun, Berlioz and the Romantic Century, I, p. 432.

63. Berlioz, letter to Joseph d'Ortigue of February 28, 1842.

64. Berlioz, Memoirs, I, p. 54.

65. Why Professor Barzun, in his profound work on Berlioz, calls Berlioz's joking letter "unlucky" (I, p. 374), is not quite clear. The reader may judge for himself. "To Chief Mendelssohn! Great Chief! We have promised to exchange tomahawks. Here is mine, which is rough; yours too is plain. Only squaws and palefaces are fond of ornate weapons. Be my brother! And when the Great Spirit has sent us to the Happy Hunting Grounds, may our warriors hang up our tomahawks together at the entrance of the council." For the comically false interpretation of the letter, see Hensel, F. M., III, p. 2.

66. The program consisted of compositions of earlier conductors or Thomas Cantors: J. S. Bach, J. A. Hiller, J. G. Schicht, M. Hauptmann, and Mendelssohn.

67. The performance was solemnized by the "grand salvo" of 101 cannon shots. Mendelssohn must have been delighted!

68. Letter of Wagner to Mendelssohn of June –, 1843 (Oxford Collection); see also R. Wagner, Mein Leben (1911), I, p. 325.

69. This report, originally bound with a sketch of the oratorio text Das Liebesmahl der Apostel, was first discovered in 1898, in the Prussian State Library in Berlin.

70. Letter from Wagner, Oxford Collection, Vol. XIX, No. 19. See also letter from Wagner to Minna, January 8, 1844.

71. L. Spohr, Selbstbiographie, II, p. 306ff.

72. February 12, 1846.

73. R. Wagner, Das Judenthum in der Musik (Leipzig, 1869), p. 25. See also Mein Leben, I, pp. 399ff., and 284, where Wagner observes that the artistic success of Mendelssohn "had characteristic features which made it somewhat frightening."

74. R. Wagner, Mein Leben (1911), I, p. 309. Shortly afterwards, Wagner reported to Minna that he had dined with Mendelssohn; the latter had come on stage after the performance of The Flying Dutchman, had embraced Wagner and congratulated him most cordially. (Letter to Minna, January 8, 1844.)

75. Hensel, F.M., III, p. 53.

76. J. Wasielewski, op. cit., p. 78.

77. F. Hiller, *Erinnerungen an F.M.B.*, p. 190. See also R. Wagner, *Mein Leben*, I, pp. 351ff.; also Wasielewski, *op. cit.*, p. 68; and R. Sietz, *Aus Hillers Briefwechsel* (Cologne, 1958), p. 54.

78. *Allgemeine Deutsche Biographie*, article on G. F. A. Strauss.

79. *Ibid.*

80. Hensel, *F.M.*, III, p. 89, 114.

81. *Ibid.*, p. 116.

82. His honorarium was £250. From this, however, he had to pay all expenses, including travel for himself and his servants; therefore, he cannot have had much left over.

83. Letter to Bunsen of May 4, 1844.

84. Unpublished letter to Fanny of May 16, 1844.

85. *Grove's Dictionary*, 4th ed., article on Mendelssohn.

86. P. Scholes, *The Mirror of Music*, I, p. 414.

87. *Ibid.*, I, p. 416.

88. *Ibid.*

89. *Ibid.*, II, p. 834.

90. A. Moser, *J. Joachim*, pp. 52-55.

91. A long list of names of English friends is found in the letter to Klingemann of July 17, 1844.

92. He had to decline an invitation to Dublin, where the University wanted to give him the honorary doctorate, because of lack of time.

93. Hensel, *F.M.*, III, p. 177.

94. Mostly recently three leaves of a symphonic score have come to light; they might be remnants of this work. One page contains a stretto-like *Presto* of a symphonic movement.

95. Hensel, who evidently knew this draft, believes that already when he "left [in April] it was decided that he would not return permanently again." (*F.M.*, III, p. 191.) Compare the detailed description of Berlin musical life in Berlioz's *Voyage Musical*. Here we sense the truth of the old saying "the grass is always greener on the other side."

CHAPTER XVII

The Works of

1841-1844

But all the story of the night told over,
And all their minds transfigur'd so together,
More witnesseth than fancy's images
And grows to something of great constancy;
But howsoever, strange and admirable.

A Midsummer Night's Dream, Act V, Scene 1

MENDELSSOHN's position as "official composer" to a romantically minded King resulted in a number of works which owe their existence to the Royal preferences. But this does not mean that they are of lesser value.

A hundred years ago, the compositions written upon commission played a much greater role in the life of the composer than we are accustomed to today. Nearly all composers of the eighteenth century, and many of the nineteenth, wrote works upon commission or for a given historical or personal occasion. The categories "occasional" and "commissioned" music do not necessarily coincide. In most cases, the large "occasional" work attained no more than an ephemeral status. If we think of Beethoven's *Wellington's Victory*—written for the Vienna Congress—and the host of its successors, engendered by "patriotism" and/or every European war thereafter until our own day, we see readily that none of these compositions has become living music.

It is different with compositions commissioned by a patron. In the first place, these works are mostly planned on a grand scale. The challenge of a large form for the composer is more important than the extraneous (or accidental) demands of the patron that it be "tailor-made." At any rate, the *sine qua non* of the success of the large form is the composer's *will to greatness*. The basically different attitude of the composer, in this case, to the greatness of his task leads to the conclusion that the success of a large form depends far more on the artist's critical insight and intensity than has been assumed up till now.[1]

In the case of Mendelssohn, one might be inclined to suspect that the works which he wrote on commission for the Prussian King would suffer from his negative reaction to the Berlin atmosphere. But, in general, this is absolutely not the case. *Antigone, A Midsummer Night's Dream*, and *Athalie* all maintain a high standard of accomplishment, and the same is true of the liturgical compositions for the Berlin Cathedral Choir.

In this chapter, we shall confine ourself to the study of the following compositions:

Theatre music: Sophocles' *Antigone;* Sophocles' *Oedipus in Colonus;* Racine's *Athalie;* Shakespeare's *A Midsummer Night's Dream.* Religious music: Psalms for the Cathedral Choir; *Sechs Sprüche;* Hymns and Motets. Instrumental music: Scotch Symphony; Violin Concerto in E minor; Piano Trio· in C minor; Six Organ Sonatas.

THEATRE MUSIC

Antigone, Oedipus in Colonus, and Athalie

ONCE MORE, Mendelssohn was confronted with an archaic subject. In a Biblical oratorio, he had been able to count on his public's familiarity with the story and the language, since he clung strictly to the words of Holy Writ. In setting a Goethe ballad—the *Walpurgisnacht*—he could easily identify himself with a style which would make elements, bound to a particular period, understandable through the transcendental power of the poetry. But, in reviving ancient Greek tragedies, there was no possibility of taking public understanding for granted. German poetry had not absorbed antique subjects and forms to the same extent as had the Romance literatures, where they had always been cultivated since the Renaissance and Humanism. Even the efforts of Goethe and Schiller could not fundamentally change this state of affairs. Quite aside from the mythological components, with which the educated classes in Germany were also familiar, Mendelssohn had to fit his music to the antique Greek meters. Anyone who has read a Greek tragedy in the original text or in a faithful metrical translation can comprehend what this requirement means for a musician. What modern composer would willingly submit himself to the Procrustean bed of meter and meaning in, say, the following verses?

> Thou comest here to the land, o friend,
> Fam'd for fleet-footed steeds and blooming meadows,
> Thou standest now in Colonos' grove,
> Where the voices of nightingales resound,
> Floating in dulcet strains
> Thro' their temples of verdure

Where the thick woven ivy clings
Spreading over the sacred aisles;
Where, in security, ripens the fruitful vine,
Unscathed by beam, or stormwind.
And here roameth the bounteous God,
Gay and good Dionysos, ever greeted in lays,
Sung by the nymphs, who rear'd him.   (tr. Bartholomew)

Two strophes and the accompanying antistrophes were to be composed in this meter! Even in the poems—conceived and executed in the spirit of the German language—of a Hölderlin, we often note the constraint of a yoke willingly borne; all the more so in the compositions of his verses by Brahms, Wolf, or others. How much more difficult was the task here, where the cramped verses, set to music, interrupt the flow of the dramatic action! So it is no wonder that even a humanistic spirit like Mendelssohn, to whom the antique world was still very much alive, had to battle with the greatest difficulties in setting individual sections. Often, he overcame them in spite of everything; but, in general, the shackles of the ancient meters perceptibly impeded the flow of his musical invention. In order to remain within the metrical bonds, he often neglected the syntactical articulation of his music. No wonder that, today, the many new editions and paraphrases of Greek tragedies dispense with all metrical form, let alone keeping the original metrical feet.

But, for Mendelssohn's time, the myth and its poetic formulation were not enough. Everything had to be there: the mythological references for which one would need an encyclopedia to understand; the old meters; the strophes and antistrophes; the *stasimon;* the *parodos* of the male chorus. Even this far-reaching authenticity was not enough for the purists: they wanted Greek instruments, the old *modi* (or *nomoi*) of ancient Greek music, and their strictly syllabic character. But, to be consistent, they would have had to dispense with all chords and content themselves with a boring *Sprechgesang* of the chorus and actors. To the credit of the philologists, let it be said that they practically all supported Mendelssohn's solution of the problem—probably because they understood the difficulties of a sensible solution better than did criticasters à la Rellstab.

The tragedy *Antigone* is preceded by an introduction. Its slow opening portion (*Andante Maestoso*) fully reflects the tragic character; the rapid second section (*Allegro assai appassionato*) cannot maintain the iron tread of the beginning and degenerates into aimless rushing, in which the endlessly long cadences contradict the sense of the fast tempo. Of the choruses, the second, *Vieles Gewaltige lebt; doch nichts ist gewaltiger als der Mensch* (Wonders in Nature we see, and scan, but the chief of them all is man") was particularly attacked. But a connoisseur of tragedy like old Boeckh observed: "It is precisely the intelligent gayety which animates it that charmed us; this music seems to breathe all the delightfulness and sweetness of the Sophoclean Muse. . . ." The Bacchus chorus (No. 6) *Vielnamiger! Wonn' und Stolz der Kadmosjungfrau* (Fair Semele's high-born son, thou many-naméd one) is a beautiful, really enthusiastic piece, in which there are fore-shadowings of the quite differently intended *War March of the Priests* in *Athalie*.

The inserted melodramas, especially the funeral march at the end, are dramatically effective. In Mendelssohn's interpretation of *Antigone*, we see how far he had come from Winckelmann's formula for the spirit of an-tiquity, "Noble simplicity and calm grandeur." His interpretation is equally far-removed from the concept of Goethe's *Iphigenie* or Gluck's work of the same name. The presentation comes close to the irrational, to the awe-somely heroic—to that meaning of the "Goat Song" which Nietzsche and Wilamowitz were the first to summon up for us.

Oedipus at Colonus more or less follows *Antigone* in style and textual treatment. However, Mendelssohn permits himself more freedom from the *Choriambus* here, through the introduction of recitative sections. By this means, *Oedipus* becomes more effective, from the purely dramatic view-point, than is *Antigone* in its metrical strait jacket. Especially successful are the choruses No. 3 and No. 6; the latter contains the hollowly echoing an-tistrophe *Nie geboren zu sein, ist der Wünsche grösster* (Never to have been born is the greatest of wishes) which proclaims a heroic pessimism.

What was the significance of this experiment with Greek tragedy for the Europe of those days? We recall that once upon a time opera had been born from a famous and fruitful misunderstanding of Greek tragedy. Now, a new way of bringing these ancient masterworks to the public was sought. However sincerely we might sympathize with the private interests of a humanistically minded King, they meant little in his time. Even the Berliners had no understanding for these royal extravagances. Their mouthpiece, the caricaturist Glassbrenner, made it quite clear, in his impudent and humorous parodies, just how anachronistic the royal enthusiasm for tragedies—or love for the Greeks—seemed to his contemporaries. Yet, in spite of all his senti-mental foolishness, the Prussian King brought more honor to the German name than did his successors on the throne, William I and II, both of whom still tried to maintain a pseudotradition of antiquity in Prussia.

Be that as it may, in Germany the enthusiasm for Hellas, which had been fed from political sources since 1821, soon subsided. Since 1810, ancient German mythology had begun to displace the classical variety. With Heb-bel's and Wagner's Nibelung tragedies, the decisive battle was won. An-tiquity and its champions had to beat a rather shamefaced retreat—at least in the German-speaking sector of Europe. In France, England, and Italy the experiment of Greek tragedy gained ground, because it had been at home since the Renaissance. In spite of naturalism and surrealism, this tradition has continued; in our time it has been championed by great French and Italian authors and has also returned to the German theatre.

We must mention here a personality which contradicts the trend away from classicism in Germany. Only one thinker, perhaps the greatest German outsider of the nineteenth century, runs a more complex course. Friedrich Nietzsche, a philologist of the highest order, had first hoped for the "rebirth of tragedy out of the spirit of music." He had all but identified himself with Wagner, his German mythology, and his dramatic solutions. Only later, when Wagner attempted the old Romantic synthesis of fictitious Germandom and fictitious Christianity, did Nietzsche turn from him to *Carmen*, which he considered a modern opera written in the spirit of Hellenic tragedy. The same Nietzsche characterized Mendelssohn in general, and the incidental music to the tragedies in particular, very well when he wrote: "In Mendelssohn, they [the Wagnerians] miss the elemental shattering force (by the way, that is the talent of the Old Testament Jew). Mendelssohn finds a substitute in what he has, freedom within the law and noble emotions within the bounds of beauty."[2]

With Racine's *Athalie*, Mendelssohn entered different territory. Because of the Biblical nature of the subject, it was more familiar to him than Greek tragedy; yet Racine's dramatic style—typical for French literature of the period—was strange to him. *Athalie* is a work of Racine's old age, originally written for the boarding school at St. Cyr. It not only permitted music and song as the Greeks did, it required them. This time, the meter is no obstacle; everything is in Alexandrines or iambic blank verse.

Mendelssohn created a successful work, which not only fulfilled its function as incidental music, but also "set forth a series of mighty scenes which could easily be filled out into a full-length oratorio."[3]

The Overture breathes a Biblical, sacred atmosphere:

Example 55

Molto allegro

With great art and wealth of dramatic understanding, the master constructs the second chorus, which, beginning with choral recitatives, resolves into an idyllic duet of two sopranos (*O wie selig ist das Kind*), and closes with the symbolically intended paraphrase of *Verleih uns Frieden gnädiglich.* Naturally, the chorale is associated with different texts here. There is even a kind of "grail motif" when the high priest Joad anounces a noble vision to the despairing Israelites. The trumpet, amidst a flurry of high string *tremoli* and quivering woodwinds, intones the chorale *Vom Himmel hoch da komm ich her* on the words

> *Quelle Jérusalem nouvelle*
> *Sort du fond du désert, brillante de clartés, . . .*
> *Lève, Jérusalem, lève ta tête altière.*

> This new Jerusalem emerges from the desert,
> shining with brilliance . . .
> Raise, Jerusalem, raise thy lofty head.

Example 56

Musically, the following women's trio is an exquisite piece, but it retards the action. On the other hand, the brilliant *War March of the Priests* has a splendid effect, and also functions as an accompaniment to the change of scene. It foreshadows motifs of the famous *Wedding March.* But the most important piece in *Athalie* is the fifth number, beginning with the prayer *Gott unsrer Väter* (God of our Fathers). It contains antiphonal and responsorial chants, solemn prayers, lamentations and blessings; it juxtaposes sharp dramatic contrasts, which are introduced and resolved with a firm hand. Never does one have the feeling of the anachronistic or archaic, as occasionally happens in *Antigone*—not even at the appearance of Protestant chorales, which had disturbed many admirers of *St. Paul.*[4] The reason for this is probably that the chorale themes are never sung *in toto,* so that they are really understood simply as leitmotif-like symbols. *Athalie* is certainly worthy of a new edition and a revival in performance; this would prove the vitality of the work.

A Midsummer Night's Dream

Mendelssohn felt completely at home again in *A Midsummer Night's Dream*, the crowning glory of his four works for the Royal Theatre. Since we may assume that our readers are at least superficially acquainted with this composition, in the following comments we shall try to point out some of the subtle details in this perfect work of art.

In the whole music to *A Midsummer Night's Dream*, we may discern a sort of *Urlinie* (basic line) which recurs in all the self-contained movements. It consists of a descending tetrachord or pentachord, which appears in major, minor, and "minor-major" (mixed). Even the four famous introductory measures of the overture contain it latently:

Example 57a,

Example 57b

Example 57c

Example 57d

Example 57e

newts and blind-worms do no wrong!

Example 57f

Intermezzo

Example 57g

Children's Song

Example 57h

Melodrama

Example 57i

Nocturno

Example 57j

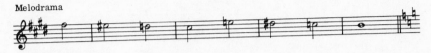

Example 57k

Example 57l

Almost all the harmony of the work is derived from the three transformations of the basic motif. This accounts for the many chromatic traits
—otherwise unusual in Mendelssohn—which are generated by the "mixed"
variant of the basic tetrachord. Other elements which Mendelssohn usually
avoided now come to the fore. Above all, we meet the "third-related"
tonalities (mediants)—for example, in the *Fairies' March*, in the *Wedding
March*—and above all in the melodramas. Also, there are Wagnerisms before
Wagner—for example, in the melancholy transition from the Intermezzo to
the merry concluding dance in A major, which contains the thematic substance of the *Wedding March*. (Example 57k.)

The motivic unity of the work is most clearly felt in its melodies, which
utilize the basic motif in the most varied transformations. A foreshadowing
of the "endless melody" in Wagner's sense may be noted here: measures
80-100 in the *Notturno*. The art of Mendelssohn displays itself—or hides
itself—most magnificently, and at the same time most subtly, in the formal
construction of the self-contained movements. Imperceptibly and surprisingly, the *Scherzo* is a real Sonata form. The *Intermezzo* is characterized
by two motifs which echo each other to which a parodistic *Nachtanz* in
2/4 time is added. The *Notturno* and *Wedding March* are in large three-part
song form; the *Rüpeltanz* (Clown's Dance) is a *Bergamasca,* just as announced by Bottom ("Will it please you . . . to hear a Bergomask dance
between two of our company?" Act V, Scene 1.) The finest subtleties

are found in No. 3, the first *Elves' Chorus*. Here, a descending minor tetrachord is used in the bass at the end of each strophe; the same tetrachord, now in major, supports the four-voiced chorus. The musical substance of the movement consists of a trill motif in the woodwinds, the tetrachord motif in the bass, and the melody of the elves' soprano—insignificant in itself, but artfully formed. (Music Example 57d.)

From these "petits riens" is spun a web that does not have its like in music literature. From here, it is only a short step to the pointillistic structure and technique of a Debussy, Ravel, or Roussel. The very sparse and transparent orchestration of the passage enhance this impression. In addition, Mendelssohn seems, consciously or unconsciously, to use the high woodwinds as a symbol of the elves, the bassoons, horns, and trumpets as representatives of mankind, and the strings as a neutral, quasi-choric background.

The music to *A Midsummer Night's Dream* has often been praised because of its close relationship in spirit with the Overture which Mendelssohn had composed seventeen years earlier. On the other hand, many critics have viewed this relationship as proof of a lack of artistic development in Mendelssohn's music. Now, this thematic relationship does exist, but, as it is usually presented, it has no decisive significance; it is rather a loose connection. Taken over into the incidental music were only the four introductory chords, the first eight measures of the Overture theme, and the motif of the Clowns' Dance. It would not have been hard for a lesser composer to evoke such associations. But the latent unity of *all the pieces*, which does not force itself on one's attention, their common origin from *one* basic idea—therein lies the charm, but also the greatness of this music. The question whether the common germ-motif was known to the artist as such, and whether he consciously formed his themes according to it, is completely irrelevant. We know that the unconscious often lends much more powerful impulses to the creative spirit than does the critical consciousness.[5] Another conclusion emerges from our analysis: the complexes of musical ideas which permeate the Overture must have lived on "underground" in Mendelssohn. They could unfold subconsciously; and, on the resumption of the familiar idea, the old associations reappeared in mysterious integration—but now on a significantly higher level of artistic power.

The atmosphere of the music is definitely Romantic in the literary sense of the word. But scarcely another Romanticist succeeded in creating such a unity of single pieces all derived from a basic motif. In comparison with this single instance, Berlioz, Liszt, and Wagner, who tried to force such unity externally by the use of leitmotifs, used a far more primitive method. It is indisputable that today we no longer understand Shakespeare in the Romantic sense that Mendelssohn did. Therefore, his incidental music has largely been lost to the theatre, but rescued in the concert hall. This state of affairs has but one disadvantage: because of it, the many clever, often enchanting melodramas have fallen by the wayside—among them, the parody funeral march of the artisans, which, in the theatre, is the perfect foil to the *Wedding March*.

RELIGIOUS MUSIC

WITH SOME EXCEPTIONS, the pieces which Mendelssohn wrote for the Berlin Cathedral Chorus at the request of the King appear in a rather ambiguous light, esthetically speaking. They correspond to the ideal of liturgical *Gebrauchsmusik* as little in his times as they do in ours; as concert music they are too liturgical, as church music too *concertante*. The same criticism has been made of the Masses of the Viennese Classicists, but unfairly. For their church music was real *Gebrauchsmusik;* in many respects, when it "sings in Austrian dialect," it is clinging to local tradition. If it was local custom that the *Christe eleison* should be sung by the solo soprano or that the *Osanna* should be written in rapid 3/4 time, the Austrian composers willingly submitted to such regional traditions; in fact, they probably created a few themselves. We can see this often enough in the masses of the Haydns (Joseph and Michael) as well as in those of Mozart. But this also means that their conception of church music was in agreement with that of the local clergy and of the faithful worshipers, or at least did not essentially deviate from it. Beethoven did not want to bow to this convention, and his successors contradicted it completely. In spite of all their love for the "folklike," in their church music they inclined towards an archaic ideal, often echoing the Palestrina style. With this, there were set up the significant pairs of opposites in church music:

> Subjective – objective
> Concertante – functional

These, as problems or as criteria for judgment, have dominated liturgical music ever since. If we think of the sacred works of Liszt, Berlioz, Brahms (*German Requiem*), Bruckner, etc., this setting up of precise concepts seems justified. As we have shown in earlier chapters, Mendelssohn was well aware of the dilemma with which the Prussian *Agende* confronted the Protestant composer. His "real" church music, that is, the music written for liturgical use, represented the watershed between two esthetic regions. As a disciple of Hegel, as a champion of Bach and Handel, he originally inclined towards the primacy of music; as the child of a puristic age, on the other hand, he had to do justice to the objective-liturgical ideal of his time. Where he tried to build a bridge between the two concepts, he could neither follow autonomous musical inspiration alone, nor retreat to the line of the merely psalmodizing or chorale-paraphrasing "official" church music director. So he simply upset the clergy, yet his music did not become "popular" as did that of Haydn and Mozart in the Austrian churches.

Catholic folk song had found, in the German and French hymn, a means of expression (if an artistically unsatisfactory one) for the congregation. For the music of the Mass itself, Latin and often polyphonic, was not very accessible to the majority of the faithful. On the other hand, in the German Protestant Church the chorale represented the only means of expression which both composer and congregation could use officially. So Mendelssohn saw himself forced, on the one hand, to use the chorale as a means of unification in the prescribed *Agende;* on the other hand, to find forms which, even without association with the chorale, could lend expression to the free religious feelings of the devout listeners. What stylistic means were at his disposal? With deep insight, Moritz Hauptmann, who, as Thomas Cantor, was quite familiar with these questions, explains the difficulties with which Mendelssohn had to struggle. He recognizes that, around 1850, everybody could imitate a Mendelssohn and do well at it; but Mendelssohn himself could imitate nobody. He knew no models which he could have followed.[6] He had only the psalm texts, and nothing else. As Hauptmann observes, his church music has no purely artistic and esthetic pretensions. Only the composer's deep religiosity and his trained artistic insight kept him on the right road. Perhaps Hauptmann should have added that Mendelssohn intuitively sought a counterpart to the refined Catholic hymn, and therefore, occasionally used folklike passages. On the whole, he remained true to the polyphonic style of Lutheran church music, but enriched it with responsorial and antiphonal forms borrowed from the repertoire of classic Italian church music.

Psalms

In the *a cappella* Psalms, Op. 78, Mendelssohn often makes use of psalmodizing text-treatment. Therefore, in these works, the word and the word accent dominate more than in his psalm-compositions with orchestra, the so-called "psalm-cantatas." But in these psalm-motets, too, the master allows himself noticeable liberties in text-treatment; especially, he is often careless in his declamation, as for example:

Example 58

Kommt, lasst uns an - be - ten

Rich - te mich, Gott.

In contrast to Liszt and the Wagnerians, Mendelssohn is no mood-composer, and disdains the musical illustration of words or phrases. Even as earlier, in his chorus *Der Jäger Abschied* (The Hunter's Farewell) at the words *aufgebaut so hoch dort droben* (built up so high there) he lets the melody and harmony *fall* gently, so now he is disinclined to deck out his music with external tone-symbolism. This strict restraint is to the benefit of the choruses. His soli or duets often suffer from a certain sentimental softness, which is explainable on the basis of the desire for sharp contrasts, but which often gives us banality instead of noble melody. On the other hand, the choruses of these Psalms belong to the best church music that Mendelssohn ever wrote. Powerful, antiphonal passages like the beginning of the second Psalm

Example 59

"founded a school" in the best sense of the word. The strictness of his concept of liturgical music is revealed in Psalm 22, which dispenses with all melodramatic effects (which could easily have been achieved in this Psalm—"My God, My God, why hast Thou forsaken me?") Here, he works with the simplest means and yet—or perhaps precisely because of this—attains a unity and purity of style which were rare in the nineteenth century.

Sechs Sprüche

On an equally high level with the Psalms stand the *Sechs Sprüche*, Op. 79. They are organized according to the Church year, and begin with Christmas. The texts consist of verses from the Psalms or the Gospels, and are set for eight-voiced double chorus *a cappella*. Such pieces easily fitted into the *Agende*, and soon became popular. The style is polyphonic, but easily accessible.

Example 60a

Mein Gott, mein Gott, wa - rum hast Du mich vor - las - sen?

heu - le, a - ber mei - ne Hil - fe ist fern.

Ich

Example 60b

Psalm 100

Mendelssohn pays more tribute to popular taste in his Psalm 100 for four-voiced mixed chorus (doubled in the middle section). The work has neither the strictness nor the strength of the psalm-motets, but, because of its elegant yet majestic character—a combination of traits which has become rare since Haydn—soon found is place. This work has an interesting previous history, unknown up till now.

In December, 1843, the *Neue Tempelverein* of Hamburg, a liberal synagogue, requested Mendelssohn to compose a psalm for the dedication of the new temple. Mendelssohn answered in the affirmative, and there followed a lively correspondence, from which we select only a few characteristic passages.[7]

Hamburg, Jan. 8, 1844

Honored Sir!

Please accept the heartiest thanks of the directorship of the New Temple Society for your kind and prompt willingness to accede to its wishes. We shall value greatly even a partial fulfillment of these wishes on your part, and shall use with great pleasure whatever psalm compositions you send us that are adaptable to our Divine service. . . .

Let us especially suggest the 24th, 84th, and 100th Psalms; especially of these Psalms, we should greatly desire the composition of a master. Our new temple building will be dedicated at Pentecost of this year, and the above-named Psalms seem to us admirably suited for this occasion. . . .

Jan. 21, 1844

The first two Psalms we named [24 and 84] should be treated as a cantata. If they are to be composed in a literal translation, the translation of your blessed grandfather (of renowned memory!) should be the basis; however, we leave it entirely up to you if you want to use a poetic version of these Psalms. . . . I must indicate the limitation that the accompaniment must be without *orchestra* and for the organ alone. . . .

Please accept, etc.

Dr. Fraenkel,
Direction of the Temple.

Mendelssohn, however, chose Psalm 100 in the translation of Luther. The *Tempelverein* accepted this choice, but asked the master to eliminate or smooth out certain "roughnesses and errors" in the text. Finally, Felix sent Psalm 100, set for four-voiced choir and small orchestra, to Hamburg, where its receipt was gratefully acknowledged on April 12, 1844. I could not ascertain the whereabouts of the manuscript of this composition. In a simplified version, the Psalm, now for chorus *a cappella,* was published without opus number by Bote and Bock in an anthology *Musica sacra.* So it appears, at any rate, since no copy of the Psalm written for Hamburg was to be found.

Psalm 98

Much more ambitious than Psalm 100 is the cantata-like composition of the 98th Psalm. Here the full orchestra goes into action, for the master wanted to do full justice to the text "O sing unto the Lord a new song." Nonetheless, in spite of the wealth of color, the work is not as good as we might hope. It is pompous in presentation, not without pretentious polyphony, but without musical substance worthy of the master. Because of the use of the harp in this work, Mendelssohn found himself in trouble with the higher clergy.[8]

English Te Deum

On the other hand, the *Te Deum* (We praise Thee), written for England, for four-voiced chorus and organ, shows Mendelssohn's art at its peak. The piece breathes a liturgical spirit without being stiff in effect, and its beauty of sound, in view of the sparse and transparant texture, comes as a pleasant surprise. This is the first of four pieces for the Anglican service; later, there followed *Nunc dimittis, Jubilate,* and *Magnificat,* all with English texts. Mature beauty and masterly economy of means speak from every line of this sacred music. (Examples 61a and 61b.)

Example 61a

Finally, let us mention a few hymns for solo voice and orchestra, which the master wrote at the King's wish. Of the occasional composition *An die Künstler (To the Artists,* Schiller) and similar purely ephemeral pieces, let us observe that they have all remained in manuscript—and rightly so.

INSTRUMENTAL MUSIC

Scotch Symphony

CERTAIN RECOLLECTIONS of the *Hebrides* remind us that parts of this Scotch Symphony had already been conceived many years before: for instance, measures 215-228, or the often criticized chromatic "wave," measures 450-475 of the first movement. Here, the master harked back to impressions and sketches from 1829. Much more than in his resumption of *A Midsummer Night's Dream*, there appear here elements of a tonal idiom which Mendelssohn had already outgrown in 1842. To this idiom belong the chromatic passages and the all-too-square symmetry of the phrases. Even the powerful, artfully developed climaxes of the first movement suffer from repetitions of certain cliché chord progressions. In spite of these retrogressions into the style of the "young" Mendelssohn, the first movement seems as if poured in a single mold, though the second theme rather lacks nobility of contour. Even a few turns of phrase which were already worn-out in that period do not really weaken the power of the movement. The effective pedal-points and the concise development of the themes certainly enhance it. In the whole first movement, we breathe the heavy, thick air of a Scottish Highland mist; accordingly, it is massively orchestrated and darkly colored. In marked contrast to this, the Scherzo (F major, 2/4) reminds us of the gay folk dances of the Scots, with their bagpipes. The theme is pentatonic, like Gaelic folk songs; it flies along in spirited and lively fashion—a perfect invention for the clari-

Example 61b

net. The movement is in sonata form, a rarity in scherzi, and attracts us
with its transparent instrumentation and variegated rhythms. Also, as is to
be expected in Mendelssohn, polyphonic subtleties are not lacking. Especially,
the clever imitations that "play tag" in measures 136-151 should be mentioned here. After a powerful reprise, which is performed by the whole
orchestra, the movement disappears in the delicate whispering of the strings,
pianissimo.

The third movement (*Adagio,* A major, 2/4) begins with a highly dramatic, recitative-like passage in the violins, which leads us to expect quite
a different sequel from the following noble, quiet song.[9] Unquestionably,
Mendelssohn here came under the spell of Beethoven's "Harp Quartet" (Op.
74), reminiscences of whose slow movement are clearly evident. The similarity does consist primarily in a cadence-motif that the two works have in
common; and yet, the whole noble, sustained mood of Mendelssohn's work
constantly reminds us of Beethoven's. Formally, the movement may best be
called a large two-part song form framed by a *ritornello*: It is especially
beautifully orchestrated, and follows well on the Scherzo. The last movement (*Allegro Vivacissimo,* A minor, C) is Mendelssohn's best symphonic
Finale. The thematic material consists of a powerful, turbulent, principal
idea, a transitional motif in eighth notes, and a sharply profiled second theme.
In this development, Mendelssohn makes use of Beethoven's "fragmenta-
tion technique" (169-182), then elaborates the transitional motif in a wonderful contrapuntal web whose art the listener hardly notices at first hearing,
and powerfully introduces the reprise with the second theme. After this,
the customary thematic coda does not follow. Instead, there is a completely new *Maestoso* in A major with a hymnic theme, a favorite idea of
the master, which he often wove into his church music:

Example 62

At first, it is played in the darker registers of the violas *divisi*, low clarinets, horns, and bassoons. But it unfolds to a triumphant apotheosis, and thus brings the symphony to an effective close. Alas, Mendelssohn did not succeed in really developing the theme of the apotheosis; it is simply repeated with increasing volume of sound. And so this splendidly constructed movement suffers from the somewhat disappointing ending, which sounds pompous enough, but whose substance is insufficient. Nonetheless, the Scotch Symphony on the whole belongs to the best symphonic music created between Beethoven and Bruckner.[10] It is no accident that Bruckner made many sketches and copies from this work and *Elijah*. In order to emphasize the unity of the work, Mendelssohn insisted that the symphony should be played without pauses between the individual movements; he felt that in this way the contrasts would show up to the best advantage.[11]

Violin Concerto in E Minor

It is not easy to say anything new about this popular work. It is a favorite of public and violinists alike. Its melodic and harmonic subtleties seem to us to deserve more thorough investigation than they have had till now, although we cannot go into too many technical details. But a few points which have scarcely been mentioned previously should be observed here. The themes of the first movement carry us away with their melodic power, yet they display astonishing simplicity and sparseness of harmonic means. The main theme is based entirely on the familiar chords of tonic, subdominant, and dominant; it permits itself a single excursion into the region of the subdominant, which gives the whole first movement its characteristic flavor. The second (lyrical) theme, in G major, uses the same simple chord progressions. Aside from a few modulations, there appear in the entire first movement only three chromatically rising bass lines, all at decisive points. These have a distinctly structural function; they are found at the end of the development, at the end of the reprise (after the famous written-out cadenza, for which Mendelssohn often called on the advice of his first interpreter, David) and at the end of the coda.[12] These chromatic passages, therefore, have a refrain-like character, and most effectively break up the otherwise purely diatonic framework of the movement. As his sketches show, Mendelssohn worked a long time on the violin part of these chromatic passages; he revised them three times, and in such a way that the formal function of these places is made as clear as possible.[13]

The subtle modulation from the end of the first movement (in E minor) to the C major of the second has often been admired. Again, it is chromatic, in contrast to the almost exclusively diatonic thematic material of the movement. The melody of the principal theme is perhaps a little too effeminate for the taste of our time; the seventh-leap at the beginning

Example 63a

Example 63b

requires great discretion and delicacy on the part of the violinist if he is not to become too "slushy"—and this must be avoided at all costs. In this middle movement, too, the subdominant region plays a significant role; it carries all the melodic high points (in F major and A minor). The transition to the brilliant Finale reminds us of the closing section of the first principal theme; it is formed with great finesse. The Finale itself is a sonata movement in form, but a firework scherzo in its musical substance. It has in common with the first movement the economy of harmonic means, as well as the contrast of diatonic themes and chromatic bass transitions. This time, such bass passages appear between first and second themes, between reprise and coda and between coda and closing cadence. Very effective for the violin virtuoso (and he must be a good one to get through the Finale at the tempo prescribed by Mendelssohn), it contains unsuspected subtleties. From this wellspring of invention, let us select just one instance. In the development, the first theme comes to G major. There, quite surprisingly, the solo violin develops a new lyrical melody, which is at once played out against the first theme in the orchestra. Later the roles are reversed, that is, the violin performs the orchestral theme and the 'celli the lyrical theme.

Example 63c

From the last movement

This is learnedly called double counterpoint; but nothing is further from dusty pedantry than this movement, sparkling with charm and wit. The superficial hearer notices none of this filigree work of graceful orchestral technique and highest thematic integration.

The Violin Concerto controls its wealth of invention in the classic spirit. It never wastes itself in "extraordinary details," "romantic extravagances," etc. Therefore, it is as alive today as it was a hundred years ago. Mendelssohn wrote it three years before his death. Under such circumstances, can we really speak of a diminution in his power of invention, or of lack of development? Yet these are the criticisms of his art made again and again by superficial authors and parroted by thoughtless readers or listeners. Let us rather point to the words of Arnold Schering, who, in his standard work on the instrumental concerto, writes:

> As, in its day, Mendelssohn's concerto was regarded as having saved the genre from the unnatural formalization which was gradually overtaking it, today it is regarded as a model of highest violinistic beauty. In its happy union of ennobled virtuosity and poetic significance of content, it has not been surpassed up till now. The former trait links it to the player, the latter to the public; the interests of both are caught by the contrasts of the movements.[14]

Piano Trio in C minor

In the case of works for the same grouping of instruments, it is always tempting to compare the later work with the corresponding earlier one. The older D minor Trio had been composed only six years before; so one might expect that present composition would be more or less similar. But it turned out quite differently; while the D minor Trio was so easily comprehensible as to approach the trivial, the later work remains free of such a popularizing attitude. Therefore, it has always been less accepted by the general public than the earlier Trio—quite unfairly! For, when we compare the two pieces movement for movement, the C minor Trio (Op. 66) surpasses the older work in all movements save the slow ones. It is much more careful in workmanship, makes greater demands on listeners and performers, and reaches a higher level.

The work was dedicated to Louis Spohr, the grand old man of German music, and Spohr himself played it with Mendelssohn. The principal theme is flexible and elastic. It develops from a so-called "open" motif; this alone makes it suitable for contrapuntal treatment. In fact, Mendelssohn made good use of polyphonic devices here, but, as always, in the most unforced and elegant fashion, without any "learned" pretensions. One might ask why a composer thinks it important to invent his themes in such a way that they are as useful as possible for contrapuntal treatment. This is a very appropriate question in applied music esthetics; for, after all, a work is not better or worse in direct ratio to the amount of polyphonic treatment. The esthetic value of contrapuntal style, above all in its imitative forms (canons, fugues, etc.), rests on three postulates of European musical esthetics, namely:

1. *Economy of means.* Obviously, this postulate is better fulfilled when all possibilities, including the contrapuntal-imitative ones, of the thematic material are fully utilized.

2. *Independence of voices in chamber music.* In a polyphonic style *each instrument* contributes essentially to the tonal fabric. If any instrument were given too much "filler" material and thus forced into a subordinate role with respect to the other instruments, neither the postulate of the equal rights of all instruments in chamber music nor the first postulate of economy could be fulfilled.

3. *Thematic integration.* It will always be the ideal of a composer to create unity in variety and vice versa. But no technique is better suited for this purpose than that of contrapuntal variation, for, through its inmost nature, it demands both thematic unity and organically necessary contrast.

Besides the adroit manner of writing and the brilliant handling of the thematic material, the strong preference for the darker sounds of the subdominant region is characteristic of this Trio, especially of the first movement. Most of the late works of our master show this inclination. In the coda of the first movement, the tonality descends from C minor to G flat major, C flat major, A flat minor, so that the hearer almost loses track of the tonal center C. Mendelssohn was aware of this, and tried to compensate for it through all-too-frequent repetition of the C minor closing cadence. The second (slow) movement is as insignificant in its invention as in its musical attitude. The spirit of Philistinism rules here; the *Gartenlaube* was not far away! On the other hand, the Scherzo is a flashing, sparkling piece, a kind of continuation of the scherzo of the Octet, but rougher, manlier, less spiderweb-like. In form, it is again a little experiment. The graceful lightness of the Trio, in G major, contrasts sharply with the frantic chase of the principal part, but is then linked with it in a radically abbreviated reprise. Therefore, we have a structure which may be diagrammed as follows:

A   B (Trio)   B–A (dovetailed and shortened)

This is certainly no conventional scheme!

By far the most significant movement of the work is the Finale. It strikes an unaccustomedly tragic note. Brahms did not like to be reminded of the similarity between his C minor Piano Quartet and this movement. He is said to have reacted mockingly to this: "Any silly ass can see that!" But what every "silly ass" cannot see is that two of the three themes of the Finale have a long history, and one of these was to have a distinguished future. The principal theme, or a variant thereof, is foreshadowed in the Gigue of Bach's English Suite in G minor. After Mendelssohn, it appears literally as the theme of the Scherzo of Brahms' F minor Sonata, Op. 5. Later, we still find hints of it in Bruckner (Third Symphony, first movement) and Mahler (Second Symphony, second movement).

In the development, Mendelssohn presents a chorale theme, *Vor Deinen Thron*, which he varies only slightly. This song of death is also known with other texts: e.g., *Ihr Knechte Gottes allzugleich* (Psalm 134), and *Herr Gott, Dich loben alle wir* (J. S. Bach). The melody comes from the Geneva Psalter of 1551. In the Coda, joined with the principal theme, it is elevated to hymnic splendor. Here, Mendelssohn, usually so sure of his sonorities, may have made a mistake in his choice of means. For this movement cries out for large orchestra: the original sounds like a piano reduction of a symphonic movement. In my opinion, it would be entirely justified to orchestrate this magnificent movement; this would enrich symphonic literature and would restore the otherwise forgotten piece to the realm of living music.

Six Organ Sonatas

Next to Bach's works, Mendelssohn's Organ Sonatas belong to the required repertory of all organists. However, one might meet with skepticism if one asserted that the purpose of the Six Sonatas and that of Bach's famous *Orgelbüchlein* was the same. And yet it is so. The English organists were deeply impressed by Mendelssohn's skill at the organ, by his independent

treatment of the pedals (derived from Bach) and by his polyphonic improvisation; they urged him to write some larger works for the organ. But
not until the publishers Coventry and Hollier concerned themselves with
the affair did the wish become reality. They commissioned the master to
compose several "Voluntaries" for the organ—this was the title which
Mendelssohn himself suggested.[15] In England, a voluntary was an organ solo
which was organically connected with the liturgy; it might be a chorale
variation, a prelude, or a little suite. Today, this expression is used only for
preludes or for postludes after a divine service.[16] The first advertisement of
the work had—with Mendelssohn's consent—the following rather commercial
text, in which the too specific expression "voluntary" was replaced by
"Sonata":[17]

MENDELSSOHN'S
SCHOOL OF ORGAN PLAYING
Messrs. Coventry and Hollier
Have the pleasure of announcing that they are about to publish,
by subscription,
SIX GRAND SONATAS FOR THE ORGAN
Composed by
Felix Mendelssohn Bartholdy

Added to this was a long "blurb" which praised Mendelssohn's achievements as composer and organist. This original title was later withdrawn by
Mendelssohn. Yet, we see that the purpose of the sonatas was, basically, as
didactic as that of the *Orgelbüchlein*, in whose title we read: "Wherein an
aspiring organist is directed how to carry out a chorale in all sorts of ways,
as well as to improve himself in the study of the pedal, since in the chorales
found herein the pedal is treated as an obligatory part."

With the exception of the Third Sonata, in which older sketches are
treated, these very diverse pieces were composed between August, 1844,
and January, 1845.

The name "sonata" is to be understood here in the broadest sense; neither
the preclassic nor the classic (Mannheim or Viennese) sonata form appears.[19]
Seen as a whole, these pieces might most appropriately be categorized as
organ suites. From the very beginning, they were widely recognized and
performed. Shortly after their appearance, one of the most important contemporary organists of England, Dr. Henry Gauntlett, reviewed them in
the *Morning Chronicle*.[20] Several observations in this review are still valid
today:

> The fourth sonata will be the favourite in England, and if not the most
> sublime or the most passionate, is yet the most beautiful of all the six.
> The first movement is a hymn of praise. It is a Bach prelude, and yet
> not Bach. Mendelssohn treats him as Melville treats the great Noncon-

formists and their Cerberus-headed orations. The epoch for expansion and extended analysis has passed away; the novelties of knotty points and subtle analogies are undesired; we want strong emotion, but it must be concentrated—it must strike sudden as the electric fluid—it must draw blood. And this is Mendelssohn. And this is the fourth sonata. Turn to the last page. Look at the second bar with its seventh on the F pedal; dwell on the heart-quivering march up the pedal from the lower E flat to the F on the second and third staves, and then "give thanks," and those "for ever!"

Schumann thought likewise. In a letter directed to the master, he admires the Sonatas unstintingly; he considers the Fifth and Sixth Sonatas the best pieces. He especially emphasizes the fine harmony: "in Mendelssohn's hands, it became ever purer and deeper in spiritual content."[21] M. Hauptmann spoke of the "artful simplicity" of the pieces, which was admired everywhere.[22] This judgment by contemporaries has not changed perceptibly in the course of a century. Even today, the Sonatas are considered *sine qua non* requirements for the organist, and the American Organists' Guild, in its admission examination, requires the performance of at least one polyphonic movement from these Sonatas.

In examining these compositions, we must ask whether their eighteen movements have elements in common, and, further, whether such or similar elements may be found in Mendelssohn's other sacred music. Six of the eighteen movements are rather folklike and songlike, ten belong to the category of strict polyphony, and two are brilliant, toccata-like concert pieces, perfectly idiomatic for the organ. (Sonata I, fourth movement; Sonata V, second movement.) We find similar proportions in the oratorios, psalms, and motets of Mendelssohn. To the songlike organ movements, there correspond the solos or duets, the arias or hymns of the religious works; to the strictly contrapuntal movements, the great choruses. The virtuosic movements have no counterpart in the sacred vocal music of the master— rather, in his concert pieces for piano or violin. This juxtaposition of almost harshly polyphonic movements on a grand scale with more delicate, rather sentimental arias is characteristic of all Mendelssohn's church music, aside from a few purely liturgical choral pieces. Nowhere is this contrast of musical expression more sharply delineated than in the Organ Sonatas. While the juxtaposition of such contrasting levels is often detrimental to the songlike pieces, it does round off the organ music (which is not really liturgical) rather nicely. After all, neither Bach nor Handel disdained to use "profane" elements in their organ music, and to ennoble them with their personal art.

The churchly spirit of the Sonatas comes most clearly to light when Mendelssohn uses chorales. The melody *Was Gott will, das g'scheh allzeit* dominates the first movement of the First Sonata; the penitential song *Aus tiefer Noth schrei ich zu dir* appears as a powerful *cantus firmus* in the Second

Sonata; a slight variation of *Dir, Dir, Jehova, will ich singen* opens the Fifth Sonata, but undergoes no further development. In grandiose fashion, the chorale *Vater unser im Himmelreich* permeates the Sixth Sonata. The first movement consists of six contrapuntal variations on it, quite in the sense of the old chorale partita; and the following fugue draws its principal theme from the intonation of the chorale. Even the closing movement in D major could have the beginning of the chorale (in major) as underlying bass. Also, the master did not hesitate to quote himself in two movements—both times with a slightly programmatic tendency. In the Third Sonata, as principal theme of the fugue in the opening movement, he introduces his own recitative from the *Lobgesang*: "Watchman, will the night soon pass?" In the developing turbulence of the fugue, he lets the chorale *Aus tiefer Noth* resound powerfully in the pedal bass. The last piece of the Six Sonatas, labelled *Finale* by Mendelssohn, is a quiet, lyrical closing piece strongly reminiscent of the beginning of the *Elijah* aria, "O rest in the Lord." The great oratorio was not yet completed at that time, but Mendelssohn was busily at work on it; it is likely that he wanted to symbolize the end of the Berlin conflicts, and his increasing resignation, in these tones.

A special word should be said about the harmony of the Sonatas. In general, it is not consistent with Mendelssohn's return to diatonicism and rejection of chromaticism; for he uses the latter extensively in many movements. The songlike movements are freer of it than are the polyphonic and virtuosic ones; thus, the splendid fugue with the *cantus, Aus tiefer Noth*, is a model of consequent chromaticism before *Tristan*. From such movements, it is only a short step to the wide-ranging chromatic organ fantasies of Max Reger, who was a greater admirer of Mendelssohn.

The organ, the polyphonic instrument *par excellence*, demands an intimate familiarity with the contrapuntal style not only from the organist, but also from the composer. Without this, organ works easily degenerate into the empty and pompous, as we can see in several impressionistic or "free" works of the nineteenth century. From his childhood, Mendelssohn had that familiarity with polyphony; already as a young lad, he acquired, through diligent practising, a specific organ technique, which is miles removed from that of the piano. In this connection, let us point out certain peculiarities of Mendelssohn's organ style:

1. The master likes stretti, that is, imitations of his themes in the same or the next measure, and he invents his motifs with this in mind.

2. The rising and falling scales in the pedal, which Mendelssohn often employs, are very effective and were, at this time, a new device.

3. The part-leading of the fugues is often very free—allowing itself many liberties, not always to the advantage of the movement in question.

Finally, let us point out several especially noteworthy movements. The first movement of the First Sonata very effectively unfolds the contrast in the sonorities of swell organ and great organ; the chorale is entrusted to the former, the figuration to the latter. The finely worked-out Adagio of the Second Sonata deserves special mention; it returns to the manner of writing of the Bach Organ Trios. In it, Mendelssohn develops a fugued duet between soprano and middle voice, against the dark background of a quietly moving contrapuntal web. The third Sonata begins festively (the movement was really intended for Fanny's wedding)[23], but the following fugue is tragic; however, it culminates in the hymnic tones of the beginning. A pastoral duet of the upper and middle voices, again set off in trio-like fashion, is the third movement of the Fourth Sonata; it requires a very skillful player. Finally, the Sixth Sonata is a masterpiece of the art of variation; not only in the chorale variations themselves, but also in the following fugue, the chorale theme is transformed. This is but one example of the high degree of thematic integration which Mendelssohn attained in the Organ Sonatas. Thus, the first two movements of the Second Sonata are founded on the basic motif C-B-C-D-E (E flat) which permeates the *Grave, Adagio,* and *Allegro maestoso.* In other movements, too, we find such "seeds," surely unknown to the composer, from which the thematic substance grows.

When we look at this significant nineteenth-century organ work as a whole, we can agree completely with the words of an English author: "So Mendelssohn here is scarcely the bright, melodious, genial Mendelssohn one finds, for example, in the 'Lieder ohne Worte'; and hardly the popular Mendelssohn, the Mendelssohn so deeply rooted in the hearts of the mass of English amateurs; but, more, the giant Mendelssohn, the wielder of the hammer of Thor. . . ."[24]

$\mathcal{N}otes$

1. Here we may appropriately cite Nietzsche's words: "The greatness of a musician . . . is measured by the intensity of his will, by the certainty with which chaos obeys his command and becomes form. . . .The greatness of a musician—in a word—is measured by his capacity for the grand style. The grand style consists in scorning little and brief beauties—it is rather the intention to develop long forms from brief motifs." (In *Kunst und Künstler,* No. 39.)

2. Nietzsche, *Nachlass 1878,* No. 129.

3. Kretzschmar, *Führer,* p. 618.

4. Contemporaries of Mendelssohn felt this way. See M. Hauptmann's letter to Hauser of February 3, 1849.

5. On this subject in a related field, see Professor Hadamard's observations in *The Psychology of Invention in the Mathematical Field* (New York, 1944).

6. Letter of Hauptmann to Hauser of January 18, 1850.

7. Oxford Collection, Vols. XV and XVI.

8. See Hensel, *F.M.,* III, pp. 114, 116.

9. The introduction of this movement also foreshadows a characteristic motif of the Violin Concerto.

10. See H. V. Bülow: "Among symphonies after Beethoven, Mendelssohn's *Scotch* Symphony occupies the highest rank as a self-contained work of art." See Bülow, *Ausgewöhlte Schriften* (Leipzig, 1896), III, p. 369-70.

11. The symphony is dedicated to Queen Victoria. However, a written agreement or thanks on the part of the Queen is to be found neither in the Royal Archives in Windsor nor in Mendelssohn's papers.

12. The chromatic bass progression even appears in the violin cadenza.

13. Sir George Grove, *Musical Times* (1906), p. 611.

14. A. Schering, *Geschichte des Instrumentalkonzerts* (Leipzig, 1906), p. 207.

15. See the correspondence between Mendelssohn and Coventry in F. G. Edwards, "Mendelssohn's Organ Sonatas," *Musical Times* (1901), December 1, p. 794ff; also, the letter of Mendelssohn to Fanny of July 25, 1844.

16. See *Grove's Dictionary*, article "Voluntary."

17. Mendelssohn received £60 as an honorarium from the publisher for this work.

18. F. G. Edwards, *op. cit.*

19. For Mendelssohn's own thoughts on the name "sonata," see R. Werner, *op. cit.*, p. 119, and the correspondence with Breitkopf and Härtel.

20. F. G. Edwards, *op. cit.*

21. Letter from Schumann, October 22, 1845. Professor Boetticher, understandably, *did not include this letter in his work*. With the worst will in the world, the Nazis could find no ammunition in it, but it does contain some harsh words about Wagner, who was sacrosanct to them.

22. Letter to Hauser, October 12, 1845.

23. The autograph of this organ piece for Fanny's wedding is found in the Library of Congress, Washington, D. C.

24. J. W. G. Hathaway, *Analysis of Mendelssohn's Organ Works* (London, 1898), p. 5.

CHAPTER XVIII *The* *Last* *Years*
and *Their* *Works*

> One so inwardly rich needs from the outside world nothing
> but a negative gift—namely, ample leisure to develop his spir-
> itual capacities and to enjoy his inner wealth; in other words,
> merely the permission to be himself all his life long. Against
> this, we must consider that those of great spiritual gifts, be-
> cause of their excessive nervous activity, are excessively sus-
> ceptible to pain in every form. Furthermore, their passionate
> temperament, caused by their sensitivity, engenders an incom-
> parably greater violence of the . . . emotions; and yet there
> are far more painful emotions than pleasant ones. . . .
> (Schopenhauer, *Aphorismen zur Lebensweisheit*, II)

IN FRANKFURT: *OTIUM CUM DIGNITATE*

FELIX had left Berlin as a free man; true, he was still in the service of the
Prussian King, but his official relationship was a very loose one. He planned
finally to carry out his dearest wish and live only for creative work and for
his family. He wanted to spend at least a year, perhaps two, in this style in
Frankfurt; to present himself occasionally before the King in Berlin; and to
look after his affairs in Leipzig.[1] Indeed, nearly a full year of such independence was granted to him before two personalities tore him away from this
idyll. We shall have more to say about them. Meanwhile, however, he refused all invitations, even one from London, where the Philharmonic Society
wanted to engage him as conductor. For the coming year, he was determined
not to be separated from his wife and children and not to undertake any
journeys even with them.[2] In fact, Mendelssohn had become so annoyed
with the London Philharmonic Orchestra, especially because of their rejection of compositions by Schubert and Bach, that he felt that "his relationship with the Philharmonic had given him an aversion to English musical
life which he could not get over easily." But he loved England as much as

ever, for "his heart is open to everything about that right little, tight little island."[3]

He did not even seriously consider a very lucrative invitation to direct a music festival in New York. He writes about it to his brother:

> I recently received an invitation to a music festival which flattered me so much that I even *look* flattered since then (as Cecile insists). To New York, it is; they tell me the friendliest things, prove that the whole trip there and return would take only four weeks, want to pay for my whole round trip, plus 1000 pounds, and arrange a concert that would bring me the same amount, assure me that my coming would elevate the whole state of music there.—What a pity that for me it is as impossible as a trip to the moon. But that I am flattered (and grateful) is not to be denied. . . .[4]

But even the Frankfurt idyll was not without its cares; the youngest son, Felix, became seriously ill, and was saved only by the tenderest care. The child always remained delicate, and outlived his father by only a few years. Excitement of another kind was caused him by the fate of his dearly beloved Klingemann. He, who had stubbornly remained a bachelor heretofore, now grew tired of being alone, and began to court Sophie Rosen, the sister of his late friend Professor Friedrich Rosen. She, in turn, looked on his suit with favor. Felix was jubilant over this good news and danced around the room when he received it. But his joy was premature. The King of Hanover, Ernst August of Cumberland—an unsympathetic figure in European history—was Klingemann's highest superior. He would give permission for the wedding only if the couple would return to Hanover to live. This would have meant severe material and social harm, even demotion, to Klingemann; therefore, he tried to have diplomatic pressure exerted on the stubborn King. At first, this was without success. For Ernst August was mixed up in an ugly legal hassle with the English Royal Family—specifically, with his cousin Victoria —concerning the Crown Jewels, which Victoria did not want to give up without concessions on his part. Therefore, Ernst August (though English himself) had no good word for anything English, including his own representatives in London. Not until he had won the lawsuit concerning the Crown Jewels did his mood improve. Then, he "graciously" gave his permission for the wedding.[5] This is a real story from the *Vormärz*; but, in Germany, many things may recur, as the prohibition of racially mixed marriages in more recent times has shown.

Mendelssohn was at this time intensively occupied with a series of works which we shall discuss later. But he tired rapidly now, and could seldom work concentratedly for an extended period of time. However, he deceived himself about his state of health, and quite consciously so, as he confirms to Droysen: "It is a virtue to deceive oneself."[6] Only when Rebecca questioned him relentlessly, he had to admit: "I myself am as you know me, but what you do not know about me is this: that for some time, I feel the need for outward repose (*not* travelling, *not* conducting, *not* performing) so strongly that I must yield to it. God willing, I hope to organize my life this way for the whole year...."[7]

He deceives himself again when he maintains that a "monotonous, quiet life" is especially pleasing to him or that he was born for such a "still, quiet existence." For a rest period, a longer period of recovery, it was certainly the right thing; as Mendelssohn's real way of life, it was completely unsuitable. But he still had sufficient sense of humor to laugh at his own self-deceptions, himself, and his work, and this gift made him—quick-tempered and irritable as he had become—bearable, especially when he laughed with all his heart. So, for example, he astonished all of his dear ones and friends with his wild merriment when he saw the *Punch* caricatures of the performance of his *Antigone* in London. He was especially amused by the leader of the chorus, "whose plaid trousers peeped out underneath his robe." That the female *corps de ballet* tripped along during the Bacchus chorus also amused him greatly, although he added that it was no joke.

From the Berlin bureaucrats, he heard but seldom. An interesting exception was the letter from Minister Eichhorn, which inquires stiffly, but politely, if Mendelssohn would be willing, in case of a reform of the Royal Academy of Arts, to take over the direction of the school for musical composition. Mendelssohn answered with a series of questions concerning the planned reform, the answers to which would determine his decision in the affair. The Minister's reply was in the highest degree discouraging, for it did not go into any of the concrete questions of the master and limited itself to platitudes in legal parlance.[8] Something else again was the letter of Cabinet Councillor von Mueller, who, in an impertinent tone which would have suited a policeman better than a Cabinet Councillor, scolded Mendelssohn for his refusal to compose *The Eumenides*. Mendelssohn was not the man to take such epistles calmly; he answered in a frigidly polite bureaucratic style, in short sentences, but does break out in one sentence. There, he says: "The condensation of the *Orestie* into one play increases these difficulties most extraordinarily, and I dare say that no musician now living would be able to fulfill this tremendous task conscientiously—let alone my being able to do it."[9]

The previously mentioned dispute with the Handel Society became quite extended, too, since Mendelssohn stuck to his resolve not to add anything to the *Urtext*, not even agogic and dynamic signs. He would not tolerate even tempo indications or suggestions. These letters are most informative, for they show Mendelssohn's conscientiousness as an editor—which, in this case, reaches the point of pedantry—and his uncommon sense of artistic responsibility.

During this time, however, he had not been idle; indeed, that was never possible for him. He worked on *Elijah*, began a Symphony (of which no trace seems to have remained),[10] finished his Second String Quintet and the great Catholic choral work *Lauda Sion*, and wrote numerous songs for single voice and chorus. And so this life "in Tusculum" could have continued beautifully, if the King of Saxony had not suddenly taken an interest in him and if Jenny Lind had not insisted on his return to public musical life.

PEGASUS YOKED ONCE MORE

MENDELSSOHN HAD BECOME an object of prestige, for the possession of whom two Kings (of Saxony and of Prussia) vied. The Saxon Minister von Falkenstein had been trying for years to lure Mendelssohn to Dresden, and these plans were now most vigorously forwarded by Geheimrat von Lüttichau, the general director of the Royal Saxon Orchestra.[11] Felix might almost have been maneuvered into an official position similar to that he had occupied in Berlin. But he had learned from experience and knew how to avoid a Saxon court position; diplomatically, he played von Falkenstein's urgent wish that he resume the leadership of the *Gewandhaus* concerts against von Lüttichau's desire to win him for Dresden. Furthermore, he emphasized, and we can imagine him winking slyly as he did so, "that he was ready to make music or play *as a private individual*, both for the King and otherwise in Dresden, with the greatest pleasure; but he would not be in a position to assume any official relationship there; indeed, as he knew musical life there, such a step would be positively *harmful*. . . ."[12] But even this wise reserve was used against him by Richard Wagner, who was not ashamed to speak of Mendelssohn as a "secret music director with a secret salary of 2000 thalers," ostensibly according to information from von Falkenstein. This poisonous slander, which Wagner did not dare publish during his own lifetime, and which attempts to brand Mendelssohn's artistic idealism as hypocrisy (Mendelssohn had given up 2000 thalers salary in Berlin!) is untrue from beginning to end. The one tiny kernel of fact is that the King of Saxony set aside a nominal salary for Mendelssohn for occasional performances in Dresden.[13]

So, in the middle of August, 1845, Mendelssohn, at the urgent wish of his Leipzig friends and of Minister von Falkenstein, returned to the familiar scene of his labors. But the daily work of the directorship bored him now, when, indeed, it did not actively irritate him. All the more was he driven towards creative work; he wanted to finish *Elijah*. Devrient, then chief director of the Dresden Theatre, visited his old friend from time to time, and remembers having explained to him that he, Mendelssohn, "confused his urge towards activity with his creative urge."[14] Now, such an observation was not tossed off casually or maliciously, and many compositions or fragments of compositions from those last years seem, indeed, to justify Devrient's warning. Mendelssohn's restlessness—after the year of rest in Frankfurt—was really strange and hard to understand. The "urge towards activity" which now appeared was no new trait in Felix's character. It may well be interpreted as an expenditure of energy motivated by the fear of not moving forward. And here, we believe we have established the psychological basis of this restless activity; it is flight, flight from death. For death is not only not-being, but also not-doing, i.e., total stillness. Not everyone reacts in like manner to so universal and elemental a feeling as the fear of death. The strict training of his parents had made the master unfit for any long period of idleness, which usually, for him, was associated with guilt feelings. So, out of fear, he sought a way out in ceaseless activity, without quite realizing it himself.

About the same time, that is, during the years 1844-47, Mendelssohn shows a distinct change in his political attitude. True, he remains a liberal; but now, he hates and fears the mob, the mass-man, as his archenemy and the enemy of every real development. There is much evidence that he abhorred a mere democracy of the majority, a tyranny of "quantity over quality."[15] For this attitude, there are, naturally, conscious motivations brought about by training and inheritance, and equally strong unconscious ones. For the political thinker Mendelssohn, the unity of aims and methods was a categorical postulate of greatest importance. Therefore, the first signs of the forthcoming revolution were distinctly unsympathetic to him; for the movement towards freedom was intimately linked with the movement towards a Greater Germany, and was, indeed, carried by it. But all "Greater German fuss and feathers" (Grossdeutsche Gethue) as he called it. was contrary to his taste, for, not without reason, he feared acts of mob violence on the part of precisely this element. He scorned mass demonstrations and all means based on mere force; in the last analysis, the wisdom of his great ancestors, which lived on in his blood, must have signified to him that great thinkers, artists, and creators of all sorts must necessarily be aristocrats— not always by birth. They stand alone, are thrown on their own resources, and may hardly ever count on the help of the great mass of people—never on its understanding.

At first, his misgiving concerned only two or three of the current controversies: the awakening of German Catholicism with a political potential, the stiffening of the Protestant Church, and the question of the "untrained representatives of the people" whom Felix considered dilettantes of public life. In contrast to the almost completely unpolitical Schumann, but equally so to the over-political Junges Deutschland, Mendelssohn sought a middle way between conservatism and liberalism. In this, he was of one mind with his friend Droysen, but quite different from Devrient, Wagner, and Laube, not to mention Heine. The path he followed was hard to define and even harder to stick to. The Mendelssohns did not have to be aroused by Bettina's secondhand descriptions of misery among the proletariat of those days; they were brought up in a spirit of social justice. They could rather sympathize with Adolf Stahr's manifestos, one of which began with the words: "Without Prussian indifference there would be no Prussian proletariat."[16]

Naturally, both Bettina and Stahr promptly fell into royal Prussian disgrace. Mendelssohn, who was basically of their opinion, was not caught; but we know how deeply he despised Berlin bureaucracy, which had discredited Bettina and Stahr.

Mendelssohn's attitude towards German Catholicism was as problematic as that towards German Judaism, to which he was bound by many relationships with family and friends. He respected the Catholic religion and its liturgy, not least because of his gratitude as a musician for the treasures of Catholic church music. His *Lauda Sion,* which he wrote for a Catholic celebration, and his readiness to write the music of dedication for the Cologne Cathedral, bear witness to this respect.[17] But he feared the Catholic Church and most of all its political machine in Germany. This was, for him, the principal reason against a monarchical or federative greater Germany, which, because of Austria's population, would have had to be strongly Catholic in orientation. He had had unpleasant experiences with the political representatives of the Protestant Church (Eichhorn, Raumer, G. A. Strauss); to the disciple of Schleiermacher, a political Catholicism must appear wholly disastrous. So, during his last years, Mendelssohn veered from radical liberalism into a monarchistic, conservatively liberal line of thought, such as was later represented by Crown Prince Frederick, the later Emperor.

JENNY LIND

Felix had met the "Swedish Nightingale," then at the beginning of her fame, in the fall of 1844 in Berlin. He frequented the house of the sculptor Professor Wichmann, whose family belonged to the singer's most intimate circle of friends. At that time, she sang the leading role in Meyerbeer's *Feldlager in Schlesien.* The relationship between the two artists became exceedingly close during the next three years. Mendelssohn actually wrote the soprano part of *Elijah* for Jenny Lind, and his unusually fine ear soon discovered the best features of her voice. He admired and valued her art more than that of any other singer, even the once-worshipped Malibran, the "flame" of his halcyon days.[18]

But the young singer loved Mendelssohn with the full devotion of her youthful soul, an *anima candida.*[19] A less honorable man than Mendelssohn might have made an "affair" out of this love and entered into an adventure with the adoring young girl. Who knows whether, in the interests of music, we should not regret Mendelssohn's integrity? But the master remained faithful to his wife and to his principle "Art and life are not divisible." So it came only to an intimate friendship between these twin souls, with Mendelssohn taking the role of the admired leader into the world of music. At least, so it appears. What was really going on in Mendelssohn's heart at the time, we do not know. A modern biography of Jenny Lind, perhaps the best and most accurate, describes this friendship:

> She could have fallen in love with Mendessohn. She had been greatly attracted by him when they met the year before. Now in the hours they spent together . . . she discovered a companionship deeper and more satisfying than anything she was ever to know for the rest of her life. Mendelssohn would sit at the piano and extemporise . . . his eyes, large and brown, always the focal centre of his beautiful, mobile, essentially Jewish face, would dilate until they turned almost black, and Jenny would be carried completely out of her self. . . . Their understanding of one another was so complete that often they knew what the other was going to say before the sentence was finished, and they soon developed private code expressions that only they understood. . . .
>
> Mendelssohn with his warm, affectionate ways had always fascinated women, and was used to it. They attracted him only in so far as they had some special talent or quality that interested him, never in themselves, except the woman he married . . . Cécile Jeanrenaud had nothing but her beauty, her charm, her distinction and her silence, and with her, a born home-maker, he was utterly happy; but he admired Jenny, as much as she admired him. He called her "as great an artist as ever lived; and the greatest I have known." He was very fond of her as a friend; no more than that.
>
> If he had not been married, she could have fallen in love with him. As it was, she clamped down on her feelings at once . . . she would not indulge in forbidden thoughts. . . . She may even have deceived herself, . . . for she spoke so openly of her feelings towards Mendelssohn that other people were sure she loved him. [e.g., Clara Schumann, and Jenny's guardian in Stockholm, H. Christian Andersen, her old friend and father confessor.] . . . Everyone knew that Mendelssohn could do anything with her: guide her career, influence her musical tastes, persuade her to sing in London or Vienna. . . . But for the present she suffered no heart-break.[20]

For reasons easy to understand, the relationship between Jenny Lind and Cecile remained cool and distant.[21] This manifested itself to the point of embarrassment when Mendelssohn invited the singer to appear in the *Gewandhaus* and to spend one or two weeks in Leipzig. The concert took place on December 4, 1845, and remained unforgettable to all hearers and participants for many years. This was not, perhaps, so much because of Lind's splendid artistic achievement as because of the attendant circumstances, which, after all (for singers) are often more important than the purely artistic event. The ticket prices were considerably raised, free admission for the conservatory students was cancelled, and the like. This led to protests on the part of the students. Their spokesman, in negotiation with Mendelssohn, was a little Jewish student with strikingly red hair. He was Otto Goldschmidt, later the faithful accompanist and husband of Jenny Lind.[22] At Mendelssohn's wish, she gave a charity concert for the benefit of the pension fund of the *Gewandhaus* musicians, and thus completely won the hearts of the Leipzigers.

After that memorable concert, the students of the University and the Conservatory serenaded the singer, who was a guest of the Brockhaus family. Mendelssohn, who was one of the party, took the somewhat shy Jenny by the arm and went with her into the garden, where a high-spirited crowd awaited her. With a few cordial words he introduced the artist, who received enthusiastic ovations. On this occasion, Fritz Brockhaus expressed an opinion about Lind which reveals deep psychological insight. He maintained that Jenny Lind was not happy, and would gladly exchange all her artistic triumphs for domestic joys such as she had seen, with yearning heart, in Mendelssohn's house.[23]

The master could exert so much influence on the singer that she often followed his advice or wishes blindly. On the other hand, we should not underestimate the importance of her mere existence for Mendelssohn. In spite of all his strict discipline and self-control (of which there are some astounding examples!), he projected the image and voice of Jenny Lind into every leading soprano part of an oratorio or opera. He writes (or sings) to the singer his familiar complaining song about "withdrawal from public life," and wants nothing but a pile of music paper and no duties as a conductor. She replies indignantly and reminds him of his operatic plans.[24] Whenever the opportunity arose, the two made music together. The second appearance of Lind in Leipzig took place on April 12, 1846, barely a half-year after the first. The program almost resembled a soirée of old friends:

Sonata for Violin and Piano in G major	Beethoven
Mendelssohn and David	
Aria from *Niobe*	Pacini
Violin Solo	David
Aria *Non mi dir*	Mozart
Sonata for Piano in C-sharp minor ("Moonlight" Sonata)	Beethoven
Mendelssohn	
Cavatinas from *Euryanthe* and *Freischütz*	Weber
	Mendelssohn
Song without Words	
Mendelssohn	
Songs with piano accompaniment	various composers
Jenny Lind and Mendelssohn	

By chance, Clara Schumann came to Leipzig on the same day, and was persuaded by Mendelssohn to take part in the concert. She played several *Songs without Words!* With the exception of the composers Mozart, Beethoven, and Pacini, all others represented here, both composers and performers, were personal friends of Mendelssohn. This was all very patriarchal and pleasant, but, as a way of educating the taste of the Leipzig public, it was certainly false and dangerous! Now Mendelssohn began to organize the *Gewandhaus* programs much like the Sunday concerts in his parents' home. He had no right to do this, nor could such one-sidedness have good results. But, if Wagner, not unjustifiably, spoke of a Mendelssohn clique, we should not forget that there was a corresponding Wagner and Liszt clan, which was no less intolerant. And so, in the confusion of these quarreling schools, the great "outsiders" Berlioz and Bruckner were neglected and overlooked.

From now on, all operatic projects are inseparably bound up with Lind, and Mendelssohn does not hesitate to initiate her into all his English operatic plans. She, the easily intimidated and often melancholy interpreter of his songs, is comforted by his reference to a verse from the *West-Oestlicher Divan* (by Goethe), which may explain to her why she, who brings so much joy to others, cannot be happy herself.[25] At the same time, he writes to his friend Hauser, who will see Lind frequently at her Viennese debut: "Tell her that no day passes during which I am not happy that we are both living at the same time . . . and that we are friends . . . and. . . ."[26]

At the Lower Rhenish Music Festival in Aachen, the last which Mendelssohn was to direct, he saw Lind again. He had put together a beautiful, but *very* conservative program:

First Day

Symphony in D major ("Haffner")	Mozart
The Creation	Haydn
(with Jenny Lind)	

Second Day

Fifth Symphony	Beethoven[27]
Motet *Ista dies*	Cherubini
Oberon Overture	Weber
Alexander's Feast	Handel
(with Jenny Lind)	

Before and after the festival, Mendelssohn and Lind, accompanied by her chaperone Louisa Johanson, made two Rhine journeys, and the master showed his friend Cologne, Bonn, the Drachenfels, and Königswinter. Significantly, in his ebullient report of the journey to Fanny, Mendelssohn mentioned Lind only in connection with rice pudding, which the French cooks in Aachen could never prepare to his liking; then he added:

"If Paul had heard Lind sing the first two arias in *Alexander's Feast*, he would have applauded again. . . ."[28] That was all that he dared to write about Lind to Fanny; not one, but two jealously loving women were watching over him! But his letters to the singer, and all related documents, show a much deeper relationship than is betrayed in these deliberately harmless *bavardages en passant*.[29]

After the parting from Jenny, the master visited Düsseldorf, where "he became serious, for the few days there tasted rather bitterly of the past."[30] From there, he went to Liège, to the first performance of his *Lauda Sion*, where he was a member of the audience. The performance was not good, because the bishops had granted insufficient means for rehearsals and orchestra.

The preliminary history of the *Lauda Sion* has become known only recently, principally through A. Van den Linden's studies in the archives.[31] It seems that St. Martin's Church in Liège asked a wealthy musical patron, M. Magis-Ghysens, to approach Mendelssohn for a solemn composition of the famous Corpus Christi sequence. The occasion for this was the 600th anniversary of this festival since its official introduction. Mendelssohn unconditionally accepted the commission, which reached him in Frankfurt, on April 26, 1845.[32] An honorarium of 400 francs (no great amount for a half-hour-long work for chorus and large orchestra) was agreed upon and paid. The original manuscript of the work is in the library of the Brussels Conservatory. It contains a note which is most unusual for Mendelssohn (original in French): "This copy of the score is the property of M. Magis-Ghysens at Liège; it is destined to be executed at the Festival of the Holy Sacrament at the Church of St. Martin in the month of June of this year and it must not be copied or multiplied *in any form without* the consent of the author."[33] The master wanted to prevent publication of the work without thorough and critical revision on his part, as appears in his letter of February 23, 1846. On the same date he sent the completed score to Liège. He could, so he writes, have completed the score long before if, "constantly troubled with business," he had not been overworked and so without the strict concentration which this work demanded. By this "business" he meant, among other things, a performance of his solemn ode *An die Künstler* to Schiller's famous verses, which was presented by the German-Flemish Singing Society in Cologne. Except for a few places which betray the master's hand, this work is both insignificant and bombastic. Mendelssohn, however, was in highest spirits, as we see from his correspondence which once again expands beyond all normal bounds. Amidst masses of trivia, there are several hitherto neglected or unknown letters, of which we shall select three for further attention. They give us intimate glimpses into the thinking and feeling of the master in the last years and are highly characteristic of him.

From the Aachen music festival, Lind had gone to Vienna, where she made her debut in the Court Opera and also wanted to give a series of concerts. Naturally, she was excited and worried, for the Viennese public was a critical, indeed, hypercritical one. In order to pave the way for her in influential musical and social circles, Mendelssohn wrote two letters to old friends: to Baroness Ertmann, the former pupil of Beethoven who was well-known to him from Milan, and to Aloys Fuchs, who was on the council of the *Gesellschaft der Musikfreunde*. Both letters, of which the first is published in part, the second is in manuscript, speak of the singer exclusively in superlatives—he calls her his "cherished friend" and "the noblest artist whom he has yet encountered."[34] Now, Mendelssohn had often been ready to help deserving people; but this almost aggressive championing of Jenny with people who would probably misinterpret his pure motives, with people whom he had to ask for favors, is something completely unusual for him. Here spoke his warm heart; we might say that here, certain of the power of his name, he held his protective and helping hands over his friend.

WORK IN LEIPZIG

As HE FOUGHT for Jenny Lind, whom he considered as his protegée, so he could take the part of other artists, too, most energetically. His high respect for Schumann's great gifts caused Mendelssohn to further his cause, too, with the full power of his reputation. We refer to a letter which Mendelssohn wrote to his English publisher Buxton in order to recommend to him Schumann's oratorio *Das Paradies und die Peri*. We shall give this letter in Mendelssohn's original English, in order once and for all to discredit the rumors spread by the Nazis and other source-corrupters that Mendelssohn thought little of Schumann's music and, at the same time, envied him his successes. Paradoxically, Mendelssohn, who had premiered two of Schumann's symphonies, is accused of hypocritical falseness, and, at the same time, of all-too-cool reserve towards Schumann. If he had behaved dishonestly, he could not very well have appeared "reserved"; if his attitude towards Schumann had been purely negative, he would scarcely have performed his symphonies. As we see, such slanders, when confronted with the facts, lead into a blind alley of contradictions from which not even the most clever Nazi musicologists could extricate themselves.[35]

The letter to Mr. Buxton is dated January 27, 1844; the original of the letter is in the Mendelssohn collection of the Library of Congress in Washington, D.C. Here is the English text:

Dear Sir,
My friend Dr. Schumann wishes for an opportunity to publish his new

work "The Paradise and the Peri" in your country, and has desired me to write you my impression of the work, which I think he intends communicating himself to you his ideas about its publication.

I must accordingly tell you that I have read and heard this new work of Dr. Schumann with the greatest pleasure, that it has afforded me a treat which made me easily foretell the unanimous applaus it has gained at the two performances at Leipzig and the performance at Dresden (which took place last month), and that I think it a very important and noble work, full of many eminent beauties. As for expression and poetical feeling it ranks very, very high, the choruses are as effective and as well written as the Solo parts are melodious and winning. In short it is a most worthy musical translation of that beautiful inspiration of your great poet Moore, and I think feeling of being indebted to that poet for that charme that pervaded the whole music has induced the composer to wish your countrymen to become acquainted with his work. He intends visiting England next year, where I am sure, he and his music will be received as they so highly deserve.

I am yours, etc.,

Felix Mendelssohn Bartholdy

About this time the *Junges Deutschland* movement began—though not yet openly—to direct malicious articles against Mendelssohn, in whom it saw, not unfairly, a symbol of the successful emancipation of the Jews. True, the *Junges Deutschland* fought bravely for its own freedom and equality, but it did not care much about that of its Jewish fellow-citizens. And more unfavorable signs began to appear; soon even the ominous word "Mosaic" was used in connection with the first performance of Schumann's C major Symphony under Mendelssohn. It was a cowardly, anonymous newspaper "smear," but it hit Mendelssohn where he was vulnerable.[36] For Schubert, too, the master stepped in with growing enthusiasm; it was a matter of making the less well-known songs and the instrumental music of the Viennese master more familiar to a public that saw Schubert's significance only in the perspective of *Die Schöne Müllerin* and *Der Erlkönig*. Thus Schubert's chamber music became generally known in Leipzig, thanks to Mendelssohn's ceaseless efforts; so did his songs, such as *Ave Maria, Der Wanderer, Am Meer, Die junge Nonne, Der Doppelgänger*, and others, especially in the deeply felt interpretation of the great artist Wilhelmine Schroeder-Devrient.[37] The great C major Symphony of Schubert, too, began but slowly to take a firm place in the concert repertoire. Even in 1847, we read in the *Signale für die Musikalische Welt* that it was performed practically nowhere else but in Leipzig, and that even Mendelssohn's effort to introduce it into England failed; "so Leipzig seems to be the Mecca to which the musician must wander in order to hear this work of genius and fantasy."[38]

Now Berlin had another commission for Mendelssohn; but this time it was not stage music that the King wanted from him. Along with Otto Nicolai and Carl Loewe, our master was commissioned to write new music for the official Protestant *Agende* (Order of Divine Service). The Royal General Intendant von Redern had approached Mendelssohn in the King's name, and Mendelssohn was glad to fulfill Frederick William's wish. On November 6, 1846, he sent the manuscript to von Redern. In his accompanying letter, he emphasized the difficulty of the task; at least on this point, he was of one mind with Nicolai and Loewe.[39] While J. Fr. Naue's *Versuch einer Musikalischen Agende* (1818-1826) looked back too much to the eighteenth century, and other composers, such as Eduard Grell, demanded and used a "pure" Palestrina style, Mendelssohn, as always in the relationship between tone and word, found the happy medium which only a composer, given to reflection can reach. But this last Berlin commission had no better lot than most of his other efforts for the music of that city; officially, that is, by the Royal Cathedral, the work was never published.[40] Only single sections, the *Ehre sei Gott* and the great *Heilig*, have been published by Bote and Bock; this and two additional pieces (*Kyrie, Segen*) are found in the large edition (incorrectly called "complete") of Breitkopf and Härtel. Also the official *Liturgischen Andachten der kgl. Hof- and Domkirche*, which were edited by Mendelssohn's old enemy G. F. A. Strauss, do not have a word to say about Mendelssohn's work. Yet, other distinctly weaker works and composers are named there.

The pieces of this "German Liturgy" are all set for eight-voiced double chorus, which is often divided, that is, used antiphonally. As always in such *a cappella* movements, Mendelssohn, here too, makes rich use of his brilliant powers of polyphonic invention. In truth, these hymnic choruses are as far removed from the banality of his contemporary Bortniansky as from the somewhat repressed orthodoxy of a Grell. Mendelssohn's liturgy has majesty, dignity, but also real warmth and euphony; above all, it is free of the "Neo-Pietism" then fashionable at court, which attracted the Quietists but often made them very noisy! The bitter mockery of the late Schleiermacher at the ministers whose partisanship of the Royal *Agende* was too vigorous and who "therefore had earned an Order *non propter acta sed propter agenda*" could be applied as well to several Royal orthodox composers, but certainly not to Mendelssohn. Until today, his beautiful German Liturgy has rested in dusty archives; perhaps these lines may help to awaken it once more to sound and life!

Ever since Mendelssohn had heard Jenny Lind at the opera, his old operatic dreams had been reawakened, and Lind did her best not to let them fade away again. Mendelssohn was so enthusiastic about her that, for her sake alone, he did not shun the troubles caused by correspondence with librettists, study of scenarios, and the like. He, who has been accused of too great reserve, went so far as to write to Lind: "I should indeed be glad if I could soon . . . write something dramatic—and especially for *you* . . . if I do not attain to the composition of a fairly good Opera *now*, and *for you* [Mendelssohn's underscoring], I shall never accomplish it at all."[41]

The same letter contains a sharp condemnation of everything French in art, life and politics. On this point, he agreed with Lind completely. But this definite aversion should not be misunderstood. Mendelssohn was always critical of French music, perhaps even unfair to it, but he had never condemned it altogether. In this letter, which could be by Hans Sachs in *Die Meistersinger* (*und wälschen Dunst mit wälschem Tand*) (For foreign fumes and foreign trash), Mendelssohn sharply attacks French trends in the contemporary literature and music of Germany.

The operatic plans which Mendelssohn now pursued, and which he wanted to protect from French influence, are quite uninteresting in themselves, the more so because none of them ever came to fruition. Nonetheless, through these plans he came into contact once more with living authors and poets, in short, with the literary successors of the once so lively Romantic movement. First he tried it out with the "theatre aunt" Birch-Pfeiffer, whose bourgeois dramas, at that time very popular, repelled Mendelssohn's classically schooled taste; she was supposed to write him a *Genoveva* drama. Then he turned to the friend of his youth, Devrient, who suggested to him a subject from the Peasants' Wars. Here too, Mendelssohn refers to Lind, who had "talked him into writing one [opera] for her, and for whom he wanted to compose something really good."[42] To Devrient's plan, he objected that in his draft there were "too many freedom-slavery-social conditions motifs."[43] The piece was to be called *Ritter und Bauer* (Knight and Peasant), and in Devrient's sketch the knight did not come off very well; Mendelssohn criticized this "trend of the times, this *captatio benevolentiae*, in which neither of us really believes."[44] But here he was wrong, for Devrient was an enthusiastic fighter for freedom and greater Germany, and, in 1848, backed up his convictions with actions.

While this correspondence between Dresden (where Devrient was working) and Leipzig was taking place, Mendelssohn had settled with Geibel on the *Loreley* subject for an opera.[45] He told this to Devrient, whereupon the latter, generous as always, put his great theatrical experience at the service of the two authors. Geibel, quite insecure as a theatrical poet, visited Devrient, in order to profit by his criticism and operatic experience. Devrient was convinced that a stageworthy scenario, which would also satisfy Mendelssohn's literary requirements, could be achieved only by a three-way collaboration. He invited Felix to come to Dresden for a few days, for the most necessary discussions with him and Geibel. Alas, the time was unfavorable, for Mendelssohn was working day and night on *Elijah* and "dared not waste an hour."[46] He cordially requested Devrient to give Geibel his best advice and expressed complete confidence in him. When, at the end of February, 1847, he received the finished libretto, he was once again disappointed and depressed by its lack of dramatic life. But the master had a few other dramatic irons in the fire. When he was shopping, he liked a "large selection," as he used to say; so he had at least two other scenarios or libretti before him. The first was written by a certain Benjamin Lumley, whom we may best characterize as a theater fan or stage adventurer. Although he was originally a lawyer, against his better judgment he let himself be talked into taking over the direction of Her Majesty's Theatre in London (1841). Since he had overestimated the drawing power of the ballet and gave it unusual prominence, by 1846 he had lost most of his singers and was near bankruptcy. Lind had promised to give him her English debut in his theater, so, for the harassed promoter, her coming was a life-and-death matter. Since everyone knew about Mendelssohn's great influence on Lind, Lumley took the liberty of asking the master to intercede with the singer in his interests. Mendelssohn promised to do so, and faithfully kept his promise.[47] On the same occasion, Lumley (who knew about the operatic plans) asked quite innocently whether Mendelssohn was interested in an operatic subject. With this began the collaboration on a new version of Shakespeare's *Tempest* as an opera. Lumley sketched a scenario and even induced Scribe, that old theatrical expert, to work out the libretto in French. Although Lumley had made no binding arrangements with Mendelssohn, he used the latter's name to advertise his theatre, in which *The Tempest*, with music by Felix Mendelssohn and sung by Jenny Lind, was to receive its world première.

It seems that, in this operatic affair, Mendelssohn was carried away by his eagerness to write an opera for Lind, and so let himself in for commitments in a way which contrasts strangely with his usualy caution. At first he thought that "Scribe is the only man who could treat this subject [*Tempest*] suitably for music."[48] And on November 1, 1846, just like a young beginner, he rashly promises Lumley, "When I think of it [the opera], I wish January had arrived and the *libretto* with it and that I could go on writing already. . . ."[49]

A month later, he writes even more impatiently:

A man like Scribe, with a subject like "The Tempest" must produce something extraordinary, something which I should feel happy and proud to combine my music with. . . . I need not tell you that I shall set all other occupations aside, if I only see the possibility of finishing it in time [i.e., for the season 1847-48]—whether I have it at New Year or not.[50]

This was the same Mendelssohn who had once damned everything French in literature! We see how the burning wish to fashion an opera especially for Lind overrode all other considerations. And so Mendelssohn, in his glowing zeal, may not have stuck strictly to the objective truth concerning another related matter; for, as we know, at this time he was already having dealings with Geibel about the *Loreley*.

On January 19, 1847, he received Scribe's complete libretto. Now he began to be afraid that he would not be ready "in time." But he added immediately: "I shall try to do it, try with all my heart, and as well as I can."[51] Only on February 21 was he certain that he would not be able to set the libretto in time, for its second part was "completely uncongenial" to him. But Scribe was ready to alter whole sections according to Mendelssohn's wishes, to please the famous composer. However, Scribe could not understand why the composer wanted to stick strictly to the formal principles of the classical drama in a "féerie," and demanded logical motivation everywhere. This finally led to the breakup of the whole project.

Now an ugly theatrical controversy developed in London. Lumley's rivals, in the best Victorian style, tried to ruin him both morally and financially. Mendelssohn took no part in the scandalous lawsuits, in which, however, his name played a considerable part. When Lumley let it be understood that Mendelssohn was working on an opera for his theatre (which was now no longer strictly true) the master sent him back the whole libretto with Scribe's drafts, accompanied by a coldly polite letter of rejection.[52] Again, Mendelssohn was not at all in the right; and once again, as formerly in Düsseldorf, there was a "tempest in a teapot."

The regular English translator of Mendelssohn's songs and oratorios, Mr. Bartholomew, also presented him with the plan for an opera, and even the critic and publicist Chorley played with an operatic subject for our master. With all these plans, it is strange that Mendelssohn never came in contact with a real dramatist, like Hebbel or Otto Ludwig, who studied in Leipzig and knew Mendelssohn personally. However, one might wonder whether Mendelssohn would have judged erotic-morbid subjects like *Judith* or *Gyges and his Ring* sympathetically as opera libretti; they would probably not have been "German" enough for him. For the same reason, he could scarcely have become enthusiastic about Ludwig's *Makkabäer*, while he would have criticized the petty bourgeois, socially problematic milieu of *Agnes Bernauerin*.

When one surveys Mendelssohn's operatic plans one must admit that only twice did the master have really usable libretti: Devrient's *Hans Heiling* and Shakespeare-Scribe's *Tempest*. He rejected both for reasons in which esthetic and ethical demands are strangely mingled. But, from Mozart, Wagner, Verdi, and Richard Strauss, we know that a composer may confront his librettist critically, but not pedantically and not burdened with doctrinaire esthetic and moral prejudices. What would Mendelssohn have said, for example, to the first act of *Die Walküre*, in which breach of hospitality, adultery, incest, and theft are musically glorified? Yet it is these very scenes, which we shudder to read, that grip the spectator as, perhaps, no other first act of Wagner can do.

THE WORKS OF 1845-46

IN THIS comparatively tranquil period, in addition to *Elijah* there were created several noteworthy, but frequently overlooked works.

Quintet in B flat major

The work, Op. 87, was composed in the carefree summer of 1845, in Frankfurt; with the exception of the slow movement, it bears many traces of those happy days. From beginning to end, it is a lyrical composition, but turns away from the stereotyped lyricisms of the *Songs without Words*.

The spirited, fiery first movement does not quite keep the promise of clear purposefulness given by the triadic theme. However, the beautiful reprise shows that the principal theme has undergone development. The fine contrapuntal coda, which carries out the second theme, brings the movement to a harmonious close. The second movement, a lyrical Scherzo (no elfin dance), a rhythmically piquant structure, makes full use of shifting accents and *pizzicati*. It is one of those Mendelssohnian movements which attract every musician by the elegance of texture. He has often been reproached for this elegance, which has unhesitatingly been dubbed "superficial." With few exceptions (some chamber music movements of Brahms, R. Strauss, Ravel, Hindemith, Poulenc, Milhaud, Tschaikowsky, and perhaps Elgar), this art of elegant and well-made quartet movements has vanished. There is nothing of this smoothness in the third movement, an adagio elegy. It begins with a theme of great pathos, which unfolds strangely in chiaroscuro sonorities. The thirds of the triads constantly fluctuate between major and minor. The movement reaches its climax in an orchestrally conceived version of the elegiac theme, and ends with dramatic tremolos. The *Finale* is not on the level of the other movements. It is rhythmically varied and rich in syncopation—it even contains many asymmetrical phrases, all too rare in Mendelssohn—but the themes are weak. Most effective is the mixture of *concertante* and contrapuntal style in the coda. Mendelssohn was very fond of this synthesis and, on occasion, executed it brilliantly. Many of his organ improvisations seem to have especially cultivated this style.

Lauda Sion

We have had occasion, when discussing the Italian journey of the young Mendelssohn, to point out the empathy of the youthful composer with the spirit of the Catholic liturgy. However, he never identified himself with it. A series of smaller Latin motets bears witness to the composer's feeling for the Roman ceremonial. But let us not forget that, even before the Italian journey, he approached Catholic liturgical texts with reverence and respect, e.g., in his great *Te Deum* (unpublished), *Tu es Petrus, Jube Domne*, and the strict antiphon for sixteen-voiced *a cappella* chorus *Hora est* (MS). Now the mature master was confronted with a text which not only emphasizes the dogmatic element of the Catholic Church, but especially glorifies the mystery of Jesus' incarnation. Alas, a great philosopher is not always a good poet! St. Thomas Aquinas, the author of *Lauda Sion*, did not entirely do justice poetically to his lofty theme. This is especially true because of the short-breathed meter of the verses:

Lauda Sion salvatorem	Praise, oh Zion, praise the Saviour
Lauda ducem et pastorem	Praise the leader and sustainer
In hymnis et canticis	With all hymns and canticles

Each line has 8 or 7 syllables, in the following accent-scheme:

$$(8) \quad \acute{}\,\_\,\acute{}\,\_\,\acute{}\,\_\,\acute{}\,\_$$
$$(8) \quad \acute{}\,\_\,\acute{}\,\_\,\acute{}\,\_\,\acute{}\,\_$$
$$(7) \quad \acute{}\,\_\,\acute{}\,\_\,\acute{}\,\_\,\acute{}$$

Each strophe consists of six such lines, and the whole sequence contains twelve such strophes, which, with few deviations, all stick to this monotonous meter.

Mendelssohn recognized this problem very well, and, in general, mastered it admirably. But, even aside from the metrical difficulties of the text, the disciple of Schleiermacher and Hegel, the son of the deist Abraham, the grandson of the traditional Jew Moses Mendelssohn had to interpret and glorify the dogmas and mysteries of the church in musical terms. We have already called attention to his demand—revolutionary for a Protestant musician—that good church music must be written "with constant remembrance of its ecclesiastical purpose." Therefore, he pointed out to his English friends who wanted to perform the *Lauda Sion* in the concert hall "that it could hardly come off well without the Catholic Church and ritual."[53]

So Mendelssohn wrote music for both the Protestant and Catholic Churches, and, as we have seen, also contributed to the Synagogue. Now, in such a case we must raise a question about the composer's sincerity. What were his true convictions? The question is, indeed, not easy to answer. Perhaps, in the case of Mendelssohn, we can resolve it as follows. He was estranged from the synagogue of his ancestors, but confronted it with the consciousness of a commitment of many thousand years' standing. The

Catholic Church was alien to him, but he respected it, and above all, its magnificent patronage of music. In the Protestant religion, he was at home. The grandson of Moses, who had preached tolerance, was still close to Judaism in a human sense; musically, he had ties with the Catholic Church; but in Protestantism, he found fulfillment.

In *Lauda Sion* he paid a splendid tribute to the Catholic Church. When K. G. Fellerer, one of the best authorities on the history of church music, observes that the "great upsurge of liturgical feeling in the Romanticism of the first half of the 19th century had become petrified in the middle of the century, and that, under these conditions, the reform of Catholic church music seemed to be able to progress only through the adoption of organizational measures,"[54] Mendelssohn, the non-Catholic, must certainly be excepted from this verdict of petrification. Among the important composers between Cherubini and Bruckner, only he succeeded in writing real liturgical music for the Catholic Church and, thereby, in enriching it with a masterpiece.

Mendelssohn organizes the twelve strophes of the text into eight sections of varying structure and mood. Rudolf Werner, with sensitive understanding for the work, observes that there are fine gradations in the choice of sonorities (choruses, soprano soli, solo quartet) and that the danger of monotony, which was near at hand because of the inflexible form and the strictly dogmatic content, was avoided.[55] In this work, Mendelssohn definitely turned his back on his usual models Bach and Handel. Instead, he revived the style of the Italians of the High Baroque—for example, Caldara, Pergolese, Jomelli—in the idiom of the nineteenth century. Alongside strictly liturgical unisons of the chorus there are enchanting quartets. The music suggests the gently curved melodic line of the Italians of the Baroque. In many places, it foreshadows the tone-color of the mature Verdi (who learned much from Mendelssohn). Here, he is closest to the religious music of Cherubini, but Mendelssohn's work is more inventive and filled with contrasts. In harmonic splendor and sonorous euphony this work surpasses all of the master's other compositions for the church. Let us mention a few of its many outstanding features.

Mendelssohn did not stick to the traditional *cantus firmus* of the sequence. However, he uses several motifs from it; recasting them, he achieves a new *cantus*, which dominates most of the work. The solemnly intoned principal theme begins, surprisingly, on the $\frac{6}{4}$ chord. The composer entrusts several of the dogmatically important sections which deviate from the regular meter, e.g., *Dies enim solemnis agitur* (For a festive day is solemnized), to the unison men's chorus in a psalmodic formula. The solo Quartet *In hac mensa novi regis* (On this table of the God-King), a melodically and contrapuntally fascinating piece, begins in *stretto*:

Example 64,1

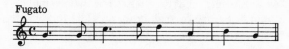

Example 64,4

Example 64,5

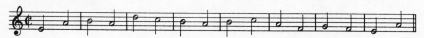

At the end of the movement, the master introduces the theme in a four-voiced canon which unfolds beautifully and naturally. The whole movement is filled with the transfigured beauty of true devotion. The following movements, in figured chorales, glorify the mystery of the Incarnation. From the above-mentioned work of Van den Linden we know that several other pieces were originally included or differently arranged here. An angel's voice (simple, tender, and pure) resounds in *Caro cibus* (His body is the food). Sharply contrasting is *Sumit unus, sumunt mille* (Summons one, a thousand summon), with its premonitions of death and the Last Judgment; rightly, R. Werner notes its *Dies irae*-like atmosphere. It reminds us even more vividly of the *Rex tremendae majestatis* in Mozart's *Requiem*. In their objective portrayal of the text, the final sections already foreshadow Fauré's sonorities and conceptions.

The powerful, stylistically pure and well-sounding work is, quite unfairly, virtually forgotten today. This is our loss, and is not to be attributed to any subjectively romantic conception of the liturgy *à la Liszt*, quite alien to our time, on Mendelssohn's part. Nothing could be further from the truth! In its well-nigh baroque boldness of conception, the *Lauda Sion* is completely equal to Bruckner's *Te Deum* and Fauré's *Requiem*.

THE GERMAN LITURGY

It sounds paradoxical, but it is true; the composition of the German Liturgy (without opus number and published only in part) was more difficult for Mendelssohn than that of the *Lauda Sion*. This was because of the very rigid Protestant liturgy, which was fixed *by law*. (The King of Prussia was simultaneously the highest bishop of his country's church.) As previously mentioned, the "new" *Agende* was a bone of contention. This *Agende* or order of the liturgy, which had been introduced under Frederick William III (1816-21) had already been attacked by Schleiermacher.[56] Nonetheless, it gradually made its way in Prussia (along with its musical version by Naue—see Chapter XVI); indeed, it was sometimes forced on opponents by administrative means.

Basically, the Prussian *Agende* (which was not drastically revised until 1894) preserves its connection with the usages of the Mass as they were at the time of the struggles of the Reformation. In the following section, we shall discuss only the musical parts of the *Agende*, or those for which music was at least permitted. These parts were:

1. Congregational singing
2. A Bible passage, with proclamation of grace
3. Chorus (Glory be to the Father)
4. Chorus (*Kyrie eleison*)

5. Hallelujah
6. Closing song (sermon chorale)
7. Chorus (Christ, thou Lamb of God)
8. Congregational singing (chorale)

Here, a fairly clear distinction is made between the choir (that is, the organized choir of laymen or professional singers who are available to the church) and congregational singing. Both the Pietism of the seventeenth and early eighteenth centuries and the Rationalism of the eighteenth and early nineteenth centuries were hostile, or, at best, indifferent, to organized professional choral singing. Many crypto-Calvinistic tendencies were concealed in the polemic writings which were ostensibly concerned with musical matters.[57] The true function of art-music in the Protestant liturgy is still disputed today by theologians, estheticians, and musicians. On the other hand, the problems of congregational singing or of the responses of the congregation were hardly ever seriously discussed.

Mendelssohn could have no doubt on which side he should stand. He was in complete agreement with Schleiermacher's viewpoint: "The choir is the artistic representation of the congregation. When music appears in a higher artistic form, this happens in the choir. We cannot assume a high degree of artistic training for the whole congregation. However, if the congregation is made up of a number of cultural levels, artistically trained individuals will not be lacking. From the gathering together of these, the choir is formed. Here, the musical elements may be stressed in more varied fashion."[58]

After the introduction of the *Agende* many musicians strove to find or write suitable music for it. For example, Fr. T. Rohleder suggests the following order:

1. Introitus (chorale prelude and chorale of the congregation)
2. Kyrie
3. Gloria or Magnificat
4. Chorale (also in the form of a Credo)
5. Gradual, Doxology, Hallelujah
6. Principal song (chorale); here the author means the chorale
   following the sermon.
7. Agnus Dei
8. Lord's Prayer (spoken or sung)
9. *Gratiarum actio*
10. Closing verse of the chorale

The author provides a Sanctus or *Heilig* only for special festival days.[59]

Rohleder was by no means the first with his suggestions. Naue's *Agende*, on which we have already reported, became the most familiar version. In his revision of the work, at the beginning of the 1840's, Naue greatly deviated from his previous rigid orthodoxy.[60] Nonetheless, he really approves only of *a cappella* singing. Both singing at the altar (*Altargesang*) and the church cantata are merely tolerated. Even congregational singing is limited to the merest essentials.[61]

In contrast to such purism, Mendelssohn saw the function of his German Liturgy as that of setting an example in the controversial realm of Protestant church music. He kept the choral movements (*a cappella*) simple and easily singable, without any turn towards Gregorian psalmody, so that, perhaps, parts of them might "eventually also be accessible to the congregation." The (unpublished) responses were intended from the beginning for congregational singing.

How closely the master clung to old liturgical conceptions, we may see in his *Heilig.* (Example 65.)

As in the other pieces of the German Liturgy, Mendelssohn, here too, used an eight-voiced double chorus. However, this was not in order to give free play to all contrapuntal devices, and also not in order to enhance the euphony of the pieces. Rather, it was in order to symbolize musically the old theological concept of the angelic choirs which praise the Lord *incessabili voce.* Therefore, this piece is miles removed from the *concertante* character of the Sanctus in Bach's B minor Mass. The harmony and the conduct of the voices are of the greatest simplicity; precisely by this means, the austere and lofty character of true liturgical music is stressed anew. At the same time, the piece has the pure sound of true *a cappella* music and is far indeed from the somewhat tiresome piety of Moritz Hauptmann's motets. It is a pity that this church music, truly Protestant in attitude and spirit, has fallen into oblivion. It seems to us that this task of reviving this great liturgical music is an obligation of the German Professing Church (*Bekenntniskirche*); for both in his oratorios and in his sacred music, Mendelssohn appears as its precursor.

In addition to making his own contributions, Mendelssohn concerned himself with stimulating other leading composers to create Protestant church music, either through his own personal intervention or through that of the Berlin officials. In a memorandum to Minister von Redern, the master, magnanimous as always, suggests a series of contemporary composers who might also write for the Cathedral chorus. He adds: "As far as the music is concerned, it might be remarked that the composition of the psalm in Luther's translation must be without all instrumental accompaniment (*a cappella*)."[62] Repetitions of words should be avoided where possible, and "figuration" (coloratura singing) should be reduced to a minimum. He suggests the following composers: L. Spohr for Psalm 47 (Ascension); C. Loewe for Psalm 68 (Pentecost); M. Hauptmann for Psalm 51 (Day of Repentance); *Musikdirektor* Neidhardt for Psalm 66 (Easter); and M. Granzin (organist in Danzig) for Psalm 8 (Sunday after Pentecost). The

Example 65

German Liturgy was his last effort for Protestant church music. Compared with the motets and cantatas of his youth, it represents a mighty step forward to a purified style of liturgical singing; but it also foreshadows the beginning of a new style of religious music for Mendelssohn himself. The renunciation of external display, the limitation to the very simplest tonal material, hints at a change to a purer, more noble style which leads us to expect great things. But, alas, the master could no longer fulfill this promise. His life was drawing to an end.

Notes

1. Letter to Klingemann of November 5, 1844.
2. Letter to Klingemann of December 17, 1844.
3. Letter to Klingemann of September 29, 1845.
4. Unpublished letter to Paul of January 11, 1845. For Mendelssohn's answer and the conditions offered, see H. E. Krehbiel in New York *Daily Tribune*, October 29, 1905.
5. This is the same Ernst August who banished the "Göttingen Seven" and was also involved in other sinister affairs.
6. Letter to Droysen of March 18, 1846.
7. Hensel, *F.M.*, III, p. 204.
8. Unpublished letter from Eichhorn to Mendelssohn of March 23, 1845.
9. Letter of March 12, 1845.
10. Letters to Klingemann of February 15 and April 15, 1845.

11. Devrient, *op. cit.,* pp. 249-255.

12. It is not hard to understand what Mendelssohn was hinting at here. Through Wagner, we learn (*Mein Leben,* I, 351) that at this time Hiller, with whom Mendelssohn had quarreled, played a considerable role in Dresden's musical life. One of his operas, a horror play by Raupach, *Der Traum der Christnacht,* was performed at this time. Besides, our master was not overanxious to be employed as young Wagner's superior. About the latter's domestic scandals, he had written to his friend Devrient that he would rather not say anything; the business repelled him, but it was not for him to judge. (Unpublished letter of October 25, 1844.)

13. See R. Wagner, *Aus Meinem Leben,* I, 377-78; also, Mendelssohn's letter to Klingemann, September 29, 1845, and Devrient's account, *op. cit.,* pp. 249-255. The Saxon archives, insofar as they were accessible to me, give no facts that would justify Wagner's assertion. How poorly informed Wagner was is obvious from the unpublished letter of Mendelssohn to an unnamed *Regierungsrat* in Leipzig (May 10, 1845), in which he says: "Now, since last December, I have free choice as to my place of residence; but since then I have heard nothing, either about the concert directorship [of the *Gewandhaus*] or from the Conservatory, or privately. So I must think that other arrangements have been made there, or that they want to detach themselves from the previous offers, as much as I should regret this. . . ." It is hard to understand how, under such circumstances and with such documentary sources, Mr. Ernest Newman can maintain: "His [Wagner's] incorruptible idealism made it impossible for him to compromise on the facts." (*Richard Wagner,* I, p. 448.)

14. Devrient, *op. cit.,* p. 260.

15. Devrient, *op. cit.,* p. 263.

16. A. Stahr, *Lebenserinnerungen* "Aus der Jugendzeit" (Schwerin, 1870).

17. Unpublished letter to J. Seydlitz of September 19, 1847 (to the Ordinariate of the Archbishopric in Cologne).

18. After Malibran's early death, Mendelssohn had planned to write a Requiem for her. Why he did not carry out this idea is unknown.

19. "Felix Mendelssohn . . . is a *man,* and at the same time he has the most supreme talent. So should it be." (Letter of Jenny Lind to her guardian in Stockholm; in Holland-Rockstro, *Jenny Lind,* I, p. 323.)

20. Joan Bulman, *Jenny Lind* (London, 1956), pp. 106ff.

21. *Ibid.,* p. 115.

22. Program of the first concert: Mozart, D major Symphony (*Prague*); Bellini, "Casta diva"; Joachim, Adagio and Rondo; Bellini, *Se fuggire,* duet (Lind and Miss Dolby); Weber, *Oberon* Overture; Mozart, *Non mi dir* (*Don Giovanni*); Ernst, Caprice for Violin on a theme by Bellini; songs (with piano), Jenny Lind and Mendelssohn. See also Reinecke, *Und manche lieben Schatten* (Leipzig, 1910), pp. 62ff.

23. Joan Bulman, *op. cit.,* p. 124. Program of the charity concert: Weber, *Euryanthe* Overture; Weber, Scene and Aria from *Der Freischütz;* Mendelssohn, G minor Piano Concerto, played by him; Weber, Finale from *Euryanthe;* N. W. Gade, Overture *Im Hochland;* Mozart, Scene and Aria of the Countess from *The Marriage of Figaro;* Mendelssohn, *Songs without Words* and free fantasy; songs with piano; finally, *Leise zieht durch mein Gemüt.* In the pieces on the program which Gade conducted, Mendelssohn played at the last desk of violas in the orchestra—a noble gesture!

24. Letter of Mendelssohn to Jenny Lind of March 18, 1846, and her answer in Holland-Rockstro, *op. cit.*.

25. Letter to Jenny Lind, May 15, 1846 (in Holland-Rockstro, I, pp. 388ff.) The reference is to the verses from *Ergebung* (*Surrender*): "Ich singe mit schwerem Herzen/ Sieh doch einmal die Kerzen/Sie leuchten indem sie vergehn." ("With heavy heart singing I go;/ See how the candles glow—/They shine as they melt away.")

26. Letter to F. Hauser, May 11, 1846.

27. On this occasion, Mendelssohn discovered mistakes in Beethoven's printed score. See also *Musical World* of May 26, 1860.

28. Hensel, *F.M.,* III, p. 240.

29. For Christmas, Mendelssohn gave Lind a little manuscript album of his own songs, an exceptional token of confidence and admiration.

30. Hensel, F.M., III, p. 241.

31. These and the following dates are drawn from the fine study of A. Van den Linden in Acta Musicologica (1954), XXVI, pp. 48-64.

32. Ibid., p. 49.

33. Ibid.

34. Letter to Baroness Ertmann, April 12, 1846, in Elise Polko, Erinnerungen an F.M.B.; letter to Aloys Fuchs, April 13, 1846 (unpublished).

35. For example, H. J. Moser, W. Boetticher, and others.

36. See also Chapter XIX.

37. Fr. Schmidt, Das Musikleben der bürgerlichen Gesellschaft Leipzigs im Vormärz (Langensalza, 1912), p. 126.

38. Signale, 1847, No. 45.

39. In "Briefe berühmter Komponisten aus dem Archiv des Hof und Domchors," ed. R. Scheumann, in Die Musik, VIII, Heft 11.

40. It is not quite clear whose negligence or even prejudice prevented the work from being printed by the Royal Cathedral. In any case, it was the King's intention to publish the work.

41. Letter to Jenny Lind of October 31, 1846. (Holland-Rockstro, op. cit., I, p. 9.)

42. Devrient, Erinnerungen, p. 257.

43. Ibid., p. 263.

44. Ibid., p. 265.

45. After a performance of A Midsummer Night's Dream, Geibel had asked Mendelssohn why he did not write an opera. The latter had answered: "Give me a good libretto and I shall start composing it tomorrow at 4 a.m." (In E. Polko, op. cit., p. 141.)

46. Devrient, p. 268.

47. See Mendelssohn's stern letter to Lind, in November, 1846 (shortly after the première of Elijah) in Holland-Rockstro, op. cit. Lind's demands were exorbitant, an honorarium of 120,000 francs was guaranteed, and, for the duration of the season, she had a whole house, numerous servants, a carriage and horses at her disposal free of charge. See B. Lumley, Reminiscences of the Opera (London, 1864), p. 163.

48. Lumley, op. cit., p. 166.

49. Ibid.

50. Ibid.

51. Ibid.

52. The authentic material and the letter of rejection in Klingemann, pp. 320-327.

53. Letter to Klingemann of January 19, 1847.

54. K. G. Fellerer, Geschichte der Katholischen Kirchenmusik (Düsseldorf, 1949), p. 154.

55. R. Werner, op. cit., p. 102.

56. In an anonymous article "Über die neue Liturgie," 1816. For the pertinent literature of this time, see G. Rietschel, Lehrbuch der Liturgik (Berlin, 1900), pp. 448ff.

57. Ibid., p. 476.

58. Schleiermacher, Praktische Theologie, p. 169.

59. Fr. T. Rohleder, Die Musikalische Liturgie (Glogau, 1828), pp. 208ff.

60. J. Fr. Naue, Versuch einer Musikalischen Agende, 2nd ed. (Halle, 1833-45).

61. See Ulrich Leupold, Die liturgischen Gesänge der evangelischen Kirche im Zeitalter der Aufklärung und Romantik (Kassel, 1933). This very thorough and informative work is indispensable for the study of the problems broached here.

62. Memorandum to Minister von Redern of February 14, 1844. (In "Briefen berühmter Komponisten aus den Archiven des kgl. Hof-und Domchors zu Berlin," presented by R. Scheumann, in Die Musik (Erstes Märzheft, 1909), VIII.

Interlude: Elijah

Night falleth around me, O Lord;
Be thou not far from me!

(Mendelssohn's paraphrase of I Kings 19:9)

Posterity has viewed *Elijah* as the *chef d'oeuvre* of Mendelssohn. Authorities of the rank of Sir George Grove, Hermann Kretzschmar, and Alfred Einstein considered it the greatest oratorio of the nineteenth century. Therefore, in order to be able to approach the oratorio objectively, we shall first investigate the history of its origin, then the principal problems of text and music.

The first indications of Mendelssohn's interest in this subject occurred ten years earlier.[1] The great success of *St. Paul* had awakened Mendelssohn's desire to follow it with a second oratorio on an even grander scale. So, he requested Klingemann to write a suitable text for him. At that time, it was virtually all the same to him whether Klingemann chose "St. Peter, Elijah, or even King Og of Bashan" as the protagonist of the oratorio. However, in the course of the correspondence, King Og of Bashan (who was mentioned only in fun, anyhow) disappears, and the choice among St. Peter, Elijah and perhaps King Saul is left to Klingemann. Unfortunately, Mendelssohn never returned to the last-named personality, whose fate offers the greatest tragic subject of the Old Testament.[2] As a wedding present from Klingemann, he asked for a libretto for his next oratorio—an original wish, at least! During his next English visit, the two friends tried to put together a usable draft of the libretto of an Elijah oratorio. But Klingemann simply could not work up any enthusiasm for the personality of Elijah. Mendelssohn was considerably depressed by this, and in the correspondence we find unpleasant traces of this passing estrangement. But Mendelssohn's interest in the Elijah subject must have become known in England, for in 1837 he simultaneously received two libretti for an Elijah oratorio. One of these was by a Mr. Charles Greville, who sent it to him in December, and added in his accompanying letter: "I know I am dealing with a gentleman of honour and may fully depend upon its being returned if not accepted

[457]

by you for setting to music."[3] An English clergyman, the Rev. James Barry, presented Mendelssohn with his version of Elijah, which he called "a metrical libretto." The composer thanked him politely, but observed that this version was too long for his purpose, and sent the manuscript back, not without expressing his lively interest.[4]

Since Klingemann still remained indifferent, Felix, though reluctantly, gave up all hope in this direction.[5] He showed the drafts which he had begun with Klingemann in London to his old friend, the theologian Schubring, who immediately became interested in them. There now unfolded a long correspondence between the two, mainly dedicated to the Elijah project. However, from 1839 onwards, Mendelssohn's interest seems to weaken, and the subject of Elijah disappears from his correspondence. Perhaps Schubring's last suggestion, that Christ should appear to Elijah, seemed so absurd to Felix that, for the moment, he simply dropped the whole plan.

Indeed, Elijah would never have been written if Mendelssohn had not been formally invited by Mr. Moore, the manager of the Birmingham Musical Festival, to write a large oratorio for that institution. Only now was the plan, which had been in abeyance for six years, revived. Once more the faithful Schubring sprang into the breach, and the text slowly took on its final German form. But the theologian kept wanting to insert more texts from the New Testament; he was also quite free with musical advice which Felix certainly did not need. For example, he suggested bringing in well-known chorales (e.g., Aus tiefer Noth) at high points of the oratorio.[6] Fortunately, Felix did not follow this advice. But he listened to Schubring's suggestion that the curse of the Prophet should precede the overture; the latter should represent the effects of the famine during the three accursed years.[7] On the other hand, Schubring gave in far too much to a whim of the composer, who wanted to dispense with all narrative means of expression. Mendelssohn sensed very accurately that

> with such a subject as Elijah . . . the dramatic must predominate—that the people must be introduced speaking and acting in a true-to-life fashion—but, for God's sake, this must not become a tone-painting, but a very clearly portrayed world . . ., and the contemplative, moving aspect which *you* demand must be conveyed to us through the words and moods of the characters.[8]

Schubring followed this suggestion so consistently that the listener can never tell exactly who is speaking or singing unless he has a libretto in front of him. This weakness of the libretto was recognized early; no one judged it with more fairness and understanding than Otto Jahn, whose review of the work we shall cite from time to time. Up till now, no one has evaluated Elijah more accurately.[9] Jahn criticizes the form of presentation, which altogether dispenses with the narrative element, in the following words:

The epic element of narration is . . . completely excluded; the *dramatis personae* are introduced speaking, without further formalities. In this respect, the form of *Elijah* approaches that of Handel's oratories; however, it distinctly differs from these in the symbolic [Christological] element (at which we have already hinted) in many choruses and solo songs. I am not at all sure that this is not an error. Perhaps, with the renouncing of the epic element which is so well suited to the nature of the oratorio, one sacrifices a real advantage for an imaginary one. The oratorio does not lend itself to truly dramatic development. What is usually called dramatic presentation is really not that at all, but merely representation of characters.[10]

How correctly Jahn judged the work's form of presentation may be seen in the following statement of Mendelssohn, which became known only in 1892: "I cannot stand the half-operatic character of most oratorio texts (where the authors help themselves out with generalized figures, as, for instance, 'an Israelite,' 'a maiden,' etc.). I consider this weak and will have none of it. But really, the eternal 'he said' etc., is not the right thing either."[11]

Here, Mendelssohn is wrong! What he considered "half-operatic" is in reality surely epic, and, therefore, far better suited to the style of the oratorio than to that of the theatre. Otto Jahn, who was equally familiar with Greek tragedy, classical opera and oratorio, speaks forcefully about the critical dividing line between oratorio and opera, which is often obscured in *Elijah*:

The more the oratorio . . . strives to approach the drama in outward form, the more obvious it will become that it lacks the essentials of drama. There can be no real plot, yet the work must not dispense with a continuing series of occurrences. Therefore one is forced to use many contrivances if one wants to avoid the natural form of narration, and yet one cannot easily attain complete clarity. The quieter mode of narration, for which the recitative is so splendidly suited a form . . . provides a background against which the characteristically developed situations are set forth. On the other hand, when everything is put as direct speech into the mouths of the characters, there is required a constantly heightened degree of characterization which often comes into conflict with its object or disintegrates into details and wearies us.[12]

Neither Mendelssohn nor Schubring went this far, but they completely avoided the narrative form. This raises the question as to the viewpoint from which Schubring actually organized the text.

Let us say it at once: the text of the oratorio does come from Holy Writ, but it is a weak potpourri of religious fanaticism and sanctimonious preacher's piety whereby both elements are torn out of their respective contexts. These two components do not blend well. An organic integration of historical texts from the wildest period of Israel's kings with Biblical poetry of a purer spirit was scarcely possible, and, furthermore, Schubring was not capable of carrying out such an assignment. Therefore, this partly bloodthirsty, partly magnificently visionary text must repel the thinking layman and alienate the theologian. For, from the theological standpoint, whether Jewish or Christian, it is not only insultingly naïve, but really untenable. It juxtaposes basically different elements of the Old Testament. Yet, in fact, the Old Testament reflects from the Book of Judges to the Psalter and Deutero-Isaiah, almost a millennium of religious and ethical development, as though these elements were completely homogeneous, and as though the Old Testament itself were an indivisible whole. If one reads a chapter from Isaiah or Psalm 23, the tremendous development of the theology of the Old Testament will immediately become clear; from Jahweh, the storm- and fire-god of a little Bedouin tribe, to the world-God, the Creator of the Universe, the Divine Lawgiver, the God of Charity. The theology of the Old Testament leads from the anthropomorphic belief in a God of the Wilderness to universal ethical monotheism. For Schubring, this development simply did not exist. Indeed, as we see in his correspondence with the master, he even wanted to confirm the theological unity of the whole Bible, which he had postulated, with a closing chorus from the New Testament. This would have been quite according to the spirit of orthodox Christology, but would have created serious confusion; principally for this reason, Mendelssohn definitely decided against it.

Our master's enthusiasm for the Biblical text misled him, who was neither a theologian nor an expert on ancient history, to accept the Old Testament quite naïvely. It would have been the duty of Schubring, the theologian, to call Mendelssohn's attention to this layman's error. The Bible may appear naïve, but this naïveté is deceptive. Many verses or whole chapters refer to specific concepts associated with a specific time and place. Therefore, a strictly historical attitude was called for; Isaiah should not be called upon as a witness for Elijah.[13] However, Schubring was not even satisfied with the limitation to the Bible, which was, for him, timeless and therefore subject to no historical differentiation. Mendelssohn's draft seemed too "objective" to him; true, it was "interesting and exciting," but it was far from "uplifting and edifying the listener and filling him with the spirit of devotion." Now, these are suitable considerations and criteria for liturgical music, but not necessary postulates for a work intended for the concert hall. Schubring did not hesitate to tell Mendelssohn that he must choose between real "church music" and a tone-painting in the manner of the *Erste Walpurgisnacht*. Mockingly and rejectingly—naturally, for the Christians do not come off well in it—he calls the latter work "Blocksberg-Cantate." Seven years later, the same comparison crops up. But this time it is

Mendelssohn who sharply defends himself against the charge of wanting to write a "Biblical *Walpurgisnacht*."[14]

When the work on the libretto was drawing to a close (1846) Mendelssohn began to feel the lack of a unifying plot, but could not think of a good solution. Thus, he asked Schubring to write many beautiful texts for "arias, meditations, pithy sayings, and everything else."[15] As we see, the librettist and the composer tackled their great task naïvely, and they were not wholly at one in their aims. Schubring wanted pure, uplifting church music, while Mendelssohn wanted dramatic religious music. Schubring did not concern himself either with historical or with esthetic questions, but vigorously emphasized theological aspects. Mendelssohn, on his part, feared churchly "uplifting" boredom and sought for lyrical and "characteristic" texts. The height of theological-historical naïveté was reached when Schubring—for the third time—suggested that the oratorio should close with a trio of Peter, John, and James. Curiously, Mendelssohn called this "too historical and too far removed from the attitude of the Old-Testament whole." He would have none of such crude anachronisms.[16] Here, symbolical and historical interpretations of Elijah's personality stood in opposition to one another. The symbolical interpretation views him as merely the forerunner of Jesus; the historical interpretation presents him as a powerful, unbending prophet from the age of Israel's kings. Felix was unable to decide on either interpretation. Therefore, the end of the work really consists of the "selection of beautiful Bible passages" for which he had asked Schubring.[17] The verses introduced here are all parts of magnificent prophetic poems, but (with the exception of No. 40) they have nothing to do with Elijah. Thus, the interpretation of the principal character, the Prophet himself, becomes problematic. In this matter, too, Jahn's observations certainly hit on one of the work's weaknesses. The Elijah presented here is not the man who firmly confronts the King and the people who have fallen away from God. Neither is he the prophet of a jealous God, nor is he the hard man who slays the priests of Baal himself. Rather, "Mendelssohn's Elijah is above all the pious man who firmly believes that God listens to his prayer . . . but zeal and hardness are not basic traits of his character. He is soft and sympathetic; he is deeply troubled that his warning is disregarded, and only the appearance of God sets him on his feet again."[18]

In view of such observations we may wonder whether Mendelssohn, consciously or unconsciously, did not see and picture himself in the character of Elijah. We may find some justification for this idea in a letter of tribute from Prince Albert to our master, in which he compares him with the prophet Elijah (see next chapter). The master's best friends, too, interpreted the resignation which is expressed in the aria "It is enough" as a personal confession of his weakening will to live. Nine years earlier, Felix had interpreted the historical Elijah as "a prophet such as we could use again today—strong, zealous, angry, and gloomy, in opposition to the courtiers, the rabble, and practically the whole world."[19] That is how the 29-year-old Mendelssohn felt; but now, at the end of his creative life, he was quite a different man. He was a creator who had mingled with "courtiers and rabble." He was no zealot, but a man who had fought and suffered for his principles. He had become famous, but "fame had become bitter in his mouth," as he admits to his brother.[20] Yet posterity saw him differently—mainly as the "always-happy" one ("after all, he never had to work for a living!"). The legend, which posterity will always prefer to facts, crept into all books on Mendelssohn and, indeed, into music history in general. Be that as it may, we can scarcely dismiss the possibility of an autobiographical element in *Elijah*—though Mendelssohn otherwise carefully avoided this.

In this connection, let us mention two other spheres upon which Elijah touches: Judaism and the mystical visionary element. Neither was actually the spiritual domain of the master. As we have seen, he was estranged from the Judaism of his time, though not from the contemporary Jewish world. Might age-old sentiments and associations have moved him to the choice of this particular subject matter? This question can certainly be answered in the negative. For Mendelssohn had long vacillated between Elijah and St. Peter as protagonists of his oratorio. Neither theological nor sentimental reasons motivated Mendelssohn's choice of Elijah rather than St. Peter; but the fact that neither in the Gospels nor in the history of the Apostles St. Peter cuts a very sympathetic figure. His Epistles are doctrinaire and dry; where he becomes dramatic and interesting, in his martyrdom, Biblical sources are lacking. But Mendelssohn rejected non-Biblical texts on principle, at least for an oratorio.

Noteworthy in the Biblical Elijah is the emphasis on the visionary element. Mendelssohn certainly had no inclination towards mysticism; his family had not especially valued this aspect of religion, nor was it stressed in his upbringing and environment. And yet, we find that in both *St. Paul* and *Elijah* the climaxes are reached in the realm of visionary mysticism. This was no accident; we hear from Hiller that Mendelssohn chose the Elijah subject because of its high point, the appearance of the Lord before the Prophet.[21] This exalted scene was elevated into a transcendental realm by Mendelssohn through the mystically intoned "Holy" of the angelic choirs. Neither his father, nor his grandfather, who thought very little of angels, would have been in accord with Felix's handling of the scene. The Biblical text, too, does not have a word about angels accompanying the Lord (I Kings 19:12, 43). Thus Mendelssohn combined the vision of Isaiah (6: 2, 3) with the image of Elijah which he had formed and which he was interpreting musically. This blunt rejection of all historical exegesis of the

Bible may be traced back to orthodox Christological ideas. However, it is more likely that Mendelssohn, when choosing texts from Isaiah for the last numbers of the oratorio, fell under the spell of the greatest seer-poet of the Bible.

Today, *Elijah* is much less familiar and popular in Germany than in England and America, where it belongs to the regular repertoire of choral festivals. Therefore, the English translation deserves a short commentary. Mendelssohn himself had entrusted it to his collaborator of many years, William Bartholomew, who had previously translated most of his songs, *St. Paul*, and the *Lobgesang* to the entire satisfaction of the composer. And this satisfaction was not easy to achieve! For, in all textual questions, whether poetic or musical, Mendelssohn was of a pedantry which would have better befitted a classical philologist. The première of *Elijah* was to take place in August, 1846; not until the middle of May did Bartholomew begin receiving the sections of the oratorio piecemeal as they were finished. His task did not consist only in creating a translation which corresponded to the rhythm and the phrasing of the music. Bartholomew's principal problem was in another area. Mendelssohn and Schubring had put together the text from Bible passages based (though not always literally) on Luther's translation. Now Bartholomew had, on the one hand, to do justice to Mendelssohn's music, but, on the other hand, to adjust his English translation as closely as possibly to the traditional English Bible translation, the King James Version. This was a very difficult task, and Mendelssohn criticized more than he helped. From the middle of May to the middle of August, Bartholomew worked on the English translation day and night, tirelessly and patiently, intelligently and conscientiously. Interesting details of his collaboration with the composer are found in F. G. Edwards's book on the origins of *Elijah*, to which we shall frequently refer.[22] The facsimile of a letter by Mendelssohn which is included there is especially impressive; it contains numerous suggestions, corrections and criticisms. In general, Mendelssohn's alterations in Bartholomew's drafts benefit the text more than the music. Again and again they show how intimately tone and word were interconnected in the creator's thinking, e.g., "Pray let always accent go first esp. in the choruses! And Songs! And Recitatives!" This is just as true for the English as for the German text; from the correspondence with Bartholomew it is clear that Mendelssohn, wherever possible, took into consideration the wording of the traditional English translation. True, not every detail could be carried over. D. F. Tovey has picked out and illuminated a particular case of this sort. The Overture, which directly follows the Prophet's curse, emphasizes the rhythm of the last words, *Ich sage es denn*. But, at the première in Birmingham, Mendelssohn had to change the text, which had preserved the German rhythm; for it would have been considered a blasphemy to cite the text otherwise than in the Authorized Version: "But according to My word." Of course, this completely destroyed the musical reference to the rhythm of the German text, which is important in the Overture.[23] (Examples 66, 1 and 66, 5.)

Example 66, 1

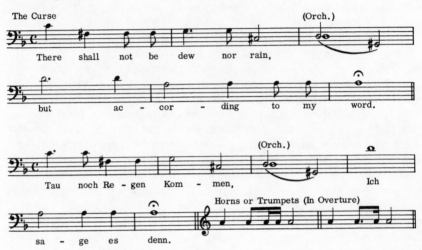

Here, we must take into consideration the haste with which some of the most important questions were decided. On July 3, Mendelssohn was still not sure of the function of the Overture and, above all, of the proper place for it. When he followed Schubring's and Bartholomew's suggestion of putting it after the curse, it was not yet written; and, when he wrote it, he was not yet fully aware of the inviolability of the Authorized Version.[24] But, on the whole, Bartholomew's achievement is admirable; and it must have been a thankless task!

As we have already observed, the oratorio does not follow a continuous story-line, but consists of individual tableaux or scenes: Nos. 1-5, 6-9, 10-20. The introductory recitative, the prophetic curse, immediately grips our attention; it enters with heavy trombone sonorities and menacing tritone skips. It is very brief and dramatic. Only now does the overture begin. It is an extensive fugal movement, strict in its thematic working out, which depicts the effect of the drought on the people of Israel. Here we see that, in the hand of a master, even a fugue can present passionate and fearful emotions. The fear of the catastrophe is also expressed with greatest forcefulness in the chorus No. 1. No. 2, a duet with chorus, is a particularly well-conceived formal experiment. Mendelssohn begins the piece with the intonation of a short Phrygian motif: (Example 67.)

Example 66, 5

Above the *ostinato* bass, there rises a charming elegiac melody, "Zion spreadeth her hands for aid" (Example 67). It is sung by two sopranos, and sparsely accompanied by the string orchestra. The following aria (No. 4), "If with all your hearts," approaches the rather sanctimonious style of the younger Mendelssohn's songs and cantatas. It is, however, immediately pushed into the background by the mighty chorus "Yet doth the Lord." This piece takes up the tritone skips of the curse and treats them like a leitmotif. It culminates in the *Grave* section, "For He, the Lord our God." At first, this section praises the jealous Jahweh who deals out justice, then,

Example 67

surprisingly, in a splendid upsurge of polyphony, it praises the Lord of mercy and forgiveness.. This dualism is discernible in the theology of the Old Testament; in the Rabbinic literature (with which neither Mendelssohn nor Schubring was familiar) it is explained by the doctrine of God's attributes. In this passage, it is somewhat contradictory in effect. The first scene ends in a majestic tribute to the love of God. This magnificently constructed scene has few equals in the oratorio literature.

The second scene (Nos. 6-9) portrays the prophet at the brook Cherith, under the protection of angels. No. 7, the double quartet "For He shall give his angels," is famous for its magical euphony. The scene is continued in Zarephath, where Elijah restores the widow's dead child to life. Mendelssohn took special pains with this section, revising it twice; yet, he was dissatisfied with his own achievement. For, unfortunately, the widow is delineated somewhat too realistically; we have the feeling that an unpleasant and querulous woman is constantly pestering the master. Somewhat more diplomatically, Otto Jahn observes "that the long-drawn-out wailings of the mother give us an unpleasant feeling. But the force of the miracle is weakened by the fact that Elijah has to repeat his prayer three times before it is answered." Here, confusing the theatrical with the dramatic, Mendelssohn gave too much of a good thing. Therefore, Jahn's criticism of the scene hits the nail on the head: "Perhaps because such things are often found in operas, Mendelssohn may have been inclined to consider this way of writing 'dramatic,' as the word is often used in excuse or criticism. One might as well call *scene-painting* dramatic."[25]

The following chorus, "Blessed are the men who fear him" (No. 9), can only partially mitigate the unsatisfactory impression of the preceding scene. Thus, the second scene is the weakest one in the whole oratorio, and perhaps it would be best to leave it out entirely.

Now the three years of drought are at an end, and the prophet sets forth to announce the longed-for rain to King Ahab. On this occasion, he challenges the priests of Baal at Ahab's court to that strange duel between Jahweh and their gods, which is universally familiar. The following choruses (Nos. 11 to 14) are among the most grippingly forceful ever to be dared in an oratorio. The foolish and vain efforts of the priests of Baal, the cutting mockeries of Elijah, the despairing prayers of the idol-worshipers, far surpass all similar passages in *St. Paul*. With fine appropriateness, the mocking speech of the prophet is set to the same motif with which the Baal-worshipers had implored, "Hear us!" In the chorus "Hear and answer, Baal!" (No. 13) every listener thrills to the breathless tension which reaches its climax in two long general pauses. These pauses portray most vividly the apprehensive waiting of the idol-worshipers. After the dignified prayer of the prophet and a weak, chorale-like little section (No. 15) which, unfortunately, is accompanied by a solo violin, there follows the miracle.

The chorus sings enthusiastically of it in "The fire descends from heav'n!" (No. 16). The licking of the flames, in this Biblical "Magic Fire Music," is represented by the polyphonically treated chorus. In somewhat forced fashion, the dramatic scene turns towards the dogmatic as the chorus sings the verse "The Lord is God." Now, the furious Elijah demands the immediate death of the priests of Baal at the hands of the uncontrolled mob; this *auto-da-fè* is promptly carried out. A rather apologetic aria of the prophet, "Is not His word like a fire?" seeks to justify the massacre; however, neither librettist nor composer seems to have felt quite at ease about it. A second elegiac and apologetic arioso, "Woe unto them who forsake Him," ends with the tritone of the curse. We seem to hear Mendelssohn's sigh of relief when he leaves this bloody scene and, in Nos. 19 and 20, describes the miracle of rain. Schubring's lack of empathy with the spirit of the Old Testament is painfully evident. At the beginning, he had the prophet pronounce the curse. Now the same Elijah prays "Regard the distress of thy people!" But this prayer does not occur in this connection in the Bible. United with the people, Elijah and his companion Obadiah pray for rain. Thrice the prophet calls on Jahweh, while a boy on a hill searches the heavens for clouds. Twice, he sees nothing; the representation of the bleak oppressive sky with the simplest means is admirable. Finally, clouds gather, and the crowd breaks into the song of thanksgiving, "Thanks be to God for all his mercies"; it culminates in the mighty chorus "Thanks be to God!" (No. 20). With Handelian breadth Mendelssohn portrays the joy of the rescued people. Here, Schubring also introduced verses from Psalm 93: "The waters gather, they rush along! They are lifting their voices!" Turning away from superficial illustration of words, the composer expresses "lifting" with *descending scales*. With the verse "But the Lord is above them, and Almighty" there commences a series of striking modulations which, in a powerful upward surge, lead to the intensified repetition of the chorus of thanksgiving. Downward-rushing scales in unison introduce the close of the first part.

The second part is divided into six groups of movements. Of these, only the second scene (Nos. 23-25) and the third scene (Nos. 30-35) further the development of the plot, which is hard to follow. The other sections consist either of pious observations and comforting Bible passages or of Messianic promises (especially No. 41 and the following quartet "O come, every one that thirsteth"). They are often interrupted by arias; only in passing does a chorus (No. 38) report the prophet's journey to heaven. Just as in *St. Paul*, the second part suffers from this lack of dramatic occurrences and the plethora of prophetic sayings.

Of the two warnings with which the second part begins, the first, "Hear ye, Israel," was, like most of the pieces for soprano, written especially for

Lind's voice, which carried beautifully even in *pianissimo*.[26] The unpretentious motifs rise to Biblical pathos, which, at the end of the aria, gives away to simple dignity. In the following chorus, "Be not afraid" (No. 22), Mendelssohn succeeded in grasping the spirit of the Old Testament, especially in the defiantly heroic passage "Though the thousands languish and fall beside thee," which, however, is carried out at too great length. Subsequently, the story continues with the appearance of the prophet before King Ahab and Queen Jezebel. Mendelssohn conceived the scene in very lively fashion. The mob, stirred up by the Queen, turns furiously on Elijah (No. 24, "Woe to him"). Here, too, this *turba* scene is far more impressive than the similar stoning chorus in *St. Paul*.

Elijah flees into the wilderness. Despondent and dejected, he longs for death. It seems as though this mood corresponded to that of Mendelssohn, who sank ever deeper into weariness and resignation; for the master portrayed this emotional state unforgettably in the aria "It is enough." The mournful melody is counterpointed by an obbligato 'cello. Just when we expect this complaint to end quietly, the prophet's anger at the vacillating people breaks out in a furious Allegro. Only towards the end of the piece does Elijah sink back into his weariness of life; he implores, "O Lord! Now take away my life." Angels appear to comfort him; they sing the famous "Lift thine eyes," unaccompanied, a daring idea in a large-scale oratorio. The contrast, however, comes off beautifully; this chorus, simple yet perfectly conceived for voices, has never failed of its effect. A comforting chorus "He watching over Israel" suffers from oversymmetrical construction. Only in a carefully balanced performance do its fine nuances really come out; then, however, they enhance the feeling of being cherished and protected which this chorus conveys.

In the recitatives (Nos. 30 and 33) which carry on the story, there are definite leitmotifs. In No. 30, the orchestral motif from "It is enough" occurs on the words "O Lord, I have labor'd in vain!" In No. 33, the melody of the first chorus, "The harvest now is over, the summer days are gone," is set to the words "My soul is thirsting for Thee, as a thirsty land." In the depths of despair, the prophet longs only for death. Then an angel calms him, and commands him to make his way to Mount Horeb, where the Lord will reveal Himself to him. This song of comfort is "O rest in the Lord" (No. 31); it is beloved by many, but scorned by others because of its "popular" quality. As Otto Jahn already recognized, it is "a representation of Elijah's inner spiritual state. He is not the only one to express it for us; rather, that which lives concealed deep within a man's unconscious here finds objective expression and thus attains the character of higher reality."[27] As we learn from the correspondence with Bartholomew, Mendelssohn wanted to omit this piece because its opening motif was

all-too-reminiscent of an old Scottish ballad.[28] After some hesitation, he altered two decisive notes and allowed the piece to remain. Here we give the original version, the Scottish ballad, and Mendelssohn's final version:
Example 68

O   rest   in   the   Lord,   wait   pa - tien - tly   Him

Young   Ja - mie loved   me   well   and   asked me   for   his   bride.

O   rest   in   the   Lord,   wait   pa - tien - tly   for   Him

As if to reinforce the "O rest in the Lord," a chorus breathing peace, "He that shall endure" (No. 32), assures the prophet of the bliss for which he longs. In this piece, it seems to me that Mendelssohn uses a characteristic motif from the chorale *O Welt, ich muss dich lassen;* here, the beautiful reminiscence intensifies the feeling of leavetaking, of transcendent resignation. The motif appears in especially impressive fashion in the basses of the closing cadence:
Example 69

Chorus

And now the work attains its towering climax in the appearance of the Lord. In a short dialogue with the angel, the prophet prepares for the Encounter. It is carried by the chorus, like the appearance of Jesus in *St. Paul.* But what a difference! There, delicate, transparent harmonies of the women's chorus, limited to a few words; here, an apocalyptic panorama of earthquake, tempest, flood, and fire. "And after the fire there came a still small voice, and in that still voice, onward came the Lord." Mendelssohn's presentation is fully worthy of the powerful scene. We know that it was the germ-cell of the oratorio; it is very strange that, here, Mendelssohn went back to a medieval tune of the German Jews. Certainly, he was not aware of the resemblance, but it seems that this scene, depicting the Holy of Holies, awakened within him associations which had slumbered since childhood. The tune is a variant of the melody to which the 13 Divine Attributes (Exodus 24:6, 7) have been sung since the fifteenth century in all German synagogues on the High Holy Days. Only on these three highest feast days of the Jewish year was the melody sung: on those days when all Jews were accustomed to assemble in the House of God. The melody, performed on the most solemn of religious occasions, with the rabbi and cantor in white robes, must have impressed itself upon the boy and associated itself with the representation of the Divine. Thus, through the mysterious workings of creative fantasy, this assocation may have been conjured from the subconscious.

Example 70

The master most felicitously chose the form of the free canon for the movement; this, as Jahn points out, "has an irresistible forward drive," and yet is firmly held together by its inner logic. The treatment of the bass deserves special admiration. First, long-drawn-out pedal-points carry the rapidly changing harmonies of the chorus (19 measures of *e*, six of *d*, five of *g*, 13 of *b*, four of *g* sharp, six of *c*, four of *f*, three of *f* sharp, four of *c*, two of *b* flat, two of *a*, two of *g*, three of *f*). Thereafter ("and the earth was shaken") the bass, which up till then was firm and steady, becomes shaky; it is really as though the ground were trembling under our feet. After this uproar, there follows the "still small voice" over pure triads in light rhythmic motion.

The following chorus "Holy is God the Lord" (No. 35) raises the dramatic vision higher yet, into a mystical realm; the hosts of angels antiphonally intone the Thrice-Holy. Only a few orchestral chords accompany the solemn chorus. With the next chorus (recitative No. 36, "Go, return upon thy way"), the second scene—and, with it, the real story—fades away. Forcefully and excitedly, the chorus does still report on the prophet's fiery journey to Heaven—and this is where Mendelssohn originally wanted to end the work. Unfortunately, he let Schubring change his mind —certainly not to the work's benefit.[29] For what now follows consists of Messianic or Christologically interpreted prophetic sayings from the last chapters of Malachi and Isaiah. Among these, the chorus "But the Lord from the north" (No. 41) is serious and on a grand scale, but the following quartet weakens this impression. The closing chorus (No. 43) "And then shall your light break forth," with the fugue "Lord our Creator," is brilliant and powerful enough, but such pious observations and joyous Bible passages have nothing to do with the personality of Elijah. They give the impression of an artificial addition, a sort of theological-musical commentary, which is superfluous and definitely harmful to the total impression of the work.

Nonetheless, if only through its great musical conception, the oratorio far surpasses the interpretation of a complex of ideas which is narrowly limited by theological considerations. In its best numbers, it rises to realms of awe which are no longer accessible to rational language. In this respect, it stands on a lonely height, near to the creations of Bach and Handel.

ℕotes

1. Letter to Klingemann of August 12, 1836.
2. Letter to Klingemann of February 18, 1837. On the contrary, Schubring believed that a character like Saul "could mean nothing to Felix."
3. Unpublished letter from Charles Greville to Mendelssohn of December 12, 1837.
4. F. G. Edwards, *The History of Mendelssohn's Oratorio "Elijah"* (London, 1896), pp. 7ff.
5. See the remark by Klingemann, the editor of the Mendelssohn-Klingemann correspondence, on p. 233. If Klingemann's draft had been followed, "the magnificent work would have taken on a dramatic form rather than the epic-lyrical form which was finally used."
6. The son of that Pastor Schubring, Dr. Julius Schubring, published the correspondence of his father with Mendelssohn (Leipzig, 1892). As the title observes, this is "a contribution to the history and theory of the oratorio." Here, see the letters of February 2, 1839, and p. 208.
7. *Ibid.*
8. Letter to Schubring of December 6, 1838.
9. Otto Jahn, "Über Felix Mendelssohn Bartholdy's Oratorium Elias," *Allgemeine Musikalische Zeitung* (1848), p. 113. (Also in Jahn's *Gesammelte Aufsätze über Musik* (Leipzig, 1866), pp. 40-63; we shall quote from this edition.)
10. Jahn, *op. cit.*, pp. 43-44.

11. Letter to Schubring of December 16, 1845 (not, as in older editions, 1842).

12. Jahn, *op. cit.*, p. 45.

13. Neither should the verses Isaiah 41:25 and Isaiah 11:2 be connected together and referred to the same person. The former passage refers to Cyrus, King of Persia, while the latter refers to the Messiah, the anointed one, the "shoot out of the stock of Jesse."

14. Letter to Schubring of December 16, 1845.

15. *Ibid.*

16. Letter to Schubring of May 23, 1846.

17. *Ibid.* The passages are: Malachi 4:5-6 (No. 40), Isaiah 41:25 and 11:2 (No. 41); Isaiah 55:1,3 (No. 41a); Isaiah 58:8 (No. 42).

18. Jahn, *op. cit.*, pp. 61ff.

19. Letter to Schubring of November 2, 1838.

20. Unpublished letter of June 28, 1846.

21. F. Hiller, *Erinnerungen an Felix Mendelssohn Bartholdy*, p. 150.

22. F. G. Edwards, *The History of Mendelssohn's Oratorio "Elijah"* (London, 1896).

23. D. F. Tovey, *The Mainstream of Music* (New York, 1949).

24. See the final passage of the facsimile letter of July 3, 1846, in F. G. Edwards, *op. cit.*

25. Jahn, *op. cit.*, p. 51.

26. It seems to me that the criticism of the soprano in the première, Mme Caradori, that the aria was not "a lady's song," emphasizes—albeit unintentionally—the living power of the piece.

27. Jahn, *op. cit.*, p. 58.

28. Edwards, *op. cit.*, pp. 63ff.

CHAPTER XIX *Triumph and Death*

The heart has its reasons, of which reason knows naught.
Pascal
O Lord, assuage the thoughts of anguish,
Illumine thou my pining heart!
(Goethe, *Faust*: among Mendelssohn's *Elijah* sketches)

THE LAST YEAR of Mendelssohn's life was filled with the obligations imposed upon him by his world fame. This observation does not touch on the essentials of these fourteen months between the première of *Elijah* and the death of its creator. In this short span of time there occurred an inner transformation which, concealed from the world at large and unrecognized by posterity, changed the man and artist Mendelssohn in his inmost being. This last year is to be called disastrous not only because of his death. What makes it tragic in the true sense of the word is Mendelssohn's decisive inner turn toward an attitude which Schopenhauer calls "heroic pessimism." We shall begin with a condensed survey of the outward occurrences, in chronological order, and then interpret the details. Only thereafter dare we approach—with all due caution—the mysterious inner transformation of the master.

Chronology of the Last Year

1. Première in Birmingham *of Elijah* (August 26, 1846)
2. Revision of the score
3. German Liturgy (October, 1846)
4. Death of Mendelssohn's servant (November, 1846)
5. Operatic plans with Lumley and Geibel (December, 1846, January-February, 1847)
6. Last birthday; drafts and work on *Christus*
7. Work for Conservatory (March, 1847)
8. Last (10th) journey to England (this and the next three events all took place in April, 1847)
9. Six performances of *Elijah* under Mendelssohn
10. Concerts in London; reception in Buckingham Palace

11. Jenny Lind's debut in London
12. Journey home; mishap in Herbesthal
13. News of Fanny's death (May 14, 1847)
14. Last stay in Switzerland (June-September, 1847)
15. Preparation for three performances of *Elijah* in Berlin, Vienna, and Leipzig.
16. Last string quartet, last songs, English motets (September, 1847)
17. Last performance on the organ in Ringgenberg; return to Leipzig
18. Concern with German domestic politics (September-October, 1847)
19. Several serious nervous attacks (October, 1847)
20. Two strokes and death (November 4, 1847)
21. Funeral services; burial in Berlin (November 7-8, 1847)

I

Mendelssohn himself considered the triumph of the première of *Elijah* as the greatest *outward* success of his artistic career. There are plenty of detailed reports by contemporaries, but they contradict each other so frequently that it is hard for us to form a clear picture of that performance.

Eight or nine days before the première, Mendelssohn had arrived in London and had immediately started rehearsing with the soloists. Since Jenny Lind had not yet appeared in England, the directors of the festival had assigned the soprano part to the 46-year-old Mme Caradori-Allan. A difference of opinion arose between her and Mendelssohn almost at once; she felt that the aria "Hear ye, Israel" (which, indeed, had been conceived for Lind) was no "lady's song," and demanded that Mendelssohn should transpose it a whole tone lower. Mendelssohn, quite the *grand seigneur*, coolly and politely informed the singer that he had no intention of altering the piece and calmly added that, if she did not want to sing it, he would ask the committee for another soprano.[1] Then, he rehearsed for two whole days with the full orchestra in the Hanover Square Hall. The faithful Moscheles helped as much as he could; at the music festival, he had to direct the whole concert of the first day and, besides, to prepare *Elijah* with the chorus and orchestra. Even before its première, this work received the unprecedented honor of being evaluated in a long analytical article in the *Times*. This was the first notable work of J. W. Davison, who was later to become a famous music critic. Three days before the performance Mendelssohn traveled to Birmingham with the whole orchestra, the soloists, and the London members of the chorus—and, naturally, accompanied by the "gentlemen of the press." At once, rehearsals were resumed, now with the full chorus; and then Mendelssohn worked with Bartholomew far into the night on correcting the choral and orchestral parts. The orchestra consisted of 125 men: 93 strings and doubled winds. The chorus comprised 271 singers: 79 sopranos, 60 altos (sung entirely by young men), 60 tenors, and 72 basses.[2] The soloists were Mme Caradori-Allan (soprano), Miss Marie B. Hawes (alto), Mr. Charles Lockey (tenor), and Joseph Staudigl (bass baritone) as Elijah. At the organ sat Mendelssohn's old friend Dr. Gauntlett; and everything had been prepared as well as possible under Mendelssohn's and Moscheles's tireless supervision.

Shortly before his appearance as conductor of the première, Mendelssohn turned to Chorley, the critic of the *Athenaeum*, with the words: "Now stick your claws into my work. Don't tell me what you like, but tell me what you *don't* like."[3] We may best hear about the success of the performance in the *Times* review, in Moscheles's letter to his wife, and, finally, in Mendelssohn's own opinion in a letter to his brother.

The *Times* wrote, at the end of its long report:

The last note of "Elijah" was drowned in a long-continued unanimous volley of plaudits, vociferous and deafening. It was as though enthusiasm, long checked, had suddenly burst its bonds and filled the air with shouts of exultation. Mendelssohn, evidently overpowered, bowed his acknowledgment, and quickly descended from his position in the conductor's rostrum; but he was compelled to appear again, amidst renewed cheers and huzzas. Never was there a more complete triumph—never a more thorough and speedy recognition of a great work of art.[4]

Moscheles to his wife:

Yes, Mendelssohn's triumph at yesterday's performance was something quite incredible, unheard of. I believe eleven numbers had to be repeated to enthusiastic applause, though usually all applause is strictly forbidden at these music festivals. . . . This time, everyone was so carried away that applause could not be restrained, and it was as noisy as in the parterre of a theatre. . . .[5]

Mendelssohn to his brother on the day after the première, August 27, 1846:

Never before has a piece of mine gone so splendidly at the first performance, and been received so enthusiastically by the musicians and the listeners, as this oratorio. It was already evident at the first rehearsal in London that they liked it and enjoyed singing and playing it; but that it would go so swingingly and vigorously in the performance, I must confess that even I had not expected. If only you had been there! The whole three-and-a-half hours that it lasted, the 2000 people in the great hall, and the great orchestra, were so concentrated on a single point that there was not the slightest sound to be heard in the audience, and that I could handle the huge choral and orchestral and organ masses exactly as I pleased. . . . . No fewer than 4 choruses and 4 arias were repeated, and in the whole first part there was not a single mistake—afterwards, in the second part, there were a few, but they were very insignificant. . . .[6]

Among these letters, reviews, and the memoirs of Chorley and Gauntlett, the single unfavorable review (in the *Musical Times*, October, 1846) is scarcely important. Nonetheless, we shall cite it:

It [the Festival] was also remarkable for the production of Mendelssohn's new work, *Elijah;* but even this work, with the advantage of the author's presence as conductor, was but imperfectly given, from the want of proper rehearsals. Many other works, the names of which in the scheme attracted visitors from a long distance, were so wretchedly mutilated, as to cause the greatest disappointment—Beethoven's Grand Mass in D [*Missa Solemnis*], for instance.[7]

In this connection, Dr. P. Scholes mentions several ·letters from contemporaries of this première, in order to criticize certain changes—not to say falsifications—of the tempi of *Elijah*. In a letter from Mr. Stanford to the *Times* (December 7, 1901) it is emphasized that Mr. Lockey, the tenor of the première, always complained that since then all the tempi were dragged, especially those of the two alto solos "Woe unto them" and "O rest in the Lord." "It is now [1901] frequently reduced to nearly half-speed. He also mentioned the prodigious pace of the final Baal chorus and of the song 'Is not his word like a fire?'; two movements of which (as my father told me) 'Mendelssohn's conducting was like whipping cream.' [i.e., very fast]"[8] As pleasant as Mendelssohn's impressions of Mr. Lockey's singing were, as unsympathetic was the soprano to him. In a letter to Frau Frege in Leipzig, an outstanding singer, he reports on the great success, but complains about the soprano, because she was "so pretty, so pleasant, so elegant, yet so impure in intonation, so soulless, so brainless, and the music took on a sort of *amiable* expression which makes my blood boil even today when I think about it. . . ."[9]

Here, we prick up our ears: had Mendelssohn ever before taken it amiss when his music was decried as elegant or amiable? Obviously, these comments are already symptomatic of the transformation which was taking place within him.

Without a doubt, *Elijah* was the center of the first day of the music festival. Yet, in spite of the triumphal ovation for Mendelssohn and his work, *Elijah* was followed in the *same* concert by arias from Mozart's *Davidde Penitente*, Cimarosa's *Abramo*, and a Handel chorus, all under Moscheles's direction.[10] On the same evening (August 26) works of Beethoven and Spohr were performed, followed by a potpourri of English glees and popular songs which was very well received. The next morning brought Handel's *Messiah*, which "the veteran Braham opened with the ruins of his voice; Staudigl raised the level of the whole."[11] In the evening followed Weber's *Preciosa* Overture, various songs and arias, Moscheles's old war-horse *Hommage a Handel* (with Mendelssohn at the second piano) and Mendelssohn's *A Midsummer Night's Dream* music.[12]

With the exception of *Elijah* and the *A Midsummer Night's Dream*, everything was directed by Moscheles. For him, the music festival represented the formal farewell to England. The Leipzig Conservatory had grown so much that Moscheles could no longer refuse Mendelssohn's repeated invitations; later, he became artistic director of the Conservatory.

Back in London, Mendelssohn tried to recuperate, in the circle of his friends, from the tremendous amount of work which lay behind him. But there was too much business to be taken care of, too many acquaintances to be visited or received. So, he was very weary when he began the journey home. He was so exhausted that he had to interrupt the journey from Ostende to Leipzig three times in order to have a good sleep.

The beginning concert season, the Conservatory, and the arrival of the Moscheles family (October 25, 1840) made renewed demands on the exhausted man. In addition he, eternally dissatisfied, had already started to revise the score of *Elijah*. What other man, blessed with fame and fortune, would have driven himself so unnecessarily?[13]

In fact, at the beginning of December he was already in the midst of revising the work. He reported to Klingemann about his changes and emphasized that he was now finally "quite through with one of the most difficult parts [the scene with the widow] and was convinced that Klingemann would approve the changes." He deceived himself, however, when he believed that "in this passage *Elijah* has become much more significant and mysterious." A comparison with the first version shows only a considerable lengthening of the scene and a more stilted musical portrayal of the prophet. But we must respect the conviction which is expressed in these words: "The pieces which I have revised up till now show me again that I am right not to rest until such a work is as good as I can possibly make it—even though most people know little and care less about these things. . . ."[14]

To all these cares and duties were now added the operatic projects, which, for the first time in many years, took on concrete form. In the previous chapter, we have discussed the Lumley-Scribe plan and also the *Loreley* plan (with Geibel's libretto to be revised by Devrient). All these projects suddenly became urgent. For into the midst of this overloaded work schedule there burst the wish (really, the command) of the Prussian King that Mendelssohn should produce a *German Liturgy*. As we have seen, the master fulfilled this wish gladly and promptly; yet until the present day this work has never been published in its entirety.

And now, as if in dark warning, death invaded his inner circle. Mendelssohn's faithful servant, or, rather, his helper of many years' standing, Johann Krebs, died after a long illness.[15] He had named Mendelssohn as his executor, and, in addition to his grief for his lost helper, the master now had his hands full with inheritance matters. Since he was not in a condition to work creatively, the restless man helped himself out with "half-mechanical tasks"; he corrected his score of Bach's B minor Mass according to the parts written by the composer. Under these circumstances, it is no wonder that he confessed to his "*one* friend" (Klingemann) that he was repelled by all conducting and public playing. "I think the time is coming, or is perhaps already here, when I shall put all this regular public music-making on the shelf, in order to make music at home, write notes, and simply let the outside world go by."[16]

As soon as he had somewhat collected himself, he began to work seriously on his third oratorio, *Christus*. Its text, again drawn from Holy Writ, was presented to him, at first, only in individual numbers. He had conceived *Christus* as the climax of his oratorio trilogy; with it, he planned to complete the musical synthesis of Old and New Testament. Strange how his theological, or, rather, religious thinking always circled around the same point! Again and again he was concerned with the transition from Judaism to universal Christian monotheism according to Schleiermacher's vision. This theology may have symbolized to him the family history, in which Moses Mendelssohn played the role of the Old Testament patriarch and Abraham, that of St. Paul, the mediator between Judaism and Christianity.

In another, most disagreeable way, he was now reminded—most publicly —of his "Mosaic" ancestry. This happened as follows: The *Gewandhaus* concerts of the season 1846-47 were nominally under Mendelssohn's direction; in reality, however, Gade and Mendelssohn alternated as conductors from concert to concert. On November 5, 1846, the master premièred his friend Schumann's Second Symphony in C major; it was planned for the second half of the concert. The first part opened with Rossini's *William Tell* Overture; the enthusiastic applause which it elicited necessitated its repetition. This was interpreted by the music critic of the *Leipzig Tageblatt* as a gesture against the novelty of the evening, Schumann's symphony. To explain the quite natural incident, he had to drag in the supposed "Mosaic" interests. To accuse a Mendelssohn of preferring Rossini to Schumann was already a piece of journalistic infamy; to deck out this accusation with anti-Semitic sentiments was a nasty demagogic trick which shows the "freedom-minded" journalism of the *Vormärz* (and probably also of the year 1848) in a most ominous light. As was to be expected, Mendelssohn took refuge in a haughty and scornful silence towards the press. He had always had serious moral reservations concerning its activities, and usually mistrusted it. When Clara Schumann wanted to give a concert of her own and begged Mendelssohn to conduct the symphony again, the furious master rejected the request. Only the combined persuasion of Clara and Cecile succeeded in changing the mind of the deeply hurt Mendelssohn; thus, on November 16, he repeated the Schumann symphony.[17]

The constant drain on his slight physical reserves now made itself felt regularly. There were few days when Mendelssohn did not suffer from headache. His doctors warned him again and again to take care of himself, but their warnings were disregarded as much as were those of his own body. Even the most tender pleas of Cecile, who was seriously concerned about Felix's health, could not accomplish much. He always had a more or less stereotyped answer at hand when he was admonished to take better care of himself: "Till my 40th birthday I'll work, after that I'll rest," or "Just let me work now, the time of rest will come for me too." But he was determined to withdraw from the "music business." Only he did not yet know where he would live. It seems that he seriously thought of moving to Berlin in order to be near his beloved brother and sisters. We must deduce this from a letter to his brother-in-law Dirichlet, which is also important for its political commentary. Felix writes:

> You will find the same bad mood and the same dissatisfaction [as in Berlin] everywhere throughout all Germany . . . and the universal sickness will not be cured by you with your move [to Heidelberg] and not by me with my subscription concerts. It can only be relieved by quite different things, or by a very severe crisis. In such a case, it is good not to find oneself in new circumstances, but, rather, in the old accustomed ones. A third thing can happen—and also, this is not too improbable in Germany: everything can remain as it was. . . .[18] I have now, I may say, definitely decided that I shall soon be spending my winters in Berlin again. . . . Under really very favorable conditions, I had preferred to remain in a smaller city [Leipzig], and am accustomed to no other. And yet, now I am drawn away from it and to the people with whom I have enjoyed my childhood and youth. . . . I think we could all have a very nice house together, such as we have not seen for a long time. . . .[19]

Devrient, on the contrary, reports that Felix wanted to built a house in Frankfurt, where he would spend spring and fall; during the winter, he planned to live in Berlin, while he had reserved the summer for Switzerland where he wanted to settle near Interlaken.[20] All this looks like a serious effort to organize a quieter and less trying life. But alas, all his plans came too late.

It is rather plain that these plans were conditioned by his political thinking. In Frankfurt, he saw a center of events in Germany, and the year 1848 proved him right. As we have already seen, Felix felt himself to be a good German, loyal to the Fatherland. Like his teacher Hegel, he, too, rejected a vague world citizenship. Though Hegel's philosophy was, much much later, set up as the oracle of German nationalism, in itself it still remained on that high level where the "philosopher may still fully believe that he is serving the idea alone," while he is, in reality, already on the way to becoming the servant of the deed. "His effort was to apply ethical principles and maxims fairly and wisely to the world of politics. So Hegel's [and Mendelssohn's] rejection of world citizenship was miles removed from that crude return to Nationalism which was to become a reality in Germany a few decades later."[21] These remarks about Hegel's system of thought also hold true for the friends Mendelssohn and Droysen, who were politically more or less of one mind. Indeed, Droysen was to succeed in taking an active part in the turbulent events; as a young man he longed for this, as an old man he smiled about it. Who knows whether Mendelssohn would have thought and acted otherwise had he experienced the 1848-50 crisis? In any case, however, he would always have agreed with Droysen's proud saying: "The lofty aim of our scholarship consists in this: that it does not merely want to make mankind more clever, but that it should and will make it better."[22] This, too, was Mendelssohn's humane belief, and, at all times, his political thinking remained under the control of his ethics. What was morally false could not be right politically. To him, this was a universal rule. Therefore, he expressed himself as forcefully about Lord Palmerstone's politics as about that of Prussia in the *Vormärz*.

Meanwhile, however, he was buried in the revisions of *Elijah* and the current affairs of Leipzig's musical life—a man world famous, yet already weary and melancholy. He had still not forgotten the wild and uninhibited laughter of his youth, but only seldom could he enjoy himself wholeheartedly. Once more it was granted him to do so to the full: on his last birthday. The celebration took place in Moscheles's house. First, a sort of prologue in Frankfurt dialect was presented by Cecile and her sister. There followed an ingenious charade on the word "Ge-wand-haus-Orchester."

The "Ge" was represented by young Joachim, who appeared in Paganini's costume and improvised in his manner on the G string. The "Wand" (wall) was that between Pyramus and Thisbe in *A Midsummer Night's Dream*. The "Haus" (house) was illustrated by Mrs. Moscheles, who, while knitting, gave orders to the cook. The word "Orchestra" was once again symbolized by Joachim, who, with a toy violin, directed Moscheles's and Mendelssohn's children playing all sorts of noisemakers. Afterwards he said it had been his finest birthday.[23] It was his last![24]

The overworked master now made a grave mistake. He had accepted the invitation of the "Sacred Harmonic Society" to conduct the new version of *Elijah* himself.[25] This one performance turned into six, all within a period of two weeks, April 16-30. In between, as usual, there were countless other duties, among them a concert of the Philharmonic in London. In addition there were private receptions and concerts in the Prussian Embassy, two appearances in Buckingham Palace before the Queen and Prince Albert, and still more concerts (with the Beethoven Quartet Society, with the Antient Concerts Society, at Baron Bunsen's, etc.).

Mendelssohn had hesitated before accepting this invitation, which would place so many obligations upon him. Even in March, he had suggested postponing the concert series till the Fall, for then everything could be better prepared and he himself would be more rested.[26] But Mr. Bartholomew and the "Sacred Harmonic Society" would not hear of a postponement. So the master, accompanied by the young Joachim, set out on his last (10th) English journey.

Many things had been changed and, on the whole, improved, in *Elijah*. The duet "Lift thine eyes" had now turned into a three-part *a cappella* chorus; the scene with the widow had been improved, though still not to the master's full satisfaction; the choruses had been tightened up and condensed. In short, the hard work had not been in vain.

On April 12, Mendelssohn arrived in London, and, as usual, stayed with his friend Klingemann. The performance of the new version of *Elijah* took place on April 16 in Exeter Hall; it was repeated on the 23rd, 28th, and 30th. The second performance was lent added lustre by the presence of the Queen and the Prince Consort.[27] On this occasion, the Prince, who had always been an admirer of Mendelssohn, wrote in his *Elijah* libretto:

> To the noble artist who, surrounded by the Baal-worship of false art, through genius and study has been able, like a second Elijah, to remain true to the service of true art; who has freed our ear from the chaos of mindless jingling of tones, to accustom it once more to the pure sounds of truly reflected emotion and regular harmony; to the Great Master, who, in a steady stream of ideas, unrolls before us the whole panorama of the elements from the gentlest rustlings to the mightiest storms; in grateful recollection,
>
> Albert.[28]

This tone is familiar to us. Do we not hear Hegel in every word, especially in the "pure sounds of truly reflected emotion?" It could be hardly otherwise; for Albert's mentor, Baron Stockmar, was a Hegelian. Albert, perhaps the most astute and statesmanlike prince of the nineteenth century, had different standards for art and scholarship than those customary in England. The "jingling of tones" which he scorned stood for the *prima donna* opera of London; the epithet "mindless" refers to the cult of "elegant" playing and singing in dilettante circles.[29] Victoria had taken over much of Albert's way of thinking; even as an old lady, she used to say proudly that Mendelssohn had been her singing teacher. Politically, too, Albert and Felix thought alike. In 1846, the Prince Consort postulated the unification of "Little Germany" under Prussia's leadership; and, in 1848, this prophetic prince calls for the unification of Germany as a federated state; not, however, in the Bismarckian sense, but, rather, through the cooperation of the princes and their parliaments.[30]

Probably, in the hours of conversation with Prince Albert, Mendelssohn touched upon the burning political questions of those days. He must have rejoiced at their agreement in these matters.

On April 20, Mendelssohn conduced *Elijah* in a performance of the Hargreaves Choral Society in Manchester; and on the 27th, in Birmingham. There, the oratorio was performed for the benefit of Mr. Stimpson, the meritorious choral director of the festivals. Therefore, our master refused any honorarium; he would not even permit himself to be reimbursed for his personal expenses. In this connection, it is interesting to see how the English copyright of *Elijah* was evaluated in England when Mendelssohn stood at the height of his fame. (The German copyright belonged to Simrock in Bonn.) Since Mendelssohn refused to name a price, his publisher and friend Buxton, of Ewer and Ewer, offered him 250 guineas (then about 5250 marks, today about four times that much in purchasing power), and the master accepted immediately. After his death, Buxton sent another 100 guineas as a "bonus" to the widow—all in all, some 7400 marks, or about 30,000 D M in modern money. This is certainly no "star honorarium" compared with the astronomical fees which a Richard Strauss or a Stravinsky demanded and got.

Between the performances in Manchester and Birmingham, Mendelssohn appeared in the Philharmonic on April 26. He conducted his Scotch Symphony and *A Midsummer Night's Dream* music and appeared as soloist in Beethoven's G major Concerto. He excelled in both capacities, for he gave of his best because he wanted to please two ladies in the audience: "the Queen and Jenny Lind."[31]

Indeed, the long-awaited London debut of Lind took place precisely during these hectic days. Mendelssohn attended it; and a whole complex of legends—doubtless apocryphal—has grown out of that brilliant performance of Meyerbeer's *Robert the Devil*.[32]

Quite different was the tone of the receptions for Mendelssohn in the Prussian Embassy. The attitude of Baron Bunsen was friendly and warm enough, but, in the reports of Baroness Bunsen and in the notes of Klingemann we sense a certain strange touchiness. It seems as though Bunsen had not quite forgiven the master for the failure of the extensive plans in Berlin, and had let him feel it a bit. On May 6, he was at the Bunsens' again and met Mr. Gladstone, later to be Prime Minister, together with his wife.[33] As usual at ambassadorial receptions, many members of the aristocracy appeared: Lords Arundel, Charles Russell, Cavendish, Ellesmere, Lady Charlotte Greville, Lady Herschel, the Bishop of London, the Gladstones, and many more.

At this last reception, shortly before his departure, Mendelssohn chose, as his final piece, the aria "Be thou faithful unto death" from St. Paul and ended with the words "We shall close with this." Then he jumped up and rushed out of the room, calling to those who wanted to follow him: "I cannot say goodbye to everyone, God bless you all!"

On May 8, he took leave of the Queen and Prince Albert, and, weary unto death, started on the homeward journey. He felt that he had already stayed too long, for he exclaimed: "Another exhausting week like this, and I'm a dead man!" Klingemann, disquieted by his friend's miserable appearance, filled with apprehensive premonitions, this time accompanied Felix across the Channel as far as Ostende and bade him a tender farewell. An ugly incident ruined the whole journey this time. In Herbesthal, he was detained and had to spend many hours satisfying official curiosity, which had confused him with a radical liberal of the same name.[34] In Frankfurt, he was not destined to enjoy the tranquil security of his family for long. On the second day, without any preparation whatsoever, he learned of the sudden death of his beloved Fanny. With a cry, he collapsed.

II

The last five months of his life were filled with the struggle of his will to live against the exhaustion of his physically and spiritually spent organism. There also occurred an inner transformation, which had already begun in 1845 and which changed the master's total personality. It appears in many traits which, for the most part, had gone unnoticed.

As he neared his end, his religious thinking took on a new dimension of mystical depth. Probably, the idea of death played an important part in this. The brighter the sun of world fame shone upon him, the more apathetic was his awareness of it. Two unpublished letters (to his brother Paul on November 27, 1846, and to Julius Rietz on February 25, 1847) leave no doubt about it. Condoling with Rietz on the death of his mother, he says:

All vitality remains in one's profession and in work; therefore, may Heaven grant you joy and strength for new creation. . . .
That's the miserable thing, that, afterwards, the Philistines cannot give you any more pleasure (with all their praise) and yet annoy you first, just as the dear arch-conservatives do now. . . .
"Crush evil and keep your head high,"[35] Beethoven closed a letter in 1809 or '10; should one not repeat this today, and be able to write it at the end of every letter? Write new things and do not let all the Philistines spoil

the pleasure which you bring to a few people. So long as you please them! For they are in the right.[36]

Though Felix tried to keep his courage up, his most intimate confidences betrayed his frightful fear of death. Thus he wrote to Klingemann: "I always have but the one thought, how short life is."[37] Even before he had received the fateful news of Fanny's death, he began to take leave of life. A letter to Droysen shows the celebrated artist full of self-doubts. He confesses resignedly:

If you only had a profession like an artisan or a doctor or a preacher! I always envied the latter because they are really necessary to humanity—they *must* help others no matter how they feel inwardly—while the artisans always *can* work. But to write a book or a symphony in days like these, to go to a lecture or a concert—for a long, long time that has seemed so inane. . . .

How everything in Berlin has changed outwardly and inwardly! And how almost everything which seemed fresh and young in our days has disappeared, become desolate, aged, and corrupted! But only *almost* everything, not everything—and somehow it comes about, thank God, that the very best things do not disappear, but eternally renew themselves, even in death. And yet there is always that sad misunderstanding: every spring, in the merry years of youth, one thought that one had the best of everything, and then one thing after the other faded away.

But the best does not fade away. God knows how that happens, but it does not fade away. . . .[38]

The "man of the world," once the hero of all salons, the most sought-after conductor during the last few years, now shies away from people. The testimonies and conversations of the last few months leave no doubt of it. Chorley speaks most clearly in his report on the master's last year.[39] He can no longer endure brilliant music, or even loud music. He now abhors what he calls "finger music," to which he himself had once paid brilliant tribute. In all music, he is now interested only in the *expression,* or, better, in the intensity of expression; no longer in the form, and not at all in the technique. Strange transformation! Therefore, after a last despairing attempt, he turns away from all instrumental music and towards vocal music; for only the latter "guarantees the expression of the artist's true feelings," as he assures Frau Livia Frege, a singer and a trusted friend of the Leipzig years. His last instrumental work, in effect a lament for Fanny, by no means gives us the feeling of closing a development. It prepares the style of a "new" Mendelssohn, only a few precious examples of which have been preserved. We shall discuss them later in detail; they reflect his inner attitude exactly. He has already given up concerts in the spring of 1847; he still teaches a few classes in the Conservatory, which he "cannot get rid of yet." Otherwise, he wants only to stay at home and work. "Everything else cometh of evil."[40] He cannot ban the fear of death completely, but he succeeds in sublimating it artistically in his last songs. Basically, he is behaving like a wounded animal that crawls away to die; and it is only his creative power which frees him again and again from the fatal spell of fear and apprehension. This power expresses itself now, too, in his painting and drawing, which attains unprecedented artistic maturity.

After he had recovered from the first and worst shock of grief over Fanny's death, Mendelssohn left Frankfurt with his family and went to Baden-Baden, where he had arranged to meet his brother Paul and his brother-in-law Hensel. But he felt uncomfortable, principally because of the silly squabbles between Cecile and Albertine, Paul's wife. So he decided once more to seek out his beloved Switzerland, which had always granted rest to the restless one, healing to the wounded one. And so it came to pass this time, too. Traveling through Lucerne and Thun, they arrived at Interlaken, where Felix settled down and remained until mid-September. Here, too, he found the place where some of his descendants would settle: Wilderswil. In a letter to Rebecca, he says: "So I marched to Wilderschwyl in a short half-hour (which is a *good* half-hour), and when, at the village, I inquired for the road once more, the people told me that I still had to walk an hour and a half [up to an Alp]. Then I walked through the long village."[41]

In Interlaken, he did not see many strangers. However, his friend Chorley visited him there, and to him we owe the best and most reliable description of Mendelssohn in his last months.[42] The master looked aged and weary; he no longer walked quite upright, but somewhat stooped-over; but his smile was more intimate and warmer than before. Naturally, there was much talk of music, and to Chorley's astonishment, Mendelssohn had become much more tolerant: pieces by Rossini, even by Donizetti, found favor with him.

He himself had important plans; they all concerned vocal music on the grand scale. In the foreground stood the opera *Loreley*, which, however, he considered as a "practice trial"; for he thought that after four or five attempts he could achieve something "really good," perhaps even for the Parisian *Grand Opéra*.[43] He took a lively interest in the music of the young Verdi; Chorley could not tell him enough about it. He had accepted the invitation to write the solemn church music for the dedication of the Cologne Cathedral, and he was already looking forward to it with pleasure. Furthermore, he was planning a German cantata after Klopstock's *Hermannsschlacht*. The Liverpool Philharmonic had asked him for a new symphony, but we do not hear a word about this; on the other hand, he said a great deal about a plan for "Swiss Music," which he was eager to compose. But the mournful refrain of all such plans was always: "I shall no longer live to see it" or "If I live to see it," and finally, "What sense is there in these projects anyhow? I shall never live to carry them out."

In strange contradiction to the far-reaching plans (which, however, he constantly negated) stands his firm resolution to settle in Frankfurt or in the Rhineland, to spend every summer in Switzerland, and occasionally to visit England. Here, he thinks very pragmatically, and his decisions seem not to have been troubled by premonitions or the fear of death. But whenever his creative work comes under discussion, fear arises.

As for politics, he feared the mob, but he criticized in the sharpest words the high officials and courtiers "who had alienated the hearts which they might so easily have attached, and who had demoralized, under pretext of educating, a great people. . . ."[44]

At Chorley's wish, the master played the organ once more—for the last time—in the little church of Ringgenberg on the *Brienzer See*. As always, he improvised in magnificent fashion.

Somewhat restored, at least calmed, Mendelssohn returned to Leipzig in the middle of September. Now he was to conduct the first German performance of *Elijah* in Berlin on November 3, and the second, in Vienna on November 14. There, the beloved Jenny Lind was to sing the part which had been written for her. He cancelled the Berlin engagement after he had visited Fanny's old home at the end of September. The excitement caused by this undid all the good of his recuperation in Switzerland.

On October 7, he wrote his last composition, the deeply sorrowful *Altdeutsches Frühlingslied* (Example 71). Its last verse reads:

> *Nur ich allein, ich leide Pein,*
> *Ohn' Ende werd' ich leiden,*
> *Seit Du von mir und ich von Dir,*
> *O Liebste, musste scheiden.*

> Ah, I alone must suffer pain,
> Forever grieves my heart,
> Since I from thee and thou from me,
> Beloved, had to part.

He brought Frau Livia Frege this song, which he had just finished, and several others which he was preparing for publication, so that she might sing them for him. He had always thought a great deal of her interpretation of his songs and had sometimes made little changes, especially of dynamic markings, according to her performance. Now, during the performance of the songs *Tröstung* and *Auf der Wanderschaft* he became very thoughtful; he felt that this would be a serious birthday present for friend Schleinitz. With the performance of the *Altdeutsches Frühlingslied*, he began to talk about Fanny. When Frau Frege sang his *Nachtlied* (Example 72), which he had written only the week before, he shuddered at the verse

Example 71

So reist die Zeit die ganze Nacht,
Nimmt manchen mit, der's nicht gedacht.

Thus travels Time throughout the night,
And many join his dreary flight.

Example 72

He cried out: "Oh, that sounds so weary, but that's just how I felt." He
turned pale, and his hands grew cold.[45] He had to lie down immediately,
but recovered and went quickly home, where the attack recurred. The

family history of the Mendelssohns shows that Moses, Abraham, and his daughter Fanny succumbed prematurely to strokes. Felix was certainly aware of this family tendency, and feared every sign of it in himself. This cannot be an empty hypothesis, for the percentage of Mendelssohn descendants who died of strokes is far above normal.

Felix now battled the dark powers with the only weapon which remained to him—with his will to live and create. Therefore, in the following days, he busied himself with preparations for the trip to Vienna. Frau Frege, who visited him and was delighted at how well he looked, was gently teased about her earlier fears for him. He could even venture a walk with Cecile (October 28). Soon thereafter, he was laid low by a severe stroke, which partially paralyzed him (November 1). He suffered dreadfully.[46] He could still see and speak to his brother Paul, who had hurried from Berlin. A second stroke (November 3) put an end to this torture. Soon thereafter he slept away (November 4). Mendelssohn's friend, the painter Bendemann, who had arrived from Dresden, reports: "The expression of his face was indescribably friendly and peaceful, so that, when one came in, one would have thought that he was asleep and not dead, if his color . . . had not revealed the terrors of death. . . ."[47]

He did not exaggerate; Mendelssohn's death mask shows a transcendent peace. A mysterious smile transfigured his features, from which the weariness and bitterness of the last year had been erased.

The two funeral ceremonies—in Leipzig and Berlin, where he was taken—were very pompous, and rather a tribute to German music, whose chief representative before the world our master was, even in death, than a simple and sincere memorial among friends such as he had always wished.

The funeral procession with the master's coffin was blessed in the *Pauliner kirche;* all the dignitaries of the city and of the kingdom of Saxony had come. Mendelssohn lay in the elaborate coffin. About his temples was twined the decoration which had always meant more to him than all other decorations and honors—a simple laurel wreath, the symbol of the Muse. At night, his body was borne by train to Berlin. On the way, the train stopped in Köthen, Dessau, and Halle, where Thiele, Fr. Schneider, and other choral directors paid their final tribute to the great man. On the morning of November 8, the train arrived in Berlin. There, the coffin was received by the Cathedral Chorus (under Neidhardt), by the *Singakademie* (under Rungenhagen and Grell), and by a great procession. He was buried in the old *Dreifaltigkeitsfriedhof,* with his parents and next to Fanny. On this occasion there came a final insult on the part of the Berliners. Grell's motet *Jesus ist die Auferstehung* (Jesus is the Resurrection) was sung, along with the chorales *Wie sie so sanft ruhen* (How Peacefully they rest) and *Jesus, meine Zuversicht* (Jesus, My Trust); and the Funeral March from Beethoven's Sonata Op. 26 was played. Of Mendelssohn's music, not a note was heard! The family was stricken when Paul and Becky remembered that the year before Felix had promised Fanny to spend her birthday (November 8) with her; he had said, "Count on it, the next time I'll be with you." He kept his word.

Everywhere in Europe and America an effort was made to pay tribute to the composer with memorial concerts. Since most of these performances, as usual, served the aims of the promoters rather than their announced purpose, we may limit ourselves here to the few celebrations that were really dedicated to the music of Mendelssohn. The most important ones took place in Leipzig, London, Vienna, Berlin, Frankfurt, and Paris.

A week after Mendelssohn's death, the first part of the regular *Gewandhaus* concert was devoted to his music. The program of the first part consisted of the Overture to *St. Paul*, the motet "Lord, now lettest Thou Thy servant depart in peace," the previously mentioned *Nachtlied* (Night Song) most beautifully sung by Frau Frege, and the overture to the *Fair Melusine*. There followed Beethoven's *Eroica*. In London, which had always considered Mendelssohn half English, the grief was deep and the memories of the master were green. On November 17, the Sacred Harmonic Society performed *Elijah* as a memorial for him; the character of the occasion was heightened and underscored by the mourning garb of the orchestra, the singers, and most of the audience. Before the beginning of the oratorio the orchestra played the Dead March from Handel's *Saul*, to which the audience listened standing and in silence. At that time—and not for the first time in England—Handel and Mendelssohn were juxtaposed as the greatest German-English composers. In Vienna, on November 12, there took place the long-planned performance of *Elijah* which Mendelssohn should have conducted. Again, a lengthy correspondence had preceded this performance. Replying to Baron Vesque's invitation to conduct his oratorio in the form of a festival, Mendelssohn wrote (letter of June 15, 1847):

> As you observed at the end of your letter, I received your invitation in a mortally afflicted state. I do what I can to tear myself away from over-indulgence in my grief, yet any thoughts of music festivals, of public conducting, are still strange to me, and I feel also that I am not physically strong enough for it. If this dispirited mood abates, then nothing will keep me from conducting my *Elijah* in Vienna, for I know for sure that it would give me the highest joy. . . .

Continuing, Mendelssohn—remembering the unpleasant bickering about his expenses on the occasion of the Vienna performance of *St. Paul*—does not wish to be compensated financially *at all*, not even for his traveling expenses. He has resolved "to refuse most definitely" any kind of fee or reimbursement, as he would consider the trip to Vienna as "a pleasure, which he wants to grant himself, and under no circumstances as a financial transaction." In later letters he makes only one stipulation: Staudigl must sing the part of Elijah. Still later he fixes the day of his arrival on October 28 or 30, and intends to hear two choral rehearsals without orchestra.

When the shocking news of his death reached Vienna, the *Musikverein* took all possible pains to transform the *Elijah* performance into a solemn demonstration of mourning for the dead master. What the Viennese had not granted to the living man, they gave in full measure to the dead one. All the participants appeared in mourning garb. Mendelssohn's conductor's desk was draped in black; on it lay a scroll of music and a green laurel wreath. The chorus master Schmidl directed the performance from a second, lower stand.

The reviews were mixed; although they paid tribute to the lofty and high standard of the work, some critics felt that Mendelssohn's kind of musical diction no longer satisfied the needs of the day, in other words, that its obsolescence had already begun. Others praised the strength, even the occasional roughness of Mendelssohn's diction, in which they acclaimed and recognized "classic purity" and his refusal to make even the slightest concession to "musical fashion or to brilliant effects."

In Berlin, the Royal Theatre Orchestra devoted the first symphony concert to Mendelssohn's memory. After the Funeral March from the *Eroica*, the dead master's *Kyrie*, the Scotch Symphony, the 43rd Psalm, and the *A Midsummer Night's Dream* and *Hebrides* Overtures were performed; at the end, the Cathedral choir sang *Es ist bestimmt in Gottes Rath*. (The Parting Hour). The performance of *Elijah* in the *Singakademie*, which still took place in November, should also be considered as a memorial concert. In Frankfurt, it was principally church music of the master which was performed. In Paris, the first concert of the *Conservatoire* bore the title À la mémoire de F. Mendelssohn Bartholdy (January 8, 1848.) The program consisted of the Scotch Symphony, the *Hebrides* Overture, the Violin Concerto, and selections from *St. Paul*.

The tribute which would have pleased Mendelssohn the most came from Jenny Lind. She was so shaken by his sudden death that for two years she was quite unable to sing his songs. A year after Mendelssohn's death, she organized a great memorial service for him. On this occasion, *Elijah* was performed in Exeter Hall; for the first time, she sang the soprano part which Felix had intended for her. The concert was so successful that a "Mendelssohn Foundation" could immediately be established, with the starting capital of 1000 pounds. This foundation encourages gifted English or Irish composers; the prize for composition which it offers was still, in 1932, the most highly regarded one in England. The first prize-winner was Arthur Sullivan, whose name became renowned not only through his operettas with Gilbert but also through his church music.

The first Leipzig presentation of *Elijah* in the *Gewandhaus* contrasted sadly with the English performances of the oratorio. The hall was half empty, the public apathetic; the many friends of the dead artist could not conceal their bitter disappointment. Perhaps this occasion foreshadowed the depreciation of Mendelssohn, which in Germany was to last till the end of the nineteenth century, indeed, till the end of World War II—given a powerful impetus by the cohorts of Wagner and his antisemitic disciples.

III

In spite of all his symptoms of illness, Mendelssohn does not seem to have believed seriously in his early death, for he left no will of any kind. This set the stage for a tragicomedy. The financial problems of the estate were quickly and smoothly settled by his brother Paul, the banker. But the personal and artistic legacy of the master caused many an ugly dispute. Worse yet, it was administered with false piety, as if Mendelssohn's work and personality were the exclusive property of his family. It is no longer worthwhile to give all the details of these tactics of concealment, or to complain about them—it is enough simply to mention them here.

When Mendelssohn died, he had just reached his Op. 72, six children's pieces for piano. They are far inferior to Schumann's *Kinderszenen*. True, he understood the world of children, but, to him, it seemed more childish than childlike. He himself had been far too precocious ever to have known the real world of childhood. The many unpublished manuscripts which were found in his legacy (Mendelssohn was as orderly as a bookkeeper in his documents and papers) were entrusted by his widow to a publication committee. It consisted of Dr. Schleinitz, the president of the governing board for the *Gewandhaus* and the Conservatory, concertmaster Ferdinand David, Ignaz Moscheles, Moritz Hauptmann, Julius Rietz (then conductor in Dresden), and Paul Mendelssohn. Here the name of Schumann is conspicuous by its absence; the reason lies in the very cool personal relation between Rietz and Schumann, which Cecile had to take into account.

Op. 72 was just in the press when Mendelssohn died. All higher opus numbers than 72 indicate the *posthumous* edition of the respective work. Until Op. 80 the manuscripts were published in more or less chronological order. And then the disorder began. In the list of works any number higher than 80 is chosen arbitrarily and without any respect to a successive order of works. Thus the Italian Symphony bears number 90, while the older Reformation Symphony has number 107.

Unfortunately it was Rietz to whom the publication of the manuscript works was finally entrusted. This was a mistake, for, after Cecile's death in 1853, the manuscripts came into the hands of Felix's eldest son, Carl Mendelssohn Bartholdy, who, together with his Uncle Paul Mendelssohn and Rietz, formed a triumvirate. Thenceforth, the committee was simply passed over, or hardly called into consultation. Since, of the three, only Rietz was a professional musician, he had a free hand to choose what he liked for publication. At first, he seems to have followed the suggestions of the committee, but we can only guess at this today; for all documents which would shed light on Rietz's editorial activity and which would justify or at least explain his choices are missing. Rietz never gave a public accounting of this highly responsible task, aside from his modest exposé at the end of the first and second editions of the letters (Leipzig 1861, 1863), in which there is not a word about his *modus operandi*. The one possible place where, perhaps, some information about Rietz's editorial activity might be found—the archives of Breitkopf and Härtel—was, unfortunately, not accessible to me; this thorny task must be left to Leipzig scholars, if they want to take it on. The viewpoint from which Rietz chose some works for publication and rejected others is incomprehensible. For important works, like the five great chorale cantatas and motets, the 8-voiced *Te Deum*, the A flat major double Concerto for two pianos and orchestra, remained unpublished until today, while insignificant pieces like the *Festgesang* for the Gutenberg Festival and occasional compositions like *Die Stiftungsfeier* or *Seemanns Scheidelied* were published early.

Mendelssohn's letters—that treasure of reminiscences, that mirror of the Biedermeier—were not very well handled, either. But here, many other motivations played a part; we have already expressed ourselves about these elsewhere. Therefore, let us here give a mere survey of the most important documents.

The first biographical documents which were made available to the general public were the "Letters from the Years 1830-32" (also "Travel Letters") edited by brother Paul. Soon thereafter appeared a second volume covering the period 1833-1847. This collection comprised letters to the family and a few to Klingemann, Pastor Bauer, Schubring, and E. Devrient, as well as a few writings concerning the Royal appointment in Berlin. Practically all later editions of the family letters are based on this one, with the exception of Hensel's worthy, bourgeois, deliberately patriotic selection of family letters combined with some gossip (*Die Familie Mendelssohn*; 1st ed., Berlin, 1879). We must point out once more that all editions of the family letters, all made by close relatives, are unreliable; for they show significant deviations from the manuscript text. They suppress and distort many passages, and sometimes reverse Mendelssohn's original meaning.[48]

It was hard to establish this definitely, for the owners of the autographs have seldom allowed "outsiders" a peep into the manuscripts. The family letters were in the possession of brother Paul, who left them to his son Ernst Mendelssohn Bartholdy. The latter, in his turn, willed them to his son Paul. After Paul's death, they came into the possession of his sisters, who put them in a Dresden bank for safekeeping. In the bombardment of Dresden, the bank was destroyed, but the safes remained intact. The occupation officers had them opened and returned the letters—which they believed to be valueless "family papers"—to the owners. They were purchased in 1960 by the New York Public Library.

The Bodleian Library in Oxford contains about 20 folio volumes—the so-called "Green Books." In these, Mendelssohn himself collected and bound all important letters to him, along with many unimportant ones. They belonged to Professor Albrecht Mendelssohn Bartholdy, whose widow left them, with other important documents, to Miss Margaret Deneke, M.A., in Oxford. This collection, too, is a rich source of documents concerning our composer. Smaller collections of the master's unpublished letters are in the Library of Congress, Washington, D. C., and in the possession of several members of the family.

The correspondence with Mendelssohn's friends has been extensively published in Hiller's and Devrient's memoirs, the exchange of letters with Droysen, the letters to Klingemann, Moscheles, and several separate publications. Among these, Schumann's recollections concerning Mendelssohn played an unfortunate part. As previously mentioned, sections of them were used as antisemitic propaganda material by Dr. W. Boetticher. In commemoration of the 100th anniversary of the master's death, the Schumann Archive in Zwickau published a photostatic edition of these memoirs.

Irrevocably lost are two of the most important and informative collections of documents: the correspondence with A. B. Marx, the friend of Felix's youth from whom he became completely estranged, and correspondence with Cecile. The latter was destroyed by her because she did not want to release it to the outside world; she felt that it belonged exclusively to her and her husband. However, a few letters from Cecile—not to Felix—do exist in various collections. They tell us less about the shy, timid, very sensitive wife and mother than do her husband's comments about her in his family letters. Marx destroyed Mendelssohn's letters to him after their break in 1839.

At Mendelssohn's death, there existed 44 volumes of his musical manuscripts, collected and bound by him. On December 23, 1877, they were deposited in the Royal Prussian State Library in Berlin, in accordance with an agreement of Mendelssohn's heirs with the Prussian State. According to this, the manuscripts were to remain in the possession of the Library; in return, the Prussian State was obliged to grant two Mendelssohn scholarships yearly, each of 1500 marks. During the inflation of the 1920's, these scholarships were suspended, and were not resumed even after the stabilization of the *Reichsmark*.[49] During the war, the manuscripts were removed from Berlin and some of them have never been returned. The publication of the most important, previously unpublished compositions of Mendelssohn would be but the first step towards the repayment of a debt that can never be cancelled. During the last years, two institutions have expressed their firm intention of rectifying this omission: the Berlin State Library (in East Germany) and the International Mendelssohn Society in Basel. While this is being written, the first two volumes of these compositions are about to appear.

IV

We must still consider Mendelssohn's last compositions. All the other works are surpassed by his Quartet in F minor, Op. 80, No. 6, an extraordinary piece which alone should negate the traditional ideas and ill-founded prejudices concerning our master's weakening powers. Granted, it is an atypical work for Mendelssohn, but it clearly shows the direction in which he would have moved had he lived longer. The Quartet is intentionally auto-biographical, a great rarity in Mendelssohn. It is one long lament for his sister; one hears everywhere the cry of grief, hardly formalized, of the suffering creature. Here, after a long time, Mendelssohn returns to the cyclic experiments of his youth. He cites scraps of the Scherzo in the last movement; in between, there glimmer ironic and sad reminiscences of a favorite old motif of Fanny's. The first movement in F minor is a purely motoric "raging" on a furious theme which scarcely maintains clear contour; it is interrupted only by the wailings of the first violin. Essentially, this movement already foreshadows forms of early Expressionism. The retransition to the principal theme is one of the strongest passages in all of Mendelssohn's music. The second movement, also in F minor, is a quite un-Mendelssohnian Scherzo. Its syncopations, its bitter, not to say gruff, chromatic harmonies, bring it into the vicinity of the macabre Scherzi in Mahler's later symphonies. The ostinato bass of the Trio intensifies the uncannily threatening monotony of the movement. The third movement, an Adagio in D flat major, unfolds as an elegy in *chiaroscuro* tones; from time to time, we seem to hear an echo of the wailings in the first movement. The movement is laid out with greatest artistic economy, and develops from an *Urlinie* of five or six notes. The last movement, again in F minor, falls back once more into the motoric, wild restlessness of the first movement, and contains distinctly orchestral effects. Three unrestrained outbursts mark the caesuras; a great weeping and a ceaseless untamed restlessness permeate the movement. We seem to see a wild animal pacing in its cage. As a whole, the magnificently conceived work does not succeed completely, for here Mendelssohn chose the wrong medium; everything in this music cries out for the orchestra. Only in symphonic garb would the work have the desired effect.

Example 73 (First movement)

Example 74 (Third movement)

Example 75 (Last movement)

The second completed work, a *Te Deum* for the Anglican Service, is on the same high level as the *German Liturgy*, but makes greater demands on performers and listeners.[50] Throughout, it is couched in a strictly polyphonic style, and strives as greatly for objective expression as the Quartet in F minor strove for the subjective. In these two works, there is a greater contrast between sacred and secular music than anywhere else in Mendelssohn's creation. Under the circumstances, we may ponder on Mendelssohn's changed relationship to an anthropomorphic divinity. What caused him, after the bitterest sorrow of his life, to which he had just consecrated unforgettable tones, to strike up a song of praise to God, in a musical language of flawless purity? And how do we reconcile this strict, almost cool attitude with the greatest of his fragments, the oratorio *Christus?*

This fragment proceeds farther along the road of *Elijah*. Perhaps it strives somewhat harder for greater intensity of musical expression, this time in the recitative, which Mendelssohn had previously treated in somewhat offhand fashion. The plan for *Christus*, for which Mendelssohn "wanted to reserve his best powers,"[51] comes from Freiherr von Bunsen, to whom the complete realization of the libretto was probably entrusted.[52] Three parts were planned; the first was to describe Christ's birth, the second the Passion, and the third the Resurrection. Again, if possible, only words from Holy Writ were to be used. Kretzschmar has said the last word about this *idée fixe*: "In particular, the effort to build up oratorio texts from the words of the Bible exclusively led to an unclearness of presentation, to a pious bombast and to an unnaturalness for which there is no counterpart in the entire earlier history of the oratorio."[53]

However, the plot is at least set forth by a narrator or Evangelist; some of his recitatives show a sharply articulated declamation which we are not accustomed to in Mendelssohn. In the first part, the words of the Evangelist are sung by a soprano, in the second part (the Passion) by a tenor. The *turba* scenes were sketched by Mendelssohn, and are distinguished for dramatic power and precise declamation; but, of course, they are far inferior to Bach's mighty frescoes. Unfortunately, it is obvious that Mendelssohn once again counted on chorales to convey symbolic-leitmotivic significance. Thus, the chorales *Wie schön leuchtet der Morgenstern* and *O Welt, ich muss dich lassen*, have already been carried out, but have not succeeded in lending the work fresh power. In his best period, Mendelssohn's gifts would not have been sufficient for a *Christus*. Now, with this work, the exhausted man wanted to crown the planned triptych which had begun with *St. Paul* and continued with *Elijah*. Here, it was not merely the limits of his specifically musical capacity which he wanted to surpass. No, he had dared to approach a task which was simply beyond the scope of his whole personality. The hypostatic combination of the human and the Divine in a single being can scarcely be hinted at, let alone represented, in the "sacred" music of an artist whose thinking was basically secular. And, indeed, no composer since Bach has succeeded in interpreting this mystery in tones.

Not much more successful was the other great fragment, that of the planned opera *Loreley*. Quite aside from the all-too-lyrical and undramatic text, Mendelssohn was not able to instill his music with dramtic breath and sensual power. Indeed, the half-finished Finale of the first act offers many lovely episodes, well-rounded ensembles and appropriate local color, but it is no operatic finale. In such a piece, it is not a question of pleasantly entertaining or edifying the listener; he wants to be stirred up, set on fire— in short, personally affected. But this task surpassed the failing strength of Mendelssohn, who, even at the height of his creative powers, had been able to strive for and attain really dramatic climaxes only in isolated cases.

So, the Finale of the *Loreley*, in which the Rhine spirits appear in chorus, is a noteworthy piece of music and is not lacking, either, in theatrical elements. But, compared with Wagner's monumental presentation of the Rhine and its underworld, Mendelssohn's effort has the effect of a pencil sketch beside a fully executed fresco. It begins in fiery and truly dramatic fashion, but the figure of Leonora has no characteristic musical contours and soon subsides into the charmingly lyrical. This is the type of woman whom Mendelssohn loved; but such a personality could not carry a serious opera or give it dramatic force. Leonora is a mixture of Cecile and Jenny Lind; but she is no Malibran, whose wild charm and sexual magnetism would have been necessary here.

So this fragment—perhaps the most ill-conceived of those which the master left behind—once again proves his faithfulness to his motto: "Art and life are not divisible." What seemed reprehensible to him in life he could not use as a subject for his art; Mendelssohn's unwillingess to compromise his deepest convictions with a *femme fatale*, effective as she might be in the theatre, can only raise him in our estimation as a man. . . .

Of his contemporaries, probably Kierkegaard alone understood the dilemma with which Mendelssohn was confronted consciously or unconsciously. The following words of the Danish thinker seem intended for Mendelssohn, the scorner of the "estheticians, without all of whom he could do very well":

> So, then, one either has to live esthetically or one has to live ethically. In this alternative . . . there is not yet in the strictest sense any question of a choice; for he who lives esthetically does not choose, and he who after the ethical has manifested itself to him chooses the esthetical is not living esthetically, for he is sinning and is subject to ethical determinants even though his life may be described as unethical. Lo, there is, as it were, a *character indelebilis* impressed upon the ethical, that though it modestly places itself on a level with the esthetical, it is nevertheless that which makes the choice a choice. . . . By the absolute choice the ethical is always posited, but from this it does not follow by any means that the esthetical is excluded. In the ethical the personality is concentrated in itself, so the esthetical is absolutely excluded or is excluded as the absolute, but relatively it is still left.[54]

With this, we—who can follow the course of estheticism from realism through "art for art's sake," through *les fleurs du mal*, to Neoclassicism and Expressionism with its problematic consequences—shall be in a better position to evaluate the relation of posterity to Mendelssohn. To this question, our final chapter is dedicated.

𝒩otes

1. Edwards, *The History of Mendelssohn's Oratorio "Elijah,"* p. 77.
2. Mendelssohn called the male altos "bearded altos." See Edwards, *op. cit.*, p. 82.
3. *Ibid.*, p. 84.
4. *Ibid.*, p. 83.
5. Moscheles's diaries (*Aus Moscheles' Leben*), II, pp. 156ff.
6. Letter to Paul Mendelssohn of August 26(?), 1846.
7. Cited from Scholes, *The Mirror of Music* (London, 1947), I, p. 80. The editor, Dr. Scholes, who knows this period thoroughly, points out, in his commentary, the discrepancy between this criticism and other contemporary reports.
8. *Ibid.*, p. 81.

9. Letter to Livia Frege of August 31, 1846. Other contemporary reports in Edwards, *op. cit.*, pp. 88ff.

10. At the performance of Handel's Coronation Anthem (*Zadok the Priest*) it was realized only at the last minute that the introductory recitative was missing. Mendelssohn leaped into the breach and, in a few minutes, composed the missing piece for tenor, strings and 2 trumpets in Handelian style. The recitative may be seen in Edwards's book, pp. 93-94; there is a facsimile of the autograph in Scholes' *Mirror of Music*, I, plate p. 80.

11. Moscheles, *op. cit.*, p. 157.

12. The last day brought a colossal concert. As a curiosity, we give the program. If there is such a thing as musical indigestion because of overstuffing, the listeners to this concert must certainly have suffered from it.

Part I.	Overture to Joseph	Méhul
	Psalm 93 for chorus, orchestra, 6 soli	Moscheles
	Kyrie, Gloria, Sanctus and Benedictus from the *Missa Solemnis*	Beethoven
Part II.	Hallelujah from *Christ on the Mount of Olives*	Beethoven
	Hymn to the Godhead (vocal soli and organ)	Spohr
	Coronation Anthem	Handel

13. His correspondence with his English publisher Mr. Buxton, most of which is in the Library of Congress, Washington, D. C., contains many self-critical observations of Mendelssohn. One of them calls his inclination to revisions "a dreadful disease"; in another letter he calls it "a veritable folly." Moscheles reacted to the revisions of *Elijah* with the words: "Your genius demands too much—turn your energies to new works now!" (Moscheles, *Diaries*, II, October 27, 1846.)

14. Letter to Klingemann of December 6, 1846. A precise list of the revised and altered places is found in Grove's article on Mendelssohn (now published separately) and in Edwards, *op. cit.*, pp. 99-100.

15. Mendelssohn's doctor wanted to send his servant to the hospital, because he did not have time for the lengthy treatment of domestics. Felix made it clear to the doctor that Krebs was a member of his household like any other and that he would consider the doctor's reluctance to treat him as a personal insult. *Noblesse oblige!*

16. Correspondence with Klingemann, p. 317.

17. In spite of all documents which testify to Mendelssohn's selfless friendship for Schumann, some of which we have presented here, the malicious gossip about Mendelssohn's two-facedness with respect to Schumann will not cease. Is there a better proof of good will than the self-denial which Mendelssohn displayed in this affair?

18. How accurately Mendelssohn foresaw here the failure of the Revolution of 1848—which he did not live to experience! And he feared the failure of every other German revolution, as we see in an unpublished letter to his brother Paul, in which he says: "We Germans are simply not good enough for a revolution, because none is good enough for us."

19. Letter to Dirichlet of January 4, 1847.

20. Unpublished letter to Becky of July 24, 1847.

21. Roland Nitsche, "Von Hegel bis Droysen: Wandlungen der deutschen Geschichtsauffassung," *Monat*, October 1960, p. 62.

22. *Ibid.*, p. 67. Prince Albert felt likewise; see Jagow, *Letters of the Prince Consort*, New York, 1938.

23. Mendelssohn believed firmly in the truth of the old saying: "Sleep yourself to health, laugh yourself to health, drink yourself to health."

24. On Good Friday (April 2) Mendelssohn still conducted his *St. Paul* in Leipzig.

25. Letter from Mendelssohn to the Society of October 7, 1846.

26. See Edwards, *op. cit.*, pp. 120ff, where several of the letters are reproduced. The reason that Mendelssohn wanted to postpone the journey was that Staudigl, the first Elijah, was not available at this time. He was replaced by Mr. Henry Philipps, by whose achievements Mendelssohn was not overwhelmed.

27. When Mendelssohn stepped before the orchestra, it spontaneously struck up the chorus from Handel's *Judas Maccabaeus* (actually from *Joshua*): "See, the conquering hero comes."

28. How much Prince Albert spoke from the very hearts of the English people, we may see from Chorley's words: "There has never been a foreigner more honest in his love for, more discriminating in his appreciation of England. . . ." (R. Elkin, *Royal Philharmonic*, London, 1947, p. 45.)

29. "A brilliant execution of a piece of music was not considered very important; for music was an 'elegant' accomplishment: touch and expression were more highly esteemed, a little tremolo in the voice was most affecting." (See F. E. Benson, *As We Were* (London, 1930), pp. 19-20. "Music, then as now, was for the majority a fashionable stunt." (*Ibid.*) In contrast, we can see how seriously Prince Albert took Mendelssohn's music from his letter to King Frederick William IV of June 13, 1842. There, he speaks at length about Mendelssohn's importance and his plans.

30. See *Letters of the Prince Consort*, ed. K. Jagow (New York, 1938), p. 138.

31. Grove, *op. cit.*, p. 413 (after W. Bartholomew).

32. Holland-Rockstro, *op. cit.*, and J. Bulman, pp. 155ff. The debut took place on the evening of May 4; on that day, Mendelssohn had already appeared before the Beethoven Quartet Society, where he played Beethoven's C minor variations and his own C minor Trio.

33. *Bunsen's Leben, op. cit.*, II, pp. 129ff.

34. That other Mendelssohn was strongly involved in the fight between the archradical Lassalle and Count Hatzfeld.

35. Indubitably a paraphrase of Voltaire's "écrasez l'infame!"

36. From the letter it is not clear whether Mendelssohn means that the Philistines or the "few people" are right. The tone of the whole letter is deeply pessimistic.

37. Letter to Klingemann of July 29, 1847.

38. Letter to Droysen of April 5, 1847.

39. Chorley, "The Last Days of Mendelssohn," *Modern German Music* (London, 1853).

40. Letter to Klingemann of October 3, 1847.

41. *Ibid.*

42. Chorley, *op. cit.*, pp. 383ff.

43. Chorley believes that preliminary negotiations between the *Grand Opéra* and Mendelssohn had already taken place; however, in the correspondence of Mendelssohn there are no indications which would substantiate this belief.

44. Chorley, *op. cit.*, II, 392.

45. Polko, *op. cit.*, pp. 178ff.

46. Moscheles, *Diaries*, II, pp. 180ff.

47. Letter of Bendemann in Droysen's correspondence, *op. cit.*, pp. 365ff.

48. Eric Werner, "New Lights on the Family Mendelssohn," *Hebrew Union College Annual* (1955); "The Family Letters of Felix Mendelssohn Bartholdy," *New York Public Library Bulletin* (January, 1961); "Mendelssohn Sources," *Notes* (March, 1955), XII; "Mendelssohn Bartholdy," *Musik in Geschichte und Gegenwart.*

49. The heirs of the composer would, therefore, have had the legal right to demand that the State Library return the manuscripts. But they were all good German patriots. As a reward for this, most of them were dispossessed or driven out under Hitler. The old firm of the Mendelssohn Bank was "liquidated"—but the manuscripts still remained in the Library!

50. Mendelssohn seems to have composed the *Te Deum* in 1832, and subjected it to a thorough revision in 1847. See his letter of August 22, 1832, in the *Musical Times* (October, 1903), p. 652.

51. See the letter of Moscheles to Professor Fischhof of November 7, 1847 (in *Die Musik*, VIII, Heft 9).

52. The autograph of the plan for *Christus* disappeared in a fire in Hamburg in 1931 or 1932.

53. Kretzschmar, *Führer*, 3rd edition, II, 2, p. 350.

54. Kierkegaard, *Either/Or*, tr. Walter Lowrie (Princeton, 1946), II, 142, 150.

CHAPTER XX

Mendelssohn

and Posterity

Question: "Why is it that his [Mendelssohn's] music has been neglected for some time now?"
Answer: "It may be because he knows too much in comparison to the apprentices of our days."
Question: "The grace, the clarity and the distinction of Mendelssohn! Some people think he is the Murillo of music."
Answer: "Yes, I have heard this comparison! But everyone can make comparisons. Personally, I prefer the musician to the painter!"

Question: "Would you say that Mendelssohn is a romantic 'without the excess or frenzy' of Romanticism?"
Answer: "Yes, a romantic who felt at ease within the mould of classicism and who was able to solve, with an elegance and imaginativeness peculiar to himself, the most difficult problems of form. . . . I feel sure he will come to his own again."

(J. M. Corredor: *Conversations with Casals*)

I

NOT MORE than a handful of composers are chosen from thousands by posterity; and, of the hundreds of compositions of such a "chosen one," only a fraction remains as living music. What forces determine this choice? Do the preferred works remain forever in the favor of posterity, or does it alter its judgment? It is impossible to answer these fundamental questions in a general way, but we know that the fluctuations of musical taste must be involved here. Nowhere can one recognize this more clearly than in the history of musical styles, especially in cases where the musical *fashion* changes. There have been such fashions in music just as in all other arts, and their fluctuations by no means always coincide with changes in style. For instance, the turn against Romanticism, which became plain in the 1920's, separated the arch-Romanticist Berlioz from his contemporaries Chopin, Mendelssohn, and Schumann, and saw in him, doubtless rightly, a champion of the modern. On the other hand, the full stature of a great master like Haydn has been appreciated only in our day, without any simultaneous change in style to account for this.

These "points of inflection" in the curve of taste, if we may use a geometrical simile, lead us to more valid conclusions concerning the evaluation of a master and posterity's image of him than do the sections of curve before and after such a point. Two examples may illustrate this assertion.

The curve of the evaluation of J. S. Bach shows three such points of inflection: 1) some 5 to 10 years before his death, when he was gradually being forgotten; 2) during the nineteenth century, when his music gradually invaded the living concert repertoire (not only that of the historical concerts); and 3) the beginning of the present century, when he began to be evaluated as the greatest composer of the Baroque. If we go by statistics, his music is still gaining in popularity.

Quite differently oriented are the points of inflection of the Wagner curve. After a rise during his lifetime which was slow at first, then meteoric, and reached its peak about the turn of the century, a slow descent began before World War I; after this, the curve sank to its lowest point in the 1920's. The strongly nationalistic tinge of Wagner's operas and writings caused his curve to rise once more, and during the Hitler years it reached an unprecedented peak; after World War II it began to fall once more, but not so low as after the first war. It now follows a steady course.

Aside from political ideas, such as those which helped to assure the success of several works of Wagner, we find that changes of interest in whole style-periods have often influenced musical fashion. At present, so-called high Romanticism, like all artistic accomplishments of the whole Victorian epoch, is out of fashion, and most composers of the first half of the nineteenth century are overshadowed by the great masters of the Baroque, of the Classic period, or of modern times (e.g., Stravinsky or Bartók). Since Mendelssohn's death there has not been *one* change of style which has not retouched posterity's picture of him, mostly to his disadvantage. It is no exaggeration to say that the fate of his music after his death was much more adventurous and controversial than ever during his life. We may distinguish no fewer than five phases in his evaluation, all in connection with changes of style *and* taste. They coincide with the rise of Wagner and his school; with the beginning of Impressionism; with Neoclassicism before and after World War I; with Expressionism; and finally, with the Nazi condemnation of all "non-Aryan" music. *Post tot discrimina rerum*, to speak with Virgil, the half-forgotten figure of Mendelssohn now seems to be awakening to new life; if the statistics of performance and recordings of his music do not deceive us, his work should find, in the near future, an appreciation commensurate with its historical importance.

II

For a millennium there has subsisted in European civilization a basic difference in rank between art-music and popular music. It has become even more pronounced since the Renaissance, and, at the end of the eighteenth century, widened to a gap that has been bridged but seldom at that time. *The Magic Flute* and *Der Freischütz* represented the last bridges between century, Verdi was still able to bridge the gulf with his operas, e.g., with the two standards of music, for many numbers of both operas are either drawn from popular music or were taken into it. In Italy of the nineteenth *La donna è mobile* and other numbers; even today they belong to the repertoire of the street-singer.

In pure instrumental music, which, after all, had originated in dance and march music, the alienation from the popular is even more clearly seen. Haydn, Mozart, and Beethoven still, to a diminishing degree, established some connections with popular music; but Schubert's instrumental music, though it was nourished by popular sources, had little effect upon the popular taste (in spite of his *German Dances* and other works of the same type). So, about 1820, we find two streams of instrumental music running side by side. On the level of "pure art" there is the Classic and Postclassic chamber and symphonic music; on the level of the popular, either the highly significant dance music of that time or the light entertainment music for piano, harp, or the little ensemble of the garden restaurants.

Popular music was then—and is still—basically more conservative than art-music. Mendelssohn was one of the few composers of the nineteenth century some of whose pieces were still taken into the popular idiom; others were Schumann, Wagner, to a lesser degree Chopin, but also Lortzing and Offenbach. In studying the vicissitudes to which Mendelssohn's music was subjected, it will be necessary to distinguish between his popular prestige on the one hand and his stature in the eyes of professional musicians, critics, and musicologists on the other hand. Here, we shall deal only with that portion of posterity which is represented by professional musicians; for in popular taste, the status of Mendelssohn did not change much after his death. The judgment and taste of these two groups, however, can hardly be brought into agreement today. This has already been expressed several times, perhaps most clearly by R. Capell:

> The day has . . . gone of the production of a music generally likeable, superior and at the same time characteristically contemporary, attracting the lay people without representing a derogation on the composer's part. . . . Much the same has happened to poetry and painting. . . . Today good poetry and popular poetry are incompatible terms. . . .[1]

Is this lamentable state of affairs so very new? Have we not already heard something very similar, and better formulated? We recall Schiller's sentences quoted in the Prologue to Chapter VIII. He also said: "Far from making the poet's task easier or sheltering mediocre talents, popularity simply presents him with one more difficulty, and, indeed, with so knotty a problem that its successful resolution can be called the highest triumph of genius."[2]

Schiller had conceived the problem in this way; yet this considered perspective was hardly acceptable to literary Romanticism which uncritically adulated everything "folklike." Neither was it acceptable to litterateurs of an esoteric bent, like Oscar Wilde and Baudelaire, who condemned all popular trends as concessions to the mob.

Mendelssohn reached, in some of his compositions, the ideal that Schiller had pointed out and set for himself. If the price that a composer must pay for complete popularity is anonymity, i.e., the forgetting of his name in certain instances, Mendelssohn duly paid this tribute. This is true not only of the universally familiar songs *Wer hat dich, du schöner Wald* and *Es ist bestimmt in Gottes Rath*, but also of the pieces which, nearly unknown in German-speaking countries, have won many hearts in English-speaking ones: for example, the Christmas carol *Hark, the Herald Angels Sing*, or the English version of Heine's *Auf Flügeln des Gesanges* (On Wings of Song). Few German, English, or American singers are aware that the composer of these pieces also wrote *Elijah* and the Scotch Symphony. This real popularity inherent in some of his pieces was already recognized very early. As sensitive a critic of culture as W. H. Riehl, a younger contemporary of Mendelssohn, expressed this very well: "He was the fortunate one, who succeeded in remaining strict, serious and pure in his creations—and yet became popular."[3] Moritz Hauptmann, the learned Thomas Cantor and musical theoretician, was of the same opinion.

Quite independent from popular taste is the evaluation of Mendelssohn by the professional critics, the musicologists, and the "estheticians" whom the master had so despised. At first, his early death was mourned as a catastrophe for music and its future, throughout Central Europe and, perhaps even more sincerely, in England. Also in the United States and Canada, whose musical centres were primarily entrusted to Germans and Englishmen, there was an overwhelming feeling of an irreparable loss. Even many years after his death (1874) a newly established, very influential, and distinguished musical society in Philadelphia took his name. The same thing happened in New York (Glee Club), Boston, where the first American chamber music society bore his name (Mendelssohn Quintette Club), Chicago (Mendelssohn Society and Club), Toronto (Mendelssohn Choir), and many more. H. F. Chorley, the English critic, spoke for many when he reported on England's mourning:

How the news of Mendelssohn's death was received in England, and by what manner of regret it was and is followed here, we know. That in his own land his fame for the future is solid, may be hoped, and, I think, believed, with good assurance. That his countrymen, however, have in the meantime done their character for good faith, constancy, and reverence for Genius and Virtue, no honour, by their change of note, after death, concerning one whom they had followed and fawned upon while he was living, is sadly true.[4]

These reproachful words were spoken exactly three years after the appearance of a work which was to prove a fateful turning point for the future of Mendelssohn's music: Wagner's pamphlet *Judaism in Music*, published under the pseudonym K. Freigedank.[5] One should not condemn this pamphlet without reading it. It contains several noteworthy ideas, and shows that the author had a certain understanding (born of his hate-love) for the problematic position of Mendelssohn and of German assimilated Jewry in general. Also, the tone of this polemic writing, though hostile enough, is still far removed from Wagner's later antisemitic fanaticism. The dangerous part of this work lies in the shifting of the critical plane from the purely musical level to that of popular, but subjectively slanted German-Aryan nationalism.

In his polemic pamphlet, Wagner started from a premise which was like an axiom to the German intelligentsia of the nineteenth century: All art has its best and strongest roots in the folk and in folk customs. Wagner himself cannot have been so naïve, at least he was not in this work, as to demand that the artistic raw material reach the composer *directly*, i.e., without any intermediary; he himself could not have fulfilled such a requirement. Yet, rather *unequivocally*, he explained that artistic achievement was dependent on the composer's bond with the folk. The further logical continuation of this thought was self-evident; since all art-music draws its best powers from its specific folk-racial sources, the assimilated Jew has nothing of importance to contribute. He falls, so to speak, between two stools; the Jewish nation, to which he no longer wants to belong, and the German, to which he never can belong.[6]

Wagner now comes to the following conclusion: if the German assimilated Jew understood his situation, he would necessarily suppress his intention of working actively at the development of German culture. Wagner illustrates this theory, which is totally unrealistic but is naïvely logical, with a specific case; and his "guinea pig" is, naturally, Mendelssohn. Now the polemicist really lets himself go:

All that offered itself to our gaze, in the inquiry into our antipathy against the Jewish nature; all the contradictoriness of this [Jewish] nature, both in itself and as touching us; all its inability, while outside our footing, to have intercourse with us upon that footing, nay, even to form a wish to further develop the things which had sprung from out our soil; all these are intensified to a positively tragic conflict in the nature, life and art-career of the early-taken FELIX MENDELSSOHN BARTHOLDY. He has shown us that a Jew may have the amplest store of specific talents, may own the finest and most varied culture, the highest and the tenderest sense of honour —yet without all these preeminences helping him, he was not able, even one single time, to call forth in us that deep, that heart-searching effect which we await from Art. . . .[7]

So began the devaluation of Mendelssohn's work under the aegis of antisemitic German nationalism. In all justice we must admit that Wagner, in his polemic pamphlet, tried to fight fairly, if not chivalrously—against a dead master and rival. Later, he wrote much more poisonous words about the Jews in general and Mendelssohn in particular. In an article "Know Thyself!" he goes so far as to praise the massacres of Jews in Russia as an example worthy of imitation ("See how it succeeded in Kiev!") and he ends his persecution with this tirade:

> Drive them out, German people—but not like the Egyptians, those Hamitic fools, who even gave them golden vessels for the journey. But they must go away empty-handed. Where to, I do not know, but I give them all the same advice. May they find no shelter, no homeland, unhappier than Cain, may they seek and not find—may they descend into the Red Sea—but may they only never, never emerge from it—German people, know thyself.[8]

Indeed, the German people imagined that it knew Wagner and itself; blindly, it followed this advice.

Thus spake the "Master." And what of his disciples?—they behaved much more stupidly; they attacked Mendelssohn where he was invulnerable, in his music. So Theodor Uhlig, a long-forgotten Wagner apprentice, tears apart the *A Midsummer Night's Dream* Overture in the following clever words:

> He [Mendelssohn] does not think that the listener can extract the essentials from a poem. . . . When Mendelssohn had not yet written the rest of the *Midsummer Night's Dream* music, the art-connoisseurs could find an obvious explanation only for the first bit of tone-painting in the overture, and called it the whispering of elves. Later, the composer sanctioned this assumption, thus showing what he wanted to accomplish in this piece of music—and could not. . . .[9]

From these lines, there speaks only the rage of artistic impotence, fanned to a white heat by the envy of the untalented.

Not everyone was inclined to subscribe to the judgment of Wagner and his faithful entourage, but without a doubt his doctrine dominated the rest of the nineteenth century. A characteristic example of this is furnished by Bernard Shaw, who swallowed Wagner's dogmas all too faithfully. In his music criticisms, where he concealed himself (with good reason) under the pseudonym "Corno di Bassetto," he always takes an ironic and condescending tone towards Mendelssohn, as though the latter were one of those dilettantes for whom he felt such deadly scorn. Shaw's judgment was too good not to have appreciated Mendelssohn's art and technical mastery. His prejudice against him was rooted, not in musical causes, but in sociological ones. He saw in Mendelssohn, as in Tennyson, above all the protagonist of that Victorian culture which he so tirelessly mocked and yet in which he himself was so intimately at home. What linked him with Wagner's belief about Mendelssohn was his conviction that Mendelssohn was unable to create truly original musical substance, and that he lacked Wagner's power of suggestion to represent intensive and passionate emotions and to awaken them in the listener. In all his music criticism, Shaw makes exactly the same basic error as do his dyed-in-the-wool Victorian colleagues: he postulates a fundamental, but completely untenable distinction between form and content of the musical work of art.

III

An opposition of quite different character grew up against Mendelssohn even during his lifetime; only after his death did it assume greater significance. Its first spokesman was A. B. Marx, once Mendelssohn's intimate friend. It is quite possible to evaluate the factual criticisms of these opponents independently of their personal resentments.

As might be expected, Marx sets himself up as the chosen defender of "true" and "original" music. He backs up his viewpoint with the terminological apparatus of a post-Kantian esthetics, maintaining it against "imitators," "inauthentic composers," and "sentimentalizers." Without a doubt, he divined a fundamental weakness of Mendelssohn's, without being able to formulate it exactly. He did not fall into the usual delusion that the content and form of a musical work of art can be considered and handled separately; but, unhesitatingly, he introduced into musical esthetics criteria (like "truth" or "longing more than feeling"), which may rightly find their place in the theory of cognition or in ethics, but not in the study of works of art. Without going into the questionable postulate that genuine art must be true, we shall merely observe here that there is no *objective* criterion for distinguishing the true from the false in a work of music.

And yet Marx sensed the truth when he wrote: "For to him [Mendelssohn] the real power and loftiness of the drama was not given; indeed, it basically contradicted his nature, which was more reserved and sensitive than originally creative. . . ."[10] Aimed at Mendelssohn (who is named later) is the following sentence: "In real contrast to it [genius] talent has the (usually happier) task of developing and imitating, improving in certain respects, beautifying, or making more acceptable. That is, it balances the demonically high-flying thoughts of genius against the weakness and fear of the world by means of intermediary formations which are imitative in character. . . ."[11]

Here, only the expression "imitative" is false and misleading; Mendelssohn was far more than a mere imitator. In connection with our own interpretation, we shall return to Marx's ideas.

Around the turn of the century—it was in every sense a *finis saeculi*—a sort of "twilight of the gods" began in all the arts. This was not exactly the "transvaluation of all values" demanded by Nietzsche, but in any case it was a revision of inherited tradition. In France Wagner's work began significantly to lose its influence (probably for political reasons as well), and the waves coming from France and Russia finally reached the citadels of European music, Germany and Austria. The most dominant musicians of the turn of the century, Debussy, R. Strauss, Mahler, Reger, Busoni, and Elgar, had all grown up "in the shadow of the Titan" (Wagner). In spite of their respect for Wagner and their admiration for his work, they followed their own paths, which led them further and further from the ideals of the Bayreuth *Festspielhaus*. The blind obedience with which the previous generation had followed the dogmas of Wagner had reached its end; often, the younger generation turned against him. As usual, the music critics and oracles followed them, though hesitantly and cautiously at first. But the image of Mendelssohn and his work did not profit by this turn of the tide. We must thank the violinists with their devotion to his Violin Concerto, and the oratorio societies with their loyalty to *Elijah*, that his name did not disappear from concert programs entirely during these lean years.

True, his hundredth birthday (1909) brought forth a goodly number of articles, and a spasmodic flareup of his music in the repertoire, combined with the usual lip-service which is one of the conventions of the European musical world. Nevertheless, despite all acclamations, it seemed that his reputation was diminishing.[12] The congratulators did not quite believe in the power of survival of the one whom they were commemorating. For instance: "If Mendelssohn's real position is sometimes unacknowledged by the younger generation, it is simply and solely because his best works have had to suffer for the reverence that has, by chance of association, been attached to some of his worst." Nonetheless, the author remains pessimistic: "But of one thing, at any rate, we may be sure, that he, one of the sincerest of men, would have preferred a thousand times over that his fame should go down with injustice rather than that it should be saved by insincerity."[13]

During World War I, the taste of the leading spirits seemed, for a short while, to turn in Mendelssohn's direction. True, the era of expressionism, which was miles removed from him, had begun; but Neoclassicists, like Busoni, Casella, and other like-minded spirits, considered him practically one of their patron saints. As is well-known, towards the end of his life Busoni was restudying Mendelssohn's *Variations Sérieuses* and *Songs without Words*. Adolf Weissmann, one of the most astute critics of that period (1916-1922) recognized that the music of R. Strauss and M. Reger owes more to Brahms and Mendelssohn than to Wagner. Shortly thereafter, Romain Rolland threw his word on Mendelssohn's behalf onto the scales. He closes his appreciation of the master with these words: "His sense of equilibrium, the purity of his taste and his severe cult of form earned him the appellation of Neo-Classicist. . . ."[14]

We meet similar ideas with Busoni; according to him, Rossini, Cherubini, and Mendelssohn were the only true disciples of Mozart.[15] On the contrary, Mendelssohn remained unacceptable to the radical Expressionists, and was therefore ignored by them, because his will to form held his impulse to express within strict bounds. If they did not reject him completely, they were indifferent and often haughty towards him. (The older Schoenberg, however, often spoke of him in tones of high respect.) The only one of that group to appreciate him then was Paul Bekker, who rightly recognized him as an independent successor of Beethoven. Nevertheless, the fleeting recollection of Mendelssohn, who momentarily escaped the beginnings of oblivion, was submerged in the current battle for the "freedom of expression," a battle to which Mendelssohn had been totally indifferent. If his memory was not kept alive in his music, the conductor and organizer was not completely forgotten. In connection with the various jubilees of the *Gewandhaus* Orchestra or the Leipzig Conservatory, we meet his name again and again. He is still surrounded with the prestige for which he had striven: to be the champion of German music before the world.

The next phase is one of shame and ineradicable disgrace. It began with a series of attacks on Mendelssohn from the German Nationalists; not surprisingly, the first shot was fired by H. J. Moser in his *Geschichte der deutschen Musik*. There, it is not Mendelssohn, but Moser's caricature of him who is dubbed a hothouse flower of the Jewish-dominated Berlin salons, and the noble Aryan Moser turns up his nose at this corrupt figure. Thereupon followed a general attack on Mendelssohn's memory. In a shameful and foolish way, Mendelssohn is accused of shallowness; this is attributed to his light way of life and his parasitic wealth. As though Mendelssohn had ever been spoiled by his wealth—so that he could, or even wanted to—live for pleasure alone! Of course, his church music and his championship of Bach and Handel are simply brushed aside; for most Protestant clergymen worried little enough about dead composers, they had their hands full with the cares of their living fellow men.

Related to this, there cropped up the old Romantic axiom that a creative artist, in order to leave enduring work behind him, must have suffered long and deeply. Indeed, an almost mathematical proportion between the suffering of the creator and the worth of his creations was considered quite natural. Yet this conception, while popular enough, did not remain undisputed:

> At that time there arose the legend that a great artist—especially a musician—must always have been a great *sufferer* in life. Whence, by God, should the convincing power of his creation derive otherwise? Beethoven was considered the classic example. But no one turned more sharply against this superstition than he, the manliest of the Classicists, when he said: "Most men are moved by something good, but these are not artists by nature. Artists are fiery, but they do not weep—that sort of emotion is fit only for women; music must strike fire from the spirit of a man."[16]

For the estheticians who revelled in suffering, Mendelssohn had not suffered enough so that he could be credited with really first-rate accomplishment! This oldmaidish attitude was ingeniously linked with popular antisemitism, and, at the law's command, Mendelssohn disappeared from concert programs and domestic music.

Similar arguments, though not obscured by racial issues, were to be heard during the 1930's even in England, Mendelssohn's true homeland of choice. As has been mentioned, the English composers of the close of the nineteenth century rebelled against the Mendelssohn tyranny to which they had been subjected by Mendelssohn pupils and admirers during their years of study. Now he was openly called "a fallen idol," again because of his popularity in the Victorian age. Since everything Victorian was suspect, so was Mendelssohn. Many, though not all, of these critics simply kept silent about the undiminished popularity of the master with the British bourgeoisie. Here, too, we occasionally meet the argument that Mendelssohn's all-too-carefree life could not have allowed him to achieve anything significant. This concept is based on the English axiom that "suffering ennobles."

As if the fate to be born a Jew in Germany, to bear a celebrated Jewish name, to think as a Protestant, to pine for freedom before 1848, was not cause enough for suffering—be it noted: silent and concealed suffering!

Today we know, having learned a frightful lesson through the experiences of millions of suffering people during and after World War II, that suffering brutalizes rather than ennobles.

A scholar of the rank of P. H. Lang has had the courage to write: "While we cannot help noting the limitations in Mendelssohn's music . . . his frail figure becomes gigantic if we glance at the musical world around him."[17]

Just before the 90th anniversary of Mendelssohn's death (1937) the city fathers of Leipzig removed the master's monument from the *Gewandhaus*, which he had made world-famous, and sold it for scrap iron. We may dispense here with the enumeration of other cultural abominations. One flower is sufficient to give us the scent of the whole bouquet: a certain K. Blessinger considered it his sacred duty to call the attention of the German people to the fact that Mendelssohn had treated Bach's work with inexcusable lack of consideration and respect.[18]

In 1945 the Thousand-Year Reich collapsed, and in 1947 the centennial of Mendelssohn's death was commemorated in festive and solemn fashion throughout the world. Again his music was tested to the utmost, but this time with somewhat more insight and with growing understanding for Mendelssohn's subtlety. The old controversial slogans such as the Wagnerian school, Romanticism, Impressionism and Neoclassicism, Expressionism and Formalism had meanwhile become uninteresting, academic, or simply musty; and, even as abstract esthetic theories became obsolete, Mendelssohn's music began to flourish once more. The statistics of the postwar years, based on record catalogues, concert performances, radio broadcasts, etc., bear witness to the steadily increasing popularity of his music. The concert programs of the last ten years alone show an increase of some 15 per cent in the number of performances. And if one could regard the catalogues of the record industry as a reliable barometer of good public taste (which is, unfortunately, by no means the case), Mendelssohn would be counted among the most popular composers. All such calculations are, however, deceptive and without any evidential value; *for they ignore the ceaseless reduplications or even tenfold performances of the same work by different conductors and ensembles.*

In reality, matters stand as follows: from the wealth of Mendelssohn's works, posterity has selected a small segment, which is constantly played and broadcast. In the last years, however, this segment has decreased rather than increased. Unfortunately works which had previously been neglected have not become available to the public: on the contrary! With the exception of the so-called "Little Violin Concerto" in D minor, which Yehudi Menuhin published (without assistance from the State Library!), and of the two Double Concerti for two pianos, which are available on records but not in score, nothing new or previously unknown had come to light—only now this neglect is in process of being remedied.

Which of Mendelssohn's works are performed again and again in monotonous exclusiveness? 1) The Violin Concerto; 2) the *A Midsummer Night's Dream, Hebrides,* and *Fair Melusine* Overtures; 3) the Italian and Scotch Symphonies and occasionally the Reformation Symphony; 4) the incidental music to *A Midsummer Night's Dream*; 5) one or two organ sonatas; 6) *Elijah;* 7) several *Songs without Words* and the, unfortunately, indestructible *Rondo capriccioso,* that bravura piece of all lady pianists, young and old. His chamber music, certainly the noblest part of his instrumental compositions, and the great sacred and liturgical compositions for chorus, especially the psalms and motets, are as good as forgotten. Not even the *Walpurgisnacht,* indisputably the finest secular oratorio of the nineteenth century, has been reawakened, not to mention the silence which shrouds great works like the *Antigone* music or the solemn choruses of *Athalie.* A hundred years ago, these musical works of high rank were to be found regularly in most concert programs. How shall we interpret this discrepancy between the growing number of Mendelssohn performances and the constantly more restricted choice of pieces to be performed?

Identical causes result in the gradual revival of Mendelssohn's music in general and the shrinking of the Mendelssohn repertoire in particular. Again, we must distinguish here between the levels of popular taste and of critical evaluation by professional musicians. The operation of the previously mentioned process of selection by popular taste, and its criteria, are mysterious. We know virtually nothing about it, but we may guess that subconscious association and certain symbolic elements play a considerable part. This is the probable cause of the shrinking of the repertoire to a few familiar favorites with their wealth of associations.

And now, the professional musicians also begin to turn their attention to Mendelssohn once more. This turn is probably to be explained by their rejection of the exaggerated subjectiveness of late nineteenth century music and Expressionism, in contrast to which Mendelssohn's music must appear to be in "objective style" compared to that of Berlioz, Schumann, Wagner, Liszt, or R. Strauss, and the early Schoenberg. To us, the concept of the "objective," borrowed from the theory of cognition, seems to be quite out of place in applied esthetics; it is vague and undefined. Nonetheless, we recognize with pleasure the genuine tone of admiration and respect in the often high-flown or *recherché* comments of the critics. These apply mostly to the elegance and perfection of Mendelssohn's construction. Even in modern harmony and counterpoint textbooks (e.g., those of Schoenberg and Hindemith), examples from his music appear as models. This matter of craftsmanship is often discussed in modern interpretation of the master:

Composer's craftsmanship having taken a new turn and reached an impasse, the ease with which Mendelssohn progressed has become an object of admiration, perhaps of envy. He has joined the elect band of composers, Mozart and Ravel among them, who knew just how many notes to write and where to put them.[19]

Perhaps still another circumstance helps to restore Mendelssohn's music to public favor. With the exception of the oratorios, it makes no pretensions; this trait corresponds to the characteristics of the social class for which it was originally written, the well-bred bourgeoisie. Unlike Haydn, Mozart, or Beethoven, who still, in the main, addressed themselves to the aristocracy, Mendelssohn speaks the language of a moderate, well-brought-up bourgeoisie. So it is only natural that this very bourgeoisie made him famous, both in Germany and in England. When, after World War I, the middle class began to disappear, Mendelssohn's popularity diminished also. Now that a new bourgeoisie has come to the fore everywhere in Europe, Mendelssohn, too, is being restored to his former position. However, we must not overlook that this arch-bourgeois music contains the danger of Philistinism; and the secret longing of man in the atomic age for the sheltered calm of the *Gartenlaube* should not prejudice the right of art to be a mirror of its times. Thus we should not pose the alternative "Mendelssohn *or* Stravinsky and Schoenberg," but should rather demand to hear Mendelssohn *and* Stravinsky *and* Schoenberg!

IV

The role of Mendelssohn in the history of musical style has always been a controversial one. Scholars by no means agree as to his historical position. Alfred Einstein calls him a "Romantic Classicist,"[20] while E. Bücken sees in him a Classically minded Romanticist,[21] and Arnold Schering refers to him as a "Neo-Romanticist of greatest restraint."[22]

Now Mendelssohn himself was well aware of this role as a "lone wolf" and often defended himself against a strict categorization of his style. This consideration cannot, however, free the music historian of our day from the obligation to attempt to give Mendelssohn his proper place in the sequence of musical styles. True, at present the nineteenth century is not fashionable, musically speaking; for more than 30 years, scholars have been passing it by or neglecting it in favor of the Middle Ages, the Renaissance, and the Baroque. It is, however, quite possible that, as our historical distance from the early nineteenth century grows, the interest of musicologists will turn once again—just as Schering wanted and expected—to the change of taste which took place in that period.

The more we try to delimit the Classic and the Romantic sharply *in music*, the more clearly we must finally realize that such an antithesis cannot be maintained *in music*. It is otherwise in literature, where it is legitimate and, in spite of all imponderables, can be demonstrated in concrete cases. Even more radical is the viewpoint of so penetrating a thinker as Theodor Haecker:

> It is not true that art swings back and forth between two poles which are called Classicism and Romanticism. Today, this is a truly outdated relativistic construction, even though Romanticism may remain a relative antipode. For it confuses the reality of becoming with that of being, and confuses the laws of both. It equates the former with the latter, and is wrong in so doing. . . .[23]

And do we not know from our own experience and that of history that things draw closer together, the greater the distance from which we observe them, even as the parallax of a star becomes smaller and smaller the further we are from it? Therefore, all efforts to construct a "useful" (for textbooks) definition of the concepts "Classicism" and "Romanticism" seem to us mere shadowboxing. We must begin elsewhere if we want to do justice to Mendelssohn and his special position.

In order, first of all, to get rid of the above-mentioned false antithesis, we shall start with Schiller's famous contrasting pair, the naïve and the sentimental. Going beyond this, we shall discover new criteria of a historic-esthetic kind. As is well known, Schiller starts from the fundamental postulate that the naïve poet *is* Nature, while the sentimental poet *seeks* lost Nature. In the latter category he also places the *elegiac* poet:

> If the poet sets nature against art and the ideal against the reality in such a way that the representation of the former preponderates, and that the pleasure taken in it becomes the dominant emotion, I call him *elegiac*. . . .
> In the elegy, sorrow should flow out from an enthusiasm awakened by the ideal. Through this alone does the elegy gain poetic content, and every other source for it is completely beneath the dignity of the art of poetry. . . .

Later, Schiller observes that "sentimentality and melancholy" alone are no fit subject for elegiac poetry if they lack "the energetic principle which must enliven the material." Schiller sees the chief danger of the sentimental poet in "eccentricity," which stems from the artist's idealizing tendency.

Mendelssohn has often been called an "elegiac artist." The expression, properly understood, is not inappropriate, and points up a certain distance from Classicism, which was but slightly elegiac. Concerning a related type of artist, the mannerist, Goethe expressed himself in several pithy sentences:

> When we now look at manner, we see that, in the highest sense and the purest meaning of the word, it can be an intermediary between simple

imitation and style. The nearer it comes, with its easier method, to faithful imitation, the more diligently it seeks, from the other side, to grasp the characteristic features of subjects and express them in a comprehensible manner, the more it links these two approaches by means of a pure, lively, active individuality, the higher, greater and more respectable it will become. . . .

And he adds: "We need not repeat here that we use the word *manner* in a high and respectable sense, and that, therefore, the artists whose works . . . fall into the area of manner need not complain about us."[24]

Not far removed from this attitude towards an evaluation of mannerism is Ernst Robert Curtius. He goes far beyond the historically limited image of the mannerist as a "transitional figure" between the High Renaissance and the Baroque. In mannerism, he sees all artistic trends "which are opposed to Classicism, whether they be pre-Classic, post-Classic, or contemporary with any form of Classicism." According to this view, mannerism is "a complementary phenomenon to Classicism of all epochs"; in other words, it is by no means bound to one period.[25]

Curtius's pupil, G. R. Hocke, starts off from the former's comprehensive observation. Hocke detects at least five "manneristic epochs" in the history of ideas during the last 2000 years: Alexandria (*ca.* 350-150 B.C.), the so-called "Silver Latinity" (*ca.* 14-138 A.D.), the late Middle Ages, the "consciously" manneristic epoch from 1520 to 1650, Romanticism from 1800 to 1830, "and finally the epoch immediately preceding ours, from 1880 to 1950. Each form of mannerism is, at first, still '*classicistically*' bound, but then its 'compulsion towards expression' becomes stronger. So it becomes '*expressive*,' finally '*distorting*,' '*surreal*,' and '*abstract*.' "[26]

Most sharply opposed to mannerism is, above all, Schopenhauer. For him, mannerists are mere imitators: "They start out with a concept in art; they make note of what is pleasing and effective in genuine works, they clarify it for themselves, comprehend it . . . abstractly, and now imitate it, openly or covertly, with clever calculation."[27]

Here, it appears that Schopenhauer, in his definition, did not mean the mannerist, but the eclectic; for good mannerists can certainly not be denied originality. For Schopenhauer, however, that is the decisive criterion.

W. Hofmann more sharply delimits the concepts "manner" and "style," which Goethe had already tried to separate. For Hofmann, mannerism develops from a "pluralism of forms," which, together with a certain turn away from nature leads to an art which is *derived* from art, or stimulated by art.[28] It was doubtless this which A. B. Marx had to criticize seriously in Mendelssohn's music: its cause is often art, seldom nature.

After this summary and fragmentary enumeration of views on the essence of mannerism and its principal epochs, let us see if Mendelssohn fits this category of mannerist, which has been so variously described and judged, and what other composers belong there. The principal criteria here are position between imitation and style; emphasis on the characteristic in detail (Goethe); a direction opposed to Classicism, at the same time a complementary phenomenon to Classicism (E. R. Curtius); conscious, skillful imitation of effective elements of other artists (A. Schopenhauer); and the turn away from nature to the construction of an art stimulated by art (W. Hofmann). The early nineteenth century, in particular, is a manneristic epoch (G. R. Hocke).

If we disregard Schopenhauer's one-sided misunderstanding of the concept, Mendelssohn would satisfy all criteria of mannerism. He stands between two directions, subscribes to neither Classicism nor Romanticism, and is thus a "complementary phenomenon" to Classicism. It cannot be denied, either, that many of his creations do not come from elemental inspiration, and that almost all of his church music represents a "derived" art. Nevertheless, these works are far more than mere imitations; indeed, in their day they formed a style and a school. But the works of Bach, Handel, and the Italian choral composers of the seventeenth century were, beyond a doubt, the decisive models for Mendelssohn. Also in the realm of the concert overture and of theatrical music, Mendelssohn fulfills the criterion of "derived" art. Shakespeare, Aeschylus, Sophocles, Racine inspired him, as did Goethe (*Calm Sea and Prosperous Voyage*)[29], and German fairy tales (*Fair Melusine*), not to forget the glees. On the contrary, he had no models for the oratorios; neither Bach's nor Handel's forms were completely adequate for him or his time. So, we may view him as a mannerist oriented to the Classical past and to his own post-Beethovenian era. Thus he becomes part of a development in music history to which many other like-minded composers also belonged, although this fact was not always fully recognized.

Monteverdi seems to belong to this category, as do all the early composers of opera, for after all, this form was derived from the Latin tradition of Greek tragedy. In like manner, at least in his dramatic works, derived from long-standing models, Berlioz inclines in the manneristic direction. But also composers like C. P. E. Bach, Tschaikowsky, Saint-Saëns, and Reger, who belong to no "school," may be better understood as manneristic artists than as eclecticists or individualists. The most significant and most clearly defined mannerist of our epoch, however, seems to be Richard Strauss. Each of the above-mentioned criteria, and most of those which we have not mentioned, apply to his work: even that of "manneredness," which is to be distinguished from mannerism. By "manneredness," we mean the preponderance of certain clichés which, deliberately or otherwise, crop up again and again in an artist's work, without, however, helping to integrate a style. The stylistic copy, brought into favor once more by Strauss (Couperin Suite, *Bourgeois Gentilhomme*, *Ariadne*, etc.), points to his manneristic

inclination. These appear most clearly in his late work *Capriccio*. There, it is not even a matter of a composition stimulated by another work of art; it is a composed *esthetic* discussion between imaginary Gluckists and their equally imaginary opponents.

Basically, however, all such classifications can never do justice to the specific genre of the artist. In Mendelssohn, we clearly recognize a *stilo misto*, a mixed style. We might compare it to an ellipse with two foci. The sensuous component belongs to the "Romantic" ideal of sound; the formal-esthetic component is of an almost classical strictness. In mannerists, we can often find this split in artistic thinking.

At this point, in literature, Manneristic and Romantic thoughts and expressions merge, or, rather, meet on common ground. Both originate in that twilight zone in which rationalistic ideas, now paradoxically transformed, pass (through an artistic medium) into the realm of communication of *emotions*. The founders of the Romantic school loved to play with such "approaches to the limit."

This last term, borrowed from mathematical analysis, most clearly describes the intellectual borderline situation. Applying such concepts to music, the literary Romanticists availed themselves frequently of such "passes over the limit." A few quotations from Novalis may illustrate this point:

> In music, it [mathematics] really appears as revelation, as creative idealism.
> All pleasure is musical, hence mathematical.
> How little has physics been used for the benefit of the soul, and the soul used for the benefit of the outside world!
> Music has to do with combinatorial analysis.

Applied to speculative philosophy, such ideas are substantiated by Friedrich Schlegel:

> Many find it strange and ridiculous when musicians speak about the thoughts in their compositions. Often it may happen that we observe that they have more thoughts *in their music* than *about it*. But anyone who has a feeling for the marvellous affinities among all arts and sciences will, at least, not regard the matter from the commonplace viewpoint of so-called "naturalness." (According to this, music should be only the language of the emotions.) Such a person will not find a certain tendency of all purely instrumental music toward philosophy impossible *per se*. Must purely instrumental music not create its own text? And, in it, is not the theme developed, confirmed, varied and stated, just like the subject of meditation in a philosophical sequence of ideas?[30]

How close is such an attitude to the anti-Romantic esthetics of Hanslick,

which postulates music as the play of forms in tonal motion! Such ideas
were conceived by *litterateurs,* not by musicians, in ruthlessly consistent
deductions and conclusions from Rationalist positions. This philosophical
view of music was, however, not at all in accord with the music of that
time, or with the views of the musicians. For they had not abandoned the
claim that music is the art which communicates and sublimates *emotions.*
This was the conception and conviction of all composers since Rousseau
and C. P. E. Bach. In no way was it a monopoly of the "Romanticists" in
music. At least during the nineteenth century there simply does not exist
a tangible dividing line between the ideas and ideals of the Classical school
and those of a style new *in principle,* which might generally and sensibly
be termed "Romantic." The breaking points, and there were a number of
them, occurred only during the twentieth century, when they were immediately noticed and understood as such.

Perhaps the Romantic emphasis on "expression" or emotional commun-
cation was more a postulate of the *litterateurs,* musical or nonmusical, than
a consistent and conscious musical practice. This aspect of musical Romanticism, more speculative than creative, becomes fully evident in the her-
meneutics of the champions of program music. These authors did not
hesitate to resuscitate the old *ars inveniendi* in the new disguise of lengthy,
dull, and tedious exercises on the emotional qualities of the Wagnerian
leitmotifs.

Again, Romantic elements were being superimposed upon music by
nonmusicians. Should we not be wary of the term "Romantic" in music
per se? Mendelssohn despised all empty speculation on musical esthetics,
unless it was applied, concrete, and pragmatic.

Far from such critical considerations, in the last few years we meet
with a rather superficial objection to Mendelssohn's music. It is said to
serve for "escape," that is, the flight from the confusion of daily life. This
effect it certainly has in common with operetta, movies, and cabaret, not
to mention anything worse. If the term "escape music" expresses nothing
but the readiness of the listener to flee from our "age of anxiety" and its
wild and undisciplined demons into a purer atmosphere, then it is quite
rightly chosen and we have nothing to say against it. For this purpose,
Mendelssohn's music certainly possesses the necessary "wings of song." But,
if, under the concept of "escape music," we were to understand a public
preference for light, shallow or even frivolous music, then we would certainly be unfair to Mendelssohn.

Escape—no, that was never Mendelssohn's resource. Scion of a highly-
bred family of German-Jewish intellectuals, he often was called a child of
fortune, because he never had to struggle for his daily bread. True, he was
wealthy; yet wealth never impaired his artistic integrity. He never spared
himself; he, the rich man, allowed himself less leisure than many a struggling

artist. Nor did he succumb to cheap acclaim: aside from a few drawing room trifles, he aspired to the most lofty, hence the least rewarding aims in art. As stern as was his sense of duty, as great was his charity. He was born an intellectual; he turned to the spiritual. To this side of his nature the older music appealed most, and his concern with it, never merely of archeological character, proved fruitful. Being a focal personality during the first half of the nineteenth century, he reintroduced many of the older masters to living music. J. S. Bach is the most striking instance of this.

In Mendelssohn's own music the styles of these older composers were transformed into a new polyphony, which is as different from that of Beethoven as Beethoven's is from that of Bach. Unlike Beethoven, Mendelssohn never arrogated to himself the right to exceed the boundaries of his chosen means. Every measure of his music suits its medium, even in works of lesser value.

In a time which cherished freedom to excess (only in art; in politics it was taboo), Mendelssohn's disciplined craft led to new heights of formal subtlety. As Nietzsche realized, there lay his true excellence. There also we can find his place in history: a contemporary of Berlioz, Liszt, Chopin, Schumann, and Wagner, he was, *au fond*, nobody's contemporary because of his overriding concern with formal balance in absolute music; then as now not a fashionable aim.

This concern may, in certain instances, have led to manneristic formulae, which by their very cliché-like nature could be used in many structures, with more or less inherent musical logic. This is the root of certain typically Mendelssohnian mannerisms, which sometimes mar his style. In the mature composer we encounter also the ever increasing urge towards intensity of expression, which is sometimes thwarted by a not fully commensurate musical substance.

As a man and artist, he may be best described in three paradoxes: a sufferer serene, an irascible angel, and a skeptical missionary. This sense of mission, however, transcended the boundaries of his era and nation. It is no coincidence that he set to music a poem by Schiller *Die Künstler* whose closing lines—also transcending all limitations of time and place— embody the supreme purpose of his life:

> *Der Menschheit Würde ist in Eure Hand gegeben;*
> *Bewahret sie!*
> *Sie sinkt mit Euch; mit Euch wird sie sich heben!*

> The state of man's entrusted to your hand;
> Protect it well!
> It may decline with you; with you it will ascend!

Notes

1. Capell, "Mendelssohn after 100 years," *Hallé Magazine* (London, August-September, 1947).
2. Schiller, *Über Bürgers Gedichte.*
3. W. H. Riehl, *Musikalische Charakterköpfe* (Leipzig, 1853), Vol. I.
4. H. F. Chorley, *Modern German Music* (London, 1854), pp. 400ff. Hauptmann expresses himself similarly in his letters to Hauser (letter of February 22, 1858).
5. Wagner availed himself of various pseudonyms for his polemic writings. They concealed him like Siegfried's *Tarnhelm.* The first example was his attack on Rellstab under the name Wilhelm Drach. His furious criticism of Rossini's *Stabat Mater* appeared under the pseudonym H. Valentin. Aside from *Judaism in Music*, we find the most cowardly and treacherous use of a pseudonym (W. Drach) in an attack on his former friend and comrade-in-arms Devrient.
6. Here Wagner permits himself a dig at the synagogue music of his times. "However sublime and noble we may be minded to picture to ourselves this musical Service of God in its pristine purity, all the more plainly must we perceive that that purity has been most terribly sullied before it came down to us." Wagner originally (1850) meant and expressed this quite naively and honestly. But, in the meantime, the poet of *Die Meistersinger* had progressed far from this naïveté. In that opera, he exclaimed:

> That by our Masters she was kept
> And cherished as their own,
> With anxious care that never slept
> This Art herself has shown.
> If not so noble as of yore,
> When courts and princes prized her more
> The troublous years all through
> She's German been and true.
> She was not always being blessed
> As now, when all men pinched and pressed,
> You see she kept our full respect.
> What more from us can you expect?

This shows that Wagner had learned to understand cultural history without a priori "postulates of value." For the parallel with synagogue music is clear here. Nonetheless, the more mature Wagner did not eliminate the passage from the pamphlet.

7. Wagner, *Das Judenthum in der Musik* (Leipzig, 1869), p. 25. (Tr. William Ashton Ellis in *Richard Wagner's Prose Works* [London, 1894], III, pp. 93-94.)
8. *Bayreuther Blätter* [February-March, 1881-2]. (This passage is excluded from Ellis's translation in *Richard Wagner's Prose Works, IV.*)
9. Uhlig, *Musikalische Schriften*, 2nd ed. (Regensburg, 1913), p. 168.
10. A. B. Marx, *Die Musik des 19. Jahrhunderts (Methode der Musik)*, 2nd ed.
11. *Ibid.*, p. 221.
12. Only Max Reger and his pupils, also perhaps Cyril Scott and Saint-Saëns, felt differently, much to their credit.
13. Ernest Walker, "Mendelssohn," *The Manchester Guardian* (February 3, 1909).
14. Rolland, "L'école romantique," in Lavignac, *Encyclopédie de la musique*, 2nd ed.
15. Dent, *Ferruccio Busoni* (London, 1933), p. 267.
16. Arnold Schering, *Vom musikalischen Kunstwerk* (Leipzig, 1949), p. 79.
17. P. H. Lang, *Music in Western Civilization* (New York, 1941), p. 811.
18. K. Blessinger, *Judentum und Musik* (1944), pp. 58ff.

19. *Musical Times* (London, October, 1947), leading article.
20. A. Einstein, *Music in the Romantic Era* (New York, 1947), pp. 124ff.
21. E. Bücken, *Die Musik des 19. Jahrhunderts* (1932), p. 105.
22. A. Schering, *Vom Musikalischen Kunstwerk* (Leipzig, 1949), p. 67.
23. Th. Haecker, *Vergil, Vater des Abendlandes*, 7th ed. (Munich, 1952), pp. 89-90. About the ambiguity of the term "musical romanticism," see also the penetrating introduction to *Romantik in der Tonkunst* by Kurt Stephenson (*Das Musikwert*), Koln, 1961; most recently the relationship between romanticism and mannerism has been seriously investigated by Marianne Thalmann in *Romantik und Manierismus*, Stuttgart, 1963.
24. Goethe, "Einfache Nachahmung, Manier, Styl" (*Über Italien, Fragmente*).
25. E. R. Curtius, *Europäische Literatur und lateinisches Mittelalter* (Bern, 1953), Ch. "Manierismus."
26. Gustav René Hocke, *Die Welt als Labyrinth* (Hamburg, 1957), pp. 10-11.
27. Cited from Hocke, *op. cit.*, pp. 212-13.
28. W. Hofmann, *Manier und Stil in der Kunst des 20. Jahrhunderts, Studium generale* (1955, Heft 1).
29. Here it should be noted that Beethoven did not take Goethe's poem merely as subject matter, but, in contrast to Mendelssohn, composed it fully.
30. *Athenaeum*, ed. F. Baader (Berlin, 1905), IV, p. 89.

Appendix

I

Excerpts from a confidential report by Varnhagen van Ense. "This article was written early in April 1836, in bed; it may be published only after my death."

Ludwig Achim von Arnim and Moritz Itzig

Arnim was engaged to Bettina Brentano, who was "brought up in Frankfurt and antisemitism." She did, however, attend the soirées and parties given by Madame Sara Levy.

Bettina was once invited by Mme Levy to a grand party with music, but not Arnim, who had never accompanied her to these parties. Suddenly it occurred to him that he might attend this time. As he did not think it necessary to appear formal in a Jewish house, he came in his ordinary clothes. A brand-new fashion of wide breeches had just emerged, but it was so conspicuous and extraordinary that it was considered impolite; at any rate, such breeches were permitted only in the mornings and on the street. Arnim appeared in this dress at the well-groomed and elegant party of Mme Levy. She, who had not expected him anyway, was somewhat embarrassed, but controlled herself admirably. Arnim, however, appeared quite at ease and did not say a word of apology or even of politeness; quite to the contrary! He cracked unpleasant jokes, offended some of the guests, and caused a painful disturbance for the whole evening.

Here the reporter, in all fairness, assumes that Arnim acted without malice and merely meant to "show-off as a genius" (*in der Anmassung, genial zu seyn*). When he had left, the indignation became general when the company heard that he had neither been invited by nor ever called upon his hostess. Mme Levy's nephew, Moritz Itzig, considered it his duty to defend her. The very next day, he wrote Arnim a grave and measured letter, reprimanding him for what he considered rude behavior towards his aunt. Arnim replied mockingly and impolitely. He thereupon received a challenge to a duel with Itzig. This seemed too much for Arnim: that a Jew boy should teach him proper deportment and should challenge him, to boot! Arnim took Itzig's letter to the officers' *casino*. There, he obtained from his comrades, noblemen and officers all, a certificate that he, Arnim, could never cross arms with a Jew. This document, together with a personal reply, he sent to Itzig. The latter answered: he who refused the sword in so cowardly a fashion would be taught better by a cane! Arnim ignored this threat.

Some time later, Arnim went to take a bath. On entering the hall, he saw a young man jump up, and a moment thereafter he found himself being soundly thrashed and caned. The giant Arnim could not defend himself, but cried for help. Meanwhile, the aggressor Itzig called him: "Infamous rascal, base poltroon!" Finally, Itzig identified himself to the witnesses and explained his action.

Arnim chose the way of redress which seemed most advantageous to him. He transmitted the case to the *Kammergericht* (Supreme Court). Varnhagen had (illegally) access to the documents of the case and reports on his findings:

> Arnim asked the court to protect him against an insane Jew-boy, whom he considered sick and hypochondriac. The Court replied that it had observed no insanity of the defendant, and that in the Court's opinion Itzig was a most reasonable man. The Court was obligated to punish him for assault and battery, but did so as leniently as possible.

Added to the records was the *votum* of Arnim's comrades that he could not give satisfaction of arms to a Jew.

> The "gentlemen" who concocted this nice testimonial were the *Junkers* von Chasot, von Quast, von Barnekow, von Rothenburg, von Bardeleben, von Moellendorf, Roeder I., and von Hedemann. The document itself is couched in an unctuous, sermonizing tone and full of bitter, sneering sarcasm. In it, pedagogic maxims are expressed; it excuses him (Itzig), it sympathizes with him because he will never be spared such insults, it blames him for his impiety in not submitting to the universal law of the world(!).

Yet he is young—he may improve—and therefore the gentlemen prefer to treat him with wise doctrines instead of with horsewhips and cudgels. . . .

It so happened that later most of the officers (not Arnim) apologized, chiefly under the influence of Rahel von Varnhagen. When Itzig entered the Prussian army as a volunteer in 1813, the case fell into oblivion. However, when Itzig was killed in the battle of Gross-Görschen, while Arnim did not even enter the army remaining comfortably on his estate, the bitter joke was propagated:

> Itzig and Arnim, both remained;
> The one dead at Lützen, the other behind his stove.

The scandal hurt Arnim even more than the former one and led to his ostracism by such men as Gneisenau. His career as officer was ruined forever.

II

Letter of Felix to his father, from Frankfurt (unpublished).

November 13, 1831.

Dear Father:

Please receive my heartiest thanks for your letter which announced Rebecca's engagement, as well as my warm congratulations. May Heaven grant you as joyous a future and as much happiness as you have merited it for all of us, and as we wish you gratefully.

With all of its gaiety, this event carries a serious significance, inasmuch as it concludes and starts another timespan in the life of our family, God willing. This also moves me to open a serious discussion with you, for which I have long been meaning to ask you. Long before the beginning of this journey you spoke of it, you established the points of view which I should bear in mind, and you kindly heard my arguments and wishes. You did likewise before any of us took an important step in life; and now, as my journey draws to its close, I should like to discuss with you the plans for the time after my return. Accordingly I should like to ask you first about your intentions in this respect, and also for your views—quite extensively; then, I'd like to submit to you my wishes and plans. For I, too, have for some time past been making plans for my life; and now the question arises how far you will concur with my ideas, and how far they agree with your decisions about me.

The only time when you spoke with me about the period [after the journey] was just before our trip to Dessau and Leipzig. Then you said quite generally that I should, after the journey, make myself independent, and you added that I own a sum of money (I do not know how much) which my grandmother left for me as a legacy. The implication was that

I could use this money to facilitate my first steps. My first question to you is, when do you want me to begin this [my independence], and when is my journey to end? Also tell me kindly: do you wish me to avail myself of this money and my accumulated fees which are in your possession, or should I start all by myself and without any auxiliary money except what I have earned? I have no fear that I should be unable to do so, and in this respect I shall follow your ideas completely. In that case, I believe I should be obliged to do things just for money which would hardly advance me, e.g., giving lessons or recitals. I think it would be advantageous for my career if I were to use whatever I own; this would spare me some inconveniences, especially in the beginning. Yet, as I said before, I await only your decision; if you consider it more profitable that I start from scratch, I shall do so, let the money lie untouched, and try my wings. Finally, I should like to hear your personal opinion concerning a position (at a theatre), if you wish that I accept or aspire to such a post, or if you wish that this position be in Berlin, etc.

And yet, if you permit me to speak of my own plans, it seems to me almost too early to accept such a position at the age of 23. As things are today, the position of a music director encompasses such a mass of small details, dissipations, intrigues, etc., that only an indisputable authority can evade or neutralize them. I do not have such authority as yet, and I do not yet have sufficient confidence in it. It could well happen that I might become involved in matters which would distract me—at least temporarily—from my main object (composition); or I might try reforming before I felt the perfection and calmness which are indispensable to every reform. This alone would keep me from applying for such a post, especially in Berlin, where because of Spontini's personality the soil is fertile for all kinds of gossip and intrigue—in short, for any so-called theatrical affairs. It would be quite different if a post were offered to me where I might put myself in a different position from the outset, and bind myself only for a limited time. Here, the question arises of how I should earn my livelihood without a position, and I cannot but say that I should prefer to do it—at least at first—with my compositions. In England, I was offered £300 for an opera; my pieces were as well paid for as I could have wished. I am quite certain that I shall be commissioned to write an opera for London; perhaps I shall attend and direct the music festivals in the summer—this is quite well-paying work. Moreover, I shall negotiate with a music dealer in Paris, and he will take in commission all the pieces written for London. If I then have an opera in London and thereafter go to Munich with another opera commission, this will be a good beginning; moreover, after the opera's performance it will be easier for me to find a position and agreeable working conditions. If I should have success with my opera for Munich, I shall go to Stuttgart, where Count Leutrum has made me some promising offers. This is all I plan for the next year and if all this should materialize, other things will be waiting for the subsequent year. At any rate, I plan to return to Berlin, when I have done my work in England and before going to the Munich opera. There [in Berlin] I would look around to see if there is something to do for me; of course, I would prefer to remain and live where you are, but I must be able to work and produce. Then I can explain and discuss all these matters with you personally, God willing, always following your will.

Finally, I am copying for you my formal commission for Munich, because I know that it will give you pleasure if one treats me as a professional musician and commissions compositions formally:

"My dear Sir,

You were kind enough to express, during our talk, your inclination to write an opera, and seemed not averse to the idea of having it first performed at the Royal Theatre here in Munich. I believe that I act in the interest of art, and not against your own desires, if I take the liberty of making the following suggestions to you:

1) You, dear Sir, will write the new opera, which you intend to compose, with regard to the present personnel and the already existing theatrical means.

2) You will be so kind as to inform the undersigned immediately after the completion of the work, and to send him the libretto and the score, so that all necessary preparations can be made with despatch and the date of the première can be set as exactly as possible. When such a date is set, you will be so kind as to state your consent, and also state whether it will be feasible for you to come here in person in order to be present at the rehearsals, the study of parts, and the première.

3) If you are in possession of a libretto which you plan to compose, I should ask you to submit it to me; if this is not the case, you will be so kind as to enter into negotiations with any German poet of renown in whom you have confidence, and to inform the undersigned about the poet, the subject of the libretto, and the honorarium desired by the poet, well in time. Thus, the Intendancy of the Opera might express its views of it, and will settle the payment of the honorarium, which will come out of the general funds of the theatre, for the poet will be obliged to consider the artistic and technical means which are at our disposal here and now.

4) The work remains your own possession, and you alone will be entitled to sell it to other theatres. The Intendancy, which commits itself to pay you that fee which is customary for outstanding composers, acquires no other privilege than that of the utilization of your work for the performance at our theatre.

Expecting your written confirmation or modification of these suggestions, I am, with the expression of my high esteem,

Baron von Poissl, Intendant."

I replied that I was delighted to accept the proposal, and that I would start the work with despatch as soon as I had a suitable libretto. I missed Uhland [celebrated German poet] in Stuttgart; he is totally mixed up with politics and aspires to become a deputy [of the parliament]. I contacted

Gustav Schwab, but doubt that he is the right man, for he is not musical at all and has never written anything for the stage. This is also the reason why I am still (Nov. 17) here; today I am supposed to receive a reply from Düsseldorf to my letter in which I asked if Immermann had returned. It would be most desirable to see him, and I would, at the same time, arrange for the edition of my church music in Bonn. Please mail the reply to this letter to Paris, because I should arrive there in about ten days. Schelble, who insisted that I live in his house and who overwhelms me with his kindness, has commissioned me to write an oratorio for the *Caecilienverein,* but I hardly know how I can approach such a task. The day before yesterday, he had some of my Roman church music performed in his *Verein,* and just now he is copying some parts of another of my pieces, which will be sung tonight at an extraordinary gathering. The other night I had to improvise there before a large audience; it was exactly like that occasion when all of you were seated below and listened.

Meanwhile, your dear letter arrived with the news about the dear aunt [Henrietta had died]. Ever since my arrival in Rome I had abandoned hope of seeing her again; but this is different now, when it is impossible. You asked me why I did not write about Betty; I have nothing to say, but I have begun a composition for her which I shall send her later, a long-promised Adagio; now it is different and more serious than I had planned it.

Now all our life goes on and we all feel deeply the incision which the last year made; but you remain well and happy! Last night Mr. André toasted your health with a warmth which reminded me of you very much. This time, it is hard for me to leave Germany; since I returned from Italy I could truly pursue the aims which you set for my journey: to establish contact with people, to befriend some of them, and to make the necessary connections for the future. Never did I feel so clearly that I am a German in my heart and must always remain one. . . ."

III

Unpublished letter of Lea Mendelssohn to K. F. Zelter.

March 10, 1829

You, my most esteemed professor, must have felt, during many years, with how great a debt you have charged a mother's heart. It is probably unnecessary that I express to you my gratitude once again and in special manner. Yet at this moment [the day before the first performance of Bach's *St. Matthew Passion*], which for me constitutes a significant time of my life, I feel the urge to assure you, as if by shaking your hand, that none of your spiritual benefits to my children has been lost or passed by unnoticed, and that I remember all of your—thanks to God!—fruitful aspirations and endeavors deeply in my heart. You were not only friend and adviser, guide and helper; you allowed every seed and every gift to develop freely and independently, and never have I seen a teacher so unselfishly wise, so free from all egotism. You know full well with how infinite a faith, love and respect your disciple is attached to you; now permit his mother, too, to express to you all her thanks and the wish that we may not wholly be forgotten in your thoughts, and that you will grant us the delightful and quickening pleasure of your presence in our home often and willingly.

Yours,   Lea Mendelssohn Bartholdy.

IV

Opinions of King Frederick William IV about Mendelssohn (from Aloys Fuchs' collection of Mendelssohniana in the possession of the abbey of Göttweig, Austria).[1]

The anonymous author opens his article with a "funny" quotation from a critique of Mendelssohn's Overture to the *A Midsummer Night's Dream* which appeared in a Vienna journal in 1837. We quote the following passage:

> Into what devious ways can the urge to be original, to be classical, lead an artist! In the overture there is too much of Mendelssohn, i.e., too much of musical philosophy and not a grain of immortality. It smacks of *Faust* and of the *Wolfsschlucht* [from Weber's *Freischütz*], and that is still the best of it. As for the rest, it is a dull aggregate of dissonances and other musico-mathematical calculations [*Rechenexempeln*]—in short, much night, a bad dream, and at best an old woman's summer [*Altweibersommer*].

Later, the author reports some remarks quoted from Rellstab's *Zwei Gespräche mit Sr. Majestät König Friedrich Wilhelm IV*, published by Decker (Berlin, 1849). We quote two characteristic and interesting passages from it:

> The King remarked: "Mendelssohn suffered from a nervous aversion against close contact with the public world [*Öffentlichkeit*], at least against contact with a large public. I made a formal contract with him, according to which the work [*Athalie*] was to be performed only in a close circle of carefully selected and invited listeners. If he were alive, I would certainly have kept my promise in accord with his inclination. Now we have lost him, and I should consider it wrong that the world should lose one of his worthiest works . . . hence, I have ordered the performance of *Athalie* for the coming season in Berlin."

The King asked if the anecdotes of Mendelssohn's fabulous memory were true. Rellstab replied:

> Beyond his other great qualities as a musician, Mendelssohn owned an extraordinary memory. He knew by heart not only his own works, but

almost *all* works of the great masters; he retained in memory, note for note, lengthy pieces of music after hearing them once, even when they did not please him especially and he had not listened to them very attentively. Because of this gift, he was accustomed not to write down his own larger compositions until and unless he had completely perfected and rounded them in his mind. . . ."

Notes

1. I am deeply indebted for this rare piece of nineteenth-century publicity to P. Maurus Grois, O.S.B.; also to Dr. Friedrich Wilhelm Riedel, Kassel, for his active interest and kind cooperation.

Index

Index